THE ALEXIAD
OF ANNA COMNENA

TRANSLATED FROM THE GREEK BY
E. R. A. SEWTER

PENGUIN BOOKS
BALTIMORE · MARYLAND

Penguin Books Ltd, Harmondsworth, Middlesex, England
Penguin Books Inc., 7110 Ambassador Road, Baltimore, Maryland 21207, U.S.A.
Penguin Books Pty Ltd, Ringwood, Victoria, Australia

—

This translation first published 1969

—

Copyright © E. R. A. Sewter, 1969

—

Made and printed in Great Britain
by Richard Clay (The Chaucer Press) Ltd,
Bungay, Suffolk
Set in Monotype Garamond

CONTENTS

THE ALEXIAD

CONTENTS

TRANSLATOR'S PREFACE

FORTY years have passed since Elizabeth Dawes produced the first English translation of the *Alexiad* in full. At the time her version was highly praised. In the following year (1929) Georgina Buckler's *Anna Comnena* appeared, an excellent study of great value but somewhat amorphous and difficult to use – a scholar's book. Unfortunately Miss Dawes hoped that her readers would find in this volume all the aid they required; consequently she provided virtually no annotation; no maps were furnished, no appendixes of any kind, no genealogical tables and no bibliography. *Anna Comnena*, though recently reissued, has long been out of print, and it had become more than ever necessary to publish a fresh version, with a brief commentary and other essential help for the reader.

The translator is at once faced with the question: How literal should it be? The old word-for-word construe, of course, was thoroughly abandoned at least a generation ago, but there are still those who like to adhere very closely to the Greek, not merely in diction but even in syntax. Miss Dawes herself preferred the almost literal interpretation, and this inevitably led to solecisms: 'If they did not whet their swords, they certainly did their souls'; 'By reason of their terror they were almost constrained to belch forth their souls into thin air.' A determination to observe hypallage in the Greek can also have bizarre results: 'Demetrius with murder in his heart whetted his sword and got his bloody right hand ready.' It could be argued that this method more truly reflects Anna's own thoughts and style, but in general the historian is best served, I think, by a straightforward modern idiom common to scholars on both sides of the Atlantic. The present volume therefore tries to express in contemporary Anglo-American the ideas and language of a Byzantine princess who wrote some eight hundred years ago – no easy task. Nothing must be omitted and at all costs obscurity must be avoided, even if

7

need be by a short paraphrase. For example, when Anna writes of Bohemond that 'by his nostrils nature had given free passage for the high spirit which bubbled up from his heart' (Dawes) – a particularly awkward sentence in Book XIII – one must make an effort to be lucid. What does Anna mean? Presumably Bohemond had broad nostrils (apparently a mark of manhood, for she mentions the fact more than once), nostrils that allowed the breath to escape from his lungs in great gusts – or should we say, allowed him to breathe deeply? The whole idea is alien to us. Maybe Normans suffered inordinately from catarrh and Bohemond was an exception. To be fair to Anna, she does not often present such difficulties, for in narrative her style is usually unaffected. She is much more forthright than Michael Psellus, whom she admired and sometimes plagiarized. Where her style becomes elevated and approaches an almost poetic diction, the English must harmonize with her mood, but with due restraint: to reproduce her exclamations, her rhetoric, her passionate outbursts in all their Byzantine glory is apt to end in bathos.

There remains the problem of archaisms. It has been said that Anna wrote in pseudo-Classical Greek, a learned language totally unknown to the ordinary people of Constantinople, 'an almost entirely mummiform school language'[1]. If this is true of Anna, then it is true of Byzantine historians from Procopius to Phrantzes. Naturally there were variations, but in essence all used the same form of Greek. There is a famous anecdote in Psellus's *Chronographia* (VI, 61) which proves how readily these same ordinary people of the capital recognized and appreciated the point of a line quoted from the *Iliad*. Nor is this really surprising: most intelligent people are bilingual. My American students at a mid-west university spoke good English; their essays differed hardly at all from those of under-graduates here; but the University *Daily News*, written in their own jargon, was esoteric in the extreme – only the initiated could have understood a quarter of it. Millions of people in these Isles speak their own dialect – Cockney, Geordie, broad Scots and so on, all mutually incomprehensible – but all can understand the B.B.C. News and write the Queen's English

1. Krumbacher, K., *Geschichte der byzantinischen Litteratur*, p. 277.

(with varying degrees of success). So it must have been in Constantinople: the Greek element (the majority) read and wrote the Byzantine form of the language; the vernacular was probably quite different. There is no need, therefore, to inject 'thou', 'thee' and 'thy' into a translation of the *Alexiad*.

The maps are not intended to be exhaustive – indeed, they cannot be, for many place-names are still unidentified – but they should enable the reader to follow Alexius's campaigns with fair ease. I am no more consistent in the matter of names than any of my predecessors: I write Dyrrachium rather than Durazzo or even Durres, but Brindisi rather than Brundisium; I retain Smyrna where the moderns would read Izmir, but prefer Joscelin of Courtenay to Iatzoulinos. The alternatives, however, are listed in the notes. In the case of the Crusaders I have for the most part followed Runciman, and where Turks or Patzinaks are concerned I accepted the lead of the *Cambridge Ancient History*. In this arbitrary behaviour euphony is bound to influence one's choice: Abul-Kasim sounds more convincing than Apelchasem and Raymond de Saint-Gilles than Isangeles. On the other hand, I have carefully retained Anna's Franks, Normans, Latins and Kelts; also her Turks, Ishmaelites, Persians, Agarenes and Saracens. These names she uses indiscriminately for the western and eastern enemies of the emperor respectively, sometimes substituting the pejorative 'barbarians'.

The translation is based on the text of Bernard Leib, who published his own French version of the *Alexiad* some thirty years ago. European scholars are much indebted to his labours. I am grateful, too, to Professor J. M. Hussey, who with Baynes, Talbot Rice, Moss and Runciman has done so much to revolutionize the British attitude to Byzantina in the post-war era. I must also thank the publishers for their unfailing courtesy and forbearance and in particular the editor of the Penguin Classics, Mrs Betty Radice. Mr Andrew Pennycook and Miss Julia Vellacott have also been helpful. Finally, I thank my wife who for two years has endured the drone of this typewriter while the book was once written and twice revised.

Newbury, Berkshire   E.R.A.S.
  March 1968

INTRODUCTION

'THE life of the Emperor Alexius has been delineated by a favourite daughter, who was inspired by a tender regard for his person and a laudable zeal to perpetuate his virtues. Conscious of the just suspicion of her readers, the Princess Anna Comnena repeatedly protests that besides her personal knowledge she had searched the discourse and writings of the most respectable veterans: that after an interval of thirty years, forgotten by, and forgetful of, the world, her mournful solitude was inaccessible to hope and fear; and that truth, the naked perfect truth, was more dear and sacred than the memory of her parent. Yet instead of the simplicity of style and narrative which wins our belief, an elaborate affectation of rhetoric and science betrays in every page the vanity of a female author. The genuine character of Alexius is lost in a vague constellation of virtues; and the perpetual strain of panegyric and apology awakens our jealousy to question the veracity of the historian and the merit of the hero. . . .'

So wrote Edward Gibbon in the ninth volume of the *Decline and Fall*. Modern critics, less hasty in judgement and turgid in declamation, pay tribute to Anna's high intelligence and good education. Runciman protests that modern historians are too ready to belittle her work; Ostrogorsky refers to the *Alexiad* as a 'historical source of first importance'; Vasiliev says it is 'extremely important from the historical point of view'; Krumbacher that her memoirs remain 'one of the most eminent works of medieval Greek historiography'[1]; Marshall that Anna is 'an outstanding figure among Byzantine historians'[2]; Hussey, more sympathetic, refers to her work as 'mature and markedly individual', the product of an unusually cultivated society. Now, nobody could deny that Anna was less than partial in the matter of her father, but there is a tendency

1. *Geschichte der byzantinishen Litteratur*, p. 276.
2. Baynes and Moss (eds.), *Byzantium*, p. 232.

now to acquit her of deliberate falsehood: her sins were sins of omission only – and the translator, who spends months, even years, in her company, has better opportunities than most of 'sensing' where she is failing to tell the whole truth; her discomfort is reflected in subtle changes of diction. She may not say that Alexius made a fool of himself in this or that situation, but one can feel the implication. Gibbon, no stranger himself to prejudice, censures her bias and treats her with scorn; maybe today's scholars are more understanding – their verdict is generally favourable, certainly not patronizing.

The *Alexiad* was not her only work. Like her father and her brother Isaac, she is said to have written poems; if it is true, they seem to have won no commendation. Some years ago Kurtz published the prologue to her Will, apparently written sometime during the interval between her father's and mother's death (1118–23).

Anna was born at dawn on a Saturday, 1 December in the seventh indiction (1083), the morning after her father 're-turned to the capital with the laurels of victory'. It was a happy moment for Alexius and Irene, disappointed though they must have been that the first-born was not a son. Anna was in fact the eldest of seven children (four daughters and three sons). Attempts have been made by some modern historians to prove that Alexius was unfaithful to his wife in these early years and seriously considered an alliance with the deposed Empress Maria – and there was some scandalous talk, which Anna quickly dismisses. But the family seems to have been remarkably united, at least while the children were young, except for one thing: Anna very soon grew to dislike her brother John. Her troubles began, she tells us, in her eighth year. She had been betrothed to Constantine Ducas, the Empress Maria's son and the rightful heir to the throne, and in the Byzantine way she had gone to live with her prospective mother-in-law. Constantine was treated with great generosity by Alexius and was allowed to share the privileges of an emperor; he was, of course, the junior partner, for at the time he must have been no more than a boy. Anna had every reason to hope that in due course she and young Constantine would follow Alexius and Irene on the throne. Whether Alexius never really intended the marriage to take place, or whether the feud between her grandmother, the formidable Anna Dalassena, and the Ducas family eventually made it impossible, we shall never know, but the engagement was broken off and Constantine's place as heir was taken by her brother John. The latter was then (1092) four or five years old, and from that moment Anna became his enemy. John was small, thin and dark-skinned – hardly a prepossessing child – but he was the emperor's eldest son. The Byzantines, who loved to give their rulers nicknames, called him Calo Johannes, 'Handsome John', and in later life, as a beloved emperor and virtuous father of his people, he retained the name. Anna says little about him in the *Alexiad*, but that little betrays her enmity, and when John did become emperor she instigated a rebellion against him; it failed, and she was sent into a comfortable exile, fortunate to escape a worse fate.

However, let us return to Constantine. The young man, no longer a public figure, retired to his estate in the country, where we find him entertaining Alexius; relations between them were still most friendly and we are told that he was loved by Alexius as his own son. The plot of Nicephorus Diogenes (1094), which was known to Constantine's mother although she took no active part in it, must have ended for ever any hopes of reinstatement. He died soon after, certainly before 1097. In that year Anna married 'her Caesar', Nicephorus Bryennius – against her wishes, if we are to believe the prologue to her Will, for she declares that she agreed to the ceremony only to please her parents: she would have preferred to live unwed. Maybe Alexius arranged it all as a political move: Bryennius was the son of his old rival.[3] Anyhow, the

3. While it is usual now to assume that the Caesar Nicephorus Bryennius (Anna's husband) was the grandson of the pretender, there is some doubt and I have followed Zonaras, who definitely states that he was a son. We know from the *History* of Michael Attaliates (Bekker, pp. 53–4) that another Bryennius rebelled in 1056 and was duly blinded; Zonaras, xviii, 2, confirms this fact, although he gives the date 1057. It may be that this man was the Caesar's grandfather; his father, Nicephorus Bryennius the elder, lost his eyes after the rebellion against Botaniates. See Anna's note

marriage proved to be happy enough; they had four children and lived together in harmony for forty years, until Bryennius contracted some illness on campaign with her hated brother and died in 1137 (he at least bore no grudge and served John faithfully). This husband of hers was a man of culture, a historian whose work is still extant and often studied for its valuable contribution to our knowledge of Botaniates' reign. If he was no great military commander (although clearly a brave one), he was a most persuasive and eloquent speaker: Alexius used his talents to win over Gregory Taronites, Bohemond and the Manichaean heretics (not always successfully, but obviously he had faith in Bryennius' oratory). His death and the loss of her parents finally embittered Anna: when she wrote the *Alexiad* (she was still engaged on the work in 1148) she was full of self-pity, a disappointed old woman. When she died we do not know.

Despite the underlying current of misery and her tendency to over-praise Alexius, the history makes good reading. Her narrative is vivid and, when the digressions are consigned to footnotes (as they are in this book, with the addition of 'A.C.'), fast-moving and interesting. Her character-sketches at their best are unforgettable (of Anna Dalassena, for example, or Bohemond, or Italus); nearly always they are shrewd and the princess clearly had a more than superficial acquaintance with human nature beyond the palace walls. She reminds us herself that she had led no cloistered existence. Of course she has her prejudices, like any historian worth his salt (only Polybius, I believe, was almost completely impartial – and nobody reads him from choice). She dislikes Armenians, loathes the Pope Gregory VII, is unfair to Mohammedans, despises the Latins in general and (somewhat reluctantly) Bohemond in particular. There is a curious love-hate in her account of him. She greatly admires physical beauty, but was not apparently much impressed by fine architecture. (In this

---

Bk X, n. 13. Buckler discusses the matter briefly (p. 33). Much depends on the interpretation of one Greek word which can mean either *descendant* or *son*.

she differs from Psellus, who delights in descriptions of magnificent buildings and their wonderful symmetry.)

She excels in her detailed accounts of machines or instruments, like the cross-bow and the various helepoleis[4] invented by allies or enemies. This was unusual in a woman, but Anna had a catholic education and was interested in science (in the narrow sense of the word). Like Psellus, she had studied medicine and was considered good enough to act as arbiter at the doctors' conference held when Alexius was on his death-bed. She knew something of astrology – enough to respect its most famous exponents; but she refused to accept the claim that the stars could in any way influence human destiny. Her religion was strictly orthodox and utterly sincere. Miracles, angels and demons are frequently mentioned, and quotations (not invariably accurate) from the Holy Scriptures are numerous; she alludes to certain superstitious beliefs, too, but mostly without comment. One has the impression that her Christian faith was based on reason and genuinely free of medieval superstition; her father, the 'thirteenth apostle', no doubt saw to it that his family eschewed all heresies. In this respect Anna is incredibly cruel; there is nothing charitable in her abhorrence of heretics. The gloating triumph in her account of Basil's death by burning is really horrible. To her the Bogomils are indeed devils incarnate.

Anna was well aware of the importance of her work. It was something more than a record of the Comnenian revival and the triumph of Byzantine arms; it vindicated the old *mores* before the rot set in. With the reign of Alexius there was a return to order and discipline, not only in the physical sense but also through the spiritual life of East Rome. At least that is how she saw it. In an age of cynicism and denigration it is perhaps no bad thing to be reminded that not all rulers are corrupt: Alexius was no plaster saint; he was cunning and 'versatile' (in the Odyssean fashion), at times harsh and uncompromising, a bit of a hypocrite, maybe, but essentially he was a good man with honourable intentions, certainly courageous and mindful of his duty to God and man. Anna's

4. See note 29, p. 94.

history has justly been described as 'the remarkable account of a remarkable man'.

But, of course, nothing in this world is perfect. Anna has her defects. Her geography is vague; there are difficulties in chronology, and in general she avoids precision in dates or even avoids them altogether; there are anomalies and contradictions (mostly in minor details); there are lacunae in the text, where she failed to give names (perhaps through forgetfulness, or lack of revision, or because, like Psellus, she prefers occasionally to tantalize the reader); her battle scenes are the least impressive passages in the history, and the famous *parataxis*, the emperor's new formation which so amazed Manalugh, seems to us nothing more than the ancient hollow square, or something so intricate as to be unworkable. There are many unanswered questions: Why did Maria adopt Alexius? How did a court eunuch prevent her remarriage and what were the timely words of wisdom he imparted to her? Why are we not told of Anna Dalassena's death? Who were the ungrateful persons Anna would dearly love to mention, but refrains from doing so? Who was the 'third cause' of the emperor's gout, the mysterious somebody who never left him? What was the true story of Alexius' last hours?

More than anything else in her writing, I suppose, the modern reader misses the evidence of a sense of humour. She derives a certain grim amusement from the predicament of Bohemond in his coffin; and the tiny Scyth leading in chains a gigantic Frank perhaps caused her to smile; but she completely lacks the light, subtle humour of Psellus and many other Byzantine writers. Tears came more easily to Anna than laughter.

Yet when all is said the *Alexiad* is eminently readable, a document more urbane, more vivid, more inspiring than any produced by her Latin contemporaries in the West.

Let her speak now for herself.

PREFACE

The stream of Time, irresistible, ever moving, carries off and bears away all things that come to birth and plunges them into utter darkness, both deeds of no account and deeds which are mighty and worthy of commemoration; as the playwright says, it 'brings to light that which was unseen and shrouds from us that which was manifest'[1]. Nevertheless, the science of History is a great bulwark against this stream of Time; in a way it checks this irresistible flood, it holds in a tight grasp whatever it can seize floating on the surface and will not allow it to slip away into the depths of Oblivion.

I, Anna, daughter of the Emperor Alexius and the Empress Irene, born and bred in the Purple,[2] not without some acquaintance with literature – having devoted the most earnest study to the Greek language, in fact, and being not unpractised in Rhetoric and having read thoroughly the treatises of Aristotle and the dialogues of Plato, and having fortified my mind with the Quadrivium of sciences[3] (these things must be divulged, and it is not self-advertisement to recall what Nature and my own zeal for knowledge have given me, nor what God has apportioned to me from above and what has been contributed by Opportunity); I, having realized the effects wrought by Time, desire now by means of my writings to give an account of my father's deeds, which do not deserve to be consigned to Forgetfulness nor to be swept away on the flood of Time into an ocean of Non-Remembrance; I wish to recall everything, the achievements before his elevation to the

1. Sophocles, *Ajax* 646.

2. The Purple (*porphyra*) was a room in the Palace set aside for the confinement of the ruling empress. Thus the children born there were called porphyrogeniti (more or less equivalent to prince or princess) (cf. p. 219).

3. The medieval curriculum comprised two parts: the *Trivium* (grammar, rhetoric and dialectic) and the *Quadrivium* (geometry, arithmetic, astronomy and music).

throne and his actions in the service of others before his coronation.

I approach the task with no intention of flaunting my skill as a writer; my concern is rather that a career so brilliant should not go unrecorded in the future, since even the greatest exploits, unless by some chance their memory is preserved and guarded in history, vanish in silent darkness. My father's actions themselves prove his ability as a ruler and show, too, that he was prepared to submit to authority, within just limits.

Now that I have decided to write the story of his life, I am fearful of an underlying suspicion: someone might conclude that in composing the history of my father I am glorifying myself; the history, wherever I express admiration for any act of his, may seem wholly false and mere panegyric. On the other hand, if he himself should ever lead me, under the compulsion of events, to criticize some action taken by him, not because of what he decided but because of the circumstances, here again I fear the cavillers: in their all-embracing jealousy and refusal to accept what is right, because they are malicious and full of envy, they may cast in my teeth the story of Noah's son Ham[4] and, as Homer says, 'blame the guiltless'.[5]

Whenever one assumes the role of historian, friendship and enmities have to be forgotten; often one has to bestow on adversaries the highest commendation (where their deeds merit it); often, too, one's nearest relatives, if their pursuits are in error and suggest the desirability of reproach, have to be censured. The historian, therefore, must shirk neither remonstrance with his friends, nor praise of his enemies. For my part, I hope to satisfy both parties, both those who are offended by us and those who accept us, by appealing to the evidence of the actual events and of eye-witnesses. The fathers and grandfathers of some men living today saw these things.

The main reason why I have to write the account of my father's deeds is this: I was the lawful wife of the Caesar

---

4. Genesis ix, 18–27.
5. *Odyssey* xx, 135 *et al.*

Nicephorus,[6] who was descended from the Bryennii, an extremely handsome man, very intelligent, and in the precise use of words far superior to his contemporaries. To see and hear him was indeed an extraordinary experience. For the moment, however, let us concentrate on what happened afterwards, lest the story should digress. My husband, the most outstanding man of the time, went on campaign with my brother, the Emperor John,[7] when he (John) led an army against other barbarians and also when he set out against the Syrians and again reduced the city of Antioch. Even in the midst of these wearing exertions the Caesar could not neglect his writing and, among other compositions worthy of honourable mention, he chose in particular to write the history of the Emperor Alexius, my father (on the orders of the empress), and to record the events of his reign in several books, when a brief lull in the warfare gave him the chance to turn his attention to historical and literary research. He did indeed begin the history – and in this, too, he yielded to the wishes of our empress – with references to the period before Alexius, starting with the Roman emperor Diogenes[8] and carrying it down to the times of his original subject. In Diogenes' reign my father was only a youth; he had done nothing worthy of note, unless childhood doings are also to be made the object of encomium.

The Caesar's plan was such as I have described; his writings make that clear. However, he was disappointed in his hopes and the history was not completed. After carrying on the account to the times of the Emperor Nicephorus Botaniates[9]

6. Eldest son of Nicephorus Bryennius, who was a rival claimant to the throne in the reigns of Michael VII and Botaniates. Anna was originally betrothed to Constantine Ducas, but after his premature death married Nicephorus in 1097.

7. Born 1088. Emperor from 1118 to 1143. Anna disliked him and her comments are unfair.

8. Romanus IV Diogenes (1068–71). Bryennius' four books cannot be compared with the *Alexiad*, but they are not without value.

9. Proclaimed emperor by the people in St Sophia on 7 January 1078 while he was still in Asia Minor. He was crowned in July and abdicated in March 1081.

he stopped writing because circumstances prevented any further progress, to the detriment of the history itself and the sorrow of its readers. That is why I have chosen to record the full story of my father's deeds myself, so that future generations may not be deprived of knowledge about them. Everyone who has encountered his literary work knows with what symmetry and grace the Caesar wrote, but having reached the point I have mentioned, he brought back to us from foreign parts his work half-finished and hastily put together, and also, I am sorry to say, an illness which was to prove fatal, caused by too much soldiering, excessive fatigue and inordinate concern for ourselves. He was by nature a worrier and a worker; he could not relax. The unpleasant changes of climate, too, contributed to his death. He was a very sick man, then, when he set out for the Syrian and Cilician wars; his health continued to fail in Syria; after Syria came Cilicia, Pamphylia, Lydia and Bithynia before he returned to us in the Queen of Cities. He was ill in all these countries, already suffering from an oedema, the result of so much fatigue. In this weak condition, although he wanted to give a graphic account of his adventures, he could not because of his illness; besides, we would not let him do it – the strain of talking might open up his wound.

At this point my mind is *distrait*; floods of tears fill my eyes when I think of Rome's great loss. His wisdom, his vast practical experience, gained over so wide a field, his knowledge of literature, the diverse learning acquired abroad and at our own Court – these were grievous losses. Charm suffused all his body and a majesty befitting not, as some say, a human throne, but something higher and more divine. My own lot has been far from fortunate in other ways, ever since I was wrapped in swaddling-clothes in the Porphyra, and I have not enjoyed good luck – although one would not deny that fortune did smile on me when I had as parents an emperor and an empress, and when I was born in the Porphyra. The rest was full of troubles, full of revolution. Orpheus with his song moved rocks and forests, even inanimate nature; Timotheus the flute-player by his Orthian strains[10] once stirred the Macedonian Alexander to take up the sword and arm himself without delay for battle; the story of my afflictions would move no one physically to arms or battle, though it would stir the reader to weep with me and wring sympathy from nature, animate and inanimate alike.

The Caesar's untimely death[11] and the suffering it brought about touched my heart deeply and the pain of it affected the innermost part of my being. The calamities of the past, in the face of this infinite disaster, I regard as a mere drop of rain compared with the whole Atlantic Ocean or the waves of the Adriatic Sea. They were, it seems, the prelude of these later woes, the warning smoke of this furnace-flame; the fierce heat was a herald of this unspeakable conflagration, the daily signal-fires of this awful funeral-pyre – a fire that lights up with torches the secret places and burns, but does not consume with burning; parching my heart imperceptibly, although its flames pierce to the bones and marrow and heart's centre.

But I see that I have been led astray by these thoughts from my subject; the Caesar stood over me and his sorrow provoked heavy sorrow in me too. I will wipe away the tears from my eyes, recover from my grief and continue my story, earning thereby a double share of tears, as the playwright says,[12] for one disaster recalls another. To put before the public the life-history of such an emperor reminds me of his supreme virtue, his marvellous qualities – and the hot tears fall again as I weep with all the world. When I remember him and make known the events of his reign, it is for me a theme of lamentation; the others will be reminded of their loss. However, this is where I must begin the history of my father, at the point where it is better to begin, where the narrative will become at once clearer and more accurate.

10. Timotheus came from Thebes. His performance of the Orthian Nome to Athena apparently had a violent effect on the young Alexander, but the story may be apocryphal; there were several men of this name. The Orthian Nome (or strain) was high-pitched and stirring, as familiar in ancient Greece as a national anthem is to us.

11. Bryennius died *c.* 1137 in Constantinople.

12. Euripides, *Hecuba*, 518.

MAPS

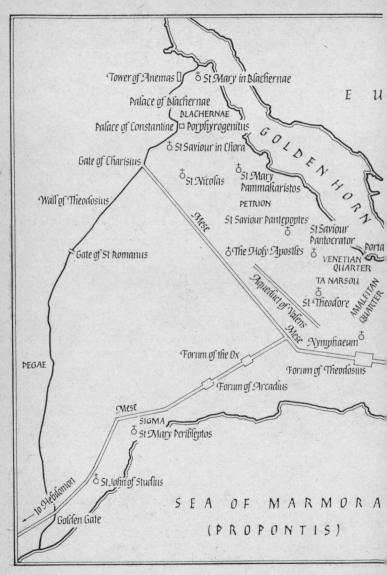

Tower of Anemas □   ♀ St Mary in Blachernae

Palace of Blachernae
BLACHERNAE
Palace of Constantine □ Porphyrogenitus

♀ St Saviour in Chora

Gate of Charisius

E   U

GOLDEN HORN

♀ St Nicolas   ♀ St Mary
Pammakaristos

PETRION

Wall of Theodosius

St Saviour Pantepoptes
♀

St Saviour
Pantocrator
♀   Porta

Mese

♀ The Holy Apostles

VENETIAN
QUARTER

TA NARSOU
♀
St Theodore

AMALFITAN
QUARTER

Gate of St Romanus

Aqueduct of Valens

Mese   Nymphaeum ♀

Forum of the Ox
Forum of Theodosius

PEGAE

Forum of Arcadius

Mese
SIGMA
♀ St Mary Peribleptos

to Hebdomon   ♀ St John of Studius

SEA   OF   MARMORA
(PROPONTIS)

Golden Gate

24

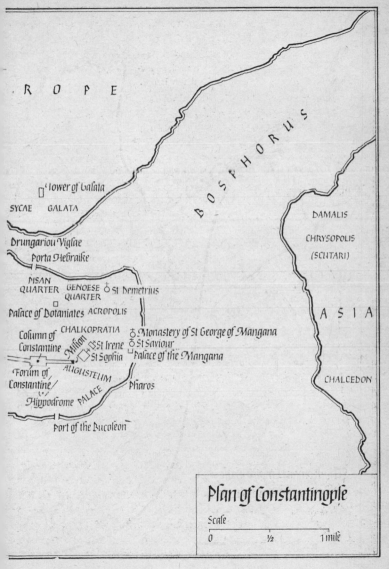

E U R O P E

Tower of Galata

SYCAE   GALATA

BOSPHORUS

DAMALIS

CHRYSOPOLIS

(SCUTARI)

Drungariou Viglae

Porta Hebraike

PISAN
QUARTER   GENOESE   St Demetrius
QUARTER

Palace of Botaniates   ACROPOLIS

Column of   CHALKOPRATIA
Constantine   Milion   St Irene
                St Sophia

ASIA

Monastery of St George of Mangana
St Saviour
Palace of the Mangana

Forum of   AUGUSTEUM
Constantine

Hippodrome   PALACE

Pharos

CHALCEDON

Port of the Bucoleon

Plan of Constantinople

Scale

0   ½   1 mile

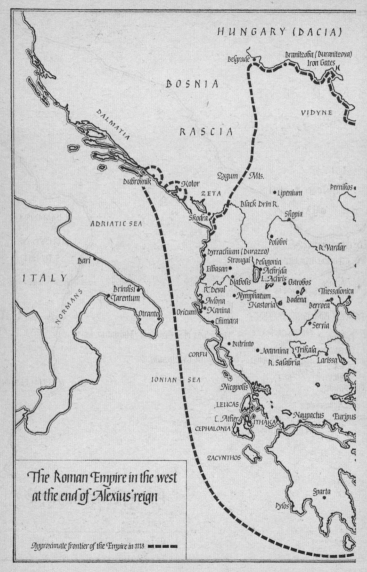

HUNGARY (DACIA)

Belgrade   Branitzoba (Duranitzova) Iron Gates

BOSNIA

DALMATIA

RASCIA

VIDYNE

Dubrovnik

Kotor

Zygum Mts.

ZETA

Lipenium

Pernikos

Black Drin R.

Skodra

Skopia

ADRIATIC SEA

Poloboi

R. Vardar

Dyrrachium (Durazzo)
Strougai

Pelagonia

Bari

Elbasan

Achrida

ITALY

Diabolis

L. Achris

Ostrobos

Thessalonica

R. Devol

Brindisi
Tarentum

Aylona

Nymphaeum

Kastoria

Bodena

Berroea

Oricum

Kanina

Otranto

Chimara

Servia

Butrinto

Joannina

Trikala

CORFU

R. Salabria

Larissa

IONIAN SEA

Nicopolis

LEUCAS

Naupactus

Euripus

L. Ather

ITHAKA

CEPHALONIA

ZACYNTHOS

The Roman Empire in the west at the end of Alexius' reign

Approximate frontier of the Empire in 1118 ▬ ▬ ▬

Sparta

Pylos

SCYTHS
PATZINAKS AND CUMANS

Peristhlaba

Danube R.   Dristra

Nicopolis   BLACK SEA

PARISTRION   Great Peristhlaba • Bitzina •
Balkan Mts. (HAEMUS)

BULGARIA   Mesembria
• Triaditza   Berroea   Anchialos

Beliatoba   Diampolis   Sozopolis

Philippopolis   R. Hebrus ('Euros)
              Blisnos   Agathopolis •
          Rhodope Mts.   Adrianople (Orestias)
                     Little Nicaea • Bulgarophygon
              Didymotichus   Tzouroulos • Selymbria
R. Strymon   Pamphilon   Rhaedestos •   Constantinople
• Serres Drama Comatine   Agora   Heraclea
       • Philippi   Mosynopolis   Cypsella   SEA OF MARMORA
              THASOS   Aenos • Koule Rousion
                                  Callipolis
                          CHERSONESE
              IMBROS

         LEMNOS   Hellespont

              AEGEAN SEA

EUBOEA
• Thebes
Athens

CYTHERA

27

The Roman Empire in the east
at the end of Alexius' reign

Approximate frontier of the Empire in 1118 ------

28

Singpe
Paurae
Trapezus
Kastamouni
PONTUS
CHALYBES
Paipert
Coloneia CHOROSAN →
PAPHLAGONIA
ARMENIAC THEME
Amasea
✗ Manzikert
R.Euphrates
R.Halys
Tebenna
ARMENIA
Sebasteia
SULTANATE OF
DANISHMENDS
Melitene
ICONIUM
(RUM)
L.Tatta
Caesarea
Mazacha Comana
Augustopolis
R.Saros
Samosata
Marash
Iconium (Konya)
Tyana
Heraclea
ROUPENIANS
Anazarbus R.Jihan
Edessa
Cilician Gates)(
Mamistra
Lampron
Adana
Harran
Taurus Mts.
Tarsos
CILICIA
R.Orontes
Seleuceia
R.Cydnus
Antioch
Chalep
St Symeon
Sycae
Laodicea
Kyrenia
LEBANON
Nicosia
Tripolis
CYPRUS
Citium
Byblos
SYRIA
Berytus
KINGDOM OF
JERUSALEM
Sidon
COELE-SYRIA

BOOK ONE

FROM THE BOYHOOD OF ALEXIUS
TO THE LAST MONTHS
OF BOTANIATES' REIGN

THE Emperor Alexius, my father, even before he seized the throne had been of great service to the Roman Empire. In fact, his military career began in the time of Diogenes Romanus, when he impressed the emperor's friends by his great courage. On that occasion, although he was only fourteen years old,[1] he wanted to serve on campaign under Diogenes, who was leading an expedition against the Persians[2] – a most important task – and this ambition of the young Alexius threatened the barbarians: he made it clear that one day he would come to grips with them, and when that happened his sword would have its fill of blood. Despite the youth's warlike fervour the emperor did not let him go on this campaign, because his mother had suffered a grievous loss. She was mourning the recent death of her eldest son Manuel, whose great and heroic deeds had made him famous in the Empire. In order that she might not be left comfortless, the young man was compelled to return to her. It was hard enough that the burial place of one son was still undecided; if another were sent off to the wars, she feared that he too might die before his time on some unknown battle-field. So he was left behind by his comrades against his will, but the future gradually opened up to him a fine opportunity for brave exploits. In the reign of Michael Ducas,[3] after the downfall of the Emperor

1. Romanus IV Diogenes set out on his expedition in 1070, which would mean that Alexius had been born in 1056. Zonaras tells us that he was seventy or thereabouts when he died in 1118 – which of course conflicts with Anna's date. Perhaps he *looked* about seventy when he died. (See Buckler, p. 264.)

2. The Turks. Romanus was campaigning against the Seljuqs, led by Alp Arslan, until his defeat and capture at Manzikert in 1071.

3. Michael VII Parapinaces (1071–8).

Diogenes, the Roussel episode proved how valiant he was. Roussel[4] was a Kelt and had previously joined the Roman army. His good fortune made him conceited and he gathered an army of his own, a considerable force made up partly of his own countrymen and partly of other nationalities. He was a formidable rebel. His attack on the Roman Empire was launched at a moment when its leadership had received many setbacks and the Turks had established their superiority. Roman prestige had fallen; the ground was giving way, as it were, beneath their feet. Roussel was in any case an extremely ambitious man, but at this crisis, when the condition of the Empire was so desperate, he was even more tempted to rebel openly. He plundered almost all the eastern provinces. The operations against him were entrusted to many generals renowned for bravery, men who had vast experience in battle as army commanders, but he was clearly master of these veterans. Sometimes he attacked in person, defeating his adversaries and falling upon them like a whirlwind; at other times, when he sought aid from the Turks, it became so impossible to withstand his onslaughts that he even took prisoner some of the greatest generals and routed their armies. My father was then serving under his brother[5] who had been put in command of all soldiers in both East and West; Alexius was in fact second-in-command. It was at this crucial moment in Roman affairs, when the barbarian was everywhere on the move, attacking with lightning speed, that the admirable Alexius was promoted to supreme command by the Emperor Michael. He was a worthy opponent for Roussel. He called on all his experience as a general and a soldier, all his wisdom (accumulated over a short period of time). Despite his youth – he had only recently shown evidence of the proverbial 'first beard' – he was even then considered by Roman experts to have attained the summit of the general's art, through devotion to sheer hard work and constant vigilance; to them he was another Aemilius, the

4. Roussel of Bailleul (called by Anna 'Urselius') was a Norman mercenary who proclaimed his own independence in Asia Minor in 1073.
5. Isaac Comnenus.

famous Roman,[6] or a Scipio,[7] or a second Carthaginian Hannibal. As Roussel was descending on our people like a flood in full spate, he was captured and within a few days the affairs of the East were settled. Alexius was quick to see the opportune course of action, even quicker in carrying it out. As to the manner in which Roussel was caught, that is described by the Caesar in his second book, but I will also give my account, as far as it concerns my own history.

Not long before, the barbarian Tutush had come down from the remoter parts of Anatolia to plunder Roman territory with a powerful army. Roussel, meanwhile, was being repeatedly hard-pressed by the Roman general and one after another his strongholds were falling, although he was at the head of a numerous force thoroughly equipped with fine and impressive weapons. My father completely outwitted him. To save himself Roussel decided to adopt a new policy, for he was now at the end of his resources. He met Tutush, made a friend of him and asked for an alliance. His scheme was thwarted by Alexius, who by cordial offers, backed persistently by arguments, gifts, and every device and stratagem, won Tutush over to our side. Nobody surpassed my father in ingenuity; under the most difficult circumstances he found ways and means. The most convincing point in the persuading of Tutush can be summarized as follows: 'Your sultan[8] and my emperor are friends. This barbarian Roussel prepares to attack both of them, and is indeed a fearful enemy of both. His incursions against the emperor are continually whittling away some part of his Roman domain, bit by bit. At the same time Persia is being deprived of all that she herself might win. His whole plan of campaign is carefully thought out: for the moment he is pursuing me with your help; later, when the time is propitious, he will leave me, thinking he is now free from danger, alter his tactics again and make war on you. My advice to you

6. There were many Aemilii. Anna is probably referring to L. Aemilius Paullus, who ended the Third Macedonian War at Pydna in 168 B.C.

7. P. Cornelius Scipio Africanus, victor of Zama (202 B.C.) and conqueror of Hannibal.

8. Malik-Shah.

is this: when he returns to you, seize him, for which we will pay you well, and send him to us in chains. You will profit from this in three ways: first, you will have more money than anyone else has ever received before; secondly, you will win the friendship of the emperor, thereby quickly attaining great prosperity; and thirdly, the sultan also will be delighted to see so formidable an enemy out of the way, an enemy who trained his men to fight both of us, Turks and Romans.' Such was the message sent to Tutush by my father, as commander-in-chief of the Roman army. At the same time he sent as hostages certain distinguished persons and persuaded Tutush's friends to seize Roussel on a predetermined day and for a set sum of money. Roussel was at once taken and sent to Amaseia to the Roman general. After that there was trouble. The money promised was slow in arriving and Alexius himself was unable to pay the full amount. The emperor took no interest in the affair. Far from coming 'with measured tread', as the tragic playwright[9] says, the money was nowhere to be seen at all. Tutush's men pressed for payment in full or the return of the captive who had been bought; he should be allowed to go back to the place where he had been seized. The agreed sum could not be paid, but Alexius, after spending the whole night in deep perplexity, decided to collect the money by contributions from the inhabitants of Amaseia. He knew it would be no easy matter. However, on the next morning he summoned the people, especially those in positions of authority and the richer folk. Fixing his eyes on the latter in particular, he made a speech. 'You all know,' he said, 'how this barbarian has treated all the cities of the Armenian province, how many townships he has ravaged, how many citizens he has cruelly subjected to intolerable persecution, how much money he has extorted from you. But now you have a chance to free yourselves from his evil deeds – if you wish. It is essential that he should not be allowed to go. As you see, he is our prisoner, thanks entirely to the Will of God and our zeal, but Tutush captured him and demands the reward from us. We are quite incapable of paying the money, being on foreign soil and hav-

9. Euripides.

34

ing already exhausted our capital on a long war against the barbarians. Of course, if the emperor were not so far away and if the Turk granted some respite, I would make haste to get the money from Constantinople, but as that is altogether out of the question (you know that yourselves) you will have to contribute the money, and the emperor will repay you in full on my promise.' Hardly had he ended this speech when the Amaseians broke into loud uproar. Openly defiant, they hissed him. The confusion was made worse by the criminal element and troublemakers expert in rabble-rousing. At any rate there was a tremendous hubbub, some wanting Roussel to be kept and urging the mob to lay hands on him, while others, in utter confusion (as is the way with the dregs of the people in a crowd), wanted to grab him and strike off his chains. Seeing the people in such a rabid mood, Alexius realized that his own position was extremely precarious. Nevertheless, he did not lose heart and bracing himself made a sign with his hand to enforce silence. After a long time and with much difficulty he stopped the uproar and addressed them. 'Men of Amaseia,' he said, 'I am amazed that you have so completely misunderstood the intrigues of these men who deceive you, buying their own safety at the cost of your blood and continually plotting your absolute ruin. What will you get out of Roussel's revolt, except massacres, blindings and mutilations? Yet the men who engineer such things for you, by courting the favour of the barbarian, made sure that their own welfare would not be affected. At the same time they were gorging themselves on the emperor's gifts and humoured him with assurances that they did not yield you, or the city, to the enemy. So far they have never given a thought to you. The reason why they want to help Roussel in his revolt, flattering him with high hopes, is that they may keep their own fortunes intact, *and* continue to beg for honours and gifts from the emperor. If their luck should somehow alter, they will withdraw from the business and stir up the emperor's anger against you. Take my advice. Tell the troublemakers to go to blazes. Now go home, every one of you, and consider what I have said. You will know who gave you the better advice.'

On hearing these words, as unaccountably as the way a potsherd falls this or that side up, they changed their minds and went home. Alexius was aware how on the slightest pretext the common folk will reverse a decision, especially when influenced by scoundrels, and he was afraid that agitators would harangue them during the night, attack him, lead Roussel from his prison and set him free. Resistance against such overwhelming numbers would be impossible. However, he devised a plan worthy of Palamedes himself.[10] He pretended to blind Roussel. The man was stretched out on the ground, the executioner brought the branding-iron near to his face, and Roussel howled and groaned; he was like a roaring lion. To all appearances he was being blinded. But in fact the apparent victim had been ordered to shout and bawl; the executioner who seemed to be gouging out his eyes was told to glare horribly at the prostrate Roussel and act like a raving madman – in other words, to simulate the punishment. So he was blinded, but not in reality, and the people clapped their hands and noisily spread the news all over the city that Roussel had lost his eyes. This bit of play-acting persuaded the whole mob, citizens and foreigners alike, to give money to the fund. They were busy as bees. The whole point of my father's stratagem was that those who were disinclined to contribute and were plotting to steal Roussel away from him might give up in despair when they were foiled; they might abandon their original plan for his and quickly become his allies. Thus the emperor's displeasure would be averted. With this in view he seized Roussel and kept him like a lion in a cage, still wearing bandages over his eyes as evidence of the supposed blinding.

Despite the glory already won, he was far from satisfied; other tasks still remained to be done. Many other cities and strongholds were subdued; those areas which had fared badly under Roussel's government were incorporated in the Empire. After that he turned his horse's head straight for the imperial city, but in his grandfather's town[11] there was a short rest from

10. Palamedes ('the crafty one') was traditionally the clever hero. He even outwitted Odysseus.

11. Kastamouni. The family came originally from Comne, near Hadrianople.

labour for himself and all his soldiers. It was here that he afterwards performed a feat worthy of the famous Hercules when he rescued Alcestis, the wife of Admetus. Doceianus, nephew of the former emperor Isaac Comnenus and cousin of Alexius, himself a man of distinction not only because of his lineage but also on account of his own worth, saw Roussel wearing the bandages, apparently blinded, and being led by the hand. He sighed deeply, shed tears and accused my father of cruelty. He even went so far as to rebuke him personally for having deprived a man so noble and a true hero of his sight; he shouted that Roussel should have been saved from punishment altogether. For the moment Alexius merely remarked, 'My dear fellow, you will soon hear the reasons for his blinding.' But not long afterwards he took him to a little room and there uncovered Roussel's head and disclosed his eyes, fiercely blazing. Doceianus was astonished at the sight; the miracle filled him with wonder and amazement. Again and again he put his hands on Roussel's eyes, to convince himself that it was not a dream or a magic trick or some other newly-invented manifestation of that sort. When he did learn of his cousin's humane treatment of the man and with his humanity his artifice, he was overcome with joy. He embraced and kissed Alexius repeatedly and his wonder turned to happiness. The members of the Court and the emperor were similarly affected; so was everybody else.

Later Alexius was sent back to the west by the Emperor Nicephorus, who was now at the head of affairs, to deal with Nicephorus Bryennius. The latter was throwing the whole of the West into confusion. He had already assumed the imperial crown and proclaimed himself emperor, although Botaniates had established himself on the throne immediately after the deposition of Michael Ducas,[12] and having won the hand of the Empress Maria[13] was governing the Empire. During Michael's reign Nicephorus Bryennius had been appointed

12. He had exchanged the diadem and cloak of an emperor for the alb and tunic of a high priest. (A.C.)

13. The story of this marriage will be told in greater detail as my history proceeds. (A.C.)

Duke of Dyrrachium and even before the accession of
Botaniates he had begun to play the part of an emperor and
planned revolt against Michael. Why and how this came about
it is unnecessary for us to explain: the Caesar's history has set
out the reason for the rebellion. But I must briefly explain –
this is most important – how he overran and subdued the
whole of the western provinces, using the city of Dyrrachium
as his operational base, and how he was captured. Those who
wish to learn the details of the revolt can refer to the Caesar's
account. Bryennius was a mighty warrior, one of the most
extraordinary men – tall, of noble lineage, very handsome,
dignified and thoughtful, physically strong – an outstanding
candidate for the imperial throne in that generation. So persuasive were his arguments and so great his ability to influence
all men, even at first sight and the beginning of their acquaintance, that everyone, both soldiers and civilians, united in
giving him precedence and judging him worthy of rule over
the whole Empire, East and West. In fact, all the cities received him at his coming with hands raised in supplication,
but sent him on his way from city to city with applause. This
worried Botaniates, threw his army into extreme confusion
and caused anxiety throughout the Empire. It was my father,
therefore, Alexius Comnenus, whom they decided to pit
against Bryennius. Alexius had recently been promoted
Domestic of the *Scholae*[14] and he had with him the available
military forces. The truth is that in this area the Empire was
reduced to its last men. Turkish infiltration had scattered the
eastern armies in all directions and the Turks were in almost
complete control of all the districts between the Black Sea and
the Hellespont, the Syrian and Aegean waters, the Saros and
the other rivers, in particular those which flow along the
borders of Pamphylia and Cilicia and empty themselves into
the Egyptian Sea. So much for the eastern armies; those in the
west joined Bryennius and left the Roman Empire with quite
small and insignificant forces. Some 'Immortals'[15] were left to

14. See Glossary on (*Domestic*).
15. A corps recruited by Michael VII to fight the Turks. The name was
no doubt inspired by Greek and Persian 'Immortals' of pre-Roman times.

fight for it, but they had only touched sword and spear a short time before. There were also a few soldiers from Choma[16] and a Keltic regiment which was far below strength. At any rate, these were the men whom they gave to my father and at the same time they (the emperor's advisers) called on the Turks to supply help. He was then ordered to set out for a campaign against Bryennius. They had less confidence in the army than in the general's own intelligence and his strategic and tactical skill. Alexius did not await the arrival of reinforcements, but hearing that the enemy was advancing rapidly at once armed himself and his followers, left the capital and in Thrace near the River Halmyros pitched camp without ditches or rampart. He discovered that Bryennius was bivouacking on the plains of Kedoktos and he wanted to keep the two armies, his own and the enemy's, a considerable distance apart, for to attack Bryennius head-on was impossible: the state of his own forces and their inferiority in numbers might become known. He would have to fight with a handful of inexperienced soldiers against a large force of seasoned veterans. Thus he gave up the idea of a bold, open attack, and planned a victory by stealth.

Now that the history has brought these men, Bryennius and my father Alexius Comnenus, both heroic men, to the point of battle, it is worthwhile to arrange them in their opposing battle-lines and then to examine the fortunes of the war. Neither was inferior to the other in bravery, nor was one surpassed by the other in experience. Certainly they were both handsome and brave, in skill and physical strength equally balanced as on a scale. Our task is to see how fortune inclined to one side. Bryennius, confident in his soldiers, relied on his own knowledge and the good discipline of his army, whereas on the other side Alexius had small hopes, and very thin hopes, so far as his own forces were concerned, but in reply put his trust in the strength of his own ingenuity and in his art as a general. When they had made contact and determined that now was the time for battle, Bryennius, who had learnt that Alexius, encamped near Kalaura, was intercepting his own line of march, moved to the attack with the following forma-

16. Not far from Laodicea ad Lycum in Phrygia.

tion. His army was drawn up on right and left: his brother
John[17] was in command of the right, where there were 5,000
men in all, Italians and members of the detachment of the
famous Maniaces,[18] as well as horsemen from Thessaly and a
contingent, by no means despicable, from the Hetaireia.[19] On
the other wing, the left, Tarchaniotis Catacalon was in command of Macedonians and Thracians, well armed and number-
ing altogether 3,000. Bryennius personally commanded the
centre of the line, where Macedonians and Thracians were posted
with the élite of all the nobles. All the Thessalians were mounted
on horseback; with their breastplates of iron and the helmets on
their heads they flashed like lightning. Their horses alert with
pricked-up ears, their shields clashing one on another, the
brilliant gleam of their armour and their helmets struck terror
into the enemy. Bryennius, circling round in their midst like
some Ares[20] or a Giant standing out head and shoulders above
all others, taller by a cubit, was in truth an object of wonder
and dread to those who saw him. Apart from the main body,
about two stades[21] distant, were some Scythian allies equipped
with barbaric weapons. They had been ordered to fall upon
the rear as soon as the enemy appeared and the trumpet
sounded the charge; they were to shoot at them and harass
them ceaselessly with showers of arrows, while the others in
close order, shield to shield, were to attack the strongest part
of their line. So much for Bryennius' formation. His adversary, after inspecting the lie of the land, stationed one part of
his army in some ravines, and the rest facing Bryennius' line.
When both the men hiding and the visible contingent had
been duly arranged, Alexius addressed his soldiers, individually inciting them to deeds of bravery. The section already
lying in ambush he ordered to fall upon the unsuspecting
enemy as soon as they found themselves in their rear; they

17. Like Alexius, he was a Domestic of the *Scholae*.
18. Maniaces had made a great name for himself as a general in the first
half of the century. No doubt these men had been enrolled by him. For
the career of George Maniaces see *Fourteen Byzantine Rulers*, Appendix III.
19. The personal bodyguard of the emperor, composed of foreigners.
(*Hetairos* is Greek for 'comrade'.)
20. Greek god of war (Mars).   21. See Glossary.

were to dash against their right wing with the maximum violence and energy. He kept for himself the so-called 'Immortals' and some of the Kelts; these he commanded in person. Catacalon was put in charge of the men from Choma and the Turks; he was to be responsible for the general surveillance of the Scyths and the repulse of their forays.

So much for the disposition of Alexius' army. Now for the battle. When Bryennius' men reached the ravines, my father immediately gave the signal and the party in ambush leapt upon the enemy with loud war-cries, each man striking and killing any who happened to come in his path. The suddenness of this attack terrified the others and they were thrown into flight. John Bryennius, the general's brother, however, 'mindful of his furious might'[22] and still courageous, turned his horse's bridle and with one blow struck down the 'Immortal' who came at him. Thereupon the breaking line was restored and discipline returned: the ambushers were driven off. The 'Immortals' in some disorder began to flee headlong, losing men at the hands of their relentless pursuers. My father hurled himself into the midst of the foe and fighting nobly spread havoc wherever he went, striking and at once cutting down all who opposed him. He hoped that some of his men were following and protecting him, and he continued to fight with unrestrained fury. But when he saw that his army was by now utterly defeated and scattered in many directions, he gathered together the more courageous men, six in number, and told them to draw sword and when they got near Bryennius to make a violent assault on him; if necessary they should die with him. This plan was thwarted by a common soldier, Theodotos, who had served my father from boyhood; he said that the enterprise was foolhardy. Alexius was persuaded, and adopted the contrary plan: he decided to retire a little way from the enemy, collect some men who were known to him from the scattered army, reorganize them and again plunge into the fray. However, before he could disengage from the enemy, the Scyths with much shouting and yelling began to harass Catacalon and his Chomatenians. They drove them

22. A common expression in Homer.

41

back and put them to flight without any difficulty, and then turned to plunder, following the national custom of the Scyths: before they are absolutely sure of the enemy's defeat and before consolidating their own advantage, they ruin their victories by carrying off the loot. Now all the camp-followers, fearing they might suffer some damage from these Scyths, caught up with the rear of Bryennius' army and mingled with the soldiers, and as others constantly joined them (having escaped the Scythian bands) they caused no little confusion in the ranks and the standards were thrown into chaos. Meanwhile, my father was cut off, as we have said above, and as he darted here and there in the enemy's ranks he saw one of the grooms dragging away a horse from the imperial stables. It was decked out with the purple-dyed saddle-cloth and had discs plated with gold; the men running beside it, too, had in their hands the great iron swords[23] which normally accompany the emperors. Seeing all this Alexius covered his face, drawing down the vizor fastened to the rim of his helmet, and with the six men I spoke of before rushed violently against them. He knocked down the groom, caught the emperor's horse and took it away together with the great swords. Then he slipped away unnoticed from the enemy. Once he reached a safe place he sent off the horse with its gold-plated bosses, and the swords brandished to the right and left of emperors. He also sent a herald, who was to run through all the army and in a stentorian voice proclaim that Bryennius had fallen. The announcement brought together crowds of hitherto scattered men (soldiers of the Great Domestic of the *Scholae*, i.e. my father). They came from all directions and marched back to their general. The news also encouraged the others (who had not fled) to stand their ground. Wherever they happened to be they stood motionless, looking back to the rear and amazed beyond all belief by what they saw. It was indeed an extra-ordinary sight: the horses on which they rode were gazing to the front, but the faces of the riders turned backwards; they neither advanced nor had they any intention of wheeling about, but just stopped, dumbfounded and utterly unable to

23. The famous *rhomphaia*.

understand what had happened. The Scyths thought of home and were already on their way; they had no further interest in pursuit, but far off from both armies wandered around at random with their booty. The proclamation of Bryennius' capture and downfall put courage into the hearts of those who only a little while before had been cowards and fugitives; moreover, the general display of the royal horse with its insignia and the sight of the great swords (which all but spoke for themselves) convinced them that the news was true: Bryennius, who was guarded by these swords, had fallen into the hands of his enemies.

Chance then took a hand in the proceedings. A detachment of Turkish allies found Alexius, the Great Domestic, and having learnt how the battle stood, they asked where the enemy had gone. Then with Alexius they climbed a little hill and when he pointed it out to them they saw Bryennius' army. They looked down on it as if from a watch-tower and the situation below seemed to be as follows: his men had not yet re-formed rank; they were disordered, apparently believing the victory was already won, and so, contemptuous of their adversaries, they thought the danger was past. The fact that my father's contingent of Franks had gone over to them after the first rout was the main reason for this attitude. The Franks had dismounted from their horses and given them their right hands (their way of pledging faith). Thereupon a crowd gathered from all directions to see what was going on, for a rumour spread through the army that the Franks had abandoned their supreme commander Alexius and actually joined Bryennius. My father and his men saw them in this state of confusion; they also took into consideration the Turks who had recently come up to them and decided to split up their combined forces into three groups: two were to stay in ambush somewhere near the hill, the third was ordered to advance against the enemy. My father was responsible for the whole idea. The Turks attacked not in one body drawn up in regular formation, but in separate units at some distance from each other. Alexius gave the signal for each unit to attack on horseback and fire thick volleys of arrows. He himself, the

deviser of the whole stratagem, followed immediately behind
them with as many soldiers collected from his scattered forces
as the circumstances demanded. At this point one of the
'Immortals' serving under him, a hot-headed, reckless fellow,
spurred on his horse in front of the rest and slackening rein
charged straight for Bryennius. He thrust his spear very hard
at Bryennius' chest, but he, drawing his sword quickly,
before the spear could be driven home cut it off above the
point, struck his attacker by the collar-bone, and as he bore
down with all his might severed his whole arm, cutting right
through his breastplate. Meanwhile the Turks riding up one
after the other covered the enemy with showers of arrows.
Bryennius' men were overwhelmed by the unexpectedness of
this onslaught; nevertheless they recovered and re-formed
ranks. Calling upon one another to endure like men they bore
the shock of the attack. The Turks, however, and my father,
after holding their ground for a little while against the enemy,
pretended to make an orderly withdrawal, gradually luring
them and cunningly drawing them into the ambush. When
they reached the first place where their men were hidden, they
wheeled about and faced them. At a given signal, from many
directions the ambushers suddenly rode out through Alexius'
men, like swarms of wasps, attacking with loud war-cries and
yelling and ceaseless volleys of arrows. The enemies' ears were
deafened, their eyes blinded by the streams of darts falling upon
them from all sides. Then, as they could not withstand them,
Bryennius' army (for by now all had been wounded, horses
and men) turned their standard back and retreated, allowing
their opponents to strike them from the rear. Even then
Bryennius showed his bravery and high spirit, hard-pressed
though he was by the battle, and he pushed on by main force.
At one moment he would turn about and strike some assailant,
at the next he would be supervising the retreat with courage
and presence of mind. On either side of him were his brother
and his son,[24] helping in the battle and in the crisis provoking

24. Nicephorus Bryennius, the future husband of Anna Comnena. It is
interesting to compare his account of this battle with the rather dramatic
story we have here.

the admiration of the foe by their heroic resistance. But when his horse grew weary, unable either to flee or even pursue (for it was almost at its last gasp through constant chargings) Bryennius reined it in, and like some noble athlete stood ready for combat, challenging two high-born Turks to fight. One struck at him with his spear, but was not fast enough to give a heavy blow; instead he received a heavier one from Bryennius's right arm, which, too quick for him, cut off his hand with his sword, and hand and spear rolled to the ground. The other Turk leapt down from his horse and panther-like jumped on to Bryennius' mount, fastening himself on its flank, and there he clung desperately, trying to climb on its back. Bryennius like a wild beast kept twisting round and tried to stab him off with his sword, but without success, for the Turk behind him kept swaying to avoid the blows. Eventually his right arm tired of striking at empty air and himself worn out with fighting, Bryennius surrendered to the main body of the enemy. They seized him and like men who have won great glory took him off to Alexius. The latter was standing not far away from the place where Bryennius was taken and was at the time marshalling the Turks and his own men, encouraging them to fight. News of the capture had arrived earlier through messengers; now Bryennius was set before the general in person, a really formidable sight, whether fighting or a prisoner. Such was the manner of his downfall. Alexius sent him as a prize of war to the Emperor Botaniates, and no attempt whatever was made to injure his eyes by Alexius. It was contrary to his nature to inflict injury on those who had fought against him, once they had surrendered; he thought capture was punishment enough for an enemy. He treated them with humanity, with acts of kindness, with munificence; in the case of Bryennius the same clemency was shown. After his capture Alexius accompanied him for some distance and when he reached the place called . . .,[25] wishing to comfort the man in his sorrow and inspire him with fair hopes for the future, he said to him, 'Let us dismount and sit down for a little rest.'

25. It appears that Anna intended to give the name, but either forgot or never revised the text. At any rate, there is a lacuna at this point.

Bryennius feared for his life; he seemed to be out of his mind and certainly in no need of leisure. How could he be when already he despaired of his very life? However, he fell in with the general's suggestion without delay – a slave readily yields to every command, even more so if he happens to be a prisoner-of-war. Well, the two leaders dismounted. Alexius immediately lay down on some green grass as though it were a couch, but Bryennius kept apart, propping his head against the root of 'a high-leafed oak'.[26] The former fell asleep but 'sweet sleep'[27] (as the charming poet calls it) did not visit Bryennius. Lifting his eyes, however, and noticing Alexius' sword hanging from the branches, as he spied no one anywhere present, he recovered from his despondency and became more composed; he would kill my father. And maybe the plan would have come off, had not some divine power from above prevented it, calming the man's savage wrath and compelling him to turn a benevolent eye on the general. I have often heard Alexius tell this story. Anyone who likes can indeed learn from it how God was reserving Comnenus, like some precious object, for a greater destiny, wishing through him to revive Roman power. Whatever unpleasing fate befell Bryennius after that must be attributed to certain people at Court; my father was blameless.

Thus ended the revolt of Bryennius. But the Great Domestic was not to rest: one struggle followed another, for Borilos, a barbarian and a great friend of Botaniates, coming from the city and meeting Alexius took over Bryennius from him and did what he did.[28] He also brought an order from the emperor to proceed against Basilacius, who had already crowned himself emperor and was triumphantly stirring up trouble in the west, like Bryennius before him. Now this Basilacius was much admired for his courageous and daring spirit as well as his great physical strength. The man was, besides, a masterful person, arrogating to himself the high offices of state; some titles he coveted, others he usurped. When Bryennius was

26. Homer, *Iliad* xiv, 398.
27. Homer, *passim*.
28. Bryennius was blinded.

removed he became leader of the whole revolutionary movement as Bryennius' successor. He started from Epidamnos
(the capital of Illyria) and came as far as the chief city of
Thessaly, crushing all opposition on the way and having himself elected and proclaimed emperor. Bryennius' wandering
forces he transported wherever he wished. The man's other
fine qualities were supplemented by an impressive physique,
great strength and a majestic presence – all of which exercise
an unusual fascination on country folk and the military class.
They do not see beyond them to a man's soul, nor do they
regard his virtue, but stand in awe only of his physical excel-
lence, his daring, his virility, his speed of running, his size, and
these they judge to be worthy of the purple robe and the
crown. Well, he had these qualities in abundance, and he had
a brave and invincible spirit; in short, there was a kingly aura
about this man Basilacius. He looked the part. With a voice
like thunder he could strike terror into a whole army and his
shout was enough to humble the boldest heart. In argument
irrefutable, he was expert alike at stirring his men to battle or
covering them in flight. Such were the natural advantages
with which he took the field and with an invincible army
occupied the city of the Thessalians, as we have said. As for
my father, he had made counter-preparations as if for a contest against a huge Typhon[29] or a hundred-handed Giant,
summoning to his aid all his general's art and courageous
spirit; he was ready to fight a worthy opponent. The dust of
former combats had not yet been shaken off, his hands and
sword not yet wiped clean of blood, when like a terrible lion
he went forth with high hopes to do battle with this long-
tusked boar, Basilacius. He arrived then at the River Vardar, as
the natives call it, which flows down from the mountains near
Mysia, and after passing by many places on its way divides the
districts round Berroea and Thessalonica in two, the eastern
and western, and finally empties itself into our Southern Sea.
It is the case with all the greatest rivers that when a pretty

29. Typhon (or Typhoeus) was a legendary monster who fought even
with Zeus. He had a hundred heads and many hands and feet (presumably
a hundred).

considerable level of earth has been built up in the form of
a deposit, they flow on to low-lying ground as if deserting
their first beds and leave the old course empty of water and
dry; the new bed they fill with abundant streams. Between the
two channels of the River Vardar, the old ravine and the
newly-formed course, Alexius, that master of strategy, saw a
piece of ground and there pitched his camp. The present
channel he thought would protect him on one side, the old
course (not more than two or three stades distant), which had
by then become a deep chasm through the action of the water,
he used as a natural trench. The whole army was at once
ordered to rest by day, to refresh themselves with sleep, and to
give the horses sufficient fodder. They were told that when
evening came they would have to be awake and ready for a
surprise attack from the enemy. These arrangements were
made, I suppose, because my father suspected danger that
evening; he thought that they would attack, either forewarned by long experience, or guessing for some other reason.
The presentiment came to him and no time was wasted in
taking the necessary action. He led his army from the camp,
fully armed, with horses and all supplies required for battle. In
the camp lights were left burning everywhere and a former
monk, now one of his servants, was put in charge of his tent
with all his mess equipment and other baggage. His name was
'Little John'. Alexius himself after going away a good distance
sat down with his soldiers ready and armed, to wait for what
would happen next. His idea was that Basilacius, finding camp-
fires lit everywhere and my father's tent bright with lamps,
would think he was there having a rest and thus in his power,
an easy prey.

Alexius' prophecy was not unjustified, for Basilacius made
his assault on the camp, as expected. It came suddenly, with
cavalry and infantry to the number of 10,000 in all. The
soldiers' living-quarters he found all lit up, but when he saw
the general's tent blazing with light, he hurled himself into it
with blood-curdling, terrible cries. But when the man he
expected to see was nowhere to be found, and no soldier, no
general at all started up from it, nobody in fact except a few

disreputable servants who had been left behind, he shouted
and bawled even louder, 'Where the hell is the lisper?' That
was his way of mocking the Great Domestic, for although my
father was in other respects a fine speaker and natural orator
who surpassed all rivals in the setting out of proofs and arguments, yet in the matter of the 'r' sound only there was a
slight stammer and his tongue would lisp almost imperceptibly; and yet he pronounced all the other letters without
hesitation. So Basilacius roared his abuse and in his thorough
search turned everything upside down, chests, camp beds,
furniture, and even my father's own couch, lest perchance the
general might be hiding in any of them. From time to time he
fixed his gaze on the monk called 'Little John'; Alexius'
mother had taken pains to insist that on all his expeditions he
should have as tent-companion one of the more highly
esteemed monks, and her dutiful son submitted to her wishes,
not merely in his baby days, but when he was a candidate for
admission to the ranks of the young men – and indeed until he
married. Basilacius made a complete search in the tent and
never relaxed his 'fumbling about in nether darkness',[30] as
Aristophanes says. At the same time he questioned 'Little
John' about his master. The monk persisted in his story:
Alexius had left the camp with all his army some time before.
Basilacius realized that he had been much deceived. In his
utter wretchedness, he changed the tone of his language,
shouting, 'Comrades, we've been cheated. The enemy is outside.' The words were not yet out of his mouth before my
father came upon them as they were leaving the camp. He
had ridden on ahead of his army at full gallop with a few companions. When he saw someone restoring the ranks to some
discipline (for the majority of Basilacius' men had given themselves up to looting and pillage, which was what my father had
planned long before) and while the line was still unready and
the men not marshalled for battle, he came upon them suddenly, a terrible threat. The man arranging their regiments he
thought was Basilacius himself, either because of his size or
because of the brightness of his armour, which reflected the

30. *Clouds*, 192.

light of the stars, and with a quick onset struck at his hand. The hand, together with the sword in it, was at once hurled to the ground – an incident which greatly dismayed the enemy. However, the person concerned was not Basilacius, but one of his retinue, a very brave man and as far as courage goes in no way inferior to him. After that Alexius continued his whirling onslaught, shooting at them with arrows, wounding them with his spear, roaring out his battle-cries, confusing them in the darkness, summoning to his aid everything – time, place, weapon – to achieve victory, and good use he made of them, with undaunted spirit and indomitable resolve. Never did he fail to distinguish friend or foe as he waylaid men flying in all directions. There was a Cappadocian, one Goules, a faithful servant of my father, a tough intrepid fighter, who saw Basilacius and making sure it was he aimed a blow at his helmet. Unfortunately his sword, 'thrice and four times shattered',[31] fell from his hand and only the hilt remained (like Menelaus' when he fought Alexander). The general saw him and straightway mocked him because he had no sword; he called him a coward, but was somewhat mollified when Goules showed him the hilt left in his hand. Another man, a Macedonian called Petros, with the surname Tornicius, fell upon the enemy's centre and slaughtered many. The army in fact was following Alexius blindly, not knowing what was really going on, for the battle started in darkness and not all were able to see its progress. Comnenus made for that part of the line which was not yet in disorder and struck at his opponents; then back he would come to his own men, urging them to break up the still coherent remnants of Basilacius' army. He sent messages to the rear, ordering them not to delay, but to follow him and catch up more quickly. While this was going on, a Kelt, one of Alexius' guards (a brave soldier full of martial zeal) saw my father just emerging from the enemy's centre with drawn sword still reeking with hot blood, and thought he was one of them. He attacked at once, striking his chest with his spear, and if the general had not seated himself more firmly in his saddle and called him by

31. Homer, *Iliad* iii, 363.

name, threatening to cut off his head with his sword there and
then, he might have been thrown from his horse. Anyway the
Kelt, when he had made some sort of excuse (inability to
recognize in the darkness and confusion of battle), was still
numbered among the living.

Such were the exploits of the Great Domestic of the *Scholae*
with a handful of soldiers during that night. Just after smiling
dawn broke and the sun peeped over the horizon Basilacius'
officers turned their whole attention to rounding up the men
who had left the battle and were busy collecting booty. Alexius
put his own army in order and then renewed his attack. Seeing
some of the enemy from afar his soldiers charged out violently
against them. They routed them and returned with some live
prisoners. Basilacius' brother Manuel climbed a small hill and
encouraged his army crying loudly that 'Today is Basilacius'
victory-day!' Whereupon a certain Basileios, surnamed
Curticius, an acquaintance and confidant of the Nicephorus
Bryennius already mentioned in my history, and an indomitable fighter, ran forward from Comnenus' battle-line and up
to the hillock. Manuel drew his sword and at full gallop rushed
at him furiously. Curticius, instead of using his sword,
snatched at the club suspended from his saddle-cloth and hit
him with it on the head, knocked him down from his horse
and dragged him back to my father a prisoner as if he were
part of the booty. While this was happening what remained of
Basilacius' army saw that Comnenus had appeared with his
own regiments, and after a brief resistance took to their heels
in flight. Basilacius fled with the rest; Alexius pursued him.
When they reached Thessalonica the townspeople immediately
received Basilacius but barred the gates to his adversary. Even
so my father did not relax: far from taking off his breastplate,
or removing his helmet, or undoing the buckler from his
shoulders, or laying aside his sword, he actually pitched camp
and warned them that he would attack their walls and completely ravage the town. Nevertheless he was anxious to spare
Basilacius and to ensure this made proposals for peace through
his companion, the monk 'Little John', who had a good
reputation for integrity. If Basilacius surrendered both him-

self and the town, he would suffer no ill-treatment. This
Alexius promised him, but the other was obdurate. However,
as the men of Thessalonica were afraid that the town would
be taken and something terrible would happen to it, they
allowed Comnenus to enter. Basilacius, seeing what they were
doing, went off to the Acropolis—'from the frying-pan into
the fire'. Although the Domestic gave his word that he would
suffer no irremediable ill, Basilacius still refused to forget
fighting and war; despite the dangers, hard-pressed though
he was, he showed himself to be a true hero. Unflinching,
always courageous, he would not yield an inch, until the
inhabitants of the citadel and the guards drove him out by
force and handed him over to Alexius. Without delay the
emperor was informed of the capture. Alexius himself stayed
on in Thessalonica for a while and settled affairs there before
he returned to the capital in triumph. Between Philippi and
Amphipolis messengers from the emperor met him with
written instructions about Basilacius, which they put in his
hands. They took Basilacius as their charge, led him away
to some place called Chlempina and near the spring of
water there put out his eyes. Ever since then to this day it
has been called 'the spring of Basilacius'. Such was the third
'labour' borne by Alexius before he became emperor, like
a second Hercules; for if you equated this Basilacius with the
Erymanthian Boar,[32] and my father with a modern and
most noble Hercules, you would not be wrong. So much
then for his successes and achievements; as reward for
them all he received from the emperor the honourable title
sebastos and was proclaimed as such by the Senate in full
assembly.

The infirmities of the body, it seems to me, are sometimes
aggravated by external causes, but there are also occasions
when the reasons for sickness emanate from the organs themselves; often we blame the vagaries of climate and certain
qualities of food for the onset of fevers, even sometimes
putrid humours. In the same way the bad condition of the
Roman state at that time produced mortal plagues – the afore-

32. The third of the twelve legendary 'labours'.

mentioned men, I mean, the like of Roussel and Basilacius
and all who filled the ranks of pretenders. Sometimes, though,
it was Fate which introduced into it from outside certain
foreign pretenders – an evil hard to combat, an incurable
disease. One such was that braggart Robert,[33] notorious for
his power-lust, born in Normandy, but nursed and nourished
by manifold Evil. This was the man whose enmity the Roman
Empire drew upon itself when it gave a pretext to our foes for
the wars he waged – a marriage with a foreigner and a barbarian, from our point of view quite inexpedient.[34] To be
more accurate, one should blame the imprudence of the
emperor then reigning, who linked our family with that of the
Ducas. Now if I should find fault with any one of my own
blood-relations (for I too on my mother's side am related to
the Ducas), let nobody be angry. I have chosen to write the
truth above all and as far as this man is concerned I have toned
down the universal condemnation of him. This particular
emperor, Michael Ducas, promised his own son Constantine
in marriage to the daughter of this barbarian Robert, and from
that sprang their hostile acts. About Constantine, the terms of
his marriage contract and the foreign alliance in general, his
handsome appearance and stature, his physical and moral
qualities, we shall speak in due course, when I relate the sorry
tale of my own misfortunes. Before that I will give an account
of this proposed wedding, the defeat of the whole barbarian
force and the destruction of these pretenders from Normandy
– pretenders whom Michael in his folly raised up against the
Roman Empire. But first I must carry my story back somewhat and describe this man Robert, his lineage and fortune; I
must show to what heights of power the force of circumstances raised him, or rather, to speak more reverently, how

33. Robert Guiscard, 'the Weasel', Duke of Apulia and Calabria, son
of Tancred.
34. Michael VII suggested that Helena, Robert's daughter, should
marry his infant son Constantine – an attempt to placate the Normans, who
had crowned a series of campaigns in Southern Italy by the capture of
Bari (1071), the last remnant of the Byzantine Empire in that area. Even
Psellus finds it hard to defend the weak, ineffective policy of his favourite
pupil Michael.

far Providence allowed him to advance, indulging his ill-natured ambitions and schemings.

This Robert was a Norman by birth, of obscure origin, with an overbearing character and a thoroughly villainous mind; he was a brave fighter, very cunning in his assaults on the wealth and power of great men; in achieving his aims absolutely inexorable, diverting criticism by incontrovertible argument. He was a man of immense stature, surpassing even the biggest men; he had a ruddy complexion, fair hair, broad shoulders, eyes that all but shot out sparks of fire. In a well-built man one looks for breadth here and slimness there; in him all was admirably well-proportioned and elegant. Thus from head to foot the man was graceful (I have often heard from many witnesses that this was so). Homer remarked of Achilles that when he shouted his hearers had the impression of a multitude in uproar, but Robert's bellow, so they say, put tens of thousands to flight. With such endowments of fortune and nature and soul, he was, as you would expect, no man's slave, owing obedience to nobody in all the world. Such are men of powerful character, people say, even if they are of humbler origin.

Robert then, being a man of such character, wholly incapable of being led, set out from Normandy with some knights; there were five of them and thirty foot-soldiers in all. After leaving his native land, he spent his time amid the mountain peaks and caves and hills of Lombardy, at the head of a band of pirates, attacking wayfarers. Sometimes he acquired horses, sometimes other possessions and arms. The start of his career was marked by bloodshed and many murders. While he loitered in the districts of Lombardy, he did not escape the notice of Gulielmus Mascabeles, who at that time happened to be ruler of most of the territory adjacent to Lombardy. From it he derived a rich income every year, and as he also recruited adequate forces from the same area he was a powerful autocrat. Having learnt what kind of man Robert was, from a moral as well as a physical point of view, he unwisely attached the man to himself and betrothed one of his daughters to him. The marriage was celebrated and

Gulielmus admired his son-in-law for his strength and military prowess, but things did not prosper for him as he had hoped. He had already given him a city as something of a wedding present and had shown certain other signs of friendship. Robert, however, became obnoxious and plotted rebellion. At first he pretended to be well-disposed while he built up his strength, trebling his cavalry and increasing his infantry two-fold. From then on the acts of kindness gradually died away and little by little his malice was laid bare. He never ceased his daily attempts to make or seize on opportunities for wrangling, continually inventing situations which usually give birth to quarrels and battles and wars. Since Gulielmus Mascabeles far excelled him in wealth and power, Robert despairing of any direct confrontation devised a wicked plot. While feigning goodwill and simulating repentance, he was secretly preparing a terrible but well-concealed trap for him, so as to seize his cities and make himself master of all Mascabeles' possessions. First he requested peace negotiations and sent an embassy asking Gulielmus to come in person to discuss them. The latter welcomed the chance of peace, because he loved his daughter dearly, and the conference was fixed for the morrow. Robert suggested a place to him in which they might conveniently come together, discuss and arrange terms mutually agreeable. There were two hill-tops rising from the level plain to an equal height and exactly opposite one another; the intervening space was marshy and overgrown by all sorts of trees and plants. The cunning Robert laid an ambush of four men in this area. They were fully armed, brave men. He told them to keep a sharp look-out in all directions. As soon as they saw him coming to grips with Mascabeles, they were to run towards him without a moment's delay. Having made these preliminary arrangements the scoundrel left the hill which he had before pointed out to Gulielmus as suitable for their meeting and took possession, as it were, of the other. He collected fifteen knights and about fifty-six foot-soldiers; with them he climbed the hill and posted them on it. The whole scheme was explained to the more reliable among them and one of these was commanded to carry his (Robert's) armour, shield, helmet and short sword, so that he might easily arm himself; the four lying in ambush were instructed, when they saw him wrestling with Mascabeles, to run up quickly to his aid. On the agreed day Gulielmus was on his way to the hill-top, to the place Robert had formerly designated, with the intention of ratifying a treaty. Robert saw him not far off, met him on horseback, and greeted him with a handshake in the most cordial manner. So, gradually moving to the slope just below the top of the hill, they both halted, talking of what they intended to do. Robert craftily wasted time, chatting about one thing after another, and then said to him, 'Why should we tire ourselves out seated on horseback? Shall we dismount and sit on the ground? Then we can consider what we have to in comfort.' Mascabeles, poor fool, unaware of his treachery and his own perilous situation, agreed. When he perceived that Robert had dismounted, he at once did likewise; he renewed the discussion, leaning with his elbow on the ground. Robert confessed that in future he would be the servant of Mascabeles, and to prove it called him 'Benefactor' and 'Lord'. Mascabeles' men had seen these two dismount from their horses and apparently begin fresh negotiations. They were tired because of the heat and the want of food and drink, for this happened in the summer time, at the hour when the sun casts its rays from directly overhead, and the temperature was becoming unbearable. Some of them, therefore, also dismounted, tied their reins to the branches of trees and lay down on the ground, cooling themselves off in the shade cast by horses and trees; others went off home. So much for them. Robert, wily as ever, now that all was ready, suddenly grabbed Mascabeles. His gentle expression changed to one of fury, and he attacked him murderously. The other struggled, pulling and being pulled; both began to roll down the slope. The four ambushers watched them, rose up from the marsh and charged on Gulielmus. They bound him well and truly, and then ran back as if to join Robert's horsemen who were stationed on the other hill and already galloping down towards them. Behind them came Gulielmus' men. For his part, Robert mounted, took helmet and spear, quickly tucking the latter under his arm, and protected himself with his shield. Then he wheeled round and struck at one of Gulielmus' soldiers with the spear. The blow killed him. This had a double effect: the onrush of his father-in-law's cavalrymen was checked and their rescue attempt was foiled. The rest, in fact, when they saw Robert's knights coming down on them from above with the advantage of higher ground, immediately turned back. In this way Robert put an end to their charge, and as for Mascabeles, he was at once led off as a prisoner-of-war in bonds to the very castle which he had given to Robert as a wedding present when he betrothed to him his daughter. So it came about that the city then had its own master as a prisoner, and naturally was thereafter called 'Phrourion'.[35] The details of Robert's cruelty are horrifying in the extreme, for when he had Mascabeles completely in his power, he first had all his teeth pulled out, demanding for each one of them an enormous sum of money and asking him where he had hidden it. As he did not cease pulling out the teeth till all had gone, and as teeth and money were exhausted at the same time, he then turned to Gulielmus' eyes. Grudging him the power of sight, he blinded him.

He was now master of all and from that time his power increased day by day. As his ambitions grew he kept adding city to city and piling up his wealth. To cut a long story short, he attained high rank and was named 'Duke of all Lombardy', which provoked the jealousy of everyone. However, being a wary fellow, he mitigated the popular movements against himself, cajoling some of his adversaries and bribing others; by his cleverness he moderated the envy of the nobles. Occasionally he had recourse to arms. By these means he brought under his personal control the whole of Lombardy and the surrounding areas. He was always thinking out some more ambitious project. He seized on the pretext of his connexion by marriage with the Emperor Michael and dreamed of ascending the throne himself. The war against the Romans was kindled anew. We have mentioned before that Michael, for some extraordinary reason, had agreed to unite his own son Constantine in marriage with Robert's daughter (the lady's name was

35. Greek for 'garrisoned fort'.

Helena). When I recall this young man again, my soul is sorely troubled and my thoughts become confused.[36] The full account of his career I defer until the appropriate time. But this at least I cannot refrain from saying, even if I speak out of place: Constantine was Nature's masterpiece, a triumph, as it were, of God's handiwork. One look at him would convince anyone that here was a descendant of the mythical Golden Age of the Greeks, so infinite was his charm. As for me, when I remember this young man after so many years, I am overcome by tears. Yet I hold back my sorrow; it shall be reserved for the 'places of honour',[37] lest by mingling my own lamentations with the historical narrative I confuse the history. This youth, mentioned by me here and elsewhere, was born before I saw the light of day and had become a suitor of Helena. He was a chaste and undefiled boy. The marriage settlement had been committed to writing, though it was not executed and consisted merely of promises, because he was still immature, and as soon as Nicephorus Botaniates became emperor the contract was torn up. But I have wandered from the point; I will go back to the place where I went astray. Robert, who from a most undignified condition had attained great distinction, having gathered about him powerful forces was aiming to become Roman emperor. Consequently he was devising plausible excuses for his hatred and warlike attitude to the Romans. At this point there are two different versions of the story. According to one, which is widespread and first reached our ears, a monk called Raiktor impersonated the Emperor Michael and fled to Robert, the father of his (supposed) daughter-in-law. He told him a pitiable tale of his own misfortunes. This Michael, you see, had seized the Roman sceptre after Diogenes and for a brief moment graced the throne, but was deprived of power by the rebel Botaniates; he submitted to the life of a monk and later wore the alb of a high priest and the mitre; you may even add the humeral.[38]

36. He was later engaged to marry Anna Comnena herself.

37. A reference from Demosthenes, 234, 14.

38. Michael abdicated on the last day of March 1078 and was allowed to retire to the Studite Monastery. He was later made Archbishop of Ephesus.

It was the Caesar John, his paternal uncle, who counselled him
to do this, for he knew the fickleness of the new emperor and
feared that some more dreadful fate might befall him. The
aforementioned monk, Raiktor, pretended that he was
Michael, but maybe I had better call him Rektes, for he was
the most brazen-faced 'doer' of them all.[39] Well, he approached Robert, because forsooth he was related to him by
marriage, and he acted out his tale of injustice, how he had
been deprived of the imperial throne and reduced to his
present state, which Robert could see for himself. For all
these reasons he challenged Robert to help him. Helena, the
lovely young wife of his son, he said, had been left defenceless,
entirely cut off from her bridegroom, for his son Constantine
and the Empress Maria, he proclaimed loudly, had been
forced against their will to join the party of Botaniates. With
these words he stirred the anger of the barbarian and drove
him to arms in a war against the Romans. Such is the story
which came to my ears and I do not find it surprising that
some persons of completely obscure origin impersonate others
of noble birth and glorious reputation. But my ears are also
assailed by another version of the affair and this is more convincing. According to the second authority it was not a monk
who impersonated Michael, nor was it any such action which
prompted Robert to make war on the Romans, but the barbarian himself with great versatility willingly invented the
whole story. The subsequent events apparently came about as
follows. Robert, they say, was a thoroughly unscrupulous rascal
and working hard for a conflict with the Romans; he had for
a long time been making preparations for the war; but he was
prevented by some of his more reputable friends and by his
own wife Gaita, on the grounds that he would be starting an
unjust war and one directed against Christians. Several times
his attempts to begin such an enterprise were put off. However, as he was determined to invent an excuse for war that
would be plausible, he sent some men to Cotrone with certain

39. The Greek pun is difficult to reproduce in English. The word implies someone who 'does' or 'contrives'; Elizabeth Dawes translates
'fabricator'.

instructions (having informed them first of his secret designs).
If they met any monk who was willing to cross from there to
Italy in order to worship at the shrine of the two great apostles,
the patron saints of Rome, and if his outward appearance did
not manifest too lowly an origin, they were to embrace him
gladly, make a friend of him, and bring him to Robert. When
they discovered the aforementioned Raiktor, who was a
clever fellow, a criminal beyond compare, they sent a message
to Robert in a letter (he was staying at Salerno at the time).
It read: 'Your kinsman Michael, deposed from his throne, has
arrived and asks for your assistance.' This was the secret code
which Robert had asked them to use. With this letter in his
hand Robert at once went to his wife and read it aloud to her
privately. Then he gathered together all the Counts and, again
privately, showed them the letter. He thought no doubt that
he had seized on a fine excuse and they would no longer
oppose his schemes. Since they all supported his plan without
hesitation, he brought Raiktor over and made his acquaintance. After that he dramatized the whole business, with the
monk at the centre of the stage. It was said that he was the
Emperor Michael; that he had been deprived of his throne;
that his wife and son and all his possessions had been taken
from him by the pretender Botaniates; that contrary to justice
and all right dealing he had been invested not with the crown
and emperor's headband, but with the garb of a monk. 'Now,'
said Robert, 'he has come as a suppliant to us.' These remarks
were made publicly by Robert and he said it was of prime
importance that he should be restored because of his kinship
with himself. The monk was every day honoured by him as if
he were indeed the Emperor Michael; he was allotted a better
seat at table, a more elevated throne and exceptional respect.
Robert's public speeches were suited to the occasion: sometimes he spoke in self-pity, bewailing the fate of his daughter;
at other times he would spare the feelings of his 'kinsman' by
not referring to the troubles which had fallen on him; and then
again he would rouse the barbarians about him and incite
them to war by cleverly promising heaps of gold which he
guaranteed to get for them from the Roman Empire. Thus he

led them all by the nose and when he set out he drew after him rich and poor alike – it might be more accurate to say that he drew away the whole of Lombardy when he occupied Salerno, the capital city of Amalfi. There he made excellent arrangements for his other daughters and then prepared for the campaign. Two of the daughters were with him; the third, of course, who had been unfortunate from the day of her betrothal, was held in Constantinople. Her young betrothed, being still a young boy, shrank from the union from the outset, just as babies are scared by Mormo.[40] One daughter he had pledged to Raymond, son of the Count Barcinon; the other he married off to Eubulus, who was himself a count of great distinction. Nor did these alliances prove unprofitable for Robert; in fact, from all sources he had consolidated and amassed power for himself – from his family, from his rule, from his inheritance rights, from all manner of ways which another man would not even consider.

Meanwhile there occurred an event which it is worthwhile to record, for this too promoted his good fortune. Indeed, I calculate that the inability of all the western rulers to attack him contributed very much to the smooth course of Robert's affairs. In everything Fortune worked for him, raised him to power and brought about whatever was to his advantage. For example, the Pope of Rome [41] (this is a noble office, protected by soldiers of many nationalities) had a quarrel with Henry, the King of Germany,[42] and wanted to draw Robert into an alliance with himself (Robert had already become very famous and attained great power). The reasons for this quarrel between pope and king were as follows: the pope accused Henry of accepting money for church livings instead of appointing incumbents freely; he also blamed him for entrusting the office of archbishop on certain occasions to unworthy men, and he brought other charges of this nature. The

40. A horrible monster used by nurses to frighten children; a bugbear or hobgoblin.

41. Gregory VII (1073–85).

42. Henvy IV. For his relations with Gregory see *CMH* vol. iv, pt. i, p. 464.

German king, on the other hand, indicted the pope of presumption, saying that he had usurped the apostolic chair without his consent. What is more, he had used the most insulting and reckless language, threatening that if he did not resign his self-appointed office, he would be expelled from it with ignominy. When the pope heard these words, he immediately expended his wrath on the envoys sent by Henry. To begin with, he outraged them savagely, then cut their hair and beards, the one with scissors, the other with a razor, and finally he did something else to them which was quite improper, going beyond the insolent behaviour one expects from barbarians, and then sent them away. I would have given a name to the outrage, but as a woman and a princess modesty forbade me. What was done on his orders was not only unworthy of a high priest, but of any man at all who bears the name of Christian. Even the barbarian's intention, let alone the act itself, filled me with disgust; if I had described it in detail, reedpen and paper would have been defiled. The very fact, that we cannot endure to disclose or describe even a small fraction of what was done, will be sufficient evidence of this barbaric outrage and the character of men ready to commit any crime, any deed of daring. It will be proof enough that Time in its flow does produce such men. And this (in the name of Justice!) was the work of a high priest. More, it was the doing of the supreme high priest, of him who presided over the whole inhabited world (according to the claims and belief of the Latins – another example of their arrogance). The truth is that when power was transferred from Rome to our country and the Queen of Cities, not to mention the senate and the whole administration, the senior archbishopric was also transferred here. From the beginning the emperors have acknowledged the primacy of the Constantinopolitan bishop, and the Council of Chalcedon [43] especially raised that bishop to

43. The famous Fourth Ecumenical Council. In the twenty-eighth canon it was laid down that patriarch and pope should have equal privileges. There were various other decisions, of great ecclesiastical and political importance, which make 451 (the date of this synod) a turning-point in the history of east and west. See *CMH*, vol. iv, pt. i, pp. 18 ff.;

the place of highest honour and subordinated to him all dioceses throughout the world. I suspect then that this outrage inflicted on the ambassadors was aimed at him who sent them, not only because they were punished, but because the particular form of chastisement was novel, the invention of the pope himself. By his actions he hinted that the state of the king was utterly despicable, as if some demi-god were holding converse with a demi-ass. Such, I think, was the purpose of these shameful acts. The pope, having used the envoys as I have described and having sent them back to the king, provoked a terrible war. To prevent Henry becoming more unbearable by an alliance with Robert, the pope anticipated him by making his own proposals for peace, though previously he was not on friendly terms with Robert. Learning that he had occupied Salerno, he set out himself from Rome and arrived at Benevento. After some communication through ambassadors they met face to face in the following manner. The pope came from Benevento with his own guard, and Robert from Salerno with his army, and when the two forces were at a reasonable distance from each other, the leaders left their ranks and met. Pledges and oaths were exchanged and the two then returned. The pope swore on oath that he would invest Robert with the rank of king and give him military aid against the Romans if need arose; the duke that he would bring help wherever the pope summoned it. In practice, however, the oaths were worthless, for Pope Gregory was violently angry with the German king and preparations against him were being hurried on, whereas Robert had his eye on the Roman Empire. Like some wild boar he gnashed his teeth and whetted his wrath against the Romans. The oaths then went no further than words, and mutual pledges quickly given by these barbarians were as quickly disregarded. Duke Robert turned his horse about and hastened to Salerno, while the abominable pope (when I think of his inhuman act there is no other word I could possibly apply to him), the abominable pope with his

Ostrogorsky, p. 55; Vasiliev, p. 106; Hussey, *Byzantine World*, pp. 17–18. Anna, it would seem, has exaggerated here.

spiritual grace and evangelic peace, this despot, marched to make war on his own kindred with might and main – the man of peace, too, and disciple of the Man of Peace! He at once sent for the Saxons and their chieftains Landulphus and Velcus.[44] Among many other enticing promises, he announced that he would make them kings of all the west and so won them to his side. It seems that he misunderstood the saying of Paul, 'Lay hands suddenly on no man',[45] for his right hand was only too ready for the laying-on of hands where kings were concerned: he bound with the kingly riband the Duke of Lombardy's head and crowned these Saxons. Each party (that is to say, King Henry of Germany and the pope) having assembled their forces and put in order their battle-lines, the horn sounded the attack and at once the two armies clashed. The battle erupted, to be fought on either side with ferocity and dogged resolution. Both displayed such courage and bore up so well though wounded by spear or arrow that in a short time all the plain beneath their feet was swamped in the blood of the dead, and the survivors were fighting on like ships on a sea of gore. In places they became entangled in masses of corpses and falling down were drowned in the torrent of blood. If, as they say, more than 30,000 men fell in that battle, how great the river of blood that flowed, how vast the area of earth stained by their gore! Each side held its head high, so to speak, in this struggle as long as Landulphus, the Saxon chief, directed the battle. But when he received a mortal wound and died instantaneously, the pope's line wavered and broke. Its flight was bloody and murderous. Henry drove them on wildly in pursuit, much heartened at the news that Landulphus had fallen and become the prize of his enemies. However, he gave up the chase and ordered his soldiers to rest. Later on, he armed himself again and hastened to Rome with the idea of besieging it. The pope thereupon recalled the agreements made with Robert and his oaths. An embassy was dispatched to him asking for help. Just at this moment Henry also, as he started for Ancient Rome, requested an alliance with Robert

44. Rudolf, Duke of Swabia; Welf, Duke of Bavaria.
45. First Epistle to Timothy v, 22.

through ambassadors. To Robert it seemed that each of them on this occasion was a fool to ask. He made some sort of verbal reply to the king, but wrote a letter to the pope. The gist of it was as follows: 'To the great High Priest and my lord from Duke Robert, by the grace of God. Although I heard of the assault made upon you by your enemies, I did not pay over-much attention to the story, knowing that no one would dare to raise his hand against you. For who would attack so great a father, unless he were mad? Be sure that I am arming myself for a most important war against a people hard to conquer, for the Romans are my enemies, the Romans who have filled every land and sea with their trophies. As far as you are concerned I owe fidelity from the bottom of my heart and will prove it when necessity demands it.' Thus he evaded the envoys of both sides when they called for his assistance, the former by this letter, the latter by certain plausible excuses; and he sent them away.

But let us not forget what he did in Lombardy before coming to Avlona with his army. In any case Robert was an over-bearing and cruel man, but at this point he emulated even Herod in his madness. Not being satisfied with the men who had served in his army from the beginning and had experience in battle, he formed a new army, made up of recruits without any consideration of age. From all quarters of Lombardy and Apulia he gathered them, over age and under age, pitiable objects who had never seen armour even in their dreams, but then clad in breastplates and carrying shields, awkwardly drawing bows to which they were completely unused and falling flat on the ground when they were allowed to march. Naturally these things provided an excuse for incessant trouble in Lombardy. Everywhere one could hear the lament-ation of men and the wailing of women who shared in the bad fortune of their menfolk, for one mourned a husband unfit for military service, another a son who knew nothing of war, and a third a brother who was just a farmer or occupied in some other job. As I said, this idea of Robert's was just as lunatic as the behaviour of Herod, or even worse, for Herod raved only against babes, but Robert against boys and older men as well.

Yet, however unused to soldiering they were (to put it thus), he trained them daily and hammered his recruits into a disciplined force. This was his business in Salerno before he arrived in Otranto. He had sent on ahead a very efficient army to await him there when he had settled all the affairs of Lombard territory and given suitable replies to the envoys. He did, however, send an additional note to the pope, saying that he had instructed his son Roger (whom he had appointed ruler of all Apulia together with his brother Boritylas) to go with the utmost zeal to the aid of the pope, whenever he called for it; he was to attack King Henry with a strong force. His younger son Bohemond he sent with powerful forces to our country. He was to descend on the districts round Avlona. Bohemond resembled his father in all respects, in daring, strength, aristocratic and indomitable spirit. In short, Bohemond was the exact replica and living image of his father. He at once attacked Canina, Hiericho and Avlona like a streaking thunderbolt, with threats and irrepressible fury. He seized them, and fighting on took the surrounding areas bit by bit and destroyed them by fire. Bohemond was in fact like the acrid smoke which preceded the fire, the preliminary skirmish which comes before the great assault. Father and son you might liken to caterpillars and locusts, for what was left by Robert, his son fed on and devoured. But we must not get him across to Avlona yet. Let us examine what he did on the opposite mainland.

Robert set out from Salerno and arrived at Otranto. There he stayed for a few days waiting for his wife Gaita[46] (she went on campaign with her husband and when she donned armour was indeed a formidable sight). She came and he embraced her; then both started with all the army again for Brindisi, the seaport with the finest harbour in the whole of Japygia. He swooped down on the city and stopped there, watching anxiously for the assembling of all his forces and all his ships, transports and long ships and fighting vessels, because it was from Brindisi that he expected to sail to these shores. While he was at Salerno, he had sent an ambassador called Raoul, a

46. Or Sigelgaita (of Salerno).

noble and one of his retinue, to the Emperor Botaniates, who
had by now seized power in succession to Ducas. Robert was
eagerly awaiting the reply. Raoul was charged to make certain
complaints and to put forward some apparently reasonable
excuses for the impending war: Botaniates had separated
Robert's daughter from her future husband Constantine (as
the history has already made clear) and had stolen from him
the imperial crown. Robert, therefore, because of this injustice, was preparing vengeance. To the Great Domestic of
that time and the Commander of the Armies of the West
(that is to say, my father Alexius) he had sent some presents
and letters promising friendship. He was now waiting at
Brindisi for his answer. Before all the contingents had been
collected or most of the ships launched, Raoul came back from
Byzantium, bringing no reply to Robert's communications –
which enraged the barbarian more than ever. What made
matters worse was the fact that Raoul pleaded vigorously
against undertaking war with the Romans. First he argued
that the monk in Robert's army was an impostor and a cheat,
impersonating the Emperor Michael, and the whole story
about him was an invention. He said that he had seen Michael
after his dethronement in Constantinople, wearing a miserable
garment of some dark colour and living in a monastery. He
had taken special care to see with his own eyes the deposed
emperor. Secondly, he reported also the event which he had
heard of on his way back. My father, you see, had seized power
(as I shall describe in detail later), had driven Botaniates from
his throne, had sent for Constantine, Ducas' son, who of all
men under the sun was the most illustrious, and had given him
for a second time a share in the government. This news Raoul
had heard on his journey and now, in an attempt to persuade
Robert to abandon his preparations for war, he informed him
of it. 'How shall we be able to make war on Alexius with any
justice,' he said, 'when it was Botaniates who started the
wrong and deprived your daughter Helena of the Roman
throne? What happens to us at the hands of others should not
bring war on those who have done no wrong; and if the war
has no just pretext, then all is lost – ships, arms, men, the

whole warlike preparation.' These words irritated Robert even
more. He raved madly and almost laid violent hands on the
ambassador. For his part, the fictitious Ducas, the so-called
Emperor Michael (whom we have called Raiktor), was
indignant and much put out. He did not know how to contain
his wrath when it was so clearly proved that he was not the
emperor, but a sham. Robert was filled with rage against Raoul
in any case, but when Raoul's brother Roger deserted to the
Romans and gave intimate details of all his preparations for
the war, in his desire to commit some dreadful crime he
threatened the man with death on the spot. Raoul, however,
wasted no time at all in fleeing to Bohemond. Finding in him
the nearest place of refuge, as it were, he became a fugitive. In
tragic fashion Raiktor, too, uttered the most bloodcurdling
threats against Raoul's brother, the deserter; with loud cries
and slapping his thigh with his right hand, he begged Robert:
'One thing only I ask of you: if I get my hands on the crown
and sit again on the throne, give me this Roger. If I don't con-
sign him to the most horrible death in the middle of the city
with instant crucifixion, then let me suffer such and such at the
hands of God.' In the midst of this story I cannot help laugh-
ing at the silly and farcical behaviour of these men, or rather
at their mutual bragging. For Robert, of course, this rogue
was a mere bait, a sort of projection of his kinsman the
emperor, and he constantly exhibited him in the cities and
stirred to rebellion all whom he could reach and persuade.
When the war and his luck went well for him, he intended to
rap him on the neck and send him off with a laugh. After all,
when the hunt is over the bait is a matter of scorn. The monk,
on his side, was being fed on false hopes: it might somehow
come true, he might have some share in power – such things
often do happen, contrary to expectation. He would certainly
grasp power with a tight fist, feeling sure that the Roman
people and army would never call the barbarian Robert to the
throne. In the meantime he would make use of him as a
tool to achieve all his wicked designs. When I think of it I
cannot but smile and a laugh rises to my lips as I slowly move
my pen in the lamplight.

Robert concentrated his whole force at Brindisi, ships and
men. The ships numbered 150, and the soldiers, all told, came
to 30,000, each ship carrying 200 men with armour and horses.
The expedition was equipped thus because they would probably meet the enemy in full armour and mounted when they
landed. He intended to disembark at the city of Epidamnos,
which in accordance with modern tradition we will call
Dyrrachium. He had thought of crossing from Otranto to
Nicopolis and of capturing Naupaktos and all the country and
forts round it, but as the distance by sea between these two
towns was far greater than the voyage from Brindisi to
Dyrrachium, he chose the latter; it was not only the fastest
route, but he was looking to the comfort of his men, for it was
the winter season and the sun being on its way to the southern
hemisphere and approaching the Tropic of Capricorn, the
daylight hours were shortened. Rather than leave Otranto at
daybreak and voyage by night with possible heavy weather,
he preferred to cross from Brindisi under full sail. The
Adriatic is not so wide at this point so the sea distance is cor-
respondingly shorter. Robert altered his mind about his son
Roger. Originally, when he appointed him Count of Apulia,
he had intended to leave him behind, but for some unknown
reason he included him in his retinue. On the voyage to
Dyrrachium a side-expedition made him master of the strongly
fortified town of Corfu and some other of our forts. He
received hostages from Lombardy and Apulia, raised money
and exacted tribute from the whole country and looked forward to a landing at Dyrrachium.

The Duke of all Illyricum at that time happened to be
George Monomachatos, who had been sent out there by the
Emperor Botaniates. Yet in the first place he had refused the
mission and it was by no means easy to persuade him to undertake this duty, but something compelled him to go. There
were two barbarian servants of the emperor, Scyths called
Borilos and Germanos, who were annoyed with Monomachatos and were always inventing some more terrible
charge against him, which they then reported to the emperor.
They strung together stories to their heart's content and so

inflamed the latter's wrath against Monomachatos that one day
he turned to the Empress Maria and said, 'I suspect this Monomachatos of being an enemy of the Roman Empire.' John, an
Alanian, heard this remark; being a friend of Monomachatos
and knowing that the Scyths in their venom brought continual accusations against him, he told him in full what had
been said. He advised him to consult his own interests. However, Monomachatos kept his head, had an interview with
Botaniates and soothed him with adulation. Then he quickly
grasped the opportunity of service at Dyrrachium. Arrangements were made for him to go to Epidamnos and he received
written instructions with regard to his ducal office. On the
next day he left Constantinople for Epidamnos and Illyricum,
the Scyths Germanos and Borilos most gladly hastening his
departure. Somewhere near the so-called Pege (Pighi) he met
my father.[47] When they saw one another, Monomachatos was
the first to speak, telling Alexius with considerable emotion
how he was being exiled because of his friendship for him,
how the Scyths Borilos and Germanos, who envied the whole
world, had set in motion against him the full force of their
jealousy and were actually banishing him on a hollow pretext
from his friends and beloved city. When he had ended his
dramatic and detailed account of the calumnies whispered in
the emperor's ear and the sufferings he had endured at the
hands of these slaves, the Domestic of the West thought it
right to comfort him to the best of his ability. Alexius was well
fitted to raise up a soul weighed down by misfortune. Finally
he told him that God would in truth avenge such wrongs and
assured him that he remembered his friendship. Thus the one
set out for Dyrrachium, the other, left behind, went back to
the imperial city.

When Monomachatos reached Dyrrachium he learnt of the
military preparations of the tyrant Robert and also the revolt
of Alexius. He carefully weighed his own situation in the
balance. To all appearances he was hostile to both, but in fact

47. At Pege a church has been built in honour of my mistress, the Virgin
and Mother of Our Lord. Among the churches of Byzantium it is much
talked of. (A.C.)

he was planning something more subtle than open warfare.
The Great Domestic had written to him about what had occurred. He said he had been threatened with blinding; because
of this and the cruel exercise of power he was resisting the
tyrants; for his friend's sake Monomachatos must rise in
rebellion and send him money, collected from any source that
was possible. 'We need money,' he wrote, 'and without it
none of the things can be done which should be done.' Well,
Monomachatos did not send the money, but he treated the
envoys with kindness and put in their hands a letter instead.
The gist of it was as follows: he still respected his old friendship and promised to do so in the future. But with regard to
the money he requested, he (Monomachatos) would very
much like to send him as much as he wanted. 'But,' he added,
'I cannot; it's a matter of principle. I was sent here by the
Emperor Botaniates. I gave him a pledge of loyalty. Even you
would not look upon me as an honourable man, devoted to
his rulers, if I yielded to your demands at once. However, if
Heavenly Providence should judge you worthy of the throne,
as I was in the first place a faithful friend, so in the future I
shall be a most faithful servant.' Monomachatos dashed off
this letter to my father. He was trying to win over both at
once – my father, I mean, and Botaniates. In addition he made
more overt proposals to the barbarian Robert and broke out
into open revolt. He is in my opinion much to be condemned
for it. But somehow it seems that men of such character are
naturally inconstant, changing colour again and again according to the changes of government. All such men contribute
nothing to the common good, but for their own good they
are most circumspect, arranging what suits their convenience
and theirs alone. Yet they generally fail. But these speculations
have carried me off the main road of my history; we must get
my horse back on the right path again – he got out of hand.
Well, Robert even before these events had been madly impatient to cross over to my country and dreamed of Dyrrachium; now he was all the more inflamed with a quite
uncontrollable desire to make the naval expedition. He hurried on his soldiers and encouraged them with buoyant

speeches. Monomachatos' scheme had worked in that direction; he proceeded to build up a similar place of refuge elsewhere. By his letters he won the friendship of Bodin and Michaelas, exarchs of Dalmatia, and influenced their judgement with gifts, thereby opening up for himself by underhand means all kinds of doors. For if he failed with Robert and Alexius, if both rejected him, he would at once ride to Dalmatia and side with Bodin and Michaelas.[48] If, in fact, the former pair should prove openly hostile, Michaelas was still available, and so was Bodin, and he placed his hopes in them; once the news from the other quarter (from Alexius and Robert, I mean) turned bad for him, safety was assured. So much for them. Now is the right moment for me to turn to the reign of my father and explain how and with what resources he came to rule. The events of his life before then I did not intend to speak of, but rather to give a full account of his successes or failures as emperor – if on the journey we are about to make we do find some temporary lapses. For if I should discover some action of his not commendable, I will not spare him because he is my father, nor shall I course lightly over his triumphs because of an under-current of suspicion that a daughter, writing of her father, may be biased. In both cases we should be doing injustice to the truth. As I have remarked on several occasions before, my object is to tell the truth and the subject of my history is my father, the emperor. Let us then leave Robert at the point where the history has brought him in, and now consider the acts of Alexius. His battles and wars against Robert we shall reserve for another book.

48. Constantine Bodin, son of Michaelas, was crowned czar of an independent *Zeta* (a Serbian principality) *c.* 1075. It is probable that he (and Michaelas) received their titles of King from Gregory VII, the pope. Bodin conquered Rascia and Bosnia, but the Roman revival under the Comneni soon undermined his authority and he was forced to acknowledge the emperor's superior position. At this point (*c.* 1080) these Serbian kings were threatening to liberate much of the Adriatic coastline from Byzantine control.

BOOK TWO

THE REVOLT OF THE COMNENI

IF the reader wishes to know the birthplace and antecedents of the Emperor Alexius, we would refer him to the writings of my husband the Caesar. From the same source he will be able to extract information about the Emperor Nicephorus Botaniates also. Isaac and Alexius had an elder brother, Manuel, the first-born of all the children descended from John Comnenus, my grandfather on my father's side. He was appointed commander-in-chief of the whole of Asia by the previous ruler Romanus Diogenes, but Isaac became Duke of Antioch after being elected by lot.[1] They fought many wars and battles and many also were the trophies they set up over their enemies. In succession to them my father Alexius was promoted supreme general by the current ruler Michael Ducas and sent out to fight Roussel. The Emperor Nicephorus too saw in him a most capable strategist, and when he heard how while serving in the east with his brother Isaac he had proved himself valiant beyond his years in different campaigns, and how he had routed Roussel, he came to treat him with marked affection, no less in fact than Isaac. Both had a special place in his heart, as he looked on them with pleasure and occasionally invited them to share his table. This inflamed jealousy, particularly in the case of the afore-mentioned Slavonic barbarians, Borilos and Germanos, who saw that the emperor was kindly disposed towards the young men – and yet, despite the darts of envy to which they were so often exposed, they still remained unharmed. The Scyths were wasting away with chagrin, for Nicephorus, recognizing the fine reputation he enjoyed among all, appointed Alexius commanding officer in the west and honoured him with the rank of proedros – and this although he was still but a youth. We have already recorded the number of his victories in the west and spoken of

1. From 1074 to 1078.

rebels subdued and brought living to the emperor as prisoners-of-war; enough has been said on that subject. But these events, far from giving pleasure to the barbarian slaves, fired their burning jealousy even more. They murmured a lot and plotted evil against Alexius and Isaac. Many things they told the emperor in private, some things they said in public and certain things were conveyed through agents; in their eagerness to rid themselves of the brothers they used any and every device, to the embarrassment of their victims. The Comneni decided that they must conciliate the officers in charge of the women's quarters and through them gain the goodwill of the empress even more than before. They had charm enough, and wit enough, to soften a heart of stone. Isaac indeed had already achieved success, for he had been chosen by her to marry her own cousin;[2] he was in word and deed a true aristocrat, in very many ways recalling my own father. Now that his own affairs prospered, he was much concerned for his brother: as Alexius had supported him in the matter of this marriage, so he was zealous that Alexius should not be less in favour with the empress. According to legend Orestes and Pylades were friends and so much affection did they have for one another that in the crisis of battle each ignored the enemies attacking himself and bore aid to his friend, shielding him with his own breast from the volleys of arrows. One could see a like affection in the case of Isaac and Alexius, for each was willing to face dangers for the other and they shared prizes of valour and honours, and in general the good fortune of each other, so great was their mutual attachment. In this way, thanks to the Providence of God, the interests of Isaac were assured. Not long afterwards the officers of the gynaeconitis[3] on the advice of Isaac cajoled the empress to adopt Alexius as her son. She listened to their words and when the two brothers on a pre-determined day came to the palace she adopted him in the ceremony long established for such cases. Thus the Great Domestic of the western armies was for the future relieved of much anxiety, and from that day they both visited the palace frequently. After performing the act of adoration due to the

2. Irene of Alania.   3. Women's quarters in the palace.

ruling couple and waiting for a short time they would go to
the empress. Thereupon the envy flared up against them even
more fiercely – as many persons made clear to them. Being
afraid therefore that both might be caught in the snares of
their enemies, with none to protect, they sought with God's
help some means of ensuring their safety. Together with their
mother they turned over many ideas; many plans were
thoroughly examined on many occasions. In the end they
found one hope (humanly speaking) of security – to approach
the empress, when some plausible excuse presented itself, and
confide in her their secret. The plan, however, was concealed
and divulged to nobody at all; like fishermen they were careful not to frighten away the catch before they were ready.
What they intended to do, in fact, was to run away, but they
were afraid to tell her; she might disclose their plan to the
emperor, being concerned for both him and them. The
original scheme was abandoned and a new idea took its place
(they were prepared to grasp any opportunity that might
occur).

By now the emperor was too old to have a son and fearing
the moment when death would inevitably cut him off, he was
looking for a successor. There was a certain Synadenos, of
Levantine origin, of illustrious descent and fine appearance, a
thoughtful youth of strong physique, on the verge of manhood, who apart from other considerations was a family
relative of Nicephorus.[4] It was to him, in preference to all
others, that the emperor planned to bequeath the imperial
throne as a family heritage. It was a bad decision. He might
have left the crown to Constantine, the empress's son, and in
a way it was his right, because of his grandfather and father.
Had he done so, he would have ensured his own safety to the
end; at the same time it would have been a just settlement;
the empress, moreover, would have had more confidence in
him; she would have been more loyal. The old man did not
realize the unfairness and inexpediency of his plans, unaware
that he was bringing evil on his own head. The empress knew

4. It has been suggested that Synadenos was a son of Theodoulos
Synadenos, who had married Botaniates' sister.

of these rumours and was much grieved at the thought of the danger which threatened her son. Although she was down-hearted, she betrayed her sorrow to no one, but it did not escape the notice of the Comneni. Here was the opportunity for which they had been waiting. They decided to approach her. Their mother gave Isaac a pretext for an interview. His brother Alexius was to go with him. When they appeared before her, Isaac spoke: 'In the last few days, Your Majesty, you have changed. It seems to us that you are worried by private cares and because you have no one to whom you can confide your secret you have lost heart.' She, unwilling as yet to reveal anything but sighing deeply, replied, 'There is no need to question a stranger[5] like that; the very fact that strangers live in a foreign land is reason enough for sorrow. Heaven knows the troubles I have had, one after another – and soon, apparently, there will be more in store for me.' The brothers kept their distance and said nothing. With eyes fixed on the ground and both hands covered, they stood there for a moment in deep thought, and then after making the usual obeisance went home much distressed. On the next day they came again to talk with her, but seeing that she was in a more cheerful mood they both approached her. 'You are our empress,' they said, 'and we your most faithful servants, prepared to suffer anything whatever on Your Majesty's behalf. We beg you not to let any worry confuse or perplex you.' By these words they gave her confidence and relieved her of all suspicion. Already they had guessed her secret, for they were quick-witted and shrewd, skilled in divining from brief remarks the hidden thoughts that lie deep in the hearts of men. Straightway they offered their help, and having given clear proof in many ways of their loyalty they promised bravely to answer her every call for aid. With great enthusiasm they agreed (following the apostle's bidding[6]) to rejoice with her

5. The empress was originally Martha of Georgia, daughter of Bagrat IV, who in 1065 sent her to be the wife of Michael Ducas. Her name was changed to Mary of Alania. When Michael abdicated in 1078 she married Nicephorus Botaniates. Psellus writes of her with great admiration (*Chronographia*, vii 9).

6. Romans xii, 15.

when she rejoiced, to feel pain with her when she was grieved. They asked her to regard them as fellow-countrymen, as friends and relatives, adding this one request, that if any information was laid against them by their jealous rivals, in her hearing or the emperor's, they might be told at once; otherwise they might fall unawares into the traps set by their enemies. They asked for this favour, bade her to be of good courage and said that with God's help they would zealously give all possible assistance; so far at least as they were concerned her son Constantine would not lose his throne. What is more, they were willing to confirm their assurances by oaths. There was no time to lose, they said, because of their detractors. It was in fact a great relief to them. They recovered their spirits and in future spoke to the emperor looking much happier. Both of them, and Alexius in particular, had the art of concealing their secret thoughts and private designs behind assumed expressions. The burning jealousy of the two powerful slaves flared up into a really great conflagration, but from now on, because of the newly made pact with the empress, none of the charges brought against them to the emperor escaped their notice. They knew that their enemies were plotting to do away with them. No longer, therefore, did they go together to the palace in their normal way, but each on alternate days. It was a wise provision, worthy of a Palamedes. If by chance one was caught through the furtive machinations of the Scyths, the other would survive; they would not both fall into the snare together. Such were the precautions they took, but things did not turn out for them as they suspected, for they proved too strong for the schemers, as the narrative will now make abundantly clear.

The city of Cyzicus was captured by the Turks and when the emperor heard the news he immediately sent for Alexius Comnenus. On that particular day it happened that Isaac was visiting the palace. When he saw his brother enter (contrary to their arrangement) he went up to him, asking why he was there. Alexius at once told him the reason. 'The emperor summoned me.' Both therefore went in and made the customary obeisance. As it was time for a meal, the emperor invited them to stay for a while and required them to share his table. They were separated, one sitting on the right, the other on the left, opposite one another. After a short pause they began to inspect the guests and noticed that they whispered together in a sullen manner. The young men feared a sudden attack: the slaves must have devised some imminent danger for them. In desperation they cast furtive glances at one another. For a long time they had been winning the friendship of the emperor's servants, by kindly words, by courtesies and all kinds of polite attentions; their affability had even persuaded the cook to regard them with a friendly eye. One of Isaac's retinue approached this man and said: 'Tell my master that Cyzicus has fallen. A letter has come from there with this news.' He at once served the food on the table and at the same time in a low voice told Isaac what his servant had said. Isaac passed on the message to Alexius by slight movements of his lips. Alexius easily grasped what he meant, as quick as lightning reading his lips. The burden of anxiety was lifted; both breathed again. When they had fully recovered, they considered what reply they should have ready, if someone questioned them about the affair; if the emperor, too, called on them for advice, what fitting counsel should they offer. In the midst of these calculations, he did look towards them and taking it for granted that they knew nothing about it told them that Cyzicus had been taken. They – ready now to comfort the emperor's soul, troubled as it was with the ravaging of cities – raised his fallen spirits and revived him with fine hopes, assuring him that Cyzicus would easily be delivered. 'All that matters,' they said, 'is that Your Majesty should be well. The besiegers of the city will surely pay sevenfold for what they have done.' At the time the emperor was delighted with their reply. He allowed them to take their leave from the banquet and passed the rest of the day freed of his worries. After that the Comneni made it their business to attend the palace regularly, to befriend the emperor's retinue even more, to give no chance whatever to their adversaries of plotting against them, no excuse at all for hating them; on the contrary they set out to win the affection, sympathy and outspoken

support of all. They were especially determined to propitiate
the Empress Maria and convince her that they were wholly
devoted to her in mind and soul. Isaac could speak freely to
her because he was a relative (he had married her cousin) and
my father had no less liberty because of his close relationship.
His adoption, in particular, furnished an excellent reason for
access to her: it was impossible to accuse him and the envy of
evil-doers was thrown into the shade – not that he was unaware of their blind fury and the feeble character of Nicephorus. Naturally the brothers were anxious not to lose Maria's
goodwill; if they did, they would fall victim to their enemies,
for weak-minded folk (and the emperor was one such) are
quite unstable, moving with the tide, first one way, then
another, like Euripus.[7]

The slaves,[8] seeing all this and realizing that their own
scheme was making no progress – men like Isaac and Alexius
could not easily be destroyed and the emperor's kindly concern for them grew daily stronger – after much debate, with
many resolutions and counter-resolutions, turned to a different
plan. Their idea was to summon the young men one night,
without the knowledge of the emperor, and get rid of them by
gouging out their eyes on a trumped-up charge. The Comneni
got to hear of it. They knew they were in imminent danger.
With great reluctance they decided their one hope of safety
lay in rebellion; hard necessity was driving them to it. Why
should they wait for the executioner to brand their eyes and
extinguish the light in them? Nevertheless, they kept their
plan strictly to themselves. Not long after, though, Alexius
received instructions to bring in a party of troops; they were
to be equipped for war against the Agarenes[9] who had sacked
Cyzicus. At the time he was Domestic of the West. Here was a
reasonable chance to summon by letter all army officers loyal
to himself, with their men. He seized it. Thus alerted they all

7. Euripus is the narrow channel between the island of Euboea and the
Greek mainland, notorious for its currents.

8. Anna constantly refers to Borilos and Germanos as 'the slaves'; the
words must not be taken literally. 'Slave' here is a term of abuse.

9. The Turks.

hurried to the capital. Meanwhile someone, prompted by one of the two Scyths (Borilos), went to the emperor and asked him if it was his desire that the Great Domestic should bring all the forces into the capital. Alexius was at once sent for and Nicephorus demanded to know if it were true. Alexius answered without hesitation: he did not deny that an army was being brought in at his command, but he argued convincingly against the story that the whole army was being concentrated in the city from all parts of the Empire. 'The army is in fact dispersed,' he said, 'and individual men have come here from all provinces on receipt of my order. Those who see them arriving here in groups from different parts of the Empire imagine that all the army is gathering; they are deceived by appearances, nothing more.' Borilos protested vigorously, but Alexius' explanation proved stronger and he won the emperor's unqualified approval. Germanos, who was a less complex character, did not attack Alexius at all. However, since even these accusations failed to stir the emperor to take action against the Domestic, the slaves, taking advantage of a moment's immunity (it was evening time) set an ambush for the Comneni. It is a fact that slaves are in any case by nature hostile to their masters, but if they cannot strike at them, they seize the chance to become intolerable to one another. Such at least was Alexius' experience of the character and spirit of these men. They were certainly not filled with animosity against the Comneni for the emperor's sake. Borilos, according to some people, coveted the throne; and as for Germanos, he was Borilos' accomplice in the plot and carefully helped him to lay the ambush. They talked among themselves about their plans and discussed how the affair would go their way. By now they were speaking openly of things hitherto whispered in secret. Somebody, an Alanian by birth, heard what they said. He had the rank of magistros, had long been attached to the emperor and was counted among his friends. In the middle watch of the night, therefore, he left home, ran off to the Comneni and told the Great Domestic everything. Some say that the empress too was not altogether ignorant of his coming to the brothers. Alexius took the man to his mother and Isaac.

When they learnt this frightful news, they decided that the
time had come to put into practice their secret plan; with God's
aid they must assure their own safety. Two days later the
Domestic heard that the army was at Tzouroulos (a small
place somewhere near the Thracian frontier) and about the
first watch of the night he went to visit Pakourianus. The
latter was 'tiny of body', as the poet says,[10] 'but a mighty
warrior', born of a noble family in Armenia. Alexius told him
the whole story – the anger of the slaves, their jealousy, their
long-continued feud against himself and his brother, their
sudden plot to blind them; it was not right, he said, to suffer
like slaves – better to do some noble deed and perish, if it
should come to that; a man of spirit should die thus. Pakourianus listened to all that he said, and knowing that in such
matters there was no time to lose and they must act bravely at
once, he said, 'If you leave here at daybreak tomorrow, I will
follow you and I will personally fight as a volunteer on your
side; but if you defer your plan to the next day, I must warn
you that I shall go to the emperor without delay and denounce
both you and your men without hesitation.' 'Since I see that
you are concerned for my safety – and that is truly the work of
God – I will not refuse your advice,' said Alexius. 'But we
must do one thing more – take oaths to give assurance to our
agreement.' So they exchanged pledges under oath. Alexius
swore that if God elevated him to the imperial throne he
would promote Pakourianus to the rank of Domestic, which
he himself then held. After that he took his leave of Pakourianus and went off to another fine soldier, Humbertopoulos.
He told him of his object, explained the reason for it and
called on him for help. He agreed at once. 'You will have my
wholehearted support,' he said. 'I too am ready to sacrifice my
life for you.' There were other factors that inclined these men
to serve Alexius, but his exceptional courage and wisdom
above all won their loyalty. They had an extraordinary
affection for him, because he was a very liberal man, with
hands unusually ready to dispense gifts (although he was not
by any means over-rich). He was certainly not a money-

10. *Iliad* v, 801.

grubber, dedicated to the amassing of a fortune. It is not customary to judge a man's liberality by the amount of money he distributes, but one naturally weighs it by his motive. One could define a person of few resources who gives within his means as liberal; on the other hand, the very rich man who buries his wealth underground, or provides for the needy less than he could afford, might not improperly be described as a second Croesus or a gold-crazy Midas,[11] a greedy niggardly skinflint. Pakourianus and Humbertopoulos[12] knew long before that Alexius was endowed with all the virtues, so that they both desired and prayed for his accession to the throne. After exchanging oaths with Humbertopoulos too, Alexius ran off home and told his friends all that had happened. It was during the night of Sunday in Cheese-Week[13] that my father made these arrangements. On the next day, just as the sun was rising, he left the city with his friends. It was because of this that the people, who admired Alexius for his dash and wit, made up a little song in his honour. It was composed in the vulgar idiom, but caught in a dexterous way the general drift of the matter, emphasizing his foreknowledge of the plot and the measures he took to combat it. The actual words of the ditty were as follows:

> On Saturday in Cheese-Week their plan went phut!
> Alexis (he's your boy) had used his nut.
> Alexis, he's your boy.
> On Monday at dawn the hawk was out of sight.
> Alexis (you're my boy) had taken flight.
> Alexis, you're my boy. Hurrah!

The meaning of this popular couplet[14] was roughly this:

11. Whatever King Midas may have been, one could hardly describe Croesus as mean.

12. He was a nephew of Robert Guiscard, a Norman in the service of the Romans.

13. *Tyrophagy*, or Cheese-Week, immediately preceded Lent; during it cheese, butter, milk, eggs and fish were eaten, but not meat.

14. A couplet in Greek, but impossible in English. The translation is no more trite than most popular ditties or school songs – they sound better to music! The Greek is pretty trite too.

'On the Saturday of Cheese-Week, Alexius, you did wonderfully well because of your wit; but on the Monday off you flew, like some falcon soaring on high, away from the scheming barbarians.'

Anna Dalassena, the mother of the Comneni, had arranged a marriage between the grandson of Botaniates and the daughter of Manuel, her eldest son. She was afraid now that the youth's tutor, if he knew of the plot, might tell the emperor. To avoid this, she devised an excellent plan. She ordered all her household to gather in the evening for a visit to the holy churches for worship; it was her custom to attend the sanctuaries regularly. The order was carried out. All were present, in the usual way, led out the horses from the stables and made a show of carefully arranging saddle-cloths appropriate for the women. Botaniates' grandson, with his tutor, was asleep (a special apartment had been set aside for them). About first watch the Comneni, who were about to arm and ride away from the capital, closed the gates and handed the keys to their mother. They also closed the doors of the room in which the young Botaniates was sleeping, without making any noise; in fact the doors were not absolutely fast-closed (they were double doors) in case the sound should wake him. Most of the night had gone by while these things were happening. Before first cock-crow they opened the gates and taking with them their mother, sisters, wives and children went off to the Forum of Constantine on foot. There they took leave of them and ran in great haste to the Palace of Blachernae, while the women hurried to the church of Santa Sophia. Botaniates' tutor meanwhile had been roused and realizing what had occurred went out to look for them with a torch in his hand. He soon found them, before they had quite reached the Church of the Forty Martyrs. Dalassena saw him. 'Some people have denounced us to the emperor, I'm sure,' she said. 'I will go to the holy churches and get what help I can from them, and when day breaks, I will come back to the palace. You go off (speaking to the tutor) and when the porters open the gates, tell them of our coming.' He at once hurried off to do so. They proceeded to the sanctuary of Bishop Nicolas, which is still called 'The

Refuge' to this day. It is near the great church and was built
long ago for the safety of people arrested on charges of crime;
in fact it is an annexe of Santa Sophia and was, I fancy,
purposely constructed by our ancestors for all accused persons,
for if they once entered its doors they were freed from the
penalty of the laws. The emperors and Caesars of old, you see,
were much concerned for the welfare of their subjects. The
verger, who lived in the place, was in no hurry to open the
doors to them; he asked who they were and from where they
came. Someone of their party answered: 'Women from the
east. They've spent all their money on necessary purchases
and want to worship quickly before going home.' Without
more ado he opened the doors and let them in. On the next
morning the emperor called a meeting of the senate (when he
had heard about Alexius and Isaac) and naturally in his speech
attacked the Domestic. At the same time he sent Straboromanos and a certain Euphemianos to the women, summoning
them to the palace. Dalassena gave her reply: 'Tell the emperor this: my sons are faithful servants of Your Majesty and
gladly bearing allegiance to you in all things they have not
spared soul or body, being always the first to expose themselves
to danger in fighting bravely for your empire. But jealousy,
which cannot bear Your Majesty's goodwill and kindness to
them, has brought them into great and hourly peril. And
when their enemies planned to gouge out their eyes, my sons,
who had discovered the plot, found the danger intolerable, as
well as unfair, and left the city, not as rebels but as faithful
servants with three objects in view: to escape imminent peril;
to convince Your Majesty of the conspiracy against them;
and to implore Your Majesty's protection.' The envoys
pressed them hard to return, but Dalassena grew angry.
'Allow me,' she said, 'to enter the church of God for worship.
It's absurd that when I have reached its gates I should be
prevented from going in and praying Our Lady, the Immaculate Mother of God, to intercede for me with God and
the emperor's soul.' It was a reasonable request and they
granted it. She was allowed to enter. As if she were weighed
down with old age and worn out by grief, she walked slowly

(in reality she was pretending to be weary) and when she approached the actual entrance to the sanctuary made two genuflexions; on the third she sank to the floor and taking firm hold of the sacred doors, cried in a loud voice: 'Unless my hands are cut off, I will not leave this holy place, except on one condition: that I receive the emperor's cross as guarantee of safety.' Straboromanos took off the cross which he wore on his breast and gave it to her. 'It is not from you,' she said, 'that I am asking for a guarantee; I want the safeguard from the emperor himself. I will not be satisfied with just any little cross offered to me; it must be a cross of reasonable size.' She demanded this, so that when the oath was taken on it all might see, if the promise were made over a small cross, the confirmation of the oath would probably be invisible to most spectators. 'It is to the emperor that I appeal for judgement and mercy. Go away and tell him so.' Her daughter-in-law, Isaac's wife (she had come into the church when the gates opened for the morning hymn), removing the veil that covered her face, spoke to them: 'Let her go, if she wishes, but we are not leaving this church without a guarantee, even if we have to die.' The envoys therefore went away and told the emperor everything. They saw how determined the women were and how their behaviour grew more reckless; moreover, they feared a commotion. Nicephorus was a good man and touched by the woman's words sent her the required cross and with it a complete reassurance. Thus she left the church. The emperor condemned her to be confined, with her daughters and daughters-in-law, in the nunnery of Petrion near the Sidera.[15] Her kinswoman, the daughter-in-law of the Caesar John, was also sent for (she had the rank of protovestiaria[16]) from the sanctuary in Blachernae, built in honour of Our Lady the Mother of God, and she too was committed on the emperor's orders to the nunnery of Petrion. Their cellars, granaries and all their store-houses were to be kept free of all interference. Every morning both women approached the guards and

15. The Iron Gate, not far from the palace of Blachernae.
16. Mistress of the Wardrobe. John Ducas was brother of Constantine X and uncle of Michael VII.

asked if any news had arrived from their sons, and the guards, who behaved towards them in a very straightforward manner, told them all they had heard. The protovestiaria, being generous of hand and heart, and wishing to conciliate the warders, instructed them to take from the food-supplies whatever they wanted for their own use (the women were allowed to import all they needed without opposition). After that the guards became more eager to supply information and thereafter the prisoners learnt all that was going on from them.

I will say no more about them. The rebels[17] reached the gate[18] near Blachernae and having forced the bolts gained free access to the imperial stables. Some of the horses they left there, after first cutting off their hind-feet with their swords; all those which seemed more useful they took. From there they rode fast to the monastery called Kosmidion[19] on the outskirts of the city. At this point I will interrupt the narrative to make the story clearer. They found there the protovestiaria, whom I have mentioned above. (This was before she had been summoned by the emperor.) They took their leave of her as they were riding off and began to persuade George Palaeologus to accompany them; actually they compelled him to do so. They had not yet revealed their plan to him, because they suspected him – for a good reason: George's father was extremely devoted to Nicephorus and to tell him of the revolt would not be without its dangers. At first Palaeologus was not amenable; he produced many objections and rebuked them for disloyalty; and told them that, on second thoughts, they would change their minds and call on the emperor for help. However, when the protovestiaria, who was Palaeologus' mother-in-law, insisted vehemently that he must go with them and even added the most awful threats, he agreed to do so. From then on he began to concern himself

17. Alexius and Isaac.
18. There is some difficulty here in the Greek, which reads 'near the "bracelet" of Blachernae'; Elizabeth Dawes translates: 'the gate in the circular walls of Blachernae', but it is not clear why the walls should be 'circular'.
19. The Monastery of SS. Cosmas and Damian, not far from Blachernae.

for the women, his own wife Anna and his mother-in-law
Maria. The latter was of Bulgarian descent, endowed with
such effortless beauty and perfect symmetry of face and form
that no woman, it seems, was more lovely than she in that
generation. It was natural then that Palaeologus and Alexius
should be concerned about her. The men of Alexius' retinue
were all of the opinion that the women should be taken away;
some wanted to take them to a fortress, but Palaeologus felt
they should go to the Church of the Theometor in Blachernae.
His advice prevailed. Without delay they took them away and
entrusted them to the care of the Holy Mother of the Word
who encompasses all. The men themselves went back to the
place from which they had set out and considered what to do.
'You must go,' said Palaeologus, 'but I will soon catch you
up, bringing my money with me.' (It happened that all his
movable wealth was deposited there.) The others therefore
lost no time in setting out on their agreed route, while he
loaded his money on the monks' baggage animals and followed
after them. He arrived safely with the beasts at Tzouroulos, a
Thracian village, and by good fortune they all joined the army
which had concentrated there on the Domestic's orders.
Thinking that they ought to inform the Caesar John Ducas of
their adventures, they sent a messenger to tell him about the
rebellion. John was living on his estate at Moroboundos.
The messenger reached it in the early afternoon and stood
outside the doors of the house asking for the Caesar. His
grandson John, who was only a young boy and for that reason
constantly with the Caesar, saw him and ran inside to rouse his
grandfather (who was asleep). He announced that a revolution
had broken out. In astonishment at these words John boxed
his ears and telling him not to talk such nonsense pushed
him away. The boy after a short interval came back again with
the same news; he also brought the message addressed to John
by the Comneni. At one point in the letter there was a very
clever veiled reference to the revolt: 'We have prepared a very
fine dish, not without rich savoury sauce. If you would like to
share the feast, come as soon as you can to sit with us at the
perfect banquet.' John thereupon gave orders to bring in the

messenger, having first seated himself, leaning on his right elbow. The man described the whole affair. The Caesar's first reaction was to cover his eyes with his hands, exclaiming, 'What a pity!' But after stroking his beard for a little while, like a man in deep thought, he came to a firm decision – to join in the revolution with them. At once he called his equerries, mounted his horse and took the road to the Comneni. On the way he met a certain Byzantios who was carrying a large sum of gold and returning to the capital. In the usual Homeric way John asked him, 'Who are you? From where do you come?' And when he learnt that the man had with him a considerable quantity of gold collected in taxes and that he was taking it to the treasury, he urged him to stay there with himself, promising that at daybreak he could go wherever he wished. The man protested angrily at this, but John pressed him more urgently and in the end persuaded him to agree. It was typical of John: he was a glib talker, had a ready wit and a convincing tongue, like a second Aeschines or Demosthenes.[20] So he took the man along with him and spent that night in a small house. With every mark of friendship he invited Byzantios to share his table. After allowing him to have a good rest, he kept him there. About dawn, when the sun was rising fast on the eastern horizon, Byzantios saddled his horses, impatient to ride straight to the capital, but the Caesar saw him. 'Wait,' he said, 'and go along with us.' Byzantios neither knew where John was going nor had he the least idea why he had been treated in such a friendly way, and he again became angry. He began to suspect the Caesar and the Caesar's friendly actions. John advanced on him and held him back. As Byzantios would not listen, he changed his tactics and spoke in a harsher tone, with threats if he would not obey. When he still refused, John commanded all his baggage to be loaded on his own animals; he then gave the order to set out along the road, but Byzantios, he said, could go wherever he wanted without interference. Byzantios had completely abandoned any intention of returning to the palace; he was afraid that when

20. Aeschines (*c.* 390–*c.* 330) and Demosthenes (384–22) were rival orators and statesmen at Athens in the fourth century B.C.

the treasury officials saw him empty-handed he would be thrown into prison. On the other hand he was unwilling to retrace his steps, because of the unsettled conditions and confusion which had affected everything since the revolt of the Comneni had come into the open. So he followed the Caesar, but against his will. John was rather fortunate at this stage, for as he set out he met some Turks who had recently crossed the River Euros. He reined in his horse and asked from where they journeyed and what was their destination. He also promised to give them much money and grant them all sorts of favours if they would join him on the march to Comnenus. The Turks agreed there and then, and John, wishing to confirm the arrangement, required their leaders to take an oath. At once they swore on oath, after their own fashion, to fight with great enthusiasm on the side of Alexius. Thus John went on his way accompanied by these Turks. The Comneni sighted him a long way off and were more than delighted by the fresh booty. My father, most of all, could not contain himself for joy. He came on ahead of the others, threw his arms round John and embraced him repeatedly. Later, at the instigation of the Caesar, who was in a hurry, they set forth on the road to the capital. All the inhabitants of the small towns met them spontaneously and acclaimed Alexius as emperor, except for the people of Orestias,[21] who remained loyal to the party of Botaniates; they had long been angry with Alexius because of the capture of Bryennius.[22] When they arrived at Athyra they rested; on the next day the march was resumed and they reached Schiza, a village in Thrace, and there camp was pitched.

Everyone was excited, anxiously awaiting the outcome and hoping to see his own favourite proclaimed emperor. The majority prayed that the throne would fall to Alexius, but Isaac's partisans had not given up hope; they did their best to win the support of all for their man. To all appearances the division was irreconcilable, some desiring Isaac to become

21. The area round Adrianople. Nicephorus Bryennius came from the district. Anna is here referring, of course, to her own father-in-law.
22. As described in Book I, p. 45.

ruler of the Empire, some Alexius. Among those present then were Alexius' closest relatives: the above-mentioned Caesar John Ducas, a man who gave good counsel and in the most competent fashion put it into practice (I myself saw a little of him in the past); Michael and John, his grandsons; and of course George Palaeologus, the husband of their sister. All these were present, working hard to canvass all votes for their own choice, pulling all the strings, as they say, and cleverly making use of every device to have Alexius proclaimed emperor. Thus they converted everyone to their way of thinking, and Isaac's party gradually diminished, for the Caesar John proved irresistible; no one could rival his fine intellect, his tremendous stature, his regal presence. The Ducas family did and said everything; there was no advantage that they did not promise to the officers, and the rank and file of the army, if Alexius ascended the throne. 'He will reward you,' they declared, 'with most magnificent gifts and honours, each according to his deserts – not haphazardly, like ignorant generals of no experience. Alexius has been your army commander for a long time, and Great Domestic of the West; he has shared salt with you, fought bravely at your side in ambush and set battle, sparing neither his body nor his limbs nor even life itself for your safety's sake, again and again crossing with you over mountain and plain, knowing the miseries of war and understanding you well, both as individuals and as an army. He is a real soldier, with a deep affection for the fighting man.' While the Ducas family was busy, Alexius himself treated Isaac with every respect, allowing him precedence at all times, whether through brotherly love or rather (this too must be said) because the whole army was rallying to his side and was eager that he should win, but entirely ignored the claims of Isaac. Alexius therefore had the power and strength; he saw the issue unexpectedly turning in his favour. Yet he encouraged his brother to seek the throne. It involved no unpleasant risk, since the army to a man was determined to promote himself to the highest office; he could afford to flatter Isaac and make a pretence of yielding authority to him. Time was being wasted then in these manoeuvres when one day the

whole army was collected round the headquarters. There was
intense excitement, every man praying that his own hopes
would be fulfilled. Isaac stood up and taking the purple-dyed
sandal tried to put it on his brother's foot. Alexius objected
again and again. 'Come,' said Isaac, 'it is through you that
God wishes to recall our family to power.' And he reminded
him of the prophecy made to him once by a man who appeared
somewhere near Karpianos as the two brothers were on their
way home from the palace. For at that place a man met them
– or maybe he was a superior being; at all events, someone
who really had exceptional clairvoyant powers. As he approached them bare-headed he had the appearance of a priest,
white-haired, rough-bearded. He grasped Alexius by the leg
and drew him down to his own level (he was on foot and
Alexius on horseback) to whisper in his ear this verse from
the Psalms of David: 'Be earnest and prosper and govern
with an eye to truth and mercy and justice,' and then he added,
'Emperor Alexius.' Having said this in the manner of an
oracle, he vanished. Alexius could not find him, although he
looked everywhere in case he might catch sight of him, and
galloped at full speed in pursuit of him in case he might lay
hands on the man, to find out who he was and whence he
came. But the apparition had completely vanished. When
Alexius returned, Isaac made many inquiries about the vision
and begged him to tell his secret. He persisted in his questions
and although Alexius at first seemed reluctant, he afterwards
betrayed the secret prophecy to him. In speaking of it openly
to his brother he explained the thing as an hallucination and
said it was humbug, but in his own heart, when he recollected
that priestly vision, he likened the old man to the Theologian,
the son of Thunder.[23] Now when Isaac saw the prophecy
being fulfilled (words translated into action) he followed a
more energetic course and forcibly put on the purple sandal,
especially when he recognized the burning zeal of the whole
army for Alexius. At that signal the Ducas family led the acclamations. Their support derived from various reasons: one
was that their kinswoman Irene (my mother) was the legal wife

23. St John the Divine. -

of my father. Their blood-relatives willingly followed their example and the rest of the army took up the cry – their shouts almost reached the heavens. It was indeed an extraordinary sight: here were men who before had divided loyalties, prepared to face death rather than disappointment of their hopes; now in one swift moment they were so united in purpose that all traces of faction were obliterated. One would have thought there never had been a difference of opinion.

While these events occurred, a rumour spread that Melissenus [24] was near Damalis [25] with a strong force, already proclaimed emperor and clothed in the purple. At the time the Comneni were not inclined to believe it, but Melissenus who had heard of their activities quickly sent ambassadors to them with letters. The envoys arrived and handed them over. They read somewhat like this: 'God has brought me safe and unharmed with my army as far as Damalis. I have learnt about your adventures: how rescued by the Providence of God from the evil designs of those slaves and from their fearful attempts on your lives, you have consulted your own safety. I myself am naturally disposed to make an alliance with you because by the will of God we are related; sentiment too plays its part and in my lasting friendship for you I yield to none of your blood-kinsmen, as God, who judges all, well knows. If we are to achieve a position of strength and absolute security, it is essential that we should decide on a common policy. Otherwise, instead of laying a firm foundation for the good government of the Empire, we shall be at the mercy of every wind of change. Good government can without any doubt be achieved if, when you by God's will have captured the city, you administer the affairs of the west (one or other of you being proclaimed emperor), while I am permitted to govern Asia as my province; if moreover I wear the diadem and purple robes and receive the acclamation in the way that emperors normally do,

24. Nicephorus Melissenus had emerged as a pretender to the throne at Nicaea towards the end of 1080. He had married Alexius' sister Eudocia.

25. The promontory on which the modern Scutari stands.

with one of you. Thus, although we shall rule over different
territories with separate administrations, we shall still pursue
an identical policy. In these circumstances the Empire, directed
by both of us, will be free from party-strife.'[26] The envoys did
not receive a definite reply to this message, but on the next day
the Comneni summoned them and after a long discussion
pointed out the impossibility of Melissenus' proposal. Nevertheless they promised to make known to them their decision
on the following day through George Manganes, who was
responsible for their welfare. Meanwhile the siege operations
were by no means relaxed; as far as possible skirmishing
attacks continued to be made on the city walls. However, on
the appointed day the envoys were informed of their decision:
Melissenus was to be honoured with the rank of Caesar; he was
to have the diadem, the acclamation and the other privileges
due to his rank; he was also to be given Thessalonica.[27] The
envoys were ill content with these offers, but as their own
terms were ignored and they saw the rebel's great preparations
for the capture of the city, not to mention the enormous army
under his command and the growing pressure on themselves,
they asked for written confirmation in a chrysobull (with
purple ink). They were afraid that once Constantinople had
fallen the Comneni in their confidence might refuse to fulfil
even their present promises. Alexius, the newly acclaimed
emperor, agreed to sign the chrysobull and immediately commissioned his secretary George Manganes to write it. For
three days Manganes, on various pretexts one after the other,
put off the task; on one occasion he said that being over-
worked all day long he could not finish the writing at night; on
another that a spark had fallen on the document in the night
and burnt it to ashes; with such excuses and others like them

26. It was not the first time that a division of power had been suggested;
Bardas Phocas and Sclerus, for example, had agreed to partition the Empire
in the civil war of 985–6, before Basil II Bulgaroktonos established himself as undisputed emperor.

27. A great city in which a very beautiful church had been built
dedicated to the famous martyr Demetrius; his tomb, much venerated,
exudes an oil which is always effecting the most wonderful cures for those
who approach it with faith. (A.C.)

Manganes, true to his name 'Cheater'[28] deferred the business from day to day. The Comneni now left Schiza and soon reached Aretai, near Constantinople and overlooking the plain. If you view it from below, it has the appearance of a hill with one side facing the sea, a second facing Byzantium, while on the north and west it is exposed to every wind. The water there is clear and drinkable at all times, but the place is utterly devoid of plants and trees; you would imagine that woodcutters had completely bared the hill. The Emperor Romanus Diogenes, because of its delightful situation and mild climate, had put up some fine buildings there, worthy of an emperor, for brief holidays. It was to this spot that the Comneni now came. Attempts were made on the walls of the capital from there, not with helepoleis[29] or machines or catapults (because time did not allow it) but by peltasts,[30] archers, spearmen and cataphracts.[31]

Botaniates realized that the rebel army of the Comneni was very numerous, extremely heterogeneous, and already hurrying to the gates of the city; he was also aware that Nicephorus Melissenus was near Damalis with an army no less powerful and with equal pretensions to the throne. His position was desperate. It was impossible to resist on two fronts. Botaniates moreover was a little chilled by old age; however brave he had been in his youth, he only breathed freely now as long as the walls encircled him and he was becoming more and more frightened. Already he was rather inclined to abdicate, which terrified and threw into chaos all his supporters. Everything pointed to a total collapse. The Comneni however were of the opinion that Constantinople would not easily be captured: their own forces were composed of different elements, native and foreign, and where there is any heterogeneous group, there discordant voices will surely be raised. Alexius recog-

28. The Greek verb *manganeuo* means 'to contrive means', 'to play tricks'.

29. A wooden tower moved on rollers or wheels and used to assault enemy walls.

30. A light-armed soldier with a round target shield.

31. A soldier armed from head to foot, sometimes riding on a horse similarly protected.

nized the hardness of his task. He also suspected the trust-worthiness of his men. So he adopted a new plan: he would tempt some of the defenders by flattery, and having stolen their allegiance so take the city. All night long he considered this scheme. At dawn he entered the Caesar's tent and told him what he had decided. At the same time he asked for John's support while he examined the walls and viewed the battle-ments and their defenders (for they too were of different nationalities); thus he would determine how the capital could be taken. John was indignant at this command, for he had only recently adopted monastic garb [32] and he knew he would be laughed at by the soldiers on the walls and ramparts if he came near them in such a dress. And that is just what did hap-pen, for when he followed Alexius under compulsion, they immediately spotted him from the walls and sneered at 'The Abbot' with certain ribald epithets. John scowled, and al-though inwardly he felt the insults, he made light of it and devoted all his attention to the task in hand. That is the way with men of strong character: they stand by their decisions, heedless of outside circumstances. He asked the men on guard at the various towers who they were. He learnt that at one point the defenders were the so-called 'Immortals' (a regiment peculiar to the Roman army); at another the Varangians [33] from Thule [34] (by these I mean the axe-bearing barbarians); at another the Nemitzi [35] (these also belonged to a barbarian race which has for a long time served in the armed forces of the Empire). He advised Alexius not to attack the Varan-gians, nor the 'Immortals', for the latter, being natives of the country, are of necessity most loyal to the emperor and would

32. John Ducas served Michael VII loyally, but his influence on the young man declined as the favourite Nicephoritzes gradually became more powerful and he was forced to become a monk. For a glowing description of the Caesar's virtues see Psellus, *Chronographia* vii, 16–17.

33. The Varangian Guard was recruited in Scandinavia, England and Russia.

34. Thule is rather vaguely used for the northern countries; it may refer here to the British Isles.

35. Germans (the name is preserved in the Slav countries today). Tradi-tionally they guarded the Gate of Charisius.

rather lose their lives than be persuaded to plan any evil
against him; and as for the Varangians, who bear on their
shoulders the heavy iron sword, they regard loyalty to the
emperors and the protection of their persons as a family
tradition, a kind of sacred trust and inheritance handed down
from generation to generation; this allegiance they preserve
inviolate and will never brook the slightest hint of betrayal.
But if Alexius put the Nemitzi to the test he would not, he said,
be far short of the mark; from the tower guarded by them he
would gain an entrance to the city. Alexius listened to the
Caesar's advice and accepted it like an oracle from God. A
man was sent therefore to the base of the wall. He was to
sound the Nemitzian leader cautiously. The latter, leaning
over the battlements, after a lengthy exchange of words
agreed to betray the city in the near future. The soldier came
back to Alexius with this news. He (Alexius) and his staff were
overjoyed at this unexpected announcement and with great
enthusiasm made ready to mount their horses.

At this very moment the envoys from Melissenus were most
insistent as they demanded the promised chrysobull. Manganes
was at once sent for and told to produce it. He said that the
chrysobull had been written, but protested strongly that the
instruments essential for the emperor's signature, including
the pen, had been lost. Manganes was a dissembler, with a
remarkable flair for discerning the future and extracting some
profit from the past; he was good at estimating accurately the
situation of the present, cunningly altering it to suit his own
purposes and obscuring certain things merely to please himself. It was in order to keep Melissenus' hopes in suspense
that he deferred the writing of the chrysobull, for he feared
that if it were sent to him before the proper time, conferring on
him the rank of Caesar, Melissenus might reject that honour
and insist without reservation on the title of emperor (as
indeed he had told the Comneni already); Melissenus might
plan some bolder action. Such was the explanation of Manganes' crafty deceit. While this was going on, it was becoming
urgent to force an entrance into the city. The ambassadors,
who were suspicious of this play-acting, pressed their demands

more vigorously. The Comneni answered, 'Now that we have
the city in our power, we are with God's help going to take
full possession of it. Go away and tell your Lord and Master
that, and add that if all goes according to our hopes, with him
at our side, everything will be arranged to suit his and our
convenience without any difficulty.' After this reply to the
envoys, they sent George Palaeologus to the leader of the
Nemitzi, Gilpractus, to find out how he stood and whether he
was prepared to accept them after giving a signal, as he had
promised. The plan was as follows: when they saw the signal,
they were to hurry inside the city the moment he went quickly
up the tower and opened the gates. George Palaeologus most
willingly undertook this mission to Gilpractus – he was never
reluctant to engage in warlike activities and the sacking of
cities. Homer called Ares 'smiter of walls' and the name fitted
George exactly. Meanwhile the Comneni armed themselves
and after marshalling the whole army with great skill advanced slowly towards the city *en masse*. In the evening George
Palaeologus approached the wall, received the signal and
climbed the tower with his men. Alexius' soldiers, during
this time, had arrived at a short distance from the walls. They
threw up a palisade and openly made camp. For a brief part of
the night they bivouacked there, but the Comneni later took
up position in the centre of the line, with the élite of the
cavalry and the better infantry; the light-armed forces were
drawn up separately. As day broke they went forward at a
walking pace and concentrated before the walls. In order to
strike terror into the defenders every man was armed and all
were at battle-stations. When Palaeologus gave the signal
from the tower and opened the gates, the rebels rushed in
pell-mell, armed with shields, bows and spears, wherever they
happened to be, regardless of discipline. It was Holy Thursday
(the day on which we sacrifice our mystic paschal lamb and
feast) in the fourth indiction in the month of April 6589.[36]
Thus the whole army, composed of foreign and native troops
collected from the country-side round Constantinople and the
neighbouring districts, very quickly poured into the city

36. 1 April 1081.

through the Charisian Gate. They knew the capital had for a long time been well stocked with all kinds of provisions, which were constantly replenished by land and sea. Once inside they scattered in all directions, in the main streets, at cross-roads and in alley-ways, in their cruelty sparing neither houses nor churches nor even the innermost sanctuaries; in fact they gathered from them heaps of booty. They did refrain from murder,[37] but all the other crimes were committed with complete and reckless disregard for decency. What was worse was the fact that even the native-born soldiers did not abstain from such excesses; they seemed to forget themselves, debasing their normal habits and unblushingly following the example of the barbarians.

Under the circumstances the Emperor Botaniates was more inclined to abdicate in favour of Melissenus. He was now in a really serious position, for the city was besieged from the west, while on the east Nicephorus Melissenus was already in camp near Damalis. The emperor had no alternative plan. After the capital had passed into the control of the Comneni, he sent for one of his more trustworthy servants and ordered him to bring Melissenus to the palace with the help of the fleet. One of the guardsmen, a fine fighting soldier, accompanied this messenger. But before the order could be carried out the city had been captured. Palaeologus with one of his men walked down to the sea and finding a boat there immediately boarded it and told the oarsmen to row to the place where the fleet was normally anchored. He was nearly across when he saw Botaniates' messenger preparing the fleet; the guardsman was on one of the warships. Palaeologus recognized him a long way off (he was an old acquaintance) and as he went by, spoke to him. He asked the usual questions, where he came from, where he was going, and then asked to be taken on board. The guardsman, with an eye on Palaeologus' sword and buckler (for he was afraid), replied, 'If I hadn't seen you armed like that, I would have taken you on board very gladly.' Palaeologus agreed to lay aside his shield, sword and helmet, provided he was allowed to join him, and when the guardsman

37. Zonaras (xviii, 20) declares that there was killing.

saw that he had done so, he at once took him aboard, put his
arms round him and embraced him with every sign of pleasure.
Palaeologus, however, being a man of action wasted little
time on this; he proceeded with the task. Leaping to the prow
he questioned the rowers: 'What are you up to? Where are
you going? You're bringing the most terrible trouble on your
own heads. You can see the city is taken. The man who was
once Great Domestic has now been proclaimed emperor. You
see his soldiers; you hear the acclamations. There will be no
room for anyone else in the palace. Botaniates is a fine man,
but the Comneni are far too strong for him; his army is
numerous, but ours easily outnumbers it. It's wrong then to
throw away your lives and betray your wives and children.
Come and look round the city – see for yourselves that the
whole army is inside the walls. See the standards. Hear the loud
cries of acclamation. See Alexius on his way to the palace,
already invested with the authority of an emperor. Turn the
prow, admit that Alexius has won and join him.' To a man they
yielded at once to these arguments, except for the guardsman;
he was disgusted. Palaeologus threatened to chain him down
on the ship's deck there and then, or throw him overboard,
and immediately led the acclamation. The rowers followed
suit, but the guardsman still angrily refused. He was put in
chains below deck. Palaeologus, after a brief voyage, resumed
his sword and buckler and moored the ship in the fleet's
anchorage. There he made a public acclamation of Alexius.
Meeting Botaniates' messenger (sent to seize the fleet and
transport Melissenus to the palace) he arrested him without
delay and ordered the sailors to loose the stern-cables. Thus
he sailed with the fleet and arrived at the Acropolis, with loud
cheers for the new emperor. The rowers were told to heave-to
and wait quietly to intercept anyone who tried to cross from
the east. Soon afterwards he saw a ship bearing down on the
Great Palace and made haste to cut it off. He spied his own
father on board. At once he stood up and gave the bow one
usually gives to fathers, but there was no happy response; unlike the Ithacan Odysseus when he saw Telemachos, he certainly
did not call Palaeologus 'his sweet light'. In Homer of

course there was a banquet, suitors, games, a bow and arrows, as well as a prize for the winner – the prudent Penelope. Moreover, Telemachos was not an enemy, but a son who came to help his father. Here it was different: battle and war, father and son on opposite sides. Each was aware of the other's loyalties, though intentions had not yet been translated into action. Looking askance at George and calling him a 'fool', the father asked him, 'What have you come to do here?' 'Since it is you who ask me – nothing.' 'Hold on a little then, and if the emperor listens to my advice, you will soon know what's to be done.' Thereupon Nicephorus Palaeologus went off to the palace, but when he saw the general dispersion of the army and the preoccupation with loot, believing it would be easy to beat them he begged Botaniates to give him the barbarians from the island of Thule;[38] with them he could thrust the Comneni from the city. But Botaniates, who had given up all hope, pretended that he wished to avoid civil war. 'If you take my advice, Nicephorus,' he said, 'now that the Comneni are already in the capital, you will go away and negotiate terms of peace with them.' Nicephorus left him, but most unwillingly.

The Comneni, having entered the city, waited confidently in the square of the great martyr George Sykeotes. They were undecided whether first to visit their mothers and pay them the usual courtesies, according to custom, and then proceed to the palace, but the Caesar heard of this and sent one of his servants to threaten and reproach them severely for dawdling. They set out at once. Near the house of Iberitzes, Nicephorus Palaeologus caught them up. 'The emperor sends you this message,' he said. 'I am a lonely old man, with neither son nor brother nor relative. If it is agreeable to you (and here he addressed himself to the new emperor) you can become my adopted son. For my part, I will take away none of the privileges granted by you to each of your comrades-in-arms, nor will I share in any way your authority as emperor, but will merely enjoy with you the title, the acclamation, the right to wear the purple buskin and to live quietly in the palace. The government of the Empire will rest entirely on your shoulders.'

38. That is to say, the English.

To this message the Comneni offered a few words which
expressed approval. When the Caesar heard of this, he soon
hastened to the palace, full of indignation. As he came in on
the right of the courtyard on foot, the Comneni, who were
going out, met him. He rebuked them soundly. Just as he
entered, his eye fell on Nicephorus Palaeologus coming back
again from the left. 'What are you doing here?' he said, 'What
do you want, kinsman?' 'Apparently I shall accomplish
nothing here,' replied Nicephorus, 'but I have come with the
same message as before from the emperor to the Comneni.
The emperor is determined to keep his promise and treat
Alexius as his son. Alexius will be invested with imperial
authority and administer the Empire according to his own
wishes, while Botaniates will share the title of emperor only,
together with the red slippers and the purple robe; he will
also live quietly in the palace, for he is now an old man and in
need of rest.' The Caesar glared fiercely at Nicephorus and
with a scowl replied, 'Go away and tell the emperor that these
offers would have been most expedient before the city was
captured. From now onwards there is no place whatever for
further negotiations. As he is an old man now, let him vacate
the throne and look to his own safety.' Borilos, meanwhile,
hearing that the Comneni had entered the city and that their
army was scattered in all directions in the search for booty
(entirely occupied in fact in the collection of spoils) decided to
attack. He thought, dispersed as they were, it would be a very
easy matter to subdue them, for the Comneni had been left
alone with their relatives, near or distant, and a mere handful
of strangers. Accordingly he concentrated the whole of the
Varangian Guard and the soldiers who had arrived from
Choma. With perfect discipline they were drawn up in line
from the Forum of Constantine as far as the Milion[39] and
beyond. They stood in close order, ready for battle but for the
time being immobile. Now the reigning patriarch[40] was a

39. A triumphal arch of elaborate design marking the starting-point of
the roads leading out from Constantinople. Sometimes called the Milliar-
ium (Milestone).
40. Cosmas, who had succeeded the famous John Xiphilinus in 1075.

saintly man, who in very truth had no possessions and had practised every form of asceticism known to the early Fathers who dwelt in deserts and mountains. He was also endowed with the divine gift of prophecy and had made many predictions on several occasions which never proved to be wrong. He was indeed a model and example of virtue to future generations. It was clear that Botaniates' misfortunes were by no means unknown to him. Maybe he was inspired by God, or perhaps he acted on the advice of the Caesar (for that too was alleged, as the Caesar had long been a friend of his because of the patriarch's exceptional virtue). At all events, he counselled Botaniates to abdicate. 'Do not engage in civil wars,' he said, 'nor transgress the will of God. Do not allow the city to be defiled with the blood of Christians, but yield to God's will. Renounce the world.' The emperor heeded these words. Fearful of the army's insolent behaviour, he wrapped his clothes round him and went down to the great cathedral with downcast eyes. In the general confusion he had not noticed that he was still wearing the robes of an emperor, but Borilos, turning on him and touching the embroidered work fastened round his arm with pearls, wrenched it off, sarcastically remarking in his mocking way, 'This sort of thing really fits us now.' Botaniates entered the great church of God, Santa Sophia, and there for a time he remained.[41]

41. The abdication took place on 4 April 1081.

BOOK THREE

THE ACCESSION OF ALEXIUS
AND THE STRUGGLE BETWEEN
THE DUCAS AND COMNENUS FAMILIES

HAVING seized the palace the Comneni at once sent Michael, their niece's husband, to Botaniates. This Michael afterwards became logothete of the *secreta*.[1] He was accompanied by Rhadenos, who was at that time eparch.[2] Michael put the emperor on a small boat and went with him to the famous monastery of the Peribleptos. There he and Rhadenos urged him to adopt the habit of a monk, but he put off the decision to the next day. As they were afraid that, in the confusion and disorder which still prevailed, some new attempt at revolution might be made by the two slaves and the men from Choma, they pressed him urgently to accept the tonsure. He obeyed and was honoured with the robes of a monk.[3] Such is the way of Fortune: when she wishes to smile on a man she exalts him on high, crowns him with a royal diadem, gives him sandals of purple; but when she frowns, instead of the purple and the crown, she clothes him in ragged garments of black. And this was the fate of Botaniates now. When he was asked by one of his friends if he found the change tolerable, he replied: 'Abstinence from meat is the only thing that worries me; the other matters cause little concern.' In the meantime the Empress Maria still remained in the palace with her son Constantine, whom she bore to the previous emperor Michael Ducas. As the poet says, she feared for her 'blond Menelaus';

1. A logothete is properly speaking an accountant; the *secreta* were the offices used by various civil authorities. Michael was a financial dignitary of high standing.
2. The eparch was the city prefect. Psellus describes the office as second only to the position of emperor: 'an imperial dignity, although it did not carry with it the privilege of wearing the purple'.
3. The Greek reads 'dress of angels' – a euphemism.

and she had a perfectly respectable excuse for staying on – the ties of kinship, although some people, activated by jealousy, surmised that she had certain other reasons. They argued that one of the Comneni was related to her by marriage and another was her adopted son. In fact though, the real cause which determined her actions was not one generally condemned by society, nor was it the attractive and friendly nature of those persons,[4] but the fact that she was in a foreign country, without relatives, without friends, with nobody whatever of her own folk. Naturally she did not wish to leave the palace hurriedly; she feared some evil might befall the child, if she went before receiving some guarantee of safety. When emperors fall, that kind of thing usually happens. The little boy,[5] apart from other considerations, was a lovely child, still quite young (he was not yet seven years old) and no one should blame if I praise my own[6] when the nature of the case compels me. It was delightful enough to hear him speak, but that was not all: his extraordinary agility and suppleness made him unrivalled at games, if one is to believe what his companions in those days said later. He was blond, with a skin as white as milk, his cheeks suffused with red like some dazzling rose that has just left its calyx. His eyes were not light-coloured, but hawk-like, shining beneath the brows, like a precious stone set in a golden ring. Thus, seemingly endowed with a heavenly beauty not of this world, his manifold charms captivated the beholder; in short, anyone who saw him would say, 'He is like the painter's Cupid.' That was the true reason for the empress's continued presence in the palace. For my own part, I am in any case naturally averse to story-telling and the fabrication of history, although I know the custom is general, especially among the jealous and spiteful. I am not quickly impressed by the slanders of the mob. As a matter of fact, I have other reasons to believe I know the truth in this affair: from my

4. Alexius and Isaac. It was hinted in some quarters that Alexius was the empress's lover (Mary of Alania).

5. Psellus is even more enthusiastic when describing the charms of the little Constantine (*Chronographia* vii, 12–3).

6. See Introduction, p. 12. Anna had been betrothed to Constantine.

early girlhood, before I was eight years old, I was brought up by the empress. She was very fond of me and shared all her secrets with me. I have heard many others speak of these things with differing accounts, as some interpreted the events of that time in one way, and others in another; each followed his own inclination, influenced by sympathy or hatred, and I saw that they were not all of one mind. Moreover, I have on several occasions heard the empress herself describe in detail all that happened to her and how frightened she was, in particular for her son, when the Emperor Nicephorus abdicated. Indeed, in my opinion and in the opinion of most people who care for the truth and are best qualified to judge, it was love for her child that kept her then for a little while in the palace. With that I end my remarks about the Empress Maria. As for Alexius, my father, who had meanwhile seized power, he came to live in the palace. His wife, fifteen years old at the time, he left in the 'lower' palace with her sisters and mother and the Caesar, her grandfather on the paternal side. This palace was so-called because of its position. Alexius himself, with his brothers, his mother and his close relatives went up to the higher palace, also called Boucoleon.[7]

As I have said, many people were suspicious when the empress stayed on there and they suggested in an underhand way that the new emperor intended to marry her. The Ducas family believed no such thing (they were not carried away by chance rumours) but they knew that the mother of the Comneni had for a long time been undisguisedly hostile to themselves. Their suspicions made them fearful, as I myself have often heard them say. Thus when George Palaeologus arrived with the fleet and began the acclamation, the party of the Comneni, leaning over the ramparts, tried to silence him from above, bidding him not to link the names of Irene and

---

7. It was called *Boucoleon* for the following reason. Near its walls a harbour had been constructed in the old days of marble and concrete, where the stone lion catches its prey, an ox; it clings to the bull's horn and having broken its neck has its teeth embedded, so to speak, in the animal's throat. The whole place (the buildings on land and the harbour itself) has been called after it Boucoleon. (A.C.)

Alexius in a common acclamation. He was extremely angry. 'It was not for your sakes,' he cried, 'that I won so great a victory, but because of the Irene you speak of.' And at the same time he ordered his sailors to acclaim both together, Irene and Alexius. All this thoroughly disturbed the Ducas faction; but it also, of course, provided the fault-finders with an opportunity to revile the Empress Maria. The Emperor Alexius had in fact no such thought in his mind (how should he?). Once he had taken over the leadership of the Romans, being always the man of action, he at once became immersed in matters of state. He became, one might say, the centre of supreme power. At sunrise he entered the palace, and before shaking off the dust of battle and resting his body, he applied himself immediately and totally to the consideration of the military position. In everything he had in his brother Isaac a partner (Isaac he respected like a father) and he shared his plans with his mother. They supported him in the administration of the Empire, although his own fine intelligence and vigour were more than equal to the government of one realm; he could have managed several empires of more than one type. However, he turned his attention to a matter of urgency: the rest of the day and all that night he spent in devising some method of ending the indiscipline and licence of the soldiers without causing a mutiny; he also wanted to relieve the population of the city from anxiety for the future. The soldiers were scattered over Byzantium in great numbers, behaving like complete hooligans. Under any circumstances he feared their wildness and all the more because of their mixed origin; there was a danger that they might even plan a coup against himself. The Caesar John Ducas had his own ideas. He wanted to expedite the Empress Maria's departure and drive her from the palace, in order to free the public from their unjustified suspicions. He proceeded therefore to win over the Patriarch Cosmas by all means. He demanded that he should support their cause and absolutely refuse to listen to Maria's arguments; next he cleverly suggested to her that she should ask the emperor for a written guarantee of safety on her own behalf and for the sake of the child, and then withdraw. It was a

Patroclus-like scheme,[8] for he had already secured a hold over her when the Emperor Michael Ducas had resigned the throne: he had advised Michael's successor, Nicephorus Botaniates, to take the lady in marriage, because she was of foreign birth and had no crowd of relatives to embarrass the emperor. He spoke to him at length of her noble birth and physical attractions; again and again he praised her. She was in fact very tall, like a cypress tree; her skin was snow-white; her face was oval, her complexion wholly reminiscent of a spring flower or a rose. As for the flash of her eyes, what mortal could describe it? Eyebrows, flame-coloured, arched above eyes of light blue. A painter's hand has many times reproduced the colours of all the flowers brought to birth each in its own season, but the beauty of the empress, the grace that shone about her, the charming attractiveness of her ways, these seemed to baffle description, to be beyond the artist's skill. Neither Apelles,[9] nor Pheidias, nor any of the sculptors ever created such a work. The Gorgon's head,[10] so they say, turned men who saw her to stone, but a man who saw the empress walking, or who suddenly met her, was stupefied, rooted to the spot where he happened to be and speechless, apparently deprived in that one moment of all feeling and reason. Such was the proportion and perfect symmetry of her body, each part in harmony with the rest, that no one till then had ever seen its like among human-kind – a living work of art, an object of desire to lovers of beauty. She was indeed Love incarnate, visiting as it were this earthly world. With such praises then the Caesar on that occasion softened the emperor's heart and won him over, although many were counselling him to marry the Empress Eudocia.[11] Some people whispered

8. Homer, *Iliad* xix, 302. The women lamented for the dead Patroclus, but it was a pretence – they were really bewailing their own lot.

9. Apelles, the famous painter of the fourth century B.C.; Pheidias, the Athenian sculptor, designer of the Parthenon sculptures (fifth century B.C.).

10. Gorgo or Medusa, a mythical monster and popular apotropaic symbol. Perseus killed her.

11. Eudocia Macrembolitissa had married Constantine X (1059–67) and later Romanus Diogenes (1067–71). Her daughter Zoe, by the former, married Alexius' brother Adrian.

that she (Eudocia) in her desire to become empress a second time tried to woo Botaniates by letters when he arrived at Damalis, hurrying to seek the throne. Others said that she wrote, not for her own sake, but on behalf of her daughter, the Porphyrogenita Zoe. And maybe she would have had her way, had not one of his servants cut short her attempt, Leo Cydoniates the eunuch, who gave her much timely advice. I am not at liberty to report in detail what he said, because I have a natural abhorrence of slander, but the chroniclers of such matters will surely make it their business to write about it. The Caesar John, however, after using every form of persuasion finally achieved his purpose: Botaniates married the Empress Maria, as I have explained in more detail before. Thereafter John enjoyed great freedom of speech in his dealings with her. These events took place in the course of several days, for the Comneni absolutely refused to drive her from the palace, for two reasons: they had received many kindnesses from her throughout the whole of her reign, and (no less important) they were on friendly terms with her because of the double relationship that bound them. At the time many rumours were put about, emanating from many sources and following one after the other in a constant stream. They plainly reflected the different policies. The interpretation given to events depended on the attitude of the individual: some were sympathetic to her, others were filled with hate; both parties were prejudiced, unwilling to judge the case on its merits. Meanwhile Alexius was crowned alone by the Patriarch Cosmas.[12] The thought that the empress was still not considered worthy of the imperial crown frightened the Ducas family more than ever; however, they insisted that the Empress Irene should be crowned. It happened that a monk called Eustratios and surnamed Garidas had his dwelling near the great church of God and derived therefrom a false reputation for virtue. This man in times past had frequently visited the

12. In the fourth year of the reign of Michael Ducas, the son of the Emperor Constantine, the Patriarch John Xiphilinus had died, on the second day of August in the third indiction, and Cosmas, a man of great virtue and much revered, was thereupon elected in his place. (A.C.)

mother of the Comneni and made prophecies about power. In
any case she was well disposed towards monks, but such words
flattered her and she made it clear that her faith in him was
increasing every day. Eventually she became eager to establish
him on the patriarchal throne. The reigning high priest, she
alleged, was of a simple nature, not a man of action, and she
persuaded certain persons to put in his mind the idea of retirement; they were to advise this because, forsooth, it was in his
own best interests. But the holy man was not deceived by this
pretext. 'By Cosmas,' he said, for he went so far as to take an
oath in his own name; 'By Cosmas, if Irene is not crowned by
my own hands, I will never resign the patriarchal throne.'
They returned to their 'sovereign' and told her what had been
said (by now they all addressed her by that name, because the
emperor, who loved his mother, wished her to be so named).
So, on the seventh day after the public proclamation of
Alexius' accession, his wife Irene was crowned by the
Patriarch Cosmas.

The physical appearance of the two rulers, Alexius and
Irene, was remarkable, indeed quite incomparable. A painter
could never reproduce the beauty of such an archetype, nor a
sculptor mould his lifeless stone into such harmony. Even
the celebrated canon of Polyclitus [13] would have seemed
utterly inadequate, if one looked first at these living statues
(the newly crowned rulers, I mean) and then at Polyclitus'
masterpieces. Alexius was not a very tall man, but broad-
shouldered and yet well proportioned. When standing he did
not seem particularly striking to onlookers, but when one saw
the grim flash of his eyes as he sat on the imperial throne, he
reminded one of a fiery whirlwind, so overwhelming was the
radiance that emanated from his countenance and his whole
presence. His dark eyebrows were curved, and beneath them
the gaze of his eyes was both terrible and kind. A quick glance,
the brightness of his face, the noble cheeks suffused with red
combined to inspire in the beholder both dread and confidence. His broad shoulders, mighty arms and deep chest, all
on a heroic scale, invariably commanded the wonder and

13. A Greek sculptor of immense repute (fifth century B.C.).

delight of the people. The man's person indeed radiated beauty and grace and dignity and an unapproachable majesty. When he came into a gathering and began to speak, at once you were conscious of the fiery eloquence of his tongue, for a torrent of argument won a universal hearing and captivated every heart; tongue and hand alike were unsurpassed and invincible, the one in hurling the spear, the other in devising fresh enchantments. The Empress Irene, my mother, was at that time only a young girl, not yet fifteen years old. She was a daughter of Andronicus, the Caesar's eldest son, and of illustrious descent, for her family derived from the famous houses of Andronicus and Constantine Ducas. She stood upright like some young sapling, erect and evergreen, all her limbs and the other parts of her body absolutely symmetrical and in harmony one with another. With her lovely appearance and charming voice she never ceased to fascinate all who saw and heard her. Her face shone with the soft light of the moon; it was not the completely round face of an Assyrian woman, nor long, like the face of a Scyth, but just slightly oval in shape. There were rose blossoms on her cheeks, visible a long way off. Her light-blue eyes were both gay and stern: their charm and beauty attracted, but the fear they caused so dazzled the bystander that he could neither look nor turn away. Whether there really was an Athena in olden times, the Athena celebrated by poets and writers, I do not know, but I often hear the myth repeated and satirized. However, if someone in those times had said of this empress that she was Athena made manifest to the human race, or that she had descended suddenly from the sky in some heavenly glory and unapproachable splendour, his description would not have been so very inappropriate. What was rather surprising – and in this she differed from all other women – was the way she humbled swaggerers, but when they were subdued and fearful restored their courage by a single glance. For the most part her lips were closed and when thus silent she resembled a veritable statue of Beauty, a breathing monument of Harmony. Generally she accompanied her words with graceful gestures, her hands bare to the wrists, and you would say it (her hand) was

ivory turned by some craftsman into the form of fingers and
hand. The pupils of her eyes, with the brilliant blue of deep
waves, recalled a calm, still sea, while the white surrounding
them shone by contrast, so that the whole eye acquired a
peculiar lustre and a charm which was inexpressible. So much
for the physical characteristics of Irene and Alexius. As for my
uncle, he was about the same height as his brother and indeed
was not very different from him in other respects, but he was
rather pale and his beard was not particularly thick; round the
jaws it was thinner than that of Alexius. Both brothers indulged often in hunting, when there was no great pressure of
work, but they found war more exhilarating than the chase.
On the battle-field no one outpaced Isaac even when he commanded regiments in person: the moment he saw the enemy's
line, heedless of all else, he hurled himself into their midst like
a thunderbolt and quickly threw their ranks into confusion – a
habit that led on more than one occasion to his capture in
battle against the Agarenes[14] in Asia. This impetuosity was
Isaac's undoing – the one fault for which he can be censured in
war.

Alexius had promised Nicephorus Melissenus (his brother-
in-law) the title of Caesar. Isaac, the eldest of his brothers,[15]
therefore had to be honoured with some higher dignity, and as
there was no such rank between that of emperor and Caesar,
a new name was invented, a compound of *sebastos* and *autocrator*. Isaac was created sebastocrator, a kind of second
emperor and senior to the Caesar, who received the acclamation in third place. In addition, Alexius decreed that both
sebastocrator and Caesar should wear crowns at public
festivals, although they were much inferior to his own. The
imperial diadem, decked all over with pearls and stones, some
encrusted, some pendent, was shaped like a half-sphere, fitting
the head closely; on either side of the temples clusters of
pearls and precious stones hung down, lightly touching the
cheeks. This diadem constitutes a unique ornament of the

14. The Turks.
15. That is, the eldest surviving brother, Manuel having died in battle
(cf. p. 31).

emperor's dress. The crowns of the sebastocrator and the
Caesar, on the other hand, are embellished with few pearls and
stones and are not cap-shaped. At the same time Taronites,
who had married the emperor's sister Maria, was also
honoured with the titles of protosebastos and protovestiarius,
and not long afterwards he was promoted to the rank of
panhypersebastos with the right to sit with the Caesar.
Alexius' brother Adrian, too, was granted the title of Most
Illustrious Protosebastos and Nicephorus, his youngest
brother, who had been made Great Drungarius of the Fleet,
was also raised to the rank of sebastos. My father was responsible for inventing these honours. Some were compound
names (like the example quoted above), others were titles put
to a new use. For names like 'panhypersebastos' and 'sebastocrator' and so on were synthetic, but the dignity of sebastos
took on a new meaning. In the old days the epithet 'sebastos'
had been applied to emperors only, a distinctive title, but
Alexius for the first time allowed it to be more widely used.
If one regards the art of ruling as a science, a kind of supreme
philosophy (the art of all arts, so to speak, and the highest
science of all), then one would have to admire him as a
scientist in a way and a leading thinker for having invented
these imperial titles and functions. Of course there was a
difference: the great logicians invented names for the sake of
lucidity, whereas Alexius, the master of the science of government, directed all his innovations towards the good of the
Empire itself, whether changes were effected in the allotment
of duties or in the granting of titles.

However, let us return to the saintly Cosmas, the patriarch.
He presided over the sacred ceremony in honour of the
Hierarch John the Theologian, in the church named after him
in the Hebdomon,[16] and a few days later resigned his high
office (which he had held with distinction for five years and
nine months) and retired to the monastery of Callias.[17] The
eunuch Eustratius Garidas succeeded to the patriarch's

16. About three miles west of the Golden Gate.
17. 8 May 1081. The resignation was probably due to Cosmas's dis-
approval of the financial policy of the Comneni.

throne. After the deposition of his father Michael Ducas, Constantine Porphyrogenitus, the son of the Empress Maria, had voluntarily set aside the purple buskins and adopted ordinary black ones, but the new emperor (Nicephorus Botaniates) ordered him to throw them away and wear silk shoes of various colours. He felt sorry for the young man and admired him no less for his handsome appearance than for his aristocratic origin. The wearing of footwear resplendent with scarlet throughout he would not countenance, but granted him the privilege of a few strands of red in the material. Later, when Alexius Comnenus was proclaimed emperor, Maria on the advice of the Caesar asked for a written pledge, guaranteed in letters of red and a golden seal, not only that she should be allowed to live in security with her son, but that he should be co-ruler with Alexius, with the right to wear the purple sandals and a crown, and the right to be acclaimed as emperor with him. Her request was granted in a chrysobull confirming all her demands. Constantine's woven silk shoes were removed and buskins wholly of red substituted for them. In the matter of donations or chrysobulls his signature now appeared immediately after that of Alexius and in the processions he followed him wearing an imperial diadem. Some people declared that even before the revolt the empress had made an agreement with the Comneni that her son should be treated in this way. Whether that was true or not, she now left the palace with an escort worthy of her rank and withdrew to the house built by the late Emperor Constantine Monomachus near the monastery of the great martyr George (still commonly known as Mangana). The Sebastocrator Isaac accompanied her.

Such were the arrangements made by the Comneni in respect of the Empress Maria. As for Alexius, who had enjoyed a good education from his earliest years and, obedient to the precepts of his mother, had the fear of the Lord deeply implanted in his soul, he was grieved and embarrassed at the plundering of the capital, which on his arrival had affected the whole population. Unbroken success can sometimes lead a man who has never met with any reverse to commit a deed of folly; if he is of a cautious, sensible disposition, his error will promptly be followed by absolute remorse and alarm as he becomes aware in his heart of the fearfulness of God, especially if he is engaged on projects of great importance and has himself attained exalted rank. An underlying dread will affect him lest by some act of ignorance or foolhardiness or pride he should call down on himself the wrath of God and be cast down from his position of authority and lose all his present possessions. Such was once the fate of Saul, for God, because of the king's foolish pride, smashed and broke up his kingdom. Distraught with these reflections and deeply perturbed, Alexius feared that somehow he might be the scapegoat, the object of divine vengeance. He regarded the evil which had befallen the whole city as his responsibility, even if it was really the work of individual soldiers, all that rabble that descended in a mighty flood on all parts of Constantinople. He was sick at heart, filled with shame, as if he, personally, had committed these frightful atrocities. Majesty and power, the royal purple and the stone-encrusted diadem, the robe adorned with gold and jewels, all these he (quite rightly) looked upon as worthless compared with the indescribable disaster that had then afflicted the capital; for no writer, however earnest, could possibly do justice to the terrors by which it was enveloped in those days. Churches, sanctuaries, property both public and private, all were the victims of universal pillage, while the ears of all its citizens were deafened by cries and shouts raised on every side. An onlooker might well have thought an earthquake was taking place. With these reflections Alexius suffered agonies of remorse and a grief beyond endurance. He was extremely sensitive at all times to wrong-doing and though he was aware that these crimes against the city were the work of other hands, engineered by other men, yet conscience told him, and that in quite unmistakable terms, that it was he himself who had afforded the pretext for such a calamity and had given it the original impetus. (The true responsibility for the revolt, of course, lay with the slaves I have referred to before.) But even so he assumed the whole burden of guilt and was anxious and willing to heal the wound, for only thus, after healing and cleansing, could he approach the task of governing the Empire or satisfactorily direct and bring to a proper conclusion his plans for the army and its wars. So he went to his mother, informed her of his anxiety (a state which did him credit), and asked how he could find relief and freedom from the cares that gnawed at his conscience. She embraced her son and gladly listened to his words. Being of one accord, therefore, they summoned the Patriarch Cosmas (he had not yet resigned his throne) and certain leading members of the Holy Synod and the monastic order. The emperor came before them as a man on trial, a person of no account, one of 'those set under authority',[18] condemned and tensely awaiting at any moment the verdict of the court. He confessed everything, passing over neither the temptation, nor the yielding to it, nor the commission of evil, nor even the responsibility for what was done. He admitted all in fear and faith, passionately demanding from them a remedy for his misdeeds and offering to undergo penance. They condemned not only Alexius but his blood-relations, as well as those who shared with him in the rebellion; all were to submit to the same punishment – fasting, sleeping on the ground and the performing of the appropriate rites to appease the anger of God. The penalties were accepted and paid with enthusiasm; in fact, their wives could not bear to stand aloof (how could they, when they loved their husbands?) and of their own free will they too submitted to the yoke of penance. The palace became a scene of tearful lamentation – a lamentation not reprehensible nor evidence of any faint-heartedness but rather to be praised and the forerunner of a higher, everlasting joy. It was typical of the emperor's own piety that he should inflict on himself a further penalty: for forty days and nights he wore sackcloth beneath the royal purple and next to his skin. At night his bed was the bare ground and while he bewailed his sins (as was only right) his head was supported on nothing more than a stone. Thereafter, when the penance was complete, he turned his attention to the administration of the Empire with clean hands.

It was his desire that his mother should govern rather than

18. St Luke vii, 8.

himself, but so far the plan had been concealed for fear that she, if she knew of it, might leave the palace (Alexius was aware that she considered withdrawal to a monastery). Nevertheless, in all matters however ordinary he did nothing without her advice: she became his confidante and co-partner in government. Gradually and surreptitiously he involved her more and more in state affairs; on occasions he even declared openly that without her brains and good judgement the Empire would not survive. By these means he bound her more closely to himself, but prevented her from attaining her own goal and frustrated it. She had in mind the last stage of life and dreamed of monasteries in which she would drag out her remaining years in the contemplation of wisdom. Such was her intention, the constant aim of her prayers. Despite this longing in her heart, despite the total preoccupation with a higher life, she also loved her son to a quite exceptional degree and wished somehow to bear with him the storms that buffeted the Empire (if I may apply seafaring metaphor to the manifold troubles and tumults to which it was exposed). She desired to guide the ship of state on the best possible course, in fair weather or in tempest (when waves crashed on to it from all sides), especially since the young man had only just taken his seat in the stern and put his hand to the tiller, with no previous experience of storms, winds and waves of such violence. She was constrained, therefore, by a mother's affection for her son, and governed with him, sometimes even grasping the reins (to change the metaphor) and alone driving the chariot of power – and without accident or error. The truth is that Anna Dalassena was in any case endowed with a fine intellect and possessed besides a really first-class aptitude for governing. On the other hand, she was distracted from it by her love for God. When in the month of August (in the same indiction [19]) Robert's crossing to Epirus compelled Alexius to leave the capital, he brought to light and put into operation his cherished plan: the whole executive power was entrusted to his mother alone and the decision was confirmed publicly in a chrysobull. As it is the historian's duty not merely to sum-

19. See Glossary.

marize the deeds and decrees of good men, but as far as he can to give some details of the former and transmit the latter in full, I myself will set out the terms of this document, omitting only the subtle refinements of the scribe. It ran thus: 'When danger is foreseen or some other dreadful occurrence is expected, there is no safeguard stronger than a mother who is understanding and loves her son, for if she gives counsel, her advice will be reliable; if she offers prayers, they will confer strength and certain protection. Such at any rate has been the experience of myself, your emperor, in the case of my own revered mother, who has taught and guided and sustained me throughout, from my earliest years. She had a place in aristocratic society, but her first concern was for her son and his faith in her was preserved intact. It was well known that one soul animated us, physically separated though we were, and by the grace of Christ that happy state has persisted to this day. Never were those cold words, "mine" and "yours", uttered between us, and what was even more important, the prayers she poured out during all that time reached the ears of the Lord and have raised me now to the imperial throne. After I took in my hand the imperial sceptre, she found it intolerable that she was not bearing an equal share in my labours, to the interests both of your emperor and of the whole people. But now I am preparing with God's help to do battle with Rome's enemies; with much forethought an army is being recruited and thoroughly equipped; not the least of my cares, however, has been the provision of an efficient organization in financial and civil affairs. Fortunately, an impregnable bulwark for good government has been found – in the appointment of my revered mother, of all women most honoured, as controller of the entire administration. I, your emperor, therefore decree explicitly in this present chrysobull the following: because of her vast experience of secular affairs (despite the very low value she sets upon such matters), whatever she decrees in writing (whether the case be referred to her by the logothete, or by his subordinate officers, or by any other person who prepares memoranda or requests or judgements concerning remissions of public debts) shall have permanent validity as if I myself, your Serene Emperor, had issued them or after dictating them had had them committed to writing. Whatever decisions or orders are made by her, written or unwritten, reasonable or unreasonable, provided that they bear her seal (the Transfiguration and the Assumption), shall be regarded as coming from myself, by the fact that they carry the "In the month . . ." of the current logothete.[20] Moreover, with regard to promotions and successions to the tribunals and fiscs, and in the matter of honours, offices and donations of immovable property, my saintly mother shall have full power to take whatever action shall seem good to her. Further, if any persons are promoted to the tribunals or succeed to the fiscs and are honoured with the highest or medium or lowest dignities, they shall thereafter retain these positions on a permanent basis. Again, increases of salary, additional gifts, reductions of tax, economies and diminution of payments shall be settled by her without question. In brief, nothing shall be reckoned invalid which she commands either in writing or by word of mouth, for her words and her decisions shall be reckoned as my own and none of them shall be annulled. In years to come they shall have the force of law permanently. Neither now nor in the future shall my mother be subjected to inquiry or undergo any examination whatsoever at the hands of anybody, whoever he may be. The same provision shall also hold good for her ministers and the chancellor of the time, whether their actions seem to be reasonable or ridiculous. It shall be absolutely impossible in the future to demand account of any action taken by them under the terms of this present chrysobull.'

The reader may be surprised by the honour conferred on his mother by the emperor in this matter, since he yielded her precedence in everything, relinquishing the reins of government, as it were, and running alongside as she drove the imperial chariot; only in the title of emperor did he share with her the privileges of his rank. And this despite the fact that he had already passed his boyhood years and was of an age which in the case of men like him is particularly susceptible to the

20. It was sufficient for the emperor to write the date in his own hand. The logothete's document would begin with these words.

lust for power. Wars against the barbarians, with all their attendant trials and tribulations he was prepared to face himself, but the entire administration of affairs, the choice of civil magistrates, the accounts of the imperial revenues and expenditure he left to his mother. At this point the reader may well censure him for transferring the government of the Empire to the gynaeconitis, but had he known this woman's spirit, her surpassing virtue, intelligence and energy, his reproaches would soon have turned to admiration. For my grandmother had an exceptional grasp of public affairs, with a genius for organization and government; she was capable, in fact, of managing not only the Roman Empire, but every other empire under the sun as well. She had vast experience and a wide understanding of the motives, ultimate consequences, interrelations good and bad of various courses of action, penetrating quickly to the right solution, adroitly and safely carrying it out. Her intellectual powers, moreover, were paralleled by her command of language. She was indeed a most persuasive orator, without being verbose or longwinded. Nor did the inspiration of the argument readily desert her, for if she began on a felicitous note, she was also most successful in ending her speeches with just the right words. She was already a woman of mature years when she was called upon to exercise imperial authority, at a time of life when one's mental powers are at their best, when one's judgement is fully developed and knowledge of affairs is widest – all qualities that lend force to good administration and government. It is natural that persons of this age should not merely speak with greater wisdom than the young (as the tragic playwright[21] says), but also act in a more expedient way. In the past, when Anna Dalassena was still looked upon as a younger woman, she had impressed everyone as 'having an old head on young shoulders'; to the observant her face alone revealed Anna's inherent virtue and gravity. But, as I was saying, once he had seized power my father reserved for himself the struggles and hard labour of war, while she became so to speak an onlooker, but he made her sovereign and like a slave

21. Aeschylus: perhaps *Persae*, 782.

said and did whatever she commanded. He loved her exceedingly and depended on her for advice (such was his affection for her). His right hand he devoted to her service; his ears listened for her bidding. In all things he was entirely subservient, in fact, to her wishes. I can sum up the whole situation thus: he was in theory the emperor, but she had real power. She was the legislator, the complete organizer and governor, while he confirmed her arrangements, written and unwritten, the former by his signature, the latter by his spoken approval. One might say that he was indeed the instrument of her power – he was not emperor, for all the decisions and ordinances of his mother satisfied him, not merely as an obedient son, but as an attentive listener to her instruction in the art of ruling. He was convinced that she had attained perfection in everything and easily excelled all men of that generation in prudence and understanding of affairs.

Such were the events that marked the beginning of the reign. One could hardly at that stage call Alexius emperor once he had entrusted to her the supreme authority. Another person might yield here to the claims of panegyric and extol the native land of this remarkable woman; he might trace her descent from the Adriani Dalasseni and Charon,[22] while he embarked on the ocean of their achievements. But I am writing history and my fitting task is not to describe her through the family and kinsmen, but by reference to her character, her virtue, and the events which form the proper subject of history. To return once more to my grandmother, I must add this: not only was she a very great credit to her own sex, but to men as well; indeed, she contributed to the glory of the whole human race. The women's quarters in the palace had been the scene of utter depravity ever since the infamous Constantine Monomachos had ascended the throne and right up to the time when my father became emperor had been noted for foolish love intrigues, but Anna effected a reformation; a com-

22. Anna Dalassena was the daughter of Charon (so-called because every time he struck his enemies they went to Hades). On the mother's side she was descended from Adrian and Theophylactus Dalassenus, both famous men. The family was prominent in the mid-eleventh century.

mendable decorum was restored and the palace now enjoyed a discipline that merited praise. She instituted set times for the singing of sacred hymns, stated hours for breakfast; there was now a special period in which magistrates were chosen. She herself set a firm example to everybody else, with the result that the palace assumed the appearance rather of a monastery under the influence of this really extraordinary woman and her truly saintly character; for in self-control she surpassed the famous women of old, heroines of many a legend, as the sun outshines all stars. As for her compassion for the poor and her generosity to the needy, no words could do justice to them. Her house was a refuge for penniless relatives, but no less for strangers. Priests and monks she honoured in particular: they shared her meals and no one ever saw her at table without some of them as guests. Her outward serenity, true reflection of character, was respected by angels but terrorized even the demons, and pleasure-loving fools, victims of their own passions, found a single glance from her more than they could bear; yet to the chaste she seemed gentle and gay. She knew exactly how to temper reserve and dignity; her own reserve never gave the impression of harshness or cruelty, nor did her tenderness seem too soft or unrestrained – and this, I fancy, is the true definition of propriety: the due proportion of warm humanity and strict moral principle. She was by nature thoughtful and was always evolving new ideas, not, as some folk whispered, to the detriment of the state; on the contrary, they were wholesome schemes which restored to full vigour the already corrupted empire and revived, as far as one could, the ruined fortunes of the people. In spite of her preoccupation with matters of government, she by no means neglected the duties incumbent on a religious woman, for the greater part of the night was spent by her in the chanting of sacred hymns and she wore herself out with continual prayers and vigils. Nevertheless, at dawn or even at second cock-crow, she was applying herself anew to state business, attending to the choice of magistrates and answering the petitions of suppliants with the help of her secretary Gregory Genesius. Now if some orator had decided to make this the subject of a panegyric, he would no doubt have exalted her and praised her to the skies (as is the way of encomiasts) for her deeds and thoughts and superiority to all others; the famous ones of old, both men and women, who were renowned for their virtue would certainly have been thrown into the shade. But such licence is not for the writer of history. Those who know her virtue, therefore, her dignified character, her never-failing sagacity and the loftiness and sublimity of her spirit, must not blame my history, if I have done less than justice to her great qualities.

But we must return now to the point where we digressed briefly to talk about her. As I said, she guided the Empire's destinies, but not all day was spent on secular matters: she still attended the prescribed services in the church dedicated to the martyr Thecla. I will now tell how this church came to be built by the Emperor Isaac Comnenus, her brother-in-law. When the Dacians [23] refused to observe any longer the ancient treaty with the Romans and deliberately broke it, the Sarmatians [24] (who used to be called Mysians in the old days) heard of their action and became restive themselves. They were not satisfied to remain in their own territory (separated from the Empire by the Ister) and when a general uprising took place they crossed the river to our lands. The reason for the migration was the deadly hostility of the Getae, who were neighbours of the Dacians and plundered Sarmatian settlements. They waited for the right moment and when the Ister was frozen the whole tribe crossed over dry-footed and dumped themselves down on our territory. Then they proceeded to spread havoc in the cities and districts of that area. At this news the Emperor Isaac decided that Triaditza must be occupied and since he had already checked the ambitions of the eastern barbarians this task presented no great difficulty. With the intention of driving them from Roman territory, he assembled the whole army and set out on the road leading to the

23. The Hungarians.
24. The Sarmatians are better known as the Patzinaks. Anna is describing the campaign of 1059. She has freely used the narrative of Psellus (*Chronographia* vii, 67 ff.).

north. The enemy, seeing the Romans in battle order, with Isaac leading the attack in person, immediately quarrelled among themselves. Isaac, who had good reason to distrust them in any case, launched a violent assault on the strongest and bravest part of their army. As he and his men drew near, the Sarmatians were filled with dismay; the sight of this 'Wielder of the Thunderbolt' and the serried ranks of his army was too much for them. They lost heart. So they withdrew a little and after challenging him to do battle with them in three days time, abandoned their tents there and then, and fled. When Isaac reached their camp, he destroyed the tents and took away the booty found there, but his triumphant return was interrupted at the foot of Mount Lobitzos; a tremendous and unseasonable snowstorm overtook him (it was 24 September).[25] The water-level in the rivers rose and they overflowed their banks; the whole plain, on which the emperor and his army were encamped, became a sea. All the supplies disappeared, swept away in the river currents, while the men and baggage-animals were numbed with cold. In the sky there were constant rumbles of thunder, with frequent lightning flashes which followed one another in quick succession and threatened to set the whole countryside on fire. The emperor did not know what to do. However, during a brief lull in the storm and after losing a great number of his men who were caught up in the whirling waters of the river, he escaped with some picked soldiers and took refuge with them under an oak tree. He could hear a tremendous roaring noise apparently coming from the tree and as the winds at that moment were becoming even more violent, he was afraid the oak might be blown down. So he moved away, just far enough to avoid being struck, and stood there speechless. At once, as though at a signal, the tree was torn up by the roots and lay in full view on the ground. Isaac stood before it marvelling at God's care for him. Later, news arrived that the east was in revolt. He returned to the palace. It was at this time that Isaac had a lovely church built in honour of Thecla, at

25. On this day the memory of the great martyr Thecla is honoured. (A.C.)

THE ALEXIAD OF ANNA COMNENA *viii–ix*

considerable expense, with magnificent decorations and works of art; there he made his thank-offering in a manner fitting to a Christian and worshipped God in it for the rest of his life. Such was the origin of this church. As I have already remarked, the empress (Alexius' mother) regularly prayed there. I myself knew her for a short time and admired her. Any unprejudiced witness to the truth knows and, if he cares to, will admit that what I have said about her was not mere empty boasting. Indeed, if I had preferred to compose a panegyric rather than a history, I would have written at greater length, adding more stories about her. But I must now return to the main narrative.

Alexius knew that the Empire was almost at its last gasp. The east was being horribly ravaged by the Turks; the west was in a bad condition, while Robert strained every nerve to put on the throne the pseudo-Michael who had taken refuge with him. In my opinion this was rather in the nature of a pretext: it was love of power that inspired Robert and never let him rest. Having found Michael he had a Patroclus-like excuse and that spark of ambition, hitherto lying hidden beneath the ashes, blazed up into a mighty conflagration. In a terrifying fashion he armed himself to do battle with the Roman Empire. Dromons, triremes, biremes, *sermones* [26] and other transport vessels in great numbers were made ready. They were equipped in the coastal areas, while from the mainland strong contingents were being assembled to aid him in the coming struggle. The brave young emperor was in serious trouble. He did not know which way to turn, for both enemies demanded the right to challenge first. He was worried and vexed. The Romans had no worthwhile forces; in fact there were no more than 300 soldiers in the capital and these were from Choma, quite unfit for war and with no combat experience; there were also a few mercenaries, barbarians whose custom it was to dangle swords from their shoulders. [27] In the imperial treasury there were no reserves of money with which he could summon allies from foreign countries. The emperors before him, having little knowledge of war and military affairs, had reduced Roman prestige to a minimum. Indeed, I

26. See Appendix II.   27. The Varangian Guard.

have heard it said by men who were soldiers themselves, and by some of the older men, that no other state in living memory had reached such depths of misery. Conditions were desperate then for the emperor, distracted as he was by anxieties of all sorts. However, being not only a courageous man and undaunted, but having excellent experience in war, he wanted to restore his Empire, to bring it again to a safe anchorage after its terrible buffeting and by God's aid to break up, like waves spent on the rocks, the enemies who in their madness had risen up against him. He realized that he must quickly summon all the toparchs [28] in the east, men who as governors of forts or cities were bravely resisting the Turks. At once, therefore, he dashed off important despatches to all of them: to Dabatenus, temporary governor [29] of Pontic Heracleia and Paphlagonia; to Burtzes, governor of Cappadocia and Choma; and to the other officers. He explained to them all what had happened to him and how by the Providence of God he had been promoted to the supreme rank of emperor, after being rescued beyond all expectations from imminent peril. He ordered them to ensure the safety of their own provinces, leaving for that purpose enough soldiers, but with the rest they were to come to Constantinople, bringing along with them as many able-bodied recruits as they could. He decided, too, that he must seize the initiative in protecting himself against Robert; the leaders and counts who were joining Robert must be diverted from their plans. A messenger had been sent to Monomachatos (before Alexius had become master of the capital) calling for help and asking him to supply the emperor with money. But the envoy returned with nothing more than a letter in which Monomachatos made excuses (as I have written earlier in the history). He said that as long as Botaniates was in control of the Empire, help was out of the question. Alexius read this reply and feared that once the fall of Botaniates became known to him Monomachatos might go over to Robert. He was filled with despair. George

28. Governor of a town.
29. Anna uses the word *topoteretes*, (one who usually commanded a fortress or strong-point).

Palaeologus, the husband of his wife's sister, was sent off to Dyrrachium [30] with instructions to drive Monomachatos from the place without bloodshed (because he had no force powerful enough to eject him involuntarily) and to counteract the machinations of Robert as best he could. Alexius insisted, too, that the ramparts should be constructed in a new way: the majority of the wooden planks were to be left unnailed, so that if the Latins did climb up on ladders, as soon as they set foot on the planks they would upset them and crash down to the ground, planks and all. Moreover, the prefects of the coastal cities and the islanders themselves were earnestly exhorted in letters not to lose heart, nor to relax their efforts in any way, but to be watchful and sober, providing all-round protection for themselves and keeping a wary eye open for Robert. A sudden attack, leading to the capture of all the towns by the sea and even of the islands, would cause trouble later to the Roman Empire.

Such were the emperor's precautions with regard to Illyricum. It was obvious that the districts lying in the direct path of the enemy and nearest to him were now well fortified. At the same time he had not been slow to stir up trouble in Robert's rear, for letters were sent first to Hermann, the Duke of Lombardy, then to the Pope of Rome, and again to the Archbishop Hervé of Capua, to the princes, and besides that to all the military leaders of the Keltic lands, courting their favour by moderate gifts, with promises of much largess and many honours in the future. Thus he incited them to enmity against Robert. Some of them at once renounced their friendship with him; others agreed to do so, if more money was forthcoming. Alexius knew that the German king [31] was more powerful than all the others; whatever policy he adopted, however Robert opposed it, would be successful. On more than one occasion, therefore, letters full of conciliatory phrases and all kinds of pledges were despatched to him, and when he was certain that the king acquiesced and was prepared to yield to his wishes, Choerosphaktes once more departed with another message for him. It read as follows: 'Most noble and

30. An Illyrian city. (A.C.)   31. Henry IV.

truly Christian brother, I pray that your mighty realm may flourish and enjoy even greater prosperity. And why not? I am myself God-fearing and recognize in you the same reverence, so that it is right to pray on your behalf for a better and more profitable future. This decision of yours, your attitude to me, and the undertaking to share in the labours of war against this evil-minded man, in order that you may punish the murderous, sinful enemy of God and the Christians in a manner worthy of his depravity – these things give clear proof of the great goodness of your heart and this brotherly deed of yours makes evident the full measure of your godly spirit. Although in other respects my affairs go well, to a very small degree they are in disarray and confusion because of the actions of Robert. Nevertheless, if there is any point in trusting God and His righteous judgements, then the downfall of that most iniquitous of men cannot be long delayed. For it is impossible that God should suffer the rod of evil to lie for ever upon His heritage. As for the presents that we agreed should be despatched to you, they are now delivered through the Protoproedros Constantine, the Catepan [32] of Dignities; namely, 144,000 pieces of gold and the hundred purple cloths of silk. This is according to the arrangement concluded with your most noble and trustworthy Count Burchard. The afore-mentioned sum, sent to you, has been made up of pieces of silver of the old quality stamped with the effigy of Romanus. [33] When you take the oath, the remaining 216,000 pieces of gold will be forwarded and the salaries of the twenty dignities conferred; your most faithful Abelard will hand them over when you come down to Lombardy. As to the manner of the oath-taking, that has been previously explained to you in detail, but the Protoproedros and Catepan Constantine will make it even clearer; he has been given my instructions on each of the main points which will be required of you and which will be confirmed by you on oath. When the agreement was made between me and the envoys you sent, certain articles of greater

32. See Glossary.
33. There had been a devaluation of currency since the reign of Diogenes Romanus.

importance were mentioned, but because your men said they had no mandate on these matters, I deferred the oath in the circumstances then obtaining. Please take the oaths, then, as the faithful Abelard promised me and as I require of you in respect of the more important addendum. It was my fault that your most faithful and noble Count Burchard has been delayed: I wished him to see my favourite nephew, the son of the sebastocrator, my own well loved brother (happy man!), so that when he returned he could tell you of the boy's intelligence, despite his tender years. (The outward appearance and physical characteristics count less, as far as I am concerned, although in these too he is abundantly blest.) Your envoy will tell you how during his visit to the capital he saw the little boy and had the usual conversation one has with a child. Since God has not blessed me with a son, this beloved nephew takes for me the place of a true heir. If it is the will of God, there is nothing to prevent an alliance between us through ties of kinship. You and I can be mutual friends as Christians, brought more closely together as kinsmen; thus deriving strength from one another, we shall be formidable to our enemies and with God's help invincible. I have now sent to you, as a pledge of my goodwill, a gold pectoral cross set with pearls; a reliquary inlaid with gold containing fragments of various saints, identified in each case by a small label; a cup of sardonyx and a crystal goblet; an astropelekis [34] attached to a chain of gold; and some wood of the balsam tree. [35] May God prolong your years. May He widen the bounds of your realm and put all your adversaries beneath your feet and bring them to shame. May your kingdom enjoy peace and may the sun shed its calm light on all your people. May your foes be destroyed by the mighty Power from on High which preserves you invincible against all attacks, because you love so dearly His true name and arm yourself against His enemies.'

After these arrangements had been made in the west,

34. A *fulmen* (or thunderbolt) bound with gold, a kind of ornament.
35. *Opobalsamum*. No doubt sweet-smelling. Dawes translates as 'balm of Mecca'. In the stench of a medieval town the odour of such wood burning would be more than welcome.

Alexius made preparations to deal with the immediate and pressing danger which threatened him from the east. Meanwhile he remained in the capital, examining every means of counteracting the enemies before his very eyes. As I have said in a previous chapter, the godless Turks were in sight, living in the Propontis area, and Sulayman, who commanded all the east, was actually encamped in the vicinity of Nicaea. His sultanate was in that city (we would call it his palace). The whole countryside of Bithynia and Thynia was unceasingly exposed to Sulayman's foragers; marauding parties on horseback and on foot were raiding as far as the town now called Damalis on the Bosphorus itself; they carried off much booty and all but tried to leap over the very sea. The Byzantines saw them living absolutely unafraid and unmolested in the little villages on the coast and in sacred buildings. The sight filled them with horror. They had no idea what to do. The emperor, aware of this, found it hard to decide what plan to adopt. However, after considering many schemes, with frequent changes and experiments, he chose the best and as far as he could put it into practice. He appointed decarchs from the men hurriedly conscripted (Romans and some recruits who came originally from Choma) and made them embark on small ships, the light-armed with bows and shields only, the rest (who had some experience of other armament) equipped with helmets, shields and spears. They were ordered to make their way secretly at night round the headlands off-shore and then, if they were sure the enemy did not greatly outnumber them, to leap from their ships and raid the Turks; they were then to re-embark and return to base at once. These men, he knew, were absolutely ignorant of warfare, so he warned them to instruct their rowers to make no noise with their oars; they were told, too, to beware of barbarians lurking in rocky inlets. After these tactics had been repeated for some days, the Turks little by little withdrew further from the coast, and the emperor seeing what was happening, ordered his men to seize the villages and buildings the enemy had formerly occupied and stay there during the night; about sunrise, when the others normally went out to forage or for some other necessary reason, they were to make a sudden attack on them and if they met with any success, however small, to be content with it, for if they ran risks, looking for some greater advantage, the Turks would take heart; our men were to return at once to the strong-points. Not long after the barbarians withdrew a second time and this encouraged Alexius. Those who up till then had been infantrymen were commanded to ride on horseback, use a lance and make cavalry excursions against the enemy, no longer in the dark and in secret, but in broad daylight. The old decarchs now became pentekontarchs[36] and instead of fighting on foot at night, with considerable apprehension, they began to make their assaults in the morning and when the sun was at its zenith confidently engaged in some glorious battles. So it came about that while things went badly for the Turks, the hidden spark of Roman prestige began gradually to burst into flame. Comnenus not only drove the enemy far away from the Bosphorus and the places by the sea, but chased them from the districts of Bithynia and Thynia altogether, not to mention the borders of Nicomedia, and the sultan was constrained to make the most urgent pleas for an armistice. Alexius gladly accepted the offer of negotiations. He had reliable information from many sources about Robert's unlimited ambitions and he knew that enormous forces had been gathered; Robert was already hurrying to the Lombardy coast. After all, if Hercules could not fight two opponents at once, as the proverb says, how much more was it true of a young general who had but recently acquired a corrupted empire, slowly perishing over a long period and now at its last gasp, without armies and without money? For all its wealth, squandered to no good purpose, had now been exhausted. By various means he had driven the Turks from Damalis and the coastal districts near it; at the same time he had won their friendship with gifts; he had compelled them to accept a treaty of peace. The River Drakon was now made the border between them, with the proviso that the Turks were absolutely forbidden to cross it and under no circumstances to invade the frontiers of Bithynia.

36. A decarch commands ten men; a pentekontarch is in charge of fifty.

In this way the east was pacified, but Palaeologus' arrival at Dyrrachium was swiftly followed by Monomachatos' defection to Bodinus and Michaelas. Palaeologus sent a fast courier to give the news to the emperor. The truth was that Monomachatos was afraid: he had refused to listen to the envoy from Alexius and when he asked for money had sent him away empty-handed (this was before the planned rebellion had come into the open). In fact, the emperor did not intend to take any reprisal, except to deprive him of his command (for the reason already stated). Hearing what he had done, he now despatched a chrysobull guaranteeing his complete safety. Monomachatos, with the letter in his hand, came back to the palace. Meanwhile Robert arrived at Otranto and after handing over all his own authority to his son Roger (including the government of Lombardy itself) he went on from there to the harbour of Brindisi. In that city he learnt that Palaeologus had reached Dyrrachium. Without delay wooden towers were constructed in the larger vessels and covered with leather hides; everything essential for a siege was hastily put on board the ships; horses and armed knights embarked on dromons; and when military supplies from all quarters had been made ready with extraordinary rapidity, Robert was anxious to make the crossing at once. His plan was to surround Dyrrachium the moment he got there with helepoleis by land and sea – for two reasons: first, he would terrify the inhabitants; secondly, having isolated them completely, he would take the city at the first assault. News of these preparations filled the islanders with consternation; people living on the coast by Dyrrachium were equally dismayed. When he was satisfied that all was ready, the stern cables were loosed and the whole fleet of dromons, triremes and monoremes, drawn up in order of battle according to naval tradition, began the voyage in disciplined fashion. Robert had a favourable wind, made Avlona on the other side, and coasted along as far as Butrinto. There he was joined by his son Bohemond, who had crossed before him and had captured Avlona without difficulty. The whole army was now divided in two: one half, under Robert himself, was to make the sea passage to Dyrrachium (that was Robert's intention);

the other, entrusted to Bohemond, was to march on the city by land. Robert had actually passed Corfu and altered course for Dyrrachium when, off a promontory called Glossa, he was suddenly struck by a tremendous storm. There was a heavy fall of snow and winds blowing furiously from the mountains lashed up the sea. There was a howling noise as the waves built up; oars snapped off as the rowers plunged them into the water, the sails were torn to shreds by the blasts, yard-arms were crushed and fell on the decks; and now ships were being swallowed up, crew and all. And yet it was the summer season; the sun had already passed the Tropic of Cancer and was on its way to the Lion – the season when the Dog-Star rises, so they say. Everybody was confused and dismayed, not knowing what to do, unable to resist such enemies. A terrible cry arose as they groaned and lamented, calling on God, imploring His aid and praying that they might see the mainland. But the tempest did not die down, as if God were venting His wrath on Robert for the unyielding, presumptuous arrogance of the man; as if He were showing by a sign at the very outset that the end would be disastrous. Anyway, some of the ships sank and their crews drowned with them, others were dashed against the headlands and broke up. The hides that covered the towers were slackened by the rain, so that the nails fell out and the hides naturally became heavier; their weight caused the wooden towers to collapse. They fell in ruins and sank the ships. Robert's own vessel, although half-shattered, barely made its way to safety, and some transport ships also escaped, unbelievably without losing their crews. Many corpses were thrown up by the waves, and not a few purses and other objects brought by the sailors of Robert's fleet were strewn on the sand. The survivors buried their dead with all due ceremony, but because it was no easy matter to inter so many they suffered horribly from the stench. They would soon have perished of hunger too, for all their supplies had been lost, if all the crops had not been ripe and fields and gardens bursting with fruits. What had happened was significant to all men of right judgement, but not to Robert. None of it frightened him, or affected his iron nerve. If he did pray that his life might be spared, it was only, I suppose, for as long as he could wage war on his chosen enemies. The disaster by no means deterred him from the immediate aim and with the survivors (for a few had been rescued from danger by the invincible might of God) he stayed for a week in Glabinitza to recover his own strength and rest his shipwrecked mariners, but also to give time to the soldiers left behind in Brindisi, and indeed to those whom he was expecting from another quarter, to arrive by sea. He was also waiting for the heavily-armed knights and infantry, together with his light-armed forces, to cross by the overland route (they had started a little before himself). When all contingents, coming by land and sea, were united, he occupied the Illyrian plain in full force. The Latin who gave me this information was with him, an envoy, he said, from the Bishop of Bari sent to Robert. He assured me that he spent time on this same plain with him. They set up huts inside the ruined walls of the city formerly called Epidamnos. It was in this place that Pyrrhus, King of Epirus,[37] once lived. He joined with the men of Tarentum against the Romans and fought a fierce campaign in Apulia. As a result there was so much carnage that the whole population was put to the sword without exception and the city was left entirely without inhabitants. In later times, however, according to Greek tradition and indeed according to the evidence of carved inscriptions there Amphion and Zethos[38] restored it to its present condition and the name was immediately changed to Dyrrachium. So much then for my digression on this place; with it I end my third book. The fourth will relate what happened thereafter.

37. Pyrrhus (319–272 B.C.) won his famous 'Pyrrhic' victory when he defeated the Romans at Heraclea in 280.

38. There is some confusion here. No other historians mention so drastic a depopulation. Amphion and Zethos, moreover, were well-known characters in Greek mythology and were credited with the building of Thebes.

BOOK FOUR

WAR WITH THE NORMANS
(1081-2)

ROBERT was already encamped on the mainland by 17 June
of the fourth indiction. He had with him a countless host of
cavalry and infantry, for the whole force coming from all
directions had once again concentrated in one place. Its appearance and soldierly demeanour alike inspired fear. On the
sea cruised his fleet, comprising every type of vessel, manned
by other soldiers with long experience of naval warfare. No
wonder then that the inhabitants of Dyrrachium, hemmed in
on either side (that is to say, by land and sea) and in sight of
Robert's forces, innumerable and surpassing all description,
were seized with the greatest dread. Nevertheless, George
Palaeologus was a brave man, thoroughly trained in the art
of leadership; he had fought on a thousand battle-fields in the
east and proved victorious; now, without alarm, he proceeded
to fortify the city. The battlements were constructed according
to the emperor's advice, catapults were set up everywhere on
the walls, the demoralized soldiers were encouraged and scouts
posted all along the ramparts. George himself moreover visited
them at all hours of day and night, exhorting the sentinels to
be extra watchful. At the same time he informed the emperor
by letters of Robert's offensive, his presence near Dyrrachium,
and preparations for the siege. Helepoleis were outside the city
and an enormous wooden tower was built, much higher than
the walls even, protected at all points by hides of leather; on
top of it stood rock-hurling machines; the whole circuit of
walls was invested. Allies flocked to Robert from all quarters,
while the towns in the vicinity were ravaged by sudden raids
and every day the number of tents multiplied. All this terrified
the people of Dyrrachium, for they knew the real aim of Duke
Robert: it was not, as his general proclamations said, to
plunder cities and lands, collect much booty in this way, and

then return to Apulia. It was not for that he had occupied the
Illyrian plain, but because he coveted the throne of the Roman
Empire; the hasty siege of Dyrrachium was merely the first
round, so to speak. Anyway, Palaeologus told them to ask
from the top of the walls why he had come. 'To restore to his
proper place of honour my kinsman Michael, who has been
expelled from his Empire; to punish the outrages inflicted on
him; in a word, to avenge him.' Palaeologus' men gave their
reply: 'If we see Michael and recognize him, we will without
hesitation make obeisance before him and surrender the city.'
Hearing this Robert at once gave orders that 'Michael' should
be dressed in magnificent robes and displayed to the citizens.
He was led out with an imposing escort, loudly acclaimed with
all kinds of musical instruments and cymbals, and shown to
them. As soon as they saw him, a thousand insults rained down
on him from above; he was a complete stranger, they yelled.
Robert made nothing of it and applied himself to the business
in hand. However, while the conversation was going on, some
men without warning made a quick sortie, joined battle with
the Latins and after doing them some slight damage re-
entered the city. With regard to the monk who accompanied
Robert, most people had different views. Some announced
that he was the cup-bearer of the Emperor Michael Ducas;
others were certain that he was in fact the Emperor Michael,
Robert's father-in-law, for whose sake, they said, the latter
had chosen to make this terrible war; others again insisted
that they knew for sure that the whole affair had been invented
by Robert, for the monk had not come of his own free will.
Through his own natural vigour and proud spirit he (Robert)
had risen from the direst poverty and an obscure origin to
become master of all the cities and lands of Lombardy, as well
as Apulia itself; he had confirmed his position as overlord, in
the way described earlier in the history. It was not long before
his ambitions grew – the normal reaction of the greedy – and
he decided that he must make a tentative assault on the
Illyrian cities; if the attempt succeeded, he would extend his
operations further. Once a man has seized power, his love of
money displays exactly the same characteristics as gangrene,

for gangrene, once established in a body, never rests until it has invaded and corrupted the whole of it.

All this was reported by Palaeologus. The emperor learnt how Robert had crossed in the month of June; how he had been thwarted by storm and shipwreck, exposed to the wrath of God but still undismayed; how with his men he had taken Avlona at the first attack; how once again countless hosts, from all directions, were rallying to him, thick as winter snow-flakes, and the more frivolous folk, believing that the pretender Michael was in truth the emperor, were joining him. Alexius saw the magnitude of his task and was afraid. He knew that his own forces were vastly outnumbered by the Latins and decided that he must call on the Turks from the east. There and then he made his views known to the sultan. He also asked the Venetians[1] for help, with promises and bribes. Some rewards were pledged, others granted at once, if only the Venetians would be willing to equip all their fleet and sail at speed to Dyrrachium, first to protect the city and secondly to engage in serious warfare with Robert's navy. If, following his own clear instructions, they undertook to do this, one of two things would happen: either they would with God's help win a victory, or of course there was the possibility of defeat; but in either case they would have their promised reward, just as if the war had been completely successful. All their desires would be satisfied and confirmed by chrysobulls, provided that they were not in conflict with the interests of the Roman Empire. The Venetians listened, made known all their requirements through the envoys and received firm pledges. Without delay a fleet was fitted out, comprising all types of ships, and sailed in good order towards Dyrrachium. After a long voyage the Venetians put in near the sanctuary of the Immaculate Mother of God at a place called Pallia, about eighteen stades from Robert's camp, which was pitched outside Dyrrachium. When they saw the barbarian's fleet on the far side of the city, protected with every sort of warlike machine, they shrank from battle. Robert, who had heard of their arrival, sent his

1. There is a tradition that the 'Blues' (*Veneti*) in the Roman horse-racing contests got their name from Venice. (A.C.)

own son Bohemond to them with a squadron and orders to acclaim the Emperor Michael, and himself. They deferred the acclamation to the next day. Meanwhile, at nightfall, since they could not get close inshore and the wind had fallen, they lashed the bigger vessels together with chains and formed a so-called 'sea harbour'. Wooden towers were then constructed at their mastheads and with the help of cables the little skiffs towed by each ship were hoisted up between them. Armed men were put in these skiffs and very thick pieces of wood cut up into lengths of not more than a cubit; into these they hammered sharp iron nails. They then waited for the coming of the Frankish fleet. Day was already breaking when Bohemond arrived and demanded that they should acclaim the emperor and his father, but they made fun of his beard. Unable to bear the insult Bohemond led the attack on them in person, making for the biggest ships; others followed him. The battle was fiercely contested. However, when Bohemond was fighting with even greater ferocity, they hurled down one of these great blocks of wood from aloft and holed the ship on which he happened to be. The water was sucking the Franks down and as they were in danger of being engulfed, some left the ship but fell into the very same trouble and were drowned; others went on fighting the Venetians and were killed. Bohemond himself, when his life was at stake, leapt into another of his ships and took refuge there. The Venetians, taking fresh heart and pressing their attack with more confidence, routed the enemy completely and pursued them as far as Robert's camp. Reaching dry land they jumped overboard and started another battle with them, and Palaeologus too, when he saw what was going on, came out of the city and joined them in the fighting. After a violent struggle which raged right up to Robert's entrenchment, many Franks were chased away from it and many were put to the sword.[2] The Venetians returned to their ships loaded with booty. Palaeologus went back to the fortress of Dyrrachium. After a few days of relaxation the victors despatched envoys to the emperor with a full report of these events. Naturally they were received with friendly greetings and

2. The battle took place in June 1081.

rewarded with a thousand kindnesses; finally he allowed them to go, taking with them large sums of money for the Doge of Venice[3] and his officers.

Robert's warlike instinct told him that the war must go on; he would have to fight hard. But there were difficulties: because of the winter he was unable to launch his ships; the Roman and Venetian fleets, tirelessly patrolling the straits, prevented reinforcements crossing from Lombardy and the delivery of necessary supplies to him from that area was impeded. But when the spring came and winter storms died down, the Venetians made the first move. They weighed anchor and took the offensive. Behind them came Maurice with the Roman fleet. Very heavy fighting ensued and Robert's men were routed again. This convinced him that all his ships would have to be dragged up on land, whereupon the islanders, the inhabitants of the little places along the coast of the mainland, and all the others who were paying tribute to Robert, becoming courageous at his misfortunes and hearing about his defeat on the sea, were not so ready to meet the heavy obligations he laid on them. Obviously he would have to plan the war with greater care; a new campaign by sea and land was inevitable. He had ideas but it was impossible to carry them out: strong winds were blowing at that time and through dread of shipwreck he lingered for two months in the port of Hiericho. Nevertheless he was making ready and organizing his forces for battle, intending to fight by sea and land. To the best of their ability the Venetians and Romans kept up their naval blockade and when there was a little improvement in the weather – enough to encourage would-be sailors – they thwarted all efforts at a crossing from the west. Robert's men, bivouacking by the River Glykys, meanwhile found it no easy matter to get supplies from the mainland, for when they left their entrenchments to forage or bring in other necessities there was interference from Dyrrachium. They began to starve. There was other trouble: the strangeness of the climate distressed them much, so that in the course of three months, it is said, up to 10,000 men perished. This disease attacked Robert's

3. Domenico Silvo (1070–84).

cavalry too and many died; in fact, of the knights as many as
500 counts and élite fighting men became victims of disease
and famine, while in the lower ranks of the cavalry the number
of dead was incalculable. His ships, as I have said, were drawn
up on land by the Glykys, but when after the winter and the
coming of spring the weather became hotter and rainless, the
water-level dropped; there was not the normal flow from the
mountain streams. Consequently he was in an awkward
situation; the ships could not now be launched in the sea
again. Despite his troubles, Robert, being a man of great
intelligence and versatility, ordered piles to be driven in on
either side of the river; these were then tightly bound together
with osiers; very tall trees were felled at the roots and laid
behind these piles, and sand was spread on them, in order to
direct the flow into one course, concentrated so to speak into
one canal formed by the stakes. Gradually pools formed and
the water filled the whole of the artificial channel until it became deep enough to raise the ships, which had rested on the
land and were now afloat. After that, when there was a good
flow of water, the vessels were easily launched in the sea.

In view of Robert's activities, the emperor wrote at once to
Pakourianus. He explained how the man's unrestrained
ambition had led to the capture of Avlona and how he had
utter contempt for the misfortunes suffered on land and sea,
not to mention the defeat inflicted on him at the very outset of
the campaign. 'There must be no delay,' he wrote; Pakourianus must assemble his forces and join the emperor with the
greatest promptitude. Accordingly in the month of August in
the fourth indiction Pakourianus quickly left Constantinople.
Isaac remained in the capital to maintain order and quash
enemy propaganda (the usual bad news). He was also to guard
the palace and city, and at the same time to comfort the women
inclined to be tearful. As far as his mother was concerned,
help was, I suppose, uncalled for – she was herself a tower of
strength and in any case a highly skilled administrator. Having
read the letter Pakourianus at once appointed Nicolas Branas
hypostrategus,[4] a man of courage with considerable experience

4. Second-in-command.

in war. He himself with all the heavy-armed infantry and the nobles hastily departed from the Orestias [5] and hurried to meet the emperor. The latter had already drawn up his entire army in battle order. The commanders, appointed from the bravest of his officers, were told to march in this formation where the terrain permitted, so that every man becoming well acquainted with the general arrangement of the troops and recognizing his own place in the line would not panic in the hour of battle, nor readily change position under different circumstances. The corps of *excubitae* [6] was led by Constantine Opus, the Macedonians by Antiochus, the Thessalians by Alexander Cabasilas, while Taticius, who was at the time Grand Primicerius, [7] commanded the Turks from the district of Achrida. The latter was a valiant fighter, a man who kept his head under combat conditions, but his family was not free-born. His father was in fact a Saracen who fell into the hands of my paternal grandfather John Comnenus when he captured him on a marauding raid. The leaders of the Manichaeans, who numbered 2,800, were Xantas and Kouleon, themselves heretics of the same persuasion. All these men were excellent fighters, more than ready to draw blood of their enemies when the opportunity occurred; I might also add that they were headstrong and devoid of shame. The soldiers of the emperor's household (commonly called *vestiaritae*) and the regiments of Franks were commanded by Panoukomites and Constantine Humbertopoulos (so-called because of his origin). When the disposition of the troops was complete, Alexius set out against Robert in full force. On the way he met a man who came from the Dyrrachium area and after questioning him had a clearer picture of what was happening there: Robert had moved all the machines required for the siege near to the walls, but Palaeologus, after working night and day to oppose his helepoleis and frustrate his schemes, had at last grown weary

5. Adrianople and the district round it.
6. Mounted troops normally stationed in Constantinople and commanded by a Domesticus.
7. One of the officers of the imperial household. The dignity was reserved for eunuchs. See *CMH*, vol. iv, pt. ii, p. 20.

of this; he had thrown open the gates, gone out and fought a determined battle with the enemy. He had suffered serious wounds in different parts of his body; the worst was when an arrow penetrated near his temple. He tried to draw it out forcibly, but was unable to do it. An expert was summoned and he cut away the end – the butt where the feathers are attached – but the rest of it remained in the wound. Palaeologus bound up his head as far as he could, and hurled himself again into the midst of the foe, fighting on till late evening without flinching. The emperor realized when he heard this story how desperately in need of help Palaeologus must be. He quickened his march. On his arrival at Thessalonica, many informants confirmed the news about Robert, and in greater detail. When Robert was ready and when he had built up his soldiers' morale, he collected a great amount of wood on the plain of Dyrrachium and pitched camp about a bow-shot's length from the walls. There was news too of Palaeologus; from several sources the emperor heard about his careful preparations. He had already made up his mind to burn the wooden tower built by Robert and on the walls there were catapults, naphtha, pitch and small pieces of dry wood. He waited for the enemy's attack. As he expected it to take place on the next day, he set up a wooden tower of his own, inside the city and directly opposite the other. It was ready well in time; in fact, all through the night he experimented with a beam placed on top of it. The intention was to thrust forward this beam against the doors of Robert's tower when it was brought to the wall. He was testing it, to find out whether it could be moved without difficulty and falling right in the path of the enemy's doors stop them from being opened in the usual way. Being assured that the beam did thrust forward easily and could successfully perform its function, he had no more worries about the coming battle. On the next day, Robert ordered all his men to take up arms; some 500, infantry and fully equipped horsemen, were led into the tower and it was brought near to the wall. They hurried to open the door on the top, intending to use it as a draw-bridge to cross over into the citadel, but Palaeologus at that very moment thrust forward his own huge

beam by means of the mechanical devices prepared in advance
and with the help of many brave men. As the beam made it
absolutely impossible to open the door, Robert's stratagem was
frustrated. Then a never-ending shower of arrows was directed
at the Kelts on the summit and they, unable to bear it any
longer, took cover. He now gave orders to set the tower
alight; before the last words were uttered the thing was on fire.
The Kelts on top threw themselves over, those below opened
up the door at the bottom and fled. Seeing this Palaeologus
immediately led out some fully-armed soldiers by the postern
gate and others with axes, to smash up the tower. Here too he
was successful, for with the top on fire and the lower parts
broken up with stone-cutters' tools, it was completely destroyed.

According to the informant Robert was hastening to build a
second tower, similar to the first, and was making ready
helepoleis against the city. Aware of the need for speedy help,
Alexius pressed on. When he arrived at Dyrrachium, he made
an entrenchment for his army by the banks of the River
Charzanes. Without delay messengers were sent to ask Robert
why he had come and what he intended to do. Alexius meanwhile went off to the sanctuary dedicated to Nicolas, the greatest of pontiffs, which was four stades from the city. He
reconnoitred the ground, hoping to pick the most favourable
site for a battle-line before Robert could do so. It was then 15
October. A neck of land extended from Dalmatia to the sea,
ending in a promontory which was almost surrounded by
water; on this the sanctuary was built. On the side facing
Dyrrachium there was a gentle slope down to the plain, with
the sea on the left and a high, overhanging mountain on the
right. At this point the Roman army was concentrated and
camp pitched. Then George Palaeologus was summoned. But
he, with long experience of such matters, refused to come,
making it clear to the emperor that he reckoned it unwise to
leave the city. Alexius again sent for him, more urgently this
time, but in vain. Palaeologus replied, 'To me it seems
absolutely fatal to leave the citadel under siege. Unless I see
Your Majesty's seal-ring, I will not come out.' The ring was

sent and he at once joined the emperor with some warships. Alexius asked him about Robert's actions and when he had received a full and accurate account went on, 'Ought I to risk a battle with him?' Palaeologus thought not, for the time being. Certain others too who had many years of experience in war earnestly opposed the idea and advised him to adopt a waiting policy; he should try to reduce Robert by skirmishing and by preventing his men from leaving camp to forage or plunder; the same plan should be forced on Bodinus and the Dalmatians and the rest of the officers in the neighbouring districts. They were sure that Robert could be easily defeated if he took these measures. The majority of the younger officers preferred to fight, especially Constantine Porphyrogenitus, Nicephorus Synadenus, Nampites the commander of the Varangians, and even the sons of the former emperor Romanus Diogenes, Leo and Nicephorus. While these arguments were going on the envoys returned from Robert and delivered his answer: 'I have not come to fight Your Majesty – that was not my intention at all – but rather to avenge the wrong done to my father-in-law. If you wish to make peace with me, I too welcome it, provided that you are ready to fulfil the conditions stated by my ambassadors to you.' He was demanding quite impossible terms, which were also harmful to the Empire, although he did promise at the same time that, if he got what he wanted, he would regard Lombardy itself as his by permission of the emperor, and he would help us when the need arose. It was a mere pretext: by demanding terms he would give the appearance of desiring peace himself; by proposing the impossible and failing to obtain it he would have an excuse to make war, and then hold the Roman emperor responsible for the fighting. Anyway his proposals were out of the question and he failed. So, having called together all the counts, he addressed them: 'You know the wrong done by the Emperor Nicephorus Botaniates to my father-in-law, and the disgrace suffered by my daughter Helena when she was thrown out of the Palace with him. Finding this intolerable, we have left our country to avenge the insult and punish Botaniates. But he has been deprived of his throne and now we have to deal with a young emperor and a brave soldier, who has acquired an experience of the military art beyond his years; we must not take up his challenge in a light-hearted manner. Where there are many masters, there will be confusion, brought about by the diverse strategies of the many. In future therefore one man among us should command the rest; he should consult all, not adopting his own schemes in an autocratic way and according to his own caprice; the others will openly express to him their own opinions, but at the same time accept the counsel of the elected leader. Here is one man who is ready to obey your unanimously elected leader – I am the first to agree.' Everyone praised this plan and complimented Robert on his speech. There and then, without any dissension, they offered him the leadership. For a while he dissembled, like a girl acting coyly, and refused to accept, but they pressed him all the more and begged him. In the end he yielded, apparently in reply to their entreaties, although he had been plotting this in fact for a long time. After an involved series of arguments and a catalogue of reasons cleverly linked together, he made it appear, to those who did not understand his mentality, that he was coming involuntarily to what he really desired with all his heart. He ended his speech thus: 'Listen to my advice, you counts and the rest of the army. We have left our own native lands and come here to fight against an emperor of great courage, one who has only recently seized the helm of power, but has won many wars in the reigns of his predecessors and brought to them most powerful rebels as prisoners of war. All our energies therefore must be devoted to this struggle. If God grants us the victory, we shall no longer be in want of money. That is why we must burn all our baggage, hole our transport ships and send them to the bottom of the sea, and take up this challenge from him as if today is the supreme decider of life and death.' They all agreed with him.

Such were the thoughts and plans of Robert; the emperor's schemes were different, but more complicated and subtle. Both generals kept their armies together while they planned their tactics and movements, so that operations might be directed in a sensible way. The emperor decided to launch a sudden night attack on Robert's camp from two sides and the whole of the allied army was ordered to surprise him from the rear. They were to go through the salt-marshes, a longer route – but Alexius did not object to that, for the sake of catching the enemy unawares. He himself intended to attack from the front when he knew the others were in position. Robert left his tents empty and crossed the bridge in the night (on 18 October in the fifth indiction). With all his forces he arrived at the sanctuary built long ago by the sea in honour of the martyr Theodorus. All that night the Normans, in an attempt to propitiate the Deity, were partaking of the holy and divine mysteries. Then Robert arranged his battle-line: he himself commanded the centre; the wing nearer to the sea was entrusted to Amiketas, a distinguished count, physically and morally courageous; the other wing was given to his son Bohemond, surnamed Saniscus. The emperor, realizing what had happened, adapted his own plans to meet the new circumstances – in moments of crisis he was expert at choosing the profitable course – and drew up his line somewhere along the slope by the sea. His army was divided, but the barbarians already on their way to attack Robert's camp were not re-called; the others, who carry on their shoulders the two-edged swords, together with their commander Nampites, were kept back. He ordered them to dismount from their horses and march forward in their ranks a short distance in front of the line. They were carrying shields, like all men of their race. The rest of the force was split up into companies. The emperor led the centre in person; on right and left respectively he stationed the Caesar Nicephorus Melissenus and Pakourianus the Great Domestic. Between himself and the barbarians on foot was a strong contingent of skilled archers. These he intended to send first against Robert, having instructed Nampites to open his ranks quickly for them (by moving to right and left) whenever they wanted to charge out against the Kelts; and to close ranks again and march in close order, when they had withdrawn. When all was ready, he himself moved to attack the Keltic front, following the coastline. As for the barbarians who had gone through the salt-marshes, they made an assault on the enemy camp just at the moment when the inhabitants of Dyrrachium, in accordance with the emperor's instructions, threw open the city gates. As the two leaders approached one another, Robert sent a detachment of cavalry with orders to manoeuvre in such a way that some of the Romans might be enticed from their line. Alexius did not fall into that trap; in fact, large reinforcements of peltasts were moved to oppose them. Both sides then indulged in some moderate skirmishing, but Robert was quietly following these horsemen and the gap between the two armies was already diminishing, when the infantry and cavalry of Amiketas' group charged ahead of the main body in an assault on the extremity of the line where Nampites was. Our men resisted bravely and the enemy turned back (they were not all picked men). They threw themselves into the sea up to their necks and when they were near the Roman and Venetian ships begged for their lives – but nobody rescued them. There is a story that Robert's wife Gaita, who used to accompany him on campaign, like another Pallas, if not a second Athena, seeing the runaways and glaring fiercely at them, shouted in a very loud voice: 'How far will ye run? Halt! Be men!' – not quite in those Homeric words, but something very like them in her own dialect. As they continued to run, she grasped a long spear and charged at full gallop against them. It brought them to their senses and they went back to fight. Meanwhile the axe-bearers and their leader Nampites had advanced a fair distance from the Roman line, carried away by their own inexperience and hot temper; they had gone too fast, eager to clash with the Kelts who were just as eager themselves. Nampites' men were passionately devoted to war, like the Kelts, and in the matter of fighting were by no means their inferiors. Robert noticed however that they were already tired and short of breath; their rapid advance, the distance they had covered and the weight of their arms were enough to convince him. He ordered a detachment of infantry to fall upon them. It seems that in their tired condition they were less strong than the Kelts. At any rate the whole barbarian force was massacred there, except for survivors who fled for safety to the sanctuary of the Archangel[8] Michael; all who could went inside the building; the rest climbed to the roof and stood there, thinking that would save their lives. The Latins merely set fire to them and burned the lot, together with the sanctuary. The remnants of the Roman army carried on the battle with courage, but Robert, like some winged horseman, with the rest of his forces charged and pushed back the Roman line, in many places tearing it apart. In the end, some fell fighting on the field of battle, others looked to their own safety and fled. The emperor, like an impregnable tower, stood his ground, though he had lost many of his companions, men distinguished alike for their birth and their experience in war. In that battle there died Constantius, the son of the former emperor Constantine Ducas, who was born after his father had ceased to be an ordinary citizen and so came into the world and was brought up in the Porphyra; at the time he was honoured by his father with an imperial diadem. Nicephorus, surnamed Synadenus, a brave man and very handsome, who was impatient to surpass all others in that day's fighting, also died. The Constantius mentioned above often spoke to him about a marriage to his own sister. Other nobles fell, including Nicephorus the father of Palaeologus;[9] Zacharias received a mortal wound in the chest and died instantly; Aspietes and many other fine soldiers were killed. The battle was not yet finished when three Latins, seeing the emperor still holding out against the enemy, detached themselves from the rest and bore down on him at full gallop with long spears at the ready. One of them was the Amiketas I spoke of; the second was Peter, who described himself as the son of Aliphas; the third was at least their equal. Amiketas missed the emperor because his horse swerved slightly. Alexius parried the spear of the second with his sword and with all his strength wounded him by the collar-bone, severing his arm from his body. The third aimed a blow directly at the emperor's forehead, but with great presence of mind Alexius, coolly and not at all alarmed,

8. In Greek *archistrategus*, 'supreme commander'.

9. He had remained faithful to Botaniates until his abdication; now he was fighting for his rival.

recognized in a flash what he had to do in that split second: as the blow fell he leaned over backwards towards his horse's tail. The sword-point just grazed his skin, immediately causing a slight cut, but was impeded by the rim of his helmet. It cut through the leather strap which fastened under his chin and knocked the helmet to the ground. The Kelt then rode on past him, thinking he was unseated, but Alexius drew himself upright and sat firmly in the saddle, with all his arms intact. In his right hand he held his unsheathed sword. He was dusty and bloodstained, bareheaded, with his bright red hair straggling in front of his eyes and annoying him (for his horse, frightened and impatient of the bit, was jumping about wildly and making the curls fall over his face), but even so he recovered as best he could and defied his adversaries. But he saw the Turks running away too and even Bodinus was withdrawing without a fight. Bodinus had put on armour and had drawn up his troops in battle array; throughout the day he stood by, apparently ready to help the emperor at any minute in accordance with the agreements made with him. Really, it seems, he was watching anxiously to discover if victory was going to the emperor; if it did, he would join in attacking the Kelts; if Alexius lost he would quietly beat a retreat. From his actions it is clear that this was his plan, for when he realized that the Kelts were now sure of victory, he ran off home without striking a single blow. Alexius knew this and when he saw nobody coming to his aid, he also retired before the enemy. Thus the Latins put to flight the Roman army.

Robert reached the sanctuary of St Nicolas, where was the imperial tent and all the Roman baggage. He then despatched all his fit men in pursuit of Alexius, while he himself stayed there, gloating over the imminent capture of his enemy. Such were the thoughts that fired his arrogant spirit. His men pursued Alexius with great determination as far as a place called by the natives Kake Pleura.[10] The situation was as follows: below there flows the River Charzanes; on the other side was a high overhanging rock. The pursuers caught up with him between these two. They struck at him on the left side with

10. 'Bad Side'.

their spears (there were nine of them in all) and forced him
to the right. No doubt he would have fallen, had not the
sword which he grasped in his right hand rested firmly on the
ground. What is more, the spur tip on his left foot caught in
the edge of the saddle-cloth (which they call a *hypostroma*) and
this made him less liable to fall. He grabbed the horse's mane
with his left hand and pulled himself up. It was no doubt some
divine power that saved him from his enemies in an unexpected
way, for it caused other Kelts to aim their spears at him from
the right. The spear-points, thrust towards his right side,
suddenly straightened him and kept him in equilibrium. It was
indeed an extraordinary sight. The enemies on the left strove
to push him off; those on the right plunged their spears at his
flank, as if in competition with the first group, opposing spear
to spear. Thus the emperor was kept upright between them.
He settled himself more firmly in the saddle, gripping horse
and saddle-cloth alike more tightly with his legs. It was at this
moment that the horse gave proof of its nobility. Under any
circumstances, it was unusually agile and spirited, of exceptional strength, a real war-horse (Alexius had actually
acquired him from Bryennius,[11] together with the purple-
dyed saddle-cloth when he took him prisoner during the
reign of Nicephorus Botaniates). To put it shortly, this
charger was now inspired by Divine Providence: he suddenly
leapt through the air and landed on top of the rock I mentioned
before as if he had been raised on wings – or to use the language of mythology, as if he had taken the wings of Pegasus.
Bryennius used to call him Sgouritzes (Dark Bay). Some of
the barbarians' spears, striking at empty air, fell from their
hands; others, which had pierced the emperor's clothing,
remained there and were carried off with the horse when he
jumped. Alexius quickly cut away these trailing weapons.
Despite the terrible dangers in which he found himself, he
was not troubled in spirit, nor was he confused in thought;
he lost no time in choosing the expedient course and contrary
to all expectation escaped from his enemies. The Kelts stood

11. The father of Anna's husband who had taken the purple when he
rebelled against Michael VII and Nicephorus Botaniates.

open-mouthed, astonished by what had happened, and indeed it was a most amazing thing. They saw that he was making off in a new direction and followed him once more. When he was a long way ahead of his pursuers he wheeled round and, coming face to face with one of them, drove his spear through the man's chest. He fell at once to the ground, flat on his back. Turning about Alexius continued on his way. However, he fell in with several Kelts who had been chasing Romans further on. They saw him a long way off and halted in a line, shield to shield, partly to rest their horses, but at the same time hoping to take him alive and present him as a prize of war to Robert. Pursued by enemies from behind and confronted by others, Alexius despaired of his life; but he gathered his wits and noting in the centre of his enemies one man who, from his physical appearance and the flashing brightness of his armour, he thought was Robert, he steadied his horse and charged at him. His opponent also levelled his spear and they both advanced across the intervening space to do battle. The emperor was first to strike, taking careful aim with his spear. The weapon pierced the Kelt's breast and passed through his back. Straightway he fell to the ground mortally wounded, and died on the spot. Thereupon Alexius rode off through the centre of their broken line. The killing of this barbarian had saved him. The man's friends, when they saw him wounded and hurled to the ground, gathered round and tended him as he lay there. The others, pursuing from the rear, meanwhile dismounted from their horses and recognized the dead man. They beat their breasts in grief, for although he was not Robert, he was a distinguished noble, and Robert's right-hand man. While they busied themselves over him, the emperor was well on his way.

In the course of this account, partly because of the nature of the history and partly because of the great importance of these events, I have forgotten that it is my father whose successes I am writing of. Often, in my desire not to incur suspicion, in the composition of my history I hurry over affairs that concern him, neither exaggerating nor adding my personal observations. I wish I were detached and free from this feeling that I have for him, so that seizing on this vast material I might demonstrate how much my tongue, when released from all restraint, could delight in noble deeds. But the natural love I have for him overshadows my personal wishes: I would not like the public to imagine that I am inventing marvels in my eagerness to speak about my own family. On many occasions when I recalled the glorious deeds of my father, if I had written down and given a full account of all the troubles he endured, I would have wept away my very soul, and I could not have passed over the story without lamentation and mourning. But so far as that part of my history is concerned, I must avoid the subtleties of rhetoric, and like some unfeeling adamant or marble pass quickly over his misfortunes. If I wanted to win a deserved reputation for loving him, I should have included his disasters in an oath, like the young man in Homer's Odyssey who swore: 'No, Agelaos, by Zeus and my father's woes.' For I am certainly no worse than that young man. But now we must leave my father's suffering; I alone must marvel at them and weep, but the reader must return to the narrative.

After this, the Kelts went on their way to Robert. When the latter saw them empty-handed and learnt what had happened to them, he bitterly censured all of them and one in particular, whom he even threatened to flog, calling him a coward and an ignoramus in war. The fellow expected to be put to horrible torture – because he had not leapt on to the rock with his own horse and either struck and murdered Alexius, or grabbed him and brought him alive to Robert. For this Robert, in other respects the bravest and most daring of men, was also full of bitterness, swift to anger, with a heart overflowing with passion and wrath. In his dealings with enemies he had one of two objects: either to run through with his spear any man who resisted him, or to do away with himself, cutting the thread of Fate, so to speak. However, the soldier whom he accused now gave a vivid account of the ruggedness and inaccessibility of the rock: no one, he added, whether on foot or on horseback, could climb it without divine aid – not to mention a man at war and engaged in fighting; even without war it was impossible to venture its ascent. 'If you can't believe a word I say,' he cried, 'try it yourself – or let some other knight, however daring, have a go. He will see it's out of the question. Anyway, if someone, I say *if* someone should conquer that rock, not only minus wings but even with them, then I myself am ready to endure any punishment you like to name and to be damned for cowardice.' These words, which expressed the man's wonder and amazement, appeased Robert's fury; his anger turned to admiration. As for the emperor, after spending two days and nights in travel through the winding paths of the neighbouring mountains and all that impassable region, he arrived at Achrida. On the way he crossed the Charzanes and waited for a short time near a place called Babagora (a remote valley). Neither the defeat nor any of the other evils of war troubled his mind; he was not worried in the slightest by the pain from his wounded forehead; but in his heart he grieved deeply for those who had fallen in the battle and especially for the men who had fought bravely. Nevertheless, he applied himself wholly to the problems of the city of Dyrrachium and it hurt him to recall that it was now without its leader, Palaeologus (for he had been unable to return – the war had moved so fast). To the best of his ability he ensured the safety of the inhabitants and entrusted the protection of the citadel to the Venetian officers who had migrated there. All the rest of the city was put under the command of Komiskortes, a native of Albania, to whom he gave profitable advice for the future in letters.

BOOK FIVE

WAR WITH THE NORMANS (1082-3) AND ALEXIUS' FIRST CONTEST WITH THE HERETICS

ROBERT, without any trouble whatsoever, seized all the booty, as well as the imperial tent, and took up position on the plain where he had formerly bivouacked during the siege of Dyrrachium. Full of pride he brought with him the trophies of victory. After pausing there for a short time he reviewed plans for the future: should he revive the assault on the walls, or should he defer it to the next spring,[1] meanwhile occupying Glabinitza and Joannina, and wintering there with his whole army stationed in the valleys which dominate the plain of Dyrrachium? The people of that city, as I have said, were mostly emigrants from Amalfi and Venice. When they learnt of the misfortunes of the emperor, the enormous casualties suffered and the death of soldiers so distinguished, not to mention the withdrawal of the fleets and Robert's decision to renew the siege in the coming spring, their own policy was thoroughly examined. How could they save themselves and avoid the recurrence of similar perils? They met in assembly. Each man expressed his own private opinion and when they failed to agree on a common course, they decided to resolve the *impasse* by submitting to Robert and surrendering the city. Instigated by the colonists from Amalfi and in obedience to their advice, they opened the gates and allowed him to enter. Once master of the place, Robert called together his forces, separating them into their several nationalities. A careful check was made of those who had received serious wounds or chance skin-grazes from a sword; he inquired into the type and number of men killed in the previous battles; at the same time he took care, since winter was already at hand, to plan the recruiting of another mercenary force and the assembling of

1. Spring 1082.

foreign contingents, so that on the arrival of spring he could march against the emperor at full strength. Robert thus laid his plans and proclaimed his own triumphs and victories. But he was not alone in preparing for the next campaign: despite this intolerable defeat, his own wound and the loss of so many noble comrades, Alexius was by no means like a man cringing before some hobgoblin; far from belittling his own chances or relaxing his efforts, he devoted himself entirely, with all his mental powers, to the avenging of defeat in the coming spring. Both leaders were prepared for all eventualities, able to comprehend at a glance every detail, acquainted with all the ruses of war; each was thoroughly conversant with siege tactics, the laying of ambushes, fighting in line of battle; in hand-to-hand combat bold and valiant, these two men, of all commanders under the sun, were worthy rivals, in wit and bravery well suited. The emperor had a certain advantage over Robert, because he was still young[2] and in no way the inferior of his adversary – although Robert was at the height of his powers and boasted that he could make the earth tremble, or nearly tremble, and cause terror among whole regiments by his battle-cry alone. However, these matters must be reserved for other works; they will surely claim the attention of would-be encomiasts. After resting for a little while at Achrida and recovering his spirits the emperor came to Diabolis. As best he could, he comforted the survivors, victims of battle fatigue; the rest he ordered through envoys to meet in Thessalonica from all directions. Now that he had experience of Robert and the boldness of his great army, he condemned the extreme naïveté and the cowardly behaviour of his own men; I will not emphasize the fact that even the men there present with him were completely untrained and ignorant of a soldier's life. It was essential therefore that he should acquire allies, but without money this was impossible. There was no money – the imperial treasury had been denuded by his predecessor on the throne, Nicephorus Botaniates, and to no good purpose. So

2. When Robert died in 1085, he was 70 years old according to Anna. Since Alexius was born in 1048 according to Zonaras, in 1056 according to Anna, there was a considerable difference in age.

bare was it indeed that even the treasury doors were unlocked; anyone who wished to walk through them could do so unhindered, for everything had been frittered away. Thus the general situation was critical. The Roman Empire was weak and at the same time crushed by poverty. What then was this young emperor, having only recently seized the helm of government, what was he to do? Briefly, he had two courses open to him: he could either abandon all in despair and abdicate, to avoid imputations of incompetent and inept leadership (although he was not responsible); or, of necessity, he could call on allies wherever available, collect from whatever source he could enough money to satisfy their demands, and recall by means of largess his army now scattered to the four points of the compass. The men still with him would thus become more confident and hold on, while the absentees would be keener to return. Under those circumstances they might resist the Keltic hordes with greater boldness. Wishing to do nothing unworthy or inconsistent with his own knowledge of military science (not to mention his own bravery), he had two objects in view: first, to summon allies from all quarters, cleverly luring them with expectations of liberal gifts; and, second, to demand from his mother and brother the provision of money – from any source whatever.

Because they were unable to find another method of providing the money, they first collected their own available resources, in the form of gold and silver objects, and sent them to the imperial mint. The empress, my mother, took the lead: all that she had inherited from her father and mother was offered, in the hope that by doing this she might inspire others to follow her example. She was much concerned for the emperor in his extremely difficult position. Afterwards there was a spontaneous and eager offering of available gold and silver by all the more loyal friends of the two rulers (Isaac and the empress); they sent contributions partly to the allies, partly to the emperor. Even so the amount was far from sufficient for their immediate needs. Some allies demanded favours on the grounds, forsooth, that they had fought on our side before; others (the mercenaries) wanted higher pay. The emperor, despairing of the goodwill of the Romans, called for greater efforts and made fresh demands. His mother and brother, now in a state of utter perplexity, discussed many proposals, in public and behind closed doors – for they knew that Robert was arming again – but there seemed to be no solution. Then they examined the ancient laws and canons on the alienation of sacred objects. Among other things they discovered that it is lawful to expropriate sacred objects from churches for the ransoming of prisoners-of-war (and it was clear that all those Christians living in Asia under barbarian rule and all those who had escaped massacre were thus defiled because of their intercourse with infidels [3]). In order to pay the soldiers and allies, therefore, they decided to convert into money a small quantity of such objects, which had long been idle and set aside as serving no purpose; in fact these objects merely tempted the majority to perform acts of sacrilege and irreverence. Once the decision was made, the Sebastocrator Isaac went to the great church of God, where he had called together the Synod [4] and all the clergy. The members of the Holy Synod, who sit in council with the patriarch on ecclesiastical matters, were amazed to see him and asked why he came. 'I have come,' he replied, 'to inform you of a proposal which will help us in this terrible crisis and save our army.' Then he quoted the canons relating to sacred objects no longer in use, and after speaking at length on the matter, he added, 'I am forced to force those whom I do not wish to force.' The bold arguments he produced seemed likely to convince the majority, but he was opposed by Metaxas, who raised certain specious objections and also poured ridicule on Isaac himself. Nevertheless the original proposal was passed. This became the subject of a very serious accusation against the emperors (for I do not hesitate to call Isaac emperor, although he did not wear the purple) not only on that occasion, but even later, right down to our own time. A certain Leo was then Bishop of

3. Anna writes obscurely. By 'defiled' she probably means that any Christian who survived was nothing better than a prisoner-of-war.

4. Anna no doubt refers to the 'resident Synod'. See *CMH*, vol. iv, pt. ii, pp. 109–110.

Chalcedon. He was not a particularly learned man nor a very wise one, but he had lived virtuously; unfortunately his manner was rough and curt. When the gold and silver on the doors of the Chalcopratia [5] were being taken away, he appeared in public and spoke freely, without the slightest concern for either the public finances or the laws relating to the sacred vessels. He behaved with inexcusable arrogance and even insubordination towards Isaac, for every time he (Leo) returned to the capital he abused his patience and courtesy. On the first occasion that Alexius left Constantinople to fight Robert, when his brother Isaac, the sebastocrator, with general consent and in accordance with the laws and justice provided him with money collected from all available sources, Leo provoked Isaac to wrath by his quite shameless conduct. After numerous defeats and thousands of daring attacks on the Kelts, the emperor by the grace of God came back crowned with the laurels of victory, but once again he heard that fresh hordes of enemies (the Scyths) were setting out against him. For the same reasons as before there was a hurried collection of money. The bishop made a ruthless attack on the emperor, who was living at the time in the capital. A long discussion followed on the sacred objects. Leo maintained that the holy images were truly worshipped by us, not merely treated with reverence. On some points his arguments were reasonable and befitting a bishop, but on others he was unorthodox, whether because of his contentious spirit and hatred for the emperor, or through ignorance I do not know. He was incapable of expressing his ideas accurately and without ambiguity, because he was utterly devoid of any training in logic. His attacks on the rulers became more and more reckless as he listened to the prompting of evil-minded men (many of whom at that time held places in the administration). They prodded him into such a state that he even became insolent and indulged in foolish calumnies, despite the fact that the emperor, who had already been commended by the more illustrious members of the Synod (men whom the Chalcedon Faction

5. The Copper-Sellers' quarter, in the vicinity of St Sophia. Anna refers to the church of St Mary there, built some 500 years before.

dubbed 'stooges'), called on him to change his mind about the images and refrain from hostile acts against himself. Moreover, the emperor promised to restore to the sacred churches images more glorious than the originals and do everything necessary by way of reparation. In the end Leo was condemned; he lost his bishopric. Far from cowering under the verdict or maintaining silence, he proceeded to stir up more trouble in the Church, and his reputation for intransigence and absolute incorruptibility won him a not inconsiderable following. Many years later he was unanimously condemned to exile. He retired to Sozopolis in Pontus, where every provision was made by Alexius for his comfort, although Leo afterwards refused to accept these courtesies, apparently because he nursed a grudge against him. There the story must end.

Recruits flocked to join the emperor when they heard that he was safe. They were carefully trained in good horsemanship, in accurate shooting with the bow, in arms drill and the best ways of setting an ambush. Envoys were once more sent to the King of Germany,[6] led by Methymnes. In a letter Alexius urged him to delay no longer, but to invade Lombardy at once, in accordance with the treaty concluded between them; thus Robert would be kept busy while he (the emperor) could with impunity collect his armies and foreign troops; Robert would then be driven from Illyricum. If the king would do this, he said, not only would he be most grateful to him, but he confirmed that the marriage alliance promised by his ambassadors would be fulfilled. After making these arrangements, Alexius left the Great Domestic (Pakourianus) somewhere in that area and returned himself to Constantinople to recruit foreigners from all quarters and to take certain other measures made necessary by the crisis and events that had occurred. The Manichaeans, Xantas and Kouleon, with their men to the number of 2,500 returned home in disorder.[7] On many occasions they were recalled by the emperor, but al-

6. Henry IV.
7. According to Zonaras the Manichaeans were forbidden to serve in the army.

though they made promises, they were constantly putting off
the day. Nevertheless he persisted, offering them gifts and
honours. The offers were made in writing, but it was all of no
avail. While Roman preparations for war were going forward,
someone came to Robert with the news that the German king
was about to arrive in Lombardy. Robert was in an awkward
position. When he crossed to Illyricum he had left Roger in
charge of his realm, but so far no land had been apportioned
to the younger son Bohemond. Now, after considering many
possible courses, with many changes of mind, he summoned
all the counts and officers of the whole army to a meeting.
Bohemond Saniscus was invited to attend it. Seating himself
in front of them Robert made a speech: 'You know, counts,
that when I was about to cross to Illyricum I appointed my
beloved son Roger, my eldest son, lord of my realm. It would
not have been right to go away on so important a campaign
and leave my own country without a leader, a ready prey for
anyone who cared to seize it. Now since the King of Germany
is already on the point of attacking it, we must do our best to
repel him, for it's wrong to lay claim to the possessions of
others and neglect one's own. That is why I am going in
person to protect my own country and to fight Henry. To
this younger son of mine I entrust Dyrrachium, Avlona and
the other cities and islands that I have won in war. I give you
an order and ask you to treat him as you would myself; fight for
him with all your heart and strength. And to you, my dear son,
(turning to Bohemond) I give this advice: honour the counts
in every way, make use of their counsel at all times, do not
dictate, but always work with them. As for yourself, make sure
you don't neglect to follow up the war with the Roman
emperor; although he has suffered a great defeat and barely
escaped with his own life; although most of his armies have
been lost in war and he himself was almost taken alive – he
barely slipped from our hands, a wounded man – yet you must
never relax. A respite might give him the chance to recover his
breath and take up the fight with greater courage than ever.
He is no ordinary enemy. From his infancy he has been brought
up amid wars and battles. He has traversed the whole of the

east and west, making prisoners of all rebels against previous emperors – you have heard with your own ears all about that often enough. In a word, if you lose courage, if you fail to march against him with total determination, all my achievements, all my efforts will be brought to nothing and you yourself will reap the fruits of your neglect in full. As for me, I go now to fight the king, to expel him from our territory and thus confirm my beloved Roger in the position of authority I gave him.' With these words he took leave of him and embarking on a monoreme crossed over to Lombardy. He quickly arrived at Salerno which had for a long time been set aside as the residence of claimants to the dukedom. He stayed there long enough to collect strong forces and as many mercenaries from other parts as he could. Meanwhile the German king, keeping his pledges to the emperor, hurried to occupy Lombardy. Robert knew this and himself lost no time in going to Rome; he wished to unite with the pope [8] and frustrate the king's immediate aims. The pope was not reluctant and both set out against Henry. However, while the latter hastened to invade Lombardy he heard of the emperor's misfortunes: that he had lost a great battle; that some of his army had been wiped out, the rest had scattered in all directions; that Alexius himself, exposed to many dangers and fighting bravely, had been seriously wounded in various parts of his body, but thanks to his daring and courage had been miraculously saved. The king thereupon turned his horse back along the path by which he had come, reckoning that victory for him meant not running personal risks for no good purpose. He took the road home. When Robert entered the king's camp, he was unwilling himself to pursue any further, but detached a strong body of his men and ordered them to hunt the Germans down. All the booty was seized and then Robert, with the pope, went back to Rome. The pope was enthroned by Robert and in return acclaimed him, after which Robert retired to Salerno in order to recover from the fatigue of his many battles.

Not long after Bohemond rejoined him; one could plainly

8. Gregory VII (1073–85).

read in his face the news of the defeat inflicted on him. How
this came about I will now explain. Mindful of his father's
precepts, Bohemond, who was in any case a warlike man and
loved danger, was tenaciously carrying on hostilities against
Alexius. He had his own troops and was also accompanied by
distinguished officers of the Roman army, as well as governors
of the countries and cities conquered by Robert. These men,
once they had given up hope for the emperor, had transferred
their loyalty altogether to Bohemond. The latter now went
through Bagenetia to Joannina, where trenches were dug by
the vineyards outside the town; all the soldiers were posted in
vantage-points while Bohemond himself had his headquarters
inside the place. After making an inspection of the ramparts
and recognizing that the citadel was in a dangerous condition,
he not only did his best to restore it, but built another of great
strength at a different section of the walls where it seemed to
him that it would be more useful. At the same time the towns
and lands in the vicinity were being plundered. The emperor,
informed of Bohemond's activities, without a moment's delay
gathered all his forces and hurriedly left Constantinople in the
month of May. When he reached Joannina the time was ripe
for campaigning, but he was well aware of his own deficiencies:
his army was vastly outnumbered and in any case the experience of the previous battle with Robert convinced him
that the first charge of Keltic cavalry was irresistible. He decided
therefore to begin operations by skirmishing with a small
group of picked men; by doing this he would gain some
indication of Bohemond's skill as a military commander and
these minor engagements would also give him an opportunity
to discover the general situation; afterwards he would be able
to use the intelligence to face the Kelt with more confidence.
Both armies were impatient, eager for battle, but the emperor,
fearing the first charge of the Latins, adopted a new strategy.
Lighter wagons, smaller than usual, were made ready and on
each four poles were fixed; armed infantrymen were stationed
near them so that when the Latins made their assault on the
Roman line at full gallop these men from underneath would
push the wagons forward. In this way the continuous line

of the enemy would be broken up. Just after the sun rose above the horizon and was shining brightly – the moment for battle – the emperor took his place in the centre of the line, prepared for combat. When the fighting began, however, it was clear that Bohemond had not been trapped; as though he had fore-knowledge of the Roman plan he had adapted himself to the changed circumstances. His forces were divided in two and swerving away from the chariots launched an attack on either flank. There was a general mêlée as the fighters met in head-on collision. The casualties on both sides were heavy, but Bohemond won. As for Alexius, he stood like some un-shakeable tower attacked from right and left, sometimes charging on horseback against the advancing Kelts and when he closed with a group of them, striking, killing and being struck; sometimes rallying the runaways with frequent cries. But when he saw his regiments broken up and scattered, he realized that he must secure his own safety, not to preserve his own life nor overwhelmed by fear, as someone might suggest, but in the hope that by avoiding the danger and recovering his strength he might resume the struggle with his Keltic adversaries more bravely another day. Fleeing with a mere handful of his men he fell in with some of the enemy and once again showed himself a dauntless leader. He encouraged his comrades and in a death-or-glory charge himself struck and killed one of the Kelts; his men, real fighters, wounded many and chased the others away. Thus, after escaping fearful dangers beyond number he reached safety again at Achrida, when he had passed through Strougai. At Achrida he rested and when a considerable force of the defeated army had been rounded up, he left them all in that district with the Great Domestic while he went on to the Vardar, but not to enjoy a period of leisure (he never allowed himself to indulge in royal pleasures and relaxations). The armies were assembled once more and when the mercenaries were ready he marched against Bohemond with a new idea for victory. He had iron caltrops made and since he expected the battle to take place on the next day, the evening before broadcast them over the plain between the two armies at the point where he guessed

that the Kelts would make a heavy cavalry attack. The plan was
to frustrate the first (and decisive) charge when the caltrops
pierced the horses' hooves. The Roman lancers in front of
them were to ride forward measured distances, avoiding
damage from the caltrops, but split up to right and left, while
the peltasts were to shoot arrows in a continuous stream at the
Kelts from afar and the wings would fall on the enemy with
terrific force from either flank. Such was my father's scheme,
but it did not deceive the enemy. It happened thus: the
emperor's plan was conceived in the evening and in the morning the Kelts discovered it. Bohemond cleverly altered his own
dispositions to thwart it. He accepted the challenge to fight,
but his attack did not follow its usual course, for the emperor's
plan was anticipated by a furious assault from the flanks, while
the enemy centre remained immobile. In the hand-to-hand
conflict which ensued the Romans were defeated and fled.
In any case they were frightened before the battle started
because of their previous disaster and did not dare to look
their opponents in the face. Our line was thrown into confusion, although Alexius stood firm, gallantly resisting with
all his strength and resolution. He wounded many, but was
himself wounded. When all his army had melted away and he
was left with few companions, he judged it to be his duty no
longer to expose himself to senseless risks (for when a man
after much suffering has no more strength to fight, he would
be a fool to thrust himself into obvious peril). The right and
left wings of his army had already taken to their heels when the
emperor was still holding his ground, courageously carrying
on the battle with Bohemond's men and bearing the whole
brunt of the fight on his own shoulders. The danger became
overwhelming and knowing that resistance was no longer
possible, he came to the conclusion that he must save himself,
in order to fight again and by really powerful opposition
prevent Bohemond from enjoying the full fruits of victory. In
defeat and in victory Alexius was always like that; whether in
flight or once more in pursuit, he never cowered, was never
caught in the toils of despair. The truth is that he had the
greatest faith in God, making Him the centre of his own life

in all things, but abstaining completely from taking oaths in His name. On this occasion, as I have said, he knew that the position was hopeless and fled, chased by Bohemond and picked counts. While this was going on he spoke to Goules, a servant of his father, and the others who were with him: 'How far shall we flee?' Then, wheeling round, he drew his sword and struck the first adversary to catch up with him in the face. The Kelts, seeing this and perceiving that he was quite reckless, halted and gave up the chase. They knew from long experience that such men are invincible. In this way he was free of his pursuers and escaped. Even in flight he did not lose heart altogether, but rallied some of the runaways and mocked others, though most of them pretended not to know him. At any rate he was saved and returned to the capital, to recruit other armies and march against Bohemond again.

When Robert returned to Lombardy, Bohemond took charge of operations against the emperor. He put into practice the advice of his father and fanned the flames of war and battle everywhere. He sent Peter Aliphas [9] with Pounteses [10] to besiege various places. Peter at once seized the two Polobi, while Pounteses made himself master of Skopia. [11] Bohemond himself arrived quickly at Achrida in answer to a summons from the townspeople there. After a short stay he departed without accomplishing anything (because Ariebes guarded the citadel) and went on to Ostrobos, where he was again repulsed. Empty-handed he left for Berroea, [12] going through Soscus and Serbia. Although a number of assaults were made on the walls at many points, he was unsuccessful and went on through Bodena to Moglena, where he rebuilt a tiny fort long since in ruins. A Count surnamed Saracenus was left there with a strong garrison, but Bohemond moved to the Vardar to a place called Asprae Ecclesiae. He remained there for three months and during this period three picked counts, Pounteses, Renaldus and another called Gulielmus formed a conspiracy

9. Peter of Aulps.
10. It has been suggested that Pounteses is Raoul, Count of Pontoise.
11. Uskub or Skoplje.
12. Verria.

to desert to the emperor. Their plot was detected, but Pounteses being forewarned ran away to Alexius; the other two
were arrested and according to Keltic custom were freed to
fight in single combat. Gulielmus lost and was therefore condemned: he lost his eyes; the other, Renaldus, was sent by
Bohemond to his father in Lombardy. Robert had him blinded
too. Bohemond, leaving Asprae Ecclesiae, went off to Kastoria. The Great Domestic[13] at this news arrived at Moglena,
seized Saracenus, put him to death immediately and completely
razed the little fort. Bohemond meanwhile left Kastoria and
moved to Larissa with the intention of wintering there. As
for the emperor, after reaching the capital, as I said, he set to
work at once, which is what one would expect of him for he
was a hard worker and never had his share of rest. He called
on the sultan[14] to supply forces with leaders of long experience.
The request was answered without delay: 7,000 men were sent
with highly skilled officers, including Kamyres, who excelled
all in his knowledge of war, acquired over a long period.
While Alexius was making these preparations, Bohemond
detached some of his men, all Kelts armed from head to foot,
and took Pelagonia by assault, as well as Trikala and Kastoria.
He himself with the whole army came to Trikala, but another
detachment, all brave men, captured Tzibiscus without difficulty. He then moved on to Larissa, arriving in full force on
St George the Martyr's Day.[15] The walls were invested and the
siege began. Leo Cephalas, son of John Comnenus'[16] servant,
was governor of Larissa then and for six months held out
bravely against Bohemond's war-engines. At the time he sent
news of the barbarian's attack in letters to the emperor, but
Alexius impatient though he was did not immediately set out
on the road to Larissa; he was collecting more mercenaries
from all directions and his departure was delayed. Later, when
all were properly armed, he left Constantinople. As he drew
near to the environs of the city and had crossed Mount
Kellion,[17] he left the public highway on his right and the hill

13. Pakourianus.   14. Sulayman, the Seljuq ruler.
15. 23 April 1083.   16. John Comnenus, the emperor's father.
17. So called because of the many monasteries in the area.

called by the locals Kissabos and descended to Ezeban, a
Vlach village lying quite close to Andronia. From there he
made his way to another small place commonly called Pla-
bitza, situated fairly near the River . . . and there, having dug
a good entrenchment, he pitched camp. From there he went on
in a hurry to the Gardens of Delphinas, then to Trikala. At
this point a messenger arrived with a letter from Leo Cephalas,
whom I have mentioned above. It was written with some
frankness, as follows: 'I would like you to know, Sir, that I
have till now preserved this fortress from capture through
my own great efforts. But we are now deprived of victuals which Christian men may eat; we have even touched
what is not lawful. Even that has failed us. If you are
willing to hurry to our aid and can drive off our besiegers,
thanks be to God. If not, I have already fulfilled my duty.
From now on we are the slaves of necessity – what can a man
do against nature and the tyranny she imposes? We have a
mind to surrender the place to the enemies who press us hard
and are clearly strangling us. If this should be our unhappy
lot – call down curses on me if you like, but I will speak
boldly and frankly to Your Majesty: unless you hurry with
all speed to deliver us from this peril (for we cannot hold out
any longer against so great a burden of war and famine) you,
our emperor, if you do not bring aid quickly when you have
the power to do so, you will be the first to be charged with
treachery.' Some other method, the emperor knew, must be
found to defeat the enemy. He was absorbed in anxious calculations; indeed, he worked hard all through the day planning
how to lay ambushes, pleading with God to help him. Help
came in this way: he summoned one of the old men from
Larissa and questioned him on the topography of the place.
Turning his eyes in different directions and at the same time
pointing with his finger, he carefully inquired where the
terrain was broken by ravines, where dense thickets lay close
to such places. The reason why he asked the Larissaean
these questions was of course that he wished to lay an ambush
there and so defeat the Latins by guile, for he had given up
any idea of open hand-to-hand conflict; after many clashes of

this kind – and defeats – he had acquired experience of the
Frankish tactics in battle. When the sun went down he retired
to his bed after working all day. He had a dream. It seemed that
he was standing in the sanctuary of the great martyr Demetrius[18] and he heard a voice say: 'Cease tormenting yourself
and grieve not; on the morrow you will win.' He thought that
the sound came to him from one of the ikons suspended in
the sanctuary, on which there was a painting of the martyr
himself. When he awoke, overjoyed at the voice he had heard
in this dream, he invoked the martyr and gave a pledge,
moreover, that if it was granted to him to conquer his enemies,
he would visit the shrine and dismounting from his horse
some stades from the city of Thessalonica he would come on
foot and at a slow pace to pay homage. A council of generals,
officers and all the relatives of the emperor was then called.
Each man was asked to give his opinion. After that Alexius
explained his strategy. He intended to hand over all the main
forces to his kinsmen. Nicephorus Melissenus and Basil
Curticius, also called 'Little John',[19] were appointed commanders-in-chief. Curticius was a famous soldier, renowned
for his bravery and knowledge of warfare. He came originally
from Adrianople. Not only did the emperor entrust to them
the army, but all the imperial standards. They were instructed
to draw up the battle-line according to the principles he himself had followed in former engagements; he advised them to
test the Latin vanguard first by skirmishes, then to advance
against them in full force with loud war-cries; but as soon as
the two lines came to close quarters, they were to turn their
backs and pretend to run pell-mell in the direction of Lykostomion. While these orders were being given, all the horses of
the army were suddenly heard to neigh – a sound which
caused general consternation. To the emperor however and to
all others of an inquiring mind it seemed a good omen. After
the meeting he left them to the right of Larissa, waited until
sunset and with certain picked men, who were to follow him,
passed through the defile of Libotanion, went round Rebeni-

18. The basilica of St Demetrius is still standing at Thessalonica.
19. See p. 49.

kon, through the place called Allage and arrived on the left of Larissa. The entire countryside was thoroughly reconnoitred and he found a low-lying spot; there he lay in ambush with his party. The Roman commanders, while the emperor was hurrying on his way and just about to enter the defile of Libotanion, sent out a detachment against the Kelts. The plan was to distract the enemy by drawing attention to themselves and thus give them no chance of finding out Alexius' final destination. These men went down on the plain and put in an attack; fighting went on for a long time until nightfall put an end to it. Thus Alexius was enabled to reach the chosen place. His men were ordered to dismount and kneel down, still holding the reins in their hands. He himself happened to alight on a germander-bed and there he spent the rest of the night, kneeling with reins in hand and his face turned towards the ground.

At sunrise Bohemond saw the Romans ranged in battle formation, the imperial standards, the silver-studded lances and the horses with the emperor's purple saddle-cloths. To the best of his ability he ranged his own army against them, dividing his forces in two, one half commanded by himself, the other by Bryennius, a Latin of distinction who had the title of constable.[20] He (Bohemond) used his normal tactics and launched a frontal attack where he saw the imperial standards, thinking that the emperor was there. He swooped down on the enemy like a whirlwind. For a little time they held out, then turned and fled. He drove on in mad pursuit. The emperor, seeing all this and judging that Bohemond was now far enough from his own camp, mounted his horse, bade his men do likewise and made for the Keltic entrenchment. Once inside it he massacred many of the Latins and took up the spoils; then he looked round for Bohemond and the runaways. The latter were still fleeing in a haphazard way, Bohemond was still pursuing and behind him was Bryennius. The emperor sent for George Pyrrhus, a famous archer, and some other great fighters and ordered them to drive hard on the heels of Bryennius (there were sufficient peltasts among them) but

20. Count of Brienne, Constable of Apulia.

not to fight at close quarters; they were to shoot great numbers of arrows from a distance and at the horses rather than the riders. Catching up with the Kelts, therefore, they rained down arrows on their mounts and thus completely upset the riders, for all Kelts when on horseback are unbeatable in a charge and make a magnificent show, but whenever they dismount, partly because of their huge shields, partly too because of the spurs on their boots and their ungainly walk, they become very easy prey and altogether different as their former enthusiasm dies down. It was this, I fancy, that led the emperor to suggest firing at the horses in particular. Bryennius' men, as their chargers fell, began to circle round and round. As they congregated in a great mass, a thick cloud of dust rose high to the heavens, so that it might have been compared with the darkness over Egypt long ago, a darkness that could be felt. The thick dust blinded their eyes and they were unable to find out from where the arrows came or who was firing them. Bryennius sent three Latins to tell Bohemond the whole story. They found him with a small group of Kelts on a tiny island in a river called the Salabria and eating grapes. He was bragging loudly, full of his own vainglory. The remark he made is repeated even today and still parodied: he kept saying, with barbaric mispronunciation of Lykostomion, 'I've thrown Alexius to the wolf's mouth.'[21] That is what happens when excessive pride blinds people to what is right under their eyes and at their feet. However, when he heard Bryennius' message and realized that the emperor had won a victory by a cunning ruse, he was naturally angry, but being the kind of man he was, by no means dismayed. Some of his Keltic cataphracts were sent off to the top of a mountain ridge opposite Larissa. The Roman soldiers, seeing them there, argued with great force and eagerness that they should fight them. The emperor tried to deter them, but they were many, a composite force from different contingents, and having climbed the ridge they put in an attack. The Kelts charged against them without hesitation and killed up to 500 of them. Afterwards, Alexius, guessing the

21. There is a play on words here in the Greek: *Lykostomion* and *Lykou stoma*.

likely direction of Bohemond's march, sent Migidenus with some good soldiers of his own and a company of Turks to obstruct him, but as soon as they approached Bohemond charged and defeated them. He chased them as far as the river.

On the next morning when the sun rose Bohemond, with his attendant counts and Bryennius, rode along the river bank until he found a marshy area on the outskirts of Larissa. Between two hills there was a wooded plain ending in a rugged defile (their name for it is *klisura*). Going through this he pitched camp on the plain, which was called the 'Palace of Domenicus'. On the following day at dawn the commander-in-chief, Michael Ducas, my maternal uncle, caught up with him there with the whole Roman army. Michael was renowned for his prudence; he surpassed others of his generation in physical stature too, as well as fine looks; in fact he excelled all men who ever lived in these respects, for everybody who saw him was overcome with admiration. Endowed with extraordinary and unrivalled powers of prevision, he was no less capable of discerning the main perils and of destroying them. To him the emperor gave instructions not to allow his men to enter this defile all at once; the main force was to remain outside the entrance and only a few Turkish and Sarmatians, all skilled bowmen, were to go in and they were to use no other weapons but their arrows. After they had entered and were charging against the Latins, the rest began to quarrel among themselves; they were impatient to join them and the question was, who should go. Bohemond, with his superb knowledge of military tactics, ordered his men to stand firm in serried ranks, protecting themselves shield to shield. The proto-strator,[22] noticing that the Romans were slipping away one by one and going into the mouth of the defile, went in himself. Bohemond 'rejoiced like a lion which has chanced upon a mighty prey'[23] (to quote Homer) when with his own eyes he saw Michael and his soldiers. He hurled himself at them in a furious assault with all his strength and they fled forthwith. Ouzas,[24] who owed his name to his race, a man famed for

22. Commander-in-chief.   23. *Iliad* iii, 23.
24. The Uzes were a tribe related to the Huns and Scyths.

courage and one who knew how to 'wield the dried bull's hide to right and left'[25] (as Homer says), when he emerged from the pass, swerved slightly to the right, swiftly turned and struck at the Latin behind him. The man at once fell head-first to the ground. Nevertheless Bohemond chased them to the River Salabria. In the flight, however, Ouzas speared Bohemond's standard-bearer, snatched it from his hands, waved it round a little and then pointed it towards the ground. The Latins, puzzled by the sight of the lowered standard, turned in confusion along another route and arrived at Trikala, which had already been occupied by some of the Kelts on their flight to Lykostomion. With them they now mingled and bivouacked in the town[26] for some time. Later they went on to Kastoria. Alexius meanwhile left Larissa and went on to Thessalonica. With his usual cleverness in such circumstances he lost no time in sending envoys to Bohemond's counts with many pledges if they would demand from their leader the pay he had promised them. If Bohemond failed to produce the money, they were to persuade him to go down to the sea and get the pay from his father Robert, actually crossing to demand it in person. Alexius assured them that if they could bring this about (that is, get rid of Bohemond) they would all be honoured by him and receive countless benefits. Those who desired to serve with pay in the imperial army, would be placed on the rolls and enjoy good wages which they themselves could determine; on the other hand if they preferred to go home, he guaranteed their safe return through Hungary. The counts followed his instructions. Implacably they demanded their pay for the last four years. Bohemond could not manage it and temporized, but they pressed him harder (their demands were reasonable) and he in desperation left Bryennius there to guard Kastoria and Peter Aliphas in charge of the two Polyboi, while he himself went to Avlona – whereupon the emperor returned in triumph to Constantinople.

He found the affairs of the Church in disarray. Not for a brief moment was he suffered to enjoy respite, but Alexius was

25. *Iliad* vii, 238. Referring, of course, to the shield of a warrior.
26. Trikala.

a true representative of God and when he saw the Church troubled by the teaching of Italos, although he was planning operations against Bryennius (the Kelt who occupied Kastoria) he did not disregard the plight of that Church. It was just at this time that the doctrines of Italos flourished. The man had a disturbing influence. I must give an account of his career from its beginning. He came originally from Italy and for a long time lived in Sicily.[27] The Sicilians revolted against the Romans and when they decided to pursue a warlike policy called in the help of their Italian allies. Among the latter was the father of Italos. The boy, although not old enough to bear arms, followed skipping along at his side. He was learning the art of war as the Italians understand it. Such were his early ventures and the first rudiments of his education. But when the celebrated George Maniaces[28] made himself master of Sicily in the reign of Monomachos, it was with difficulty that father and son escaped from the island. They both became refugees in Lombardy, which was at that time still subject to the Romans. From there in some mysterious way he migrated to Constantinople, a not inconsiderable centre for all branches of learning and literary studies. In fact, from the reign of Basil the Porphyrogenitus[29] until that of Monomachos, letters although treated with scant regard by most folk at least did not die out, and once again they shone in bright revival when under Alexius they became the object of serious attention, to those who loved philosophical argument. Before then the majority had lived a life of luxury and pleasure; because of their wanton habits they concerned themselves with quail catching[30] and other more disreputable pastimes, but all

27. An island lying off Italy. (A.C.)

28. Psellus gives a lengthy account of the career and revolt of Maniaces in the *Chronographia* (vi). Constantine IX Monomachos reigned from 1042 to 1055.

29. Basil II Bulgaroktonos, 976–1025. Psellus naturally has much to say on this subject; see vi, 37. It was his proudest boast that he took the leading part in the revival; he was chosen Professor of Rhetoric ('consul of the philosophers') in the new University of Constantinople (1045).

30. There is nothing exceptionally immoral in the hunting of quail. Anna uses the expression to signify a lazy, ineffectual existence.

scientific culture and literature to them were of secondary importance. Such was the character of the people whom Italos found here. He conversed with school-men who were both cruel and rough natured (for in those days there were men of that kind in the capital) and from them he received a literary education. Later he came into contact with the famous Michael Psellus,[31] who, because of his own native intelligence and quickness of apprehension, had not often attended the lectures of the 'learned'. Psellus, moreover, had the help of God, apart from those mentors, for his mother[32] with passionate supplication kept constant vigil in the sanctuary of the Lord before the sacred image of the Theometor,[33] with hot tears interceding for her son. He attained the perfection of all knowledge, having an accurate understanding of both Hellenic and Chaldaean science, and so became renowned in those times for his wisdom. Italos, although he was a disciple of Psellus, was unable with his barbaric, stupid temperament to grasp the profound truths of philosophy; even in the act of learning he utterly rejected the teacher's guiding hand, and full of temerity and barbaric folly, believing even before study that he excelled all others, from the very start ranged himself against the great Psellus. With fanatical zeal for dialectic he caused daily commotions in public gatherings as he poured out a continuous stream of subtle argument; subtle propositions were followed in turn by subtle reasons to support them. The then emperor, Michael Ducas, was a friend of his, as were Michael's brothers, and although they considered him inferior to Psellus, yet they gave him their patronage and took his part in literary debate. The Ducas family were in fact great patrons of literature (I am referring here to the brothers and Michael himself). Italos invariably regarded Psellus with a

31. Constantine (Michael) Psellus was born in 1018 of a noble but poor family; he died about 1078. During his life he served in high offices of state under many rulers, exercising a decisive influence in numerous crises, but he is best known for his voluminous writings and of course for his history (the *Chronographia*) which is a most important document.

32. Psellus owed much to her sacrifices; she procured for him the best tutors.

33. Mother of God.

turbulent frenzy, but the other winged his way, like some eagle, far above the petty subtleties of Italos. You will want to know what happened afterwards. In their struggle against the Romans, the Latins and Italians planned to take over the whole of Lombardy and indeed of Italy too. The emperor (Michael) looking upon Italos as a personal friend, a good man and an expert on Italian affairs, sent him to Epidamnos. To cut the story short, it was discovered that he was betraying our cause there and an envoy was commissioned to remove him. Italos knew what was happening and took refuge in Rome. Then, true to character, he repented, appealed to the emperor and was on his instructions permitted to live in Constantinople at the Pighi monastery and the Church of the Forty Saints. When Psellus withdrew from Byzantium after his ton-suration,[34] Italos was promoted to the Chair of General Philosophy, with the title 'Consul of the Philosophers'. He devoted his energies to the exegesis of Aristotle and Plato. He gave the impression of vast learning and it seemed that no other mortal was more capable of thorough research into the mysteries of the peripatetic philosophers, and more particularly dialectic. In other literary studies his competence was not so obvious: his knowledge of grammar, for example, was defective and he had not 'sipped the nectar' of rhetoric. For that reason his language was devoid of harmony and polish; his style was austere, completely unadorned. His writings wore a frown and in general reeked of bitterness, full of dialectic aggression, and his tongue was loaded with arguments, even more when he spoke in debate than when he wrote. So power-ful was he in discourse, so irrefutable, that his opponent was inevitably reduced to impotent silence. He dug a pit on both sides of a question and cast interlocutors into a well of diffi-culties; all opposition was stifled with a never-ending string of questions, which confounded and obliterated thought, so skilled was he in the art of dialectic. Once a man was engaged in argument with him, it was impossible to escape the man's

34. Psellus accepted the monk's tonsuration in the reign of Constantine IX, but Anna is here referring rather to his disgrace and deposition at the hands of the ungrateful Michael VII (*c.* 1078).

labyrinths. In other ways, though, he was remarkably un-
cultured and temper was his master. That temper, indeed,
vitiated and destroyed whatever virtue he had acquired from
his studies; the fellow argued with his hands as much as his
tongue; nor did he allow his adversary merely to end in failure –
it was not enough for him to have closed his mouth and
condemned him to silence – but at once his hand leapt to the
other's beard and hair while insult was heaped on insult. The
man was no more in control of his hands than his tongue.
This alone would prove how unsuited he was to the philosopher's life, for he struck his opponent; afterwards his anger
deserted him, the tears fell and he showed evident signs of
repentance. In case the reader may wish to know his physical
appearance, I can say this: he had a large head, a prominent
forehead, a face that was expressive, freely-breathing nostrils,
a rounded beard, broad chest and limbs well compacted; he
was of rather more than average height. His accent was what
one would expect from a Latin youth who had come to our
country and studied Greek thoroughly but without mastering
our idiom; sometimes he mutilated syllables. Neither his
defective pronunciation nor the clipping of sounds escaped
the notice of most people and the better educated accused him
of vulgarity. It was this that led him to string his arguments
together everywhere with dialectic commonplaces. They were
by no means exempt from faults of composition and there was
in them a liberal sprinkling of solecisms.

This man then occupied the Chair of General Philosophy
and it was to his lectures that the young men flocked. He
elucidated the works of Proclus[35] and Plato, the teachings of
the two philosophers Porphyry[36] and Iamblichus,[37] and above

35. Proclus flourished in the fifth century after Christ. He was given
the surname Diadochus, because it was commonly thought that he was
Plato's successor.
36. Porphyry of Tyre (A.D. 232–c. 305) wrote voluminously on many
subjects, but without originality.
37. Iamblichus was born at Chalcis, in Koele-Syria, about A.D. 250.
His main interest lay in thaumaturgy. No doubt Italus inherited some of
his material from Psellus, who had studied these writers (see *Chronographia* vi, 38).

all the technical treatises of Aristotle. He gave lectures on
Aristotle's system to those who wished to use it for practical
purposes; it was on the utility of his work that he prided himself especially and on this he spent much time. Yet he was
unable to help his students very much owing to his own hot
temper and the general instability of his character. And who
were his pupils? Here are the names of some: John Solomon,
men like Iasitas and Serblias and others who maybe were
industrious in their studies. Most of them were frequent
visitors to the palace and I myself perceived later on that they
had acquired no accurate systematic knowledge of any kind:
they played the role of dialectician with chaotic changes and
frenzied metaphors, but they had no sound understanding.
They propounded their theories, even at that time putting
forward their ideas on metempsychosis in rather veiled terms
and on certain other matters of a similar nature and almost as
monstrous. It was natural that men of culture should attend the
palace when the devoted pair (my parents, I mean) were themselves labouring so hard night and day in searching the Holy
Scriptures.

I will digress here for a moment – the law of rhetoric will
not grudge me that privilege. Many a time when a meal was
already served I remember seeing my mother with a book in
her hands, diligently reading the dogmatic pronouncements
of the Holy Fathers, especially of the philosopher and martyr
Maximus.[38] Inquiries into the physical nature of things did not
interest her so much as the study of dogma, for she longed to
reap the benefits of true wisdom. It often occurred to me to
wonder at this and as a result I once asked her: 'How could
you of your own accord aspire to such sublimity? For my
part, I tremble and dare not give ear to such things even in the
smallest degree. The man's writing, so highly speculative and
intellectual, makes the reader's head swim.' She smiled. 'Your
reluctance is commendable, I'm sure,' she replied, 'and I

38. Maximus the Confessor (*c.* 580–662) was an important theologian
and an uncompromising adversary of the monothelete heretics. Anna may
well have found him a hard teacher to follow, for his style is involved and
at times obscure.

myself do not approach such books without a tremble. Yet I
cannot tear myself away from them. Wait a little and after a
close look at other books, believe me, you will taste the sweet-
ness of these.' The memory of her words pierces my heart and
plunges me into a sea of other reminiscences. But the law of
history forbids me: we must return to the affairs of Italos.

   At the height of his popularity among the disciples I have
already spoken of, he treated all with contempt; most of the
thoughtless he incited to revolt and not a few were encouraged
to become seditious. I could have named many of them, had
not age dimmed my memory. These events, you see, took
place before my father was raised to supreme power. When he
found here a general neglect of culture and literary skills (for
letters had been banished far from the city) he was eager to
revive whatever sparks still remained hidden beneath the ashes.
All those who had any inclination for learning were unceasingly urged by him to study (there were some, only a few,
and those stood merely in the forecourt of Aristotelian philosophy), but he did advise them to devote attention to Holy
Scripture before turning to Hellenic culture. Noting that
Italos was everywhere causing trouble and leading many
astray, he referred the man for preliminary examination to the
Sebastocrator Isaac, who was himself a great savant with high
ideals. Isaac, satisfied that Italos was indeed a trouble-maker,
publicly refuted him at this inquiry and later, on instructions
from his brother (the emperor), committed him to appear
before an ecclesiastical tribunal. It was impossible for Italos to
conceal his ignorance and even before that gathering he
belched out doctrines foreign to Church teaching; in the
presence of Church dignitaries he persisted in ridicule and
indulged in other things of a boorish and barbaric nature.
At that time Eustratios Garidas [39] presided over the Church
and he, in order to convert him to a better frame of mind
·if he could, kept Italos near the precincts of St Sophia. But
the patriarch himself would sooner have come to share the
heresies of Italos than impart to him a saner doctrine. Italos,
so they say, almost made Garidas his own dedicated

39. Patriarch from 1081 to 1084.

disciple. As a result of all this, the whole population of Constantinople moved in a body to the church looking for him. He would probably have been hurled from the galleries into the centre of the church if he had not hidden himself by climbing on to the roof and taken refuge in some hole. His evil doctrines were a common topic of conversation among many people in the palace and not a few nobles were corrupted by these pernicious ideas, to the great grief of the emperor. Accordingly his heretical teachings were summarized in eleven propositions and these were sent to Alexius.[40] He ordered Italos to retract these propositions from a pulpit in the great church, bareheaded and in the hearing of all the congregation, which was to repeat after him the anathema.[41] Although this was done, Italos proved to be incorrigible and once more he openly preached these same doctrines in public and when he was warned by the emperor, rejected advice in barbaric and lawless fashion. He was therefore personally sentenced to excommunication, though afterwards, when he had recanted for a second time, the penalty was moderated. His teachings were anathematized, but his own name was inserted in a somewhat oblique manner, veiled and not easily recognized by the mass of people. Later he did indeed change his ideas about dogma and repented of his former errors. He repudiated the transmigration of souls and the ridicule of sacred images of the saints; he was eager to re-interpret the theory of ideas[42] so that it should in some way be rendered orthodox, and it was clear that he condemned his early deviations from the truth.

40. The trial (for heresy) took place early in 1082. It has been suggested that Alexius' involvement may have been inspired by political motives, for the philosopher was friendly with the Ducas family. See *CMH*, vol. iv, pt. i, p. 213, and also 217.

41. Curse.

42. Platonic.

BOOK SIX

NORMAN DEFEAT AND THE DEATH
OF ROBERT GUISCARD – THE TURKS

As we have noted, Bryennius occupied Kastoria. The emperor, being anxious to drive him out and seize the town himself, again called up his army. It was completely equipped for siege warfare and for fighting in open country. After preparations had been duly made, Alexius set out. The position of Kastoria is as follows: there is a lake, named after the place, and a promontory broadening at the tip and ending in rocky cliffs juts out into it; on the promontory towers and battlements had been built by way of fortifications – hence the name, Kastoria.[1] The emperor found Bryennius in occupation and decided that he must first test the fortifications with helepoleis. However, as it was impossible for the soldiers to get near except from some base, he built a palisade to begin with and then wooden towers; the whole construction was held together tightly with iron chains to form a kind of stronghold and from this he commenced operations against the Kelts. Helepoleis and rock-throwing catapults were set up outside the walls and fighting went on all night and day. The circumference of the walls was breached, but the defenders resisted even more vigorously (although the rampart was smashed they still refused to surrender) and as he was unable to achieve his object, Alexius made a bold, and at the same time a wise decision. His idea was to make war on two fronts simultaneously, from the mainland and from the lake; the lake assault would be made by soldiers from ships, but as they were non-existent he had some tiny skiffs transported on wagons and launched them in the lake from a small mole. He noticed that the Latins climbed up one side of the promontory quite quickly, but came down more slowly on the other side. He embarked George Palaeologus with fighting-men, therefore,

1. Anna derives the name from Latin *castra*, a camp.

and ordered him to moor his skiffs at the foot of the rocks; he was also instructed to seize the summit in the rear of the enemy when he had seen the agreed signal, climbing up there by the unfrequented but easier route. Moreover, when he saw the emperor had attacked the Latins from the land side, he was to hurry on as fast as he could, for they would be incapable of fighting with equal determination against two attackers: resistance must grow feebler on one or the other front and at that point they would be vulnerable. Palaeologus moored off the cliffs and stood to under arms, with a sentinel posted above to watch for the emperor's signal; he was to inform Palaeologus when he saw it. At daybreak Alexius and his men charged into battle from the mainland, uttering their war-cries. The scout, seeing the signal, passed it on to Palaeologus with another of his own. At once the summit was secured and ranks formed there. Despite the fact that Bryennius knew he was under siege[2] from the land and realized too that Palaeologus was gnashing his teeth against them from the other side, he still would not give in. In fact, he ordered the counts to fight back with greater courage. Their reply was abominable: 'You see how our troubles multiply. It is right then that each one of us should from now on look to his own safety, some by joining the emperor, others by returning to their native land.' Without hesitation they put their scheme into practice and asked the emperor to set up two standards: one, close to the sanctuary of the great martyr George (this church had been built there in the saint's honour), the other on the road to Avlona. 'Those of us who wish to serve under Your Majesty,' they said, 'will go to the standard close by the sanctuary, and those who prefer to return to their own country will approach the other, on the Avlona road.' With these words they promptly went over to Alexius. Bryennius was a brave man and had no intention of joining him, but he did swear never to take up arms against him, provided that safe conduct was granted him as far as the frontiers of the Empire and if permission was given to return freely to his home. The emperor

2. Anna is our only source for this siege.

very readily agreed. After that he took the road to Byzantium, a glorious victor.[3]

At this point I must interrupt the narrative briefly to describe how he also overcame the Paulicians.[4] To him it was intolerable not to put down these rebels before entering the palace again. One success, he thought, should be followed by another and the people of the Manichaeans should be made to round off the cycle of his triumphs. To allow these men, descended from the Paulicians, to constitute a blot, as it were, on the splendid roll of his victories over the western enemies, was unbearable. Nevertheless, he did not wish to bring this about by war and battle, because many men on either side might well be wiped out in the fighting. He knew them of old as desperate warriors, full of loathing for their opponents. It was desirable that the ringleaders should be punished, but he hoped to enrol the others in his own army. He set about the task with a trick. Recognizing their love of danger and their incurable delight in wars and battles, he was afraid they might in a crisis meditate some awful crime. At the moment they were quietly living in their own territories and so far they had not turned to fresh robberies and plundering raids. On his return to Byzantium therefore he summoned them in letters full of promises. For their part, they had heard of his victory over the Kelts and feared his letters were merely flattering them with fine hopes. However, much against their will, they came to him. After reaching Mosynopolis, he had halted in the vicinity, pretending to stay on there for some other reasons but really to await their arrival. When they did arrive he feigned a desire to meet them personally and enter their names in the register. He took his seat in front of them, a most impressive figure, and directed that their leaders should come forward, not in a disorderly fashion, but in groups of ten.

---

3. Kastoria was taken in October or November 1083.

4. The Paulicians derived their religious ideas from the old Manichaeism, but the sects are not identical. Because of their warlike activities they had been transported from the eastern borders of the Empire to Thrace; Philippopolis, in particular, became a centre of Paulicianism (cf. pp. 160 and 463 ff).

Arranged thus they were to be registered and then enter the
gates of the town. A general review of the rest was promised
for the next day. Men had already been posted to relieve them
of their horses and arms, to put them in chains and lock them
up in selected prisons, but the groups, following in due order,
had no knowledge whatever of this. They went inside ignorant
of their fate. So he arrested them. Their property was confiscated and divided among the brave men who had shared his
privations in the battles and perils of the past. The officer in
charge of this duty left to drive the Manichaean women from
their homes; they too were held in custody in the citadel. Not
long after, the emperor thought it right to exercise clemency
and all those who preferred holy baptism were not denied it.
After a thorough investigation the ringleaders were identified
– those responsible for their absurd behaviour – and these he
condemned to exile and imprisonment on islands. The others
were granted an amnesty and allowed to go away wherever
they wished. They chose their own country before all others
and returned there at once to manage their affairs as best they
could.

   Alexius went back to Constantinople.[5] He was not unaware
of the whispering campaign against himself in the highways
and byways of the city, but it hurt his feelings to hear these
things. After all, the deed was not so very heinous. Yet the
number of his accusers, eager to bring charges, was greatly
multiplied. His offence had been committed under the pressure
of circumstances, in a national emergency when the imperial
treasury had failed him, and he regarded the money as a loan;
to him the transaction was neither brigandage, as his detractors
claimed, nor the treacherous plot of a tyrant. His intention had
been, after winning the wars that menaced him then, to restore
to the churches the precious objects taken from them. Now
that he had returned to the capital the thought that would-be
censurers of his acts had any pretext was unbearable. Accordingly he announced that a most important meeting would take
place in the palace of Blachernae (at which he proposed to
appear as defendant and so offer his own explanation). There

5. On 1 December 1083.

were present the whole senate, military commanders and all the dignitaries of the Church, all impatient to know the purpose of a full assembly. It was in fact nothing more than the emperor's reply to the rumours against him. On this occasion, therefore, the priors of the sacred monasteries attended and the books (commonly called *brevia*) were produced for inspection; in these the treasures in each sanctuary were recorded. One would imagine that the emperor, seated on the imperial throne, was presiding as judge but in reality he was about to subject himself to cross-examination. The objects presented to the sacred houses by many persons long ago were scrutinized in the records, to see if they had been removed by the said persons later on or by the emperor himself, but it was proved that nothing had been taken, with one exception: the gold and silver ornament which lay on the coffin of the famous Empress Zoe,[6] and certain other small objects no longer in use at divine worship. Thereupon the emperor publicly submitted himself to judgement, accepting the verdict of anyone there present who was willing to serve as juror. Then, after a short pause, he went on with a change of tone: 'It was my misfortune to find the Empire surrounded on all sides by barbarians, with no defence worthy of consideration against the enemies who threatened it. You know the many dangers I faced, almost myself becoming a victim of the barbarian's sword. Those who drew bow on us from east and from west vastly outnumbered our forces – you cannot be ignorant of the Persian invasions and the raids of the Scyths; you cannot have forgotten the sharp-pointed spears of the Lombards. With the arms we provided our money disappeared and the circle of empire was drawn close, indeed to its irreducible limit. You are aware how our entire army was built up, recruited from all sides and trained, and there is no one here who does not know that all these things involved great

6. Zoe died in 1050 at the age of 72. She was the second daughter of Constantine VIII and wife of three emperors, Romanus III, Michael IV and Constantine IX. For a short period in 1042 she shared the throne with her sister Theodora. A most interesting and full account can be found in Psellus (*Chronographia*).

expenditure of money; what was removed has been spent on necessities (after the manner of the great Pericles[7]) and it has been used to safeguard our honour. However, if the censorious see in our actions some offence against the canons, that is not surprising. For we hear that even the prophet-king David, when he was reduced to the same necessity, ate of the sacred bread with his warriors, although it was forbidden for an ordinary person to touch the food reserved for the priests. Anyway, the sacred canons palpably allow the holy objects to be sold for the ransoming of prisoners-of-war (among other things). But if the whole country is being taken prisoner, if its cities and Constantinople itself are already in danger of becoming captives, if then we, in such a moment of peril, laid our hands on a few objects, not really worthy of the name "sacred", and used them to secure our freedom, surely we leave no reasonable excuse to our detractors for charging us.' Having said this he altered the argument, assumed responsibility for what had occurred and condemned himself; after which he told those who had the inventories to read them again, so that it might be quite clear what had been removed. He then immediately calculated an adequate sum of gold to be paid annually by the treasury officials to the Chapter of the Antiphonetes [8] – a custom which has persisted without interruption even to this day. It was there that the coffin of the Empress Zoe lay. To the church in the Chalcopratia[9] he ordered a yearly income of gold to be allotted from the treasury for payment to those who usually sing hymns in the holy sanctuary of the Theometor.

Meanwhile it became apparent that a plot was being made against the emperor by leading members of the senate and the great military commanders. He was at once informed. Accusers came before him and the conspirators were con-

7. Pericles was prepared in a crisis to borrow from the Goddess Athena (Thucydides ii, 13).

8. The Antiphonetes is the Saviour (the Greek word means 'surety'). Three churches in Constantinople were dedicated to the Saviour: St Saviour in Chora, St Saviour Pantepoptes and St Saviour Pantocrator.

9. The Chalcopratia is the district near St Sophia. The church referred to here is doubtless the St Mary.

victed. Although their guilt was established and the penalty laid down by law was a severe one, Alexius was not at all eager to pass the full sentence: the ringleaders were merely condemned to lose their property and go into exile. He pursued the matter no further than that. However, let us return to the point where we digressed. When Alexius was promoted to the rank of Domestic by Nicephorus Botaniates, he had taken with him a certain Manichaean called Traulos and made him one of his family servants. The man was considered worthy of holy baptism and was married to one of the empress's maids. Traulos had four sisters and when he found out that they had been carried off to prison with the others and deprived of all their possessions, he could not contain his indignation. He sought a way of escaping from the emperor's service. His wife had by now discovered his plan and seeing that he was about to run away, told the man who was at that time charged with supervision of the Manichaeans. Traulos knew what she had done and straightway called on his confidants to meet him in the evening. All those who were relatives obeyed and together they went off to Beliatoba (a small place on the ridge which dominates the valley of the same name). They found it uninhabited, looked upon it as their own and proceeded to make their dwelling there. Every day they made sorties and returned with much booty from as far away as our Philippopolis. But Traulos was not satisfied with these achievements. He made a treaty with the Scyths [10] of Paristrion and won the friendship of the chiefs in Glabinitza, Dristra and the neighbouring area. At the same time he married the daughter of a Scythian chieftain. By every means he strove to foster a Scythian invasion in order to hurt the emperor. Daily reports of his doings kept the emperor informed and he did his best to avert catastrophe. He foresaw the evil likely to result and wrote conciliatory letters full of promises. He even sent a chrysobull guaranteeing Traulos an amnesty and full liberty. But the crab refused to learn how to walk straight: he remained what he had been the day before and the day before that, intriguing

10. The Patzinaks, or as *CMH* has it, the Pechenegs. These events took place in 1084.

with the Scyths, sending for more of them from their own
lands and plundering all the vicinity.

In the end the emperor, who had regarded the Manichaean
affair as of minor importance, again brought them under his
control. But Bohemond was still waiting at Avlona. Let us
get back to him. When he heard of the fate of Bryennius and
the other counts, some of whom had chosen to serve under
Alexius, while the rest dispersed in all directions, he left for
his own country and crossed to Lombardy. At Salerno he met
his father Robert (as I have already described) and with many
charges he tried to stir up resentment against the emperor.
Robert, who saw the terrible news in his son's face and knew
that the glorious hopes he had placed in him had gone
completely astray (like a coin falling wrong way up), stood for
a long time speechless, as if struck by a thunderbolt. When he
had learnt all and fully realized how his expectations had been
disappointed, he was in the depths of despair. Yet no ignoble
thought unworthy of his own bravery and daring entered his
head. On the contrary he was more than ever eager for battle,
more occupied with plans and ideas for war. Robert was a
determined champion of his own designs and prejudices,
absolutely resolved never to give up a decision once taken:
in a word, indomitable – for he believed that his first assault
could win anything. He quickly regained his composure; his
terrible gloom passed. Heralds were sent everywhere proclaiming a general mobilization and a fresh attack on the
emperor in Illyricum. All men were required to join Robert.
So a host of soldiers, cavalry and infantry, soon gathered from
all directions, all finely armed, thinking only of battle. They
flocked to join him from the neighbouring cities and no less
from foreign countries, coming as Homer would have said
'like buzzing swarms of bees'. Robert therefore had the military power to avenge his son's defeat. Now that sufficient
forces had assembled he sent for the two other sons, Roger
and Guy. The emperor had secretly made overtures to Guy,
with offers of a marriage alliance and the prospect of exceptional honour and generous largess. He hoped to tempt him
from allegiance to his father. Guy listened to the proposals and

accepted, but for the moment kept his own counsel. To Roger and Guy, then, Robert handed over all his cavalry and sent them off to seize Avlona without delay; the city was taken at once. They left a handful of soldiers there to protect the place and with the rest went on to Butrinto and captured that too without any difficulty. As for Robert, he sailed with his whole fleet along the coast opposite Butrinto until he reached Brindisi, intending to cross from there. However, when he discovered that the voyage would be shorter from Otranto, he sailed from that place to Avlona. After coasting along as far as Butrinto he rejoined his sons. Corfu, previously subdued by him, had again rebelled; accordingly he left Roger and Guy in Butrinto and himself sailed to the island. During these operations he personally commanded the whole fleet.[11] So much for Robert. The emperor meanwhile was informed of his movements, but was far from shaken. Having decided to accept the enemy's challenge, he urged the Venetians to equip a strong naval expedition. He promised that they would be re-imbursed; he would pay their expenses many times over. He himself made ready biremes, triremes and all kinds of pirate vessels. With soldiers on board experienced in naval warfare they sailed against Robert. The hostile manoeuvres of these fleets were known to Robert and, characteristically, he seized the initiative: weighing anchor he sailed with his entire force to the harbour of Kassiopi. The Venetians had not been long in the harbour of Passaron (to which they had sailed) before they heard of his move. Immediately they too made for Kassiopi. In the tremendous struggle that took place at close quarters Robert was defeated, but remained utterly undaunted. He prepared for a second conflict of even greater ferocity – it was typical of the man's combative, war-loving spirit. The admirals of the allied navies, knowing of his preparations, but confident after their own triumph, attacked him three days later and won a resounding victory, after which they withdrew again to the harbour of Passaron. It may be that they over-estimated the importance of their successes (under the circum-

11. If we are to believe the Latin sources, Robert had with him some 150 ships (in the autumn of 1084).

stances a reaction normal enough) or perhaps they believed their opponents were really down and out; anyway, they relaxed as if the business was completely finished and treated Robert with thorough contempt. A squadron of fast ships was despatched to report these events and describe the absolute rout of the enemy in Venice. A certain Venetian called Pietro Contarini, who had recently taken refuge with Robert, told him what they had done. The news plunged him into a worse despair; for a time he lost all energy, but better counsels prevailed and once more he assailed the Venetians. The latter were astounded by the unexpectedness of it, but lost no time in linking their bigger vessels with iron chains in the port of Corfu, with the smaller ships inside this compact circle (the so-called 'sea harbour'). All anxiously awaited his onslaught under arms. In the ensuing battle – terrible and more violent than the two previous encounters – both sides fought with unprecedented passion and neither would give way; indeed they collided head on. The Venetians had already exhausted their supplies, however, and there were no reserves of men – they had only the soldiers on the ships. The latter, because they had no cargo, floated on the surface as if buoyed up by the waves (the water did not even reach the second line) so that when the men all rushed to one side to oppose the enemy, the boats immediately sank. Up to 13,000 were drowned. The other vessels were captured, with their crews. Unfortunately Robert behaved in cruel fashion after his famous victory. Many of the prisoners were treated with hideous savagery: some were blinded, others had their noses cut off, others lost hands or feet or both. As for the remainder, he sent heralds to their fellow-countrymen widely advertising their sale: anyone who wished to buy a relative for a price could come and do so with impunity. At the same time he had the effrontery to suggest negotiations for peace. They rejected the idea: 'Duke Robert, you can be sure of this: even if we saw our own wives and children having their throats slit, we would not denounce our treaty with the Emperor Alexius. What is more, we will certainly not cease to help him and fight bravely on his behalf.' Not long afterwards they made ready dromons, triremes and

some other ships (small, fast sailers) and attacked Robert in
greater force. They caught up with him off Butrinto (where
he was encamped) and joined battle. The Venetians won,
killing many of their adversaries and throwing more into the
sea. They very nearly captured his (Robert's) own son Guy,
as well as his wife. The report of this fine success was sent in
full to the emperor, who rewarded them with many gifts and
honours. The Doge of Venice [12] was personally honoured with
the rank of protosebastos and the appropriate pension. The
patriarch, too, received the title of hypertimos, also with the
corresponding pension. Apart from that, all the churches in
Venice were allotted an annual payment of gold – a considerable sum – from the imperial treasury on the emperor's orders.
To the church of St Mark the Apostle and Evangelist [13] all
the Amalfitani [14] who had workshops in Constantinople were
to pay tribute, and he made a present to it of the workshops
from the ancient quay of the Hebrews as far as the Vigla,
including the anchorages between these two points, not to
mention the gift of much real property both in the capital and
in the city of Dyrrachium and wherever else the Venetians
demanded it. But the main reward was the free market he
afforded them in all provinces under Roman control, so that
they were enabled to trade without interference as they wished;
not a single obol [15] was to be exacted by way of customs
duties or any other tax levied by the treasury. They were
completely free of Roman authority.

Now we must go back to the point where we digressed and
take up the main thread of the narrative. Even after this defeat
Robert did not return to peaceful ways. He had already sent
some of his ships, under the command of his son Roger,
against Kephalonia. He was eager to capture the city. The rest
of the fleet anchored off Vonitsa with all the army. He himself
boarded a galley with one bank of oars and sailed to Kephalonia,

12. Domenico Silvo.
13. The famous Cathedral of St Mark in Venice.
14. Amalfi had trading interests in the east, but was steadily losing
influence as Venice became more powerful.
15. A small Greek coin (equivalent to a farthing, say).

but before he could join the other forces and his son, while he was still waiting near Ather (a promontory of the island), he was attacked by a violent fever.[16] Unable to bear the burning heat, he asked for some cold water. His men, who had scattered everywhere in search of water, were told by a native: 'You see the island of Ithaka there. On it a great city was built long ago called Jerusalem, now in ruins through the passage of time. There was a spring there which always gave cold drinkable water.' Robert, hearing this, was at once seized with great dread, for a long time before some persons had uttered a prophecy (the kind of prediction sycophants usually make to the great): 'As far as Ather you will subdue everything, but on your way from there to Jerusalem, you will obey the claims of necessity.' Whether it was the fever that carried him off, or whether he suffered from pleurisy I cannot say with certainty. He lingered on for six days and then died.[17] His wife Gaita reached him as he was breathing his last, with his son weeping beside him. The news was given to the other son,[18] whom he had named heir to his domains previously. He was heart-broken at the time, but reason prevailed and when he had recovered his self-composure he called a general meeting. First of all, he announced what had happened, shedding tears copiously over his father's death; then he compelled all to take the oath of allegiance to himself. With them he crossed to Apulia, but ran into a terrific storm on the voyage (although it was the summer season). Some ships were sunk, others were cast up on the beach and wrecked. The vessel carrying the dead man was half destroyed; it was with difficulty that his friends saved the coffin with the body inside and brought it to Venusia. He was buried in the monastery built long ago in honour of the Holy Trinity, where his brothers had also been laid to rest before him. Robert died in the twenty-fifth year of his ducal reign, having lived in all seventy years. The emperor was relieved at the news of his sudden death, like a man throwing off a great load from his shoulders. He immediately set about the enemies still occupying Dyrrachium, attempting to sow dissension among them by letters and every other method.

16. In the summer of 1085.   17. On 17 July 1085.   18. Roger.

He hoped that by doing this he would capture the city easily. He also persuaded the Venetians resident in Constantinople to write to their fellow-countrymen in Epidamnos, and to the Amalfitani and all other foreigners there, advising them to yield to his wishes and surrender the place. Unceasingly, with bribes and promises, he worked to this end. The inhabitants were in fact persuaded, for all Latins lust after money: for one obol they would sell even their nearest and dearest. In their desire for great rewards they formed a conspiracy, wiped out the man who first led them to betray the city to Robert and killed his partisans with him. They then approached the emperor and handed over Dyrrachium; in return they were granted a complete amnesty.

A certain mathematician called Seth,[19] who boasted loudly of his knowledge of astrology, had foretold Robert's death, after his crossing to Illyricum. The prediction, set out in the form of an oracle on paper and sealed, was handed to some of the emperor's closest friends. Seth told them to keep the document for some time. Then, when Robert died, on his instructions they opened it. The oracle ran thus: 'A great enemy from the west, who has caused much trouble, will die suddenly.' All wondered at the skill of the man; he had indeed reached the peak of this science. For a brief moment let us leave the main narrative for a short digression on the nature of oracles.

The art of divination is a rather recent discovery, unknown to the ancient world. In the time of Eudoxus,[20] the distinguished astronomer, the rules for it did not exist, and Plato had no knowledge of the science; even Manetho[21] the astrologer had no accurate information on the subject. In their attempts to prophesy they lacked the horoscope and the fixing

19. Symeon Seth was a contemporary of Michael Psellus and like him wrote pseudo-scientific works. For the whole subject of superstition and mysticism see *CMH*.

20. Eudoxus of Cnidus (*c*. 408–355 B.C.) studied under Plato and wrote widely on astronomy and mathematics. His greatest distinction was his hypothesis of concentric spheres.

21. Manetho (fl. 280 B.C.) was an Egyptian priest; he dedicated a history of Egypt to Ptolemy II. The astrological poem ascribed by the ancients to him was almost certainly a forgery.

of cardinal points; they did not know how to observe the
position of the stars at one's nativity and all the other things
that the inventor of this system has bequeathed to posterity,
things intelligible to the devotees of such nonsense. I myself
once dabbled a little in the art, not in order to make use of any
such knowledge (Heaven forbid!) but so that being better
informed about its futile jargon I might confound the experts.
I write this not to glorify myself, but to point out that in the
reign of this emperor many sciences made progress. He
honoured philosophers and philosophy itself, although it was
obvious that he adopted a somewhat hostile attitude towards
this study of astrology, because I suppose it diverted most of
the more simple-minded from their faith in God to a blind
belief in the influence of the stars. That was the reason for
Alexius' war on the pursuit of astrology. You must not
imagine, however, that there was any dearth of astrologers in
this period – far from it. Seth, whom I have already mentioned,
flourished then and the famous Egyptian [22] from Alexandria
devoted much of his time to the revelation of the mysteries of
astrology. Many people interrogated him and he gave extra-
ordinarily accurate forecasts in some cases without using an
astrolabe; he relied for his predictions on some form of pebble-
casting. [23] There was no magic whatever in this, but merely a
certain numerical skill on the part of the Alexandrian. When
the emperor saw young people flocking to consult him as
though he were a prophet, he himself put questions to him on
two occasions and each time received a correct reply. Afraid
that Seth might do harm to many and that the public might
turn to the unprofitable pursuit of astrology, he banished him
from the city and made him live at Rhaidestos, but took great
care that his wants should be generously provided for at the
expense of the imperial treasury. Then there was the case of the
famous dialectician Eleutherios, also an Egyptian, who
attained great proficiency in the art, which he practised with a
wonderful skill. He was undoubtedly the supreme exponent.

22. Seth.
23. Lecanomancy presumably. It appears that three pebbles were
thrown into a bowl in some way and a demon or spirit invoked.

In later times, too, there was an Athenian, one Katanankes, who came from his native city to Constantinople with the ambition to surpass all his predecessors. He was asked by some people about the emperor, 'When will he die?' He forecast the date according to his calculations, but proved to be wrong. However, it happened at that moment that the lion living in the palace after a fever of four days breathed its last and most people thought that Katanankes' prediction referred to that. Some time afterwards he again foretold the emperor's death wrongly, but on the very day he had mentioned the Empress Anna, his mother, died. Alexius, although the man had been in error both times, was unwilling to remove him from the city, even if he was self-convicted; moreover, he wished to avoid any appearance of resentment. It is time now for us to return to the narrative: I would not like to acquire a reputation for 'star-gazing' and darkening with the names of astrologers the main theme of my history.

It was generally agreed and some actually said that Robert was an exceptional leader, quick-witted, of fine appearance, courteous, a clever conversationalist with a loud voice, accessible, of gigantic stature, with hair invariably of the right length and a thick beard; he was always careful to observe the customs of his own race; he preserved to the end the youthful bloom which distinguished his face and indeed his whole body, and was proud of it – he had the physique of a true leader; he treated with respect all his subjects, especially those who were more than usually devoted to him. On the other hand, he was niggardly and grasping in the extreme, a very good business man, most covetous and full of ambition. Dominated as he was by these traits, he attracted much censure from everyone. Some people blame the emperor for losing his head and starting the war with Robert prematurely. According to them, if he had not provoked Robert too soon, he would have beaten him easily in any case, for Robert was being shot at from all directions, by the Albanians and by Bodinus' men from Dalmatia. But of course fault-finders stand out of weapon range and the acid darts they fire at the contestants come from their tongues. The truth is that Robert's manliness, his marvellous skill in war and his steadfast spirit are universally recognized. He was an adversary not readily vanquished, a very tough enemy who was more courageous than ever in the hour of defeat.

The emperor, accompanied by the Latins of Count Bryennius who had deserted to him, returned to the capital with the laurels of victory. The date was the first of December in the seventh indiction. He found the empress in the throes of childbirth, in the room set apart long ago for an empress's confinement. Our ancestors called it the *porphyra* – hence the world-famous name *porphyrogenitus*. At dawn (it was a Saturday)[24] a baby girl was born to them, who resembled her father, so they said, in all respects. I was that baby. On several occasions I have heard my mother tell how, two days before the emperor's return to the palace (he was coming back then after his battle with Robert and his other numerous wars and labours) she was seized with the pains of childbirth and making the sign of the Cross over her womb, said, 'Wait a while, little one, till your father's arrival.' Her mother, the protovestiaria, so she said, reproached her soundly: 'What if he comes in a month's time? Do you know when he'll arrive?' she said angrily. 'And how will you bear such pain?' So spoke her mother; but her own command was obeyed – which very clearly signified even in her womb the love that I was destined to have for my parents in the future. For thereafter, when I grew to womanhood and reached years of discretion, I had beyond all doubt a great affection for both of them alike. Many folk, certainly all those who know my history, are witnesses of this deep feeling of mine and their evidence is supported by the numerous struggles and labours I have endured on their behalf, as well as those dangers to which I have exposed myself because of that love, unmindful of honour, of money, of life itself. My love for them burned so fiercely that many a time I was ready to sacrifice my very soul for them. But it is not time to speak of that yet. I must tell the reader of the events that followed my birth. When all the ceremonies usual at the birth of royal children had been faithfully performed (the

24. 1 December 1083.

acclamations, I mean, and gifts and honours presented to leaders of the Senate and army) there was, I am told, an unprecedented outburst of joy; everyone was dancing and singing hymns, especially the close relatives of the empress, who could not contain themselves for delight. After a determined interval of time my parents honoured me too with a crown and imperial diadem. Constantine, the son of the former emperor Michael Ducas, who has on many occasions been mentioned in this history, was still sharing the throne with my father; he signed notices of donations with him in purple ink, followed him with a tiara in processions and was acclaimed after him. So it came about that I too was acclaimed and the officers who led the acclamations linked the names of Constantine and Anna. Often in later times I have heard my relatives and parents say that this practice continued in fact over a long period. Maybe it foreshadowed what was about to befall me afterwards, for good or ill. When a second daughter[25] was born, very like her parents and at the same time showing clear signs of the virtue and wisdom which were to distinguish her in later years, they longed for a son and he became the object of their prayers. Thus in the eleventh indiction a boy[26] was indeed born to them – an event immediately followed by great rejoicing; not a trace of disappointment remained now that their desire was fulfilled. The entire people, seeing the pleasure of their rulers, made merry; everyone was pleased and all together were glad. The palace then was a place of perfect happiness, all sorrow and worries of all kinds banished, for the loyal showed a genuine, heartfelt pleasure, and the rest pretended to share their joy. For ordinary folk are in general not well-disposed to their rulers, but usually counterfeit loyalty and by flattery win the favour of their betters. Anyway on this occasion the universal delight was there for all to see. The little boy was of a swarthy complexion, with a broad forehead, rather thin cheeks, a nose that was neither flat nor aquiline, but something between the two, and darkish eyes which, as far as one can divine from the

25. Maria, who later married Nicephorus Catacalon Euphorbenus.
26. John, who became emperor as John II.

appearance of a newborn baby, gave evidence of a lively spirit. Naturally my parents wanted to promote the little one to the rank of emperor and leave to him the empire of the Romans as a heritage; in the great church of God, therefore, he was honoured by the rite of holy baptism and crowned. Such were the events that befell us, the porphyrogeniti, from the very moment of our birth. What happened to us later on will be told in the appropriate place.

As I have said before, after driving the Turks from the coastal districts of Bithynia and the Bosphorus itself, as well as the parts further inland, the emperor concluded a peace treaty with Sulayman.[27] He then turned to Illyricum, thoroughly defeated Robert and his son Bohemond (not without much suffering) and rescued the provinces of the west from utter disaster. On his return from that campaign he found that the Turks of Abul-Kasim were not merely invading the east again, but had even reached the Propontis and the places on the coast there. I must now describe how the Emir Sulayman, having left Nicaea, appointed this Abul-Kasim governor of the city; how Pouzanus was sent by the Persian sultan to Asia and vanquished by the brother of the sultan, Tutush; and how he was killed by him, but Tutush after the victory was strangled by Pouzanus' cousins. An Armenian called Philaretos, highly respected for his bravery and intelligence, had been promoted to the rank of Domestic by the former emperor Romanos Diogenes, and when he saw Diogenes' downfall and knew moreover that he had been blinded,[28] it was more than he could bear, for he had a deep affection for this emperor. He organized a rebellion and seized power for himself in Antioch. As the Turks plundered the area round the city every day and there was no respite at all, Philaretos decided to join them and offered himself for circumcision, according to their custom. His son violently opposed this ridiculous impulse, but his good advice went unheeded. After a journey of eight days he arrived in a state of extreme distress at Nicaea and approached

27. By the treaty (June 1081) Sulayman, sultan of Iconium, agreed not to molest Bithynia. The border was recognized as the river Dracon.
28. Romanos IV Diogenes was blinded and deposed in 1071.

the Emir Sulayman,[29] who had just been promoted to the rank of sultan. He urged him to besiege Antioch and prosecute the war against his father. Sulayman agreed and as he was about to leave for Antioch appointed Abul-Kasim governor of Nicaea with overriding authority over all other military commanders. After a march of twelve nights (with rest by day) Sulayman and Philaretos' son reached Antioch without being seen and took it at the first assault. Meanwhile Charatikes, who had discovered that a large sum of gold and currency from the imperial treasury had been deposited in Sinope, made an unexpected attack on the place and captured it. Tutush, the brother of the great sultan,[30] ruler of Jerusalem, the whole of Mesopotamia, Aleppo and the territory as far as Bagdad, also coveted Antioch, and when he saw the Emir Sulayman in revolt and laying claim to the governorship of that city, he took up position with his whole army between Aleppo and Antioch. Sulayman advanced to meet him and a fierce war broke out at once. However, when it came to fighting at close quarters Sulayman's troops turned and fled in disorder. He made strenuous efforts to inspire them with courage, but in vain, and seeing that his life was in imminent danger he left the battle-field. Maybe because he felt that he was now safe, he put his shield on the ground and sat down there beside it. But his fellow-countrymen had seen him. Some of the satraps came near and told him that his uncle Tutush was sending for him. Suspecting some danger from this invitation he refused. They pressed him and as he had no power to resist Tutush anyway (he was alone), he drew the sword from its sheath and thrust it into his own entrails. The sword passed clean through him and the wretched man perished wretchedly. His death was

29. After the death of Alp Arslan in 1072 (the victor over the Romans at the Battle of Manzikert) his son Malik-Shah appointed Sulayman ibn Kutlumish commander of the Turkish forces in Anatolia. Taking advantage of the Roman civil wars, Sulayman extended his dominions considerably. Both Cyzicus and Nicaea were taken from the Byzantines (Nicaea became his headquarters). After the treaty of 1081 he turned his attention to the east, took Antioch, but was killed in battle against Tutush in 1086.

30. Malik-Shah, Seljuq of Rum.

inevitably the signal for his surviving forces to join Tutush. This news alarmed the great sultan – Tutush was becoming too strong – and he despatched Siaous to the emperor with proposals for a marriage alliance; he promised that if this were arranged he would force the Turks to withdraw from the coastal regions and hand over to the emperor the fortified places; he would lend his whole-hearted support. Alexius received Siaous, read the sultan's letter privately, but made no reference to the question of a marriage. He noticed that Siaous was a sensible man and asked him where he came from and who his parents were. On his mother's side, he told Alexius, he was an Iberian,[31] but he admitted that his father was a Turk. The emperor was much concerned to have him baptized and Siaous consented to this. He gave pledges, moreover, that he would not return to the sultan once he had obtained the inward grace of that holy rite. He had a written order from the sultan which gave him the right to remove all satraps from the coastal cities they had occupied. All he had to do was to produce this document, if the emperor showed himself willing to conclude the marriage agreement. The emperor suggested to Siaous that he should make use of the sultan's order, and when he had by means of it removed the satraps, he should come back to the capital. With great enthusiasm Siaous visited Sinope first, revealed the sultan's letter to Charatikes and made him leave the place without taking possession of a single obol of the imperial money. Then the following incident took place. As Charatikes left Sinope he smashed the sanctuary built in honour of the Mother of God, our Immaculate Lady, and by Divine Providence he was delivered to a demon, as to some avenger, and fell to the ground frothing at the mouth. And thus he left, possessed by a devil. Siaous then handed over Sinope to its new governor, Constantine Dalassenus, who had been sent by the emperor for that very purpose. In the same way Siaous visited the other cities, showing the sultan's order, removing the satraps and reinstating the emperor's nominees. Having completed his task, he came back to Alexius, received holy baptism and was

31. From Iberia in the Caucasus region.

promoted Duke of Anchialos, with the added enjoyment of
many gifts.

When the murder[32] of the Emir Sulayman became known
throughout Asia, all those satraps who happened to be
governors of cities or fortresses seized the places for themselves. For at the time when Sulayman departed for Antioch,
he had left the protection of Nicaea in the hands of Abul-
Kasim and various other satraps, so it is said, were entrusted
with the coastal region, with Cappadocia and with the whole
of Asia, each being required to guard his own particular area
until Sulayman's return. But Abul-Kasim was at the time
Archisatrap of Nicaea and having control of this city (which
also happened to be the headquarters of the sultan) and having
ceded parts of Cappadocia to his brother Poulchases, he had
no qualms in claiming for himself the title of sultan: indeed, he
believed he already had power in his hands. He was a clever
man, prepared to run risks and his ambition was by no means
satisfied. He sent out raiding parties to plunder the whole of
Bithynia right down to the Propontis. The emperor pursued
his former policy: the raids were checked and Abul-Kasim
was constrained to seek terms of peace. But Alexius knew well
enough that the man continued to cherish secret designs
against himself and deferred the signing of any treaty; it was
clearly necessary to send out a really strong force to make war
on him. Taticius (often mentioned before), in command of a
powerful army, was despatched to Nicaea with instructions to
engage whatever enemies he met outside the walls with circumspection. He departed and when he was just outside the
city, as no Turks appeared then, marshalled his troops in
battle array. Suddenly a band of 200 Turks rode out against
him. The Kelts (who were not outnumbered) armed with long
lances charged into them head-on with terrific force; they
wounded many and drove the rest back into the citadel.
Taticius stood to arms in the same formation until sunset, but
as no Turk showed himself outside the gates, he moved away
to Basileia and pitched camp there, twelve stades from
Nicaea. During the night a peasant came with definite

32. Strictly speaking it was suicide.

information that Prosouch was on the way there with 50,000 men sent by the new sultan Barkiyaruq.[33] The news was confirmed by others and since Taticius was greatly inferior in numbers he altered his plans: it seemed more desirable to look to the safety of his whole army than to fight against overwhelming odds and lose everything. His intention was to retire to the capital through Nicomedia. Abul-Kasim from the city ramparts saw the direction of his march (Taticius was already on the road to Constantinople) and left the city in pursuit, with the idea of attacking when he encamped in some place which gave the Turks an advantage. He caught him at Prenetos, took the initiative and engaged in a violent conflict. Taticius was very quick in drawing up a battle-line and ordered the Kelts, in reply to this onslaught, to make the first cavalry charge against the barbarians. With their long lances at the ready they swept down on the enemy at full gallop like a flash of lightning, cut through their ranks and put them into headlong flight. Thus Taticius returned to the capital through Bithynia. Abul-Kasim, however, was far from spent. He coveted the sceptre of the Roman Empire, or failing that control of the whole seaboard and even of the islands. With this in mind, he decided first to build pirate-vessels, since he had captured Kios (a town situated on the coast of Bithynia). While the ships were being completed, his scheme was going well or at least he thought so, but the emperor was not unaware of his activities. A fleet of the available biremes, triremes and other ships, under the command of Manuel Boutoumites, was immediately launched against Abul-Kasim with orders to lose no time in burning his half-built navy, in whatever condition they found it. Taticius was also to attack him from the mainland with a strong force. Both commanders left the city. Abul-Kasim, seeing that Boutoumites was already on his way by sea and crossing at great speed, and learning moreover that other enemies were arriving by land, struck camp. He was looking for a better position; the old site, he thought, was not in his favour, too rugged and narrow, quite unsuited to the

33. Malik-Shah died in 1092. Barkiyaruq was his son. Anna's account is difficult to follow and there appear to be discrepancies in the chronology.

archers and giving them little chance against the Roman
cavalry charges. The new place was called by some Halykai,
by others Kyparission. Once he was over the sea Boutoumites
very quickly burnt their ships. On the day after, Taticius also
arrived, from the landward side, pitched camp in a good
strategic position and for fifteen whole days, from early morning till evening, kept up unceasing attacks on Abul-Kasim,
sometimes skirmishing, sometimes in regular battles. Abul-
Kasim never gave in; in fact he resisted vigorously, to the dis-
comfiture of the Latins, who begged Taticius to let them fight
the Turks on their own despite the unfavourable terrain. It
seemed to him an unwise move, but he knew that every day the
Turks were reinforcing their general. He yielded to the Latins.
About sunrise he drew up his forces and joined battle. Many
of the Turks were killed in this engagement, very many were
taken prisoners, but the majority fled without a thought for
their baggage. Abul-Kasim himself drove straight for Nicaea
and barely escaped with his life. Before they returned to their
own camp the men serving with Taticius had helped themselves to much booty. The emperor, expert in winning the
heart of a man and softening the hardest nature, at once sent
Abul-Kasim a letter in which he advised him to give up such
useless schemes, to stop beating the air and make terms with
himself (the emperor); by doing this he would relieve himself
of much labour and enjoy instead liberal gifts and honours.
Abul-Kasim knew that Prosouch was besieging the strong-
points held by some satraps and would soon approach Nicaea
for the same purpose, so that he made a virtue of necessity, as
they say, and welcomed peace with the emperor confidently,
for he had a shrewd idea of his intentions. A treaty of peace
was concluded between them, but Alexius was eager to obtain
a further advantage, and since there was no other way of
achieving his goal, invited the Turk to the capital; he would
receive money, sample the delights of the city to his heart's
content, and thus rewarded go home. Abul-Kasim accepted
the offer and was welcomed in the capital with every mark of
friendship. Now the Turks who controlled Nicaea had also
occupied Nicomedia (the capital city of Bithynia) and the

emperor wished to eject them; in order to do so, he thought it was essential to build a second stronghold[34] by the sea, while the 'love-scene' was being played out in Constantinople. All the construction materials needed for the building of this fortress, together with the architects, were put on board transport ships and sent off under the command of Eustathios, the Drungarius of the Fleet, who was to be responsible for the building and to whom the emperor confided his secret plan. Eustathios was to receive in the most friendly fashion any Turks who happened to pass that way, supply their needs with the utmost generosity and inform them that Abul-Kasim knew of the project; all ships were to be barred from the coastal areas of Bithynia, to prevent him from finding out what was happening. Every day the emperor continued to give Abul-Kasim presents of money, to invite him to the baths, to horse-races and hunts, to sight-seeing tours of the commemorative columns set up in public places; to please him the charioteers were ordered to organize an equestrian display in the theatre built long ago by Constantine the Great and he was encouraged to visit it daily and watch the horses parade for inspection – all in order to waste time and allow the builders a free hand. When the fortress was finished and his aim achieved, Alexius presented the Turk with more gifts, honoured him with the title of sebastos, confirmed their agreement in greater detail and sent him with every sign of courtesy back over the sea. When Abul-Kasim eventually heard about the building, although he was deeply distressed, he pretended ignorance and maintained a complete silence on the subject. A similar anecdote is recorded of Alcibiades.[35] He too in the same way deluded the Lacedaemonians, when they had not agreed to the rebuilding of Athens after its destruction by the Persians. He told the Athenians to rebuild the city, then went away to Sparta as an envoy. The negotiations took time and gave the

34. Civetot or Kibotos, on the sea of Marmora, near Helenopolis.
35. The story is told in Thucydides (I, 90) but Anna has confused Alcibiades with the real hero Themistocles. Alcibiades was no less capable of deceiving the Lacedaemonians (Spartans) and would have appreciated the compliment.

restorers a good opportunity. The Lacedaemonians only heard of the restoration of Athens after the ruse had fully succeeded. The Paeanian,[36] in one of his speeches, recalls this beautiful trick of Alcibiades. My father's scheme was indeed like it, but one must admit that it was more worthy of a general, for by humouring the barbarian with horse-races and other pleasures and by putting off his departure from day to day he allowed the job to be finished, and then, when the whole work was completed, he let the man go free from the capital.

According to expectations Prosouch arrived with an impressive force to besiege Nicaea, exactly as Taticius' night visitor had said, and for three months he never relaxed his efforts. The inhabitants of the city, and indeed Abul-Kasim himself, saw that their condition was really desperate – it was impossible to hold out against Prosouch any more. They got a message through to the emperor asking for help, saying that it was better to be called his slaves than to surrender to Prosouch. Without delay the best available troops were sent to their aid, with standards and silver-studded sceptres. The emperor's aim in this was not to help Abul-Kasim directly, but he calculated that the relieving force would work rather to the destruction of the man. For when two enemies of the Roman Empire were fighting one another, it would pay him to support the weaker – not in order to make him more powerful, but to repel the one while taking the city from the other, a city which was not at the moment under Roman jurisdiction but would be incorporated in the Roman sphere by this means; little by little a second would be taken, and then another, so that Roman influence, which was then reduced to almost nothing, especially since Turkish military strength had increased, would be much extended. There was a time when the frontiers of Roman power were the two pillars at the limits of east and west – the so-called Pillars of Hercules in the west and those of Dionysos not far from the Indian border in the east. As far as its extent was concerned, it is impossible to say how great was the power of

36. Demosthenes of the Paeanian deme refers to the story in his speech *Against Leptines* (20, 73) delivered in 354 B.C., but D. attributes the deception rightly to Themistocles. Obviously Anna is quoting from memory.

Rome: it included Egypt, Meroë, all the land of the Troglodytes, the countries near the Torrid Zone; on the other side, the famous Thule and all the peoples who live in the region of the North, over whom is the pole-star. But at the time we are speaking of, the boundary of Roman power on the east was our neighbour the Bosphorus, and on the west the city of Adrianople. The Emperor Alexius, fighting two-fisted against barbarians who attacked him on either flank, manoeuvred round Byzantium, the centre of his circle as it were, and proceeded to broaden the Empire: on the west the frontier became the Adriatic Sea, on the east the Euphrates and Tigris. He would have revived the ancient prosperity of the empire, too, had not a succession of wars and constant dangers and troubles checked his ambitions, for he was always taking risks and exposing himself to great perils. However, as I said at the beginning of this episode, when he sent an army to Abul-Kasim, the ruler of Nicaea, it was not to rescue him, but to win a victory for himself. Nevertheless, fortune did not smile on his efforts. It happened like this. The expeditionary force reached the place called St George and the Turks without hesitation opened the gates to them. The soldiers climbed up to the ramparts above the east gate and put their standards and sceptres all together there, at the same time making a great hullaballoo and shouting their war-cry over and over again. The besiegers outside were terrified by these noises and thinking that the emperor had come in person they went away in the night. But the Roman army returned to the capital, too outnumbered to resist another Persian invasion expected from the deep interior of the Turkish Empire.

The sultan waited for the return of Siaous, but when he saw how dilatory he was and learnt moreover what had happened to him: how he had driven Charatikes out of Sinope by a trick, how he had received holy baptism and how he had been sent to the west by the emperor with the title 'Duke of Anchialos'; he was annoyed and distressed. Anyway he decided that Pouzanus must this time[37] be sent to attack Abul-Kasim. At the same time he entrusted to him a letter

37. In 1092/3.

addressed to the emperor about a marriage alliance. The message read as follows: 'I have heard, Basileus, of your troubles. I know that from the start of your reign you have met with many difficulties and that recently, after you had settled the Latin affairs, the Scyths were preparing to make war on you. The Emir Abul-Kasim, too, having broken the treaty which Sulayman concluded with you, is ravaging Asia as far as Damalis itself. If therefore it is your wish that Abul-Kasim should be driven from those districts and that Asia, together with Antioch, should be subject to you, send me your daughter as wife for the eldest of my sons. Thereafter nothing will stand in your way; it will be easy for you to accomplish everything with my aid, not only in the east, but even as far as Illyricum and the entire west. Because of the forces which I will send you, no one will resist you from now on.' So much for the Persian sultan's [38] proposal. Pouzanus meanwhile reached Nicaea. Several attempts were made on the city without success, for Abul-Kasim fought back bravely; he asked for and obtained help from Alexius. In the end, Pouzanus left hurriedly to attack the other towns and fortresses. He pitched camp by the Lampe, a river near Lopadion. When he had gone, Abul-Kasim loaded gold on fifteen mules, as much as they could carry, and went off to the Persian sultan, hoping that with this bribe he would not be relieved of his command. He found him bivouacking near Spacha and, as a personal interview was denied him, he sent intermediaries who pleaded earnestly on his behalf. The sultan replied: 'I have given authority, once and for all, to the Emir Pouzanus; it is not my wish to deprive him of it. Let Abul-Kasim take his money then and give it to him. Let him tell Pouzanus whatever he likes. What Pouzanus decides will be my decision.' So, after waiting there for a long time and after much suffering and nothing accomplished, he set off to find Pouzanus. On the way he met 200 satraps sent out by the latter to arrest him (Abul-Kasim's departure from Nicaea had not gone unnoticed). These men seized him, made a noose of twisted bowstring, put it round his neck and strangled him. In my opinion the whole business

38. The Sultan of Rum (Iconium) – in this case Barkiyaruq.

was not the doing of Pouzanus but of the sultan, who gave orders to deal with Abul-Kasim in this way.[39] So much for him. Let us return to the emperor. Having read the sultan's letter he had no intention whatever of accepting his proposal. How could he? His daughter, the bride sought for the barbarian's eldest son, would have been wretched indeed (and naturally so) if she had gone to Persia, to share a royal state worse than any poverty. But that was not the will of God, nor did the emperor dream of going so far, however desperate his position. At the first reading of the letter he immediately burst into laughter at the Turk's presumption, muttering, 'The devil must have put that into his head.' Despite his attitude to the marriage, he still thought it advisable to keep the sultan in suspense by offering vain hopes. He summoned Kourtikios with three others and sent them as envoys furnished with letters in which he welcomed the idea of peace and agreed with the sultan's propositions; at the same time he himself made certain demands which would prolong the negotiations. Actually the ambassadors had not yet arrived in Chorosan when they heard that the sultan had been murdered.[40] They came back to Byzantium. Tutush, after the killing of the Emir Sulayman, his own son-in-law, who had marched against him from Arabia, was full of arrogance. He had heard that the sultan, his full brother, was already seeking peace terms with the emperor and he now planned to murder him. To this end he summoned twelve bloodthirsty individuals called in the Persian dialect Chasioi[41] and sent them at once as envoys to him. He gave them instructions as to the killing: 'Go,' he said, 'and first of all make an announcement that you have certain secret information for the sultan, and when you are granted the right of entry, approach as if you desire to speak

39. There is some doubt whether the sultan was in fact Barkiyaruq at this time. He may have been Malik-Shah (the father). All the Christian writers regard the latter as singularly tolerant in his dealings with enemies (including Christians); he seems to have been a model of chivalry.

40. There is confusion here. It appears that Anna is describing the murder of Nizam-al-Mulk, the sultan's vizier, about a month before Malik-Shah was poisoned (19 November 1092).

41. The Assassins.

with him privately, and then massacre him at once.' The
ambassadors, or rather murderers, as if setting out for some
dinner or festive occasion, most gladly departed to commit
this crime. They found the victim in his cups and when they
could do it with impunity (the sultan's guards were standing
some way off) they went near, drew their scimitars from under
their arm-pits and straightway cut the wretched man to pieces.
The Chasioi delight in that sort of bloodshed; their idea of
pleasure is merely the plunging of a sword into human entrails.
As for the future, if some other folk happen to attack them at
the very same moment and cut them up into mincemeat, they
regard such a death as an honour, passing on these bloody
deeds from one generation to another like some family heritage. At all events, not one of them returned to Tutush, for
they paid for their crime with their own violent deaths. At the
news Pouzanus with all his forces retired to Chorosan. The
brother of the murdered man, Tutush, met him as he was
nearly at the end of his journey. A battle was fought at once
at close quarters, both armies showing great spirit and neither
yielding the victory to the other. Pouzanus played a gallant
part in the struggle and spread confusion in the enemy ranks
everywhere, but fell mortally wounded. His men, each looking
to his own safety, fled in all directions, so that Tutush returned
in triumph to Chorosan as if he had already won the title of
sultan. In reality, he was in imminent peril. Barkiyaruq, son of
the murdered Sultan Taparas,[42] encountered him 'like a lion
rejoicing when he lights upon some mighty prey', as Homer
says, and attacking with might and main tore his army apart
again and again. Tutush himself, who was puffed up with the
pride of Nauatus,[43] was killed. At the time when Abul-Kasim
went off with the money to the Sultan of Chorosan (as I have
already said), his brother Poulchases came to Nicaea and
occupied it. The emperor, hearing of this, offered bribes on a
liberal scale if he would hand over the city and leave. Poulchases
was willing, but kept putting off the decision, again looking to
Abul-Kasim; a continuous stream of messages to the emperor

42. Another name for Malik-Shah.
43. Nauatus was apparently a heretic whose pride became a by-word.

left him in suspense, but in fact the man was waiting for his brother's return. While this was going on, an incident took place which I will outline as follows: the Sultan of Chorosan who was murdered by the Chasioi had previously held the two sons of the great Sulayman; after his death they ran away from Chorosan and soon arrived in Nicaea. At the sight of them the people of Nicaea ran riot with joy and Poulchases gladly handed over the city to them, as if it were a family inheritance. The elder son, Kilij Arslan by name, received the title of sultan. He sent for the wives and children of the soldiers present in Nicaea and they set up home there; the city became what one might call the official residence of the sultans. After arranging the affairs of Nicaea thus, Kilij Arslan forced Poulchases to re-sign his governorship, promoted Muhammad archisatrap, left him behind in the vicinity of Nicaea and himself went off to attack Melitene.

Such was the history of the sultans. Elkhanes the archisatrap with his men occupied Apollonias and Cyzicus (both these cities are on the coast) and ravaged all the districts by the sea. This led the emperor to equip a fair number of the available boats (the fleet had not yet mobilized) and put on board helepoleis and good fighting men under the command of Alexander Euphorbenus, a nobleman and famed for his bravery. The object of the expedition was to come to grips with Elkhanes. They arrived at Apollonias and at once began to besiege it. At the end of six consecutive days, during which the assault on the walls continued even during the night, Euphorbenus controlled the outer periphery of the citadel (nowadays this is usually called the *exopolos*) but Elkhanes stubbornly defended the acropolis, hoping for reinforcements from outside. Alexander did in fact sight a barbarian force of considerable strength on its way to help and as his own army was equivalent to a mere fraction of the enemy, he thought it wiser, if he could not win, to keep his own troops out of danger. His position was one of extreme peril and it was impossible to achieve any safety there. He decided to make for the sea, embarked his men on the ships and sailed down the river. Elkhanes, however, had guessed his plan. He anticipated

it by seizing the entrance to the lake and the bridge over the
river, at the place where in olden times a sanctuary had been
built by St Helena [44] in honour of the great Constantine (hence
the bridge's name, which still persists to this day). At the
entrance to the lake, then, and on the bridge itself, to right
and left he posted his most experienced soldiers with orders to
surprise the Roman ships on their way through. In fact they
all fell into the trap as they reached that point in small boats.
When they saw the danger, they made for the shore in desperation and leapt from the boats on to dry land, but the Turks
caught up with them and a fierce battle ensued. Many of the
officers were captured, many fell into the river and were swept
away by the current. The news of this disaster annoyed the
emperor intensely; he sent a powerful force under Opus overland against the Turks. Opus reached Cyzicus and took the
place at the first assault, then detached from his own regiments
about 300 men used to siege warfare and ready to face any
danger, for an attempt on Poimanenon. That too was easily
captured; some of the defenders were killed there, others were
taken prisoners and sent to Opus, who promptly forwarded
them to Alexius. Then, leaving Poimanenon, he went on to
Apollonias and began a determined siege. Elkhanes had too
few men there to resist and voluntarily surrendered the city.
Together with his closest relatives he deserted to the emperor
and was rewarded with countless gifts, including the greatest
of all – the holy rite of baptism. All those unwilling to follow
Opus, Skaliarios, for example, and . . . who was afterwards
honoured with the title of hyperperilampros (they were
archisatraps and distinguished men), when they heard of the
emperor's friendly overtures to Elkhanes and how generous
he had been, also came to Alexius and received what they
wanted. One can truly say that this emperor was a most
saintly person, both because of his virtues and in his manner
of speaking – a high priest, as it were, of perfect reverence.
He was an excellent teacher of our doctrine, with an apostle's

44. Helena was the mother of Constantine the Great. According to
tradition she made a pilgrimage to the Holy Land and found the true
Cross.

faith and message, eager to convert to Christ not only the nomad Scyths, but also the whole of Persia and all the barbarians who dwell in Egypt or Libya and worship Mahomet with mystic rites.

I need say no more on that subject, but as I wish to describe a more terrible and greater invasion of the Roman Empire, it will be advisable to tell the story from its beginning, for these invaders followed one another in succession like the waves of the sea. A Scythian tribe, having suffered incessant pillaging at the hands of Sarmatians, left home and came down to the Danube. As it was necessary for them to make peace with the people living near the river and everyone agreed, they entered into negotiations with the chiefs: Tatos, also called Chales; Sesthlavos and Satzas (I have to mention the names of their leading men, even if it spoils the tone of my history). One controlled Dristra, the other two Bitzina and the remaining areas. A treaty was concluded and the Scyths in future crossed the Danube with impunity and plundered the country near it, so that they even seized some fortresses. Later, as they enjoyed a period of peace, they tilled the soil and sowed millet and wheat. But the notorious Traulos, the Manichaean, with his followers and some men of the same religious persuasion who had occupied the stronghold on the hill-top of Beliatoba (a fuller account of this was given earlier in the history), learning about the activities of these Scyths,[45] brought to light a scheme long and painfully elaborated hitherto only in their minds: they manned the rough tracks and mountain passes, called in the Scyths and proceeded to ravage Roman territory. The Manichaeans, of course, are by nature a bellicose people, always ravening like dogs to gorge on human blood. Alexius, being informed of this, ordered the Domestic of the West, Pakourianus, to march with his army against them. Branas, himself a first-class soldier, was to accompany him. Pakourianus, he knew, was an extremely able commander with unusual powers of organization where masses of men were concerned, whether in battle-line or in intricate manoeuvres.

45. Anna is vague. The Scyths here were the Patzinaks, or Pechenegs. She is equally vague when she refers to Latins, Kelts, Franks and Normans.

He discovered that the Scyths had passed through the defiles
and pitched camp not far from Beliatoba, in such vast numbers
that war was out of the question: the very thought of it
numbed him. The more profitable course, he believed, was for
the present to keep his troops out of harm's way without risking an engagement; better that than to fight a losing battle and
suffer annihilation. But Branas, who was a bold man and foolhardy, disapproved; the Domestic, to avoid any imputation of
cowardice if he refused the challenge, gave way to his impulsive colleague. Everyone was ordered to arm. When the preparations for battle were complete, they advanced against the
Scyths, with Pakourianus at the centre of the line.[46] The
Romans were vastly outnumbered and the sight of the enemy
filled all of them with dread. Nevertheless they attacked. Many
were slain and Branas was mortally wounded. The Domestic,
fighting furiously and charging the Scyths with great violence,
crashed into an oak tree and died on the spot. After that the
rest of the army dispersed in all directions. Alexius mourned
all those who had fallen, individually and as a body, but in
particular he lamented the death of Pakourianus, for even
before his accession he had loved him dearly. He shed many
tears for the Domestic. However, there was no lessening of
effort on that account. Taticius was sent with large sums of
money to Adrianople to pay the soldiers their annual wages
and draw recruits from everywhere for a new army, worthy of
battle. Humbertopoulos was to hurry, with only the Kelts, to
join Taticius and he was to leave a moderate garrison in
Cyzicus. Taticius, full of confidence on the arrival of these
Latins and their commander, lost no time, once the force was
strong enough, in marching against the Scyths. Near Philippopolis, by the banks of the river which flows past Blisnos, he
pitched his camp, but before all the baggage could be stored
inside the entrenchments, the enemy came into sight on their
way back from a marauding raid with much booty and many
prisoners. A powerful detachment was sent against them;
Taticius followed later with the main body, all fully armed and
arranged in line. When the Scyths with their spoils and

46. This battle took place in 1086.

captives joined the rest of their forces near the banks of the Euros,[47] the Romans were divided in two and ordered to shout their war-cry. The attack went in from either flank with tremendous yells and clamour. Most of the enemy fell in the bitter fighting, but many saved their lives in scattered flight. Taticius, with all their booty, returned to Philippopolis. At this new headquarters he planned a second attack; the question was, from where and how was it to be launched. They had enormous resources of manpower. Taticius, realizing this, deployed his scouts in all directions – he wanted continuous information of all their movements. The scouts reported the presence of a large army of Scyths concentrated near Belia-toba; the neighbourhood of the place was already being plundered. Taticius, despite his complete inability to match their numbers, awaited the Scythian onslaught, but he was really at his wits' end and in a most embarrassing situation. However, he sharpened his sword and encouraged his men to fight. When someone came to announce that the barbarians were on the march and emphasized that they were near, he immediately donned his own armour, gave the general call to arms and at once crossed the Euros. On the far side the line was drawn up for battle, with the battalions in due order. He personally commanded the centre. The enemy arranged themselves in their Scythian fashion, obviously spoiling for a fight and provoking the Romans. Even so, both armies were afraid and put off the moment of conflict, the Romans because they trembled before the overwhelming numbers of the Scyths; the Scyths because they feared the sight of all those breastplates, the standards, the glory of the Roman armour and the brightness reflected from it like rays of star-light. Of all those men only the Latins were venturesome and daring enough to seize the initiative, sharpening teeth and sword alike, as they say. But Taticius restrained them – he was a level-headed man and knew well what was likely to happen. Thus both sides stood firm, waiting for their adversaries to make the first move. Not a man from either line dared to ride out into the no-man's-land between them, and when the sun was going down both

47. The Danube.

generals went back to their encampments. This was repeated on the two following days. The leaders prepared for combat and each day the troops were drawn up in battle order, but, since no one had the courage to attack, at dawn on the third day the Scyths withdrew. Thereupon Taticius at once set out in pursuit, but it was a case of the proverbial footslogger chasing the Lydian chariot. The Scyths crossed the Sidera first (the name of a valley) and Taticius retired with his whole army to Adrianopolis. The Kelts he left in that area; the soldiers he told to go home individually, while with one detachment he himself came back to the capital.

BOOK SEVEN

WAR WITH THE SCYTHS
(1087–90)

At the beginning of the spring[1] Tzelgu, the supreme commander of the Scythian army, traversed the upper Danube valley at the head of a mixed force. He had about 80,000 men, Sarmatians, Scyths and a large contingent of Dacians led by one Solomon.[2] Tzelgu proceeded to ravage the towns of the Charioupolis area, and even reached Charioupolis itself. After taking much plunder he established himself in a place called Skotinos. When Nicolas Maurocatacalon heard of this, he and Bempetziotes (who revealed by that name his country of origin)[3] occupied Pamphilon with their own forces, but left when they saw that the villagers from the surrounding districts were hurrying to the towns and strongholds in panic; the whole of their army was moved to the little town of Koule. Behind them came the Scyths, who had realized that the Romans were 'browned-off' (to use an expression known to soldiers) and they closely followed their tracks. It was already light when Tzelgu drew up his forces to fight Maurocatacalon. The latter climbed with some picked men to a narrow defile which dominated the plain; from there he could observe the barbarian's army. Eager though he was to join battle, the sight of the Scythian host persuaded him to put it off: it was obvious that the Romans were greatly inferior in number. However, on his return to camp he consulted the officers of the whole army and Joannaces himself. He asked whether an attack should be made. They encouraged him to do so, and as he was

1. In 1087.
2. Solomon became King of Hungary in 1063; he lost his throne to Géza I (1074–7), who married a niece of Nicephorus Botaniates. He was hostile to Byzantium for this reason among others. See *CMH*, vol. iv, pt. i, p. 578.
3. It is said that there was a town of this name on the Euphrates

more inclined to that course anyway, the Roman forces were divided into three, the order to sound the attack was given and the battle began. In the struggle many of the Scyths fell wounded; just as many were killed, among them Tzelgu. He received a mortal blow while fighting bravely and spreading confusion everywhere in the Roman ranks. Most of the enemy fell in their flight into the mountain torrent between Skotinos and Koule, were trampled under foot by their own comrades and drowned. The emperor's men after this glorious victory entered Constantinople, where they received from him appropriate rewards and honours. Afterwards, with Adrian Comnenus the emperor's own brother, now promoted to the rank of Great Domestic of the West, they retired from the city.

Although the enemy had been driven from Macedonia and the area round Philippopolis, they returned to the Danube and made their camp there. Living alongside our territories they treated them as their own and plundered with complete licence. The news that they were living inside the Roman borders was reported to Alexius. He thought the position was intolerable, but he was also afraid they might make their way over the mountain passes again and turn bad to worse. Accordingly preparations were made and the army was well equipped before he made for Adrianople; from there he went on to Lardea, a place lying between Diampolis and Goloë. At Lardea George Euphorbenus was appointed general and sent by sea to Dristra. The emperor himself spent forty days in the district, summoning forces from all parts until an army strong enough to fight the Scyths had been assembled. A decision was then made about the advisability of marching north through the defiles. Alexius remarked that no truce whatever should be given to the Scyths – a reasonable comment on these barbarians, for Scythian incursions did not begin in any one of the four seasons only to end in the next, lasting from the start of summer, for example, till autumn, or even to late autumn and the cold weather; the Scyths did not limit their evil activities to a whole year even, but in fact troubled Rome over a long period, although I have mentioned only a few out of many such invasions. Specious arguments failed to divide them and, despite the emperor's repeated efforts to win them over by all kinds of enticement, no deserter came to him, even in secret, so inflexible was their determination. Nicephorus Bryennius and Gregory Maurocatacalon on this occasion were by no means in favour of making war on them in the Paristrion.[4] On the other hand, George Palaeologus and Nicolas Maurocatacalon and all the other young and vigorous officers inclined to the emperor's idea and urged him to cross the pass over the Haemus and join battle with them near the Danube. The two sons of the Emperor Diogenes, Nicephorus and Leo, were also of the same opinion.[5] Anyway, when a loud blast from the trumpet gave the signal to cross the Haemus, Bryennius tried hard to dissuade Alexius from the enterprise. When all his arguments failed, he ended solemnly with these words: 'I tell you this, Sir: if you cross the Haemus, you will appreciate the fastest horses.' Someone asked him what he meant. 'For the flight,' he replied, 'all of them.' This Bryennius, although he had lost his eyes because of a revolution, was recognized to be a foremost authority and expert on strategy and tactics. If anyone wants to know in greater detail how he lost his eyes (through some revolt or uprising against the Emperor Botaniates) and how he was taken prisoner by Alexius Comnenus, at that time Great Domestic of the western and eastern forces, and afterwards handed over to Borilos with his sight undamaged, then we must refer him to the illustrious Caesar Nicephorus. He was the son of Bryennius, and after Alexius became emperor, he married his

4. Gregory had been captured by them and was ransomed by the emperor for 40,000 pieces of money. (A.C.)

5. They had been born in the porphyra after their father's elevation to the throne and for that reason had the title porphyrogeniti. This porphyra is a room in the Palace built in the form of a complete square from floor to ceiling, but the latter ends in a pyramid. The room affords a view of the sea and harbour where the stone oxen and the lions stand. Its floor is paved with marble and the walls are covered with marble panels. The stone used was not of the ordinary kind, nor marble which can be more easily obtained but at greater expense; it was in fact casually acquired in Rome by former emperors. This particular marble is generally of a purple colour throughout, but with white spots like sand sprinkled over it. It was for this, I suppose, that our forefathers called the room porphyra. (A.C.)

(Alexius') daughter.[6] But these memories upset me; my heart is filled with sorrow, for the Caesar was a man of learning and in his writings gave excellent proof of it. Everything – strength, agility, physical charm, in fact all the good qualities of mind and body – combined to glorify that man. In him Nature brought to birth and God created a unique personality, outstanding among his fellows; just as Homer sang the praises of Achilles among the Achaeans, so might one say that my Caesar excelled among all men who live beneath the sun. He was a magnificent soldier, but by no means unmindful of literature; he read all books and by closely studying every science derived much wisdom from them, both ancient and modern. Later on he devoted himself to writing and even dashed off a history which is of value and deserves to be read. He did this on the order of my mother, the Empress Irene, and in it gave an account of my father's exploits before he seized the reins of power. He describes in detail the Bryennius episode, telling the story of his own father's sufferings and at the same time writing of the noble deeds of his father-in-law. As a relative of the one by marriage and a kinsman of the other by birth, he would not have lied about these two men. I too in the early books of this history have mentioned these matters. The Scyths saw George Euphorbenus coming down the Ister[7] against them, accompanied by a strong naval and military force. They also learnt that the emperor was on the march by land with a very large army. As they realized that to fight both was impossible, they looked for a way of escape – the danger was acute. Ambassadors were sent, 150 Scyths who were maybe to ask for peace terms, but at the same time to

6. Anna herself. The marriage lasted from 1097 to at least 1137, when Bryennius died of an illness contracted on campaign in Asia. There were four children, two sons (Alexius and John) and two daughters (one of whom was called Irene).

7. This river flows from high ground in the west and after a series of cataracts issues through five mouths into the Black Sea; it is long and wide, traversing vast plains, and it is navigable, so that even the biggest merchantmen can sail on it. It has not one name, but two: the upper reaches to the source are called Danube; the part near the mouth and the lower reaches have the name Ister. (A.C.)

introduce a certain menace into the discussions; they might even make occasional promises to aid the emperor, whenever he wished, with 30,000 horsemen, provided that he agreed to their demands. Alexius saw through the Scythian fraud: their embassy was an attempt to evade the imminent peril, and, if they were granted a general amnesty, it would be a signal for the underlying spark of evil to be kindled into a mighty conflagration. He refused to hear the envoys. While these exchanges were taking place, a man called Nicolas, one of the under-secretaries, approached the emperor and gently whispered in his ear, 'Just about this time, Sir, you can expect an eclipse of the sun.' The emperor was completely sceptical about it, but the man swore that he was not lying. With his usual quick apprehension, Alexius turned to the Scyths. 'The decision,' he said, 'I leave to God. If some sign should clearly be given in the sky within a few hours, then you will know for sure that I have good reason to reject your embassy as suspect, because your leaders are not really negotiating for peace; if there is no sign, then I shall be proved wrong in my suspicions.' Before two hours had gone by there was a solar eclipse; the whole disc of the sun was blotted out as the moon passed before it.[8] At this the Scyths were amazed. As for Alexius, he handed them over to Leo Nicerites with instructions to escort them under strong guard as far as Constantinople. This Nicerites, a eunuch, had from his earliest years spent his life among soldiers and was a man of proved reliability. He started on the road to the city with great enthusiasm, but the barbarians, whose one ambition was to recover their own freedom, when they arrived at Little Nicaea murdered their guards in the night. The sentinels had been careless. After that the Scyths by devious paths made their way back to those who had sent them. Nicerites barely escaped with his life. He rejoined the emperor with three companions at Goloë.

The news alarmed Alexius. He was afraid that the Scythian ambassadors would stir up their whole army against him and launch an attack. Unlike Atreus' son Agamemnon he needed

8. 1 August 1087.

no dream to urge him to battle – he was longing for a fight.
With his troops he crossed Sidera and set up camp near the
Bitzina, a river which flows down from the neighbouring
hills. Many Romans who left the encampment there in search
of food went too far and were massacred, many others were
captured. The emperor left hurriedly for Pliscoba about first
light and from there climbed a ridge called Simeon's (the
native name for it was 'Meeting-place of the Scyths'). Those
who went far from the stockade for supplies suffered the same
fate as their comrades. On the next day he came to a river
which flows close by Dristra and there, at a distance of about
twenty-four stades, put down his baggage and pitched camp.
Suddenly the Scyths made an attack from the rear on the
emperor's tent; several light-armed soldiers were killed and
some of the Manichaeans, who fought with exceptional fury,
were taken captive. There was much confusion and uproar
among the soldiers because of this and the imperial tent
actually collapsed when the horses galloped about in panic –
to those not well-disposed to Alexius a sure sign of ill-omen.
However, with a band of men he drove off the intruders far
from the tent and then, to quell the tumult, mounted his horse,
restored order and marched out with his forces in disciplined
ranks to Dristra. He intended to besiege the place with helepoleis.[9] The work was indeed begun. The city was invested on
all sides and a breach was made at one point. The emperor
with the whole army had entered the perimeter, but the two
citadels of Dristra still remained in the hands of Tatou's kinsmen. He (Tatou) had already departed to win over the Cumans and hoped to bring them back with him to help the Scyths.
At his departure, when he took leave of his friends, he told
them: 'I know quite well that the emperor will besiege this
town. When you see him marching on to the plain, make sure
you seize the ridge that dominates it before he can do so.
It's the finest position of all. Make your camp there. In that
way he'll have no free hand in besieging the garrison; he'll be
forced to look out for his rear, watching for trouble from you.
Meanwhile you keep up incessant attacks on him, all day and

9. Dristra is a celebrated place, situated by the Ister. (A.C.)

all night, with relays of men.' The emperor had to yield to
necessity. The investment of the citadels was abandoned and
he left Dristra. Near the Ister he had a stockade built by a
mountain stream and there he took counsel: should he attack
the Scyths? Palaeologus and Gregory Maurocatacalon were
for deferring a war with the Patzinaks; they advised a military
occupation of the great town of Peristhlaba. 'If the Scyths see
us marching fully armed as we are and in good order,' they
said, 'they will certainly not dare to attack us. And if their
cavalry were to risk an engagement without chariots, you can
be sure that they will be defeated, and we shall take permanent
possession of Great Peristhlaba. It will be an impregnable
stronghold.[10] Maurocatacalon and his partisans went on: 'If
we use this place as a secure base of operations, we shall inflict
continual losses on them with daily guerilla warfare. They
will never be allowed to leave their own camp to get provisions or collect supplies.' The argument was still going on
when Diogenes' sons, Nicephorus and Leo, dismounted from
their chargers, took away their bridles, gave them a slap and
drove them off to graze in the millet. 'Have no fear, Sir,' they
said, 'we'll draw our swords and cut them to pieces.' They
were young men and for that reason had no experience of the
misery of war. The emperor himself loved to take risks and
was naturally inclined to provoke battle; he completely ignored the arguments for restraint, entrusted the imperial tent
and all the baggage to George Koutzomites and sent him off to
Betrinos. Having done this he gave orders that no lamp, no
fire whatever was to be lit in camp that night; the army was to
have the horses ready and stay awake until sunrise. About first
light he left the camp, divided his forces and drew up his
ranks for battle. After that he reviewed them quickly. He

10. Now this city is a famous place, lying near the Ister. Originally it
had a Greek name 'Great City' (which indeed it was), not its present
barbarian name. But after Mokros, the king of the Bulgars, and his descendants, and after Samuel, the last of the Bulgar dynasty (as Zedekiah was
the last of his dynasty among the Jews) – after they invaded the west, the
name was changed. It became a compound of the Greek word for 'great'
and a word from the language of the Slavs; the addition made it 'Great
Peristhlaba' and everybody thereabouts calls it by that name. (A.C.)

stationed himself at the centre of the line with a group of near- or blood-relations; there too was his brother Adrian, at that time in command of the Latins, and other brave warriors. The left wing was directed by the Caesar, Nicephorus Melissenus, who had married a sister of the emperor. On the right the leaders were Castamonites and Taticius, but the allies were commanded by Ouzas and Karatzas, who were Sarmatians. Six men were picked out by the emperor to act as a personal bodyguard; they were told to watch him and pay attention to nobody else at all. The men chosen were Romanus Diogenes' two sons; Nicolas Maurocatacalon (who had long and varied experience in war); Joannaces; Nampites (commander of the Varangians) and a certain Goules (a retainer of the family). The Scyths also prepared for the battle. War is in their blood – they know how to arrange a phalanx. So, after placing ambuscades, binding together their ranks in close formation, making a sort of rampart from their covered wagons, they advanced *en masse* against the emperor and began skirmishing from a distance. Alexius, who had linked the infantry and the cavalry squadrons, gave instructions that no soldier was to advance in front of the line, which must remain unbroken, until the Romans were near the enemy; then, when they saw the distance between the two charging lines was no more than enough to rein in a horse, they were to close with the Scyths. The Roman preparations were actually still going on when the enemy appeared in the distance with their covered wagons, their wives and their children. Battle was joined and from early morning till late in the evening the casualties on both sides were extremely heavy. Leo, Diogenes' son, charged furiously against the enemy and being swept on further than he should have been in the direction of the wagons was mortally wounded. Adrian, the emperor's brother and temporary commander of the Latins, seeing that it was impossible to stem the Scythian onslaught, rode at full gallop and forced his way right up to the wagons. After a gallant struggle he returned with only seven survivors; all the others had either been slain or were captured. The battle was still evenly balanced, with both armies fighting bravely, when some Scythian officers appeared in the distance with 36,000 men. At last the Romans gave ground; further resistance in the face of so many was out of the question. The emperor, however, still stood with sword in hand beyond his own front line. In the other hand he grasped like a standard the Cape of the Mother of the Word.[11] He had been left behind with twenty horsemen, all brave men. They were Nicephorus, the other son of Diogenes, the Protostrator Michael Ducas, brother of the empress, and some family servants. Some Scythian infantrymen leapt upon them. Two (there were three of them in all) seized his horse's bit, one on either side; the third grabbed him by the right leg. Alexius immediately cut off the hand of one and raising his sword and roaring loudly made the second withdraw hurriedly. The man who was clinging to his leg he struck on the helmet, but the blow, delivered with less than his whole strength, was too light to do damage. Alexius was in fact afraid that one of two things might happen: the sword, when too much violence is used, generally swerves and he might either strike his own foot or the horse on which he was riding, and so he would be taken prisoner by his enemies. He delivered a second blow, but this time took careful aim. In all his deeds and words and movements Alexius let reason be his guide; he was never carried away by anger or swept off his feet by passion. At the first blow the Scyth's helmet had been thrust backwards and he now struck at the man's bare head. In a second he was lying speechless on the ground. At this point the protostrator, who had seen the disorderly flight of the Romans (the lines were by now completely broken up and the rout was uncontrollable), addressed the emperor. 'Why, Sir,' he said, 'are you trying to hold out here any longer? Why lose your life, without a thought for your own safety?' 'Better to die fighting bravely than win safety by doing something unworthy,' replied Alexius. But the protostrator persisted, 'If you were just an

11. The sacred *pallium* (a kind of veil or cape) of the Virgin, which was normally kept in the church of Blachernae. Alexius had at least some portion of it with him in battle, as Romanus Lecapenus had before him. For a long discussion of the relic see Buckler's *Anna Comnena*, pp. 77–8.

ordinary soldier, those would be fine words; but when your
death involves danger for everybody else, why not choose the
better course? If you are saved, you will make war again, and
win.' Alexius saw the danger that now threatened him; the
Scyths were boldly attacking and all hope of saving the day
had gone. 'This is the moment,' he said, 'when with God's
help we must look to our own safety. But we must not go by
the same way as the rest; the enemy might meet us on their
return from the pursuit.' Then, waving his hand toward the
Scyths standing at the end of their line, 'We must ride hell for
leather at them. With God's aid we'll get round behind and go
by another path.' So, after encouraging the others, he led the
way himself, charging at the enemy like a flash of lightning.
He struck at the first man to meet him. The fellow was un-
horsed and fell instantly to the ground. In this way they cut
through the Scythian line and reached a place in their rear.
So much for the emperor. The protostrator had the ill luck to
fall when his horse slipped, but one of his servants at once
gave him his own mount. He rejoined the emperor and afterwards, so great was his affection for his brother-in-law, never
left his side; there was not a foot's breadth between them. In
the great confusion, with some fleeing and others chasing,
other Scyths again caught up with the emperor, who quickly
wheeled round and hit his pursuer. Nor was he the only one to
be killed by the emperor; according to the evidence of eye-
witnesses, others met the same fate. One Scyth came up on
Nicephorus Diogenes from behind and was about to strike,
when the emperor saw him and shouted to Diogenes, 'Look
out! Behind you, Nicephorus!' Turning swiftly Nicephorus
hit hard at the man's face. In later years we have heard Alexius
tell that story; never, he said, had he seen such agility and
speed of hand. 'If I that day had not held the standard,' he
went on, 'I would have smitten and killed more Scyths than I
have hairs on my head' – and he was not bragging. Never was
there a man who went to such lengths of modesty. However,
when the conversation and the subject of discussion compelled it, he would sometimes tell of his adventures to us, his
relatives, in our own circle (if we put much pressure on him).

But nobody ever heard the emperor say anything boastful in public. A strong wind was blowing and with the Patzinaks charging against him he no longer had the strength to hold the standard [12] firmly. One of the Scyths grasped a long spear in both hands and struck him on the buttock. The blow did not break the skin in any way, but caused excruciating pain which persisted for many years afterwards. In his agony he had to hide the standard in a bush of germanders, where it could no longer be seen by anyone. During the night he arrived safely in Goloë and the next day went on to Beroë where he stopped to ransom the prisoners. [13]

On the same day that the Romans were defeated and put to flight Palaeologus was thrown from his horse and lost it. It was a precarious situation for him; he realized the hazard and looked everywhere for the animal. Then he saw [14] Leo, the Bishop of Chalcedon (whom we have mentioned before). He was dressed in his priestly robes and was offering him his own horse. On that Palaeologus made his escape. He never set eyes on the reverend bishop again. Leo was a man who spoke his mind, in very truth a leader of the Church, but he was a rather simple-minded man and his enthusiasm was occasionally based on insufficient knowledge; he had not even a profound grasp of Holy Scripture. It was for that reason that the disgrace I mentioned before came upon him and he was dethroned. Palaeologus always regarded him with affection and continued to honour him greatly for his outstanding virtue. Whether it was because of his passionate belief in this man that Palaeologus was favoured with a divine visitation, or whether the apparition was in some other way concerned with this archbishop and due to the mysterious working of Providence, I cannot say. Anyway Palaeologus arrived at a marshy area covered with trees, still pursued by the enemy. There he found 150 soldiers, surrounded by Scyths and in a desperate position. Seeing that they were not strong enough to resist such a

12. The *Omophoros*, or Pallium of the Virgin.
13. The *Epitome* adds: The inhabitants told him, 'From Dristra to Goloë is a good stretch even for an unwounded man, Comnenus.'
14. Or rather, *thought* he saw.

multitude, they depended on him for advice. In the past they had recognized his fortitude and the dauntless spirit of the man. He advised them to attack, utterly regardless of their own personal safety – no doubt by that they would ensure it. 'But,' he added, 'we must confirm this plan by oaths: no one must shirk the attack against the enemy. We are now all of one mind, we must look upon the safety or danger of all as the concern of each.' He himself charged on horseback furiously and struck the first man to stand in his path; stunned by the blow he fell at once to the ground. But Palaeologus' companions rode half-heartedly and when some died the rest returned to the dense undergrowth (as if it were a hole in the ground) and there saved themselves by hiding. While Palaeologus, again chased by Patzinaks, was riding to a hill-top his horse was wounded and fell; he made his way to a mountain near there. For eleven days he wandered seeking a way to safety – no easy task – but finally met a soldier's widow and found lodging with her for some time. Her sons, who had themselves escaped danger, pointed out the path to freedom and he got away. Such were the adventures of Palaeologus. Meanwhile the Scythian leaders planned to kill their prisoners, but the majority of the ordinary warriors opposed the idea altogether: they wanted to sell them for ransom, and this scheme was approved. The emperor was notified through letters from Melissenus, who although he was a prisoner himself did much to provoke the Scyths *against* selling their captives. The emperor (still in Beroë) sent for a large sum of money from Constantinople and bought the men.

At this moment Tatou reached the Ister with the Cumans he had won over. When they saw the enormous booty and the multitude of prisoners, they told the Scythian chieftains, 'We have left our homes. We have come a great distance to help you, with the purpose of sharing your danger and your victory. Now that we have contributed all that we could, it is not right to send us away empty-handed. It was not from choice that we arrived too late for the war, nor are we to be blamed for that: it was the emperor's fault – he took the offensive. Either therefore divide up all the booty in equal shares with

us, or instead of allies you will find us ready to fight you.' The
Scyths refused and, as the Cumans thought that unbearable, a
fearful battle took place, in which the Scyths suffered complete disaster and barely saved themselves by fleeing to
Ozolimne.[15] There they were hemmed in by the Cumans for a
long time, not daring to move. When their provisions were
exhausted, they went home. They intended to return, after
making up their deficiencies, to fight the Scyths.

In the meanwhile the emperor was concentrating his forces
at Beroë, his headquarters. The prisoners of war and all the
rest of the army were thoroughly equipped. At Beroë the
Count of Flanders, who was then on his way back from
Jerusalem, met Alexius and gave him the usual oath of the
Latins: he promised that on his arrival in his own country he
would send the emperor allies, 500 horsemen. Alexius received him with honour and sent him on his journey satisfied.

15. The lake now called by us Ozolimne is in diameter and circumference very big, in surface area not inferior to any other lake described by
geographers. It lies beyond the 'Hundred Hills' and into it flow very
great and noble rivers; many ships and large transport vessels sail on its
waters, from which one can deduce how deep the lake is. It has been
called Ozolimne, not because it emits an evil or unpleasant odour,[16] but
because an army of Huns once visited the lake and the vernacular word
for Huns is '*Ouzi*'. The Huns bivouacked by the banks of this lake and the
name Ouzolimne was given it, with the addition of the vowel 'u'. No
congregation of Huns in that area has ever been mentioned by the ancient
historians, but in Alexius' reign there was a general migration there from
all directions – hence the name. However, let us leave the question of the
lake with some such explanation. I am the first to write about it in this
book, and I did so in order to demonstrate how places acquired many
names because of the frequent and widespread expeditions of the emperor. Some were named after him, some after the enemies who assembled
to fight him. I understand that some such thing happened in the time of
Alexander, the Macedonian king: Alexandria in Egypt and the Indian
Alexandria were both named after him. We know too that Lysimachia
got its name from one of his generals, Lysimachos. I would not wonder,
then, if the Emperor Alexius, rivalling him, bestowed new names on
places, either from the peoples who united against him, or were summoned by him, or because of his exploits gave his own name to them. So
much for this Ozolimne – supplementary details of some historic interest.
(A.C.)

16. The Greek root '*oz*' means 'smell'; '*limne*' is Greek for 'lake'.

From Beroë after this interlude the emperor went on to Adrianople with the new forces he had collected. The Scyths had crossed the valley between Goloë and Diampolis, and fixed their camp near Marcella. They were expected to return, but news of their movements alarmed the emperor. He summoned Synesios, furnished him with a chrysobull for the Scyths and sent him to find them. The instructions were as follows: if the enemy could be persuaded to negotiate and give hostages, Synesios was to prevent their further advance, to make sure that they remained in the area already occupied by them, and (provided these terms were acceptable) to give them ample supplies at his expense. The emperor's policy was to make use of the Scyths against the Cumans, if the latter again approached the Ister and tried to seize territory beyond it. On the other hand, if the Scyths proved obdurate, Synesios was to leave them there and return to camp. The envoy made contact and after the normal conversation persuaded them to make a truce with the emperor; he stayed with them for some time, treated all of them with courtesy, avoided every pretext for offence. The Cumans did return, again prepared to fight the Scyths, and when they failed to meet them, but learnt that they had gone over the passes and on their arrival at Marcella had concluded a treaty with Alexius, they demanded the right to pursue and attack them. Alexius refused, because peace had been made. He sent his reply: 'We do not for the present require your help. Take these gifts and go home.' Their ambassadors were honourably received and before they were dismissed peaceably generous gifts were handed over to them. Emboldened by this the Scyths broke the treaty. With their old savagery they murdered the neighbouring cities and country districts. The truth is, all barbarians are usually fickle and characteristically unable to keep their pledges. Synesios witnessed their actions and of his own free will came back to give proof to the emperor of their reckless transgression. The news that they had seized Philippopolis was embarrassing: the forces available to Alexius were insufficient to start a general war against such overwhelming numbers. But, being the kind of man who in difficulties finds ways and means, having accustomed himself never to lose heart, however hard the circumstances, he decided to practise the art of destroying the enemy by light skirmish and ambuscade. He conjectured what places and cities they were likely to occupy in the morning, and himself anticipated them the evening before; if he discovered that they were going to seize a place in the evening, he got there before them in the morning. Thus by guerrilla tactics and making best use of his forces he made war on them at a distance; they were unable to get possession of the forts. Now it happened that both parties arrived at Cypsella, both the emperor and the Scyths. As the expected mercenaries had not yet come, Alexius was in a quandary. He knew that the Scyths could move very fast; he also saw that they were already on their way to Constantinople itself, at great speed; he was, moreover, vastly outnumbered and battle was out of the question. Calculating that the lesser of two evils is the better, he once more sought refuge in peace talks. Envoys were sent to confer and for a second time the barbarians yielded to his wishes. Before the truce was made, however, Neantzes deserted to the Romans. Meanwhile Migidenus [17] was collecting large contingents from the neighbouring districts. The Scyths were not content with peace for long: like dogs they 'turned again to their own vomit'. Setting out from Cypsella they seized Taurocòmus, where they spent the winter in ravaging the nearby villages.

At the beginning of spring [18] they went on to Charioupolis. The emperor was at that time in Bulgarophygon, but he hesitated no longer. A considerable part of the army was detached, all young men and specially picked, the Archontopuli. The morale of this corps was very high. [19]

17. It was his son who in the war which broke out later charged fiercely against the Patzinaks at . . . . As he swept past, he was dragged by an iron grapple inside the circle of wagons by a Scythian woman and so made prisoner. His severed head was bought by Alexius at his father's request, but Migidenus, unable to bear his affliction, died after beating his breast for three days and nights with a huge block of stone. (A.C.)

18. 1090.

19. This company of Archontopuli was first recruited by Alexius. Because of the neglect of preceding emperors the Romans tolerated exemp-

Alexius ordered them to attack the Scyths from the
rear (the Scyths were standing on their wagons). The newly
recruited Archontopuli went off in full fighting order, but the
enemy were lying in ambush at the foot of a hill watching
their advance and, when they saw them rushing against the
wagons, charged into them with terrific impetus. In a hand-
to-hand struggle about 300 Archontopuli fell fighting valiantly. For a long time the emperor grieved deeply for them,
shedding hot tears and calling upon each one by name as if
he were merely absent from parade. After defeating these
opponents the Patzinaks went through Charioupolis and then
turned off to Aspra, ravaging everything on the way. The
emperor followed the same system as before, getting to
Aspra first (as I have said more than once, his forces were
inadequate for a set battle). He knew the Scyths left their
camp to forage about sunrise. So Taticius, with the bravest of
the young soldiers, all the Latins and the élite of Alexius' own
personal bodyguard, was ordered to keep careful watch on the
Scythian movements just before dawn; when it was reasonable
to suppose that they were well away from camp on their
foraging expedition, they were to charge down on them at
full gallop. Taticius carried out instructions, killed 300 and
took numerous prisoners. Later on the chosen knights sent
by the Count of Flanders arrived; there were about 500 of
them and they brought a gift for Alexius, 150 selected horses.
What is more, they sold to him all the other horses not required by themselves for immediate use. They were received
with due honour and warmly thanked. Afterwards, when the

---

tion from military service, but he regularly enrolled sons of soldiers who
had lost their lives, trained them in arms and war and gave them this
name, as if they were sons born of leaders. The name would inspire them
to emulate the nobility and valour of their forefathers; they would be
mindful of the 'furious battle-spirit' and when the moment called for
daring and strength they would fight all the more bravely. Such in brief
was the company of Archontopuli, made up to the number of 2,000 men,
like the Sacred Band invented by the Lacedaemonians. (A.C.)

The name Archontopuli means 'sons of leaders'. Anna is of course
wrong when she ascribes the invention of the Sacred Band to Sparta. The
honour should have gone to Thebes.

news came from the east that Abul-Kasim, the governor of
Nicaea,[20] was preparing an offensive against Nicomedia,
Alexius sent them to protect that area.

At this moment Tzachas, being informed of the emperor's
manifold difficulties in the west and of his frequent encounters
with the Patzinaks, decided that he must have a fleet – the
omens were propitious. He met a certain man from Smyrna
who had considerable experience in such matters and to him
he entrusted the business of constructing pirate vessels. Somewhere near Smyrna a large fleet was equipped. In addition to
the pirate vessels there were forty decked ships and on them
crews of efficient sailors. They put to sea and dropped anchor
again off Clazomenae, which was at once captured. From there
Tzachas went on to Phocaea. That also was taken at the first
assault. A messenger was then despatched to Alopus, the
curator appointed to govern Mitylene. He was threatened with
the most frightful vengeance if he did not immediately abandon Mitylene; Tzachas added that he wished him well and
because of that was forewarning him of the terrible fate which
would follow disobedience. Alopus, thoroughly scared by
these intimidations, boarded a ship in the night and made for
Constantinople. Not a moment was lost by Tzachas at this
news. He landed at once and took the city by storm. However, Methymna (which is situated on a promontory of the
same island) did not come over to Tzachas and this was made
known to Alexius. He at once sent a powerful force by sea and
strongly fortified the place. Contrary to expectations Tzachas
ignored Methymna and making straight for Chios took it
without difficulty, but was confronted by Nicetas Castamonites with a second Roman expeditionary force. Nicetas had
enough men and ships to fight the enemy. In the ensuing
engagement, however, he was promptly worsted and many of
the ships which had put to sea with him were captured by

20. Abul-Kasim is usually called by the Persians 'satrap', but by the
Turks who now follow the Persian tradition 'emir'. (A.C.)

In Book VI Anna has told us of Abul-Kasim's unhappy death. She
may have been anticipating events in 1092 in order to finish the story, or
there may have been two Abul-Kasims.

Tzachas. The emperor, when news came of this misfortune, sent another fleet, this time with Constantine Dalassenus as admiral, a valiant fighter and a relative on his mother's side. As soon as he had landed on the shore of Chios he invested the fortress with great spirit, hurrying to take the city before Tzachas arrived from Smyrna. The walls were battered with a host of helepoleis and stone-throwing catapults, and the ramparts between two towers were destroyed, but the Turks inside, knowing what had happened and realizing that further resistance was impossible, began to call upon the Almighty to have pity on them, uttering their prayers in the Roman tongue. The soldiers of Dalassenus and Opus in their eagerness to break into the citadel could not be held back, though their leaders tried to restrain them, fearful no doubt lest once inside they might lay hands on all the booty and wealth previously deposited there by Tzachas. 'You can hear the Turks,' they said, 'clearly acclaiming the emperor already; they have surrendered to us. It is wrong then that you should go in and massacre them without mercy.' The whole of that day passed and it was almost nightfall; by then the Turks had put up another wall to replace the ruined battlements. On the outside of it they hung mattresses, hides of leather and all the clothing they could gather, so that the violence of the bombardment might be deadened, however little. Tzachas meanwhile made ready his fleet, enlisted some 8,000 Turks and set them on the road to Chios by land. The fleet followed him, keeping close inshore. Dalassenus, aware of this, ordered his ship's captains to take on board a large number of soldiers with their leader Opus and to weigh anchor. He wanted to join battle with Tzachas wherever he might meet him at sea. Tzachas left the mainland and sailed directly to Chios; when Opus did meet him, about midnight, it was clear that the enemy had adopted a new form of anchorage. By means of a very long chain Tzachas had tied together all his ships, so that those who were minded to run away could not do so, nor could the others who wanted to sail out in front break up the line of vessels. Opus was terrified at the sight. He had not the confidence even to approach them, and making a complete

turn sailed back to Chios. Tzachas cleverly followed him,
rowing without a rest. When they were both nearing Chios,
Opus was first to anchor his ships in the harbour (Dalassenus
had already occupied it), but Tzachas sailed past and brought
his own ships to land by the wall of the fortress. It was the
fourth day of the week. On the Thursday he disembarked all
his men, counted them and entered their names on a list.
Dalassenus for his part found a small village by the harbour
and took up position there. First he destroyed his old entrenchment and dug another, with a wide ditch, at this place.
Then he moved his army there. On the following day both
forces, in full armour, prepared for action. The Romans stood
immobile (Dalassenus had given orders that the battle-line
must be unbroken). Tzachas, on the other hand, prompted the
bulk of his infantry to attack, with a small body of horsemen
in support. The Latins, seeing this, charged the Turks with
their long lances. It was not at the Kelts, however, that the
enemy fired their arrows, but at their horses; some were also
wounded by spear-thrusts. Casualties were very heavy and
the cavalry were driven back in a crowd inside their own
entrenchment; from there they tumbled into the ships in
headlong panic. The Romans witnessed this disorderly retreat
and in great alarm themselves withdrew slightly to the wall of
the village. There they halted. Thereupon the barbarians came
down to the shore and seized some of the ships. The crews slipped the stern-cables, pushed off from land, dropped anchor
again and stood off waiting anxiously to see what happened.
Dalassenus ordered them to sail along the coast westwards to
Bolissos and wait for him there. (Bolissos is a small place near
the promontory of Chios.) But certain Scyths came to Tzachas
and told him beforehand of Dalassenus' plan. Tzachas immediately sent out fifty scouts, with orders to give him warning instantly when the Roman fleet was ready to sail. After
that he sent a message to Dalassenus, perhaps because he wanted
to discuss terms of peace; in my opinion he had given up all hope
of victory when he saw his brave opponent was prepared to
face danger. The latter promised Tzachas that on the morrow
he would come to the edge of his camp, to discuss whatever

terms might be agreeable to both. Tzachas accepted the offer
and early in the morning the leaders met. Tzachas, addressing
Dalassenus by name, began the conversation: 'Let me introduce myself. I am the young man who in the old days made
incursions into Asia. I fought with great spirit, but because of
my inexperience I was deceived and captured by the famous
Alexander Kabalika. He offered me as a prisoner of war to the
Emperor Nicephorus Botaniates. I was at once honoured with
the title of protonobilissimus and after being rewarded with
liberal gifts I promised obedience to him. But ever since
Alexius Comnenus seized power, everything has gone wrong
for me. That is why I have come in person now to explain the
reason for my enmity. Let the emperor know this, and if he
wishes to put an end to the hostility which has sprung up,
let him restore to me in full the rightful possessions of which I
have been deprived. As for you, if you approve of a marriage
alliance between our families, let the marriage contract be
committed to writing, agreeable to both parties, as is the
custom of the Romans and of us barbarians. After that, when
all these aforementioned terms have been fulfilled, I will hand
over to the emperor, through you, all the islands invaded by
me and taken from the Roman Empire; moreover, when I
have observed all the conditions of my treaty with him, I will
return to my own country.' Dalassenus had long experience of
the Turks: he knew their treacherous nature. The proposals of
Tzachas he regarded as hypocritical and so deferred for the
time being the ratification of his demands. Nevertheless, he
laid bare his suspicions: 'You,' he said, 'will neither restore
the islands to me, as you said, nor can I, without the emperor's
consideration, decide the terms which you ask for from him
and from me. But when the Great Duke John, the emperor's
brother-in-law, arrives soon with all the fleet, bringing with
him massive forces by land and by sea, let him hear your
proposition. Under those circumstances you can be sure that a
treaty will be successfully concluded with the emperor – provided that John acts as arbitrator to bring about the peace.'[21]

21. This Duke John had been sent by the emperor to Epidamnos with
a considerable army, for two purposes: to concern himself diligently with

viii–ix   BOOK SEVEN

While Dalassenus waited for his arrival, in his conversations with Tzachas he made it clear that the whole business was to be referred to Ducas. Tzachas gave the impression that he was quoting Homer's line, 'Night is already upon us: it is good to heed the night.'[22] He promised that when day broke he would furnish much of the provisions. However, it was all a lie and deceit. In fact, Dalassenus was not far from the mark in his judgement, for in the grey of the dawn Tzachas went secretly down to the Chian shore and as the wind was favourable set sail for Smyrna, to collect greater forces and return to the island. His opponent, though, was no less crafty: he embarked with his men on the available ships and made for Bolissos; he acquired a fleet, made ready other helepoleis, and after giving his soldiers a rest and enrolling more of them, he went back to his original starting-point. There followed a bitter clash with the Turks, in which the ramparts were destroyed and the town fell into Dalassenus' hands. Tzachas was still in Smyrna. Afterwards, when the sea was calm, Dalassenus sailed on a straight course to Mitylene with his whole fleet.

Such was the action taken by the emperor against Tzachas. Next he discovered that the Scyths were again on their way to Rousion and had pitched camp at Polybotos. Without

---

the protection of Dyrrachium, and to make war on the Dalmatians. A certain man called Bodinus, a combative and thoroughly unprincipled rascal, had refused to stay inside his own borders and made daily attacks on the towns nearest to Dalmatia. These he annexed. For eleven years Duke John had remained in Dyrrachium. Many of the defended places under the control of Bolkan he recovered, and many Dalmatian prisoners were sent to Alexius. In the end he clashed with Bodinus in a fierce battle and took him too. Thus the emperor had good reason to recognize the warlike qualities of this John Ducas; he knew his skill as a strategist, he knew also that John would under no circumstances disregard his instructions. Since he needed such a man to deal with Tzachas, he recalled him from Dyrrachium and sent him as Grand Admiral of the Fleet with strong land and naval forces to make war on him. How many battles he fought with Tzachas and to what dangers he exposed himself before emerging undisputed victor will be made clear in the subsequent pages of this history. (A.C.)

22. Homer, *Iliad* vii, 282. The point is that he pretended to obey necessity.

hesitation he left Constantinople and arrived himself at Rousion, accompanied by the renegade Neantzes, who was devising a terrible and deep-laid plot against him, and also by Kantzes and Katranes, who had great affection for Alexius and were already tried soldiers. At a distance a fairly large detachment of Scyths was sighted and the emperor prepared to do battle. In the fighting many Romans fell, some were taken prisoners and later put to death by their captors, but several got as far as Rousion. However, that was merely a skirmish with Scythian foragers. The arrival of the so-called Maniacate Latins put new heart into the emperor and he decided to fight a pitched battle on the next day.[23] As the space between the two armies happened to be rather small, he dared not allow the trumpet to sound the alert, for he wanted to take the enemy by surprise. The man in charge of the imperial falcons, one Constantine, was summoned and told to obtain a drum in the evening; all night long he was to walk round the camp beating this drum, warning all to be ready because at sunrise the emperor planned to do battle with the Scyths and there would be no trumpet-call. The enemy, coming from Polybotos, had already reached a place called Hades and made camp there. On the Roman side preparations went on from the evening and, when the sun rose, Alexius arranged his army in companies and ranks for the battle. The struggle had not yet begun (both armies were still forming up) when Neantzes climbed a hill in the vicinity in order, as he said, to spy out the Scythian lines and bring back information to the emperor, but in fact his intention was quite different. He advised the enemy, speaking in his native language, to set their wagons in rows and not to be afraid of Alexius: he had been beaten before and was beaten and ready to run now, he said, with too few soldiers and not enough allies. Having delivered this message he returned to our lines. But a half-caste who knew the Scythian language had understood Neantzes' conversation with them and reported the

23. Maniaces had died in battle in 1043 and his soldiers were Greek rather than Latin or Italian. If these men had fought with George Maniaces, they must have been veterans indeed by 1088. It is more likely that the corps inherited Maniaces' name.

whole matter to Alexius. Neantzes heard of this and demanded proof. The half-caste unashamedly came forward and proceeded to give proof in public. All at once Neantzes drew his sword and cut off the man's head, in the presence of the emperor and with ranks of soldiers on either side of him. When Neantzes tried in this way to avert suspicion (by killing the informer), I imagine he made himself more suspect. Otherwise he would surely have waited for the proof. His desire to quash in advance the evidence of his own treachery, it seems to me, caused him to do something even more perilous and daring, a deed worthy of a barbarian, but as foolhardy as it was suspicious. Nevertheless the emperor did not immediately take action against Neantzes, nor punish him according to his deserts, but for the moment he controlled his rising indignation and anger; he did not want to frighten away his quarry too soon and upset the soldiers, but his wrath, though concealed, was reserved for the future – from former actions of the man, and for other reasons, he had foreseen his treachery and insubordination. The war stood in the balance and on account of that he checked his consuming rage temporarily, not knowing at present what to do with him. For all that Neantzes soon afterwards approached him, dismounted from his horse and asked the emperor for another; without hesitation Alexius gave him one, a fine beast, with the royal saddle. Neantzes mounted it, waited until the two lines were already marching towards one another across the battle-field and then made a pretence of charging. With spear-point reversed he went over to his fellow-countrymen and gave them much information about our army. They made use of his advice. In the hard struggle which followed the Scyths routed the Romans; they all fled in disorder and the lines were torn apart. The emperor saw this. He was in a dangerous situation and, as he was unwilling to run foolish risks, he turned his horse's head and rode off to the river which flows near Rousion. There he drew rein and with some chosen soldiers drove off his pursuers as best he could. Charging on horseback he actually killed many of them, and sometimes was hit himself. When from another direction George Pyrrhus fled to the river,

Alexius rebuked him and called him back. Later, when he saw how reckless the enemy were and how day by day their numbers grew as others came to their aid, he left this same George on the spot with the remainder of his troops, telling him to resist with discretion until he (Alexius) returned. Then, quickly turning his horse's bridle, he crossed the river and entered Rousion. All fugitive soldiers found there, the whole native population capable of bearing arms and even the peasants with their own wagons were ordered to leave the city at once and take up position on the river bank. This all happened more quickly than I can write it down. Alexius, having arranged them in some sort of line, recrossed the river and hurried back to George although he was troubled by a quartan fever, so bad that his teeth chattered from the shivering cold. By now the whole Scythian army had concentrated, but when they saw a double line and the emperor exerting himself in this way, they halted, not daring to risk a clash with him. They knew that he was prepared to face dangers and that both in victory and in defeat he remained true to himself; his attack would be overwhelming. Alexius was to a certain extent restrained by his shivering, but in particular because all the fugitives had not yet rejoined him. He too stayed where he was, but moved along the ranks, rode a little and displayed his own confidence before the enemy. Thus it came about that both armies stood motionless until evening. When night was actually falling, each side withdrew to its own camp without fighting, afraid to engage in a battle which seemed too hazardous. Little by little the men who had scattered in all directions after the first battle came back to Rousion; the majority of them had taken no part at all in the fighting. Monastras, Ouzas and Synesios, 'men dear to Ares' and fine warriors, went through Aspron at this time and they also arrived at Rousion without striking a blow against the enemy.

As I said, the emperor was afflicted by the fever and in order to get relief he was forced to take to his bed for a while. Nevertheless, ill though he was, he never ceased making plans for the next day. A Scyth called Tatranes approached him with an idea. This man had many times deserted to the emperor

and later gone back to his home; on each occasion he was
pardoned and because of the emperor's extraordinary forbearance Tatranes conceived a great affection for him. Tatranes in fact was for the rest of his life wholly devoted, body
and soul, to Alexius. 'I expect, sir,' he said, 'that the Scyths
will surround us tomorrow and having done that they will
challenge us to battle. If that is so, we must be outside the
walls by sunrise with the battle-line ready before they come.'
Alexius commended him, adopted his plan and agreed to put
it into operation at dawn. Tatranes then went off to the
Scythian commanders and spoke to them: 'Don't be elated,'
he said, 'by the previous disasters suffered by the emperor and
when you see how outnumbered we are, don't go into battle
full of confidence. His power is invincible; even now he
awaits the arrival of a strong mercenary force. If you won't
make peace with him, birds will devour your bodies.' So much
for Tatranes. Meanwhile the emperor considered the possibility of seizing their horses, which were grazing on the plain
(there were very many of them), for the Scyths every day and
night were raiding our territory. He sent for Ouzas and
Monastras. They were to take picked horsemen, he said, and
make their way to the rear of the enemy; about first light they
must be on the plain and capture all the horses and other
animals, together with their herdsmen. 'Don't be afraid,' he
added, 'we shall be attacking from the front. You will easily
carry out this order.' Nor was he wrong – the plan was immediately successful. He had no sleep that night as he awaited
the Scythian onslaught; there was not even any dozing.
Throughout the hours of darkness he was summoning his
soldiers, especially the expert archers. He talked much with
them about the Scyths, stimulating them to battle, as a trainer
encourages athletes before a contest. He gave them useful
advice for the struggle expected to take place the next day –
how to bend their bows and fire their arrows, when to rein in
a horse, when to relax the bridle, and when to dismount, if
indeed they had to. This went on during the night, but he did
have a brief nap before, as day was now breaking, the élite
of the Scythian army crossed the river *en masse*, apparently

provoking the Romans to battle. The emperor's forecast was already proving correct. He had indeed great prescience of the future, acquired from long experience of continual warfare. He at once mounted his horse, ordered the trumpeter to sound the alert, and drew up his ranks, with himself in front. Seeing that the enemy were attacking with more boldness than before, he commanded the archers to dismount without delay and advance on foot, pouring volleys of arrows into the Scyths all the time. The rest of the line followed them. As Alexius controlled the centre in person, the archers bravely pressed on. The battle was sternly contested, but the Scyths, partly because of the continuous showers of arrows, partly because they saw the unbroken line of the Romans and the emperor himself engaging in fierce conflict, turned back in flight, panic-stricken and hurrying to cross the river behind them to find refuge in their covered wagons. The Roman line pursued at full gallop, some piercing the enemies' backs with spears, others shooting at them with arrows. Many fell in death before they ever reached the bank of the river; many fleeing in haste fell into the whirling streams, were swept away by the water and drowned. On that day the emperor's retinue surpassed all others in valour; they were tireless, all of them. As for Alexius, he was clearly the bravest of all. He returned to his own camp, the undisputed victor on that battlefield.

For three days he had a rest in that area, then left for Tzouroulos. Thinking it was essential not to move from there quickly, he had an entrenchment dug towards the east side of the village big enough for the forces he had with him, and placed inside it the imperial tent and all the baggage. The Scyths also advanced on Tzouroulos, but when they heard that he had anticipated them, they crossed the river flowing through the plain not far from the village (the natives call the place Xerogypsos[24]) and pitched camp between the river and Tzouroulos. They were in a circle outside it, so that the emperor was cut off and practically besieged. When night came, 'the others, both gods and warriors with horse-hair crests, slept' (to quote Homer's muse), but 'sweet sleep did

24. 'Dry chalk'.

not embrace' Alexius.[25] He lay awake, turning over in his
mind schemes by which he might outwit and overcome the
boldness of the enemy. Well, he noticed that this village
Tzouroulos had been built on a steep hill and the entire barbarian force was encamped down below on the plain. It was
impossible for him to fight with any confidence in close combat, for he was greatly outnumbered, but he conceived a most
ingenious plan. He requisitioned the wagons of the inhabitants, separated from the upper parts the wheels and their
axles, and had them carried up to the ramparts. They were then
suspended by ropes, just as they were, on the outside of the
wall in a row from the battlements; the ropes were made fast
to the parapets. No time was wasted in putting the plan into
action: in one hour the wheels, with the axles, hung round the
wall like a series of circles, touching each other and still
attached to the axles. The emperor rose early next morning,
armed himself and his men, led them away from the wall and
set them directly in front of the Scyths. It happened that our
men took up position on the side where the wheels had been
suspended; just opposite them were the enemy in one line.
At this point Alexius, standing in the centre, warned his men:
when the trumpet sounded the attack, they were to dismount
and advance slowly on foot towards the enemy, shooting at
them with their bows again and again, skirmishing at a distance and provoking the Scythians to attack. When they saw
them moving forward and shouting at their horses to charge,
then the Romans were to turn away in disorder; gradually
they must split up into two groups, going right and left,
giving ground to the Scyths until they came up close to the
wall. Orders had been given to men standing on the walls that
when this happened – that is, when they saw the ranks moving
apart – they were to cut the ropes with their swords and let
wheels and axles crash headlong down. This was done. The
Scythian horsemen bursting out in a mass descended on our
lines with barbaric yells. The Romans were advancing on foot
and slowly, all together, with only the emperor on horseback.
Little by little, following the emperor's plan, they 'slowly

25. *Iliad* ii, 1–2.

changed knee for knee',[26] and like men on a retreat became
separated from each other, to the enemies' surprise, as if
opening up a wide door for them to enter. When the Scyths
were in fact inside this gap, with our lines on either side, the
wheels crashed down with a loud whirring noise, all of them
rebounding more than a cubit from the rampart as the curving
wheels were thrust away like bullets from a sling, and down
they rolled into the midst of their horsemen as they gathered
additional impetus. The normal weight of the wheels, falling
in this mass descent, acquired tremendous momentum from
the downward slope of the ground. They toppled down on the
Scyths with great violence, crushing them in all directions and
cutting off their horses' legs like mowers in a harvest-field;
with fore- or hind-legs severed (they were struck from front
and from rear) the horses sank down and threw their riders
forward or backward. The horsemen fell in great numbers,
one on top of another, and from either flank our infantry
advanced towards them. The Scyths were threatened on all
sides by the terrors of battle. Some were massacred by flying
arrows, others were wounded by our lances, but of the remainder most were hurtled in a crowd by the violent down-
rush of the wheels to the river and there drowned. On the
next day, seeing the survivors preparing to renew the conflict,
the emperor mobilized all his army – he knew they were
confident now. He himself donned armour and after arranging
the line went down to the plain. Then he turned his forces to
face the enemy and waited, ready to join battle as best he could.
He was at the centre of the line. It was a bitter contest, but the
Romans (unexpectedly) won the day and pursued the Scyths
madly. When he realized the chase had gone far enough,
Alexius rode again and again to warn his soldiers to draw rein
and give their horses a chance to cool off; he was afraid that
some enemy, lying in ambush, might suddenly fall upon them
and turn the Scythian rout into a victory; with the reinforce-
ment of the fugitives they might bring the Roman army into
great peril. At any rate, that is how the two forces parted that
day, one in flight, the other returning to camp rejoicing in a

26. Homer, *Iliad* xi, 547; i.e. stepped cautiously backwards.

notable triumph. After their crushing defeat the enemy
pitched tents between Bulgarophygos and Little Nicaea. Winter
had now started and the emperor decided that he must return
to Constantinople; both he and most of his army were in need
of rest after their many struggles. Having divided his forces in
two, therefore, he picked out the most courageous fighters to
watch the enemy. They were under the command of Joannaces and Nicolas Maurocatacalon. These officers were instructed to bring into each town enough soldiers to protect
the place and to round up infantry from the whole district,
with wagons and their ox-teams. He intended to carry on the
war with more vigour at the approach of spring. He was already planning and making preparations essential for the
victory. When all these arrangements were complete, he
returned to Byzantium.

BOOK EIGHT

THE SCYTHIAN WAR (1091) –
VICTORY AT LEVUNIUM (29 APRIL 1091)
– PLOTS AGAINST THE EMPEROR

THE emperor learnt that a Scythian detachment was on its way to attack Chirovachi; their arrival was imminent. Apparently always prepared even when faced with the unexpected, Alexius with typical speed assembled the garrison troops and all the new recruits, about 500 in number. All through the night he was attending to their equipment. (He had not had even a week's relaxation in the palace, nor enjoyed a bath, nor shaken off the dust of battle.) About first light on the next morning he left the city. At the same time he informed his kinsmen by birth or marriage and all the nobles enrolled in the army that he was going out to do battle with the Scyths. The following instructions were issued to them (it was then the Friday of Carnival Week, just before Lent[1]): 'I have been informed that the Scyths are moving swiftly on Chirovachi. I am leaving now, but you will join us in Quinquagesima Week. The days between the Friday of Carnival and the Monday of Cheese-Week I am allowing you for a short rest – otherwise I might seem harsh and unreasonable.' He then rode straight for Chirovachi, entered the gates of the town and locked them; he himself kept the keys. On the battlements he stationed all the servants loyal to himself and told them not to relax, but to keep awake and patrol the walls; nobody must be allowed to climb up there, or lean over and talk with the Scyths. At daybreak the enemy arrived, as expected, and took up position on a high place near to the wall. About 6,000 of

1. Cheese-Week ends in Quinquagesima Sunday; during this week 'cheese, butter, milk, eggs and fish are allowed, but not butcher's meat' (Sophocles' *Greek Lexicon*) – hence its Greek name, *Tyrophagia*. The week before it was Carnival (the Greek word implies an abstention from meat). Thus Alexius here was allowing only three days of rest.

247

them were then separated from the rest and dispersed to look for plunder, getting as far as Dekatos (which is about ten stades from Constantinople – hence, I suppose, its name[2]). The remainder of the Scyths stayed in the district of Chirovachi. The emperor climbed to the parapet to examine the plains and hills in case another force was on its way to reinforce them; maybe the Scyths had laid ambushes to trap any potential attacker. There was no evidence of any such thing, but about the second hour of the day he noticed that they were in no state for battle; they were in fact getting ready for a meal and a rest. Because of their great numbers he knew that a fight at close quarters was out of the question, but the thought that they might ravage the countryside and approach the walls of the capital itself horrified him – especially as he had left it to scare them away. At once therefore he called together his soldiers and addressed them (he wanted to test their morale): 'We mustn't be overawed by Scythian numbers, but put our trust in God and fight them. If we are all of one mind, I am absolutely confident of victory.' When they rejected the idea out of hand and refused to listen, he struck greater fear into them; trying to rouse them to face facts, he went on: 'If those who went off to plunder come back again and unite with the Scyths here, the danger is obvious: either the camp will be captured and we shall be massacred, or they will treat us as of no consequence, march to the walls of the capital and prevent us from entering by bivouacking somewhere near the gates. Our only hope is to take risks. We must do that and not die like cowards. For my part I am going out now. I shall ride on ahead and burst into the enemy's midst. All you who are willing can follow me; those who either cannot or don't want to, must not move outside the gates.' At all events he wasted no more time. In full armour he went out through the gate opposite the lake. He moved fast along the walls, then making a slight detour climbed the hill from the far side, for he was certain that his army would not fight the enemy in close combat. At the head of his men he forced his way spear in hand into the centre of the Scyths, hitting the first man who opposed

2. Greek *dekatos* = tenth.

him. The others were no less eager to fight; they captured
some and killed more. Then, resourceful as ever, Alexius
clothed his soldiers in the Scyths' uniforms and told them to
ride the Scythian horses. Their own mounts and the standards
and the severed heads of their enemies he handed over to a
few of the more reliable men, with instructions to take them
back to the fort and await him there. Having taken these precautions, he went down with the Scythian standards and his
men clad in Scythian uniforms to the river which flows near
Chirovachi. He thought the enemy would cross at this point
on their return from plundering. The Scyths saw them standing there and believing that they were fellow countrymen ran
towards them without reconnoitring first. Some were wiped
out, others were captured.

When evening fell (it was the Saturday) the emperor
returned with his prisoners. The next day he rested, but at sunrise on the Monday he left the fort. The army was divided: in
front were the men holding the Scythian standards, in the rear
the captives, each guarded by natives of the country; others
held aloft the severed heads on spears. Such was the order of
march. Behind these again, at a moderate distance, came the
emperor himself with his men and the usual Roman standards.
Early in the morning of Sexagesima Sunday Palaeologus,
eager for military fame, left Byzantium at the head of other
troops. Knowing the impulsive nature of the Scyths, he
marched with circumspection: a few of his retinue were
detached with orders to go on ahead and reconnoitre the
plains and woods and roads of the district; if any Scyths
appeared, they were to turn round quickly and report to him.
The march was proceeding in this formation when in the
plain of Dimylia they saw men clothed in Scythian uniforms
and carrying Scythian standards; so, turning back, they
reported that the Scyths were already on the way. At once
Palaeologus took up arms. Close on their heels came another
messenger who insisted that behind the men (who might be
Scyths) there appeared to be Roman standards and soldiers
following them at a fair distance. The messengers were of
course partly right and partly wrong: the army at the rear was

truly Roman, in appearance and in fact, and it was led by the emperor; but the vanguard, dressed like Scyths, was also indeed wholly Roman (according to the emperor's instructions they were wearing the same garb as they had when the real Scyths were deceived). On this occasion the use of Scythian uniforms tricked and deceived our own folk. Alexius did it so that the first men to meet our troops might be filled with dread, thinking they were Scyths – a general's joke, mild but grim as well; before there was any real terror, however, they were reassured at the sight of himself behind the 'Scyths', so that playing 'hobgoblin' caused no panic among the scouts. The rest were upset by what they saw, but Palaeologus, who had far more experience than anyone else and knew the emperor's inventive genius, immediately realized that this was one of his stratagems; he recovered his own nerve and told the others to do the same.

By now all the crowd of kinsmen and relatives of the emperor had joined them from the rear; they were hurrying, as they imagined, to meet him according to the arrangements previously made – that is, after the week of abstinence from meat in the Tyrophagy. In fact they had not left the city when he returned in triumph. Meeting him under these circumstances they could not believe that he had so quickly won a victory and returned with the trophies, until they saw the Scythian heads impaled on the end of spears and the survivors, not yet beheaded, being led with hands tied behind their backs and in chains, driven and trailing along one after the other. The rapidity of this campaign caused a sensation. In one quarter, though, it was unpopular: I heard that George Palaeologus (eye-witnesses told us about it) complained angrily and was annoyed with himself for being too late to fight in the war; he would have liked to be with the emperor when he won such glory with this unexpected triumph. He had longed with all his heart to share in such fame. As for the emperor, one might say that on this occasion the verse of Deuteronomy was visibly fulfilled in him: 'How should one chase a thousand, and two put ten thousand to flight?' For in that crisis the Emperor Alexius, by opposing himself to so great a multitude of barbarians, gloriously bore almost the whole brunt of the war, up to the moment of victory itself. In fact, if one considers the soldiers who were with him and reflects on their numbers and quality, and then compares with them the stratagems of the emperor, his versatility, his strength, his boldness in the face of all the barbarian host and its might, he would conclude that Alexius alone brought about the victory.

That at any rate was how God gave the victory – an extraordinary one – to our ruler that day. When the Byzantines witnessed his arrival in the city they rejoiced. Amazed by the speed, the boldness, the skilfulness of the enterprise, and the suddenness of his triumph, they sang, they danced, they praised God for vouchsafing them such a saviour and benefactor. Nicephorus Melissenus, though, hurt by these demonstrations and unable to bear them – such is the way with human-kind – remarked that this victory was a profitless joy to us, to them a harmless pain. For despite it all the Scyths in their countless hosts continued to ravage everything, scattered throughout the west, and nothing whatever of the mishaps that had befallen them checked their brazen audacity. In several parts of the west they seized some small towns, not even sparing the larger places near Constantinople. They got as far as the so-called 'Deep Torrent', where there is a church built in honour of Theodore, the greatest of all martyrs. Many people used to visit this place every day in order to pray to the saint, and when Sunday came round the devout made their way in crowds to the holy shrine; all day and all night they stayed there, either outside the building, or in the vestibule, or in the back of the church. But the unchecked violence of the Scyths had such an overwhelming effect that would-be pilgrims dared not even open the gates of Byzantium because of these frequent assaults. Such were the terrible disasters which fell upon the emperor in the west; on the sea, too, there was no freedom from trouble, for Tzachas had acquired a new fleet and was overrunning all the coastline. The situation was extremely dangerous, and these blows coming from all directions caused Alexius deep concern. He was vexed and harassed everywhere. The news came that Tzachas' fleet, recruited from the maritime districts, was bigger than ever; the rest of the islands previously taken by him had been sacked; he planned to attack the western provinces and his envoys advised the Scyths to occupy the Chersonese. Worse still, he would not let the mercenary force (the Turks from the east who had come to the emperor's aid) keep their treaty with Alexius inviolate. To make them desert him and come over to his own side, Tzachas promised fine rewards once he had his hands on the loot.[3] Alexius knew what was going on. His cause was faring very ill on sea and land, and the severe winter[4] blocked the exits at all points; in fact, the doors of houses could not be opened for the heavy weight of snow (more snow fell that year than anyone could remember in the past). Still, he did what he could by summoning mercenaries by letter from all quarters. Just after the spring equinox, when the threat of war from the clouds had vanished and the sea lost its fury, although his enemies attacked on two fronts, he thought it wiser to get control of the sea coast first; by doing that he could easily withstand the onslaught of enemy fleets and conveniently dispose of attacks by land. At once, therefore, he sent a message to the Caesar Nicephorus Melissenus, calling on him to take Aenos. Before this he had sent written instructions to him to recruit as many men as he could, not from the veterans (for he had already dispersed them generally among the cities of the west, to guard the more important places), but to enrol new men for a term of duty from the Bulgars and the nomads (commonly called Vlachs) and any others who came from any province, both cavalry and infantry. The emperor himself summoned the 500 Kelts of the Count of Flanders from Nicomedia, and leaving Byzantium quickly arrived at Aenos with his kinsmen. There he boarded a boat and explored the geography of the river from end to end, thoroughly examining the bed of the stream from both banks and deciding where it was best to encamp. Then he

3. There are two possible translations. If Anna is to be taken literally, we must read it thus: 'once he had got in the barley crops'; but this may have been a proverbial phrase, like 'got the swag'.
4. The winter of 1090-91.

returned. During the night he called a meeting of the army
officers and gave them a lecture on the river and the conditions
on either bank. 'You must cross the river tomorrow,' he said,
'and carefully reconnoitre the whole plain. Maybe you will
find the place I point out to you not unsuitable for a camp.'
All agreed and at daybreak the emperor was the first to make
the crossing; he was followed by the whole army. Again, with
the officers, he examined the banks of the river and the
adjacent plain. He pointed out to them the place he had chosen
(near a small town called by the natives Chireni, with the
river on one side and on the other a swamp). As the position
seemed to everyone satisfactory, a trench was quickly dug and
the whole force settled down inside it. Alexius himself went
back to Aenos with a strong body of peltasts to repel Scythian
attacks from that quarter.

Later the men at Chireni heard that countless hordes of the
enemy had arrived. They informed Alexius (who was still
at Aenos). He at once boarded a scout-ship,[5] sailed along the
coast and after crossing the river mouth rejoined the others.
He saw that his own forces were incapable of matching even a
tiny part of the Scythian multitude; with no one to aid him
(humanly speaking) he was in a serious and frightening situation. Nevertheless, there was no loss of heart, no weakening of
resolve; on the contrary, his mind was bubbling over with
ideas. However, four days later a Cuman army of about 40,000
was sighted in the distance coming towards him from another
direction. If they joined the Scyths, they might wage a fearful
war on himself, the outcome of which could be nothing but
total destruction. To avoid this, he thought it wise to win
them over by intrigue. He took the initiative by calling on
them to meet him. In the Cuman army there were numerous
chiefs, but the outstanding leaders were Togortak, Maniak
and some others noted for their warlike qualities. The sight of
the multitude of Cumans who had already assembled was
distinctly alarming, for Alexius had long experience of their

5. Dawes translates the Greek word (an unusual one) as 'coracle'. It is
unlikely that he would sail along the coast in a craft so frail, but no doubt
this was a small boat. See Buckler, p. 384.

vacillation: these allies might well become enemies, and as adversaries they could be the cause of very considerable harm to himself. It would be more prudent, he decided, to cross with all his army to the other bank of the river, but it was imperative to summon their leaders first. They soon accepted the invitation. Maniak refused at first, but he came too, though later than the rest. Alexius ordered the cooks to put before them a splendid banquet, and after they had feasted, he treated them with cordiality and gave them all kinds of presents. Then he requested them to take an oath and give hostages (distrusting their irresponsible nature). They readily complied with this demand and gave the pledges. They asked to be allowed to make war on the Patzinaks for three days, and if God granted them the victory, they promised to divide all the booty that fell to them and set aside one half of it for the emperor. He gave them permission to attack the enemy not merely for three days, but for ten whole days if they so wished, and if God did indeed grant them the victory, he relinquished all claim on the booty; they could have it all. Meanwhile both forces remained where they were (Scyths and Cumans), but the latter tested their opponents with skirmishing raids. Before three days had passed the emperor sent for Antiochus, one of the nobles and a man distinguished among his fellows for his lively intelligence. He was ordered to build a bridge. It was quickly constructed by means of boats fastened together with exceptionally long planks of wood. After that the protostrator [6] and the Great Domestic [7] were summoned. Their duty was to take up position on the river bank and prevent infantry and cavalry crossing over in general confusion: the infantry was to have precedence with the baggage-wagons and pack mules. When the infantry had crossed, Alexius, fearing the powerful Scythian and Cuman armies and suspicious of the Cumans' secret plans, had a trench dug at great speed. Inside it all his men were then congregated. After that the cavalry were given the signal to cross. Alexius himself stood by the bank and watched the whole operation. In the meantime in accordance

6. Michael Ducas, the emperor's brother-in-law. (A.C.)
7. Alexius' own brother Adrian. (A.C.)

with the emperor's written instructions, Melissenus had collected recruits over a wide area. The foot-soldiers whom he
rounded up from the vicinity piled their baggage on ox-
wagons, together with all necessary supplies, and were sent in
haste to Alexius, but when they were just near enough for a
man to see them, they were thought by most of the scouts to
be a detachment of Scyths on their way to attack the Romans.
One scout pointed them out to Alexius and confidently
declared them to be Scyths. The emperor believed him, and
because he was heavily outnumbered was at a loss what to do.
Rodomer [8] was immediately sent to spy on the approaching
force. He soon returned with the news that they were sent by
Melissenus, to the intense joy of the emperor, who after
awaiting their arrival for a short time crossed over the bridge
with them and without delay increased the area of the
entrenchment, for they joined the rest of the army. The former
camping place, from which he had set out before crossing the
river, was soon reached by the Cumans and they took it over.
On the next day Alexius left with the idea of seizing a ford
down-stream, called by the natives' Philokalos', but he fell in
with a strong body of Scyths. He attacked at once and a bitter
fight ensued. Many men on both sides were killed, but the
Scyths were heavily defeated. After the struggle, both armies
withdrew to their own camps. The Romans stayed on in the
area all through that night, but at daybreak they left for a place
called Levunium, a hill dominating the plain. Alexius climbed
it, but finding that the hill-top could not accommodate all the
army, he had a trench dug round the lower slopes. The whole
of his force was established inside this entrenchment, which
was big enough to protect them all. It was at this moment that
the deserter Neantzes again presented himself to the emperor,
accompanied by a few Scyths. The sight of him reminded
Alexius of the man's former ingratitude; there were certain
other considerations, too, which he took into account, and
Neantzes, with his companions, was put under arrest and
thrown into chains.

8. Rodomer was a nobleman of Bulgarian extraction and a relative on
his mother's side of our own mother the Augusta. (A.C.)

While the emperor was engaged in these operations, the Scyths, encamped by a mountain stream called Mavropotamus, secretly tried to win over the Cumans. Despite this they did not cease making peace proposals to Alexius. He, guessing their unscrupulous dealings, gave them appropriate replies; he hoped to keep them in suspense until the mercenaries expected to arrive from Rome could reach him. The Cumans, finding the Patzinak pledges ambiguous, were by no means inclined to support them. One evening they notified the emperor: 'How long are we to put off the battle? Be sure of this: we will not wait any longer. At sunrise we intend to decide the matter, one way or the other.'[9] Hearing these words the emperor, who thoroughly understood the passionate nature of the Cumans, no longer deferred the contest. He gave his word that on the next day battle would be joined with the enemy (and that day, he determined, would be the turning-point of the whole war). Without delay the generals and company commanders and other officers were told to spread throughout the camp the news that battle was fixed for the morrow. In spite of these arrangements he still feared the countless hordes of Patzinaks and Cumans; he suspected a covenant between them. He was still examining that possibility when some highlanders came to join him, bold men 'full of warlike frenzy'. As many as 5,000 of them had deserted to the Roman side. There was no longer any pretext for delay. Alexius invoked the aid of God. As the sun was setting he led the prayers; a brilliant torch-light procession took place and suitable hymns, also led by him, were chanted to the Lord. Nor did the emperor allow the rest of the camp to enjoy repose: the more intelligent were enjoined to follow his example, the more boorish he commanded to do so. At the moment when the sun set below the horizon, one could see the heaven lit up, not with the light of one sun, but with the gleam of many other stars, for everyone lit torches, or wax-tapers (according to their means) fixed on their spear-points. The prayers offered up by the army no doubt reached the very vault of heaven, or shall I say that they were borne aloft to the

9. Literally, 'we shall eat the flesh of wolf and lamb' – a proverbial expression.

Lord God Himself. The fact that the emperor did not believe he could attack the enemy without the help of God is proof, I think, of his piety, for his confidence was stayed neither on men nor on horses nor on machines of war, but all his faith was placed in the power of the Lord on High. Until midnight these ceremonies went on. Then, after resting his body for a short time he leapt up from his sleep to arm the light troops for battle. In some cases he even made cuirasses and caps out of silken garments, since there was insufficient iron for all, and the silk resembled iron in colour. These were worn by some of his men. The equipping was completed, and just as the morning sun was shining brightly he left the entrenchment, after ordering the alert to be sounded. At the foot of Levunium (the name of this place) the army was divided up and the ranks were massed. He himself took his place in front 'breathing the fierce spirit of battle'.[10] On the right and left wings George Palaeologus and Constantine Dalassenus were in command. To the right of the Cumans Monastras stood in full armour with his men on higher ground. The Cumans, seeing the emperor drawing up the Roman ranks, were already arming their own forces and preparing the battle-line according to their own fashion. On their left was Ouzas and towards the west Humbertopoulos with the Kelts. Thus the emperor's army was like a bastion, with its ranks of infantry tightly enclosed by squadrons of cavalry on either wing. Once again the trumpeter was ordered to sound the call to battle. In their dread of the numberless host of Scyths and their terrifying covered wagons (which served as ramparts for them), the Romans with one voice called upon the Lord of all to have pity and then, at full gallop, rushed to do battle with their enemies.[11] Riding in front of all was the emperor. When the line had become crescent-shaped, as if at one word of command, the whole army (including the Cumans) surged forward against the Scyths. One of the enemy, in command of their picked men, foreseeing the outcome of the struggle seized the opportunity to save his own life and with a few others approached the Cumans, whose language he spoke. Although

10. Homer, *Odyssey* xxiv, 319.   11. On Tuesday, 29 April 1091.

257

the latter, too, were engaged in a ferocious conflict with his people, he had more faith in them than in the Romans. He surrendered, hoping they would act as intermediaries with the emperor. Now Alexius saw this incident and he was afraid that other Scyths might come over to them; the Cumans might be persuaded to take their part against the Romans: feelings, as well as bridles, might change direction. He was the kind of man who quickly decides in a crisis what course will be expedient. So, without losing a moment, he ordered the ensign to take up position with the Cuman army, grasping in his hands the imperial standard. By this time the Scythian line was in complete disarray, and as each army fought at close quarters there was slaughter such as no one had ever seen before. While the Scyths, like men already forsaken by Almighty God, were being terribly massacred, their slayers grew weary, worn out with the violent, continual sword-blows, and they began to lose impetus. But Alexius, charging into the midst of the enemy, threw whole regiments into confusion, hacking at his immediate adversaries and with loud cries striking terror into those far off. However, when at mid-day he saw the sun shedding its rays directly overhead, he had the good sense to despatch scouts to round up the peasants; they were to fill wine-skins with water, load them on their own mules and bring them to the army. Their neighbours, even those not bidden to do this, followed their example, eager to refresh with water those who delivered them from the dread power of the Scyths, some with water jars, some with wine-skins, others with whatever vessel came to hand. The fighters sipped a drop of water, then returned to the fray. It was an extraordinary spectacle. A whole people, not numbered in tens of thousands, but in countless multitudes, with their women and children was utterly wiped out on that day. It was the twenty-ninth of April, a Tuesday. Hence the burlesque chanted by the Byzantines: 'All because of one day the Scyths never saw May.' When the sun was just about to set and all [12] had been

12. Anna exaggerates, as she often does, and she contradicts herself in the next breath. The Patzinaks were not annihilated. According to Bury their extermination was the work of John Comnenus in 1123. Zonaras

smitten by the sword (and I include children and mothers in this number), and many also had been taken captive, the emperor ordered the recall to be sounded and returned to the Roman camp. It was an amazing sight to anyone who recollects how in the old days our soldiers left Byzantium to fight these Scyths, buying ropes and leather thongs with which to bind their Scythian prisoners, only to be captured themselves and put in chains by the enemy. That was what happened when we fought them near Dristra, for on that occasion God humbled the pride of the Romans; but later, at the time I am now dealing with, knowing that they were fearful, that they had lost hope of safety, helpless in the face of such multitudes, He granted them the victory beyond all expectation, so that they enchained and massacred and took captive their enemies. Nor was that all, for perhaps in minor campaigns some such outcome is not uncommon; but in this case a whole people, comprising myriads of men, women and children, was blotted out in one single day.

The Cuman and Roman forces separated and as darkness fell the emperor prepared to dine. An angry Synesios appeared before him. 'What's this nonsense? What's the meaning of it?' he cried. 'Every soldier has up to thirty and more Scythian prisoners. The Cumans are near us and if the soldiers fall asleep, as they no doubt will, for they're completely worn out, and the prisoners set each other free, draw their daggers and kill them, what will happen then? I demand that you order most of the prisoners to be destroyed at once.' The emperor looked at him sternly. 'Scyths they may be,' said he, 'but human beings all the same; enemies, but worthy of pity. I don't understand what makes you talk such rubbish.' Synesios persisted and Alexius angrily dismissed him, but he did cause

---

speaks of a Patzinak settlement in Moglena in his time (twelfth century). For a modern example of this kind of confusion see Vasiliev, p. 385: 'The Patzinaks were crushed (at Levunium) and mercilessly annihilated'; p. 413: 'The Patzinaks . . . at the beginning of the reign of John . . . somewhat recovered from their defeat, crossed the Danube and invaded the Byzantine territory.' We are told that some of them afterwards fought for the emperor.

a proclamation to be made all over the camp: every weapon was to be taken from the Scyths and deposited in one place; the captives were to be securely guarded. After issuing that decree he spent the rest of the night in peace. Sometime in the middle watch the soldiers, as if acting under orders, killed nearly all of them. Whether they did this in response to some divine bidding, or how they came to do it, I cannot say. The emperor heard about it at dawn and immediately suspected Synesios. He was at once called. Alexius blamed him and uttered violent threats. 'This is your doing,' he said. Although Synesios protested on oath that he knew nothing about it, Alexius had him arrested and thrown into chains. 'Let him learn,' he said, 'how horrible it is merely to be chained, so that he never again passes such a verdict against his fellow-men.' Maybe he would have punished him further, had not the leading officers, close relatives of his, intervened with a common plea for mercy. Meanwhile most of the Cumans, fearful of the emperor's intentions (they thought he might plot some evil against themselves in the night) took up all the booty and went off in the darkness on the road to the Danube. As for Alexius, he also departed at daybreak because of the abominable stench of the corpses. He left for a place called Kala Dendra, eighteen stades from Chireni. While he was on his way there Melissenus joined him. He had not been able to take part in the battle, because he was busily engaged in sending off the multitude of new recruits. They greeted one another with mutual congratulations and naturally spent the rest of the march in conversation about the events which led up to the Scythian defeat. When he reached Kala Dendra, Alexius heard of the Cuman exodus. By the terms of the agreement made between him and the Cumans, the latter were entitled to certain articles; all these were now loaded on mules and forwarded to them. Instructions were given that the Cumans must be found quickly and the property delivered, even on the far side of the Danube if possible. To Alexius a lie, even an apparent lie, was a very serious thing and he often denounced in public the practice of lying. So much for the fugitive Cumans. The rest, who followed him, were entertained at a magnificent banquet for the remainder of the day, but he thought it wiser not to give them their due rewards at that moment; after a sleep, when the effects of the wine had worn off, with their wits fully recovered they could better appreciate what was being done. Next day they were all assembled and given payments far in excess of what was promised before. He wished to send them home, but was anxious lest they should roam widely in search of loot and so damage the townships on their route. So he took hostages. They in their turn asked for assurances of safe-conduct. He gave them Joannaces, a man of outstanding bravery and prudence; he was to arrange everything and make certain that the Cumans reached Zygum unharmed. So the emperor's affairs prospered, thanks to Divine Providence. When all was fully settled, he returned to Byzantium in the latter half of May, a triumphant victor. At this point I must leave the history of the Scyths, although I have said little in comparison with what might have been said, dipping the tip of one finger in the Adriatic Sea, as they say. As to the emperor's glorious victories, the partial setbacks at the hands of his enemies, his individual feats of valour, the events that occurred meanwhile, the way in which he adapted himself to every circumstance and by different means broke up the terrors which threatened us, not even a second Demosthenes, nor indeed the whole chorus of orators, nor all the Academy [13] and Stoa [14] united in one effort to do justice to the achievements of this emperor, would have had the ability to succeed.

Not many days after his return to the palace, the Armenian Ariebes and the Kelt Humbertopoulos, both distinguished officers and brave men, were discovered in the act of conspiring against him. They dragged into their plot quite a large number of other men of not ignoble birth. The proofs were there and the truth was freely acknowledged. They were

13. Founded by Plato *c.* 385 B.C. on the outskirts of Athens. It survived until A.D. 529, when it was finally dissolved by Justinian. Both Academy and Stoa played the role of a university in the ancient world.

14. Named after the Stoa Poikilé at Athens, it was founded as a philosophical school by Zeno of Citium *c.* 300 B.C. and lasted for at least five and a half centuries.

convicted and condemned to exile; their property was to be confiscated at once, but the emperor resolutely opposed the extreme penalty demanded by the laws. There was also talk at this time of a Cuman invasion. The news reached Alexius and information came later that Bodinus and his Dalmatians planned to violate their treaty and march on our territory. It was difficult to decide against which of the two enemies he should move first. In the end he judged it essential to deal with the Dalmatian threat first; he must seize the initiative by making as safe as possible the valleys between their lands and our own. A general conference was called, at which he explained his purpose, and as everyone agreed, he left the capital to settle affairs in the west. On his arrival soon after at Philippopolis, he received a written message from the then Archbishop of Bulgaria[15] who gave him advice about his nephew John, the Sebastocrator Isaac's son, Duke of Dyrrachium. He was accused of plotting a revolt against the emperor. All that night and all day long Alexius was worried about this news. Because of his father he was for putting off the inquiry into the affair; on the other hand, he feared that the rumour was true. John was only a youth, and the emperor knew that such persons are usually the victims of overwhelming impulses, so that he had reason to suspect some revolt. The youth could be the cause of unbearable grief to both father and uncle. It was necessary, therefore, to thwart the plan quickly by any method, for he had a very real affection for the boy. He sent for the officer who was Great Hetaeriarch at that time, Argyrus Karatzes, a Scyth by birth, but a man of wisdom, a lover of virtue and truth, and to him he entrusted two letters. One, addressed to John, read as follows: 'Having learnt of the hostile movement of barbarians through the passes, I, your emperor, have left the City of Constantine to ensure the frontiers of the Roman Empire. You are required to come in person to render account of the province under your government. You must, moreover, report to me on the situation in Dalmatia and say whether Bolkan himself respects the treaty of peace (for the information brought to me daily about him is

15. Theophylact, Archbishop of Achrida.

not satisfactory and I fear that he is an enemy and may be plotting against us). When we have a clearer picture of what is going on, we can prepare more fully to combat his schemes and after advising you on the proper course of action send you back to Illyricum. Thus, with God's aid, fighting our enemies on two fronts, we may have the victory.' Such was the gist of the letter written to John. The second, to be delivered to the magistrates of the city of Dyrrachium, ran thus: 'Since we have learnt that Bolkan is again plotting against us, we have left Byzantium to ensure the safety of the valleys between Dalmatia and our frontiers, and at the same time to obtain accurate information about the activities of the man and his people. For these reasons we deemed it necessary to summon your duke, the beloved nephew of your emperor. We have therefore sent this envoy who delivers to you this letter and have promoted him to the rank of duke. Do you yourselves receive him and in every way obey his commands.' These letters were then placed in the hands of Karatzes and he was bidden to leave. First he was to give John the letter addressed to him, and if he willingly followed its instructions, to send him on in peace. Karatzes was then to assume the government of the country until such time as John returned. If, however, John remonstrated and would not obey, Karatzes was to call for the leading citizens of Dyrrachium and secretly read to them the second letter, so that they might help in arresting John.

Isaac the sebastocrator heard of these things while in Constantinople. He left the city in haste and after a journey of two days and two nights arrived at Philippopolis. The emperor was sleeping in his imperial tent, but Isaac went in noiselessly and lay down on the second of his brother's beds, and after making a sign with his hand to the chamberlains to be quiet, he fell asleep too. When Alexius awoke, he was surprised to see his brother, but said nothing for a while and ordered the others who happened to be there to do likewise. Later Isaac woke up, to find Alexius had already risen and was watching him. They embraced and greeted one another. The emperor asked what on earth he wanted and why he had come. 'You,' he replied, 'are the reason for my visit.' 'You have worn your-self out with all this exertion to no purpose,' said Alexius. The sebastocrator had no answer to this for some time – he was deep in thought about information he expected from Dyrra-chium. (As soon as he had heard the rumours about his son, he had sent a messenger with a short note urging him to visit the emperor soon; he himself had left the capital at the same time as this envoy and was hurrying to Philippopolis to refute the accusations made against John; he intended to talk with Alexius and suggest likely reasons for them; meanwhile he would await John's arrival there.) Isaac took his leave of the emperor and withdrew to the tent specially assigned to him-self. But not long afterwards the messenger arrived from Dyrrachium in haste with the news that John was on his way. The sebastocrator, relieved at once of his suspicions, recovered his self-confidence. Full of wrath against those who had first denounced his son, he appeared before the emperor in a highly agitated frame of mind. The moment he saw him Alexius knew the cause of it, but merely asked him how he was. 'Rotten!' replied Isaac, 'And it's your fault.' The truth is that he was boiling over with uncontrollable anger, misled by a chance phrase unsupported by evidence. He went on: 'I'm not so much hurt by Your Majesty as by the calumnies of him' (pointing at Adrian). The emperor, a mild and gentle man, made no reply whatever to this, for he knew a better way to check his brother's seething rage. Both of them sat down together with Nicephorus Melissenus and certain other close relatives, and had a private conversation about the charges brought against John. When Isaac saw Melissenus and his own brother Adrian attacking his son in a sly, affected way, he was once again unable to restrain his bubbling wrath. Fixing his baleful gaze on Adrian, he threatened to tear out his beard: he would teach him not to try by brazen lies to deprive the emperor of such kinsmen. In the midst of this John arrived and was straightway ushered into the imperial tent. He heard all the accusations made against him. However, he was not subjected to any inquiry at all. The defendant stood free while the emperor addressed him: 'In consideration of your father, my brother, I cannot bring myself to listen to these rumours. Forget your cares and go on living as you have done in the past.' Now all this was said inside the imperial tent; only relatives were present, no strangers. What was said, therefore, or what maybe was intended, was hushed up, but the emperor certainly did send for his brother (Isaac the sebastocrator, I mean) and his nephew John. After a long conversation, he said to Isaac, 'Go in peace now to Constantinople and tell our mother what has passed between us. As for this young man (and here he pointed to John) I shall again, as you see, send him out to Dyrrachium, to devote his energies faithfully to the affairs of his own province.' So they parted, Isaac leaving for Byzantium on the next day, and John being sent to Dyrrachium.

However, that was not the end of the emperor's troubles. Theodore Gabras was living in Byzantium and the emperor, knowing his passionate nature and love of action, planned to drive him from the capital. He was promoted Duke of Trapezus, a city which he had previously recaptured from the Turks. This man Theodore Gabras came originally from Chaldaea. An aristocrat, he was also a famous soldier, of exceptional intelligence and bravery. Whatever he attempted, he was almost always successful, and he was victorious in all his wars. After capturing Trapezus he regarded the city as his own property and was invincible. The sebastocrator Isaac Comnenus had destined Gabras' son Gregory to marry one of his own daughters, but as both were merely children the union for the time being was only promised. Gabras entrusted Gregory to the care of the emperor, so that when the children attained the legal age, the marriage might be celebrated. He then took his leave of the emperor and returned to his own country. Not long after his wife died[16] and he married a second time. The new wife was an Alan, of noble blood. It happened that she and the sebastocrator's wife were daughters of two brothers. When this became known, since by law and the canons of the Church the union of the children was for-

16. Anna uses the more picturesque phrase 'paid the common debt of us all'.

bidden, the contract was broken. The emperor was aware of Gabras' military reputation and of the great harm he could cause. Consequently he was unwilling that Gregory, now that the marriage agreement was rescinded, should return to his father. He wished to keep him in Constantinople, for two reasons: first, he could hold him as a hostage; and, second, he might win Gabras' friendship. Thus, if Gabras did harbour some evil design, he might frustrate it. He intended to marry Gregory to one of my sisters. [17] These were the reasons why the boy's departure was delayed. The elder Gabras again visited Constantinople and ignorant of the emperor's plans looked for a secret way of recovering his son. You see, although Alexius had spoken in an enigmatic way about his idea and had partially clarified the situation, nothing as yet had been made public. Gabras, whether because he did not know, or because he had grown indifferent after the recent break-down of the former marriage contract (I do not know what the reason was), demanded that his son should be restored to him when he went back. The emperor refused. Gabras then pretended to leave him behind voluntarily and in deference to the emperor's wishes allow him (Alexius) to settle the boy's affairs. Having said farewell to Alexius he was just about to leave Byzantium when he was received hospitably by Isaac, partly because of their close relationship and also because of the intimacy to which it led. He entertained Gabras in a very beautiful house in the suburbs near the Propontis, where the church of the great martyr Phocas is built. After enjoying a magnificent banquet there, Isaac was going to the capital when Gabras asked that his son might be allowed to be with him on the next day. Isaac at once consented. However the notorious Gabras, when on the morrow he was about to be parted from the boy, begged his tutors to accompany him as far as Sosthenion, for he intended to rest there. They agreed and went with him. Then, in the same way, as he was again about to take his leave, he begged that his son should go with him to Pharos. They said 'No'. Whereupon he made excuses – a

17. Gregory Gabras in fact married Maria, Anna's younger sister, but according to Zonaras the union was annulled.

father's affection, a long separation and so on – and his persistence so touched the hearts of the tutors that they again gave in to his arguments and continued the journey. When he arrived at Pharos, though, he brought his plan into the light, took up the boy, put him on board a merchantman and committed both himself and Gregory to the waves of the Black Sea. When the emperor heard of it, without a moment's hesitation he despatched fast boats after him. The sailors were ordered to deliver a written message to Gabras and quickly take the boy with his father's consent; if he objected, Gabras must be made to realize that the emperor was his enemy. They caught up with him after leaving the city of Aeginus, near a place called by the natives Karambis. The royal message was delivered (in which Alexius disclosed that he desired the boy to marry one of my sisters) and after a long parley Gabras was persuaded to hand over his son. The marriage contract was soon ratified in the usual legal terms – nothing more – and Gregory was then entrusted to a tutor, one of the empress's retinue, the eunuch Michael. Spending his time thus in the palace he was honoured with much attention; he was given a good moral education and a thorough grounding in all aspects of military science. But as is the way with the young he absolutely refused to be subject to anyone; he felt grieved because he was not thought worthy, if you please, of the respect which he considered proper to him. At the same time he was at loggerheads with his tutor. He made up his mind therefore to abscond to his father, although he should have been grateful rather for the great care lavished on him. The plan did not turn out to be as successful as he hoped, but he actually tried it. He approached certain persons and confided in them. These gentlemen were George Dekanos, Eustathius Kamytzes and Michael the Cup-bearer, usually called *pincerna*[18] by the courtiers at the palace. They were all great warriors, among the closest associates of the emperor. One of them, Michael, went to Alexius and told him everything. Alexius was quite unable to believe the story. When Gabras insisted on hastening his escape, those who remained loyal to the emperor

18. The Latin name for 'cup-bearer'.

told him, 'Unless you confirm your plan to us by an oath, we will not help you.' He agreed, and they secretly indicated to him where the Sacred Nail [19] lay, with which the impious pierced my Saviour's side. They planned to remove it and bring it out so that Gabras might swear in the name of Him who was wounded by it. Gabras obeyed them, entered the place [20] and stealthily removed the Holy Nail. Then one of those who had before informed the emperor of the plot ran to him; 'Here's the proof,' he said, 'here is Gabras and the Nail concealed in his clothes.' At once the emperor commanded him to be led in and the relic was extracted at once from its hiding-place in his clothes. He was questioned and without hesitation admitted everything; he gave the names of his accomplices and confessed all his plans. Alexius condemned him and handed him over to the duke of Philippopolis, George Mesopotamites, with instructions to keep him under guard and in chains in the citadel. George Dekanos he sent with letters to Leo Nicerites, who was at that time Duke of Paristrion. Apparently he was to assist him in protecting the Danube area, but in fact he was sent so that Nicerites might keep an eye on him. Eustathius Kamytzes himself and the rest were banished and imprisoned.

19. There is much difficulty here. It has been pointed out that a spearpoint pierced Our Lord's side, not a nail. The Sacred Lance was believed to have been brought to Byzantium long before this time, and it is tempting to translate the Greek word by 'spear-point', but *helos* (the word used) does mean 'nail'. It would also have been easier to conceal a nail than a lance or spear or even the point of a spear. Buckler devotes two pages to the problem (467–8).

20. Probably the Church of the Pharos.

BOOK NINE

THE TURKISH WAR AND A
DALMATIAN INTERLUDE (1092–4)
– THE CONSPIRACY OF
NICEPHORUS DIOGENES (1094)

HAVING settled the affairs of John and Gregory Gabras, the emperor left Philippopolis for the valleys lying between Dalmatia and our own territory. He traversed the whole ridge of the Zygum (as the natives call it), not on horseback but on foot, for the country was very rugged, full of ravines, covered with forests and almost impassable. He visited all parts and saw everything with his own eyes, lest any point should inadvertently be left unguarded to give the enemy easy access to our side. At one place he commanded trenches to be dug, at another wooden towers to be erected; where the terrain permitted, small forts were to be built of brick or stone, and he personally fixed their size and the distance between them. At some points he ordered very tall trees to be felled at the roots and laid across the enemies' path. Then he returned to Constantinople. My words may perhaps give the reader the impression that these measures were easy, but many eye-witnesses, still alive today, bear evidence to the strain caused by that tour on Alexius. Soon after he had come back, more detailed news arrived of Tzachas. It was reported that defeat by land and sea had not diverted him from his previous intentions: he was wearing the imperial insignia, calling himself emperor and living at Smyrna as though it were an imperial residence. A fleet was being equipped to ravage the islands afresh, for Tzachas hoped to reach Byzantium itself and attain supreme power, if that were possible. Every day the emperor received confirmation of these reports. Under the circumstances, it was clearly essential that there should be no weakening, no relaxation of effort; he would have to prepare for a war throughout the remainder of the year – the time between the end of spring and the last days of winter – and then oppose Tzachas with strong forces; the man's ambitions, his plans, his hopes, his enterprises would have to be quickly and completely crushed; he must be driven out of Smyrna itself and all the other places he had seized in the past must be wrenched from his grasp. At the conclusion of winter, therefore, when the fine weather of spring began, John Ducas, the emperor's brother-in-law, was summoned from Epidamnos and appointed Grand Duke of the Fleet. He was given an army of picked landsmen and ordered to march against Tzachas by the overland route, while Constantine Dalassenus was to control the fleet and sail along the coast. The idea was that they should arrive simultaneously at Mitylene and converge on Tzachas by land and sea. The moment Ducas reached the place he had wooden towers constructed and using the town as a base of operations began the campaign in earnest. Tzachas had left his brother Galabatzes in charge of the garrison there and since he knew that the force was inadequate for battle against a man of Ducas' experience, he hurried back, formed a line and attacked. It was a stern contest, but night put an end to it. For the next three lunar months daily assaults were made on the walls of Mitylene and every day, from dawn to sunset, continual war was waged on Tzachas. It was brilliant, but for all his great efforts Ducas made no progress. The emperor was becoming annoyed and exasperated. Then one day he questioned a soldier on leave from Mitylene and having discovered that Ducas did nothing but fight and make war, he asked the man about the circumstances: 'At what time of the day do these battles with Tzachas take place?' – 'About sunrise.' – 'And which side faces the east?' – 'Ours,' said the man. At once Alexius recognized the reason for their failure and, as usual, found the remedy in a moment. He dashed off a letter to Ducas, advising him to refrain from dawn encounters with the enemy. 'Don't fight one against two,' he added, meaning of course the rays of the sun and the barbarians. He told him that when the sun had passed the meridian and was inclining to the west, that was the time to attack. This letter was put in the soldier's hands, with

many admonitions; finally, the emperor said with emphasis,
'If you make the assault as the sun goes down, you will win
at once.' Ducas received the letter from his man, and as he
never neglected the emperor's advice, even on quite ordinary
matters, when the barbarians on the next day armed for battle
in the normal way, no opponents were to be seen. (The Roman
troops were resting in accordance with Alexius' suggestion.)
The enemy gave up all hope of a clash for that day, piled their
arms and stayed where they were. But Ducas was not resting.
When it was mid-day he and all his men were ready, and as the
sun began to decline they were in battle formation. He charged
the barbarians suddenly, with tremendous war-cries and
shouts. It appears, however, that Tzachas was not caught unawares. He called his men to arms and without delay joined in
a fierce counter-attack. At the time a strong wind was blowing
and when they came to close quarters a dust cloud rose high in
the air. The barbarians had the sun glaring into their faces and
the dust, blown into their eyes by the wind, partly blinded
them; worse still, the Roman attack was more vigorous than
ever. They were defeated and fled. After that, Tzachas, unable
to support the siege any more and too weak to carry on incessant warfare, sued for peace, only asking to be allowed to sail
away unharmed to Smyrna. Ducas agreed and took as hostages
two of the leading satraps. Tzachas asked for hostages himself.
On condition that he (Tzachas) would wrong none of the
Mitylenians when he left, nor take them away with him to
Smyrna, Ducas gave him Alexander Euphorbenus and Manuel
Boutoumites, who were both excellent fighters and men of
courage. On his part he guaranteed to escort Tzachas in safety
on his return to Smyrna. Pledges were then exchanged. Thus
Ducas was relieved of anxiety, because Tzachas would inflict
no injury on the Mitylenians when he went; and Tzachas was
satisfied with the promise that the Roman fleet would not
molest him on his voyage. But the crab never learns to walk
straight – no more did Tzachas forget his evil designs. He
tried to carry off all the people of Mitylene, including the wives
and children. While this was going on, Constantine Dalassenus, the thalassocrator at that time, moored his ships off a

promontory (he had been ordered by Ducas to come, but had not yet arrived). Seeing now what Tzachas had done, he came to Ducas and begged to be allowed to fight him. Ducas, out of respect for the oath he had taken, for a time put off any decision. But Dalassenus persisted. 'You have sworn,' he said, 'but I was not present. As far as you are concerned, keep the assurances you gave inviolate. But I will strip for action against Tzachas. I wasn't present; I gave no solemn word; I know nothing of what you two agreed.' Tzachas, slipping his stern-cables, made straight for Smyrna just as he was, but Dalassenus overtook him at great speed. The attack went in at once and Tzachas was chased. The rest of the enemy fleet was caught as it was weighing anchor; Ducas captured their ships and rescued all the prisoners-of-war and other captives held by them in chains. Dalassenus took many of Tzachas' pirate vessels too and had their crews massacred, together with the rowers. Tzachas himself would also have been made prisoner, had not the rascal, foreseeing what was likely to happen, boarded one of the faster ships and thus, unseen and unsuspected, got safely away. Because he had guessed the outcome, he had Turks standing by on a headland watching for him until he reached Smyrna without mishap; if, on the other hand, the Romans should intercept him, he would steer his boat towards these Turks and so find refuge. He was successful, too, for he came to anchor there, linked up with the Turks and finally made his way back to Smyrna. Dalassenus, his conqueror, rejoined the grand duke, who was strengthening the defences of Mitylene. After Dalassenus returned home, Ducas detached an important part of the Roman fleet to liberate the places held by Tzachas (he had already gained control of a fair number of islands). Samos and certain other islands were quickly taken before Ducas himself withdrew to Constantinople.

Not many days later the emperor heard of Karykes' revolt and his seizure of Crete. It was reported also that Rhapsomates had taken Cyprus. John Ducas was sent with a large fleet against them. When the Cretans received the news that Ducas had arrived at Carpathos, which they knew was not far away,

they attacked Karykes and cruelly murdered him, after which
they handed over the island to the grand duke. Having made
sure that Crete was now in safe hands, Ducas left a force
strong enough for a garrison and sailed on to Cyprus. Immediately he landed, Kyrenia was captured at the first assault,
but Rhapsomates, inspired by the news, took up arms against
him. It was for the sake of these great preparations that he left
Nicosia and occupied the heights above Kyrenia; in that area
he pitched camp, but for the time being refused to fight –
which proved his inexperience of war and ignorance of the art
of strategy, for he should have fallen upon the Romans while
they were unready. His procrastination was not due to any
lack of preparedness on his side; it was not that he was ill-
fitted for the clash – in fact he was very well prepared and had
he wished he could have waged war at once. The truth is that
he did not want to commit himself to hostilities at all; he had
started the war as a game, like small boys at play. Feebly he
kept sending envoys to the Romans, apparently expecting to
win them over with soothing phrases. In my opinion he did
this because of his ignorance, for according to the information
I received about him, he had only recently laid hand on a
sword and spear and did not even know how to mount a
horse; if by some chance he did succeed in mounting and then
essayed to ride, he was seized with panic and vertigo. That
shows how inexperienced Rhapsomates was in soldiering.
Anyway he lost his head, whether for these reasons or because
he was completely taken by surprise when the Romans
attacked. Somewhat disheartened, he did make an attempt to
fight, but things did not go well for him, for Boutoumites
enticed away some of his soldiers and when they deserted enrolled them in his own army. On the following day Rhapsomates arranged his line and challenged Ducas to battle,
marching at a slow pace down the slope of a hill. When the two
armies were only a short distance apart, a group of Rhapsomates's men, a hundred strong, broke away, seemingly with
the intention of charging against Ducas, but they reversed
their spears and went over to the Romans. At this Rhapsomates immediately galloped off at full speed towards Nemesos,

hoping no doubt to find a ship there on which he could flee to
Syria; there he would be safe. But Manuel Boutoumites
pressed hard on him in pursuit. Disappointed of his hopes and
with Manuel close on his heels, he reached the mountain on
the other side and took refuge in the ancient Church of the
Holy Cross. Boutoumites (who had been assigned the task of
pursuing him) caught up with him near there, spared his life
and took him back to the grand duke. Later they all arrived at
Nicosia and after subduing the whole island assured its defence
as far as they could. A full account of the campaign was sent to
Alexius. He was well pleased by their efforts, but realized that
the security of the island required special attention: it was an
urgent matter. Kalliparios was forthwith appointed judge and
assessor of taxes. He was not a nobleman, but had given ample
proof of fair dealing; he was both modest and incorruptible.
Since a military governor was also needed, Eumathios
Philokales was designated stratopedarch with responsibility
for its defence by land and sea. He was given warships and
cavalry. As for Boutoumites, he returned to Ducas with
Rhapsomates and the Immortals who had rebelled with him,
and then made his way to Constantinople.

   Such were the events that took place in the islands (Cyprus
and Crete). Let us go back to Tzachas. Too warlike and enter-
prising to remain inactive, he soon attacked Smyrna and
established himself there. Again pirate vessels were thoroughly
equipped, as well as dromons, biremes, triremes and other fast
ships, with the same object in view. The news, far from dis-
couraging the emperor or causing him to delay, convinced him
that Tzachas must be speedily crushed by land and sea. So
Constantine Dalassenus was appointed thalassocrator and at
once sent to sea with all the fleet. It would also be expedient,
Alexius thought, to stir up trouble for him with the sultan.
A letter was therefore sent, reading as follows: 'Most Illustrious Sultan Kilij Arslan, you know that the dignity of sultan
is yours by right of inheritance. But your kinsman Tzachas,
although apparently preparing for war against the Roman
Empire (for he calls himself emperor) is in reality using this as
a pretext – an obvious pretext, for he is a man of experience

and he knows perfectly well that the Roman Empire is not for him: it would be absolutely beyond his power to seize a throne so exalted. The whole mischievous plan is directed against you. If you are wise, therefore, you will not endure this. There is no need for despair, however, but rather for vigilance; otherwise you will be driven from your sultanate. For my part, I will with God's help expel him from Roman territory and as I care for your interests, I would advise you to consider your own authority and power, and quickly bring him to heel, by peaceful means or, if he refuses, by the sword.' After the emperor had taken these precautions Tzachas appeared with an army on the landward side of Abydos and laid siege to the place with helepoleis and all kinds of rock-throwing engines. He could do no more, for his pirate ships, not yet ready for action, were not with him. Dalassenus, who loved a fight and was in fact a very courageous man, marched with all his forces along the Abydos road. The Sultan Kilij Arslan also set out on the road to Tzachas with his army immediately after receiving the emperor's message. He was eager for action – like all barbarians, always lusting after massacre and war. When the sultan drew near, Tzachas saw himself menaced by land and sea; he had no ships, because his navy was still unseaworthy; his land forces were outnumbered by the Romans and the army of his kinsman Kilij Arslan; his position was desperate. He was afraid, too, of the inhabitants of Abydos, as well as the garrison. Not unnaturally, he decided that it was better to approach the sultan, knowing nothing himself of the emperor's intrigue with him. The sultan received him graciously with a pleasant smile, and when his table was laid ready in the usual way, he shared it with Tzachas at dinner and compelled him to drink more heavily than he should have done. Then, seeing him in a fuddled state, he drew his sword and thrust it into his side. Tzachas fell dead on the spot. The sultan then made overtures to the emperor for peace in the future and his proposals met with success, for Alexius consented and a treaty was concluded in the normal way. Thus peace was restored to the maritime provinces.

However, before he could find relief from these great anxieties or purge away the ill effects caused by Tzachas (for even if Tzachas was not always present in person, yet he played his part and lent aid in all the decisions and plans), he was hurried into fresh troubles. Bolkan, two solar years after the destruction of the Scyths, crossed his own frontiers and ravaged the neighbouring towns and districts. He even got as far as Lipenium, which he deliberately burnt down. This Bolkan was ruler of all Dalmatia, a fine orator and a man of action. The emperor was informed of his doings and decided that he must be punished. Collecting a strong army he marched against the Serbs on the direct route to Lipenium, a small fortified post lying at the foot of the Zygum (which separates Dalmatia from Roman territory). He intended, if he had the opportunity, to meet Bolkan[1] in battle and, provided that God gave him the victory, to rebuild Lipenium and all the other places; the *status quo* would be restored. Bolkan, when he heard of the emperor's arrival, left for Sphentzanium, a tiny fort north of the Zygum lying in the no-man's-land between Roman and Dalmatian territory. After Alexius reached Skopia, however, Bolkan sent ambassadors to arrange peace terms. At the same time he protested that he himself was not responsible for the evil things that had occurred; he laid all the blame on the Roman governors. 'Unwilling to remain inside their own borders,' he said, 'they make repeated raids and have brought no little trouble on Serbia. As far as I am concerned, nothing of this kind will happen again, for I will go home, send members of my own family as hostages to Your Majesty, and never cross the boundaries of my land in the future.' Alexius accepted this explanation and after leaving men behind to rebuild the ruined cities and take hostages, he went back to Constantinople. But Bolkan, despite the demand for hostages, did not hand them over. Day after day he procrastinated and when less than twelve months had passed he again invaded Roman territory. He received several letters from the emperor reminding him of the treaty and promises made by him, but he was still unwilling to fulfil his obligations. Accordingly, the

1. Referred to as Vukan, the Župan (Prince) of Rascia, by Ostrogorsky.

emperor summoned John[2] and sent him with a powerful army
to deal with the man. John had no experience in war and like
all young men was impatient to get at the enemy. He crossed
the river which flows past Lipenium and pitched camp by the
foothills of the Zygum opposite Sphentzanium. His movements were noted by the enemy, who once again inquired
about terms of peace. Bolkan went on to promise that the
hostages would be delivered and in future peace with the
Romans would be scrupulously respected. In fact, these were
nothing more than empty pledges; he was arming to attack us
unawares. While Bolkan was on the march, a monk came on
ahead and warned John of his plot; he told him emphatically
that the enemy was already near. John angrily dismissed him,
calling him a liar and a humbug. But facts soon proved that
the monk was right, for during the night Bolkan did attack and
many of the Romans were massacred in their tents; many fled
in haste and being caught up in the eddies of the river below
were drowned. The more steadfast made for John's tent and
after some hard fighting managed to save it. Most of the
Roman army by then had disappeared. Bolkan rallied his own
men, climbed to the ridge of the Zygum and established himself in Sphentzanium. John's staff advised him to recross the
river, for they were too few to fight it out with Bolkan. He
took their advice and headquarters was moved to Lipenium,
about twelve stades further on. After such heavy casualties
more resistance would have been impossible. So he set out on
the road to the capital. His adversary, much encouraged
because no one had been left behind to oppose him, proceeded
to plunder the surrounding countryside and its towns. He
demolished the environs of Skopia completely and even burnt
some part of it. Not content with that, he went on to Polobos
and as far as Branea, destroying everything and carrying off
vast quantities of booty. He then returned to his own country.

The situation was intolerable and the emperor, realizing
this, immediately equipped another expedition; unlike
Alexander, who waited for the high-pitched strain of the
'Orthian' mode, he needed no urging from the flute-player

2. Son of his brother the sebastocrator. (A.C.)

Timotheus.[3] So he armed himself and all other available troops in the city, then marched quickly by the direct route to Dalmatia. His object was two-fold: to rebuild and restore to their former condition the ruined forts, and to take strong reprisals for Bolkan's evil deeds. He started from the capital, reached Daphnutium, an ancient city forty stades away, and waited there for those of his relatives who had not yet arrived. On the following day Nicephorus Diogenes came, in a thoroughly bad mood and very supercilious, but as usual putting on a cheerful expression; the sly fox pretended that he was behaving sincerely in his dealings with the emperor. How-ever, he had his tent pitched, not at the customary distance from Alexius' sleeping-quarters, but close to the passage lead-ing up to it. When Manuel Philokales observed this, he was like a man struck by lightning and stood there dumbfounded (for he was not unaware of Diogenes' schemes). With great difficulty he recovered his presence of mind and lost no time in reporting to the emperor. 'It seems to me,' he said, 'that there is something not straight here. I am afraid that an attempt may be made on Your Majesty's life in the night. Anyway, I will have a talk with him and see that he moves.' But Alexius, imperturbable as ever, would not allow him to interfere. Philokales became more insistent. 'Leave him alone,' said Alexius. 'We must not afford him a pretext against me. He alone must be responsible, before God and man, for the evil he plans.' Philokales left the tent in anger, wringing his hands and declaring that the emperor had grown foolish. Not long after, when Alexius and the empress were peacefully asleep, about the middle watch of the night, Diogenes rose, came to the threshold of their tent and stood there, with a sword con-cealed under his arm. (When the emperor was sleeping, the doors were not fastened nor was a guard on duty outside.) Such was the position now, but Nicephorus was deterred from the crime at that moment by some divine force. He caught sight of the little girl who was fanning them and driving away mosquitoes; at once 'a trembling seized on his limbs and a pale hue spread over his cheeks',[4] as the poet says. He put off the

3. See Preface, p. 21, n. 10.   4. Homer, *Iliad* iii, 34–5.

assassination to the next day. Unceasingly he plotted the murder, although he had no excuse for it, but his schemes were by no means undetected: the little maid soon went to the emperor and told him what had happened. In the morning he left that place and began the day's march, but pretended to know nothing; in fact, though, enough precautions were taken to ensure his safety without at the same time giving Nicephorus any reasonable cause for complaint. When he arrived in the area of Serres, Constantine Ducas the porphyrogenitus, who was accompanying the emperor, invited him to stay on his personal estate, a delightful place with a good supply of cold, drinkable water and apartments big enough to receive an emperor as guest. Its name was Pentegostis. Alexius accepted the invitation and stayed there. He wanted to leave on the following day, but the porphyrogenitus would not hear of it: he begged him to stay on, at least until he had recovered from the fatigue of his march and washed off the dust of travel in the bath. A costly banquet had in fact already been prepared in his honour. Once more Alexius let himself be persuaded. Nicephorus Diogenes, still lusting for power, carefully awaited the chance to kill the emperor with his own hands and when he heard that Alexius had washed and left the bath, girded on a short sword and went into the house, as if he were returning from the chase in the usual way. Taticius saw him and because he had known for a long time what Nicephorus was planning, pushed him away. 'What's the meaning of this? Why do you come here in this unmannerly fashion? – and wearing a sword? This is the bath-hour, not the time for marching or hunting or battle.' So Nicephorus went and his opportunity was lost. He realized that he was now a marked man (conscience is a terrible accuser) and decided to save his skin by running away to the estates of the Empress Maria in Christopolis, either to Pernikos or Petritzos;[5] afterwards he could restore his fortunes as circumstances permitted. Maria had taken a personal interest in him, because he was the brother of her husband, the former Emperor Michael Ducas,

5. We know from Zonaras that she owned two convents and a palace at least.

on the mother's side, though they had different fathers. On the third day Alexius left Pentegostis, but Constantine remained there to rest; the emperor was concerned for the young man's delicate constitution – he was unused to military expeditions and this was his first travel abroad. He was also his mother's only son and a particular favourite of the emperor, who allowed him to enjoy all the rest he needed with her. He loved him deeply, as if he were really his own son.

In order to avoid confusion at this point in the history, I will give an account of Nicephorus Diogenes' career from its very beginning. The elevation of his father Romanus to the imperial throne and the manner of his downfall have been described by several historians[6] and anyone who wishes to read about him will find the details in their works. In any case Romanus died when Leo and Nicephorus were still children. At the outset of his reign Alexius found them reduced to the status of ordinary citizens, for when Michael ascended the throne, although he was their brother, he deprived them of the red sandals, took away their diadems and exiled them with their mother (the Empress Eudocia) in the monastery of Cyperoudes. Alexius thought it right to give them every consideration, partly in pity for their sufferings, partly because they were exceptionally handsome and strong, on the threshold of manhood, tall and finely proportioned, with all the promise of youth; their very appearance, to anyone not blinded by prejudice, manifested a spirit that was both passionate and brave. They were like lion cubs. Apart from these qualities (for Alexius was not the man to judge anyone superficially, being neither blind to the truth nor a prey to base passions, but the kind of person who weighs facts in the fair balance of his own conscience) he took into account the degradation they had endured. He befriended them as though they were his own sons. He never lost a chance to speak well of them, to promote their welfare and provide for their future, although the envious continually attacked them. Many people, indeed, tried to provoke him to enmity against the young men,

6. In particular Michael Psellus, whose account in the *Chronographia* is most vivid and interesting.

but that made him more than ever determined to help them in
every way; invariably he had a smile for them, apparently
taking a real pride in their achievements, and always gave
advice which looked to their best interests. Another would
probably have regarded them with suspicion and made it his
business to put power out of their reach completely, but this
emperor made light of the charges brought by many against
Leo and Nicephorus. He had a deep affection for both of them
and for their mother Eudocia; she was thought worthy of
gifts and lacked no honour befitting an empress. Nicephorus
himself was made governor of the island of Cyprus, which he
could use as his own private property. Such were the arrangements of Alexius. As to Leo, he was a good-hearted man, of a
generous disposition, conscious of the emperor's benevolent
attitude to himself and his brother, and grateful for his lot. He
accepted the old saying,[7] 'Sparta is your inheritance; glorify
her'. He was content to remain as he was. But Nicephorus was
an ill-tempered, acrimonious fellow, cherishing secret designs
against the emperor, incessantly scheming for power; nevertheless, his plan remained a secret. However, when the business was really afoot, he spoke more freely about it to some
of his companions; a great many people got to hear of it and
through them it reached the ears of the emperor. He reacted
in rather a novel way: he summoned them at appropriate
moments and although he did not disclose what he had
heard, he gave them shrewd advice and offered useful suggestions. The more he got to know of the conspiracy, the
more liberal his treatment of them became; it was in this way
that he hoped to make progress. But 'the Ethiopian cannot
make himself white'.[8] Nicephorus remained what he was and
communicated infection to all with whom he came in contact,
winning over some by oaths, others by promises. He was not
so much concerned with the ordinary soldiers, for they already favoured him to a man, but he devoted all his energies

7. Quoted from a fragment of Euripides.
8. Reminiscent of Jeremiah xiii, 23: 'Can the Ethiopian change his
skin or the leopard his spots?' But the sentiment was common in the
ancient world.

to canvassing the aristocracy, paying special attention to the superior officers and leading members of the senate. He had a mind sharper than a two-edged sword, but he was extremely fickle – except in one respect: he displayed uncompromising resolution in his quest for power. He was a charming conversationalist, pleasant in his social life, sometimes wearing a cloak of modesty to deceive, occasionally showing the spirit of a lion. He was physically strong and boasted that he rivalled the Giants; a broad-chested, blond man, a head taller than others of his generation. People who saw him playing polo on horseback, shooting an arrow or brandishing a spear at full gallop, stood open-mouthed, almost rooted to the spot, thinking they were watching a genius never seen before. It was this, more than anything else, that won him the favour of the people. His advance to the coveted goal prospered so well that he even beguiled the husband of the emperor's sister, Michael Taronites, who had been honoured with the title of pan-hypersebastos.

But we must return to the point at which we digressed and follow the chain of events. When he discovered Diogenes' conspiracy, the emperor reviewed the whole situation; he recalled his treatment of the brothers from the beginning of his reign, the kindness and care he had lavished on them for so many years. None of this had changed Nicephorus for the better – a very depressing thought. The consideration of all these events was indeed immensely disturbing – Nicephorus' second attempt after an initial failure, his repulse by Taticius, the knowledge that he was sharpening his murderous weapon, eager to stain his hands with innocent blood, still lying in wait, watching by night for an opportunity to commit his crime and now openly pursuing it. He did not want to punish Diogenes in any way because he was very fond of him; he had in fact an extraordinary affection for the man. But when he summed it all up, realizing how far the evil might go and knowing that imminent danger threatened his own life, he was terribly worried. After weighing up all the evidence, he decided that he must be arrested. Nicephorus was hurrying on preparations for his flight (according to plan) and as he wished to take the road to Christopolis by night, in the evening he sent a messenger to Constantine Porphyrogenitus to beg the loan of the racehorse given to him by the emperor. Constantine refused, saying that he could not let a gift of such value from the emperor go to someone else – he had only received it that very day. In the morning Alexius set out on the day's march and Diogenes followed him with the rest. God, who frustrates the plans and brings to naught the designs of whole peoples, confounded this man too, for after debating in his mind the question of flight, he put it off from hour to hour. Such are the judgements of God. So Diogenes encamped near Serres where the emperor also was. As usual he imagined that he was already a marked man and became fearful of the future. At this point Alexius called for his brother Adrian, the Great Domestic. It was the evening on which honour is paid to the memory of the great martyr Theodore.[9] Alexius again communicated to him the facts about Diogenes (Adrian knew them before this): he spoke of Diogenes' armed intrusion into the house, his repulse from the door, his eagerness to commit even now, if possible, the deed he had so long planned. Then he instructed Adrian to invite him to his own tent, to persuade him with kind words and all manner of promises to reveal the whole plot; he was to guarantee him an amnesty, with full forgiveness for his crimes in the future, if only he would uncover everything, including the names of all his accomplices. Adrian was full of despair, but carried out the order. He used threats, he made promises, he gave advice, but he failed completely to induce Diogenes to reveal even one of his plans. Thereupon the Great Domestic grew angry and worried, having a good idea of the dangers to which he was being exposed. Diogenes had in the past chosen him as husband for the youngest of his step-sisters, and because of this relationship he persisted, even entreating him with tears, but there was no success whatever, despite pathetic reminiscences of the past. Adrian reminded him how one day the emperor was playing polo in the riding-school of the Great Palace when a barbarian of mixed Armeno-Turkish descent approached

9. 8 February 1094.

him with a sword hidden in his clothes. He saw that the emperor had been left by the other players when he drew rein to give his panting horse a rest; he fell on his knees and pretended to ask a favour. Alexius immediately stopped his horse, turned round and inquired what he wanted. The murderer – for that is what he was, rather than a suppliant – thrust his hand under his clothes, grasped his sword and tried to draw it from the scabbard, but it would not budge. Again and again he tugged at it while mouthing out a series of imaginary requests, then in desperation threw himself to the ground and lay there begging for mercy. The emperor turned his horse round towards him and asked for what he was begging forgiveness. The barbarian then showed him the sword still in its scabbard; at the same time he beat his breast and in his distress cried in a loud voice: 'Now I know that you are a true servant of God; now I have seen with my own eyes the Almighty protecting you. For I got ready this sword here to murder you; I brought it from home and here I am, prepared to plunge it into your heart. Once, twice, then once again I tugged at it, but it wouldn't yield to force.' The emperor meanwhile stood there in the same position, unafraid, as though he had not heard anything unusual, but all the others ran up to him in haste, some to hear what was being said, others in alarm. The more loyal men tried to tear the barbarian in pieces and would have done it too, if Alexius had not by signs and gestures and frequent rebukes prevented them. After that the assassin was granted a full pardon on the spot, and not only forgiveness, but magnificent presents; besides, he was allowed to enjoy his freedom. At that many exclaimed that the murderer should be expelled from the capital. They became importunate, but all to no purpose. 'Unless the Lord guards the city,' said Alexius, 'the sentinels keep vigil in vain. In future, then, we must pray to God and implore Him to grant us safety and protection.' Some whispered that the attempt on his life had been made with the connivance of Diogenes. The emperor himself refused altogether to listen to these rumours; in fact, he became more angry than ever, so tolerant of Diogenes that he feigned ignorance until the dagger-point was almost at his throat. So much for that incident. The Great Domestic reminded Diogenes of it, but made no impression on him, so he went to Alexius and told him of the man's stubbornness. 'Again and again I've begged him to speak,' he said, 'but he's absolutely determined to say nothing.'

The emperor called for Mouzakes and ordered him with other armed men to remove Diogenes from the Great Domestic's tent to his own and there detain him in safe custody, but without putting him in chains or ill-treating him in any way. The order was carried out without delay. All through the night Mouzakes pleaded with Diogenes and warned him, but his efforts failed; worse, he found the man's behaviour really offensive. In the end he became very angry and was driven to exceed the emperor's commission, for he thought fit to torture him. The process had hardly begun when Diogenes, incapable of resisting even the preliminaries, declared that he would admit everything. He was at once set free from his chains and a secretary was called, pen in hand.[10] Diogenes confessed all, including the attempted murder. In the morning Mouzakes collected the written confession, as well as other documents found when he searched him. They were addressed to Diogenes by certain people and from them it was clear that the Empress Maria knew of the conspiracy, but strongly disapproved of the plan to murder the emperor; she was obviously trying hard to dissuade him, not merely from the crime, but from the very thought of it. Mouzakes conveyed these papers to Alexius, who read them privately and when he discovered the names of several suspects mentioned in them – they were all persons of distinction – he found himself in a difficult situation. Diogenes had not cared much about the rank and file – to them he had long been a hero and they gazed on him with open-mouthed admiration – but he had been anxious to conciliate all leaders of the army and prominent civilians. The emperor decided that the references to the Empress Maria should remain secret, although he carefully

10. The man's name was Gregory Kamateros, recently appointed as under-secretary to the emperor. (A.C.)

examined them. He pretended to know nothing because of the faith he had in her and a bond of sympathy which he had felt even before his accession to the throne. A general rumour was spread that Constantine Porphyrogenitus, her son, had informed Alexius of the plot, although this was not so, for the facts were supplied piecemeal by the accomplices themselves. After Diogenes had been convicted, put in chains and exiled, those ringleaders who had not been arrested, knowing that they were under suspicion, showed every sign of alarm as they considered the next step. The emperor's friends noted their perturbation, but seemed themselves to be in difficulties. Alexius, they knew, was in extreme peril; his supporters were now limited to a handful of men and his life was in danger. He too was seriously troubled when he cast his mind over all these events – the numerous attempts by Diogenes to kill him, frustrated by Divine Power, and the fact that Diogenes had tried to assassinate him with his own hands. There was much to worry him. Time after time he altered his plans as some new idea occurred to him. He realized that both civilians and military had been thoroughly corrupted by the seductions of Diogenes; he was aware too that his own forces were inadequate to guard so many prisoners; he was certainly unwilling to mutilate a great host of people. In the end he banished Diogenes and Cecaumenus Catacalon, the principal conspirators, to Caesaropolis, to be kept in chains there and under guard. No further punishment was contemplated for the moment, although everyone advised him to have them mutilated. Alexius would not agree, for he had a great love for Diogenes; he was as concerned as ever for his welfare. Michael Taronites, his sister's husband, was also sent into exile and . . . Their property was confiscated. As for the others, he judged the safe course would be not to examine them at all, but rather to soften their hearts by a show of mercy. In the evening therefore each of the exiles heard the place allotted to him. Diogenes was to go to Caesaropolis; of the rest, none left his own district: all remained where they were.

In the midst of this crisis the emperor decided to call a general meeting for the next day and effect his plan. All his relatives, by blood or marriage, were present (those, that is, who were really devoted to him) and all the family servants. They were tough men, quick to gauge the outcome, with enough shrewdness to achieve in the shortest possible time the most profitable result. They were afraid that when the crowd assembled on the following day some men might rush against the emperor and cut him to pieces on the throne.[11] There was only one way to prevent this – to dash the people's hopes, which were centred on Diogenes, by spreading a rumour that he had been secretly blinded. Men were collected and sent to proclaim this news in all directions privately, though as yet Alexius had no inkling of the idea at all. However bare the rumour was at the time, it succeeded in its purpose, as the history will demonstrate later on. When the sun peeped over the horizon and leapt into the sky in glory, all those members of the imperial retinue not infected with Diogenes' pollution, as well as the soldiers who had long served as the emperor's bodyguard led the procession to his tent; some wore swords, others carried spears, others had heavy iron axes on their shoulders. At some distance from the throne they arranged themselves in a crescent-shaped formation, embracing him as it were in outstretched arms. They were all moved by anger and if they did not actually work on their swords, they were certainly worked up themselves.[12] Near the throne on either side stood the emperor's relatives, and to right and left were grouped the armour-bearers. Alexius, looking formidable, took his seat, dressed rather as a soldier than an emperor.[13] Because he was not a tall man, he did not tower above the rest, but it was an impressive sight, for gold overlaid his throne and there was gold above his head. He was frowning and the ordeal had brought an unusual tinge of red

11. They often carried daggers under their clothes, like the soldier who approached him in the guise of a suppliant when he was playing polo. (A.C.)

12. A difficult phrase. Anna's zeugma is almost impossible in English. Dawes has 'if they did not whet their swords, they certainly did their souls'.

13. The tent scene here owes something to Psellus (*Chronographia* vii, 20 ff.). For plagiarism in general see Buckler, p. 191–3.

to his cheeks; his eyes, fixed in concentration, gave a hint of the cares that beset him. Everybody hurried to the tent, all in a state of alarm and almost on the point of collapse through fear, some pricked by an evil conscience (more effectively than by any weapon), others dreading unwarranted suspicion. Not a sound was heard from any of them as they stood with beating hearts, their eyes fixed on the officer in charge by the tent's door (Taticius, a clever orator and powerful man of action). With a glance the emperor signalled to him that the crowd was to be admitted. He obeyed and they, frightened, came in with eyes averted and walking slowly. When they had been marshalled in lines, they waited anxiously, each fearful lest his own last moment was at hand. The emperor himself was not altogether confident (humanly speaking, for he had committed his cause entirely to God). He was apprehensive lest in a gathering so heterogeneous there might be some who planned another horrible and unforeseen crime. Reassured by firm logic and at last ready for the struggle he began to harangue them. They meanwhile were as silent as fish, as if their tongues had been cut out. 'You know,' he said, 'that Diogenes has never suffered ill at my hands. It was not I who deprived his father of this Empire, but another. Nor have I been the cause of evil or pain of any sort so far as he is concerned. Moreover, when, by the will of God alone, I became ruler of the Empire not only did I give my protection equally to him and his brother Leo, but I loved them and treated them as my own sons. Every time that Nicephorus was caught plotting against me I forgave him, and though he never mended his ways, I bore with him and concealed most of his offences, knowing the general detestation they would cause for the brothers. Yet none of my favours has succeeded in altering his perfidy. Indeed, by way of gratitude he sentenced me to death.' At these words they all shouted that they would not wish to see anyone else in his place on the imperial throne; most of them did not mean it, but they flattered, hoping thereby to escape the immediate danger. Alexius seized on the opportunity and proclaimed a general amnesty for the majority of them, since those responsible for the plot had been sentenced to banishment. Thereupon a great hubbub arose, such as none of those present there had ever heard before and have never heard since (at least, they say so); some praised the emperor and marvelled at his kindness and forbearance, while others abused the exiles, insisting that they should be punished by death. Such is the way of men – today they cheer, escort, treat with honour, but once they see the fortunes of life reversed, they act in the opposite manner, without a blush. The emperor silenced them with a gesture and continued. 'There is no need for commotion, nor must you confuse the issue. As far as I am concerned, as I said, I have granted a general amnesty, and I shall treat you just as I did before.' While he was pardoning them, certain men who had made the infamous decision sent emissaries, without the emperor's knowledge, to blind Diogenes. The same decision was made in respect of Cecaumenus Catacalon, because he had shared responsibility with him. It was the day on which the memory of the Great Apostles is honoured.[14] These events have been the subject of controversy ever since. Whether Alexius was informed of the plan by them and then gave his consent, or was himself the author of the whole idea, God alone knows. For my own part, I have been unable so far to discover anything for certain.

Such were the troubles that befell the emperor because of Diogenes. He was rescued from instant peril contrary to all expectations by the invincible hand of the Lord on High. Despite all this, he did not lose his nerve. Instead, he drove straight for Dalmatia. When Bolkan learnt of Alexius's arrival at Lipenium and saw with his own eyes that he had occupied the place, he despatched envoys without delay to offer terms of peace, promising at the same time to deliver the hostages he had agreed to hand over before, and to cease hostilities in the future. The Roman battle lines, their famous formation and their military equipment were more than he could bear to look upon. Alexius gladly accepted the proposal, for he was weary and loathed civil war. The men were Dalmatians, but they were still Christians. Soon Bolkan presented himself confidently before the emperor, accompanied

14. Peter and Paul. 29 June 1094.

by his kinsmen and the leading župans.[15] The hostages (his
own nephews Uresis and Stephen Bolkan, with others to
the total of twenty) were promptly handed over. The truth is,
of course, that he could not make any other arrangements for
the future. Thus Alexius had settled by peaceful means all that
is normally accomplished by war and strife. He returned to
Constantinople. In spite of all he still cared much for Diogenes. Often he was seen in tears and heard sighing deeply
because of the young man's misfortunes. He displayed great
friendship for him and in his anxiety to relieve Diogenes'
sufferings installed him again in most of his confiscated property. Frantic with pain and reluctant to live in the great city,
Diogenes found satisfaction on his own estates, devoting all
his energies to the study of ancient literature, read to him by
others. Deprived of his own sight, he used the eyes of
strangers for his reading. He was a man of such extraordinary
ability that, blinded though he was, he could readily comprehend things which sighted people found hard to understand.
Later he covered the whole syllabus of education and even
studied the celebrated geometry (an unprecedented feat) by
getting a philosopher he had met to prepare the figures in
relief. By touching these with his hands he acquired knowledge of all the geometrical theorems and figures. Thus he
rivalled Didymus,[16] who by sheer intellectual power and
despite his blindness attained the highest standards in the arts
of geometry and music; unfortunately after this achievement
Didymus was driven into an absurd heresy, his mind darkened
by conceit as his eyes were by disease. Everyone who hears
this about Diogenes is astonished, but I myself have seen the
man and marvelled at him as he talked about these things. As I
too am not altogether untrained in such matters, I recognized
in him an accurate understanding of the theorems. Yet,
busied as he was with literary studies, he would not forget his

15. A high-ranking official.
16. Didymus of Alexandria wrote in the fourth century and some of
his treatises are preserved in the Latin translation of St Jerome. He was
condemned for heresy, in company with Origen and Evagrius, apparently
for supporting the theory of metempsychosis.

old antipathy, but to the end maintained that smouldering lust for power. However, he confided his secret once more to certain individuals, and one of them went to Alexius and told of his plans. Diogenes was summoned and questioned about the plot and his accomplices. He immediately confessed everything and was immediately forgiven.

BOOK TEN

ANOTHER HERESY – THE CUMAN WAR – THE FIRST CRUSADE (1094–7)

NOT long after the doctrine of Italus had been condemned the infamous Nilus[1] appeared, descending on the Church like some evil flood, to the great consternation of all. Many were swept away in the currents of Nilus' heresy, in fact, for he put on a good show of virtue. Where he came from I know not, but for a time he frequented the capital, living in obscurity alone, no doubt, with God and himself. All his time was devoted to the study of Holy Scripture. He had never been initiated into Hellenic culture, nor had he any tutor to give him an elementary insight into the deeper meaning of the Bible. The result was that he examined the works of the Saints, but as he was completely devoid of a training in logic, his interpretation of Scripture went astray. However, he did attract a not inconsiderable band of adherents and wormed his way into great houses as a self-appointed teacher, partly because of his own apparent virtue and austere way of life, partly maybe because of the knowledge with which he was supposed to be secretly endowed. Nilus' ignorance led him to misapprehend the union of the human and divine natures in the one Person[2] of Christ (as taught in our doctrine). He could

1. In this episode Anna uses several theological terms well known to the Byzantines of her time, but unintelligible to the ordinary reader of today. Thus a rather fuller translation has been preferred here.

2. Anna's word is *hypostasis*, defined in Murray's Dictionary as 'personality, personal existence, person'; thus Christ has one *hypostasis*, but two natures (human and divine) which are united (not, as Nestorius taught, *conjoined*, nor *commingled* according to the doctrine of Eutyches). The orthodox view was that the one Person of Christ was composed of Godhead and Manhood, each retaining its own nature. Just as iron when heated still remains iron, so the human element in Christ when united in His one Person with the divine still retained its humanity. The theology of this Mystery was the subject of the great Maximus' works, which Anna tells us were so avidly read by her mother Irene – hence maybe her own

not clearly understand the meaning of 'union', nor had he any idea at all of the meaning of 'person', nor had he learnt from holy men how the flesh assumed by Our Lord was made divine. Thus he erred far from the truth and in his delusion supposed that His flesh changed its nature and thus became divine. The heresy did not escape the emperor's notice, and when he realized what was going on he lost no time in applying a remedy. The man was called into his presence; his boldness and ignorance were severely censured. On several points he was refuted and Alexius taught him clearly the meaning of the union of divine and human in the Person of the Word; he set before him the interpretation of the two natures, how they were united as one indivisible Person and how the human flesh assumed by Christ was made divine by the grace from above. But Nilus clung rigidly to his own false teaching and was quite prepared to undergo any ill-treatment – torture, imprisonment, mutilation – rather than give up his doctrine that the human flesh altered its nature. At that time there were in the capital many Armenians; [3] their wickedness received a new impetus when Nilus held frequent conferences with the notorious Arsaces and Tigranes. By his teachings Nilus incited them to further impiety. Later, when the emperor perceived that this evil was corrupting many souls; that Nilus and the Armenians were equally involved, proclaiming openly on all occasions that the human part of Christ had been deified in nature; that the pronouncements of the holy fathers on this subject were being put aside; and that the doctrine of the two natures united in one Person was being almost unrecognized, he decided to counteract the violent course of the heresy. So the leading members of the Church were brought together with the idea of holding a public synod to debate the matter. At this meeting the full complement of bishops was present, together with the patriarch Nicolas. Nilus, accompanied by the Armenians, appeared before them and his doctrines were

---

interest. For a close study of the pitfalls waiting for heretics like Nilus see Buckler, pp. 324 ff.

3. It is clear from other references in the *Alexiad* that Anna had no liking for Armenians as a race.

revealed. In a clear voice he expounded and vigorously defended them at greater length than before. In the end the synod, in order to save many souls from this corrupt teaching, imposed on Nilus an eternal anathema and proclaimed even more lucidly the union of the two natures according to the tradition of the saints. Afterwards (to be more exact, about this same time) Blachernites was also condemned for holding irreverent views contrary to Church teaching, although he was an ordained priest. He had in fact had dealings with the Enthusiasts[4] and infected with their impurity was deceiving many, undermining great houses in the capital and transmitting his evil dogma. On several occasions he was urgently summoned by the emperor, who personally instructed him, but since he absolutely refused to abandon his particular brand of heresy he too was brought before the Church. The bishops examined his case in more detail and when they recognized the incorrigibility of the man, an eternal anathema was put on him and his teachings also.

In this way the emperor like a good helmsman guided his craft safely through constant battering of the waves. Scarcely had he cleansed himself of the thick layers of brine (that is, set in good order the affairs of Church and State), when he was called upon to embark on fresh seas of tribulation. Indeed, there was a never-ending succession of woes – an ocean of trouble, as it were – so that he was allowed no breathing-space, no chance whatever to rest. Our outline of a few of his deeds in this crisis (for it was an outline and no full description) might well be compared to a tiny drop from the whole Adriatic Sea, for he braved all tempests, all storms, till he brought the ship of state to a calm anchorage with a following breeze. Truly neither the fine voice of Demosthenes, nor Polemo's[5] impassioned style, nor all the Muses of Homer could do justice to his exploits. I myself would go further and say that even Plato himself, even the sum total of Porch[6] and

4. The Enthusiasts may be identified with the Massalians, from whom the Bogomile heresy was derived.
5. Polemo of Laodicea (A.D. 88–145) was a noted sophist.
6. Better known as the Stoa Poikile which gave its name to the Stoics. The Academy was founded by Plato at Athens *c.* 385 B.C.

Academy acting in unison would have proved unequal to the task of describing the emperor's spirit, for before the storms had time to die down and the tempests had done their worst, before the multiple wars had ended, he was faced with another trial as bad as any before it. A man, not a member of the aristocracy, but a person of humble origin, an ordinary soldier, announced that he was the son of the Emperor Diogenes – although that son had been killed long ago when Isaac Comnenus, the emperor's own brother, fought against the Turks near Antioch.[7] Many people in vain tried to gag him (he was too determined). He had come from the east, penniless and clad in goat's skin, a thorough-going rascal full of twists and turns, and made his rounds in the city, street by street and quarter by quarter, boasting about himself and saying that he was the famous Leo,[8] son of the former emperor Diogenes who was reported to have died of an arrow-wound at Antioch. At any rate the fellow brought Leo to life again and boldly adopted his name. It was obvious that his aim was imperial power. He was winning support among the more irresponsible element of the people. This was a new danger to add to the emperor's difficulties. Fortune, one might say, was composing a new tragic play on this ill-starred fellow for the emperor's viewing. Just as gourmets, I understand, after eating their fill have honey-cakes brought on as dessert, so now it was the destiny of the Roman people, after triumphing over many evils and being sated with disaster, to tantalize their emperor with pretenders to the throne. All these rumours were treated with contempt by Alexius, but when this scum of the army persisted in his folly, losing no opportunity to spread these stories in every street and on every highway in the city, the matter came to the ears of Theodora, the emperor's sister, who was the widow of Diogenes' murdered son. This rubbish was m re than she could bear; she was very annoyed. After

7. How he met his end, if anyone wishes to know the details, can be read in the pages of the illustrious Caesar's book. (A.C.)

8. We know from Nicephorus Bryennius that it was Constantine (not Leo) who was killed. They were sons of Diogenes Romanus, emperor from 1067 to 1071.

her husband's death she had chosen to live as a nun, following a regimen of the strictest self-denial and total dedication to God. As the fool still would not hold his tongue after a second and third warning from the emperor, he was sent off to Cherson; orders were given that he was to be kept in custody. While he was there the pretender climbed to the rampart during the night and leaning over had talks on more than one occasion with the Cumans who normally visit the place to trade with the locals and purchase necessities. They exchanged pledges with him and one night he let himself down from the wall by ropes. The Cumans carried him off to their own country and there he lived with them in camp for a fairly long time, so far gaining their confidence that they were already addressing him as emperor. The Cumans, who were longing to gorge themselves on human blood and human flesh and were more than ready to amass booty from our territories, found in the pseudo-Diogenes a 'Patroclus-excuse'[9]; they decided to march in full force against the Roman Empire. Their intention was to establish him on his ancestral throne, but for the time being the plan was merely in the air. The emperor, however, was not unaware of it. Accordingly he armed his troops as best he could and made preparations for war. As I have said before, the mountain-passes (known to the ordinary people as *clisurae*) had already been fortified. Some time later, when Alexius discovered that the Cumans had occupied Paristrion with the pretender, he assembled the leading officers of the army, together with his own relatives by blood or marriage, and debated the advisability of taking the initiative against them. With one accord they opposed the idea. Alexius, unable to trust his own judgement and unwilling to rely on his own unaided calculations, referred the whole matter to God and asked Him to decide. All the churchmen and soldiers were summoned to an evening meeting in Santa Sophia. The emperor himself attended and so did the Patriarch Nicolas.[10]

9. See Bk III, note 8.

10. He had succeeded to the patriarchal throne in the course of the seventh indiction in the year 6592 [i.e., in August 1084] after the abdication of Eustratius Garidas. (A.C.)

On two tablets Alexius wrote the question, 'Should I go out to attack the Cumans?'; on one 'Yes' was added, on the other 'No'. They were then signed and the patriarch was commanded to place them on the Holy Table. After hymns had been sung all through the night, Nicolas went to the altar, picked up one of the papers and brought it out. In the presence of the whole company he broke the seal and read aloud what was written there. The emperor accepted the decision as though it derived from some divine oracle. All his energies were now concentrated on the expedition. The army was summoned by letters from all parts of the empire and when everything was ready he set out to fight the Cumans. At Anchialus, which he had reached with all his forces, he sent for his brother-in-law, the Caesar Nicephorus Melissenus, and George Palaeologus, and his nephew John Taronites.[11] They were despatched to Beroë, with instructions to maintain a vigilant guard over that city and the neighbouring districts. The army was then divided, with the other generals as separate commanders: Dabatenus, George Euphorbenus and Constantine Humbertopoulos.[12] They were to protect the mountain-passes through the Zygum. Alexius went on to Chortarea (itself a pass in that area) and inspected the whole range to see if all his previous orders had been faithfully carried out by the officers entrusted with the task; where the fortifications were half-finished or incomplete, he insisted that they should put things right: the Cumans must be denied an easy passage. When all precautions had been taken, he returned from Chortarea and pitched camp by the Holy Lake near Anchialus. During the night a certain Poudilus, one of the leading Vlachs, came and reported that the Cumans were crossing the Danube. Alexius thought it essential to hold a council of war with the more important of his kinsmen and the officers. At daybreak, therefore, they were sent for. Since all agreed that Anchialus must be occupied, he personally set

11. Son of the Michael Taronites who had plotted against Alexius (see p. 286).

12. He had been exiled for plotting against the emperor (see p. 261). Alexius showed remarkable clemency to his foes.

out for the town after despatching Cantacuzenus and Taticius
with some mercenaries (Skaliarius Elkhan and other high-
ranking officers) to a place called Therma. They were to secure
the safety of that district. At this point, however, information
was received that the Cumans were making for Adrianople.
Alexius assembled all the leading citizens. Prominent among
them were Catacalon surnamed Tarchaniotes and Nicephorus,
son of the Bryennius who had once aspired to the throne.[13]
They were ordered to guard the citadel with great determination; if the Cumans did come, they must be engaged in battle
with no half-hearted measures; he advised them to take careful
aim, shoot their arrows at long range and keep the gates closed
most of the time. Many rewards were promised if these
instructions were properly carried out. Bryennius and his
companions returned to Adrianople full of confidence. Written
orders were also sent to Euphorbenus Constantine Catacalon.
He was to take with him Monastras[14] and Michael Anemas,
together with the forces under their command, and when they
heard that the Cumans had passed through the defiles they
were to follow them closely and then make a sudden attack
from the rear.

As it happened the Cumans were shown the way through
the passes by the Vlachs and so crossed the Zygum without
any trouble. As soon as they approached Goloë the inhabitants
threw into chains the commander of the garrison and handed
him over to them. In fact they gladly welcomed the Cumans.
Catacalon, with the emperor's instructions still fresh in his
mind, fell in with a party of them on a foraging raid and after
launching a vigorous attack soon led off a hundred prisoners.
He was honoured by the emperor in person with the title of
nobilissimus on the spot. The people of the neighbouring towns,
Diabolis and the rest, seeing the Cumans in possession of
Goloë, willingly approached them with offers of surrender;
they provided hospitality and acclaimed the pseudo-Diogenes.
He, once control of all these places was assured, marched with

13. When he himself had also tried to seize power he had been blinded.
(A.C.)
14. A semi-barbarian with considerable experience of war. (A.C.)

the entire barbarian army on Anchialus, intending to make an
assault on the fortifications at once. The emperor was inside
the town. A life-long experience of war told him that the
Cumans would be deterred by the natural strength of its
position, which made the walls even more impregnable. He
divided his forces, opened the gates of the citadel and drew
up his companies in close formation outside the walls. One
part of the Roman army hurled itself on the extremity of the
Cuman line with terrible cries, routed them and pursued them
all the way to the sea.[15] Alexius saw what had happened, but
knowing that his forces were hopelessly outnumbered and
quite unable to withstand the enemy, he gave orders that in
future the serried ranks should remain absolutely unbroken
and immobile. The Cumans took up position in line opposite
them, but they too made no move to attack. For three days
from early morning to evening this arrangement was repeated;
however eager the enemy were for battle, they feared the unfavourable terrain and were put off because no Roman broke
ranks to charge out against them. The fortress of Anchialus
was situated thus: on the right lay the Black Sea; on the left
rough ground, impassable and overgrown with vines,
affording no opportunity for cavalry manoeuvres. The result
was that the barbarians, in view of the emperor's stubbornness, abandoned their plans in desperation and took the road
to Adrianople. The pretender was responsible for this: he
tricked them, saying that when Nicephorus Bryennius heard of
his arrival at Adrianople, he would open up the gates and very
gladly receive him. 'He will give me money,' he said, 'and
show every sign of friendship. He used to look on my father
as a brother, though he was not really a kinsman. Yet he chose
to regard him as such. And when the citadel is handed over to
us, we shall resume our march to the capital.' He used to call
Bryennius his 'uncle'. It was untrue, but there was some
foundation for it in fact: the former emperor Romanus
Diogenes had recognized Bryennius' quite outstanding
intellectual powers; he knew with good reason that he was

15. Probably the meaning of this sentence, but there are lacunae in the
text.

straightforward and absolutely sincere in word and deed. It
was his desire therefore to adopt Bryennius as his own brother.
Both parties were willing and the adoption was confirmed.
These facts are undisputed and common knowledge, but the
impostor had the supreme effrontery to address Bryennius as
his real uncle. So much for his schemes. The Cumans, like all
barbarians, being fickle and inconsistent by nature, listened to
his arguments and retired to Adrianople. They bivouacked
outside the city. For forty-eight days there were daily clashes
while the young men, eager for action, regularly went out to
fight the barbarians. During this time the pretender, at the foot
of the wall, asked to see Bryennius. The latter leant over the
rampart and declared that as far as he could judge from the
man's voice he was not Romanus Diogenes' son;[16] he had
undoubtedly been killed at Antioch. With these words he
rejected the usurper with ignominy. However, as time went on
provisions in the city began to fail and help had to be requested
of the emperor. He immediately ordered Constantine Euphorbenus to take a strong detachment of counts who were under
his command and make his way by night into Adrianople from
the side of Kalathades. Catacalon was soon on the road to
Orestias,[17] confidently expecting that he would escape the
vigilance of the Cumans. But he was wrong; they saw him and
charged in overwhelming numbers. The Romans were pushed
back and hotly pursued. His son Nicephorus seized a long
spear, wheeled round and met his Scythian pursuer face-to-
face. He struck him in the chest and the man fell dead on the
spot. Nicephorus was an expert with the lance and knew how
to protect himself with a shield.[18] On horseback he gave the
impression that he was not a Roman at all, but a native of
Normandy. The young man was certainly remarkable for his
horsemanship – a natural genius, in fact. In the presence of
God Nicephorus was most reverent, in dealings with his

16. Who, as I have said, was his adopted brother. The practice of adoption was not infrequent. (A.C.)

17. The old name of Adrianople.

18. He afterwards became my brother-in-law when he married my
younger sister Maria Porphyrogenita. (A.C.)

fellow-men courteous and pleasant. Before the forty-eight days had passed, Nicephorus Bryennius (who was invested with overriding authority in Adrianople) ordered the gates to be suddenly thrown open and fighting-men went out to do battle with the enemy. It was a bitter conflict and although many Romans fell in the struggle, risking their lives with no thought for their own safety, at least they killed more of the Cumans. Marianus Mavrocatacalon caught sight of Togortak, their commander-in-chief, and armed with a long spear charged against him at full gallop. He would almost undoubtedly have killed him, had not his Cuman bodyguard rescued him in time – nearly killing Marianus in the process. This Marianus was only a youth, who had recently taken his place among the young men, but he often made a sortie from the gates of the city and every time wounded or killed some enemy and returned in triumph. He was a really fine soldier, worthily upholding the ancestral reputation for bravery, the most courageous member of a very courageous family. Full of rage at his narrow escape from death, he now made his way towards the pseudo-Diogenes, who was standing on the far bank of the river just where Marianus had fought with the barbarians. Seeing him clothed in purple, with the insignia of an emperor but deserted by his bodyguard, Marianus raised his whip and beat him mercilessly about the head, at the same time calling him 'King Humbug'.

Reports of Cuman obstinacy before Adrianople and the frequent battles there convinced the emperor that he must leave Anchialus and go in person to help. The senior officers and chief citizens were summoned to a council of war, which was interrupted by a man called Alakaseus. 'It so happens,' he said, 'that my father was friendly in the old days with the pretender's father. If I go there, I can take advantage of this. I will get him inside one of the fortresses and detain him.' When he was asked how this could be managed (it was a big undertaking), he suggested to Alexius that he (Alakaseus) should imitate the stratagem of Zopyrus [19] in Cyrus's reign: he would

19. Herodotus (iii, 154–8) tells of the extraordinary feat of this Zopyrus, a Persian satrap. Zopyrus cut off his own nose and ears, and generally

disfigure himself, shave off his hair and beard, and then
present himself to pseudo-Diogenes as a victim of the
emperor's punishment. He kept his word too, for no sooner
was the plan approved by Alexius than he shaved himself
completely, maltreated his body and went off to the pretender.
He reminded him of other matters, then recalled the old
friendship, adding these words; 'I have endured many
outrages at the hands of the Emperor Alexius. That is why I
have come to you now, trusting in the ancient friendship
between my father and Your Majesty, to help you in your
enterprise.' (Flattery was a more effective way of winning
'Diogenes'' favour.) In order to enlarge somewhat on
Alakaseus' activities, I must remark here that he took with
him a safe-conduct from Alexius and a letter for the military
governor of a stronghold called Poutze which read as follows:
'Pay attention to the bearer of this note and do promptly
whatever he proposes.' (The emperor had guessed correctly
that the Cumans would make for this place when they left
Adrianople.) When these arrangements had been completed,
Alakaseus appeared, just as we have said, before 'Diogenes'.
'It is because of you,' he said, 'that I have suffered so terribly.
Because of you I have been insulted and thrown into chains.
Because of you I was imprisoned for many days – in fact, ever
since you crossed the Roman frontiers – for on account of my
father's friendship for you I was suspected by the emperor. I
escaped and now I have fled to you, my lord, after freeing myself from my bonds. I bring you advice that will be profitable.'
'Diogenes' received him warmly and asked what steps he
should take to achieve his aim. 'You see this fortress of
Poutze,' answered Alakaseus, 'and this broad plain. There is
enough pasture to feed your horses here for as long as you
choose to rest yourself and your army. Well, for the time being
we should go no further than this. Stay here for a little while,
seize the fortress and rest. Meanwhile the Cumans can go out

---

mutilated himself to win the confidence of the Babylonians and so deliver
the city to Darius (521–485), not to Cyrus, as Anna says. Cyrus had died
some years before.

to forage and afterwards we can set out for Constantinople. If you agree I will see the garrison commander, an old and dear friend of mine, and I will arrange for him to surrender the place to you without bloodshed.' The idea pleased 'Diogenes'. So, during the night, Alakaseus tied his letter to an arrow and fired it into the citadel. The governor read it privately and prepared to hand over the place. Early next morning Alakaseus was the first to approach the gates. He pretended to chat with the governor, having formerly arranged a signal with 'Diogenes'; when he saw it he was to march straight into the fort. After Alakaseus had carried on his feigned conversation for a reasonable time, he gave the signal. The pretender thereupon took with him a few soldiers and boldly entered the gates. The inhabitants received him with delight and the governor of Poutze invited him to take a bath. On the advice of Alakaseus he immediately accepted the invitation. Later, a magnificent banquet was made ready for him and his Cumans. They all feasted together to their hearts' content and after drinking their fill of wine, gulping it down from full wine-skins, they lay down and snored. Alakaseus and the governor with some others then went round, took away their horses and arms, left 'Diogenes' himself where he was, snoring away, but killed his attendants and straightway hurled them into trenches which served as natural graves. Meanwhile Catacalon, who was following the Cuman army as the emperor had ordered, when he saw that the pretender had gone into the fort and saw too that the Cumans had dispersed to look for plunder, left for a place in the vicinity of Poutze and there pitched his camp. With Cumans scattered all over the countryside Alakaseus dared not report his capture to the emperor, but took 'Diogenes' off with him and drove straight for Tzouroulos on his way to the capital. Nevertheless, the emperor's mother, acting as regent in the palace, heard about it and sent the Drungarius of the Fleet, the eunuch Eustathius Kymineianus, in great haste to arrest the prisoner and bring him to Constantinople. The Drungarius had with him a Turk called Kamyres to whom he entrusted the task of blinding 'Diogenes'. As for the emperor, he was still waiting at

Anchialus, but hearing that Cumans were roaming all over the neighbouring districts in search of booty he went on to Little Nicaea. There he was informed that Kitzes, one of the Cuman leaders, with a force of 12,000 men engaged in general pillaging had collected all his booty and occupied the ridge of Taurocomus. Alexius thereupon led his own forces down to the bank of the river which flows across the plain below it, a place covered with germander-bushes and young trees. He halted his men there. A strong contingent of expert Turkish archers was sent to join battle with the enemy and entice them on to level ground by making cavalry charges. In fact, the Cumans took the initiative and pursued them hotly as far as the main Roman army. At this point they reined in their horses a bit, re-formed their ranks and made ready for an assault. Alexius spied a Cuman horseman arrogantly leap ahead of his own line, ride along their ranks and apparently all but challenge anyone to come and fight him. The Romans on right and left did nothing, but the emperor impatiently galloped out in full view of all and struck the first blow. He used his spear, then drove his sword right through the Cuman's chest and knocked him down from his horse. Thus on this occasion he showed himself more of a soldier than a general. Anyway the deed at once put great heart into the Romans and induced a corresponding dread in the Scyths. Moving towards them like a tower of strength, Alexius broke their army up; they scattered in all directions as the line was torn apart and fled pell-mell. In the battle the Cumans lost some 7,000 men; another 3,000 were taken alive. Their entire booty was seized by the Romans, but they were not allowed to share it out among themselves in the normal manner; it had only recently been stolen from the natives of the district and had to be restored to them. The news spread like wild-fire throughout all the countryside and individuals who had been robbed came to the camp, recognized their possessions and took them away. Beating their breasts and raising their hands in supplication to heaven they prayed for Alexius' prosperity; the loud cries of men and women alike might well have been heard in the moon itself. So ended this campaign. As for Alexius, he joyfully returned with his men to Little Nicaea and after staying there for a couple of days on the third left for Adrianople, where he remained for some time in the house of Silvester. It was at this moment that the Cuman leaders separated from the rest of their army and came *en masse* to the emperor, really hoping to deceive him, but pretending to be deserters anxious for an immediate peace settlement. Their idea was that negotiations would waste time; their fellow-countrymen would thus get a flying start on their march. So having waited three days, on the night of the third they set out for home. Alexius saw through the trick and sent fast couriers to warn the officers on guard at the paths over the Zygum: they were to be constantly alert for an opportunity to intercept them; there must be no relaxation. But news came that the whole Cuman army was already well on its way. All available Romans were rushed to a place called Scutari, eighteen stades from Adrianople, and on the next day arrived at Agathonike. There Alexius discovered that the enemy were still in the Akrilevo district (not very far from both these places). Accordingly he went in that direction and from a long way off he saw innumerable camp-fires which they had lighted. After reconnoitring the position he called for Nicolas Mavrocatacalon and other senior officers. With them he debated what to do. It was decided to summon the leaders of the mercenaries, Ouzas (a Sarmatian), Karatzes (a Scyth) and the half-caste Monastras. They were instructed to have fifteen or more watch-fires lighted at every tent so that when the Cumans saw them they would believe the Roman army was enormous; they would then become panic-stricken and lose courage for any future attack. The orders were carried out and the Cumans were duly frightened. Early next morning the emperor armed himself and began the battle with an assault. Both sides fought well, but eventually the Cumans turned away. The Romans thereupon split up: the light-armed were sent on ahead to pursue the enemy, while Alexius himself, when they were already in headlong flight, also took up the chase. He caught up with them near the 'Iron Defile'. Many were slain, but most were captured alive. The Roman vanguard returned with

all the Cuman booty. The whole of that night was spent by
Alexius on the mountain-ridge of the Iron Defile while a
violent storm raged, but by daybreak he arrived at Goloë.
There he stayed for a day and a night in order to honour all
those who had distinguished themselves in the battle; they
were handsomely rewarded. Now that the plan had been
successfully accomplished, he cheerfully dismissed them all to
their respective homes and two days and nights later he was
back in the palace.

After a brief rest from his many labours the emperor discovered that the Turks were engaged in general plunder, overrunning the interior of Bithynia. On the other side the affairs
of the west claimed his attention, but he was more concerned
with the Turks (the trouble there was more urgent). To deal
with them he conceived a project of really major importance,
worthy of his genius: the plan was to protect Bithynia against
their incursions by a canal. It is worthwhile to describe how it
was done. The coastline runs straight for the village of Chele,
while another stretch of coast turns towards the north; these,
with the River Sangaris, enclose a considerable tract of land.
Because there was no one to oppose them the Ishmaelites,[20]
who have been bad neighbours to us for a long time, easily
ravaged it. They made their incursions through the Maryan-
deni and from beyond the river, and when they crossed it
Nicomedia in particular suffered from their attacks. Naturally
Alexius wished to check such raids and prevent the devastation; above all he wanted to ensure the safety of Nicomedia.
South of Lake Baane he noticed a very long trench and when
he followed its course to the end he concluded from its position and shape that the excavation had not been merely
accidental, nor was it the result of some natural process, but
the deliberate work of some human hand. After much
investigation he was told by some persons that Anastasius
Dikouros[21] had indeed superintended its digging. What his
purpose had been they could not say. To Alexius anyhow it
seemed clear that Anastasius wanted to divert water from the
lake into this artificial gully. Once he had been led to the same

20. Another name for Turks.   21. Emperor from 491 to 518.

idea he ordered the trench to be dug to a great depth, but fearing that at the point where lake and canal met it might be possible to get across, he built an extremely strong fort there, completely secure and proof against all assaults, not only because of the water, but also because of the height and thickness of its walls – for which reason it was called the Iron Tower. Even today it constitutes a city in front of a city, an outlying bastion to protect a wall. The emperor himself directed its construction from early morning till evening, despite the soaring temperatures (the sun was passing the summer solstice). He had to endure both scorching heat and the dust. Enormous sums of money were spent to ensure that the walls should be really strong and impregnable. He paid generous wages to the men who dragged the stones, one by one, even if fifty or a hundred workers were involved at a time. The money attracted not casual labourers, but all the soldiers and their servants, natives and foreigners alike; they were glad to move stones for such liberal pay under the direction of the emperor in person. To them he seemed like a prize-giver at the Games. He made skilful use of the crowds who flocked to help and the transport of these huge blocks of stone was made easier. It was typical of Alexius: he thought deeply about a project and then worked with tremendous energy to complete it. Such were the events of the emperor's reign up to the . . . indiction of the . . . year.[22] He had no time to relax before he heard a rumour that countless Frankish armies were approaching. He dreaded their arrival, knowing as he did their uncontrollable passion, their erratic character and their irresolution, not to mention the other peculiar traits of the Kelt, with their inevitable consequences: their greed for money, for example, which always led them, it seemed, to break their own agreements without scruple for any chance reason. He had consistently heard this said of them and it was abundantly justified. So far from despairing, however, he made every effort to prepare for war if need arose. What actually happened was more far-reaching and terrible than rumour suggested, for the whole of the west and all the bar-

22. Anna forgot the dates, or maybe never revised the text.

barians who lived between the Adriatic and the Straits of
Gibraltar migrated in a body to Asia, marching across Europe
country by country with all their households. The reason for
this mass-movement is to be found more or less in the following
events. A certain Kelt, called Peter, with the surname Koukoupetros,[23] left to worship at the Holy Sepulchre and after
suffering much ill-treatment at the hands of the Turks and
Saracens who were plundering the whole of Asia, he returned
home with difficulty. Unable to admit defeat, he wanted to
make a second attempt by the same route, but realizing the
folly of trying to do this alone (worse things might happen to
him) he worked out a clever scheme. He decided to preach in
all the Latin countries. A divine voice, he said, commanded
him to proclaim to all the counts in France that all should
depart from their homes, set out to worship at the Holy
Shrine and with all their soul and might strive to liberate
Jerusalem from the Agarenes.[24] Surprisingly, he was successful. It was as if he had inspired every heart with some divine
oracle. Kelts assembled from all parts, one after another, with
arms and horses and all the other equipment for war. Full of
enthusiasm and ardour they thronged every highway, and with
these warriors came a host of civilians, outnumbering the sand
of the sea-shore or the stars of heaven, carrying palms and
bearing crosses on their shoulders. There were women and
children, too, who had left their own countries. Like tributaries joining a river from all directions they streamed towards
us in full force, mostly through Dacia. The arrival of this
mighty host was preceded by locusts, which abstained from
the wheat but made frightful inroads on the vines. The pro-
phets of those days interpreted this as a sign that the Keltic
army would refrain from interfering in the affairs of Christians
but bring dreadful affliction on the barbarian Ishmaelites, who
were the slaves of drunkenness and wine and Dionysos. The

23. Steven Runciman suggests that *chtou* or *kiokio* (Picard words)
meaning 'little' may be the origin of this name. He was known to his
contemporaries as Peter the Little but we know him as Peter the Hermit.
24. Another name (like Ishmaelites) for the Turks, i.e. descendants of
Hagar.

Ishmaelites are indeed dominated by Dionysos and Eros; they indulge readily in every kind of sexual licence, and if they are circumcised in the flesh they are certainly not so in their passions. In fact, the Ishmaelites are nothing more than slaves – trebly slaves – of the vices of Aphrodite.[25] Hence they reverence and worship Astarte and Ashtaroth, and in their land the figure of the moon and the golden image of Chobar[26] are considered of major importance. Corn, because it is not heady and at the same time is most nourishing, has been accepted as the symbol of Christianity. In the light of this the diviners interpreted the references to vines and wheat. So much for the prophecies. The incidents of the barbarians' advance followed in the order I have given and there was something strange about it, which intelligent people at least would notice. The multitudes did not arrive at the same moment, nor even by the same route – how could they cross the Adriatic *en masse* after setting out from different countries in such great numbers? – but they made the voyage in separate groups, some first, some in a second party and others after them in order, until all had arrived, and then they began their march across Epirus. Each army, as I have said, was preceded by a plague of locusts, so that everyone, having observed the phenomenon several times, came to recognize locusts as the forerunners of Frankish battalions. They had already begun to cross the Straits of Lombardy in small groups when the emperor summoned certain leaders of the Roman forces and sent them to the area round Dyrrachium and Avlona, with instructions to receive the voyagers kindly and export from all countries abundant supplies for them along their route; then to watch them carefully and follow, so that if they saw them making raids or running off to plunder the neighbouring districts, they could check them by light skirmishes. These officers were accom-

25. Anna is unfair to the Mohammedans, but other authors accuse them of excessive wine-bibbing. She seems to be unaware that Aphrodite, Astarte and Ashtaroth are identical goddesses of love.

26. Chobar (or Chabar), meaning 'The Great', was the name given by the Saracens to the goddess of love. 'Moon' should perhaps be supplanted by 'star' (the Greek *astron* may refer to Lucifer). For the whole passage see Buckler, pp. 330–32.

panied by interpreters who understood the Latin language; their duty was to quell any incipient trouble between natives and pilgrims. I would like here to give a clearer and more detailed account of the matter.

The report of Peter's preaching spread everywhere, and the first to sell his land and set out on the road to Jerusalem was Godfrey.[27] He was a very rich man, extremely proud of his noble birth, his own courage and the glory of his family. (Every Kelt desired to surpass his fellows.) The upheaval that ensued as men *and* women took to the road was unprecedented within living memory. The simpler folk were in very truth led on by a desire to worship at Our Lord's tomb and visit the holy places, but the more villainous characters (in particular Bohemond and his like) had an ulterior purpose, for they hoped on their journey to seize the capital itself, looking upon its capture as a natural consequence of the expedition. Bohemond disturbed the morale of many nobler men because he still cherished his old grudge against the emperor. Peter, after his preaching campaign, was the first to cross the Lombardy Straits, with 80,000 infantry and 100,000 horsemen. He reached the capital via Hungary.[28] The Kelts, as one might guess, are in any case an exceptionally hotheaded race and passionate, but let them once find an inducement and they become irresistible.

The emperor knew what Peter had suffered before from the Turks and advised him to wait for the other counts to arrive, but he refused, confident in the number of his followers. He crossed the Sea of Marmora and pitched camp near a small place called Helenopolis. Later some Normans, 10,000 in all, joined him but detached themselves from the rest of the army and ravaged the outskirts of Nicaea, acting with horrible cruelty to the whole population; they cut in pieces some of the babies, impaled others on wooden spits and roasted them over a fire; old people were subjected to every kind of torture. The

27. Godfrey of Bouillon, Duke of Lower Lorraine.
28. The Crusaders arrived at Constantinople on 1 August 1096. They crossed the Bosphorus on 6 August. The attack on Nicaea, which was the headquarters of the Seljuq sultan (Kilij Arslan), took place in September.

inhabitants of the city, when they learnt what was happening, threw open their gates and charged out against them. A fierce battle ensued, in which the Normans fought with such spirit that the Nicaeans had to retire inside their citadel. The enemy therefore returned to Helenopolis with all the booty. There an argument started between them and the rest (who had not gone on the raid) – the usual quarrel in such cases – for the latter were green with envy. That led to brawling, whereupon the daredevil Normans broke away for a second time and took Xerigordos by assault. The sultan's reaction was to send Elkhanes with a strong force to deal with them. He arrived at Xerigordos and captured it; of the Normans some were put to the sword and others taken prisoner. At the same time Elkhanes made plans to deal with the remainder, still with Koukoupetros. He laid ambushes in suitable places, hoping that the enemy on their way to Nicaea would fall into the trap unawares and be killed. Knowing the Keltic love of money he also enlisted the services of two determined men who were to go to Peter's camp and there announce that the Normans, having seized Nicaea, were sharing out all the spoils of the city. This story had an amazing effect on Peter's men; they were thrown into confusion at the words 'share' and 'money'; without a moment's hesitation they set out on the Nicaea road in complete disorder, practically heedless of military discipline and the proper arrangement which should mark men going off to war. As I have said before, the Latin race at all times is unusually greedy for wealth, but when it plans to invade a country, neither reason nor force can restrain it. They set out helter-skelter, regardless of their individual companies. Near the Drakon they fell into the Turkish ambuscade and were miserably slaughtered. So great a multitude of Kelts and Normans died by the Ishmaelite sword that when they gathered the remains of the fallen, lying on every side, they heaped up, I will not say a mighty ridge or hill or peak, but a mountain of considerable height and depth and width, so huge was the mass of bones. Some men of the same race as the slaughtered barbarians later, when they were building a wall like those of a city, used the bones of the dead as pebbles to fill up the cracks. In a way the city became their tomb. To this very day it stands with its encircling wall built of mixed stones and bones. When the killing was over, only Peter with a handful of men returned to Helenopolis. The Turks, wishing to capture him, again laid an ambush, but the emperor, who had heard of this and indeed of the terrible massacre, thought it would be an awful thing if Peter also became a prisoner. Constantine Euphorbenus Catacalon (already mentioned often in this history) was accordingly sent with powerful contingents in warships across the straits to help him. At his approach the Turks took to their heels. Without delay Catacalon picked up Peter and his companions (there were only a few) and brought them in safety to Alexius, who reminded Peter of his foolishness in the beginning and added that these great misfortunes had come upon him through not listening to his advice. With the usual Latin arrogance Peter disclaimed responsibility and blamed his men for them, because (said he) they had been disobedient and followed their own whims. He called them brigands and robbers, considered unworthy therefore by the Saviour to worship at His Holy Sepulchre. Some Latins, after the pattern of Bohemond and his cronies, because they had long coveted the Roman Empire and wished to acquire it for themselves, found in the preaching of Peter an excuse and caused this great upheaval by deceiving more innocent people. They sold their lands on the pretence that they were leaving to fight the Turks and liberate the Holy Sepulchre.

A certain Hugh,[29] brother of the King of France, with all the pride of a Nauatos in his noble birth and wealth and power, as he was about to leave his native country (ostensibly for a pilgrimage to the Holy Sepulchre) sent an absurd message to the emperor proposing that he (Hugh) should be given a magnificent reception: 'Know, Emperor, that I am the King of Kings, the greatest of all beneath the heavens. It is my will that you should meet me on my arrival and receive me with the

29. Hugh of Vermandois, younger son of Henry I of France and Anne of Kiev. Despite his extraordinary bombast he had made little mark in French politics. See Runciman, p. 142.

pomp and ceremony due to my noble birth.' When this letter
reached Alexius, John the son of Isaac the sebastocrator happened to be Duke of Dyrrachium, and Nicolas Mavrocatacalon, commander of the fleet, had anchored his ships at
intervals round the harbour there. From this base he made
frequent voyages of reconnaissance to prevent pirate ships
sailing by unnoticed. To these two men the emperor now sent
urgent instructions: the Duke was to keep watch by land and
sea for Hugh's arrival and inform Alexius at once when he
came; he was also to receive him with great pomp; the
admiral was exhorted to keep a constant vigil – there must be
no relaxation or negligence whatever. Hugh reached the coast
of Lombardy safely and forthwith despatched envoys to the
Duke of Dyrrachium. There were twenty-four of them in all,
armed with breastplates and greaves of gold and accompanied
by Count William the Carpenter [30] and Elias (who had deserted
from the emperor at Thessalonica). They addressed the duke
as follows: 'Be it known to you, Duke, that our Lord Hugh is
almost here. He brings with him from Rome the golden
standard of St Peter.[31] Understand, moreover, that he is
supreme commander of the Frankish army. See to it then that
he is accorded a reception worthy of his rank and yourself
prepare to meet him.' While the envoys were delivering this
message, Hugh came down via Rome to Lombardy, as I have
said, and set sail for Illyricum from Bari, but on the crossing
he was caught by a tremendous storm. Most of his ships, with
their rowers and marines, were lost. Only one ship, his own,
was thrown up on the coast somewhere between Dyrrachium
and a place called Pales, and that was half-wrecked. Two
coastguards on the lookout for his arrival found him, saved by
a miracle. They called to him, 'The duke is anxiously waiting
for your coming. He is very eager to see you.' At once he
asked for a horse and one of them dismounted and gave him
his own gladly. When the duke saw him, saved in this way,
and when he had greeted him, he asked about the voyage and

30. William of Melun. Apparently surnamed 'the Carpenter' because
of his strength.
31. Given by the pope to soldiers leaving to fight the infidels.

heard of the storm which had wrecked his ships. He encouraged Hugh with fine promises and entertained him at a
magnificent banquet. After the feasting Hugh was allowed to
rest, but he was not granted complete freedom. John the duke
had immediately informed the emperor of the Frank's adventures and was now awaiting further instructions. Soon after
receiving the news Alexius sent Boutoumites to Epidamnos
(which we have on numerous occasions called Dyrrachium) to
escort Hugh, not by the direct route but on a detour through
Philippopolis to the capital. He was afraid of the armed Keltic
hordes coming on behind him. Hugh was welcomed with
honour by the emperor, who soon persuaded him by generous
largess and every proof of friendship to become his liege-man
and take the customary oath of the Latins.

This affair was merely the prelude. Barely fifteen days later
Bohemond made the crossing to the coast of Kabalion.[32] Hard
on his heels came the Count Richard of the Principate.[33] He
too when he reached the Lombardy coast wanted to cross over
to Illyricum. A three-masted pirate vessel of large tonnage
was hired for 6,000 gold staters. She carried 200 rowers and
towed three ship's boats. Richard did not make for Avlona, as
the other Latin armies had done, but after weighing anchor
changed direction a little and with a favourable wind sailed
straight for Chimara (he was fearful of the Roman fleet).
However, in escaping the smoke he fell into the fire: he
avoided the ships lying in wait at different points in the
Lombardy straits but crossed the path of the commander-in-
chief of the whole Roman fleet, Nicolas Mavrocatacalon himself. The latter had heard of this pirate vessel some time before

32. This place is near Boüsa. Kabalion and Boüsa are names of towns
in that area. I hope that nobody will rebuke me for using such barbaric
names, thereby defiling the text of my history. Even Homer did not reject
the use of Boeotian names and for the sake of accuracy he mentioned
certain barbaric islands. (A.C.)

33. There is some doubt about the identity of this man (called Pre-
bentzas by Anna). Some scholars think that he is none other than Raymond
of Provence (called by Anna 'Isangeles' – a corruption of St Gilles), but
there are good reasons to prefer Richard of the Principate. See Buckler,
p. 465.

and had detached biremes, triremes and some fast cruisers from the main force; with these he moved from his base at Ason to Kabalion and there took up station. The so-called 'second count' was sent with his own galley (*Excussaton*[34] to the ordinary seamen) to light a torch when he saw the rowers loose the stern-cables of the enemy ship and throw them into the sea. Without delay the order was carried out and Nicolas, seeing the signal, hoisted sail on some of his ships, while others were rowed with oars – they looked like millipedes – against Richard, who was now at sea. They caught him before he had sailed three stades from the land, eager to reach the opposite coast by Epidamnos. He had 1,500 soldiers on board, plus eighty horses belonging to the nobles. The helmsman, sighting Nicolas, reported to the Frank: 'The Syrian fleet is on us. We're in danger of being killed by dagger and sword.' The count at once ordered his men to arm and put up a good fight. It was mid-winter – the day sacred to the memory of Nicolas, greatest of pontiffs[35] – but there was a dead calm and the full moon shone more brightly than in the spring. As the winds had fallen completely the pirate ship could no longer make progress under sail; it lay becalmed on the sea. At this point in the history I should like to pay tribute to the exploits of Marianus. He immediately asked the Duke of the Fleet, his father, for some of the lighter vessels and then steered straight for Richard's ship. He fell upon the prow and tried to board her. The marines soon rushed there when they saw that he was fully armed for battle, but Marianus, speaking in their language, told the Latins there was no need for alarm; he urged them not to fight against fellow-Christians. Nevertheless one of them fired a cross-bow and hit his helmet.[36] The arrow

34. From the Latin *excusatum*. The boat was apparently reserved for the second in command.
35. 6 December 1096.
36. The cross-bow is a weapon of the barbarians, absolutely unknown to the Greeks. In order to stretch it one does not pull the string with the right hand while pushing the bow with the left away from the body; this instrument of war, which fires weapons to an enormous distance, has to be stretched by lying almost on one's back; each foot is pressed forcibly against the half-circles of the bow and the two hands tug at the bow,

drove clean through the top of it without touching a hair on
his head – Providence thwarted it. Another arrow was quickly
fired at the count, striking him on the arm; it pierced his
shield, bored through his breastplate of scale-armour and
grazed his side. A certain Latin priest who happened to be
standing in the stern with twelve other fighting-men saw what
had occurred and shot several times with his bow at Marianus.
Even then Marianus refused to give up; he fought bravely
himself and encouraged his men to follow his example, so that
three times the priest's comrades had to be relieved because of
wounds or fatigue. The priest, too, although he had been hit
again and again and was covered with streams of blood from
his wounds, still was undaunted.[37] After a bitter contest which
went on from evening till the next mid-day the Latins yielded

---

pulling it with all one's strength towards the body. At the mid point of the
string is a groove, shaped like a cylinder cut in half and fitted to the string
itself; it is about the length of a fair-sized arrow, extending from the string
to the centre of the bow. Along this groove arrows of all kinds are fired.
They are very short, but extremely thick with a heavy iron tip. In the firing
the string exerts tremendous violence and force, so that the missiles
wherever they strike do not rebound; in fact they transfix a shield, cut
through a heavy iron breastplate and resume their flight on the far side, so
irresistible and violent is the discharge. An arrow of this type has been
known to make its way right through a bronze statue, and when fired at
the wall of a very great town its point either protruded from the inner side
or buried itself in the wall and disappeared altogether. Such is the cross-
bow, a truly diabolical machine. The unfortunate man who is struck by
it dies without feeling the blow; however strong the impact he knows
nothing of it. (A.C.)

37. The Latin customs with regard to priests differ from ours. We are
bidden by canon law and the teaching of the Gospel, 'Touch not, grumble
not, attack not – for thou art consecrated.' But your Latin barbarian will
at the same time handle sacred objects, fasten a shield to his left arm and
grasp a spear in his right. He will communicate the Body and Blood of
the Deity and meanwhile gaze on bloodshed and become himself 'a man
of blood' (as David says in the Psalm). Thus the race is no less devoted to
religion than to war. This Latin, then, more man of action than priest,
wore priestly garb and at the same time handled an oar and ready for naval
action or war on land fought sea and men alike. Our rules, as I have just
said, derive from Aaron, Moses and our first high priest. (A.C.)

Note that Anna misquoted Colossians ii, 21 (Touch not, *taste* not,
handle not); the reference is not apt in any case.

much against their will to Marianus, when they had asked for and obtained an amnesty from him. The warrior-priest, however, even when the armistice was being arranged, did not cease from fighting. After emptying his quiver of arrows, he picked up a sling-stone and hurled it at Marianus, who protected his head with a shield, but that was broken into four and his helmet was shattered. The blow stunned him; he lost consciousness at once and for some time lay speechless, just as the famous Hector lay almost at his last gasp when struck by Ajax's stone. With difficulty he recovered his senses, pulled himself together and firing arrows against his enemy wounded him three times. The polemarch[38] (he was more that than a priest) was far from having had his fill of battle, although he had exhausted the stones and arrows and was at a loss what to do and how to defend himself against his adversary. He grew impatient, on fire with rage, gathering himself for the spring like a wild animal. He was ready to use whatever came to hand and when he found a sack full of barley-cakes, he threw them like stones, taking them from the sack. It was as if he were officiating at some ceremony or service, turning war into the solemnization of sacred rites. He picked up one cake, hurled it with all his might at Marianus' face and hit him on the cheek. So much for the story of the priest, the ship and its marines. As for Count Richard, he put himself in the hands of Marianus, together with his ship and her crew, and thereafter gladly followed him. When they reached land and were disembarking, the priest kept on making inquiries about Marianus; he did not know his name, but described him by the colour of his garments. When at last he found him, he threw his arms round him and with an embrace boasted, 'If you had met me on dry land, many of you would have died at my hands.' He drew out a large silver cup, worth 130 staters, and as he gave it to Marianus and uttered these words, he died.

It was at this time that Count Godfrey made the crossing with some other counts and an army of 10,000 horsemen and 70,000 infantry. When he reached the capital he quartered his men in the vicinity of the Propontis, from the bridge nearest

38. The *polemarch* is an army rank – a commander-in-chief of soldiers.

the Kosmidion[39] as far as the Church of St Phocas. But when the emperor urged him to go over to the far side of the Propontis he put off the decision from day to day; the crossing was deferred with a series of excuses. In fact, of course, he was waiting for Bohemond and the rest of the counts to arrive. Peter had in the beginning undertaken his great journey to worship at the Holy Sepulchre, but the others (and in particular Bohemond) cherished their old grudge against Alexius and sought a good opportunity to avenge the glorious victory which the emperor had won at Larissa. They were all of one mind and in order to fulfil their dream of taking Constantinople they adopted a common policy. I have often referred to that already: to all appearances they were on pilgrimage to Jerusalem; in reality they planned to dethrone Alexius and seize the capital. Unfortunately for them, he was aware of their perfidy, from long experience. He gave written orders to move the auxiliary forces with their officers from Athyra to Philea *en masse* (Philea is a place on the coast of the Black Sea). They were to lie in wait for envoys from Godfrey on their way to Bohemond and the other counts coming behind him, or *vice versa*; all communications were thus to be intercepted. Meanwhile the following incident took place. Some of the counts who accompanied Godfrey were invited by the emperor to meet him. He intended to give them advice: they should urge Godfrey to take the oath of allegiance. The Latins, however, wasted time with their usual verbosity and love of long speeches, so that a false rumour reached the Franks that their counts had been arrested by Alexius. Immediately they marched in serried ranks on Byzantium, starting with the palaces near the Silver Lake;[40] they demolished them completely. An assault was also made on the city walls, not with helepoleis (because they had none), but trusting in their great numbers they had the effrontery to try to set fire to the gate below the palace,[41] near the sanctuary of St Nicolas.[42] The vulgar mob of Byzantines, who were utterly craven, with no

39. The Monastery of St Kosmas.   40. Unidentified.
41. The Palace of Blachernae.
42. Built long ago by one of the emperors. (A.C.)

experience of war, were not the only ones to weep and wail and beat their breasts in impotent fear when they saw the Latin ranks; even more alarmed were the emperor's loyal adherents. Recalling the Thursday on which the city was captured,[43] they were afraid that on that day[44] (because of what had occurred then) vengeance might be taken on them. All the trained soldiers hurried to the palace in disorder, but the emperor remained calm: there was no attempt to arm, no buckling on of scaled cuirass, no shield, no spear in hand, no girding on of his sword. He sat firmly on the imperial throne, gazing cheerfully on them, encouraging and inspiring the hearts of all with confidence, while he took counsel with his kinsmen and generals about future action. In the first place he insisted that no one whatever should leave the ramparts to attack the Latins, for two reasons: because of the sacred character of the day (it was the Thursday of Holy Week, the supreme week of the year, in which the Saviour suffered an ignominious death on behalf of the whole world); and secondly because he wished to avoid bloodshed between Christians. On several occasions he sent envoys to the Latins advising them to desist from such an undertaking. 'Have reverence,' he said, 'for God on this day was sacrificed for us all, refusing neither the Cross, nor the Nails, nor the Spear – proper instruments of punishment for evil-doers – to save us. If you must fight, we too shall be ready, but after the day of the Saviour's resurrection.' They, far from listening to his words, rather reinforced their ranks, and so thick were the showers of their arrows that even one of the emperor's retinue, standing near the throne, was struck in the chest. Most of the others ranged on either side of the emperor, when they saw this, began to withdraw, but he remained seated and unruffled, comforting them and rebuking them in a gentle way – to the wonder of all. However, as he saw the Latins brazenly approaching the walls and rejecting sound advice, he took active steps for the first time. His son-in-law Nicephorus (my Caesar) was summoned. He was ordered to pick out the best

43. A reference to the revolt of the Comneni.
44. 2 April 1097 (also a Thursday).

fighters, expert archers, and post them on the ramparts; they were to fire volleys of arrows at the Latins, but without taking aim and mostly off-target, so as to terrify the enemy by the weight of the attack, but at all costs to avoid killing them. As I have remarked, he was fearful of desecrating that day and he wished to prevent fratricide. Other picked men, most of them carrying bows, but some wielding long spears, he ordered to throw open the gate of St Romanus and make a show of force with a violent charge against the enemy; they were to be drawn up in such a way that each lancer had two peltasts to protect him on either side. In this formation they would advance at a walking pace, but send on ahead a few skilled archers to shoot at the Kelts from a distance and alter direction, right or left, from time to time; when they saw that the space between the two armies had been reduced to a narrow gap, then the officers were to signal the archers accompanying them to fire thick volleys of arrows at the horses, not at the riders, and gallop at full speed against the enemy. The idea was partly to break the full force of the Keltic attack by wounding their mounts (they would not find it easy to ride in this condition) and partly (this was more important) to avoid the killing of Christians. The emperor's instructions were gladly followed. The gates were flung open; now the horses were given their head, now reined in. Many Kelts were slain, but few of the Romans on that day were wounded. We will leave them and return to the Caesar, my lord. Having taken his practised bowmen, he set them on the towers and fired at the barbarians. Every man had a bow that was accurate and far-shooting. They were all young, as skilled as Homer's Teucer in archery. The Caesar's bow was truly worthy of Apollo. Unlike the famous Greeks of Homer he did not 'pull the bow-string until it touched his breast and draw back the arrow so that the iron tip was near the bow';[45] he was making no demonstration of the hunter's skill, like them. But like a second Hercules he shot deadly arrows from deathless bows and hit the target at will. At other times, when he took part in a shooting contest or in a battle, he never missed his aim: at

45. Homer, *Iliad* iv, 123.

whatever part of a man's body he shot, he invariably and immediately inflicted a wound there. With such strength did he bend his bow and so swiftly did he let loose his arrows that even Teucer and the two Ajaxes were not his equal in archery. Yet, despite his skill, on this occasion he respected the holiness of the day and kept in mind the emperor's instructions, so that when he saw the Franks recklessly and foolishly coming near the walls, protected by shield and helmet, he bent his bow and put the arrow to the bow-string, but purposely shot wide, shooting sometimes beyond the target, sometimes falling short. Although, for the day's sake, he refrained from shooting straight at the Latins, yet whenever one of them in his foolhardiness and arrogance not only fired at the defenders on the ramparts, but seemingly poured forth a volley of insults in his own language as well, the Caesar did bend his bow. 'Nor did the dart fly in vain from his hand',[46] but pierced the long shield and cleft its way through the corselet of mail, so that arm and side were pinned together. 'Straightway he fell speechless to the ground', as the poet says,[47] and a cry went up to heaven as the Romans cheered their Caesar and the Latins bewailed their fallen warrior. The battle broke out afresh, their cavalry and our men on the walls both fighting with courage; it was a grim, dour struggle on both sides. However, when the emperor threw in his guards, the Latin ranks turned in flight. On the next day Hugh advised Godfrey to yield to the emperor's wish, unless he wanted to learn a second time how experienced a general Alexius was. He should take an oath, he said, to bear his true allegiance. But Godfrey rebuked him sternly. 'You left your own country as a king,' he said, 'with all that wealth and a strong army; now from the heights you've brought yourself to the level of a slave. And then, as if you had won some great success, you come here and tell me to do the same.' 'We ought to have stayed in our own countries and kept our hands off other peoples',' replied Hugh. 'But since we've come thus far and need the emperor's protection, no good will come of it unless we obey his orders.' Hugh was

46. Homer, *Iliad* v, 18. But Anna misquotes.
47. Another misquotation, if by 'the Poet' she means Homer.

sent away with nothing achieved. Because of this and reliable information that the counts coming after Godfrey were already near, the emperor sent some of his best officers with their troops to advise him once more, even to compel him to cross the straits. No sooner were they in sight when the Latins, without a moment's hesitation, not even waiting to ask them what they wanted, launched an attack and began to fight them. In this fierce engagement many on both sides fell and all the emperor's men who had attacked with such recklessness were wounded. As the Romans showed greater spirit the Latins gave way. Thus Godfrey not long after submitted; he came to the emperor and swore on oath as he was directed that whatever cities, countries or forts he might in future subdue, which had in the first place belonged to the Roman Empire, he would hand over to the officer appointed by the emperor for this very purpose. Having taken the oath he received generous largess, was invited to share Alexius' hearth and table, and was entertained at a magnificent banquet, after which he crossed over to Pelekanum and there pitched camp. The emperor then gave orders that plentiful supplies should be made available for his men.

In the wake of Godfrey came Count Raoul,[48] with 15,000 cavalry and foot-soldiers. He encamped with his attendant counts by the Propontis near the Patriarch's Monastery;[49] the rest he quartered as far as Sosthenion along the shore. Following Godfrey's example he procrastinated, waiting for the arrival of those coming after him, and the emperor who dreaded it (guessing what was likely to happen) used every means, physical and psychological, to hurry them into crossing the straits. For instance, Opus was summoned – a man of noble character, unsurpassed in his knowledge of things military – and when he presented himself before the emperor he was despatched overland with other brave men to Raoul. His instructions were to force the Frank to leave for the Asian side. When it was clear that Raoul had no intention of going,

48. Nothing certain is known of this Raoul.
49. Dedicated to St Michael. The abbot had once been St Ignatius, Patriarch of Constantinople, and he was buried there.

but in fact adopted an insolent and quite arrogant attitude to
the emperor, Opus armed himself and set his men in battle
order, maybe to scare the barbarian. He thought this might
persuade him to set sail. But the Keltic reaction was immediate: with his available men he accepted the challenge,
'like a lion who rejoices when he has found a huge prey'.
There and then he started a violent battle. At this moment
Pegasios arrived by sea to transport them to the other side and
when he saw the fight on land and the Kelts throwing themselves headlong at the Roman ranks, he disembarked and himself joined in the conflict, attacking the enemy from the rear.
In this fight many men were killed, but a far greater number
were wounded. The survivors, under the circumstances, asked
to be taken over the straits; reflecting that if they joined
Godfrey and told him of their misfortunes he might be stirred
to action against the Romans, the emperor prudently granted
their request; he gladly put them on ships and had them transported to [50] the Saviour's tomb, especially since they themselves wanted this. Friendly messages, offering great expectations, were also sent to the counts whom they were awaiting.
Consequently, when they arrived, they willingly carried out
his instructions. So much for Count Raoul. After him came
another great contingent, a numberless heterogeneous host
gathered together from almost all the Keltic lands with their
leaders (kings and dukes and counts and even bishops). The
emperor sent envoys to greet them as a mark of friendship
and forwarded politic letters. It was typical of Alexius: he had
an uncanny prevision and knew how to seize a point of
vantage before his rivals. Officers appointed for this particular
task were ordered to provide victuals on the journey – the
pilgrims must have no excuse for complaint for any reason
whatever. Meanwhile they were eagerly pressing on to the
capital. One might have compared them for number to the
stars of heaven or the grains of sand poured out over the
shore; as they hurried towards Constantinople they were
indeed 'numerous as the leaves and flowers of spring' [51] (to
quote Homer). For all my desire to name their leaders, I prefer

50. Or 'on their way to' (the Greek is ambiguous).
51. *Iliad* ii, 468; *Odyssey* ix, 51.

not to do so. The words fail me, partly through my inability
to make the barbaric sounds – they are so unpronounceable –
and partly because I recoil before their great numbers. In any
case, why should I try to list the names of so enormous a
multitude, when even their contemporaries became indifferent
at the sight of them? When they did finally arrive in the capital,
on the emperor's orders they established their troops near the
monastery of Saint Cosmas and Saint Damian, reaching as far
as the Hieron. It was not nine heralds, after the old Greek
custom, who 'restrained them with cries', but a considerable
number of soldiers who accompanied them and persuaded
them to obey the emperor's commands. With the idea of
enforcing the same oath that Godfrey had taken, Alexius
invited them to visit him separately. He talked with them in
private about his wishes and used the more reasonable among
them as intermediaries to coerce the reluctant. When they
rejected advice – they were anxiously waiting for Bohemond
to come – and found ingenious methods of evasion by making
new demands, he refuted their objections with no difficulty at
all and harried them in a hundred ways until they were driven
to take the oath. Godfrey himself was invited to cross over
from Pelekanum to watch the ceremony. When all, including
Godfrey, were assembled and after the oath had been sworn
by every count, one nobleman dared to seat himself on the
emperor's throne. Alexius endured this without a word, knowing of old the haughty temper of the Latins, but Count
Baldwin went up to the man, took him by the hand and made
him rise. He gave him a severe reprimand: 'You ought never
to have done such a thing, especially after promising to be the
emperor's liege-man. Roman emperors don't let their subjects
sit with them. That's the custom here and sworn liege-men of
His Majesty should observe the customs of the country.' The
man said nothing to Baldwin, but with a bitter glance at
Alexius muttered some words to himself in his own language:
'What a peasant! He sits alone while generals like these stand
beside him!' Alexius saw his lips moving and calling one of the
interpreters who understood the language asked what he had
said. Being told the words he made no comment to the man at

the time, but kept the remark to himself. However, when they were all taking their leave of him, he sent for the arrogant, impudent fellow and asked who he was, where he came from and what his lineage was. 'I am a pure Frank,' he replied, 'and of noble birth. One thing I know: at a cross-roads in the country where I was born is an ancient shrine; [52] to this anyone who wishes to engage in single combat goes, prepared to fight; there he prays to God for help and there he stays awaiting the man who will dare to answer his challenge. At that cross-roads I myself have spent time, waiting and longing for the man who would fight – but there was never one who dared.' Hearing this the emperor said, 'If you didn't get your fight then, when you looked for it, now you have a fine opportunity for many. But I strongly recommend you not to take up position in the rear of the army, nor in the van; stand in the centre with the *hemilochitae*.[53] I know the enemy's methods. I've had long experience of the Turk.' The advice was not given to him alone, but as they left he warned all the others of the manifold dangers they were likely to meet on the journey. He advised them not to pursue the enemy too far, if God gave them the victory, lest falling into traps set by the Turkish leaders they should be massacred.

So much for Godfrey, Raoul and those who came with them. Bohemond arrived at Apros with the other counts. Knowing that he himself was not of noble descent, with no great military following because of his lack of resources, he wished to win the emperor's goodwill, but at the same time to conceal his own hostile intentions against him. With only ten Kelts he hurried to reach the capital before the rest. Alexius understood his schemes – he had long experience of Bohemond's deceitful, treacherous nature – and desired to talk with him before his companions arrived; he wanted to hear what Bohemond had to say and while he still had no chance of corrupting the rest (they were not far away now) he hoped to persuade him to cross over to Asia. When Bohemond came into his presence, Alexius at once gave him a smile and

52. It is probable that the sanctuary was at Soissons.
53. Junior officers in the army.

inquired about his journey. Where had he left the counts? Bohemond replied frankly and to the best of his knowledge to all these questions, while the emperor politely reminded him of his daring deeds at Larissa and Dyrrachium; he also recalled Bohemond's former hostility. 'I was indeed an enemy and foe then,' said Bohemond, 'but now I come of my own free will as Your Majesty's friend.' Alexius talked at length with him, in a somewhat discreet way trying to discover the man's real feelings, and when he concluded that Bohemond would be prepared to take the oath of allegiance, he said to him, 'You are tired now from your journey. Go away and rest. Tomorrow we can discuss matters of common interest.' Bohemond went off to the Cosmidion, where an apartment had been made ready for him and a rich table was laid full of delicacies and food of all kinds. Later the cooks brought in meat and flesh of animals and birds, uncooked. 'The food, as you see, has been prepared by us in our customary way,' they said, 'but if that does not suit you here is raw meat which can be cooked in whatever way you like.' In doing and saying this they were carrying out the emperor's instructions. Alexius was a shrewd judge of a man's character, cleverly reading the innermost thoughts of his heart, and knowing the spiteful, malevolent nature of Bohemond, he rightly guessed what would happen. It was in order that Bohemond might have no suspicions that he caused the uncooked meat to be set before him at the same time, and it was an excellent move. The cunning Frank not only refused to taste any of the food, but would not even touch it with his finger-tips; he rejected it outright, but divided it all up among the attendants, without a hint of his own secret misgivings. It looked as if he was doing them a favour, but that was mere pretence: in reality, if one considers the matter rightly, he was mixing them a cup of death. There was no attempt to hide his treachery, for it was his habit to treat servants with utter indifference. However, he told his own cooks to prepare the raw meat in the usual Frankish way. On the next day he asked the attendants how they felt. 'Very well,' they replied and added that they had suffered not the slightest harm from it. At these words he revealed his hidden fear: 'For my own part,' he said, 'when I remembered the wars I have fought with him, not to mention the famous battle, I was afraid he might arrange to kill me by putting a dose of poison in the food.' Such were the actions of Bohemond. I must say I have never seen an evil man who in all his deeds and words did not depart far from the path of right; whenever a man leaves the middle course, to whatever extreme he inclines he takes his stand far from virtue. Bohemond was summoned then and required, like the others, to take the customary Latin oath. Knowing what his position was he acquiesced gladly enough, for he had neither illustrious ancestors nor great wealth (hence his forces were not strong – only a moderate number of Keltic followers). In any case Bohemond was by nature a liar. After the ceremony was over, Alexius set aside a room in the palace precincts and had the floor covered with all kinds of wealth: clothes, gold and silver coins, objects of lesser value filled the place so completely that it was impossible for anyone to walk in it. He ordered the man deputed to show Bohemond these riches to open the doors suddenly. Bohemond was amazed at the sight. 'If I had had such wealth,' he said, 'I would long ago have become master of many lands.' 'All this,' said the man, 'is yours today – a present from the emperor.' Bohemond was overjoyed. After accepting the gift and thanking him for it, he went off to rest at his lodging-place. Yet when the things were brought to him, although he had expressed such admiration before, he changed. 'I never thought I should be so insulted by the emperor,' he said. 'Take them away. Give them back to the sender.' Alexius, familiar with the Latins' characteristic moodiness, quoted a popular saying: 'His mischief shall return upon his own head.' Bohemond heard about this, and when he saw the servants carefully assembling the presents to carry them away, he changed his mind once more; instead of sending them off in anger he smiled on them, like a sea-polypus which transforms itself in a minute. The truth is that Bohemond was an habitual rogue, quick to react to fleeting circumstance; he far surpassed all the Latins who passed through Constantinople at that time in rascality and courage, but he was equally inferior in wealth and resources. He was the supreme mischief-maker. As for inconstancy, that followed automatically – a trait common to all Latins. It was no surprise then that he should be overjoyed to receive the money he had formerly refused. When he left his native land, he was a soured man, for he had no estates at all. Apparently he left to worship at the Holy Sepulchre, but in reality to win power for himself – or rather, if possible, to seize the Roman Empire itself, as his father had suggested. He was prepared to go to any length, as they say, but a great deal of money was required. The emperor, aware of the man's disagreeable, ill-natured disposition, cleverly sought to remove everything that contributed to Bohemond's secret plans. When therefore Bohemond demanded the office of Domestic of the East, he was not granted his request; he could not 'out-Cretan the Cretan',[54] for Alexius was afraid that once possessed of authority he might use it to subjugate all the other counts and thereafter convert them easily to any policy he chose. At the same time, because he did not wish Bohemond to suspect in any way that his plans were already detected, he flattered him with fine hopes. 'The time for that is not yet ripe, but with your energy and loyalty it will not be long before you have even that honour.' After a conversation with the Franks and after showing his friendship for them with all kinds of presents and honours, on the next day he took his seat on the imperial throne. Bohemond and the others were sent for and warned about the things likely to happen on their journey. He gave them profitable advice. They were instructed in the methods normally used by the Turks in battle; told how they should draw up a battle-line, how to lay ambushes; advised not to pursue far when the enemy ran away in flight. In this way, by means of money and good advice, he did much to soften their ferocious nature. Then he proposed that they should cross the straits. For one of them, Raymond the Count of Saint-Gilles,[55]

54. As we say, 'out-Herod Herod'.
55. Anna calls him Isangeles. He was Count of Toulouse and Marquis of Provence, hoped to lead the Crusaders in the field and was a rival of Bohemond.

Alexius had a deep affection, for several reasons: the count's superior intellect, his untarnished reputation, the purity of his life. He knew moreover how greatly Raymond valued the truth: whatever the circumstances, he honoured truth above all else. In fact, Saint-Gilles outshone all Latins in every quality, as the sun is brighter than the stars. It was for this that Alexius detained him for some time. Thus, when all the others had taken their leave of him and made the journey across the straits of the Propontis to Damalion,[56] and when he was now relieved of their troublesome presence, he sent for him on many occasions. He explained in more detail the adventures that the Latins must expect to meet with on their march; he also laid bare his own suspicions of their plans. In the course of many conversations on this subject he un-reservedly opened the doors of his soul, as it were, to the count; he warned him always to be on his guard against Bohemond's perfidy, so that if attempts were made to break the treaty he might frustrate them and in every way thwart Bohemond's schemes. Saint-Gilles pointed out that Bohemond inherited perjury and guile from his ancestors – it was a kind of heirloom. 'It will be a miracle if he keeps his sworn word,' he said. 'As far as I am concerned, however, I will always try to the best of my ability to observe your commands.' With that he took his leave of the emperor and went off to join the whole Keltic army.[57] Alexius would have liked to share in the expedition against the barbarians, too, but he feared the enormous numbers of the Kelts. He did think it wise, though, to move to Pelekanum. Making his permanent headquarters near Nicaea, he could obtain information about their progress and at the same time about Turkish activities outside the city, as well as about the condition of the inhabitants inside. It would be shameful, he believed, if in the meantime he did not himself win some military success. When a favourable opportunity arose, he planned to capture Nicaea himself; that would be preferable to receiving it from the Kelts (according to the agreement already made with them). Nevertheless he kept the idea to himself. Whatever dispositions he made, and the

56. In April 1097.   57. In May 1097.

reasons for them, were known to himself alone, although he did entrust this task to Boutoumites (his sole confidant). Boutoumites was instructed to suborn the barbarians in Nicaea by all kinds of guarantees and the promise of a complete amnesty, but also by holding over them the prospect of this or that retribution – even massacre – if the Kelts took the city. He had long been assured of Boutoumites' loyalty and he knew that in such matters he would take energetic measures. The history of the foregoing events has been set out in chronological order from the beginning.

BOOK ELEVEN

THE FIRST CRUSADE
(1097–1104)

BOHEMOND and all the counts met at a place from which they intended to sail across to Kibotos, and with Godfrey they awaited the arrival of Saint-Gilles who was coming with the emperor. Thus with their forces united they would set out along the road to Nicaea. However, their numbers were so immense that further delay became impossible – the food-supplies were deficient. So they divided their army in two: one group drove on through Bithynia and Nicomedia towards Nicaea; the other crossed the strait to Kibotos and assembled in the same area later. Having approached Nicaea in this manner they allotted towers and intervening battlements to certain sections. The idea was to make the assault on the walls according to these dispositions; rivalry between the various contingents would be provoked and the siege pressed with greater vigour. The area allotted to Saint-Gilles was left vacant until he arrived. At this moment the emperor reached Pelekanum, with his eye on Nicaea (as I have already pointed out). The barbarians inside the city meanwhile sent repeated messages to the sultan [1] asking for help, but he was still wasting time and as the siege had already gone on for many days, from sunrise right up to sunset, their condition was obviously becoming extremely serious. They gave up the fight, deciding that it was better to make terms with the emperor than to be taken by the Kelts. Under the circumstances they summoned Boutoumites, who had often promised in a never-ending stream of letters that this or that favour would be granted by Alexius, if only

[1]. Kilij Arslan, the Seljuq Sultan, was away in the east, fighting Danish-mends for Melitene. He probably underestimated the Frankish threat and put overmuch faith in stories of differences between Alexius and the Crusaders. His wife, his children and his treasures were actually in Nicaea at this time – sure proof that he believed the city was impregnable.

they surrendered to him. He now explained in more detail the emperor's friendly intentions and produced written guarantees. He was gladly received by the Turks, who had despaired of holding out against the overwhelming strength of their enemies; it was wiser, they thought, to cede Nicaea voluntarily to Alexius and share in his gifts, with honourable treatment, than to become the victims of war to no purpose. Boutoumites had not been in the place more than two days before Saint-Gilles arrived, determined to make an attempt on the walls without delay; he had siege engines ready for the task. Meanwhile a rumour spread that the sultan was on his way. At this news the Turks, inspired with courage again, at once expelled Boutoumites. As for the sultan, he sent a detachment of his forces to observe the Frankish offensive, with orders to fight if they met any Kelts. They were seen by Saint-Gilles's men from a distance and a battle took place – but it went ill for the Turks, for the other counts and Bohemond himself, learning of the engagement, set aside up to 200 men from each company, thus making up a considerable army, and sent them immediately to help. They overtook the barbarians and pursued them till nightfall. Nevertheless, the sultan was far from downcast at this setback; at sunrise the next morning he was in full armour and with all his men occupied the plain outside the walls of Nicaea. The Kelts heard about it and they too armed themselves for battle. They descended on their enemies like lions. The struggle that then ensued was ferocious and terrible. All through the day it was indecisive, but when the sun went down the Turks fled. Night had ended the contest. On either side many fell and most of them were killed; the majority of the fighters were wounded. So the Kelts won a glorious victory. The heads of many Turks they stuck on the ends of spears and came back carrying these like standards, so that the barbarians, recognizing afar off what had happened and being frightened by this defeat at their first encounter, might not be so eager for battle in future. So much for the ideas and actions of the Latins. The sultan, realizing how numerous they were and after this onslaught made aware of their self-confidence and daring, gave a hint to the Turks in Nicaea: 'From now on do just what you consider best.' He already knew that they preferred to deliver up the city to Alexius than to become prisoners of the Kelts. Meanwhile Saint-Gilles, setting about the task allotted to him, was constructing a wooden tower, circular in shape; inside and out he covered it with leather hides and filled the centre with intertwined wickerwork. When it was thoroughly strengthened, he approached the so-called Gonatas Tower.[2] His machine[3] was manned by soldiers whose job was to batter the walls and also by expert sappers, equipped with iron tools to undermine them from below; the former would engage the defenders on the ramparts above, while the latter worked with impunity below. In place of the stones they prised out, logs of wood were put in and when their excavations reached the point where they were nearly through the wall and a gleam of light could be seen from the far side, they set light to these logs and burnt them. After they were reduced to ashes, Gonatas inclined even more, and merited its name even more than before. The rest of the walls were surrounded with a girdle of battering-rams and 'tortoises'; in the twinkling of an eye, so to speak, the outer ditch was filled with dust, level with the flat parts on either side of it. Then they proceeded with the siege as best they could.

The emperor, who had thoroughly investigated Nicaea, and

2. This building acquired its name long ago, when the famous Manuel, father of the previous emperor Isaac Comnenus and his brother John (who was my grandfather on the paternal side), was promoted supreme commander of all the east by the then emperor Basil. His purpose was to put an end to hostilities with Sclerus, either by opposing him with force, or by driving him to seek peace terms through diplomatic means. Sclerus being a man of war and delighting in bloodshed, invariably welcomed battle rather than peace, so day by day there were violent clashes. Not only did Sclerus reject an armistice, but even fought bravely to capture Nicaea with helepoleis and battered down the ramparts. The greater part of this tower was cut away at its base and it sank down: it seemed to be bending its knee – hence its name, Gonatas. (A.C.)

Manuel Eroticus was a distinguished prefect under Basil II Bulgaroktonos (976–1025). The campaigns against Sclerus are described in outline by Psellus (*Chronographia*, i).

3. Called by specialists in the construction of war-machines a 'tortoise'. (A.C.)

on many occasions, judged that it could not possibly be captured by the Latins, however overwhelming their numbers. In his turn he constructed helepoleis of several types, but mostly to an unorthodox design of his own which surprised everyone. These he sent to the counts. He had, as we have already remarked, crossed with the available troops and was staying at Pelekanum near Mesampeloi, where in the old days a sanctuary was built in honour of George, the great martyr. Alexius would have liked to accompany the expedition against the godless Turks, but abandoned the project after carefully weighing the arguments for and against: he noted that the Roman army was hopelessly outnumbered by the enormous host of the Franks; he knew from long experience, too, how untrustworthy the Latins were. Nor was that all: the instability of these men and their treacherous nature might well sweep them again and again, like the tides of Euripus,[4] from one extreme to the other; through love of money they were ready to sell their own wives and children for next to nothing. Such were the reasons which prevented him then from joining the enterprise. However, even if his presence was unwise, he realized the necessity of giving as much aid to the Kelts as if he were actually with them. The great strength of its walls, he was sure, made Nicaea impregnable; the Latins would never take it. But when it was reported that the sultan was bringing strong forces and all necessary food supplies across the lake,[5] with no difficulty at all, and these were finding their way into the city, he determined to gain control of the lake. Light boats, capable of sailing on its waters, were built, hoisted on wagons and launched on the Kios side. Fully-armed soldiers were put on board, under the command of Manuel Boutoumites. Alexius gave them more standards than usual – so that they might seem far more numerous than they really were – and also trumpets and drums. He then turned his attention to the mainland. He sent for Taticius and Tzitas. With a force of brave peltasts, 2,000 in all, they were despatched to Nicaea;

4. The narrow channel between the island of Euboea and the Greek mainland, notorious for its currents.
5. The Ascanian Lake, to the west of the city.

their orders were to load their very generous supply of arrows on mules as soon as they disembarked and seize the fort of St George; at a good distance from the walls of Nicaea they were to dismount from their horses, go on foot straight for the Gonatas Tower and there take up position; they were then to form ranks with the Latins and acting under their orders assault the walls. Obedient to the emperor's instructions Taticius reported to the Kelts that he had arrived with his army, whereupon everyone put on armour and attacked with loud shouts and war-cries. Taticius' men fired their arrows in great volleys while the Kelts made breaches in the walls and kept up a constant bombardment of stones from their catapults. On the side of the lake the enemy were panic-stricken by the imperial standards and the trumpets of Boutou-mites, who chose this moment to inform the Turks of the emperor's promises. The barbarians were reduced to such straits that they dared not even peep over the battlements of Nicaea. At the same time they gave up all hope of the sultan's coming. They decided it was better to hand over the city and start negotiations with Boutoumites to that end. After the usual courtesies Boutoumites showed them the chrysobull entrusted to him by Alexius, in which they were not only guaranteed an amnesty, but also a liberal gift of money and honours for the sister and wife of the sultan.[6] These offers were extended to all the barbarians in Nicaea without exception. With confidence in the emperor's promises the inhabitants allowed Boutoumites to enter the city. At once he sent a message to Taticius: 'The quarry is now in our hands. Preparations must be made for an assault on the walls. The Kelts must be given that task too, but leave nothing to them except the wall-fighting round the ramparts. Invest the city at all points, as necessary, and make the attempt at sunrise.' This was in fact a trick to make the Kelts believe that the city had been captured by Boutoumites in fighting; the drama of be-trayal carefully planned by Alexius was to be concealed, for it was his wish that the negotiations conducted by Boutoumites should not be divulged to the Kelts. On the next day the call

6. The latter, it was said, was a daughter of Tzachas. (A.C.)

to battle was sounded on both sides of the city: on one, from the mainland, the Kelts furiously pressed the siege; on the other Boutoumites, having climbed to the battlements and set up there the imperial sceptres and standards, acclaimed the emperor to the accompaniment of trumpets and horns. It was in this way that the whole Roman force entered Nicaea. Nevertheless, knowing the great strength of the Kelts, as well as their fickle nature and passionate, impulsive whims, Boutoumites guessed that they might well seize the fort if they once got inside. The Turkish satraps in Nicaea, moreover, were capable, if they wished, of throwing into chains and massacring his own force – in comparison with the Romans they were numerous. Therefore he took possession of the keys of the city gate at once. There was at this time only one gate allowing people to enter or leave, the others having been closed through fear of the Kelts just beyond the walls. With the keys of this particular gate in his hands, he determined to reduce the number of satraps by a ruse. It was essential to have them at his mercy, if he was himself to avoid a catastrophe. He sent for them and advised a visit to the emperor, if they wanted to receive from him large sums of money, to be rewarded with high distinctions and to find their names on the lists of annual pensioners. The Turks were persuaded and during the night the gate was opened; they were let out, a few at a time and at frequent intervals, to make their way across the nearby lake to Rodomer[7] and the half-caste Monastras, who were stationed by St George's fort. Boutoumites' orders were that the satraps should be forwarded to the emperor immediately they disembarked; not even for a brief moment were they to be detained, lest uniting with the Turks sent on behind them they might plot some mischief against the Romans. This was in fact a simple prediction, an intuitive remark which could only be attributed to the man's long experience, for as long as the new arrivals were quickly sent on to Alexius the Romans were secure and no danger whatever hung over them; but when Rodomer and Monastras relaxed their vigilance they found themselves in peril from the

7. Rodomer the Bulgarian was a cousin of Anna.

barbarians whom they kept back. The Turks, as their numbers
grew, planned to take one of two courses: either in the night
they would attack and kill the Romans, or they would bring
them as prisoners to the sultan. The latter was unanimously
decided to be the better idea. They did attack in the night and
took them away as their captives. The place they made for was
the hill-top of Azala, . . .[8] stades from the walls of Nicaea.
Having arrived there they naturally dismounted to rest their
horses. Now Monastras was a half-caste and understood the
Turkish dialect; Rodomer, too, having been captured by the
Turks long ago and having lived with them for a considerable
time, was himself not unacquainted with their language. They
tried hard to move their captors with persuasive arguments.
'Why are you mixing a lethal potion for us, as it were, without
deriving the slightest benefit for yourselves? When the others
without exception are enjoying great rewards from the
emperor and having their names enrolled for annual pensions,
you will be cutting yourselves off from all these privileges.
Well now, don't be such fools, especially when you can live in
safety without interference and return home exulting in riches.
You may perhaps acquire new territory. Don't throw yourselves into certain danger. Maybe you'll meet Romans lying
in ambush over there,' pointing to mountain streams and
marshy parts; 'if you do, you'll be massacred and lose your
lives for nothing. There are thousands of men lying in wait for
you, not only Kelts and barbarians, but a multitude of Romans
as well. Now if you take our advice, you will turn your
horses' heads and come to the emperor with us. We swear, as
God is our witness, that you will enjoy countless gifts at his
hands, and then, when it pleases you, you will leave as free
men, without hindrance.' These arguments convinced the
Turks. Pledges were exchanged and both parties set out on
their way to Alexius. On their arrival at Pelekanum, all were
received with a cheerful smile (although inwardly he was very
angry with Rodomer and Monastras). For the present they
were sent off to rest, but on the next day all those Turks who
were eager to serve him received numerous benefits; those

8. There is a lacuna in the text here.

who desired to go home were permitted to follow their own
inclination – and they too departed with not a few gifts. It was
only later that Alexius severely reprimanded Rodomer and
Monastras for their folly, but seeing that they were too
ashamed to look him in the face, he altered his attitude and
with words of forgiveness strove to conciliate them. We will
leave Rodomer and Monastras there. Let us come back to
Boutoumites. When he was promoted Duke of Nicaea at that
time by the emperor, the Kelts asked him for permission to
enter the city: they desired to visit the sacred churches there
and worship. Boutoumites, as I have already remarked, was
well aware of the Keltic disposition and a visit *en masse* was
refused. However, he did open the gates for groups of ten.

The emperor was still in the vicinity of Pelekanum. He
wished those counts who had not yet sworn allegiance to give
him their pledges in person. Written instructions were issued
to Boutoumites to advise all counts not to begin the march to
Antioch before doing homage to the emperor; this would be
an opportunity for them to accept even greater gifts. Hearing
of money and gifts, Bohemond was the first to obey Boutoumites' advice. He immediately counselled all of them to return. Bohemond was like that – he had an uncontrollable lust
for money. The emperor welcomed them with great splendour
at Pelekanum. He was most sedulous in promoting their welfare. Finally he called them together and spoke: 'Remember
the oath you have all sworn to me and if you really intend not
to transgress it, advise any others you know, who have not
sworn, to take this same oath.' They at once sent for these men
and all, with the exception of Tancred, Bohemond's nephew,
assembled to pay homage. Tancred, a man of independent
spirit, protested that he owed allegiance to one man only,
Bohemond, and that allegiance he hoped to keep till his dying
day. He was pressed by the others, including even the
emperor's kinsmen. With apparent indifference, fixing his gaze
on the tent in which the emperor held the seat of honour (a
tent more vast than any other in living memory) he said, 'If
you fill it with money and give it to me, as well as the sums
you have given to all the other counts, then I too will take the

oath.' Palaeologus, zealous on the emperor's behalf and finding Tancred's words insufferable and hypocritical, pushed him away with contempt. Tancred recklessly darted towards him, whereupon Alexius rose from his throne and intervened. Bohemond, for his part, calmed down his nephew, telling him it was improper to behave with disrespect to the emperor's relatives. Tancred, ashamed now of acting like a drunken lout before Palaeologus and to some extent convinced by the arguments of Bohemond and the others, took the oath. When all had taken their leave of the emperor, Taticius (at that time Great Primicerius) and the forces under his command were ordered to join the Franks; Taticius' duty would be to help and protect them on all occasions and also to take over from them any cities they captured, if indeed God granted them that favour. Once more therefore the Kelts made the crossing on the next day and all set out for Antioch. Alexius assumed that not all their men would necessarily follow the counts; he accordingly notified Boutoumites that all Kelts left behind were to be hired to guard Nicaea. Taticius, with his forces, and all the counts, with their numberless hosts, reached Leukai in two days. At his own request Bohemond was in charge of the vanguard, while the rest followed in column of march at a slow pace. When some Turks saw him moving rather fast on the plain of Dorylaeum [9] they thought they had chanced upon the whole Keltic army and treating it with disdain they at once attacked. That crazy idiot, Latinus, who had dared to seat himself on the imperial throne, forgetting the emperor's advice stupidly rode out in front of the rest (he was on the extreme end of Bohemond's line). Forty of his men were killed then and he himself was seriously wounded. He turned in flight and hurried back to the centre – visible proof, although he would not admit it in words, of Alexius' wise counsel. Bohemond, seeing the ferocity of the Turks, sent for reinforcements, which quickly arrived. From then on the battle was hotly contested, but the terrible conflict ended in a

9. The modern Eskishehir. The battle took place on 1 July 1097. Bohemond had begun his march on 26 June; the other contingents on 28 and 29 respectively.

victory for the Romans and Kelts. After that the march continued, but with the contingents in touch with one another. They were met near Hebraike[10] by the Sultan Tanisman[11] and Hasan, who alone commanded 80,000 fully-armed infantry. It was a hard-fought battle, not only because of the vast numbers involved, but also because neither side would give way. However, the Turks were fighting with more spirit and Bohemond, commanding on the right wing, realized this. So, detaching himself from the rest of the army, he made a headlong onslaught on Kilij Arslan himself, charging 'like a lion exulting in his might',[12] as the poet says. This had a terrifying effect on the enemy and they fled. The Kelts, remembering the emperor's instructions, did not pursue them very far, but they occupied the Turkish entrenchment and rested there for a short time. They again fell in with the Turks near Augustopolis, attacked and routed them completely. After that the barbarians faded away. The survivors from the battle were scattered in all directions, leaving behind their women and children and making certain of their own safety in flight; in future they had not even the strength to look the Latins in the face.

What happened then, you ask. Well, the Latins with the Roman army reached Antioch by what is called the 'Quick Route'. They ignored the country on either side. Near the walls of the city a ditch was dug, in which the baggage was deposited, and the siege of Antioch began. It lasted for three lunar months.[13] The Turks, anxious about the difficult position in which they found themselves, sent a message to the Sultan of Chorosan, asking him to supply enough men to help them defend the people of Antioch and chase away the besieging Latins. Now it chanced that a certain Armenian[14] was on a tower of the city, watching that part of the wall allotted to

10. Heraclea.

11. Probably Malik Ghazi Gümüshtigin, son of Malik Danishmend who died *c.* 1084.

12. Homer, *Iliad* v, 299.

13. The army arrived before Antioch on 21 October 1097; the city fell on 3 June 1098.

14. His name was Firouz. He had become a Mahommedan, pretended to be loyal to Yaghi-Siyan (governor of Antioch), but bore him a grudge.

Bohemond. This man often used to lean over the parapet and Bohemond, by flagrant cajolery and a series of attractive guarantees, persuaded him to hand over the city. The Armenian gave his word: 'Whenever you like to give some secret sign from outside, I will at once hand over to you this small tower. Only make sure that you, and all the men under you, are ready. And have ladders, too, all prepared for use. Nor must you alone be ready: all the men should be in armour, so that as soon as the Turks see you on the tower and hear you shouting your war-cries, they may panic and flee.' However, Bohemond for the time being kept this arrangement to himself. At this stage of affairs a man came with the news that a very large force of Agarenes was on the point of arriving from Chorosan; they would attack the Kelts. They were under the command of Kourpagan.[15] Bohemond was informed and being unwilling to hand over Antioch to Taticius (as he was bound to do if he kept his oaths to the emperor) and coveting the city for himself, he devised an evil scheme for removing Taticius involuntarily. He approached him. 'I wish to reveal a secret to you,' he said, 'because I am concerned for your safety. A very disturbing report has reached the ears of the counts – that the sultan has sent these men from Chorosan against us at the emperor's bidding. The counts believe the story is true and they are plotting to kill you. Well, I have now done my part in forewarning you: the danger is imminent. The rest is up to you. You must consult your own interests and take thought for the lives of your men.' Taticius had other worries apart from this: there was a severe famine (an ox-head was selling for three gold staters) and he despaired of taking Antioch. He left the place, therefore, boarded the Roman ships anchored in the harbour of Soudi[16] and sailed for Cyprus. After his departure Bohemond, who was still keeping secret the Armenian's promise, battened on fine hopes, reserving to himself the future governorship of Antioch. He addressed the counts: 'You see how long a time already we have spent here in misery. So far we have made no good progress. Worse

15. Kerbogha, the Emir of Mosul.
16. St Symeon, the port of Antioch.

still, we may soon become the victims of famine, unless we make some better provision for our safety.' When they asked him what he suggested, he went on: 'Not all victories are granted by God through the sword, nor are such results invariably achieved through battle. What the moil of war has not produced is often gladly given after negotiation, and friendly diplomatic manoeuvres many a time have set up finer trophies. In my opinion it's wrong to waste our time to no purpose; we should hurry to invent some sensible and bold scheme to save ourselves before Kourpagan arrives. I suggest that each of us should try hard to win over the barbarian watching his particular section. And if you approve, let a prize be awarded to the first man who succeeds in this – the governorship of the city, say, until the arrival of the emperor's nominee, who will take over from us. Of course, even in this we may not make any good progress.' The cunning Bohemond, who loved power, loved it not for the sake of the Latins or their common interests, but to glorify himself. His plans and intrigues and deceptions did not fail – the story as it unfolds will make that plain. The counts unanimously approved of his scheme and set to work. As day broke Bohemond immediately went off to the tower; [17] the Armenian, according to his agreement, opened the gates. Bohemond leapt at once with his followers to the top of the tower as fast as he could. Besiegers and besieged alike saw him standing there on the battlements and ordering the trumpeter to sound the call to battle. An extraordinary sight could then be seen: the Turks, panic-stricken, without more ado fled through the gate at the other side of the city; a mere handful, brave warriors, were left behind to guard the citadel; the Kelts outside followed in the steps of Bohemond as they climbed the ladders to the top and straightway occupied the city. Tancred, with a strong force of Kelts, lost no time in pursuing the runaways, killing and wounding many of them. When Kourpagan arrived with his countless thousands to help, he found the place already in

17. The Tower of the Two Sisters. The full story of the assault is magnificently told in Runciman's *History of the Crusades* (vol. i) where he makes use of the much fuller evidence from the Latin historians.

the hands of the enemy. He dug a trench, deposited in it his baggage, pitched camp and prepared to invest the city, but before he could begin the Kelts made a sortie and attacked. There was a tremendous struggle, in which the Turks were victorious; the Latins were penned up inside the gates, exposed to danger from two sides – from the defenders of the citadel (the barbarians still controlled that) and from the Turks encamped beyond the walls. Bohemond, being a clever man and wishing to secure for himself the first place in the government of Antioch, again addressed the counts: 'It's not right,' he said, 'that the same men should have to fight on two fronts – with enemies outside and in the city at the same time. We ought to divide up our forces in two unequal groups, proportionate to the enemies opposed to us, and then take up the challenge against them. My task will be to fight the defenders of the citadel, if, that is, you agree. The others will be concerned with the enemy outside. They will launch a violent attack on them.' Everyone agreed with this idea of Bohemond. He immediately built a small counter-wall facing the citadel and cutting it off from the rest of Antioch, a very sturdy line of defence if the war went on. After it was completed he established himself as its guardian, ever watchful, never relaxing the pressure on the defenders at every available opportunity. He fought most bravely. The other counts devoted careful attention to their own sectors, protecting the city at all points, examining the parapets and the battlements that crown the walls, making sure that no barbarians from outside should climb up by ladders and so capture the city, that no one from inside should furtively make his way on to the walls and then, after parley with the enemy, arrange to betray it.

While these events were taking place at Antioch, the emperor was much concerned to bring help personally to the Kelts, but the despoiling and utter destruction of cities and districts by the sea held him back, however impatient. For Tzachas held Smyrna as though it were his own private property, and Tangripermes retained a city of the Ephesians near the sea, in which a church had once been built in honour of the apostle St John the Divine. One after the other the satraps occupied fortified posts, treating the Christians like slaves and ravaging everything. They had even taken the islands of Chios and Rhodes (in fact, all the rest) and there they built their pirate vessels. As a result of these activities the emperor thought it best to attend first to the sea-board and Tzachas. He decided to leave sufficient forces on the mainland, with a strong fleet; they would serve to throw off and contain barbarian incursions. With the remainder of the army he would take the road to Antioch and fight the Turks on the way as chance offered. John Ducas, his brother-in-law, was summoned and to him were entrusted troops drawn from different countries and enough ships to lay siege to the coastal towns; he also took charge of Tzachas' daughter, held prisoner along with the others who happened at that time to be in Nicaea. John's instructions were to make a general proclamation of the capture of Nicaea; if it was not believed, he was then to exhibit the lady herself to the Turkish satraps and the barbarians living in the coastal areas. He hoped that the satraps, then in control of the places I have mentioned, seeing her and being convinced that the city had really fallen would surrender without a struggle in sheer despair. So John was sent, well equipped with supplies of all kinds. How many triumphs he achieved in the fight against Tzachas and how he drove him out of Smyrna will be described hereafter. He took his leave of the emperor, left the capital and crossed at Abydos. Kaspax became admiral, with total responsibility for the naval expedition. John promised him that if he fought well he would be appointed governor of Smyrna itself (when that city was taken) and of all the neighbouring districts. While Kaspax sailed as commander of the naval forces, John remained on land as tagmatarch. The inhabitants of Smyrna saw Kaspax and John approaching simultaneously; Ducas pitched camp a short distance from the walls, while Kaspax ran his ships aground in the harbour. The men in Smyrna already knew that Nicaea had fallen and they were in no mood for fighting: they preferred to start negotiations for peace, promising to give up their city to John without a struggle and with no bloodshed, if he would swear on oath to let them go home unharmed. Ducas agreed, giving his word that Tzachas' proposal would be carried out to the letter. Thus the enemy was peacefully ejected and Kaspax became supreme governor of Smyrna. At this point an incident took place which I will outline now. When Kaspax had left John Ducas, a certain Smyrnaean came to him with a complaint. He said that 500 golden staters had been stolen from him by a Saracen. Kaspax ordered the two parties to appear before him for judgement. The Syrian[18] was forcibly dragged in and thought he was being hauled off to execution. In desperation for his life he drew his dagger and plunged it into Kaspax's stomach; then, wheeling round, he struck at the governor's brother and wounded him in the thigh. In the great confusion that followed the Saracen ran off, but all the sailors of the fleet (including the rowers) entered the city in a disorganized mob and massacred everyone without mercy. It was a pitiable sight – some 10,000 slain in the twinkling of an eye. John Ducas, deeply moved by the murder of Kaspax, once again, and for some time, devoted his whole attention to the affairs of Smyrna. He came to the city, made a thorough inspection of its defences and received accurate information from experts about the feelings of its people. The situation called for a man of courage and John appointed as the new governor a brave soldier, Hyaleas, in his opinion the outstanding candidate for the post. All the fleet was left behind to protect Smyrna, but John himself drove on to Ephesus with the army. Ephesus was then held by the satraps Tangripermes and Marakes. The enemy knew of his approach and arranged their forces, fully armed and in battle formation, on the plain outside the place. Losing not a minute the duke bore down on them with his men in disciplined ranks. The battle that ensued lasted for most of the day. Both sides were locked in combat and the issue was still undecided, when the Turks turned away and fled at speed. Many of them were killed there and prisoners were taken, not only from among the ordinary soldiers, but from the satraps, most of whom were captured. The total number reached as many as 2,000. When the emperor heard of this victory, he gave orders

18. That is, the Saracen.

that they were to be scattered among the islands. The Turkish survivors went off across the River Maeandros towards Polybotos and adopted a contemptuous attitude, thinking they had seen the last of Ducas. But it did not turn out like that. John left Petzeas to govern the city and taking with him all the infantry at once set out in pursuit. His troops marched in good order; there was no confusion. In fact, John followed the emperor's precepts well and controlled the advance in a manner worthy of a highly experienced general. The Turks, as I have said, had made their way across the Maeandros and through the towns in that vicinity; they reached Polybotos. The duke, however, did not take the same route: he followed a shorter track, seizing Sardes and Philadelphia by surprise. Michael Cecaumenus was detailed to guard them afterwards. When John arrived at Laodicea the whole population immediately came to meet him. He treated them as deserters from the enemy, encouraged them and allowed them to dwell on their own land without interference. He did not even appoint a governor. From there he went through Choma and took Lampe, where Eustathius Kamytzes was made military commander. When he finally came to Polybotos he found a strong body of Turks. An attack was launched on them just after they had deposited their baggage and in a clash a quick and decisive victory was won. Many Turks were killed and much booty, proportionate to their numbers, was recovered.

John had not yet returned and was still struggling against the Turks when the emperor was ready to march to the aid of the Kelts in the Antioch region. After wiping out many barbarians en route, he arrived at Philomelion with his whole army. Many towns formerly held by the Turks had been sacked. It was here that he was joined by Guillaume de Grantmesnil; Etienne, Count of France and Pierre d'Aulps [19] from Antioch. They had been let down by ropes from the battlements of the city and had come by way of Tarsus. By them he was assured that the Kelts had been reduced to a state of extreme peril; in fact, they affirmed on oath that the

19. That is, William of Grantmesnil; Stephen of Blois; and Peter Aliphas. They came to him about the middle of June 1098.

collapse was complete. The emperor was all the more anxious to hurry to their aid, despite the general opposition to the enterprise. But there was a widespread rumour of an imminent attack from countless hordes of barbarians: the Sultan of Chorosan, learning that Alexius had set out to help the Kelts, had sent his son Ishmael with very strong forces from Chorosan and even more distant parts, all well armed, to stop him. Ishmael was ordered to overtake the emperor before he could reach Antioch. The news brought by the Franks from Antioch and information received about Ishmael's approach checked the plans for rescuing the Kelts, however much Alexius longed to crush the furious Turkish onslaught and of course to put an end to their leader Kourpagan. As to the future, he drew the conclusion one would expect: to save a city recently captured by the Kelts, but still unsettled and immediately besieged by the Agarenes, would be impossible; the Kelts moreover had given up hopes of saving themselves and were planning to desert the fortifications and hand them over to the enemy, intent only on the preservation of their own lives by running away. The truth is that the Keltic race, among other characteristics, combines an independent spirit and imprudence, not to mention an absolute refusal to cultivate a disciplined art of war; when fighting and warfare are imminent, inspired by passion they are irresistible (and this is evident not only in the rank and file, but in their leaders too), charging into the midst of the enemy's line with overwhelming abandon – provided that the opposition everywhere gives ground; but if their foes chance to lay ambushes with soldier-like skill and if they meet them in a systematic manner, all their boldness vanishes. Generally speaking, Kelts are indomitable in the opening cavalry charge, but afterwards, because of the weight of their armour and their own passionate nature and recklessness, it is actually very easy to beat them. The emperor, having neither sufficient forces to resist their great numbers, nor the power to change the Keltic character, nor the possibility of diverting them to some expedient policy by more reasonable advice, thought it wise to go no further. He might lose Constantinople as well as Antioch in his eagerness to succour them. He was afraid that if the enormous hosts of Turks came upon him now, the people living in the area of Philomelion might fall victims to the barbarian sword. Under the circumstances he decided to make a general proclamation about the Agarene advance. It was immediately announced that every man and woman should leave the place before their arrival, thus saving their own lives and as much of their possessions as they could carry. Without delay the whole population, men and women alike, chose to follow the emperor . . . .[20] Such were the measures taken by Alexius with regard to the prisoners. One part of the army was detached and then subdivided into many companies; they were sent out in several directions to fight the Agarenes, wherever they were discovered making forays; they were to hold up the Turkish advance by force. Alexius himself, with all the barbarian prisoners and the Christians who had come over to him, prepared to return to Constantinople. The Archsatrap Ishmael had been informed of the emperor's departure from the capital; he had heard of the great slaughter that followed it and of the utter destruction of many townships on his march; he also knew that Alexius was about to return with much booty and many captives. Ishmael was in a difficult position: there was nothing left for him to do – he had lost the quarry, as it were. He changed his line of march and decided to besiege Paipert, which had been taken and occupied shortly before by the famous Theodore Gabras. The whole Turkish force halted by the river which flows near this place, but the move was not unknown to Gabras, who planned a surprise attack in the dark. The end of the Gabras affair, his origin and character are subjects reserved for the appropriate point in the history; we must now resume the narrative.

The Latins, being dreadfully harassed by the famine and the unrelenting siege, approached Peter,[21] their bishop, who

20. There is a lacuna in the text here. Incidentally, it prevents us from knowing what Alexius did with the prisoners.

21. The Latin historians have a very different version of this affair (see Runciman, vol. i, pp. 241–6, where the real hero is the peasant Peter Bartholomew, not the Bishop of Puy).

had been defeated formerly at Helenopolis (as I have already made clear) and asked for his advice. 'You promised,' he replied, 'to keep yourselves pure until you arrived at Jerusalem. But you have broken that promise, I think, and for that reason God no longer helps us as He did before. You must turn again to the Lord and weep for your sins in sackcloth and ashes, with hot tears and nights passed in intercession, proving your repentance. Then, and only then, will I join in seeking Divine Forgiveness on your behalf.' They listened to the high priest's counsel. Some days later, moved by some Divine oracle, he called to him the leading counts and recommended them to dig to the right of the altar[22] and there, he said, they would find the Holy Nail.[23] They did as he said, but found nothing, and returning to him in dismay told him of their failure. He prayed even more earnestly and commanded them to make a close examination with greater care. Again they carried out his orders exactly. This time they found what they were looking for and running brought it to Peter,[24] overcome with joy and religious awe. After that the Revered and Holy Nail was entrusted by them in their battles to Saint-Gilles, for he was purer than the rest. On the next day they made a sortie from a secret gate against the Turks. This was the occasion when the Count of Flanders[25] asked the others to grant him one request – to be allowed to ride out at the head of their force against the enemy, with only three companions. The request was granted, and when the rival armies were drawn up in ranks ready for battle, he dismounted, knelt down on the ground, and three times in prayer implored God for help. And when all cried aloud, 'God with us!' he charged at full gallop at Kourpagan, who was standing on a hill-top. Those who opposed them were straightway speared and hurled down. This struck terror into the hearts of the Turks and before battle was even begun they fled. A Divine Power was

22. In the Cathedral of St Peter, Antioch.
23. Anna writes of a 'nail'; the Latins speak of a 'Holy Lance' or 'Spear'.
24. Anna confuses Peter Bartholomew and Adhemar, Bishop of Puy.
25. Robert, Count of Flanders.

manifestly aiding the Christians.[26] What is more, in the confusion of their flight most of the barbarians were caught up in
the currents of the river and drowned; their bodies served as a
bridge for those who came after them. When the pursuit had
gone on for a fair distance the Kelts returned to the Turkish
entrenchment. The baggage was found there and all the booty
they had brought with them. Although the Kelts would have
liked to take it up at once, so enormous was the plunder that
they barely had the strength to bring it into Antioch in thirty
days. For a short while they remained there, recovering from
the tribulations of war. At the same time they were concerned
for Antioch – a new governor had to be appointed. Their
choice fell on Bohemond, who had asked for the post before
the fall of the city. He was given overriding authority, after
which the others set out on the road to Jerusalem. Many
coastal strong-points were captured along the route, but the
most powerful places (which would require a longer siege)
were for the time being ignored. They were in a hurry to
reach Jerusalem. The walls were encircled and repeatedly
attacked, and after a siege of one lunar month it fell.[27] Many
Saracens and Hebrews in the city were massacred. When
submission was complete, when all opposition ended, Godfrey
was invested with supreme power and nominated king.

Amerimnes, Exousiast of Babylon,[28] was informed of the
Keltic invasion. He heard that Jerusalem had been taken by
them and that they had occupied Antioch itself and many
other cities in that region. Accordingly he collected a huge
force composed of Armenians, Arabs, Saracens and Agarenes.
This force was sent out to fight the Kelts. Godfrey warned
them. At once they took up arms and descending to Jaffa
awaited the attack. Later they moved to Ramleh, the place
where the great George suffered martyrdom, and there they
fought a battle against Amerimnes' army. The Kelts won a
quick victory, but on the next day, when the enemy's van-

26. The battle took place on 26 June 1098.
27. On 15 July 1099.
28. That is, Sultan of Egypt. Cairo was regularly known as Babylon in
medieval times. In this passage the 'Babylonians' are Egyptians.

guard caught them from the rear, they were beaten and ran for their lives to Ramleh. The only count not present was Baldwin; he had escaped, not from cowardice, but to find some better means of securing his own safety and that of the army against the Babylonians. The latter surrounded and besieged Ramleh. It was soon taken. Many of the Latins were killed at the time, but more were sent as prisoners to Babylon.[29] From Ramleh the whole enemy force was hurriedly diverted to the siege of Jaffa – a typical manoeuvre of the barbarians. Baldwin visited all the townships captured by the Franks and collected a not inconsiderable number of cavalry and infantry troops, a force to be reckoned with. He marched on the Babylonians and routed them severely. The news of the Latin disaster at Ramleh was a grievous shock to the emperor; the thought of the counts being held in captivity was intolerable. To him these men, in the prime of their life, at the height of their strength, of noble lineage seemed to rival the heroes of old. They must no longer remain as prisoners in a foreign land. He called for Bardales and gave him plenty of money to ransom them. Before sending him off to Babylon he gave him letters addressed to Amerimnes about the counts. Amerimnes read the message and released the captives without payment, gladly freeing them all – except Godfrey, who had been sold at a price to his brother Baldwin. The counts were received with honour by the emperor at Constantinople. He gave them large sums of money, and after they had rested sufficiently sent them home, delighted with the treatment they had received at his hands. As for Godfrey, he was restored as King of Jerusalem and sent Baldwin to Edessa. At this point the emperor instructed Saint-Gilles to hand over Laodicea to Andronicus Tzintziloukes and the districts of Marakes and Valania to the officers of Eumathius, who was then Duke of Cyprus. Saint-Gilles himself was to proceed further and fight to the best of his ability for control of the other fortified places. The orders were carried out to the letter. After handing

29. From Book XII, 1, we learn that 300 counts were carried off to Egypt, if the two accounts do indeed refer to the same event (there is a difficulty, in that the names of the emperor's envoys are different).

over the places to the aforementioned officers, he departed for Antaras which he took without bloodshed. News of this spurred Atapakas of Damascus to march against him. Saint-Gilles was outnumbered by his opponent's strong forces, but devised a plan notable rather for its ingenuity than for any show of bravery. Putting his faith in the inhabitants of Antaras, he told them that he would conceal himself in some corner of the huge fortress. 'You,' he said, 'must not admit the truth when Atapakas arrives, but tell him I was frightened and ran away.' Well, Atapakas came and asked about Saint-Gilles; he was persuaded that he had indeed run away. Then, tired out after his march, he pitched his tent near the walls. As the natives showed him every mark of friendship, the Turks had no reason whatever to suspect any hostile intentions from them. They confidently set their horses free on the plain. At mid-day, when the sun's rays were directly overhead, Saint-Gilles in full armour with his men (they numbered up to four hundred) suddenly opened the gates and charged through the middle of their camp. Those who normally fought valiantly stood up and gave battle, forgetful of their own safety, but the rest attempted to escape with their lives by fleeing. The width of the plain and the absence of any marsh or hill or ravine betrayed them all into the hands of the Latins; they were all slain by the sword, except for a few who were captured. Saint-Gilles, having outwitted his adversaries in this manner, went on to Tripolis. As soon as he arrived, he climbed and seized the summit of the hill which lies opposite the city and which forms a part of the Lebanon; it would serve as a fortress and he could cut off the water flowing down from the Lebanon into Tripolis over the slopes of this hill. After informing the emperor of these actions, Saint-Gilles asked that a very strong fort should be constructed there before bigger forces turned up from Chorosan (which he would have to fight). Alexius entrusted to the Duke of Cyprus the task of building such a strong-point at whatever site the Frank might choose.[30] Such was the situation at this moment.

30. The castle was built on Mount Pilgrim (called by the Arabs Qalat Sanjil).

Meanwhile Saint-Gilles was encamped outside Tripolis, relentlessly straining every nerve to capture the place. Let us return to Bohemond. When he learnt of Tzintziloukes' arrival at Laodicea, he brought into the open the hatred he had long cherished against the emperor and sent his nephew Tancred with an adequate force to besiege the city. A rumour of it soon reached the ears of Saint-Gilles, too, and he lost not a minute in coming himself to Laodicea and entering into negotiations with Tancred. He produced all kinds of argument to dissuade him, but it was clear, after numerous meetings, that Tancred was not to be convinced – Saint-Gilles was, so to speak, 'singing to the deaf'. He returned to Tripolis. Without the slightest relaxation Tancred pressed the siege and Tzintziloukes, whose position was by now critical and who was impressed by the enemy's determination, asked for aid from Cyprus. It came too slowly and he, reduced to helplessness partly because of the siege, but also because of the distress brought about by famine, decided to surrender Laodicea.

While these things were going on, it became essential to choose a successor to Godfrey as king (he had died).[31] At once the Latins in Jerusalem sent for Saint-Gilles from Tripolis, desiring to put him on the throne, but he refused to make the journey at this time. Later he went to the capital and as the people of Jerusalem realized that he was still obdurate, they sent for Baldwin[32] and elected him king.[33] Saint-Gilles had been gladly welcomed by the emperor, but when Alexius heard of Baldwin's accession, he kept him at Constantinople. It was at this moment that the army of Normans[34] arrived under the command of the Count of Biandrate and his brother. The emperor on several occasions earnestly advised them to follow the same route as their predecessors (through the coastal areas) and so link up with the rest of the Latin army in Jerusalem. They would not listen, being reluctant to

31. On 18 July 1100, probably of typhoid. He was buried in the Church of the Holy Sepulchre.

32. Who was then in the district of Edessa. (A.C.)

33. On 25 December 1100.

34. They appear to have been mostly Lombards.

join the Franks.[35] They wanted to traverse another road to the east, going straight towards Chorosan, which they intended to conquer. The emperor knew their plan would be utterly disastrous, but since he was unwilling to see an army so numerous suffer extinction (there were 50,000 cavalrymen and 100,000 infantry) and since persuasion was impossible, he tried a new tack, as they say, and summoned Saint-Gilles and Tzitas to go with them. They were to give suitable advice and as far as they could restrain them from foolish enterprises. So they crossed the straits to Kibotus, hurried on to the Armeniac theme and took Ancyra[36] by surprise. Crossing the Halys they reached a small township held by Romans. Trusting the Normans as Christians, the priests in sacred vestments and carrying the gospel and crosses, approached them, but the invaders not only massacred the priests with inhuman cruelty, but the rest of the Christians. Then they dismissed them completely from their minds and carried on with their march in the direction of Amaseia. The Turks, who are skilled in warfare, occupied all the villages on their route and burnt all food-supplies before they arrived, then quickly attacked them. It was on a Monday that the Turks overwhelmed them. On that day they encamped somewhere in the region of Amaseia, with their baggage stored inside the rampart, but on the Tuesday the battle was renewed. The Turkish encampment surrounded the Normans, so that opportunity for foraging was denied them; nor could they lead out their horses and baggage-animals to water. By now the Kelts saw with their own eyes that annihilation awaited them. On the following day (Wednesday), fully armed and heedless of their personal safety, they engaged in a fierce battle with the barbarians. The Turks, having them in their grip, no longer relied on lance or bow, but seizing and drawing their swords fought at close quarters. The Normans were soon put to flight. Back in their own camp they looked for advice, but the finest of emperors, who had put before them a better course and whom they had refused to

35. They were anxious to rescue Bohemond, who had been captured by the Turks in August.
36. Ancyra (Ankara) was taken on 23 June 1101.

hear, was not with them any more. Their only recourse was to ask the opinions of Saint-Gilles and Tzitas. At the same time they inquired whether there was any territory in that area under the emperor's control: they might find refuge there. In the end they abandoned baggage, tents and all the infantry, mounted their horses and galloped off as fast as they could [37] to the coastal regions of the Armeniac theme and Pauraë. [38] The Turks made a mass attack on their encampment and took away everything. Afterwards they pursued and caught up with the infantry; they were all massacred, except for a handful of men who were carried off to Chorosan to be exhibited. So much for the brave exploits of the Turks in their battles against the Normans. As for Saint-Gilles and Tzitas, they made their way to Constantinople with the few survivors from the cavalry. The emperor received them there and after presenting them with generous gifts of money and allowing them to rest, he asked them where they would like to go for the future. They chose Jerusalem. Their request was granted in full: they were provided with a ship and sent off with great munificence. Saint-Gilles left Constantinople also, to rejoin his own army at Tripolis, eagerly seeking for a way to capture the city. Later he met with a fatal illness and as he was breathing his last [39] sent for his nephew Guillaume. [40] To him he bequeathed as a heritage all the strong-points taken by himself and appointed him commander-in-chief of his forces. At the news of his death Alexius at once wrote to the Duke of Cyprus, instructing him to send Nicetas Chalintzes with large sums of money for Guillaume; he was to win him over and persuade him to take a firm oath of allegiance to the emperor, an allegiance which his dead uncle Saint-Gilles had faithfully observed to the end of his life.

News also reached the emperor of Tancred's occupation of Laodicea. He sent a letter to Bohemond, which ran thus: 'You

37. The Battle of Mersivan (autumn 1101). Some four-fifths of the army died.
38. Bafra, at the mouth of the River Halys.
39. In his fortress on Mount Pilgrim (28 February 1105).
40. Guillaume-Jordan, Count of Cerdagne.

are aware of the oaths and promises made to the Roman Empire, not by you alone, but by all the other counts. Now you are the first to break faith. You have seized Antioch and by underhand methods gained possession of certain other fortified places, including Laodicea itself. I bid you withdraw from the city of Antioch and all the other places, thereby doing what is right, and do not try to provoke fresh hostilities and battles against yourself.' Bohemond read this letter in private. It was no longer possible to defend himself with his usual deceit, for his deeds bore clear evidence of the truth; in theory, therefore, he admitted the letter was justified, but blamed the emperor for his own evil doings. 'I myself,' he wrote, 'am not responsible for these things, but you. You promised to follow us with a strong force, but you were unwilling to back your pledges by action. As for us, after our arrival at Antioch, for three months with great suffering we contended with the enemy and with a famine unsurpassed in living memory, so bad that most of us were even reduced to eating meats forbidden by the law. Nevertheless, we held on as best we could, and while we were doing that, Your Majesty's most faithful servant Taticius, who had been appointed to help, abandoned us in our peril and went away. Contrary to expectation we did take the city and routed the forces which came from Chorosan to aid the men of Antioch. How, tell me, can it be right for us so lightly to renounce what we have won by our own sweat and toil?' When the emperor's ambassadors returned and he read Bohemond's reply, he realized that Bohemond was his old self again, incorrigible as ever; clearly the frontiers of the Roman Empire must be firmly held and Bohemond's unbridled ambition must somehow be checked. For these reasons Boutoumites was despatched with numerous troops to Cilicia.[41] With him he had the élite of the army, magnificent fighters, every one a 'guardsman of Ares'; also with him were Bardas and Michael the Chief Cupbearer, both in the prime of life 'just growing their first beards'. When these young men were small children the emperor had taken

41. Cilicia was clearly a province of great strategic value, the gateway to Syria.

them under his personal protection and had given them a good military education. Now, since he had more faith in their loyalty than in that of the others, he sent them to serve under Boutoumites with thousands of other fine soldiers, both Kelts and Romans. They were to accompany Boutoumites and obey him in everything, but at the same time the emperor relied on them to keep him informed by secret letters about ordinary things which happen from time to time. He was anxious to secure the whole of Cilicia; it would be easier then to prepare for operations against Antioch. Boutoumites therefore set out with all his forces and had reached Attalia when he discovered that Bardas and Michael were not obeying his orders. To prevent a mutiny among the soldiers – which would cause all his enthusiasm to end in nothing and force him to evacuate Cilicia without accomplishing anything – he at once informed Alexius of their activities. He begged to be relieved of their company. The emperor, aware of the damage likely to be done by such men, sharply diverted them and all the other suspects to a different task. They were told in writing to report without delay to Constantine Euphorbenus in Cyprus and to obey whatever orders he gave them.[42] The young men gladly read their instructions and sailed with all speed to the island. They had only spent a short time with the duke there before they were behaving with their usual arrogance towards him also. Naturally he regarded them with suspicion, while they wrote letters to the emperor full of recriminations against him. They remembered the emperor's solicitude for themselves and made constant references to Constantinople. Alexius was alarmed by their letters: with them in Cyprus were certain nobles whose loyalty he doubted and whom he had exiled; it was possible that these men might also be disaffected by their bad feeling. Because of this he at once ordered Cantacuzenus to take the young men with him. He came to Kyrenia, summoned them and took them away. Such was the story of Bardas and the Chief Cupbearer Michael. As for Boutoumites, he arrived in Cilicia with Monastras and the other commanders who had been left behind with him, and when he found that the

42. Constantine was at the time duke of the island. (A.C.)

Armenians had come to terms with Tancred, he by-passed them and took Marash, together with all the neighbouring townships and small places. A force capable of guarding the whole countryside was left under the command of the semi-barbarian Monastras. Boutoumites himself returned to the capital.[43]

When the Franks set out for Jerusalem with the intention of conquering the cities of Syria, they made fine promises to the Bishop of Pisa,[44] if he would help them to attain their goal. He was convinced by their arguments and incited two of his colleagues living by the sea to the same course of action. There was no delay. He equipped biremes, triremes, dromons and other fast vessels to the number of 900, and so left for Syria. A fairly strong squadron of this navy was detached to ravage Corfu, Leucas, Kephalonia and Zacynthos. The emperor thereupon ordered all provinces of the Roman Empire to provide ships. Many were also made ready in Constantinople itself. From time to time he used to board a ship with one bank of oars and give advice himself to the shipwrights about their construction. He knew the Pisans were masters of naval warfare and he feared a sea battle with them. Accordingly, on the prow of each vessel he had the heads of lions and other land animals affixed; they were made of bronze or iron, and the mouths were open; the thin layer of gold with which they were covered made the very sight of them terrifying. The [Greek] fire to be hurled at the enemy through tubes was made to issue from the mouths of these figure-heads in such a way that they appeared to be belching out the fire. When all was ready, Alexius sent for Taticius, who had recently come from Antioch, and entrusted this fleet to him with the title of Most Illustrious Admiral, but Landulf[45] was put in charge of the whole navy. He was promoted to the rank of grand duke,

43. In the following chapter Anna recounts events which had occurred in 1098–9; she goes back some years – an unfortunate habit of hers.

44. Daimbert, Archbishop of Pisa, appointed Patriarch of Jerusalem by Pope Urban in 1098 on the death of Adhemar of Le Puy. Anna, who has no love for Latin prelates, makes it appear that Daimbert organized the Pisan fleet.

45. Landulf had been born in Italy and no doubt understood the Latin naval strategy.

because he was the greatest expert in warfare at sea. They left the capital in the latter half of April [46] and arrived at Samos. The ships were anchored near the shore and they landed. The ships were then hauled up on the beach and thoroughly tarred to make them more seaworthy. However, when they heard of the voyage of the Pisans, they cast off and chased them as far as Cos. The Pisans reached the island in the morning, the Romans in the evening. Finding no Pisans, they sailed away to Knidus, which lies off the Anatolian mainland. While they were there they discovered a few Pisans who had been left behind (the main quarry had escaped them) and asked them where the Pisan fleet had gone. They said, 'Towards Rhodes.' At once the Romans cast off again and soon caught up with them between Patara and Rhodes. Spying the enemy the Pisans immediately made ready for battle, with sharpened swords and hearts prepared for combat. The Roman fleet drew near and a Peloponnesian count called Perichytas, who specialized in naval ambush, as soon as the enemy came in sight rowed hard and fast in his monoreme against them. He went through the Pisan centre like a flash of lightning and returned to the Romans, who unfortunately did not enter the battle in a disciplined manner – they made sharp, disorderly attacks. Landulf himself was the first to make contact with the enemy, but his fire missed the target and all he did was to squander the fuel. The count called Eleemon boldly made for a very large vessel by the stern, but fouled its rudders and found it hard to disengage. He would have been caught, too, if he had not quickly remembered the fuel prepared for his tubes and scored a direct hit with Greek fire. He then deftly manoeuvred his ship in either direction and immediately set light to three very big vessels of the Pisans. At the same time there was a sudden squall of wind which descended violently on the sea and whipped it up; the ships were dashed together and all but threatened to sink – the waves crashed down on them, the yard-arms creaked and the sails were torn. [47] The barbarians were frightened out of their wits, partly because of the fire being directed at them (they were unaccustomed to

46. 1099.   47. Anna uses language reminiscent of Homer.

such equipment: fire naturally rises upwards, but this was
being shot in whatever direction the Romans wished, often
downwards and sideways, to port or starboard [48]), partly
because they were thrown into confusion by the heavy seas.
They decided to flee. So much for them. As for the Roman
fleet, it was beached on a tiny island with a name something
like 'Seutlos'. When day broke it sailed on to Rhodes. The
Romans disembarked and led out their prisoners, including
Bohemond's nephew. They tried to scare them with threats
either to sell them all as slaves or kill them. When they saw
that the latter fate had no terrors for them and the prospect of
slavery made no impression at all, they wasted no more time –
they massacred them with swords. The survivors of the Pisan
expedition turned to plundering the islands that lay on their
course, and Cyprus. Eumathios Philokales, happening to be
there, attacked them. Their naval crews, overcome by fear and
without a thought for their shipmates who had gone ashore
for rapine, abandoned most of them on the island and weighing anchor in a state of panic sailed away to Laodicea with the
idea of rejoining Bohemond. In fact they did reach the place
and went to him, declaring their desire for friendship. He,
being Bohemond, was pleased to receive them. The others,
who had been marooned, when they returned to collect their
plunder and saw their fleet had gone, recklessly hurled themselves into the sea and were drowned. The Roman admirals
and Landulf, once they were in Cyprus, held a conference
about possible overtures for peace. As they were all agreed
that such a course was desirable, Boutoumites became their
emissary to Bohemond. He was detained by him for fifteen
whole days. Laodicea was now in the grip of famine and
Bohemond was his old self again, not changed a whit, a man
who had never learnt what it was to keep the peace. He sent
for Boutoumites. 'It wasn't for friendship's sake nor in search
of peace that you came here,' he said, 'but to set fire to my
ships. Be off with you – and think yourself lucky that you're
allowed to go away unmutilated.' So Boutoumites went. His

48. For the details of Greek fire and its use see Partington's *A History of
Greek Fire and Gunpowder*, a modern work of great value, and p. 517 below.

sponsors he found in the harbour of Cyprus. Bohemond's wicked intentions were now much clearer after these revelations and a treaty with the emperor was obviously out of the question. The Romans therefore weighed anchor again and crammed on all sail for the capital 'over the watery ways'.[49] Off Syke,[50] however, in a tremendous storm which lashed the waves into fury, the boats were cast up on the beach and all, except the ships under the command of Taticius, were half-wrecked. Such were the results of this naval war against the Pisans. Meanwhile Bohemond, being himself a thorough rogue, was afraid of the emperor's intentions: he might anticipate himself in seizing Kourikos,[51] then moor a Roman fleet in the harbour, thus guarding Cyprus and preventing the approach of hoped-for allies from Lombardy along the Anatolian seaboard. Under the circumstances he decided to rebuild Kourikos and occupy the port. In former times it had been a very strong city, but later fell in ruins. Now the emperor, foreseeing Bohemond's strategy, had taken his own precautions. The eunuch Eustathius was promoted from the office of kanicleios [52] to that of Grand Drungarius of the Fleet and was sent with instructions to seize Kourikos without delay. He was to lose no time in rebuilding the place itself and also the fort of Seleuceia, six stades away; in both places a strong force was to be left and Strategius Strabo was to be appointed duke, physically a little man but in the arts of war a person of very great importance. Moreover, an adequate fleet was to lie at anchor in the port and a proclamation was to be made warning sailors to be on their guard, to lie in wait for Bohemond's reinforcements coming from Lombardy and to give help to Cyprus. The drungarius sailed, thwarted Bohemond's schemes and restored Kourikos to its former condition. At once, too, Seleuceia was rebuilt and strengthened with ditches all round the city. Strategius had enough men to deal with

49. Homer, *Odyssey* iii, 171 *et al.*
50. In western Cilicia.   51. The modern Korgos.
52. Custodian of the Imperial Inkstand (which is said to have been shaped in the likeness of a dog – hence the name). The office was by no means a sinecure and its holders seem to have had the power to sign important documents.

any emergency in both Seleuceia and Kourikos, with a sufficient number of ships in the harbour. Eustathius returned to the capital, to be highly praised and generously rewarded by Alexius.

Such were the actions taken at Kourikos. A year [53] later the emperor learnt that a Genoese expedition was about to sail to the help of the Franks. He foresaw that the Genoese, like the others, would cause no little trouble to the Roman Empire. Cantacuzenus was accordingly sent overland with a considerable army and Landulf sailed with a fleet, hastily equipped. Landulf's task was to make full speed to the southern coast; [54] the Genoese on their voyage past Cilicia must be attacked. Both went off to their appointed tasks, but a terrible storm overwhelmed and broke up many of the ships. They were hauled up on the beach again and carefully treated with liquid pitch. While this was going on, Cantacuzenus was informed that the Genoese fleet was in the neighbourhood. He suggested that Landulf should take eighteen ships (as it happened they were the only ones seaworthy at the time – the rest were on land) and sail for Cape Maleos; he could moor the ships there (as the emperor had advised) and when the enemy sailed by, if he felt confident enough to risk a conflict, he could attack at once; if not, he could look to his own safety and the safety of his ships and crews by landing at Korone. Off he went and seeing the huge Genoese fleet he decided not to fight. Instead he sailed quickly to Korone. Cantacuzenus took over the whole Roman naval force (it was essential that he should do so), embarked what troops he had with him and pursued the enemy as fast as he could. He failed to overtake them, but reached Laodicea, eagerly looking forward to a trial of strength with Bohemond. He set to work occupying the harbour and keeping up ceaseless attacks on the walls by day and night. However, no progress was made. Hundreds of assaults went in and hundreds were repelled; his attempts to win over the Kelts were frustrated, his battles against them failed. In the end he built a small circular wall of dry rocks

53. In this chapter Anna deals with the events of 1104, although it is true that Genoese ships had been cruising in the area since 1097.
54. Of Asia Minor.

between the sands and the walls of Laodicea. The work took
up three whole days and nights. When it was completed, he
used it as a protective covering while another strong-point of
concrete was erected inside it, a base of operations for even
fiercer attacks on the city defences. Two towers, moreover,
were set up on either side of the harbour mouth and an iron
chain was stretched across the intervening space. Thus help
from the sea was excluded. At the same time he seized many of
the forts along the coast: Argyrocastron, Marchapin, Gabala
and certain others as far as the borders of Tripolis, places
which formerly paid tribute to the Saracens, but afterwards
were reunited with the Roman Empire by Alexius at the cost
of much sweat and toil. Alexius reckoned that Laodicea should
be invested from the land side as well. He had long experience
of Bohemond's cunning and his stratagems (Alexius had a
genius for appreciating a man's character quickly) and the
count's traitorous, rebellious nature was well understood.
Monastras was therefore sent overland with a powerful
contingent to besiege Laodicea from land while Cantacuzenus
shut it in by sea. But before Monastras arrived, his colleague
had occupied both harbour and town; only the citadel (nowadays commonly referred to as the *koula* [55]) was still in the hands
of 500 Keltic infantry and a hundred of their knights. Bohemond heard of this and he was also told by the count responsible for the defence of the citadel that provisions were scarce.
He concentrated all his own forces, therefore, with those of
Tancred and Saint-Gilles and all kinds of edible supplies were
loaded on mules. When he reached the city it was not long
before they were transported to the *koula*. Bohemond also had
an interview with Cantacuzenus. 'What's the idea of building
these earthworks?' he asked. 'You know,' replied Cantacuzenus, 'that you and your fellow counts swore to serve the
emperor and agreed under oath to hand over to him whatever
cities were captured by you. Later on you yourself lied about
the oaths, set aside even the treaties of peace; you took this
city and handed it over to us, then changed your mind and

55. No doubt derived from the Arabic. Perhaps it still survives in
modern army slang ('put him in the "cooler"!').

kept it, so that when I came here to accept the cities taken by you my visit was useless.' 'Have you come here hoping to take it from us with money or by force?' asked Bohemond. 'Our allies have received the money,' answered the Roman, 'for their gallantry in battle.' Bohemond was filled with wrath. 'Be sure of this: without money you wouldn't be able to capture even a watch-post.' Whereupon he provoked his troops to gallop right up to the gates of the city. As the Franks got near the walls they were driven back a little by Cantacuzenus' men guarding the ramparts, who fired arrows at them thick as snowflakes. Bohemond promptly rallied them and all (including himself) made their way into the citadel. The count defending Laodicea and his Kelts being suspect, Bohemond dismissed them and appointed a new commander. At the same time he destroyed the vineyards near the walls, so that his Latin cavalry should have freedom of movement. Then, having made these arrangements, he left the city and went off to Antioch. As for Cantacuzenus, he carried on the siege by every means available; hundreds of devices were tried, sudden assaults were made and helepoleis brought up to confound the Latins in the citadel. Monastras was also busy. Coming overland with the cavalry he occupied Longinias, Tarsus, Adana, Mamistra and indeed the whole of Cilicia.

Bohemond shuddered at the emperor's threats. Without means of defence (for he had neither an army on land nor a fleet at sea, and danger hung over him on both sides) he invented a plan,[56] not very dignified, but amazingly crafty. First he left the city of Antioch in the hands of his nephew Tancred, the son of the Marquis Odo; then he spread rumours everywhere about himself: 'Bohemond,' it was said, 'is dead.' While still alive he convinced the world that he had passed away. Faster than the beating of a bird's wings the story was propagated in all quarters: 'Bohemond,' it proclaimed, 'is a corpse.' When he perceived that the story had gone far enough, a wooden coffin was made and a bireme prepared.

56. This extraordinary story is not known to the Latin historians. Anna may have invented it; she certainly enjoys telling it and Bohemond was no doubt capable of such a ruse.

The coffin was placed on board and he, a still breathing 'corpse', sailed away from Soudi, the port of Antioch, for Rome. He was being transported by sea as a corpse. To outward appearance (the coffin and the behaviour of his companions) he was a corpse. At each stop the barbarians tore out their hair and paraded their mourning. But inside Bohemond, stretched out at full length, was a corpse only thus far; in other respects he was alive, breathing air in and out through hidden holes. That is how it was at the coastal places, but when the boat was out at sea, they shared their food with him and gave him attention; then once more there were the same dirges, the same tomfoolery. However, in order that the corpse might appear to be in a state of rare putrefaction, they strangled or cut the throat of a cock and put that in the coffin with him. By the fourth or fifth day at the most, the horrible stench was obvious to anyone who could smell. Those who had been deceived by the outward show thought the offensive odour emanated from Bohemond's body, but Bohemond himself derived more pleasure than anyone from his imaginary misfortune. For my part I wonder how on earth he endured such a siege on his nose and still continued to live while being carried along with his dead companion. But that has taught me how hard it is to check all barbarians once they have set their hearts on something: there is nothing, however objectionable, which they will not bear when they have made up their minds once and for all to undergo self-inflicted suffering. This man Bohemond was not yet dead – he was dead only in pretence – yet he did not hesitate to live with dead bodies. In the world of our generation this ruse of Bohemond was unprecedented and unique, and its purpose was to bring about the downfall of the Roman Empire. Before it no barbarian or Greek devised such a plan against his enemies, nor, I fancy, will anyone in our lifetime ever see its like again. When he reached Corfu, as if he had reached some mountain peak, as if the island were a place of refuge and he was now free from danger, he rose from the 'presumed dead', left the coffin where his 'corpse' had lain, enjoyed the sunshine to the full, breathed in a cleaner air and walked round the city of

Corfu. The inhabitants, seeing him dressed in outlandish, barbarian clothes, inquired about his family, his condition, his name; they asked where he came from and to whom he was going. Bohemond treated them all with lofty disdain and demanded to see the duke of the city. He was in fact a certain Alexius who came originally from the Armeniac theme. Coming face to face with him, Bohemond, arrogant in look and attitude, speaking with an arrogant tongue in a language wholly barbaric, ordered him to send this communication to the emperor: 'To you I, Bohemond, famous son of Robert, send this message. The past has taught you and your Empire how formidable are my bravery and my opposition. When I turn the scales of fortune, as God is my witness I will not leave unavenged the evils done to me in the past. Ever since I took Antioch on my march through Roman territory and with my spear enslaved the whole of Syria, I have had my fill of misery because of you and your army; my hopes, one after another, have been dashed; I have been thrust into a thousand misfortunes and a thousand barbarian wars. But now it is different. I want you to know that, although I was "dead", I have come back to life again; I have escaped your clutches. In the guise of a dead man I have avoided every eye, every hand, every plan. And now I live, I move, I breathe the air, and from this island of Corfu I send to Your Majesty offensive, hateful news. It will not make very pleasant reading for you. I have handed over the city of Antioch to my nephew Tancred, leaving him as a worthy adversary for your generals. I myself will go to my own country. As far as you and your friends are concerned, I am a corpse; but to myself and my friends it is manifest that I am a living man, plotting a diabolical end for you. In order to throw into tumult the Roman world which you rule, I who was alive became "dead"; now I who "died" am alive. If I reach the mainland of Italy and cast eyes on the Lombards and all the Latins and the Germans and our own Franks, men full of martial valour, then with many a murder I will make your cities and your provinces run with blood, until I set up my spear in Byzantium itself.' Such was the extreme bombast in which the barbarian exulted.

BOOK TWELVE

DOMESTIC TROUBLES –
SECOND NORMAN INVASION
(1105–7)

THE events that took place during Bohemond's first crossing; his many and obvious plots against the emperor; his attempts to win Roman domination for himself; the circumstances of his secret departure from Antioch, carefully prepared and carried out with ease and, one must admit it, with success; his voyage in the role of a corpse and his arrival at Corfu – all these have been described in sufficient detail. Let us now resume the narrative with his subsequent actions. When the stinking 'corpse' had reached Corfu, as I have said, he uttered threats against the emperor through the duke there (all this has been described); Bohemond then sailed on to Lombardy and set to work. His intention was to re-occupy Illyricum and for the purpose quickly to collect an army of allies greater than before. He entered into negotiations with the King of France[1] for a marriage and took as wife one of his daughters; the other he sent across the sea to Antioch to be united in wedlock to his nephew Tancred. Then, having gathered together enormous forces from every country and city, he summoned the counts with their several contingents and hurried on the crossing to Illyricum. The emperor, having received the communications sent to him through Alexius, at once wrote letters to all the countries, to Pisa, to Genoa and to Venice, forewarning them not to be carried away by Bohemond's insidious tales and thereafter join his expedition. Bohemond was in fact going round all these cities and provinces, making violent attacks on the emperor, calling him a pagan and an enemy of the

---

1. Philip I (1060–1108). The daughters were Constance, who married Bohemond and became the mother of his son Bohemond II (subsequently Prince of Antioch); and Cecilia, who married Tancred.

Christians. Now it happened that the Babylonian,[2] at the time
when the endless hordes of Kelts, after crossing into Asia
from the west, were striking at Antioch, Tyre and all the
places and districts in that area, had captured 300 counts. He
kept his prisoners under guard, and their imprisonment was
as terrible as any of ancient times. The news of their capture
and the dreadful things that befell them afterwards worried
the emperor. He devoted himself entirely to their rescue.
Nicetas Panoukomites was despatched with sums of money to
the Babylonian. Alexius also entrusted to him a letter, in which
he demanded the release of the counts and promised many
favours if they were set free from their bonds and allowed to
go. The Babylonian listened to Panoukomites as he delivered
this message; he also read it himself. The counts were then
without more ado set free and led out of their prison, but not
given complete freedom, for they were handed over to the
envoy and returned to the emperor. Not a penny of the money
offered was accepted by the Babylonian, whether because he
thought it an unsatisfactory ransom for captives so important,
or because he wished to avoid any imputation of bribery and
wanted it to be known that he was not selling them, but doing
the emperor a genuine, straightforward favour, or even
because he wanted more, God knows. On their arrival in
Constantinople Alexius saw them. He was overjoyed at the
barbarian's decision, and surprised too. When they were
interrogated closely about their experiences, he learnt how
they had been kept in prison for so long a time, for months in
fact, and had not once seen the sun nor been loosed from their
chains; during all that time they had been denied every kind of
nourishment except bread and water. Their sufferings excited
his pity and he shed tears of sympathy. They were at once
treated with much kindness; money was given them; all kinds
of raiment were provided for them; they were invited to the
baths and in every way attempts were made to ensure their
recovery from such ordeals. As for them, they were delighted
with the emperor's friendly attitude. These men, formerly our

2. The Fatimid caliph al-Amir or possibly the vizier who ruled in his
name, al-Afdal.

enemies and active opponents, transgressors of the oaths and pledges made to him, observed well his extraordinary forbearance to themselves. After some days he sent for them. 'I am granting you freedom of choice,' he said. 'You can stay as long as you like with us in the city. But whenever one of you, mindful of his own family, wishes to go away, he can take his leave of us without impediment and start on his homeward journey, generously provided for with money and all kinds of other necessities for the voyage. I want you to have absolute freedom of choice, to stay here or to go away; I want you to follow your own inclination as free men, according to your own opinion.' For a while the counts, treated with every kind of consideration by the emperor, were reluctant to tear themselves away. But the situation changed when Bohemond arrived in Lombardy, an occurrence I have already described. Bohemond was eager to recruit greater forces than ever, and on his visits to every city and district he often disparaged the emperor, loudly proclaiming in public that he was a pagan, aiding the pagans wholeheartedly. Now when Alexius heard of this, he presented the aforementioned counts with magnificent presents and sent them home – for two reasons: they were now themselves earnestly looking forward to the homeward voyage, and they would personally refute Bohemond's calumnies against himself. He then left hurriedly for Thessalonica, partly to give military training to the new recruits and partly to check Bohemond – news of his move would hold up Bohemond's crossing from Lombardy. The counts, then, departed from Constantinople and furnished undeniable evidence against Bohemond. They stigmatized him as a charlatan, incapable of telling the truth even about ordinary, everyday things; on many occasions they convicted him to his face and in every quarter denounced him, bringing forward witnesses worthy of credence – themselves.

Everywhere there was talk of Bohemond's invasion. If the emperor was to oppose the Keltic hordes, he would require numerous soldiers and an army of similar proportions. There was no hesitation, no delay. His officers in Koele-Syria, Cantacuzenus and Monastras, were summoned; the former

guarded Laodicea, the latter Tarsus. At their departure their
provinces were not abandoned: Petzeas with fresh troops was
despatched to Laodicea and Monastras' place at Tarsus was
taken by Oshin,[3] who came of a noble Armenian family. He
had a great reputation for bravery, according to report at the
time, although the present crisis absolutely belied it, at least as
far as his leadership was concerned. Tancred was now governing Antioch (we left him in Syria). He was constantly spreading underhand stories that he would soon be in Cilicia to lay
siege to it and wrest it from the hands of the emperor, because
it was his, won from the Turks by his spear. Propaganda of
this type was sent out in all directions; nor was that all – he
made even worse threats in letters delivered daily to Oshin.
Nor did he confine himself to threats: he gave certain preliminary examples of them and promised further action. Forces of
Armenians and Kelts were conscripted over a wide area and
these men were being trained daily. His army was thoroughly
drilled in battle formations and generally prepared for war.
Occasionally it was sent out to forage – the smoke that pre-
cedes the flames, so to speak. Siege engines were made ready
and in all kinds of ways Tancred busied himself in organizing
the assault. While he was engaged thus, the Armenian Oshin
was idly taking his ease, devoting himself to heavy drinking
bouts by night, as if nobody threatened him, as if there were
no cause for alarm, no great peril hanging over him. And yet
he was a very courageous man, a fine 'guardsman of Ares';
but when he came to land in Cilicia, far from his master's
control and invested with full authority, he completely
abandoned himself to a life of luxury; he became effeminate,
spent his time in perpetual debauches, and when the hour of
trial struck, it was clear that he had no stomach for a fight
against his tough, soldier-like adversary. The thunderous
menace of Tancred fell on deaf ears, and when Tancred came,
armed with the thunderbolt and ravaging Cilicia, Oshin's
eyes never saw the lightning flashes. All at once Tancred was
on the march from Antioch. His enormous army was divided
in two: one contingent was sent overland to attack the cities

3. Anna calls him Aspietes. He was Prince of Lampron.

of Mopsos; the other embarked on triremes and sailed under
Tancred's command to the River Saron,[4] then upstream as far
as the bridges which join the two cities. In this way Mamistra
was encircled and attacked by Tancred's forces from two sides:
one party was able to launch an assault from the river without
difficulty, while the other put pressure on the city from the
land. Oshin behaved as if nothing unusual was happening;
the noise of soldiers all round his city, like the buzzing of a
huge swarm of bees, left him almost unmoved. What was
wrong with him I do not know, but he was in a condition unworthy of his normal bravery, which caused him to be heartily
detested by his army. The Cilician cities were bound to suffer
when a man like Tancred outmanoeuvred them. Apart from
other considerations, Tancred was one of the strongest men of
his time; he was also among those most admired for their
quality and skill as leaders; when Tancred led the attack a
beleaguered town had very little chance of escape. At this
point, the reader may well wonder how Oshin's military
ineptitude escaped the emperor's notice. My reply in defence
of my father would be as follows: Alexius was impressed by
the distinction of Oshin's family: I believe that his glorious
lineage and the celebrity of his name contributed much to
Oshin's appointment as governor. After all, he was the head of
the Arsacids,[5] descended from royal stock. For that reason he
was deemed worthy of high military command throughout
the east and promoted to the most exalted ranks. Above all
Alexius had evidence of his personal courage, for when he was
waging war with Robert Guiscard, in one of the engagements
a certain Kelt, who towered head and shoulders above the
rest, spurred his horse and with levelled spear fell upon Oshin

4. The Saron has its source in the Taurus Mountains, flows between
the two cities of Mopsos (the one in ruins and the other still standing) and
empties itself into the Syrian Sea. (A.C.)

Anna is incorrect here. Mopsuestia (or Mamistra) stands not on the
Saron, but on the Jihan. For the two cities see *CMH*, vol. iv, pt. i, p. 706–7.

5. The Arsacids were Persian in origin and had long played a prominent
role in the history of the Middle East. A thousand years before Anna's
time an Iranian Arsacid had been placed on the throne of Armenia by the
Romans.

like a thunderbolt. Oshin took the violent impact just as he was drawing his sword. He received a very serious wound, for the spear passing by the lung forced its way right through him. Far from being thrown into confusion by the blow or even crashing to the ground, he actually seated himself more firmly in his saddle and struck at the barbarian's helmet. Both helmet and head were cleft in two. They fell then from their horses, the Kelt dead and Oshin still breathing. His friends took him up, by then completely unconscious, and after tending him carefully carried him to the emperor. They showed him the spear and the wound, and told the story of the Kelt's death. For some reason or other the emperor recalled the bravery and daring of Oshin on that occasion and the feat, plus the man's lineage and the glory of his family, persuaded him to send Oshin to Cilicia, a commander worthy to oppose Tancred. He was, as I have already said, given the rank of stratopedarch.

However, that is enough on the subject of Oshin. The officers in the west received other letters ordering them to march directly to Sthlanitza. Why? Was the emperor calling on the front-line fighters while he himself in retirement enjoyed a life of ease and took pleasure in baths (like some emperors who prefer and usually follow an animal existence)? Not a bit of it. Even the thought of continuing to live in the palace was repugnant. He left Byzantium and passing through the centre of the western provinces arrived at Thessalonica. It was September, in the fourteenth indiction and the twentieth [6] year after his accession to the throne. The Augusta,[7] too, was compelled to leave with him. Her natural inclination would have been to shun public life altogether. Most of her time was devoted to household duties and her own pursuits – reading the books of the saints, I mean, or turning her mind to good works and acts of charity to mankind, especially to those who from their mien and way of life she knew were serving God, monks who persevered in prayer and in the singing of hymns.[8]

6. This should read 'twenty-fourth': we are dealing here with the events of 1105.

7. That is to say, the Empress.

8. Antiphonal hymns. (A.C.) Anna refers to the alternate chanting by semi-choirs.

Whenever she had to appear in public as empress at some important ceremony, she was overcome with modesty and a blush at once suffused her cheeks. The woman philosopher Theano [9] once bared her elbow and someone playfully remarked, 'What a lovely elbow!' 'But not for public show,' she replied. Well, the empress, my mother, the image of majesty, the dwelling-place of saintliness, so far from being pleased to reveal to the common gaze an elbow or her eyes, was unwilling that even her voice should be heard by strangers. Her modesty was really extraordinary. But since not even gods, as the poet [10] says, fight against necessity, she was forced to accompany the emperor on his frequent expeditions. Her innate modesty kept her inside the palace; on the other hand, her devotion to him and burning love for him compelled her, however unwillingly, to leave her home. There were two cogent reasons: first, because the disease which attacked his feet necessitated most careful attention; he suffered excruciating pain from his gout and my mother's touch was what he appreciated most, for she understood him perfectly and by gentle massage relieved him of the anguish to some extent. In what I am going to say, let no one accuse me of exaggeration, for I do admire the domestic virtues; and let no one suspect that I lie about the emperor, for I am speaking the truth; it is true that this great man considered all his own personal affairs and the things that concerned himself as of less consequence than the safety of the masses. Nothing in fact stood between him and his love for the Christians – neither griefs, nor pleasures; neither the ravages of war, nor any other thing; neither great, nor small; neither the burning heat of the sun, nor the bitter cold of winter, nor the manifold assaults of the enemy. [11] Against all these he held fast his course, and if he yielded before the confusion of his illnesses,

9. Theano was wife or pupil of Pythagoras. Several books were ascribed to her in antiquity.

10. Simonides.

11. A reminiscence of St Paul's, 'Who shall separate us from the love of Christ . . .?' Anna's quotations from Scripture are often inaccurate and confused.

he made up for it by leaping to the defence of his Empire. The second and most cogent reason why the empress accompanied him was this: a multitude of conspiracies sprang up against him and it called for great vigilance, a power in fact endowed with a hundred eyes, for night was a time for plots, and so was mid-day, and the evening brought to birth some new evil; worst were the intrigues of the morning – God is my witness. Was it not right, therefore, that the emperor, assailed by evils so numerous, should also be protected by a thousand eyes, while some fired arrows at him, others sharpened their swords and others, when action became impossible, indulged in calumny and abuse? Who then had a better right to be at his side than his natural adviser? Who rather than the empress would keep stricter watch over him or regard with more suspicion the plotters? Who would be quick to discern what profited him, quicker to observe the intrigues of his enemies? It was for these reasons that my mother was all in all to the emperor. By night she was the unsleeping eye, by day his most conspicuous guardian, the good antidote to the perils of the table and the salutary remedy against poisoned food. These were the reasons that thrust aside her natural reserve and gave her courage to face the eyes of men. And yet, even then, she did not forget her customary decorum: a look, a silence, the retinue about her were enough to ensure that to most of them she remained inaccessible. The litter borne by two mules and over it the imperial canopy alone showed that she accompanied the army; otherwise her royal person was screened from view. It was well known among all that some excellent provision was made for the emperor's gout, some sleepless vigil guarded him, an eye wide open and never drowsy watched over his affairs – but nothing more was known. We, who were loyal to him, shared in this labour with our mistress and mother to protect him, each according to his or her ability, with all our heart and soul, never once relaxing our vigil. I have written these words for the edification of those who delight in scoffing and raillery, for they bring to judgement the guiltless (a human trait known to Homer's Muse too) and they belittle noble deeds, subjecting the blameless to reproach. On this particular

expedition [12] she went with him to some extent against her will,
and yet voluntarily. It was not necessary for the empress to
join in hostilities against the barbarian army. How could she?
That was well enough for Tomyris [13] and Sparethra the Mas-
sagete,[14] but not for my Irene. Her courage was turned elsewhere and if it was fully-armed, it was not with the spear of
Athena, nor with the cap of Hades: [15] her shield, round or
oblong, and her sword, with which she nobly ranged herself in
battle-line against the misfortunes and vicissitudes of life
menacing, as she knew, the safety of emperors, were hard
work, an absolutely relentless fight against the passions, and a
sincere faith (thereby following the counsel of Solomon).[16]
Such was the armour of my mother in this warfare, but in all
else, as befitted her name, she was a most peaceable [17] woman.
When hostilities were imminent, Alexius made preparations
for the struggle, taking care to ensure the safety of some
strong-points and fortifying others. He was anxious in general
to bring all defences to a state of complete readiness against
Bohemond's invasion. It was partly for his own sake and for
reasons already given that he took the empress with him,
partly also because there was as yet no danger and the moment
for battle had not arrived. She took what money she had in
gold or in other precious metal and certain other personal
possessions when she left the capital. Afterwards, on the
journey, she gave liberally to all beggars, clad in goat-hair
cloaks or naked; no one who asked went away empty-handed.
And when she arrived at the tent set apart for her and went
inside, it was not to lie down at once and rest, but she opened

12. I am writing of the emperor's attack on Bohemond. (A.C.)
13. Queen of the Massagetae, who fought Cyrus the Great. According
to Herodotus (I, 205 ff.) she destroyed the majority of the Persian invaders
and Cyrus was killed. She threw his severed head into a skin filled with
human blood (she had promised that he would have his fill of blood!).
14. Sparethra was a Scyth from the Caspian Sea region, who also fought
Cyrus.
15. Athena in her role of warrior-goddess, the protector of the city.
Hades had a special interest in the battlefield.
16. A confused memory of the Book of Wisdom.
17. Irene is the Greek for 'peace'.

it up and all the mendicants were allowed free access. To such persons she was very approachable and showed herself ready to be both seen and heard. Nor was it money alone that she gave to the poor; she also dispensed excellent advice. All who were obviously fit and strong (but preferred to be lazy) were exhorted to work and become active; she urged them not to beg from door to door, but to earn their own keep; not to lose heart because they were neglected. No circumstances deterred her from such good work. David is depicted mixing his cup with lamentation; but this empress every day could be seen mixing both food and drink with pity for others. There is much that I could say about her, if it were not that being her daughter I might be suspected of lying to gratify a mother. However, to those who entertain such thoughts I will corroborate my words with good evidence.

When it was known that the emperor had reached Thessalonica, the men of the western provinces all flocked to him as to a centre of gravity. The locust did not precede the Kelts as on previous occasions, but a great comet[18] appeared in the sky, greater than any seen in the past. Some likened it to a small beam, others to a javelin. Of course it was natural that the strange events about to take place should in some way be heralded by signs in the heavens. It was visible, shining brightly, for forty whole days and nights, moving across the sky from west to east. All who saw it were terrified and asked what it portended. Alexius, however, absolutely unmoved by such fears was of the opinion that the comet had some natural cause; nevertheless he did question experts on the subject. Basil, recently appointed Prefect of Byzantium and a man of undoubted loyalty, was summoned and asked about it. He promised an answer on the next day and retired to his lodging-place, the ancient monastery of the Evangelist John. When the sun was on the point of setting, he examined the star. At a loss to understand it and weary of his calculations, he fell asleep and had a vision of the saint, wearing priestly garb. Basil was overjoyed and imagined that he was seeing a real person. Recognizing the saint with fear and trembling he begged him

18. In February–March 1106.

to make known the meaning of the star. 'It foretells an invasion of the Kelts,' replied the Evangelist, 'and its extinction
prophesies their dismissal from here.' We will leave the
comet and return to the emperor. As I have said, he arrived at
Thessalonica and preparations were made for Bohemond's
coming. Recruits were trained thoroughly in the use of the
bow and in marksmanship. They were taught to defend themselves with the buckler. Moreover, Alexius despatched letters
about the enrolling of foreign troops from different countries,
so that when the crisis came they might quickly bring aid. He
also took elaborate precautions for Illyricum; the city of
Dyrrachium was fortified and the second son of the Sebastocrator Isaac was named as governor. At the same time orders
were given for a fleet to be equipped from the Cyclades Islands,
the cities on the coast of Asia and from Europe itself. But the
building of the fleet met with many objections on the ground
that Bohemond was not yet in a hurry to cross. Alexius, un-
impressed by these arguments, insisted that a commander
must be continually on his guard, not preparing merely for the
immediate future, but looking far ahead; he should certainly
not be caught unawares in the moment of crisis through
cutting down expenses – above all when he saw the enemy
about to attack. These matters were handled most cleverly.
Later he moved on to Stroumpitza and from there again as far
as Slopimus. News came of the defeat of John, the sebastocrator's son, who had been sent on ahead against the Dalmatians. The emperor sent a considerable force to help him now,
but Bolkan very craftily made inquiries at once about peace
negotiations. He provided the hostages Alexius had demanded. For a year and two months the emperor stayed in that
area, all the time being fully informed of the whereabouts of
Bohemond, who was still in the province of Lombardy. The
winter was now coming on and after dismissing his soldiers to
their own homes he himself retired to Thessalonica. While he
was on his way there, the first of the sons of the Basileus John
the porphyrogenitus[19] was born at Balabista with a twin

19. John the basileus had married a daughter of the Hungarian king.
They eventually had eight children, four boys and four girls.

sister. In Thessalonica Alexius attended a ceremony in honour of the great martyr Demetrius[20] and then proceeded to Constantinople. There then occurred the following event. In the centre of Constantine's Forum there was a bronze statue, facing the east and standing on a conspicuous column of porphyry, holding in its right hand a sceptre and in its left a sphere made of bronze.[21] It was said to be a statue of Apollo, but the inhabitants of the city called it, I think, Anthelios. The great Emperor Constantine, father and lord of the city, altered it to his own name: the monument was now called the Statue of the Emperor Constantine, but its ancient and first title persisted, and it was known by everybody as Anelios or Anthelios. South-west winds blowing over a wide area from Africa suddenly blew this statue off its pedestal and hurled it to the ground. At the time the sun was in the sign of Taurus. To most people this seemed no good omen, especially to those not well-disposed to the emperor. They whispered in secret that this accident portended his death. He made light of it: 'I know of one Lord of life and death. The collapse of images, I am absolutely certain, does not induce death. Come, tell me now, when a Pheidias or one of the stone-masons works at the marble and turns out a statue, will he produce living beings, will he raise up the dead? And suppose he does, what then will be left for the Creator of all things? He says, "I will destroy and I will make to live." That cannot be said of the fall or setting up of this or that statue.' In fact, he ascribed everything to the mighty Providence of God.

Fresh troubles had been stirred up against the emperor, but the agitators were not on this occasion ordinary folk. They were men proud of their valour and famous lineage; they plotted with murderous intent. Now that I have reached this point in my history, I wonder from where so great a multitude of troubles came to surround the emperor, for everything – yes, everything – and from every quarter assailed him. Inside the city there were numerous defections; outside it, revolts

20. On 25 January 1107.
21. The monument, now called the Burnt Column, can still be seen in Istanbul. It stands 115 ft high; the statue has gone.

abounded. The emperor had barely taken a stand against the troubles, when all burst into flames outside, as if Fate itself were propagating at one and the same moment barbarians and revolutionaries, like some spontaneous generation of Giants. And yet his government and general administration were in all ways more than usually gentle and humane, and all his subjects benefited immensely; some were honoured with posts of dignity and continually enriched with great liberality. And as for the barbarians, wherever they were, he gave them no pretext for war and did not use compulsion on them; nevertheless, if they did cause trouble, he checked them. After all, it is the mark of a bad general, when all is peaceful, purposely to provoke his neighbours to war – for peace is the end of all wars. Invariably to prefer war instead of peace, always to disregard the good end, is typical of foolish commanders and foolish political leaders, the mark of men who work for the destruction of their own state. The policy of Alexius was absolutely opposed to this: he cultivated peace to an unusual degree; its presence was always and by every means cherished and its absence worried him, so that he often spent sleepless nights wondering how it might return. By nature, then, he was a man of peace, but when circumstances forced him he would become most warlike. For my own part I would say confidently of this great man that in him and in him alone the true character of an emperor was seen again in the Roman court – after a long interval; it was as if then, for the first time, the imperial dignity dwelt like some guest in the Empire of the Romans. But, as I said at the beginning of this chapter, I cannot help feeling astonished at the veritable flood of hostile movements. Abroad and at home everything was visibly in turmoil. Yet he foresaw the furtive designs of his enemies, their private intentions, and by various manoeuvres prevented the mischief from coming too close. In his struggle with traitors at home and barbarians abroad he always outwitted them; their plots were thwarted and their onslaughts cut short. The facts themselves, it seems to me, give a clue to the destiny of the Empire: there was an accumulation of perils from all quarters, the body politic was in confusion, the

whole outside world raged against us; it was as if a man were
sick, assailed by forces from without and exhausted by physical
pain within, but revived by Providence, so that he might find
strength to combat all his troubles, whatever their origin.
The analogy was certainly not inapplicable in this crisis, with
Bohemond making ready for war with an enormous army
from without and a host of rebels being stirred to action within
the city. There were four ringleaders in all: they were called
Anemas (Michael, Leo, . . . and . . .).[22] They were brothers by
birth and on this occasion by intent, for all had the same object
in view – to murder Alexius and seize the throne. Other nobles
joined them in secret: the Antiochi, who were of an illustrious
family; the Exazeni, Ducas and Hyaleas, the most courageous
fighters who ever lived; Nicetas Castamonites, a certain
Curticius and George Basilacius. These men were leading
figures in the army, but another conspirator, John Solomon,
was a distinguished senator. Because of his great wealth and
noble birth, Michael, the foremost of the Anemas tetrarchy,
had deceitfully promised to anoint Solomon as emperor. In
the senatorial order Solomon was a member of the first rank,
but a small man – in fact, the smallest of them all, especially of
those who conspired with him; he was also the feeblest in
character. He imagined that he had attained the pinnacle of
Aristotelian and Platonic studies, but in reality his knowledge
of philosophy was not far advanced; he had been blinded by
his own triviality. Already he was aiming wholeheartedly at
the throne, helped by the Anemas brothers, who were undoubtedly thorough rascals, for Michael and his friends did
not propose to raise him to imperial power – far from it. They
made use of the man's folly and his wealth to promote their
own scheme. Always they were helping themselves to that
golden stream and, by building up his hopes of empire, they
subjugated him entirely. Their idea was this: if all went well
and Fortune smiled on them rather more, they would elbow
him out, sending him away on a pleasant sea-voyage, while
they would lay hands on the sceptre, allot him some minor
dignity and wish him good luck. Although they spoke to him

22. There are lacunae in the text here.

of the plot, there was no talk of murdering the emperor, no
mention of sword-drawing or battle or wars (lest they should
frighten the man). They knew him of old – the very idea of
war made him an arrant coward. Anyway, they took this
Solomon to their arms, as if he were indeed head of the
conspiracy. Others were drawn into it – Sclerus and Xeros,
who had just completed his term of office as Prefect of
Constantinople. I have already written of Solomon's rather
pusillanimous nature; since he knew nothing about the plans
being carefully laid by Exazenus, Hyaleas and the Anemas
brothers, he believed supreme power was already in his grasp,
and when he had a conversation with certain persons in an
attempt to win their goodwill, he promised gifts and positions
of dignity. On one occasion Michael Anemas, the leading
actor in the drama, visited him and saw him talking to someone. He asked what the subject of the conversation was and
Solomon, with his customary simplicity, answered, 'He
demanded from us a place of special honour and when I gave
him an undertaking he agreed to join us in the general
conspiracy.' Michael condemned his folly, and because he
was afraid (for he knew well enough that Solomon was
constitutionally unable to hold his tongue) he no longer
visited him as before.

The soldiers (the Anemas brothers, the Antiochi and their
accomplices) plotted their mischief; when a favourable
opportunity came they intended to proceed without delay to
the murder. But when Providence afforded them no chance
and time was slipping away, discovery of the plot became an
alarming possibility. However, they thought they had found
the moment they were seeking. When the emperor woke up in
the early afternoon, he liked sometimes to play chess with one
of his kinsmen; it sweetened the bitterness of his many
worries. The rebels armed themselves for the crime. They
intended to pass through the emperor's bedroom, a small
room, as if they were looking for him; really, they were hoping
to murder him. Now this bedroom, where my mother and
father happened to be sleeping, lies on the left side of the
palace chapel built in honour of the Theometor, although

most people said it was dedicated to the great martyr Demetrius. On the right there was a marble pavement in the open
air, and the door of the chapel which gave access to it was free
to all who wished to go there. It was from that place that they
planned to enter the chapel, break down the doors shutting
off the imperial bedroom and then, after getting inside in this
way, kill the emperor with their swords. Such was the fate
planned by these guilty men for one who had done them no
wrong. But God frustrated their plot. Somebody informed the
emperor and they were immediately sent for. First John
Solomon and George Basilacius were to be brought to the
palace to undergo examination (they were nearer the small
room where he happened to be with his kinsmen). From long
experience Alexius knew that they were rather unsophisticated
and therefore imagined that he would easily obtain information about their scheme. They were frequently questioned,
but denied any knowledge of the conspiracy. At this point the
Sebastocrator Isaac went out and spoke to Solomon: 'You are
well aware, Solomon, of the goodness of my brother the
emperor. If you give us all the details of the plot, you will be
granted an immediate pardon. If not, you will be subjected to
unbearable tortures.' Solomon gazed at him. Then, seeing the
barbarians who surrounded the sebastocrator, with the one-
edged swords on their shoulders, he began to tremble and
without more ado told him everything. He denounced his
fellow-conspirators but insisted that he himself knew nothing
about the murder. After that they were handed over to the
palace guard and imprisoned separately. The rest were later
interrogated about the business. They made a full confession,
not even concealing the intention to kill. It was known that the
soldiers had plotted the assassination, in particular Michael
Anemas the ringleader and instigator. They were all banished
and their property was confiscated. Solomon's house, a
magnificent mansion, was given to the Augusta, but she
characteristically had pity on Solomon's wife and made a
present of it to her. She removed nothing from it, however
trifling, for herself. Solomon was imprisoned at Sozopolis.
Anemas and the other prominent rebels, after having their

heads completely shaved and their beards cut, were paraded
on the emperor's orders through the Agora. Then their eyes
were to be gouged. The persons in charge of the show laid
hands on them, clothed them in sackcloth, decorated their
heads with ox and sheep entrails (to imitate crowns), put them
on oxen (not astride the beasts, but riding sideways) and drove
them through the palace court. In front of them rod-bearers
charged, bawling a comic ditty with alternate refrains suited to
the occasion. It was a vulgar song in the dialect of the common
people and its main theme was as follows: it called on everyone to . . .[23] and see the rebels wearing horns, the rebels who
had whetted their swords against the emperor. People of all
ages hurried to see the show; we too, the princesses, came out
for the same purpose secretly. However, when they saw
Michael fixing his gaze on the palace and raising his hands in
prayer to heaven, begging in pantomimic gesture that his
arms should be severed from his shoulders, his legs from his
body, and that he should be beheaded, every living person was
moved to tears and lamentation. We, the emperor's daughters,
were affected more than anyone. I myself, wishing to save the
man from such a fate, called more than once on my mother to
watch them being subjected to ribald jokes. The truth is, we
cared for the men for the emperor's sake: it hurt us to think
that he was being deprived of such brave men, especially of
Michael, because the punishment in his case was so much
heavier. Seeing how much he was being humiliated by his
suffering, I kept putting pressure on my mother: there might
be some way of rescuing him from imminent peril. The
organizers of the march set a rather leisurely pace, in an effort
to win some pity for the criminals. My mother hesitated to
come, for she was seated with the emperor and together they
were offering prayers to God before the Theometor. I went
down and stood terrified outside the doors. I had not the
courage to go in, but called her by signs. She understood and
came up to watch, and when she saw Michael she wept tears of
compassion for him. Back she ran to the emperor and pleaded
with him again and again to stop the public executioners and

23. There is a lacuna here.

save Michael's eyes. At once a man was sent and by running fast caught them inside the place called 'The Hands';[24] he handed over to Michael's escort the notice of pardon before they left the arch on which the bronze hands were fixed and so was able to bring Michael back with him. When he reached the tower built near to the palace, he imprisoned him there, according to instructions received beforehand.

Michael had not been released from prison before Gregory in his turn was shut up in the same place. It was a tower on the ramparts of the city near the Blachernae Palace and it was named after Anemas. It acquired this name because he was the first person to be incarcerated and spend a long time there. In the course of the twelfth indiction[25] this Gregory, who had been promoted Duke of Trapezus, brought to light a rebellion he had long been planning. On his way to Trapezus he met Dabatenus, the outgoing duke, and immediately made him his prisoner and shut him up in Tebenna. Nor was Dabatenus the only victim: a considerable number of the leading citizens of Trapezus, including the nephew of Bacchenus, were also thrown into gaol. As they were not freed from their chains, they agreed among themselves to make a concerted attack on their guards (posted there by the rebel). They mastered them,

24. Those who pass through 'The Hands' can no longer be rescued from their punishment. The emperors, who fixed these bronze hands on a very lofty vantage-point and on a high arch of stone, wanted it to be understood that if any man condemned by law to die was on this side of the bronze hands, and if on his march he met with clemency from the emperor, he was to be freed from punishment. The hands signified that the emperor took such a man under his protection again, held tight in his hands – he was not yet released from his merciful grasp. If however the condemned passed beyond the hands, it was an outward sign that hereafter even the emperor's power rejected him. The fate of men under sentence of death therefore depended on Fortune (which I consider to be the Will of God) and it is right to call on her for succour. Either the pardon arrives on the near side of the hands, in which case the unfortunate criminals are snatched from danger; or they pass by the hands, and there is no more hope. For my part, I attribute everything to the Providence of God, which on that occasion rescued the man from blinding. For it was God, it seems to me, who on that day moved us to pity him. (A.C.)

25. September 1103–September 1104.

led them outside the ramparts and drove them far from the city; then they gained control of Tebenna. The emperor wrote frequently to Gregory. Sometimes he tried to recall him, sometimes advised him to give up his wicked enterprise if he wanted a pardon and restoration to his old position; there were times when he actually threatened him if he refused. However, Gregory would not listen. He even sent off a long letter to Alexius in which he abused not only members of the senate and prominent soldiers, but also close relatives and kinsmen by marriage of the emperor. From the contents of this message Alexius realized that Gregory was rapidly deteriorating; he was in fact on the verge of complete mental breakdown. All hope for him was abandoned, but in the fourteenth indiction[26] John, the emperor's nephew, son of his eldest sister and a cousin on the paternal side of the rebel, was sent to give him sound advice. That was John's first task, and Alexius thought Gregory might be persuaded by him because of their ties of kinship, both of them being descended from the same ancestors. If Gregory refused, John was to recruit strong forces and attack him boldly by land and sea. His coming was reported to Gregory Taronites, who set out in the direction of Coloneia (an exceptionally well fortified place, considered impregnable) with the idea of calling on Malik Ghazi Gümüshtigin[27] for help.

John heard about the move as he was about to leave. He separated the Kelts from the rest of his army and sent them after him together with picked Roman soldiers. They overtook him and in a bitterly contested battle two noblemen attacked Gregory with their lances, knocked him off his horse and captured him. Later on John carried off the prisoner alive to the emperor. John swore that he would neither see him, under any circumstances, nor speak a word to him on the journey. Nevertheless he defended him vigorously before Alexius, who pretended that he wished to blind Gregory. Reluctantly he allowed himself to be persuaded by John's pleading and admitted that the blinding was a mere pretence,

26. September 1105–September 1106.   27. Anna's Tanismanes.

but urged him most earnestly not to divulge the verdict. Three days later he ordered Gregory's hair and beard to be shaved to the skin and himself to be led through the middle of the Agora; later, in this condition, he was to be brought to the Anemas Tower. In prison Gregory's stupidity continued; every day he uttered mad prophecies to his guards, but the emperor with great forbearance considered it worthwhile to treat him with much kindness – one day he might mend his ways and show a measure of repentance. It failed, because he remained inexorable, but he did often call for my Caesar – in the old days he had been our friend. When that happened, the emperor gave permission for the Caesar to visit him in an attempt to overcome Gregory's terrible melancholia, and also to give him useful advice. However, progress was apparently slow and his period of incarceration was accordingly prolonged. After a time he was pardoned and enjoyed more consideration, more honour and gifts than ever before. That was typical of my father in cases like his.[28]

Having dealt thus with the conspirators and the rebel Gregory Taronites, the emperor did not forget Bohemond. Isaac Contostephanus, promoted Grand Duke of the Fleet, was sent to Dyrrachium, with the threat that his eyes would be gouged if he failed to arrive there before Bohemond crossed the Adriatic. Letters were sent frequently to Alexius, the emperor's nephew and Duke of Dyrrachium, preparing him for the coming war and warning him to maintain a constant vigil and exhort the coastguards to do likewise; Bohemond must not cross unobserved and immediate information about him must be sent in writing. Such were the precautions taken. Contostephanus' instructions were merely to keep a careful watch over the straits between Lombardy and Illyricum; to stop Bohemond's convoys, sent to Dyrrachium with all his

28. The whole story of Gregory's rebellion is strange. The emperor's extraordinary leniency is suspicious and so is the pretended desire to blind Gregory; was he placating public opinion? Why was this obdurate rebel treated with unusual honour after the prison sentence? There is no hint of any recantation on his part. Why should Dabatenus be attacked? For a discussion (inconclusive) on these and other difficulties see Buckler, p. 276.

baggage; and to allow nothing whatever to be transported to him from Lombardy. Unfortunately, when Contostephanus went off he was ignorant of the natural landing-place for sailors coming over from Italy. Nor was that all: he overlooked his orders and sailed to Otranto, a city on the coast of Lombardy. The place was defended by a woman, the mother, so it was said, of Tancred, though whether she was a sister of the notorious Bohemond or not I cannot tell, for I do not really know if Tancred was related to him on his father's or his mother's side. Contostephanus, having arrived there, anchored his ships and proceeded to attack the walls. He almost succeeded in taking the place, but the defending commander, who was a highly intelligent and level-headed woman, had seen this possibility when he brought his ships to rest and had already sent a message to one of her sons asking for assistance quickly. The Roman fleet was full of confidence – the place was seemingly about to fall – and all acclaimed the emperor. The woman, who was herself in grievous straits, ordered her own people to do likewise. At the same time she sent ambassadors to Contostephanus acknowledging her allegiance to the emperor and promising to negotiate for peace; she would come to him and together they would discuss terms, so that full details might be given to Alexius. She was contriving to keep the Roman admiral in suspense and playing for time: her son would have a chance to arrive. Then, as they say of the tragic actors, she could throw off the mask and start the fighting. The mingled acclamations of those within and without echoed all round the city, while this woman gladiator by her talk and lying promises kept Contostephanus' plans in abeyance. Meanwhile the son for whom she was waiting did arrive, with attendant counts. He fought Contostephanus and beat him conclusively. All the sailors, having no experience of land warfare, threw themselves into the sea, and the Scyths (several were serving with the Roman force) rode off in the moment of battle to plunder, as barbarians are wont to do. By chance six of them were captured. They were sent to Bohemond and regarded by him as a great prize; he at once took them to Rome. There he presented himself before the

apostolic throne and in an interview with the pope[29] stirred
him to bitter anger against the Romans. These barbarians had
an ancient hatred for our race and he fostered it. In fact, in
order to enrage the Italian retinue of the pope even more, he
exhibited his captured Scyths, as if providing concrete evidence that the Emperor Alexius, of all people, was hostile to
the Christians because he set against them barbarian infidels
and fearful horse-archers, brandishing arms and firing arrows.
Every time he mentioned the subject, the Scyths were slyly
exhibited to the pope, equipped after their fashion and glaring
fiercely, as barbarians will. Following Latin custom he
persisted in calling them 'pagans', making fun of their name
and appearance alike. Not surprisingly, his references to the
war against the Christians were cunningly designed to convince even a high priest that his (Bohemond's) activities were
justified; it was the Romans who were hostile. He was at the
same time canvassing for a large volunteer force of the
rougher and more stupid element. For what barbarian, from
near or far, would not enrol of his own free will in a war
against us, if the pontiff approved and the apparent justice of
it called to arms every knight, every soldier, every bit of their
strength? The pope, cajoled by Bohemond's arguments and
taking his part, encouraged the crossing to Illyricum. We
must now return to the battle. The mainlanders fought with
great spirit, but the others were swallowed up in the sea
waves. After that the Kelts had a glorious chance of victory;
however, the braver soldiers and in particular the men of
higher rank thwarted them. Most prominent were the famous
Nicephorus Exazenus Hyaleas, his cousin Constantine
Exazenus, called Ducas, and the bravest of all, Alexander
Euphorbenus; there were others, too, of the same rank and
fortune. These men, 'mindful of their furious might' turned,

29. Unlike his predecessor Urban II, who followed a moderate policy
in his dealings with the eastern Christians, Paschal II was already prejudiced against the emperor. He was soon persuaded to back the Normans
and the papal legate who went with Bohemond to France was instructed
to proclaim a Holy War against the Byzantines. The Crusade had the
official support of the pope, not to rescue the Holy Places so much as to
break the Eastern Roman Empire. It was a turning-point in history.

drew their swords and with all their heart and soul did battle with the enemy. They bore the whole brunt, routed them and won a splendid triumph over the Kelts. Contostephanus therefore had a breathing-space from Keltic aggression. He weighed anchor and with all the fleet sailed to Avlona.[30] News reached him that Bohemond was speeding up preparations for the landing and he guessed that the voyage would most probably end at Avlona rather than Dyrrachium, the former being nearer to Italy. Avlona, he decided, must be more strongly defended. Accordingly he left with the other dukes and kept careful watch on the straits at that place. On the summit of the so-called Jason's Hill scouts were posted to observe the sea and keep an eye open for ships. A Kelt who had recently made the crossing confirmed that Bohemond was on the point of sailing. The men of Contostephanus, hearing this and terror-stricken at the thought of a sea battle with Bohemond (for the very mention of his name was enough to scare them), pretended to be ill; they said they needed treatment at the baths.[31] Landulf, who led the whole fleet and had vast experience of surprise attacks in naval warfare over a long period, emphasized his order to be continually on guard and watch closely for Bohemond's coming. The Contostephani, when they sailed for Chimara to take their baths, left behind the officer called Second Drungarius of the Fleet with the monoreme *Excusatum* to keep watch near Cape Glossa, not far from Avlona. As for Landulf, he stayed in the same vicinity with a fair number of ships.

Such were the naval dispositions when Contostephanus' men went off to take the baths, or on the pretext of bathing.

30. When he first arrived at Dyrrachium he had dispersed the warships under his command from that place as far as Avlona and Chimara. Avlona is a hundred stades from Dyrrachium and Chimara a further sixty from Avlona. (A.C.)

31. One is constantly reminded in the *Alexiad* of the importance of baths. Honoured guests are invited to take a bath and bathing has a recognized place in medical treatment. Almshouses and hospitals often had baths attached to them; so had convents and monasteries. In Irene's *Typikon* it is expressly laid down that the nuns of her foundation should bath at least once a month.

Bohemond, on his side, arranged about him twelve corsairs, all of them biremes with many rowers, so that there was a deafening, echoing noise from the continuous strokes of their oars. Around these ships and on either side he posted transport vessels, a circle inside which was the war-fleet. Had you seen it, you would have said, looking at it from some far-off outpost, that this armada under sail was a floating city. Fortune helped Bohemond somewhat, for the sea was calm except for a light breeze from the south which made a ripple on the surface and bellied out the sails of the merchantmen. It was enough to make them run with the wind and the rowing ships kept a straight course with them. The noise they made, even in the middle of the Adriatic, could be heard echoing on both mainlands. This fleet of Bohemond was indeed an astonishing sight and if the men of Contostephanus shrank from it in dread, I would not blame them for it, nor would I accuse them of cowardice. For even the famous Argonauts would have feared Bohemond and his fleet thus arranged, let alone the Contostephani and Landulfs and their like. Landulf, in fact, when he spied Bohemond crossing with his merchantmen of enormous tonnage and in such an awe-inspiring manner, since it was impossible to fight against so many, altered course slightly from Avlona and gave his enemy the right of way. Bohemond had been fortunate. He transported the whole of his army from Bari to Avlona and landed on the opposite shore.[32] First of all he ravaged all the seaboard with a countless host of Franks and Kelts, together with the entire contingent of men from the Isle of Thule[33] who normally serve in the Roman army but had through force of circumstances then joined him; not to mention an even stronger force of Germans and Celtiberians. All these men, united in one army, were spread along the whole Adriatic coastline.

32. The crossing was made on 9 October 1107.

33. Thule is a name for all the countries bordering the North Sea, but Anna here must be referring to Britain. It is hard to reconcile the behaviour of these men with what she tells us elsewhere about their undoubted loyalty to the emperor. We know from Ordericus Vitalis that Bohemond did not recruit men in England, but they may well have come over to him in Normandy.

Everything was systematically plundered. Then he attacked Epidamnos, which we call Dyrrachium. It was his intention to take this place and then to pillage the land beyond it as far as Constantinople. Bohemond was outstanding as a besieger of cities, surpassing even the famous Demetrius Poliorcetes.[34] Concentrating all his attention now on Epidamnos, he brought up every engineering device to capture it. First the army surrounded the city, while other places in the neighbourhood, near and further away from it, were invested. Sometimes Roman forces opposed him, sometimes there was no resistance at all. After many battles and encounters with much bloodshed, he considered the actual operations against Epidamnos. But before we come to the well-known Battle of Dyrrachium, I must comment on the site. The place, an ancient Greek city-state, lies on the coast of the Adriatic Sea,[35] to the south-west of Elissos,[36] which is small but absolutely impregnable on its hill and according to report it overlooks Dyrrachium on the plain. Its own invulnerability affords considerable protection to Dyrrachium both from the mainland and from the sea. The emperor took advantage of this, fortifying Dyrrachium on the landward side and opposite the River Drymon,[37] which

34. Demetrius I Poliorcetes (336–283 B.C.), son of Antigonus, tried to reunite the Empire of Alexander. He was unsuccessful, but in his early career deservedly won fame for his victories. Despite his nickname ('The Besieger') he failed to capture Rhodes in the siege of 305 and gradually declined in power and importance.

35. A vast expanse of water almost land-locked, of great length, dividing our land from Italy. It extends as far as the barbarian Vetones with a bend to the north-east. Opposite them lies the land of the Apulians. (A.C.)

The Vetones were the Narantian pirates of the Illyrian (Croatian) coast, who were traditional enemies of Venice. Anna's geography is vague and like most ancient historians she finds it difficult to give a clear and accurate description, but it is true that there is a slight bend to the north-east beyond Dyrrachium. One might say that Apulia is 'opposite' the Vetones – it depends how you hold the map.

36. Elissos may have been named after some River Elissos, a tributary of the great River Drymon; or it may just have been called that; I do not know the real reason. (A.C.)

37. This river, if I may make further remarks about its course, rises in the highlands starting from Lake Lychnis (the name has now been corrupted to Achris) and from Mokros it flows by some hundred channels,

happened to be navigable. Thus supplies were brought in by land and sea, food for the soldiers there and also for the inhabitants of the place, as well as everything necessary for the soldiers' war equipment. Alexius was still in Constantinople when he learnt from the duke's letters that Bohemond had crossed. He hastened his own departure. The duke had indeed kept careful watch, denying himself all sleep, when he discovered that Bohemond had made the voyage, disembarked, and pitched his camp on the Illyrian plain. A Scyth was sent (the proverbial 'winged messenger') to bear the news to the emperor. He met him returning from the chase. Running in and prostrating himself, with his head to the ground, the man cried in a loud, clear voice that Bohemond had arrived. All the others who were present stood rooted to the spot, stupefied at the very mention of the name, but Alexius, full of spirit and courage, merely remarked as he unloosed the leather strap of his shoe, 'For the moment let us have lunch. We will attend to Bohemond's affairs later.'

---

or as we call them, 'dykes'; the streams, up to a hundred in number, flow separately from the lake as though from different sources and continue thus until they unite in the river near Deure, after which it has the name Drymon. The addition of these streams makes it broad; indeed it becomes a very great river. It skirts the borders of Dalmatia, turns northward, and then bends to the south, washes the foothills of Elissos and finally empties itself into the Adriatic Sea. (A.C.)

The Drymon is the Black Drin; Achris is known today as Achrida.

There is considerable difficulty in this passage: the codices read, 'from Mokros, King of the Bulgarians, who was born in the time of the emperors Constantine and Basil the Porphyrogeniti, and whose name was later changed to Samuel.' It has now been generally accepted that this is an interpolation.

There is also trouble over the word translated above as 'dykes'; the Greek word *gephyras* normally means 'bridges', which seems inappropriate and this has led to emendations of the text. However, there is good authority for 'dykes' and it makes sense.

BOOK THIRTEEN

THE CONSPIRACY OF AARON–
THE FINAL DEFEAT OF BOHEMOND–
THE TREATY OF DEVOL
(1107–8)

AT the time we were all amazed at the emperor's self-control. In fact, although he appeared to belittle the news (for the sake of those who were present) inwardly he was much perturbed by it. Indeed, he came to the conclusion that he must again leave Byzantium. He knew that once more his cause was going badly at court; nevertheless, after setting the affairs of palace and capital in good order and after appointing as governors the Great Drungarius of the Fleet, the eunuch Eustathius Kymineianus, and Nicephorus, the son of Dekanos, he left with a few companions (close relatives) on the first day of November in the first indiction,[1] and reached the imperial tent of purple outside the town of Geranion. But he was alarmed because at his departure the Theometor had not performed the usual miracle.[2] He waited therefore four days in the place, and then as the sun was setting went back with the empress. They entered the holy shrine of the Theometor secretly with a few others. He sang the usual hymns and prayed with great fervour. There followed the customary miracle and so with good hope he left the sanctuary. On the next day he was on the road to Thessalonica. When he arrived at Chirovachi, he promoted John Taronites[3] eparch. John was an aristocrat who from his early childhood had been under the emperor's protection and for a long time served him as an

1. 1 November 1107.
2. Every Friday a mysterious unveiling of the Virgin's ikon took place in the church of St Mary in Blachernae. The interruption of this miracle was regarded as a bad omen. For a long discussion of the subject see Buckler, pp. 77–8.
3. He was first cousin of Anna.

under-secretary. He was a man of active mind, with a sound knowledge of Roman law, prepared to extol the emperor's ordinances as long as they were written in language worthy of his Imperial Majesty. If he spoke freely, his censures were not devoid of tact: he was what the Stagirite [4] bids a dialectician to be. After Alexius left Chirovachi, he sent frequent letters to Isaac Contostephanus, duke of the fleet, and his colleagues (Exazenus Ducas and Hyaleas) with instructions to be constantly on the watch and to stop all attempts to cross to Bohemond from Lombardy. When they arrived at Mestos, the Augusta wanted to return to the palace, but Alexius compelled her to go further; they both crossed the River Euros and pitched camp at Psyllos. Alexius, having escaped one assassination, would have fallen victim to a second, had not some divine hand stayed the murderers from their crime. It happened thus. A man who traced his ancestry back to the famous Aronii [5] on one side (although he was of illegitimate birth) invited the emperor's political opponents to kill him. His secret plan was shared with his brother Theodorus. I prefer not to say whether others of the faction were accomplices in this. In any case they suborned a Scythian slave called Demetrius to do the killing (the slave's master was Aaron himself). The time agreed for the crime was to be the moment of the empress's departure. The Scyth was then to seize some good opportunity – meeting the emperor in a narrow passage or even catching him unawares in his sleep – and plunge the sword into his side. Demetrius, full of murderous thoughts, sharpened his blade and practised his hand for the bloodshed. At that point, however, Justice brought a new element into the drama, for when the empress did not immediately leave Alexius, but continued to accompany him while he from day to day kept her back, the criminals lost heart. They saw the emperor's unsleeping guard (my mother) still lingering on, and they wrote some *famosa* which they threw into his tent. At the time it was not known who threw these *famosa* (the word means 'scurrilous writings'). They warned the emperor

4. Aristotle (384–22 B.C.) was born at Stagira in northern Greece.
5. A former Bulgarian dynasty.

to march on and the Augusta to take the road to Byzantium. The writers of such missives are dealt with very severely by our law: the letters themselves are burnt in the fire, the perpetrators subjected to the most painful chastisement. The conspirators, having failed in their attempt to kill, had been foolish enough to write this stuff. One day, after the emperor had lunched, most of his retinue withdrew and the only persons remaining with him on this particular occasion were Romanus the Manichaean, Basil Psyllus the eunuch, and Theodorus, Aaron's brother. Once again a lampoon was found, thrown under the emperor's couch; it made a violent attack on Irene because she accompanied Alexius and would not go back to the capital. This, of course, was their object: they would then have perfect freedom to do what they wanted. The emperor (who knew the person responsible) was very angry. 'Either you or I,' he said, turning to the empress, 'or someone here present threw this object.' At the bottom of the note was a postscript: 'I, the monk, write this. For the moment, emperor, you do not know me, but you will see me in your dreams.' A certain eunuch called Constantine, who had been a servant of the emperor's father and in charge of his table, but was at this time one of Irene's retinue, was standing outside his tent about the third watch of the night; he was just finishing the usual hymn when he heard somebody cry out, 'If I don't go to him and tell him everything about your plans – yes, *and* denounce the *famosa* you keep on throwing at him, then you can count me a dead man.' At once Constantine ordered his own man-servant to find out who was speaking. Off he went and recognizing Strategius, Aaron's retainer, took him back to the Officer of the Table. Without delay Strategius told all he knew. Constantine thereupon went with him to the emperor, but Their Majesties were sleeping. However, he met Basil the eunuch and forced him to tell Alexius what information Strategius had given. Basil obeyed instantly, taking Strategius into the emperor's tent with him. Strategius under interrogation revealed the whole story of these absurd lampoons and clearly named the ringleader of the attempted assassination and the man destined to do the killing. 'My master Aaron,' he said, 'with others not altogether unknown to Your Majesty plotted against your life. He sent Demetrius to murder you. Demetrius is a fellow-servant, a Scyth by birth, a bloodthirsty fellow, strong in the arm, ready for any bold deed you like to name, savage and cruel. They put a two-edged sword in his hand and gave their brutal order: "Get close and, recklessly forgetting all restraint, plunge the weapon into the emperor's heart."' Alexius was not easily convinced by such stories. 'Make sure,' he said, 'that you are not inventing this accusation through some hatred of your masters and fellow-slave, but tell the whole truth and clearly describe what you know. If you are convicted of lying, these charges will do you no good.' The man insisted that he was telling the truth and was handed over to Basil the eunuch; he was to give Basil the ridiculous papers. He took him to Aaron's tent, where they were all asleep, picked up a soldier's leather wallet which was full of such scribblings and handed them over. Day was already breaking when Alexius examined them. He recognized the man who was planning his death and instructed the police officials in Constantinople to exile Aaron's mother to Chirovachi, Aaron himself to . . .[6] and his brother Theodorus to Anchialos. The emperor's march had been delayed for five days by these events.

While he was on his way to Thessalonica, as the contingents drawn from all parts were concentrating in one area, he though it a good idea to arrange them in battle formation. The phalanxes at once halted by companies, the commanders in front and the officers of the rearguard behind; making up the middle of the phalanx stood the mass of the soldiers with their flashing arms, ranged side by side like some city wall. It was a frightening experience to gaze on that parade. You would have said they were statues of bronze, metal soldiers, for they all stood motionless on the plain, only their spears quivering, as if eager to draw blood. When all was ready he put them in motion, experimenting with methods of deploying to right or left. Then the recruits were separated from the rest of the army and the men personally trained by Alexius, to

6. A lacuna here in the text.

whom he had given a thorough military education, were appointed officers. There were 300 of them in all, young men, very tall, in excellent physical condition; each man had but recently 'grown his first beard'[7] and all were good bowmen and strong, expert javelin-throwers. Despite their different places of origin, they were by now one composite body, the élite of the whole Roman army serving under their general the emperor (for to them he was both general and instructor). Once more a selection was made: the more efficient were promoted battalion commanders and sent to the valleys through which the barbarians would have to pass. The emperor himself wintered in Thessalonica. Bohemond, as we have said, had crossed the Adriatic with a very powerful fleet and the entire Frankish army had poured out over our plains. Now he gathered them together and marched against Epidamnos, hoping to take it at the first assault, if he could; if not, he intended to force the whole city to surrender by using siege-engines and rock-throwing catapults. He bivouacked opposite the east gate (over which there is a bronze horseman) and after a reconnaissance he began the siege. For a whole winter he laid his plans and examined every point where Dyrrachium is vulnerable, but when spring began to smile again, as soon as the crossing was completed, he burnt his cargo ships, and his horse-transports – in fact, all the vessels that had brought over his military expedition. It was good strategy: in the first place, his army would not look to the sea; and, in the second, the Roman fleet compelled him to do it anyway. He devoted himself entirely to the siege. First the barbarian force spread out all round the city. There were skirmishes when detachments of Franks were sent out to fight, but the Roman archers shot at them, sometimes from the towers of Dyrrachium, sometimes from more distant places. Bohemond assailed the enemy and was himself assailed. He gained control of Petroula and the place called Mylos on the far side of the River Diabolis. Other places like them in the neighbourhood of Dyrrachium all fell into his hands by right of conquest. These successes

7. The proverbial Byzantine expression for a young man who has just passed adolescence.

were the result of skilful tactics. At the same time he was building machines of war, making movable sheds which carried towers and were equipped with battering-rams; others were constructed to protect sappers or men filling up the enemy's ditches. Throughout the winter and summer he was hard at work. By threats and by his actions he terrorized the inhabitants of the city. Nevertheless, he was by no means able to break their spirit. Problems of food supply, too, caused him great difficulty, for everything plundered from the area round Dyrrachium had now been exhausted and the Roman army was cutting off other prospective sources because the valleys and defiles had already been seized. The Romans moreover controlled the sea. Hence came famine which continually affected horses and men alike. They died, the horses having no fodder, the men no food. Bohemond's army suffered also from dysentery; it was apparently caused by some unsuitable diet (I am referring to millet), but the truth is that this countless, invincible multitude was visited by the wrath of God, and they died like flies.

But to a man of his proud spirit, one who threatened to destroy a whole land, this misfortune seemed but a small matter; despite all his troubles he continued to make plans and like a wounded animal gathered himself together, prepared to spring.[8] All his attention was focused on the siege. First of all a portable shed was made, carrying a battering-ram, an extraordinary, indescribable object. It was pushed up to the eastern side of the city. Its very appearance inspired terror. It had been constructed as follows. A small 'tortoise' was made in the shape of a parallelogram; wheels were put under it and it was completely covered, on top and on every side, by ox-hides sewn together at all points, so that roof and walls of the machine were indeed, as Homer says, 'of seven bull's-hides'.[9] Then inside the rams were suspended. When the machine was completed, Bohemond had it brought close to the city wall, pushed forward from inside by a great number of men armed

8. A reminiscence of Plato, *Republic*, 336 B.
9. A well-known expression (applied to a warrior's shield) in both *Odyssey* and *Iliad*.

with poles. When it was near enough, at just the right distance, they removed the wheels and made it firm on all sides by wooden props in the ground, so that the roof would not sway with the constant pounding. After that men of great strength took up position on either side of the ram and began a violent assault with a regular, rhythmical battering of the wall; each time they pushed with tremendous momentum the ram leapt forward tearing at the wall, then rebounded, only to be thrust at the wall again, trying to make a breach. The action was repeated many times, the ram keeping up its pounding, never ceasing the work of boring into the wall. Probably the ancient engineers who invented this device near Gadeira[10] called it a *ram* after the animals we know, which exercise by butting one another. Anyway, the inhabitants of Dyrrachium laughed at the barbarians and the men who handled it; this goat-like method of attacking a city wall was in their opinion ridiculous, and the enemy's siege efforts were coming to nothing. They threw open their gates and invited them in, as they mocked the repeated blows of the ram. 'Pounding away at the wall with that,' they said, 'will never make as big a hole as the gate offers.' The bravery of the defenders and the confidence of Alexius the general (the emperor's nephew) proved the futility of their tactics at once and the Franks themselves relaxed their efforts, despairing of taking the city, at least by this method. The defenders' courage and the fact that they had enough confidence to open the gates in their faces disheartened them; they abandoned the use of the ram and its portable shed stood idle. But idle and immobile though it was, for reasons I have given, fire was hurled on to it from above and it was reduced to ashes. The Frankish army tried another, more terrifying device. It was moved away towards the northern parts opposite the ducal residence, which is called the *praetorium*.[11] I will describe the site. Rising ground ended in a hill, not of rock but of soil; on this hill the city wall had been built. Opposite it, as we said, Bohemond's men started to dig

10. Gadeira (Latin *Gades*) is the modern Cadiz.

11. It is interesting to note that the Latin *praetorium* (general's head-quarters) had survived to Anna's time.

in a most expert manner – another invention of the besiegers
for the downfall of cities. The crafty scheme was now put into
operation against Dyrrachium. The sappers dug a mine, advancing like so many moles as they bored their underground
tunnel. Above ground they were protected by sheds with high
roofs against the showers of rocks and arrows; below they
made progress with their digging in a straight line, propping
up their tunnel roof with wooden posts and making a very
broad, long passage. All the time the soil was being carried
away in wagons. When the mine had gone far enough, they
congratulated themselves as if some great work had been
accomplished. But the defenders had not been negligent. Some
way off they dug their own trench, and when it was really
large, they sat down along its whole length, listening to find
out at what point the besiegers were likely to tunnel. It was
not long before they discovered a place where the enemy was
striking with spades and digging at the foundations of the
wall; they now knew their direction, even more so when they
opened up a hole just in front of them and saw the crowd of
Franks from their own tunnel. The defenders attacked with
fire [12] and severely burnt the enemies' faces and beards. Like
a swarm of bees pursued with smoke they could be seen
fleeing in disorder from their tunnel (which they had entered
in such a disciplined way). So their hard work on this scheme
too was in vain and another idea had ended to no good purpose. Thereupon a third invention was tried – a wooden tower.
According to report this siege-weapon was not constructed
for the first time after the failure of the others; in fact, this
tower was begun a full year before them. It was the main
weapon; the others I have mentioned were merely incidental.

12. Now this fire was chemically prepared in the following manner.
From the pine and other similar evergreen trees they gather resin, which
burns easily. This is rubbed with sulphur and introduced into reed tubes.
A man blows on it with a strong, sustained breath, as though he were
playing a pipe, and it then comes in contact with the fire at the end of the
tube, bursts into flames and falls like a flash of lightning on the faces in
front of it. This was the fire used by the defenders of Dyrrachium when
they came close to the enemy. (A.C.) See Appendix I, and for an excellent
description of Greek fire, Partington's recent book.

First, however, I must explain briefly the plan of the city of
Dyrrachium. Its wall is interrupted by towers which all round
the city rise to a height of eleven feet above it (the wall). A
spiral staircase leads to the top of the towers and they are
strengthened by battlements. So much for the city's defensive
plan. The walls are of considerable thickness, so wide indeed
that more than four horsemen can ride abreast in safety. My
passing remarks about the walls have been made in order to
clarify to some extent what is going to be said later. It is hard
to picture in words the construction of Bohemond's new
weapon; his barbarians devised it as a kind of mantelet with a
tower. According to eye-witnesses its appearance was terrifying, and certainly to the Dyrrachines threatened by it it was a
most awe-inspiring sight. It was made in the following manner. A wooden tower was built to a considerable height on a
four-sided base. So high was it that the city towers were
overtopped by as much as five or six cubits. It was essential
to make it so, in order that when the hanging drawbridges
were lowered the enemy ramparts might be easily overrun;
the natives, being continually pushed backwards, would not
be able to resist a violent attack launched in this way. It seems
likely that the besiegers of Dyrrachium had an excellent knowledge of optical theory, for without such expertise they would
not have judged the height of the walls. If they were ignorant
of optical theory, at least they knew how to use a Jacob's
staff.[13] The tower was indeed a terrible sight, but it seemed
even more terrible in motion, for its base was raised on many
rollers and this was done by soldiers inside who jacked it up
with levers; as the cause of the movement was invisible, the
onlookers were amazed. Like some giant above the clouds it
was apparently self-propelled. On all sides it had been covered
from base to top, and there were many storeys with embrasures
of every type all round it from which showers of arrows could
be fired. On the topmost floor were brave men, completely
armed, sword in hand and well trained for defence. When this
dread spectacle drew near the wall, Alexius, the governor of

13. The *dioptra*, used in surveying, had a level and a micrometer
screw for fine adjustment (*CMH*, vol. iv. pt. ii, p. 302).

Dyrrachium, and his soldiers were not caught unprepared. At the same time as Bohemond's structure, like some inescapable helepolis, was being put up outside the city, another was being made to oppose it inside. When the defenders saw how tall the enemy's self-moving tower was and where, after removing the rollers, they had brought it to a standstill, they set up opposite it four very long poles like a scaffolding, with a four-sided base; then they put floors at intervals between the poles; the whole thing was built to a height one cubit above the outside wooden tower. It was completely open, for except at the top (where it was covered with a roof) there was no need of protection. Alexius' men carried up there the liquid fire, intending to aim it from the highest storey. But when their plan was put into practice it failed to destroy the tower completely, for the jets of fire barely reached their objective. What were they to do? Well, they filled the gap between the two structures with all kinds of combustible material, on which great streams of oil were poured. The fire was started with brands and torches. For a little time it burned slowly, then caught a slight puff of air and burst into a bright flame as the torrents of liquid fire helped on the work. The whole frightful contraption with its abundance of wood was alight. It burned noisily – a horrible sight, visible up to thirteen stades away in all directions. The barbarians inside were desperate because of the uproar and great confusion; some were cut off by the conflagration and reduced to ashes, others hurled themselves from the summit to the ground. The tumult was tremendous and there was blind panic as the barbarians outside joined in the shouts.

So much then for the enormous wooden tower and the barbarians' attempt to take the walls. Now we must continue the story of the emperor. When spring came, the Augusta returned from Thessalonica to the capital, while Alexius marched on to Diabolis through Pelagonia. The place is in the foothills and after that the tracks (which I mentioned before) become impassable. The emperor conceived a new plan of campaign: he was quite convinced that there should be a rest from large-scale fighting for a time, and he was for that reason unwilling to risk a hand-to-hand battle with Bohemond. However, after leaving the impenetrable valleys and the roads that led nowhere as a kind of no-man's-land between the two armies, he did post along the mountain ridges all the officers he could trust with ample forces. The object of this new strategy was to prevent easy access from our side to the Franks, and also to stop letters reaching our army from the enemy or the sending of friendly greetings. Deep affection usually depends on such greetings; as the Stagirite says, a want of communication has proved the end of many friendships.[14] Bohemond, the emperor knew, was a man of great cunning and energy, and although he was prepared to meet him face to face in battle, as indeed I have said, he was perpetually seeking ways and means of dealing with him which were entirely different. For reasons already mentioned, despite the fact that he was most impatient for war – my father loved danger and had long experience of it – he acknowledged the rule of reason in everything and his desire was to conquer Bohemond by another method. The general (I think) should not invariably seek victory by drawing the sword; there are times when he should be prepared to use finesse, if the opportunity occurs and events allow it, and so achieve a complete triumph. So far as we know, a general's supreme task is to win, not merely by force of arms, but also by relying on treaties; and there is another way – sometimes, when the chance offers itself, an enemy can be beaten by fraud. The emperor seems to have employed fraud on this occasion. He wished to stir up discord between the counts and Bohemond, to shake or break their harmony. The stage was set, the play began. He called for Sebastos Marinos from Naples, a member of the Maistromili family,[15] who had not been entirely faithful to his oath of allegiance, being led astray by deceitful arguments and promises, but Alexius was confident that at least as far as Bohe-

14. The quotation from Aristotle (*Nicomachaean Ethics* viii, 6) is not quite accurate, but Anna may have been relying on memory alone.

15. Maistromili is a corruption of the old Latin *magistri militum*. The family had appropriated the Roman title – they were no doubt hereditary rulers of Naples.

mond was concerned he could tell him his secret plan. Roger, a Frankish nobleman, and Peter of Aulps, a man of great renown for his warlike exploits, whose loyalty to the emperor was absolutely dependable, were also summoned.[16] Alexius asked for their advice. What steps should he take to defeat Bohemond? What men were most faithful to him? How many shared his views? They gave the information and Alexius impressed on them the necessity of winning over these men by every means. 'If this should happen,' he said, 'the Keltic army will be torn by discord and through these men their common purpose will be smashed.' After telling them of his plan, he required each of them to provide one of his most faithful servants, a man who knew how to hold his tongue. They readily agreed. The servants arrived and the emperor proceeded with the plan. He composed letters as though in reply to some of Bohemond's most intimate friends; one would suppose on reading them that these men had written to the emperor, trying to win his friendship and disclosing the private intentions of Bohemond. In his 'answer' he thanked them and gladly acknowledged their good wishes. The persons to whom he wrote were Guy, Bohemond's own brother; one of his most distinguished soldiers, a man called Coprisianus; Richard and Principatus,[17] a brave man and high-ranking officer in his army. There were several others. The letters sent to them were fraudulent, for the emperor had received no communication at all of this kind from them. Neither Richard nor any other person like him had expressed good wishes and loyalty in a note. His 'answers', in fact, were an invention of his own. This play-acting had a purpose: if it came to Bohemond's ears that such men were traitorous, that they had been seduced and had made overtures to the emperor, he would at once be thrown into confusion. His barbaric nature would assert itself, he would maltreat them, and force them to break away; thanks to Alexius' cunning, they would rebel against

16. It is noteworthy that western soldiers were serving the emperor loyally.

17. That is, Richard, son of Rainulf of Salerno; and Richard of the Principate, a cousin of Bohemond.

Bohemond – a thing that had never entered their heads. The general knew, I think, that the opposition is strong when the whole body is welded together and of one mind; but let there be faction, and it splits up into many parts and becomes feebler, an easy prey to its enemies. This was the underlying plan and the secret treacherous intent of the letters. It was put into practice as follows. The messengers were instructed to deliver them to the individuals concerned, each letter to the respective addressee. Not only did the missives contain expressions of gratitude, but they also promised donations, gifts from the emperor and extraordinary guarantees; he invited them in future to be loyal, to show their loyalty, to conceal nothing of their secret designs. After the messengers he sent one of his own most trustworthy men, who was to follow them undetected and when he saw them getting near to Bohemond, he was to drive on past them, make his approach ahead of them to the Frank and pretend that he was a deserter, adding that he was joining the other side because he hated being with the emperor. He was to feign friendship for Bohemond and even a certain cordiality by openly accusing the persons to whom the letters were addressed, saying that this one and that one (giving their names in detail) had sworn allegiance to Bohemond, but had now become friends and allies of Alexius; they had become his adherents and Bohemond should beware lest they planned some sudden attack on himself, an attack meditated long before. It had to be done in this way, in case Bohemond did something dreadful to the letter-carriers. The emperor regarded it as his duty to protect these men (whom he had suborned) from harm, but also to reduce Bohemond's affairs to chaos. Nor was this a matter merely of words and counsel – action followed, too. The man I have mentioned approached Bohemond, and after ensuring the safety of the messengers by persuading him to take an oath, told him everything according to the emperor's instructions. When he was asked where he thought they were, he said they had passed through Petroula. Bohemond sent men to arrest the envoys. He opened the letters and becoming faint almost collapsed, for he believed they were genuine. The men he kept under close guard, but he himself for six days never left his tent. He was debating what ought to be done, turning over in his mind numerous possible courses: should the constables appear before him? Should he openly tell his brother Guy of the prejudice caused against him? Should they appear before him after the inquiry or without inquiry? Moreover, whom would he appoint constables in their place? Such men, he knew, were courageous and their withdrawal would consequently cause much harm. He settled the affair as best he could, and I fancy he suspected the underlying intention of the letters.[18] Anyway he treated them with good humour and confidently allowed them to remain at their posts.

The emperor had anticipated the enemy in establishing a considerable force in all the passes, under picked leaders, and every route was denied to the Kelts by means of the so-called *xyloklasiai*.[19] Without delay Michael Cecaumenus became the vigilant governor of Avlona, Hiericho[20] and Canina; Alexander Cabasilas was made governor of Petroula, with a mixed corps of infantry, a brave soldier who had put to flight many Turks in Asia; Leo Nicerites defended Deure with an adequate garrison; and Eustathius Kamytzes was detailed to guard the passes of Arbanus. Right from the starter's signal, as they say, Bohemond had sent his brother Guy, a count called Saracenus, and Contopaganus to deal with Cabasilas. Some little places in the neighbourhood of Arbanus had previously come over to Bohemond and their inhabitants, who were thoroughly acquainted with the tracks, came to him, explained the exact position of Deure and pointed out the hidden paths. Thereupon Guy divided his army in two: he himself undertook to fight Kamytzes from the front, while Contopaganus and the Count Saracenus with Deuriot guides were ordered to fall upon him from the rear. Both of them approved of this plan, and when Guy launched his frontal attack the others struck at Kamytzes from behind. He suffered

18. Anna's pride in her father's duplicity is clear enough, but she cannot help respecting Bohemond's commonsense.

19. Barricades of felled timber.

20. Hiericho is the ancient Oricum.

terrible casualties, for he could not fight against all of them at once, and when he saw his men in flight he followed them. In this engagement many Romans fell, including Karas who as a young boy had been accepted and enrolled by the emperor among his nobles, and Skaliarius, a Turk who in the old days had been a famous general in the east but deserted to the emperor and was baptized as a Christian. While Kamytzes was faring thus, Alyates, who was guarding Glabinitza with other picked men, came down to the plain. Whether he did this in order to fight, or to make a reconnaissance of the ground, God knows. By chance some Kelts not long afterwards met him. They were brave men, in full armour, and at the time divided into two groups: one, fifty in number, made a violent onslaught on his front, charging at full gallop; the other quietly followed him from the rear (there was no noise because the area was marshy). Alyates, knowing nothing of the threat from behind, fought against the others with might and main; he did not realize into what danger he had put himself. The enemy coming from behind fell upon him with great ferocity. In the battle a count called Contopaganus hit him with his spear and Alyates, felled to the ground, died instantly. Not a few of his men fell with him. When the news reached him, the emperor summoned Cantacuzenus, recognizing his outstanding qualities as a soldier. As I said before, he had been recalled from Laodicea and had rejoined Alexius. Because an attack on Bohemond could no longer be deferred, he was now sent out with a strong force. The emperor also left camp after him, giving him added encouragement, as it were. He reached a mountain pass called Petra by the natives and near it he halted. The strategy of the campaign was explained in great detail to Cantacuzenus; he was then sent on his way to Glabinitza with excellent advice and words of high hope. The emperor returned to Diabolis. On his march Cantacuzenus approached a small place called Mylos. At once he made ready all kinds of helepoleis and besieged it. The Romans moved boldly to the walls and soon got on to the parapets. The Kelts, encamped on the far side of the River Bouse, saw what had happened and ran to help. Cantacuzenus' scouts (they were barbarians, as the reader will already know) seeing the enemy movement, came back to him in disorder and instead of telling him privately what they had observed, began shouting some way off that the enemy were about to attack. When the soldiers heard this, even though they had climbed the walls, even though they had burnt the gates and already had the place in their grasp, they were panic-stricken. Every man ran for his horse, but in their mad frenzy and terror they grabbed any horse that came their way. Cantacuzenus fought hard and made repeated charges into the crowd of frightened men. 'Be men,' he shouted (quoting the poet). 'Recall the spirit and fury of war.'[21] They would not listen. But he overcame their fear by a clever ruse. 'It would be wrong,' he said, 'to leave the siege-engines to the enemy. They'll be used against ourselves. Set fire to them and then go away in good order.' These words had an immediate effect. With great zeal the instructions were carried out; and not only were the machines burnt, but also the boats on the river, to make it hard for the Kelts to cross. Cantacuzenus withdrew a short distance until he came to a plain; on the right was the River Charzanes, on the left a muddy swamp. Taking advantage of river and marsh, which afforded protection, he pitched camp on this plain. The Kelts arrived at the river-bank, but their boats had already been destroyed and they went back, disappointed of their hopes and downcast. Bohemond's brother Guy learnt from them what had happened. He changed direction and picking out his best men sent them to Hiericho and Canina. They found the valleys guarded by Michael Cecaumenus (the emperor had given him that task) and taking advantage of the terrain, which was in their favour, made a confident attack on the Romans and routed them. The Keltic soldier, when he catches his enemies in a narrow gorge, is irresistible; on flat ground it is easy to deal with him.

Encouraged by this success they returned to face Cantacuzenus again. However when they discovered that the place where he had encamped was of no assistance to themselves, they timidly put off the battle. He knew of their advance and throughout the night he was moving with all his army to the

21. Homer, *Iliad* vi, 112 and elsewhere.

other bank of the river. Before the sun had risen over the horizon, he was himself fully armed and his whole force stood ready for the fight. He took up position in front of the line at the centre, with the Turks on his left and the Alan Rosmikes in command of the right wing with his own compatriots. The Scyths he sent on ahead against the Kelts, with instructions to draw them forward by skirmishing; at the same time they were to bombard them continually with arrows, but to withdraw again and then once more move back. The Scyths went off eagerly, but they accomplished nothing, for the Kelts kept their ranks absolutely unbroken and advanced slowly in perfect order. When both armies were close enough for battle, the Scyths could no longer fire their arrows in face of the enemy's violent cavalry charges and they fled before them at once. The Turks wanted to help them and put in an attack on their own account, but the Kelts, not in the least worried by their intervention, fought even more fiercely. When Cantacuzenus saw the rout, he at once brought the Exousiocrator[22] Rosmikes into action (you will remember that he was on the right with his Alans, who were great fighters). Even his effort proved abortive, although he roared defiance at them like a lion. Cantacuzenus, when he also was in retreat, took fresh courage, as if the battle were just beginning, hurled himself at the Keltic front and split their army into many fragments. The enemy were utterly beaten and pursued as far as Mylos. Many of the ordinary soldiers were wiped out, as well as officers; some even of the distinguished counts were taken prisoner: Hugh,[23] his brother Richard, and Contopaganus. Cantacuzenus returned in triumph, but wishing to impress the emperor even more by his victory, he had the heads of many Kelts stuck on the ends of spears and the most illustrious of his captives, Hugh and Contopaganus, were at once sent to him. As I write these words, it is nearly time to light the lamps; my pen moves slowly over the paper and I feel myself almost too drowsy to write as the words escape me. I have to

22. A title. Anna is fairly accurate in the matter of rank.

23. Presumably Hugh of St Pol, who was one of Bohemond's leading officers.

use foreign names and I am compelled to describe in detail a mass of events which occurred in rapid succession; the result is that the main body of the history and the continuous narrative are bound to become disjointed because of interruptions. Ah well, ''tis no cause for anger'[24] to those at least who read my work with good will. Let us go on.

The warrior Bohemond realized that his affairs were in a really serious condition: he was under attack from sea and land; now that his supplies were failing, too, he was in the greatest difficulty. However, a strong detachment was sent to all the towns near Avlona, Hiericho and Canina for plunder. The move did not catch Cantacuzenus off-guard: as Homer says, 'nor did sweet slumber hold back the man'.[25] Quickly Beroites was despatched with a considerable force to oppose the Kelts and he soon beat them. For good measure on his way back he set fire to Bohemond's fleet. The great man heard of this setback, but so far from being downcast, he became even more bold, as if he had suffered no casualties at all. Another contingent, of 6,000 infantry and cavalry most eager to do battle, was put in the field against Cantacuzenus. Bohemond thought that the Roman army and its general would be taken without a blow. But our general had scouts continually on the watch for the Keltic multitudes and when he knew they were on the march, he armed himself and his soldiers during the night, impatient for the assault at first light. The Kelts, worn out with marching, lay down for a brief rest by the bank of the Bouse and there, just as day was breaking, he found them. He went into the attack at once. Many prisoners were taken, but more were killed; the rest, swept away by the river currents, were drowned – they 'escaped the wolf only to meet the lion'. All the counts were sent off to the emperor, after which he (Cantacuzenus) returned to Timoros, a place which was marshy and almost inaccessible. During the week in which he remained there a fair number of scouts, posted in different places, were observing Bohemond's movements. Reports came in, so that he was better able to make his decisions. As it happened, the scouts found a hundred Kelts making rafts;

24. A reminiscence of Homer.   25. Homer, *Iliad* ii, 2.

they intended to cross the river on them and capture a village on the far side. The Romans fell upon them unexpectedly and took almost all of them alive, including Bohemond's cousin, a gigantic man ten feet tall and as broad as a second Hercules. It was indeed an extraordinary sight – this huge giant, a really monstrous man, the prisoner of a tiny Scyth, a pygmy. Cantacuzenus gave orders, when they left, that the pygmy Scyth should lead the monster on a chain into the presence of the emperor, probably by way of a joke. When Alexius heard that they had arrived, he took his seat on the imperial throne and commanded the prisoners to be brought in. In came the Scyth leading this tremendous Kelt on a chain. He was not even tall enough to reach his captive's buttocks. Of course there was an instant outburst of laughter from all. The rest of the counts were committed to prison . . . .[26]

The emperor barely had time to smile at the success of Cantacuzenus, when more news arrived, an ill-omened report that the Roman regiments of Kamytzes and Cabasilas had suffered enormous losses. The emperor did not in any way lose heart, but he was deeply distressed and hurt; he grieved for the dead and for some individuals even shed tears. Nevertheless, Constantine Gabras,[27] a fine soldier and bitter adversary of the Kelts, was commissioned to take up position at Petroula. His task was to find out where the enemy got into the valleys to carry out such a massacre, and then to bar their way for the future. Gabras was annoyed; the thought of the enterprise worried him – he was a conceited fellow, ambitious to undertake only important commands. Without delay the emperor turned to Marianus Mavrocatacalon, the husband of my Caesar's sister, a man of great courage, proved by many brave honest deeds and much liked by Alexius. A large force made up of the best soldiers was put under his command, supplemented by many servants of the porphyrogeniti and my husband, who were glad of an opportunity to fight. Marianus, however, also had reservations about the expedition; never-

26. There is a lacuna here in the text.
27. Son of Theodore Gabras and brother of Gregory. They were a turbulent family.

theless, he did retire to his tent to consider the matter. About the mid-watch of the night, a letter arrived from Landulf, who was at the time with Isaac Contostephanus, the thalassocrator. In this message he made accusations against the Contostephani, Isaac, his brother Stephanus, and Euphorbenus: they had been neglectful in guarding the Lombardy strait and sometimes had landed for a rest. There was a postscript: 'You, Sir, would have prevented the marauding incursions of the Kelts with every ounce of strength and all the resources of your mind, but these men have given up and are still sleeping at their post. Because they neglect their duty at sea, the sailors bringing supplies to Bohemond inevitably have time on their side, for those who have recently made the crossing from Lombardy have waited for a favourable wind; then they crowd on sail and boldly make the voyage.[28] Even so, a blustery south wind never allows them to anchor in Dyrrachium; they are forced to coast along and put in at Avlona. The enemy anchor their transports there, ships of great tonnage bringing over heavy reinforcements of infantry and cavalry, and all the food supplies necessary for Bohemond. After landing they organize a number of markets at which the Kelts can buy plenty of produce for the table.' The emperor was extremely angry and Isaac was severely censured. By threatening him with punishment if he did not mend his ways, Alexius brought about a change – Isaac became a most vigilant guard. But things did not go according to plan for him: on more than one occasion he tried to prevent the enemy from crossing, but failed. The trouble was this: he sailed midway between the two coast-lines, but when he spied the Kelts under full sail with a following wind and moving fast in the opposite direction, he could not fight both them and the head winds at the same time. Not even Hercules (as they say) can take on two at once. He was blown back, therefore, by the force of the wind – and the emperor was disgusted. As he knew that Contostephanus was stationing the Roman fleet in the wrong area, so that the south winds which blew

28. To those sailing from Lombardy to Illyricum the strong winds from the south are favourable, but the northerlies are the reverse. (A.C.)

against him were making the voyage easier for the enemy, he drew him a map of the coasts of Lombardy and Illyricum, with the harbours on either side. This he sent to him, adding written instructions. He advised him where to moor his ships and from what place to set sail if the wind was favourable, in order to attack the Kelts at sea. Thus he put fresh hope into Contostephanus and persuaded him to act. Isaac, confident again and going where the emperor had told him, ran his ships ashore. There he awaited his chance and when the enemy were out at sea with a great convoy and the wind was in the right quarter, he intercepted them in mid-straits. Some of their pirate ships he burnt; more were sent to the bottom of the sea with all hands. Before news of this reached Alexius, he was much concerned at letters from Landulf and the Duke of Dyrrachium and he changed his plans. Marianus Mavrocata-calon (whom I mentioned above) was immediately summoned and appointed duke of the fleet; the Petroula mission was entrusted to somebody else. Marianus departed and by some chance at once fell in with the corsairs on their way from Lombardy to Bohemond. There were also some cargo vessels. He captured all of them, fully loaded with all kinds of food-supplies. After that the straits had a tireless guardian, for Marianus gave the Kelts no opportunity whatever for further crossings.

The emperor bivouacked at the foot of the passes near Diabolis, keeping a tight hand on would-be deserters. Messages poured out from his headquarters in a continuous stream to the commanders on the passes: he advised them about the number of men required on the plain of Dyrrachium to fight Bohemond and the type of battle formation they should adopt as they came down from the hills: they were to make frequent charges on horseback and then withdraw; this manoeuvre was to be repeated often while they fired arrows, but the lancers were to move slowly in their rear, so that if the archers should be swept back too far they might help and at the same time strike at any Kelt who by chance came within reach. They were issued with a plentiful supply of arrows and told not to be at all niggardly in their use; but they were to shoot at the horses rather than the Kelts, for he knew that cuirasses and coats of mail made them almost, if not entirely invulnerable; to shoot at the riders, therefore, would in his opinion be a waste of arrows and absolutely ridiculous. Keltic armour consists of a tunic interwoven with iron rings linked one with another; the iron is of good quality, capable of resisting an arrow and giving protection to the soldier's body. This armour is supplemented by a shield, not round but long, broad at the top and tapering to a point; inside it is slightly curved; the outside is smooth and shiny, and it has a flashing, bronze boss. Any arrow, whether it be Scythian or Persian or fired by the arms of a Giant, will be repelled by that shield and rebound against the firer. It was for these reasons, I fancy, that the emperor (having experience of Keltic armour and our arrows) ordered them not to worry about the men but rather to attack the horses. 'Give them wings,' he said (referring to the arrow-feathers, of course). There was another reason for shooting at the horses: the Kelts, when they dismounted, would be easily handled. A mounted Kelt is irresistible; he would bore his way through the walls of Babylon; [29] but when he dismounts he becomes anyone's plaything. Knowing the perverse nature of his followers Alexius was unwilling to go over the passes, despite his own intense desire to fight it out with Bohemond in a general battle (on many occasions I have emphasized this in earlier chapters of the history). On the battle-field more incisive than any sword, a man of fearless disposition, absolutely indomitable, he was yet deterred from this enterprise by the terrible events which were now oppressing his spirit. While Bohemond was being cramped by land and sea, the emperor sat like a spectator, watching what was happening on the plains of Illyricum, although he was heart and soul with his fighting men, sharing in their sweat and toil – there were times when one might say he had more than his share – stimulating the officers posted above the mountain passes to battle and war, and giving advice on methods of attacking the enemy. Marianus, guarding the sea routes from Lombardy to Illyricum, effectually stopped all movement eastwards: no three-master, no heavy merchant-

29. The ancient Babylon, capital of Chaldaea.

man, no little two-oared boat was given the slightest chance of
reaching Bohemond. Food-supplies brought over by sea,
therefore, had failed him and so had those extra provisions
acquired on the mainland. He realized that the war was being
successfully pursued by the emperor with much skill; for
example, every time his men left camp for forage or any
other necessities, or even led out the horses for drink, the
Romans would attack and kill most of them, so that his army
was gradually wasting away. Under the circumstances he sent
proposals for peace to Alexius, the Duke of Dyrrachium. One
of Bohemond's counts, William Clarelès, a man of noble
lineage, saw that the whole Keltic force was being wiped out
by famine and plague (for some terrible illness had visited them
from above) and for his own safety deserted to the emperor
with fifty horses. He was welcomed and when Alexius asked
him how Bohemond was faring, he confirmed the distress
caused by the plague and the extreme harshness of their plight.
He was thereupon rewarded with the title of *nobilissimus* and
showered with gifts and favours. From the letters of his
namesake Alexius also learnt that Bohemond had sued for
peace through his envoys, but as he was aware that his own
entourage were always plotting some new mischief against
himself (every hour he saw them rebelling and himself more
impugned by his own flesh and blood than by foreign enemies)
he decided to fight no more with both hands against both
adversaries. Making a virtue of necessity, as somebody once
said, he thought the wiser course was to accept peace with the
Kelts and not to reject Bohemond's proposals. On the other
hand, he was afraid to advance any further – for the reason I
have already mentioned. He stayed where he was, therefore,
facing the enemy on two sides, but his letters to the duke
instructed him to address Bohemond thus: 'You know perfectly well how many times I have been deceived through
trusting your oaths and promises. And if the Holy Gospel did
not command Christians in all things to forgive one another,
I would not have opened my ears to your proposition. But it is
better to be deceived than to offend God and transgress His
holy laws. I do not therefore reject your plea. If you do in

THE ALEXIAD OF ANNA COMNENA   *viii–ix*

truth desire peace, if you do indeed abominate the absurd and impossible thing that you have attempted, and if you no longer take pleasure in shedding the blood of Christians, not for the benefit of your own country nor for that of the Christians, but to satisfy the whim of yourself alone and of nobody else, then come in person with as many companions as you like. The distance between us is not great. Whether in the course of negotiations we agree on the same terms, or even disagree, you will in any case return to your camp unharmed according to my promise.'

At this reply Bohemond demanded that noble hostages be given to him; they would be free, but guarded by counts in his own camp, until he himself returned; otherwise he would not dare to go to the emperor. Alexius chose the Neapolitan Marinus and the Frank Roger (who was renowned for his bravery). Both men were intelligent and well versed in the Latin customs. A third member of the party was Constantine Euphorbenus, brave in action and brave of heart, a man who never failed the emperor in any undertaking entrusted to him; and the fourth was a certain Adralestos, who understood the Keltic language. These men were sent to Bohemond. They were to cajole him by every argument and persuade him to come of his own free will to Alexius. He could say whatever he wished and required of Alexius, and if the emperor gave his unqualified approval, he would have his way; if not, then he would return unscathed to his own encampment. Such were the instructions given to the envoys before they were released for the journey. They set out on the road to Bohemond. When he heard of their arrival he was alarmed lest, noting the sickness-rate in his army, they might tell the emperor; so he rode out far from the camp to meet them. They delivered their message thus: 'The emperor has by no means forgotten the promises and oaths given by you and all the other counts who passed through Constantinople. No doubt you see how badly the transgression of them has turned out for you.' At this Bohemond interrupted. 'Enough of that. If the emperor had anything else to tell me, I would like to hear it.' The envoys went on: 'The emperor, desirous of your safety and the safety of the army under your command, makes this proclamation to you through us: "You know perfectly well that after much suffering, you have proved incapable of taking Dyrrachium. Moreover you have profited neither yourself nor your men. Nevertheless, if your desire is not to bring utter destruction on yourself and your people, come to me, the emperor, without fear; thus you may reveal all your own ambitions and listen in turn to my adjudication. If our views coincide, thank God; if not, I will send you back to your own camp unhurt. Another point: all those under your command who desire to visit the Holy Sepulchre for worship will be given safe-conduct by me; those who prefer to go back to their homes will be free to do so, after receiving liberal gifts from me."' Bohemond replied, 'Now I know in very truth that skilled debaters have been sent to me by Alexius. I ask you then for a full assurance that my reception by the emperor will in no way whatever be dishonourable; that six stades before I reach him his closest blood relatives will come to meet me; that when I have approached the imperial tent, at the moment when I enter its door, the emperor will rise from his throne to receive me with honour; that no reference whatever shall be made to our past agreements and that I shall in no way be brought to trial; that I shall have absolute freedom to say whatever I wish, as I wish. Moreover I ask that the emperor shall take my hand and set me at the place of honour; that I, after making my entrance with two officers, shall be completely excused from having to bend my knee or bow my head to him as a mark of respect.' The envoys listened to these requests. They refused his demand that the emperor should rise from his throne, saying that it was presumptuous. Nor was this their only refusal. The request that he should not kneel or bow to the emperor in obeisance was also vetoed. On the other hand, they accepted that some of the emperor's distant relatives should go a reasonable distance to meet and escort him when he was about to enter the emperor's presence, as a ceremonial mark of respect; he could, moreover, enter with two officers; also (and this was important) the emperor would take his hand and seat him in the place of honour. After these exchanges the ambassadors withdrew to the place already prepared for them to rest, guarded by a hundred sergeants.[30] This was to prevent them going out in the night to examine the condition of the army, thus becoming more inclined to treat Bohemond with contempt. On the next day, with 300 knights and all the counts, Bohemond arrived at the spot where on the day before he had talked with the envoys. Then, with a retinue of six chosen men, he went to find them, leaving behind the rest who were to await his return. The envoys and Bohemond discussed again what had previously been said, and when the latter became threatening, one count called Hugh, who was of most noble lineage, addressed him thus: 'Not one of us who intended to join battle with the emperor has up till now struck anyone with his lance. An end, then, to most of this talk. It is peace that we must make instead of war.' A long argument ensued on both sides. Bohemond was angry, feeling that he had suffered outrageous treatment because not all his requests were granted by the envoys; to some they assented and where they refused, Bohemond making a virtue of necessity (as they say) withdrew his objections. But he asked them to swear that he would be received with honour and that if the emperor would not meet his wishes, he would be escorted in safety to his own camp. The Holy Gospels were produced therefore and he formally asked for hostages to be handed over to his brother Guy, to be guarded by him until his (Bohemond's) return. The ambassadors agreed to this and in turn made counter-demands, asking for the swearing of oaths for the safety of their hostages. When Bohemond agreed to this, oaths were taken on both sides and the hostages, the Sebastos Marinus and the man called Adralestos and the Frank Roger were handed over to Guy, on condition that when a treaty of peace was concluded with the emperor, or even if their efforts failed, he would send them back to Alexius unharmed, according to their solemn guarantee.

When Bohemond was about to start on his journey to the

30. The Greek *sergentioi* is said to derive from Latin *servientes*, and in that case could be translated by *infantrymen*. But it seems more likely that Anna is using the word as a rank.

emperor with Euphorbenus Constantine Catacalon, because
the camp was fetid with a most horrible odour – the army had
been in the same area for a long time – he wished to move his
men and said he was unwilling to do even that without their
permission. That is typical of the Kelts: they are inconsistent,
changing to opposite extremes in a moment. You can see one
and the same man boasting that he will shake the whole world
and the very next minute cringing prostrate in the dust – and
this is even more likely to happen when they meet stronger
characters. The envoys agreed that the camp should be moved,
but not more than twelve stades. They added: 'If you wish to
do this we will come along with you and see the place ourselves.' Bohemond made no objection to this. They immediately informed the officers who were watching the passes
not to make sorties or do them any harm. Euphorbenus
Constantine Catacalon in his turn asked Bohemond to allow
him to visit Dyrrachium. The request was granted and
Catacalon quickly arrived there. Having found Alexius, the son
of Isaac the sebastocrator and the commander of the garrison,
he delivered the emperor's message entrusted to him and also
to the picked men who had come down there with him. The
garrison troops were unable to lean over the walls because of
a device invented before by the emperor for use on the ramparts of Dyrrachium. Planks of wood were cleverly laid along
the parapets of the citadel. They were not nailed, for this
reason: any Latins who happened to try clambering up
ladders would find no firm foothold if they reached the ramparts; in fact, they would slip and fall inside the walls, planks
and all. Euphorbenus had a conversation with them, gave them
the emperor's instructions and filled them with confidence.
He also asked questions about conditions in the fort. After
being assured that their affairs were going very well, as they
had enough provisions and were in no way worried by
Bohemond's schemes, he went away. He found Bohemond
had set his new encampment in the agreed place. Together
they set out on the road to the emperor while the rest of the
envoys, according to the promises given beforehand, were
left with Guy's men. Catacalon sent Manuel of Modena on

ahead to announce Bohemond's coming to the emperor (this Manuel was one of his most trustworthy and faithful servants). The arrangements for his reception, when he drew near the imperial tent, had been carried out in the manner settled by the envoys. Bohemond went inside, the emperor extended his hand, grasped Bohemond's and after the words of welcome usually spoken by emperors, placed him near the imperial throne. Bohemond's appearance was, to put it briefly, unlike that of any other man seen in those days in the Roman world, whether Greek or barbarian. The sight of him inspired admiration, the mention of his name terror. I will describe in detail the barbarian's characteristics. His stature was such that he towered almost a full cubit over the tallest men. He was slender of waist and flanks, with broad shoulders and chest, strong in the arms; in general he was neither taper of form, nor heavily built and fleshy, but perfectly proportioned – one might say that he conformed to the Polyclitean ideal. His hands were large, he had a good firm stance, and his neck and back were compact. If to the accurate and meticulous observer he appeared to stoop slightly, that was not caused by any weakness of the vertebrae of the lower spine, but presumably there was some malformation there from birth. The skin all over his body was very white, except for his face which was both white and red. His hair was lightish-brown and not as long as that of other barbarians (that is, it did not hang on his shoulders); in fact, the man had no great predilection for long hair, but cut his short, to the ears. Whether his beard was red or of any other colour I cannot say, for the razor had attacked it, leaving his chin smoother than any marble. However, it *appeared* to be red. His eyes were light-blue and gave some hint of the man's spirit and dignity. He breathed freely through nostrils that were broad, worthy of his chest and a fine outlet for the breath that came in gusts from his lungs. There was a certain charm about him, but it was somewhat dimmed by the alarm his person as a whole inspired; there was a hard, savage quality in his whole aspect, due, I suppose, to his great stature and his eyes; even his laugh sounded like a threat to others. Such was his constitution, mental and physical, that in him both courage and love were armed, both ready for combat. His arrogance was everywhere manifest; he was cunning, too, taking refuge quickly in any opportunism. His words were carefully phrased and the replies he gave were regularly ambiguous. Only one man, the emperor, could defeat an adversary of such character, an adversary as great as Bohemond; he did it through luck, through eloquence, and through the other advantages that Nature had given him.

After a brief and somewhat discreet review of what had happened in the past, Alexius turned the conversation in another direction. Bohemond, under the influence of a guilty conscience, studiously avoided any attempt to answer his words and merely remarked, 'I have not come to defend myself against such objections. In fact, I could have said much myself. Now that God has reduced me to this state, I put myself entirely in your hands for the future.' 'Let us forget the past now,' said the emperor. 'But you, if you want to make peace with us, must first of all become one of my subjects; then you must inform your nephew Tancred of this and instruct him to hand over the city of Antioch to my emissaries in accordance with our first agreement; moreover you must respect, both now and in the future, all the other pacts made by them.' After much further conversation, in which both had their say, it became clear that Bohemond was still his old self: he had not changed. 'It is impossible,' he declared, 'for me to give such an undertaking.' When the emperor made certain other demands, he asked to be allowed to return to his own camp. (It was stipulated in the terms agreed by the ambassadors that he had this right.) However, the emperor told him, 'I have no one who can better guarantee your safety than myself.' With these words he ordered his commanders in a loud voice to make ready the horses for the road to Dyrrachium. When Bohemond heard this, he left Alexius and withdrew to the tent set apart for him. He asked to see Nicephorus Bryennius, my Caesar, who had then been promoted to the rank of panhypersebastos. Nicephorus arrived and after exerting all his powers of persuasion (and he was unrivalled in discourse and public oratory) he convinced

Bohemond that he should consent to most of the emperor's terms. Thereupon he took him by the hand and led him into the imperial tent. On the next day, under oath and of his own free will, because he considered it the best course, he accepted the terms in full. They were as follows:

When with my multitudinous army of Franks I came to the imperial city, on my way from Europe to Asia for the liberation of Jerusalem, an agreement was made with Your Majesty, the divinely appointed Emperor. That agreement, in consequence of certain unexpected events, has since been violated; it must therefore be in abeyance and of no validity, no longer effective and abrogated because of changed circumstances. Your Majesty can legally have no due claims against me relying on that agreement, nor can there be any contention about what was stipulated and committed to writing in it. For when I declared war against Your Majesty, the divinely appointed Emperor, and when I violated the agreed terms, the charges brought by you against me likewise became null and void. But now that I have come to repentance and like some fisherman [31] caught unawares by a storm have learnt my lesson; now that I have regained my senses and almost at spear-point recovered my sanity; with the memory of defeat and former wars, I beg to make another agreement with Your Majesty. By the terms of this second pact I shall become the liege-man of Your Highness; if I may speak in terms more explicit and more definite, I shall be your servant and subject, for you have been willing to extend to me your protection and accept me as your liege. By the terms of this second agreement, which I hope to keep for ever – I swear it by God and all his Saints, since the terms agreed are committed to writing and recited with them as my witnesses – I shall be, from this moment, the loyal man of Your Majesty and of your much-loved son, the Basileus Lord John, the Porphyrogenitus. And I shall arm my right hand against all who oppose your power, whether the

31. The point of the 'fisherman' has been the subject of much debate. The proverbial expression was clearly equivalent to our 'once bitten, twice shy'. For a full discussion see Buckler, pp. 514–5.

rebel be of the Christian persuasion or a stranger to our faith, one of those whom we call pagans. One clause, therefore, contained in the aforementioned accord and accepted by both parties, by Your Majesties and by me, this one clause alone (all the others having been made null and void) I extract and stoutly uphold and cling fast to, namely, that I am the servant and liege-man of both Your Majesties, renewing as it were that which has been rescinded. Whatever happens, I shall not violate this; nor shall there be any reason or method, manifest or obscure, which shall make me appear to be a transgressor of the articles of this present covenant. But since I am to receive now a region (to be duly specified hereafter in this agreement) by a chrysobull to which Your Majesty will append his signature in purple ink and a copy of which has been given to me, I accept these lands in the east as a gift from Your Majesties, the chrysobull being the guarantee of the validity of this gift. In exchange for lands and cities so extensive I pledge my loyalty to Your Majesties, to you the Great Autocrator and Lord Alexius Comnenus, and to your thrice-beloved son, the Basileus and Lord John the Porphyrogenitus, and I promise to preserve that loyalty unshaken and immovable as a sure anchor. Let me repeat what I have said in clearer terms and establish the identity of the signatories. I, Bohemond the son of Robert Guiscard, make this agreement with Your Highnesses, and I intend to keep this agreement inviolate with Your Majesties; that is to say, with you, the Autocrator of the Romans, the Lord Alexius, and with the Basileus, your son the Porphyrogenitus; and I will be your liege-man, sincere and true, as long as I breathe and am numbered among the living. And I will arm my hand against any enemies that may hereafter rise up against the Romans and you, the ever-august Rulers of the Roman Empire. And when I am commanded by you, with all my army I will be your faithful servant, without evasion, in the hour of need. And if there should be any ill-disposed to your power, unless they are the like of the immortal angels, impervious to wounds inflicted by our weapons or endowed with bodies hard as steel, I will fight them all for Your Majesties. And if I am fit in body and free from wars against barbarian and Turk, I myself with my own hands will fight on your behalf with my army behind me. If I am held fast by some serious illness (the kind of thing that oft-times befalls mankind) or if impending war drags me to itself, then – yes, even then – I promise to send what help I can through the brave men about me; they shall make amends for my absence. For true allegiance, which today I give to Your Majesties, entails the meticulous observance of the terms of agreement, either through my own efforts or, as I have said, through the efforts of others. I swear to be truly faithful, in general and in particular, to your sovereignty and I pledge my protection for your life – that is, your life here on earth. To guard your life I shall be under arms, like a statue hammered out of iron. But I extend my oath to include your honour and Your Majesties' persons, in case some mischief is plotted against you by criminal foes whom I can destroy and repel from their evil enterprise. I swear too to defend every land that is yours, cities great and small, the islands themselves – in brief, all land and sea under your jurisdiction from the Adriatic Sea as far as the whole East and the territories of Great Asia included in the Roman boundaries. Moreover I agree, and God shall be the Witness and Hearer of my agreement, never to control and hold any land, any city, any island which either now or in the past was subject to your authority; in a word, all those territories which the Empire of Constantinople held or now holds, both in the east and in the west, with the exception of those areas duly given me by Your Highnesses crowned by God, which areas shall be expressly named in the present document. If I am able to subjugate any land once upon a time paying tribute to this Empire by driving out its present rulers, then I must refer the question of its government to your decision; and if you wish me to act as regent of the conquered land, me your liege-man and loyal servant, it shall be so; but if you decide otherwise, I shall hand over the territory to whatever man Your Majesties desire, without any equivocation. I shall accept neither any land betrayed to me by any other person, nor any city, nor any village once subject to you, as though they were my property; but what is acquired, by siege or without a siege, was yours in the past and shall again be yours in the future, and I shall in no way whatever lay claim to those places. Nor shall I accept the oath of any Christian or myself take an oath to another person; nor shall I make any agreement whatever which is likely to hurt you or inflict loss on you and your Empire. I shall become the liege-man of no one else, of no other power greater or smaller, without your permission. The one sovereignty to which I pledge my allegiance is that of you and your thrice-beloved son. If men approach me who have rebelled against the authority of Your Majesty and wish to become my slaves, I shall express my loathing of them and reject them – more than that, I shall take up arms against them. As for the other barbarians who are yet willing to submit to my spear, I shall receive them, but not in my own name; on behalf of you and your much-loved son I shall compel them to take oaths, and I shall take over their lands in the name of Your Majesties. Whatever instructions you give with regard to them, therefore, I undertake to carry out with no evasion. These promises concern all cities and countries which happen to be under the jurisdiction of Roman Destiny; with regard to those which have not yet become subject to Roman Power I make the following promises under oath. All those lands which come under my control without war, or even with war and battle, I shall reckon as coming from Your Majesties, whether they be Turkish or Armenian; whether, as one who understands our language would say, they are pagan or Christian; the people of these nations who come to me and wish to be my slaves I shall receive, on condition that they also become liege-men of Your Majesties. My agreement with the sovereign power shall extend to them also, and so shall the oaths ratified. Of these men those whom you, the Basileus ever-august, wish to be subject to me, shall be so subject; but those whom you desire to add to your domain I shall refer to you, if they acquiesce; and if they do not acquiesce, but reject your over-lordship, I shall not even in those circumstances receive them. With regard to Tancred, my nephew, I shall wage relentless war against him unless he is willing to become somewhat less hostile to Your Majesties and relax his grip on the cities which belong to you. And when with his consent or against his will the cities are liberated, I shall myself with your authority become lord of the places granted me by the chrysobull, which places will be set out in due order. Those cities, including Laodicea in Syria, which are not among this number, will be attached to your realm. Nor shall I on any occasion receive fugitives from your Empire, but I shall force them to retrace their steps and return to Your Majesties. Moreover, in addition to the promises mentioned before, I make further pledges to strengthen the agreement: I undertake to use as guarantors of these terms, so that they may remain for ever unbroken and inviolate, those men who will take possession in my name of the land given to me by Your Majesties and the cities and strong-points to be named. I will ensure that they swear with the most solemn oaths to keep strict faith with your government, in all respects observing Roman law, and to adhere with punctilious care to all the provisions set down in writing here. I will make them swear by the heavenly powers and the ineluctable wrath of God that if ever I plot against Your Majesties – and may that never come to pass, never, O Saviour, never, O Justice of God! – they will first for a period of forty days endeavour by all means to break my rebellious spirit and restore me to my allegiance to Your Majesties. Such a thing would happen – if indeed it were possible for it ever to happen – only when sheer madness and lunacy took hold of me or if I were manifestly driven out of my mind. However, if I should persist in my folly and remain obdurate in face of their advice, and if the turbulent blast of lunacy does blow upon my soul, then they shall disown me upon oath and in every way reject me, transferring to your service their own power and allegiance, and the lands which in my name they control shall be torn from my hands and given up to your jurisdiction. They shall be compelled to do these things under oath and they shall observe the same loyalty and obedience and good-will towards you as I have promised; for your life and for your temporal honour they shall take up arms; they shall always be ready to welcome battle for Your Majesties' life and limb lest they suffer at the hands of some enemy, as long as they are aware of conspiracies and perils. These things I swear and call to witness both God and men and the angels of Heaven that I shall indeed force them by frightful oaths to do and practise them to the best of their ability. They shall agree to the same terms under oath as I have about your forts and cities and lands – in brief, about all the provinces which belong to Your Majesties both in the east and in the west. And these things they shall do both in my life-time and after my death; they shall be subjects of your Empire and serve it faithfully. All those who happen to be here with me will at once take the oath of allegiance and loyalty to Your August Majesties, the Lord Alexius, Autocrator of the Romans and your son the Basileus and Porphyrogenitus; but all those of my horsemen and men-at-arms (whom we usually call *caballarii*) who are not here, if Your Majesty sends a man to the city of Antioch, will there take the same oaths and your man will administer the oaths to them, while I (I swear this) will urge them to pledge adherence and consent to these same provisions unaltered. Moreover I agree and swear that if it is Your Majesties' wish that I should take up arms and wage war against those who hold the cities and lands which once were subject to the Empire of Constantinople, I will do this and I will bear arms against them. But if it is not your will that I should declare war, then we will not march against them. For in all things we desire to support your authority and to make every deed and every policy dependent on your consent. All those Saracens and Ishmaelites who congregate in your Empire, coming over to your side and surrendering their cities, I will neither prevent nor will I zealously try to win them over to myself, unless indeed when hard-pressed by my forces and driven everywhere into desperate straits they turn under the imminent threat of danger to you for help, thus ensuring their own safety. In the case of all men, who through fear of Frankish warriors and the nearness of death turn away to Your Majesties for succour, you will not for this reason lay claim to our prisoners-of-war, but naturally to those only who of their own free will become your servants, without toil and trouble on our part. Moreover,

I agree to the following: all those soldiers of Lombardy who are willing to cross the Adriatic with me shall also take the oaths and agree to serve Your Majesty; the oaths shall of course be administered to them by some man of your Empire, whom you yourselves shall send for this very purpose from the other side of the Adriatic. If they reject the oath, they shall in no circumstances be allowed to cross, because of their hostility to our common policy. As for the lands granted to me in a chrysobull by Your Divinely-appointed Majesties, it is essential that they should be set out in the present document, as follows: the city of Antioch in Koele-Syria with its fortifications and its dependencies, together with Souetios, which is situated by the sea; Doux with all its dependencies, together with the castles of Kauka and Loulou, the castle of 'Wondrous Mountain' and Phersia, with all its territory; the military district of St Elias, with its dependent small villages; the military district of Borze and its dependent villages; all the country in the neighbourhood of the military district of Sezer (which the Greeks call Larissa); likewise the military districts of Artach and Telouch with their respective fortifications, and with these Germaniceia and the small villages which belong to to it; Mount Mauros and all the castles dependent on it, as well as all the plain lying at its feet, except of course the territory of the Roupenians, Leo and Theodorus, the Armenians who have become your liege-men; in addition to the above-mentioned, the strategat [32] of Pagras, the strategat of Palatza, the theme of Zoume, together with all their dependent castles and small villages, and the country which belongs to each. For all these are included in the chrysobull of Your Majesties as granted to me by the divine power until the end of my life, and as reverting of necessity after my departure from this world to the Empire of New Rome, the Queen of Cities, Constantinople, on condition that I keep my faith absolutely unspotted and preserve my loyalty to its sovereignty faultless, in the person of Your Ever-august Majesties, and provided that I am the servant and liege-man of its throne and imperial sceptre. I agree and swear by the God worshipped in the church of

32. That is, the military district.

Antioch that the Patriarch of that city will not be of our race, but a man whom Your Majesties will promote, one of the clergy of the Great Church in Constantinople. For in future the throne of Antioch will be occupied by such a man; he will carry out all the duties of an archbishop, the laying on of hands and the other business of the church, according to the privileges of this cathedral. There were also certain parts cut off from the jurisdiction of the Duke of Antioch by Your Majesties, since you wished to appropriate them entirely: they are as follows: the theme of Podandon . . .[33] the strategat of the city of Tarsus, the city of Adana, the city of Mopsuestiae and Anabarza – in short, the whole territory of Cilicia which is bounded by the Cydnus and the Hermon; likewise the military district of Laodicea-in-Syria and, of course, the strategat of Gabala, which we with our rather broken foreign accent call Zebel; the strategats of Balaneus, Marakeus and Antaras with Antartes, for both the latter are military districts. These are the places which Your Majesties have separated from the general jurisdiction of the Duke of Antioch and brought under your own sphere of influence. And I am content with both alike – with your concessions and with your annexations. To the rights and privileges which I have been granted by you I will cling, but I will not lay claim to those which I have not received. Nor will I cross the frontiers, but will remain in the territories given me, ruling them and enjoying the free use of them as long as I live, according to my previous declaration. After my death (and this too has already been stipulated in writing) they will revert to their own governments, from which they were transferred to me. I will make sure of this by instructing my governors and my men to hand over all the lands in question to the Roman authorities without fuss; there will be no equivocation. These instructions will be given as my last wish. I swear this, and ratify this clause of the treaty: they will carry out the command without delay and without ambiguity. However, let the following addendum be made to the agreement: let it be stated that when your government detached the territories from the jurisdiction of the Duke of

33. There is a lacuna here.

Antioch, I personally made an urgent request to Your Majesties to grant some compensation, and this request was supported by the pilgrims; that Your Highnesses agreed, and certain themes, lands and cities in the east were granted as compensation. It is necessary that these should be named here, in order to avoid any ambiguity on the part of Your Majesties and so that my own claims can be justified. They were as follows: the entire theme of Casiotis, whose capital is Berroea (called by the barbarians Chalep); the theme of Lapara and its dependent small towns – that is to say, Plasta, the castle of Chonios, Romaïna, the castle of Aramisos, the small town of Amira, the castle of Sarbanos, the fort of Telchampson together with the three Tilia (Sthlabotilin and the other two, the fort of Sgenin and the castle of Kaltzierin); moreover, the following small towns: Kommermoeri, the district called Kathismatin, Sarsapin, and the little village of Mekran. These places are situated in Nearer Syria. The other themes are in Mesopotamia, in the neighbourhood of the city of Edessa, namely, the theme of the Limnii and the theme of Aetos together with their respective fortifications. There are other points which should not be passed over in silence, concerning Edessa and the annual payment of talents in cash to me by Your Majesties; I refer to the 200 pounds stamped with the effigy of the Emperor Michael.[34] Apart from that payment, according to the terms of Your Majesties' esteemed chrysobull the dukedom of . . .[35] has been granted to me in its entirety, with all its dependent forts and lands, and this authority has not been vested in my person only, for by that same document I am allowed to bequeath it to any person I wish, on the understanding, of course, that he too will bow to the orders and desires of Your Majesties; he will be the liege-man of the same authority and the same Empire; he will voluntarily subscribe to the same agreement as I. Hereafter, since I have become your man once for all and have become one of your subjects, it will be my due every year to receive from the imperial

34. The coinage had been devalued. Michael VII had issued comparatively 'good' money.
35. There is a lacuna here. The dukedom of Edessa is probably meant.

treasury the sum of 200 talents, in coin of good quality stamped with the effigy of the Lord Michael, the former emperor, and this payment will be made through some agent of ours, sent from Syria with my letters to you in the imperial city so that he may accept these monies in our name. And you, emperors ever-revered with the titles of Sebastos and Augustus of the Roman Empire, will doubtless observe the clauses written in the chrysobull of Your Majesties and will keep your promises to the letter. For my part, I confirm the agreements I have made with you by this oath:

I swear by the Passion of Christ Our Saviour who suffers no longer, and by His invincible Cross, which for the salvation of all men He endured, and by the All-holy Gospels here before us, which have converted the whole world; with my hand on these Gospels I swear; in my mind I associate with them the much honoured Cross of Christ, the Crown of Thorns, the Nails, the Spear that pierced Our Lord's side, giver of life; by these I swear to you, our Lord and Emperor Alexius Comnenus, most powerful and revered, and to your co-Emperor, the thrice-beloved Lord John the Porphyrogenitus, that all the agreements made between us and confirmed by me verbally I will observe and will for ever keep absolutely inviolate; that as I support Your Highnesses now, so I will support you in the future, with no malignity, no treachery – the mere thought of them is abhorrent – for I will abide by the undertakings I have given and will in no manner whatsoever violate my oath to you, nor will I proceed to disregard my promises, nor attempt to evade my responsibilities in any way under the treaty – and this applies not only to myself but also to all those with me, who are under my jurisdiction and make up the numbers of my army. Moreover, we shall arm ourselves against your enemies with breastplate, weapons and spears, and we shall clasp the right hand of your friends. In thought and in deed I shall do everything to help and honour the Empire of the Romans. So may I enjoy the aid of God, of the Cross, of the Holy Gospels.

These words were committed to writing and the oaths were administered in the presence of the under-mentioned witnesses in the month of September of the second indiction, in the year 6617.[36] The names of the witnesses present, who signed

36. That is, 1108 of the Christian era.

beneath and before whom the treaty was concluded, are as follows:

Maurus of Amalfi and Renard of Tarentum, bishops dearly-beloved of God, together with the clergy who accompanied the latter.

The most reverend Abbot of the Holy Monastery of St Andrew in Lombardy, on the island of Brindisi, and two monks from that monastery.

The leaders of the pilgrims, who made their marks with their own hands and whose names have been written beside those marks in the handwriting of the Bishop of Amalfi, dearly-beloved of God, who came as papal legate [37] to the Emperor.

From the imperial court the following signed:

The sebastos Marinus,

Roger, son of Dagobert,

Peter Aliphas,

William of Gand,

Richard of the Principate,

Geoffrey of Mailli,

Hubert, son of Raoul,

Paul the Roman,

the ambassadors who came from the Dacians on behalf of the kral,[38] kinsman of the Basileus John's wife (they were the župans[39] Peres and Simon),

the ambassadors of Richard Siniscard[40] (they were the Nobilissimus Basil the eunuch and the notary Constantine).

This oath, set down in writing, Alexius accepted from Bohemond and in return gave to him the above-mentioned chrysobull, signed in purple ink according to custom by the hand of the emperor.

37. From Paschal II.
38. By Dacia Anna means Hungary. The kral's daughter Irene had been betrothed to the future emperor John II. The kings of Hungary had the title 'kral'.
39. Župan was a title, roughly equivalent to 'prince'.
40. A nephew of Robert Guiscard.

BOOK FOURTEEN

TURKS, FRANKS, CUMANS
AND MANICHAEANS
(1108–15)

THE emperor had achieved his purpose. Bohemond under oath had confirmed the written agreement set out above, swearing by the Holy Gospels put before him and by the spear with which the impious pierced the side of Our Saviour. Now, after handing over all his troops to the emperor to command and use as he wished, Bohemond asked for permission to return home. At the same time he requested that his men should be allowed to winter inside the Roman Empire, that they should be plentifully supplied with necessities, and that when the winter passed and they had recovered from their many exertions, they might be granted the privilege of leaving for any destination they wished. The emperor at once gave his consent. Bohemond was thereupon honoured with the title of sebastos and provided with adequate funds. He retired to his own camp. With him went Constantine Euphorbenus, surnamed Catacalon, whose duty it was to prevent harm coming to him on the road from certain soldiers of our army; another, more important, task was to supervise the siting of Bohemond's camp in a favourable and safe place, and also to satisfy his soldiers' reasonable demands. Having arrived at his own headquarters, Bohemond handed over his forces to officers sent for the purpose by Alexius and then, boarding a monoreme, sailed for Lombardy. Not more than six months later he died.[1]

The emperor was still concerned about the Kelts, however; he did not set out on the road to Byzantium before he had

1. There is some doubt about the chronology. Some historians believe that he died in March 1111. The contempt with which Anna dismisses Bohemond recalls Caesar's abrupt reference to the murder of Pompey (Civil War Bk III).

made a good settlement of their affairs. When he did return it was not entirely for relaxation and pleasure, for he was again confronted with the problem of barbarian attacks on the sea-board of Smyrna, even as far as Attalia; the devastation wrought by them was complete. Not to restore these cities to their former condition, in his opinion, would be a terrible disgrace; their old prosperity must be revived, their inhabitants, scattered in all directions, must be brought back. Far from being insensible to the fate of Attalia, he did in fact devote much attention to its problems. Eumathius Philokales approached him with an earnest appeal that he might become its governor. This Eumathius was a man of considerable attainments; his birth gave him a special place among the illustrious, but that was not all: he excelled most of them in intellect too. Free-spirited and free of hand, he was most faithful to God and his friends, loyal if ever a man was to his masters. On the other hand, he was utterly ignorant of the ordinary soldier's training. The art of holding a bow, of drawing it to the fullest extent, of defending oneself with a buckler was unknown to him, although in other respects he was extremely proficient – in laying an ambush, for example, and outwitting the enemy by all kinds of stratagem. The emperor, recognizing his manifold talents, intellectual and practical, listened to his arguments and gave him the necessary forces, together with much advice. He was told in all cases to temper his undertakings with discretion. There was another reason for Alexius' faith in the man: Fortune, whoever she may be in fact or fancy, invariably accompanied Eumathius and he had never failed in any task to which he put his hand. He now arrived at Abydos and without delay sailed across the sea to Adramyttium. This city had formerly been a very populous place, but Tzachas, when he ravaged the Smyrna area, had reduced it to rubble and wiped it out entirely. Eumathius saw the devastation, which was so complete that one would have thought no man had ever lived there, and at once began to restore the city. It resumed its old appearance and all survivors of the original inhabitants were recalled. They came from all quarters of the compass and with them came many strangers, summoned by Eumathius as colonists. Adramyttium's old prosperity had returned. He made inquiries about the Turks and when he discovered that they were at that time in Lampe, he detached some of his forces to attack them. Contact was made with the enemy and in the stern battle which ensued the Romans soon won a victory. They treated the Turks with such abominable cruelty that they even threw their new-born babies into cauldrons of boiling water. Many Turks were massacred, others the Romans brought back in triumph to Eumathius as prisoners. The survivors dressed themselves in black, hoping by this sombre garb to impress on their fellow-countrymen their own sufferings. They traversed all the territory occupied by Turks, wailing mournfully and recounting the horrors that had befallen them. Their sad appearance moved all to pity, stirred all to vengeance. Eumathius meanwhile arrived at Philadelphia, well pleased with his good progress. An archsatrap called Asan, the governor of Cappadocia, who used the natives as though they were his slaves bought with money, heard what had happened to the Turks I have already mentioned and mobilized his own forces; to these were added many others called up for service from other areas, so that his army totalled 24,000 men. He set out against Eumathius. The latter was, as I have said, a clever man; he did not sit idly by in Philadelphia, nor did he relax his efforts once he was inside the walls of the city. On the contrary, scouts were sent out in all directions and in order that they might not be careless they were supervised by others. Thus Eumathius kept them on the alert. In fact they watched all night, keeping roads and plains alike under close surveillance. One of these men spotted the Turkish army some way off and ran to tell him. Now Eumathius was an intelligent officer, quick to appreciate the right course of action and ready to take instantaneous decisions. Since on this occasion he knew that his own forces were outnumbered, he at once ordered the gates of the city to be strengthened; nobody, under any circumstances, was to be allowed to climb to the battlements; there was to be no noise at all, no playing of flutes or lyres. In a word, he ensured that passers-by would think the place was absolutely deserted. Asan reached Philadelphia, surrounded the walls with his army and stayed there for three days. As no one appeared to be looking over the walls and the besieged were well protected by the gates; as moreover he had no helepoleis and no catapults, and as he came to the conclusion that Eumathius' army was insignificant and for that reason lacked the courage to make a sortie, he turned his attention to another scheme, condemning the enemy's thorough cowardice and treating him with utter contempt. He divided his army, sending off 10,000 men against Kelbianos, others to attack Smyrna and Nymphaeon, while the rest were to advance on Chliara and Pergamon. All were to engage in plunder. Finally he joined the detachment on its way to Smyrna. Once Philokales recognized Asan's policy, he launched all his troops in an attack on the Turks. Pursuing the group unconcernedly making its way to Kelbianos the Romans caught up with them, put in an offensive at daybreak and mercilessly slaughtered them. All the prisoners held by the Turks were liberated. Then they set out in pursuit of the others moving towards Smyrna and Nymphaeon; some actually ran on ahead of the vanguard and joined battle with them on either flank. They won a complete victory. Many Turks were killed, many taken captive; the mere handful who survived fell in flight into the currents of the Maeander[2] and were promptly drowned. The Romans, gaining confidence from this second triumph, chased the remainder, but nothing came of it, the Turks having gone too far ahead. They returned, therefore, to Philadelphia, where Eumathius learnt how courageously they had fought and how determined they had been to let no one escape from their clutches. He rewarded them liberally and promised generous favours in future.

After Bohemond's death Tancred seized Antioch, dispossessing the emperor and regarding the city as his own undisputed property. It was now clear that these barbarian Franks were violating the oaths taken by them with respect to Antioch. Despite the large sums of money Alexius had person-

2. This Phrygian river has the most winding course of all, with continuous turns and bends. (A.C.)

ally spent, despite the many perils he had faced in transporting these enormous armies from the west to Asia, he had always found them a haughty, embittered race. He had sent many Romans to help them against the Turks, for two reasons: first, to save them from massacre at the hands of their enemies (for he was concerned for their welfare as Christians) and secondly, that they, being organized by us, might destroy the cities of the Ishmaelites or force them to make terms with the Roman sovereigns and thus extend the bounds of Roman territory. In fact, however, his great generosity, his toils and troubles, had won no advantage for the Roman Empire. On the contrary, the Franks were clinging stubbornly to Antioch and debarred us from the other townships. The situation was intolerable. Reprisals were absolutely inevitable and they would have to be punished for behaviour so inhuman. The emperor had made countless gifts, expended heaps of gold, devoted time beyond measure to their interests, sent hosts of men to aid them – and Tancred was reaping the benefit, while the Romans got nothing; the Franks looked upon the final victory as theirs, violating their treaties with him and their pledged word, regarding them as worth nothing. To him their conduct was heart-rending, their insolence quite unbearable. An ambassador was accordingly despatched to the governor of Antioch (Tancred), charging him with injustice and perjury; he was told that the emperor would not for ever submit to his scorn, but would repay him for his ingratitude to the Romans. It would be disgraceful – more than disgraceful – if after the expenditure of vast sums of money, after the aid rendered by the élite Roman divisions in order to subdue the whole of Syria and Antioch itself, after his own wholehearted efforts to expand the bounds of Roman power, Tancred was to enjoy luxury – as the result of *his* spending and *his* labours. Such was the emperor's communication. The barbarian lunatic in his frenzied rage absolutely refused to listen; he could not bear either the truth of these words or the frankness of the envoys, and immediately reacted in the Frankish way: glorying in his own boastfulness he babbled that he would set his throne high above the stars and threat-

ened to bore with his spear-point through the walls of Babylon;[3] he spoke with emphasis of his might, mouthing out the
words like a tragic actor – how he was undaunted, how no one
could withstand him; he confidently assured the envoys that
whatever happened he would never release his grip on
Antioch, even if his adversaries came with hands of fire; he
was Ninus the Great, the Assyrian, a mighty irresistible giant,
with his feet firmly planted on earth like some dead weight,[4]
but all Romans were to him nothing more than ants, the
feeblest of living things. When the envoys returned and gave
a graphic account of the Kelt's madness, Alexius, full of
wrath, could no longer be restrained: he wanted to make for
Antioch at once. He held a conference of the most distinguished soldiers and all members of the senate. He asked for
their advice. All agreed that for the moment the emperor's
expedition against Tancred must be postponed; first, they
said, he must win over the other counts who controlled the
places near Antioch, and in particular Baldwin, the King of
Jerusalem, and put them to the test. Would they be willing to
help him if he left the capital to make war on Antioch? If they
were known to be hostile to Tancred, then the expedition
should be undertaken with confidence; if their attitude was
doubtful, the Antioch problem should be solved in some
other way. Alexius commended this plan and without delay
summoned Manuel Boutoumites and another man, who
understood the Latin tongue. They were sent to the counts
and the King of Jerusalem. The emperor gave them much
advice on the negotiations they would have to conduct with
them. Inevitably money was required for this mission because
of the Latin greed; Boutoumites was therefore entrusted with
orders for the officer who was then Duke of Cyprus, Eumathios Philokales. He was to supply them with as many ships
as they needed and at the same time great sums of money of

3. Babylon, the capital of Chaldaea, noted in antiquity for its powerful
fortifications.
4. The Greek expression (Homeric in origin, found in both *Iliad* and
Odyssey) is sometimes used proverbially for an idler, a wastrel, a good-for-
nothing.

all types, of every kind, stamped with any effigy and of all values, to serve as gifts for the counts. The envoys in question and especially Manuel Boutoumites were commanded, after accepting the money from Philokales, to moor their ships at Tripolis. There they were to visit Count Bertrand, the son of Saint-Gilles (who has been mentioned in my history on several occasions). He was to be reminded of his father's loyal service to the emperor and letters from Alexius were to be handed to him. The envoys were to address him thus: 'It is not right that you should be inferior to your father; your allegiance to us must be as firm and lasting as his. The emperor informs you that he is already on his way to Antioch, where he will exact vengeance for the breaking of fearful oaths to God and himself. As for you, make sure that you help Tancred in no way, and do your best to win over the counts to our side, so that they also may give him no comfort whatever.' After their arrival in Cyprus and after they had the money from Philokales and all the ships they required, the envoys sailed directly to Tripolis. They anchored in the harbour, disembarked, found Bertrand and delivered by word of mouth the emperor's message. They saw that Bertrand was sympathetic, prepared to satisfy any demand made by the emperor, even if need be to face death gladly on his behalf. He promised solemnly that he would come to pay him homage when he arrived in the Antioch region. With his consent, therefore, they deposited in the bishop's palace at Tripolis the money they had brought with them. In this they were following Alexius' advice, for he had feared that if the counts knew who had the money they might seize it, send the envoys away empty-handed and use it for their own and Tancred's pleasure. He judged it wise that they should leave it behind; later, when they had discovered how the others stood, they were to give them the emperor's message, and simultaneously pledge donations and exact oaths – provided of course that the counts were willing to yield his demands. Only under those conditions could they be given money. Boutoumites and his companions accordingly left the cash in the bishop's residence at Tripolis. When Baldwin heard of the arrival of these envoys at Tripolis, he lost no time in sending them an invitation in advance through Simon, his brother's son. Of course he was greedy for gold. They accompanied Simon (who had come from Jerusalem) and met Baldwin outside Tyre,[5] which he was besieging. He was delighted to welcome them with every sign of friendship. It was the season of Lent and throughout the forty-day period[6] he kept them with him while the siege continued. The city was protected by impregnable walls, but the defences were further strengthened by three outworks which completely encircled it. They were concentric, with a space between each. Baldwin had decided to destroy these outworks first, and then capture the city itself; they acted as a kind of breastwork, shielding Tyre and averting siege operations. By means of war-machines the first and second circles were demolished; he was now attempting to throw down the third. Its battlements were in fact already in ruins, when he began to relax his efforts; he could have taken it, had he really exerted himself. He thought that later he would climb into the city by ladders; as far as he was concerned, Tyre was already won and the work slackened. This proved to be the salvation of the enemy: he, with victory at hand, was thoroughly repulsed, while the Saracens, who found themselves in the hunter's net, jumped clear of its toils. For during Baldwin's holiday they used the respite in careful preparation. They tried a clever stratagem. They pretended to seek a truce and sent ambassadors to Baldwin, but in reality while the peace negotiations were going on they perfected their defence; while his hopes were encouraged they were planning methods of attack on him. They had seen much warlike activity, and then the besiegers apparently had lost heart; so one night they filled many earthenware jars with liquid pitch and hurled these at Baldwin's machines which threatened their walls. The jars of course were shattered and the liquid poured over the timber frames. Lighted torches were then flung on them, together

5. Tyre had been captured by the Crusaders in 1097, but was left in Turkish hands and threatened the Frankish supplies. Baldwin had arrived there late in November 1111.
6. Ending in April 1112.

with other jars containing a good supply of naphtha, which caught fire. At once it flared up into a conflagration and their machines were reduced to ashes. As the light of day spread, so the fiery light of flames from the wooden 'tortoises' spread into the city like a tower. Baldwin's men had the due reward for their carelessness, and when the smoke and flames warned them what had happened they were sorry. Some of the soldiers on the 'tortoises' were taken prisoner and when the governor of Tyre saw them, six in number, he had their heads cut off and slung into Baldwin's camp by catapults. The sight of the fire and the severed heads affected the whole Frankish army. They fled on horseback in terror, as if stricken with panic, despite all Baldwin's efforts to recall them and restore their courage. He rode everywhere, trying all he knew, but he was 'singing to the deaf', for once they had abandoned themselves to flight nothing could stop their running — faster, it seemed, than any bird. Eventually they came to a halt, at a garrisoned place called by the natives Acre; to these craven runners it was a place of refuge. Naturally Baldwin was discouraged. There was nothing for it but to follow them there, although it was against his wishes. He too ran away. As for Boutoumites, he embarked on Cypriot triremes (there were twelve in all) and sailed along the coast in the direction of Acre, where he met Baldwin and delivered the emperor's message in full, according to instructions. He provided a postscript: the emperor, he said, had reached Seleuceia. In fact this was not true; he was trying to frighten the barbarian into leaving Acre quickly. However, Baldwin was not deceived by this play-acting and charged him roundly with lying. He had already been informed by someone about the emperor's progress; he knew he had advanced a long way down the coast, had taken the pirate vessels which were ravaging the places by the sea and had returned through illness (details of that will be given later in the history). Baldwin told Boutoumites all this and accused him of prevarication. 'You must come with me to the Holy Sepulchre,' he said, 'and from there my envoys will inform the emperor of our decisions.' As soon as he arrived in the Holy City, he asked them for the money sent for him by

Alexius, but at this point Boutoumites had something to say:
'If you promise to help against Tancred, keeping the oath you
swore to the emperor when you passed through Constantinople, then you shall have the money.' Baldwin wanted it; on
the other hand, he was eager to help Tancred, not Alexius.
Still, it grieved him not to get the money. That is the way of all
the barbarians: their mouths gape wide for gifts and money,
but they have no intention whatever of doing the things for
which the money is offered. So Baldwin entrusted non-
committal letters to Boutoumites and let him go. The envoys
also fell in with Count Joscelin,[7] who had come to worship at
the Holy Sepulchre on the day of the Saviour's resurrection.
They had the usual conversation with him, but as his replies
were like Baldwin's, they returned with nothing accomplished.
Bertrand,[8] they discovered, was no longer alive, and when
they asked for the money deposited in the bishop's palace his
son[9] and the bishop[10] again and again put off the moment of
restitution. The envoys used threats: 'If you don't give back
the money to us, you are no true servants of the emperor. It
seems you have not inherited the loyalty of Bertrand and his
father Saint-Gilles. So in future you will have neither plentiful
supplies from Cyprus nor the helping hand of its duke. After
that you will die, the victims of famine.' Every method of
persuasion was tried: sometimes they spoke mildly, sometimes
with menaces, but no progress was made. In the end they
thought it necessary to force Bertrand's son to swear a solemn
oath of allegiance to the emperor and then to present him with
the gifts destined originally for his father alone; namely,
coined money of gold and silver and robes of all kinds. On
receipt of these he swore a solemn oath of allegiance to Alexius
and they, having carried off the remainder of the money to
Eumathius, bought with it pedigree horses from Damascus,
Edessa and even Arabia. From there they passed by the Syrian

7. Joscelin of Courtenay, a poor cousin of Baldwin. Anna calls him
Iatzoulinos.
8. Bertrand died in January or February 1112.
9. Pons, who had no great liking for Byzantines.
10. That is, of Tripolis.

Sea and the Pamphylian Gulf, but begged to be excused from sailing because they considered the mainland safer. They made for the Chersonese, where the emperor was, and after crossing the Hellespont rejoined him.

As thick and fast as snowflakes troubles descended on the emperor: from the sea the admirals of Pisa, Genoa and Lombardy were making ready an expedition to ravage all our coasts; on the mainland the emir Saisan [11] had once more come from the east and was already threatening Philadelphia and the maritime provinces. Alexius knew that he must leave the capital and station himself where he could fight on two fronts. Thus he came to the Chersonese. From everywhere military forces were gathered by land and sea. A strong detachment was placed on the far side of the Scamander at Adramyttium and indeed in the Thracesian theme or province. At that time the military commander at Philadelphia was Constantine Gabras, who had enough men to protect the city; Pergamon, Chliara and the neighbouring towns were under the authority of Monastras. [12] The other coastal cities, too, were controlled by officers distinguished for their boldness and experience as leaders. They received constant directives from Alexius, who exhorted them to be on their guard, to send out reconnaissance parties in all directions to watch for enemy movements and to report them immediately. After strengthening the Asian front, Alexius turned his attention to the war on the sea. Some sailors were told to moor their ships in the harbours of Madytos and Koiloi, to maintain a ceaseless patrol of the straits with light dromons and protect the sea-routes at all times as they awaited the Frankish navy; others were to sail among the islands and guard them. This latter force was also to keep an eye on the Peloponnese and give it adequate protection. As Alexius wanted to spend some time in the area, [13] he had temporary buildings erected in a

11. Saisan was Kilij Arslan's eldest son, Malik-Shah, who was liberated from the Persians in 1110. After defeating the Emir Asan, he established his capital at Iconium (Konya) and became powerful enough to challenge the Byzantines.

12. The half-breed often mentioned before in this history. (A.C.)

13. That is, the area of the Chersonese. (A.C.)

suitable place and wintered there. The allied fleet sailed from
Lombardy and other parts in excellent condition; once at sea
the admiral in charge detached a squadron of five biremes to
take prisoners and gain information about the emperor. They
were already off Abydos when four were captured with all
their crews; the survivor managed to return to the admiral. It
brought news of the emperor's activities: careful security
measures had been taken by land and sea and he was spending
the winter in the Chersonese to encourage his men. Because
these dispositions made victory impossible, the enemy
changed course and steered their ships elsewhere. One Kelt in
the service of these admirals left the main fleet with his
monoreme and sailed off to Baldwin, whom he found besieging Tyre. He gave him a full account of the emperor's
affairs (just as I have described above) and told him how the
Romans had taken the dromons sent out to reconnoitre. It is
not improbable, I believe, that this Kelt went off with the
consent of the admirals. Anyway, he admitted unblushingly
that the Keltic commanders, knowing that Alexius was so well
prepared, had withdrawn; they had thought it better to sail
away with nothing accomplished than to fight and be defeated.
As he said this to Baldwin the man still trembled slightly at
the dreadful recollection of the Roman fleet.

So much for the Keltic adventures on the sea; by land the
emperor was not without his own worries and troubles. A
certain Michael from Amastris, who governed Akrounos,
organized a rebellion, seized the city for himself and ravaged
the neighbouring lands with a reign of terror. The emperor
reacted to the news by sending George Dekanos to fight him
with a strong army. George took the city after a siege of three
months and the traitor was soon on his way to the emperor,
who appointed another man in his place. Alexius glared at the
rebel angrily, threatened numerous punishments and when to
all appearances sentence of death was already pronounced
threw the man into utter panic – but not for long: the sun had
not yet sunk below the horizon when the cloud of fear was
lifted – he was a free man, loaded with countless gifts. My
father was always like that, even if later he was repaid by

all of them with base ingratitude. In the same way long ago the
Lord, Benefactor of the whole world, caused manna to rain
down in the desert, fed the multitude on the mountains, led
them through the sea dry-footed – yet afterwards He was
rejected and insulted and smitten and finally condemned to be
crucified by wicked men. But when I reach this point the tears
flow before my words; I long to speak of these things and
compile a list of these unfeeling men, but I check my tongue,
bear with my impatience and over and over again quote to
myself the words of Homer: 'Endure, my heart; thou hast
suffered other, worse things before.'[14] I will say no more
about that ingrate. Of the men sent from Chorosan by the
Sultan Malik Shah, some went through the district of Sinaos,
while others came through Asia properly so called. Constantine Gabras, governor of Philadelphia at the time, heard
about it and with his troops made contact with the Turks at
Kelbianos. He was the very first to charge at full gallop
against them, calling on the rest to follow, and he vanquished
the barbarians. The sultan, when news arrived of this setback,
made overtures for peace. He admitted, through his ambassadors, that for a long time he had longed to see peace established between Roman and Muslim; from afar he had heard
men speak of the emperor's glorious deeds in war against all
his enemies; now he had made trial of him, so to say, and
recognizing the robe from its hem, the lion from his claws, he
turned away, even against his will, to sue for peace. When the
envoys from Persia arrived the emperor was seated on his
throne, an impressive figure, and the officers in charge of
ceremonial arranged in order the soldiers of every nationality,
together with the Varangian Guard. The envoys were then
ushered in and placed before the imperial throne. Alexius
asked the usual questions about the sultan and heard their
message. He acknowledged that he welcomed and desired
peace with all; but the sultan's objectives, he realized, would
not all be in the interests of the Empire. With much persuasive
skill and great cleverness he defended his own position before
the envoys and after a long discourse brought them round to

14. *Odyssey* xx, 18.

his point of view. They were then allowed to retire to the tent prepared for them and told to consider what had been said; if they wholeheartedly agreed with his proposals, on the next day the treaty would be concluded. They were apparently eager to accept the terms and on the following day a pact was signed. The emperor was not concerned merely with his own advantages; he also had in mind the Empire itself. He cared more, in fact, for the general welfare than for his own. All the negotiations, therefore, were conducted in the light of Roman sovereignty; that was the criterion for all decisions. His purpose was to ensure that the treaty would last after his death and for a long time. It failed, because when he died affairs took a different course and ended in confusion. However, in the meanwhile the troubles subsided and there was great harmony. Thereafter we enjoyed peace until the end of his life, but with him all the benefits disappeared and his efforts came to nothing through the stupidity of those who inherited his throne.[15]

As I have said, the survivors of the five dromons informed the Frankish admirals of the Roman naval dispositions. They knew that the emperor had equipped a fleet and was in the Chersonese awaiting their arrival. They abandoned their previous aim and decided to avoid Roman territory altogether. Alexius, after wintering in Calliopolis with the empress (for she, as I have often explained, was accompanying him because of his gout) and after watching carefully for the moment when the Latin fleet usually sailed home, returned to the capital. Not long after it was announced that the Turks were on the move from all lands of the east, even from Chorosan, to the number of 50,000. Indeed, throughout the whole of his reign Alexius had little opportunity for rest, as enemies one after another sprang up in constant succession. On this occasion the armies were completely mobilized everywhere. Guessing

15. Anna no doubt hoped that she herself and her husband would succeed Alexius. She cannot conceal her jealousy of the new emperor John (her brother) although it was agreed by Cinnamus and Choniates the Byzantine historians that he was a man of high ideals and a great ruler. Modern scholars acknowledge that Alexius was right in making John his heir.

that the time was ripe (the time when the barbarians normally launch their attacks on the Christians) he crossed the straits between Byzantium and Damalis. Not even a painful onset of the gout deterred him from this campaign. This malady had afflicted none of his ancestors, so that it was certainly not an inherited disease; nor was it due to indulgence in luxury (gout usually attacks libertines and lovers of pleasure). In his case the trouble originated in an accident. One day he was exercising at polo, his partner being the Taticius I have often mentioned. Taticius was carried away by his horse and fell on the emperor, whose knee-cap was injured by the impact (Taticius was a heavy man). The pain affected the whole of his foot and although he did not show that he was in distress – he was used to bearing pain – he did receive some minor treatment. Little by little the trouble wore off and disappeared, so that his normal habits were resumed. That was the prime origin of his gout, for the painful areas attracted rheumatism. There was a second, more obvious cause of all this illness. Everyone knows that countless multitudes of Kelts came to the imperial city, having migrated from their own lands and hurried from all directions to us. It was then that the emperor was plunged into a vast ocean of worries. He had long been aware of their dream of Empire; he was aware too of their overwhelming numbers – more than the grains of sand on the sea-shore or all the stars of heaven; the sum total of Roman forces would equal not one tiny part of their multitudes, even if they were concentrated in one place – much less when they were dissipated over wide areas, for some were on guard in the valleys of Serbia and in Dalmatia, others keeping watch near the Danube against Cuman and Dacian incursions, and many had been entrusted with the task of saving Dyrrachium from a second Keltic victory. Under the circumstances he devoted his whole attention now to these Kelts and all else was considered of secondary importance. The barbarian world on our borders, which was restless but had not yet broken out into open hostility, he kept in check by granting honours and presents, while the ambition of the Kelts was confined by all possible means. The rebellious spirit of his own subjects caused no less trouble – in fact he suspected them even more and hastened to protect himself as best he could. Their plots were skilfully averted. But no one could adequately describe the ferment of troubles which descended on him at this period. It compelled him to become all things to all men, to accommodate himself as far as he could to circumstances. Like a trained physician (following the rules of his craft) he had to apply himself to the most pressing need. At daybreak, as soon as the sun leapt up over the eastern horizon, he took his seat on the imperial throne and every day on his orders all Kelts were freely admitted to his presence. The purpose of this was twofold: he liked them to make their own requests, and he strove by various arguments to reconcile them to his wishes. The Keltic counts are brazen-faced, violent men, money-grubbers and where their personal desires are concerned quite immoderate. These are natural characteristics of the race. They also surpass all other nations in loquacity. So when they came to the palace they did so in an undisciplined fashion, every count bringing with him as many comrades as he wished; after him, without interruption, came another and then a third – an endless queue. Once there they did not limit the conversation by the water-clock, like the orators of ancient times, but each, whoever he was, enjoyed as much time as he wanted for the interview with the emperor. Men of such character, talkers so exuberant, had neither respect for his feelings nor thought for the passing of time nor any idea of the by-standers' wrath; instead of giving way to those coming behind them, they talked on and on with an incessant stream of petitions. Every student of human customs will be acquainted with Frankish verbosity and their pettifogging love of detail; but the audience on these occasions learnt the lesson more thoroughly – from actual experience. When evening came, after remaining without food all through the day, the emperor would rise from his throne and retire to his private apartment, but even then he was not free from the importunities of the Kelts. They came one after another, not only those who had failed to obtain a hearing during the day, but those who had already been heard returned as well, putting forward this or that excuse for more talk. In the midst of them, calmly enduring their endless chatter stood the emperor. One could see them there, all asking questions, and him, alone and unchanging, giving them prompt replies. But there was no limit to their foolish babbling, and if a court official did try to cut them short, he was himself interrupted by Alexius. He knew the traditional pugnacity of the Franks and feared that from some trivial pretext a mighty blaze of trouble might spring up, resulting in serious harm to the prestige of Rome. It was really a most extraordinary sight. Like a statue wrought by the hammer, made perhaps of bronze or cold-forged iron, the emperor would sit through the night, often from evening till midnight, often till third cock-crow, sometimes almost until the sun was shining clearly. The attendants were all worn out, but by frequently retiring had a rest and then came back again – in bad humour. Thus not one of them would stay motionless as long as he did; all in one way or another kept changing position: one would sit down, another turned his head away and rested it on something, another propped himself against a wall. Only one man, the emperor, faced this tremendous task without weakening. His endurance was truly remarkable. Hundreds of people were talking, each one prattling on at length, 'brawling away unbridled of tongue'[16] as Homer says. As one stood aside he passed the conversation on to another, and he to the next, and so on and on. They stood only in these intervals but he all the time, up to first or even second cock-crow. After a brief rest, when the sun rose he was again seated on his throne and once more fresh labours and twofold troubles succeeded those of the night. It was for this reason, then, that the emperor was attacked by the pain in his feet. From that time to the end of his life the rheumatism came on at regular intervals and caused him dreadful pain. Despite this he bore it so well that not once did he murmur in complaint; all he said was, 'I deserve to suffer. This happens to me justly because of the multitude of my sins.' And if by chance a cross word did escape his lips he immediately made the sign of the Cross against the assault of the evil demon. 'Flee from me, wicked one,' he would say.

16. *Iliad* ii, 212.

'A curse on you and your tempting of Christians!' I will say no more now about the pain that afflicted him. Maybe there was someone who contributed to this malady of his and increased the sufferings he bore (and surely his cup of bitterness was already full). I will give a brief outline of the story, not the full details. The empress smeared the rim of the cup with honey, as it were, and contrived that he should avoid most of his troubles, for she unceasingly watched over him. The man I am speaking of must be introduced at this point and considered a third reason of the emperor's illness, not merely as the immediate cause, but also the most effective cause (to use the doctors' terms). He did not attack once and for all and then disappear, but remained with him, a constant companion like the most pernicious humours in the veins. Worse than that, if one reflects on the man's character, he was not only a cause of the disease, but he was himself a malady and its most troublesome symptom. But I must bite my tongue and say no more. However eager I may be to jump on these scoundrels, I must not run off the main highway. I will reserve what I have to say about him to the appropriate time.

Let us return to the Kelts. The emperor was in camp on the opposite coast, at Damalis. It was there, in fact, that we left him. While he was staying there awaiting the arrival of all his retinue and hoping, too, to get relief from his terrible pain, they all crossed, descending on him thick as snowflakes. The Augusta was with him, tending his feet and by all kinds of care lightening his anguish. When he saw that the moon was already at the full, he remarked to her, 'If ever the Turks wanted to make a raid, this is a good opportunity for them. I'm sorry I missed the chance.' It was evening when he said this. The next morning at dawn the eunuch in charge of Their Majesties' bedchamber announced that the Turks had attacked Nicaea and showed him a letter from Eustathius Kamytzes, who was governor of the city at that time. It gave a full report of their actions. Without a moment's hesitation or the slightest delay, as if he had completely forgotten the incessant pain, the emperor mounted a war-chariot and set out on the road to

Nicaea, holding a whip in his right hand. The soldiers, taking up their spears, went on either side of him, arranged by companies in ordered ranks. Some ran alongside him, others went on ahead, others followed in the rear. All rejoiced at the sight of him marching out against the barbarians, but grieved at the thought of the pain which prevented him from riding on horseback. But he put heart into all of them by his gestures and words, smiling pleasantly and chatting with them. After a three days' march he arrived at a place called Aigialoi, from which he intended to sail over to Kibotos. As she saw that he was in a hurry to make the crossing, the Augusta took her leave of him and set out for the capital. On his arrival at Kibotos someone came with the news that the leading satraps of the 40,000 had separated: some had gone down to Nicaea and the neighbouring districts to plunder, while Manalugh [17] and . . . had ravaged the coastal area. Those who had devastated the country near the lake of Nicaea and Prusa, as well as Apollonias, had encamped by the latter town and collected all their booty there. They had then marched on in a body pillaging Lopadion and all the land round it; even Cyzicus, they said, had been attacked from the sea and had fallen at the first assault; its governor had put up no resistance at all and had fled in disgrace. Kontogmen and the Emir Mahomet, moreover, archsatraps of the best troops, were on their way through Lentianoi to Poemanenon, bringing with them much booty and a host of captives, men, women and children who had escaped massacre. As for Manalugh, after crossing a river called by the natives Barenus, which flows down from Mount Ibis,[18] he had turned off to Parion and Abydos on the Hellespont; later he had passed through Adramyttium and Chliara with all his prisoners without shedding a drop of blood or fighting a single battle. The emperor's reaction to this news was to give Kamytzes, Duke of Nicaea at the time, written instructions to keep in touch with the barbarians and inform

17. Anna calls him Monolykos. There is a lacuna immediately after the name.

18. Many other rivers have their source there, the Scamander, the Angelokomites and the Empelos. (A.C.)

him of their activities by letter, but to avoid all combat. He
had 500 men for the purpose. Kamytzes left Nicaea and caught
up with Kontogmen, the Emir Mahomet and the others at a
place called Aorata. Apparently oblivious of the emperor's
orders he attacked at once. The enemy thought that he was
the emperor in person (they were expecting him) and fled in
terror. At the time, however, they had captured a Scyth and
from him they learnt that Kamytzes was the general. Thereupon they crossed the mountains, gaining courage from the
sound of their drums and war-cries. Their fellow-tribesmen,
scattered all over the countryside, were recalled (they recognized the signal) and the army gathered afresh, now at full
strength. So they descended to the plain at the foot of Aorata.
Kamytzes, who had seized all their plunder, did not wish to go
on to Poemanenon, where he could have taken proper
measures for security – Poemanenon was a very strongly
fortified town – but he marked time round Aorata, not realizing that he was doing himself a disservice, for the enemy
being now out of danger, instead of forgetting all about him,
were constantly lying in wait. They knew that he was still in
Aorata making arrangements about all the booty and the
prisoners. Without delay they drew up their forces in companies and soon after mid-day fell upon him. At the sight of
the barbarian multitude the greater part of Kamytzes' army
thought it wise to look to their own safety in flight; he himself, with the Scyths, the Kelts and the more courageous of the
Romans fought on bravely. Most of them died there. Even
then Kamytzes still continued the battle with a handful of
survivors. He was thrown to the ground when his horse was
fatally wounded, but his nephew Katarodon dismounted and
offered him his own charger. But Kamytzes, who was a large,
heavy man found it difficult to mount and instead withdrew a
little and stood with his back to an oak-tree. With drawn
sword (he had given up all hope of saving his life) he struck at
any barbarian who dared to attack him, hitting out at helmets,
shoulders or even hands. He would not give in. This went on
for a long time and many Turks were killed or wounded, so
that they were astonished at his bravery. In admiration for his

tenacity they decided to spare him. The Archsatrap Mahomet, who knew him of old and recognized him now, stopped his men fighting (they were locked in close combat with him) and dismounted from his horse. His companions did the same. Mahomet then approached Kamytzes. 'Don't prefer death to your own safety,' he said. 'Give me your hand and live.' Kamytzes, surrounded as he was by so many barbarians and quite unable to resist any more, gave his hand to the Turk, who put him on a horse and shackled his feet to prevent an easy escape. Such were the adventures of Eustathius. The emperor meanwhile, guessing the path by which the enemy would go, chose a different route by Nicaea, Malagina and the so-called Basilika (these are valleys and inaccessible ways on the ridges of Mount Olympos). He then came down to Alethina and went on to Akrokos, hurrying to a position from which he could attack the Turks from their front. He hoped to fight a pitched battle with them. The latter, with no thought at all of the Roman army, discovered a part of the valley covered by reeds. They scattered there and lay down to rest. As Alexius was on the point of leaving to attack them, he was told that they were in the lower parts of the valley. He drew up his battle-line some distance away. In front he stationed Constantine Gabras and Monastras. On the two wings the troops were arranged in squadrons. The rearguard was entrusted to two officers who had a long and considerable experience of warfare, Tzipoureles and Ampelas. The centre he led himself, with an overall supervision of the line. In this order he swooped down on the Turks like a thunderbolt. In the stern conflict that followed many of the barbarians died in close combat, many were led away as prisoners. Some took refuge in the reeds and were safe for a time, but after a notable victory was assured Alexius turned on them. He was anxious to drive them out of their hiding-place, but the soldiers were non plussed: the marshy ground and the thickness of the reeds made it impossible to get near them. After surrounding the area with soldiers, the emperor gave the order to start a fire on one side of the reeds. The flames leapt to a great height. The enemy, running away from the fire, fell into the hands of the Romans. Some were cut down by the sword, others were led off to Alexius.

Such was the fate of the barbarians who had come down from Karme. The Emir Mahomet, hearing of this Moslem disaster, at once joined the Turcomans who dwell in Asia and the others in pursuit of the emperor. Thus Alexius was both chasing the enemy and being chased himself, for Mahomet and his barbarians were following his tracks from behind while he himself was tracking down the others from Karme. He was caught between the two. One group he had already beaten, the other (in the rear) was still unimpaired. Mahomet launched a sudden assault on the Roman rearguard, where for the first time he clashed with Ampelas. Ampelas, being in sight of the emperor, had more confidence than usual; in any case, he was a bold man and now, without waiting a moment for the men behind to join him, he charged against the Turk. Had he delayed they could have borne the brunt of the Turkish assault in good order. Tzipoureles followed him into battle. Before their men could catch up with them, the two generals had reached an ancient fortification and there Mahomet met them. He was in a very determined mood. He shot Ampelas' horse with an arrow (but not the rider). Ampelas was thrown to the ground, surrounded by Turks on foot and killed. Then they spied Tzipoureles charging recklessly on them. His horse they winged, as it were, with their arrows, unseated him and in a minute despatched him with their swords. The soldiers posted in the rear, whose duty it was to protect the tired baggage-men and the horses, as well as to repel attacks to the best of their ability, charged these Turks and routed them completely. Kamytzes was there with them, a prisoner, and when he saw the confusion as the two armies clashed, with some running away and others in pursuit, being a level-headed man he planned his own escape and took to the road. A fully-armed Kelt met him on the way and gave him his horse. On the lower part of the valley he found the emperor encamped between Philadelphia and Akrokos. The place was large enough to accommodate not one army, but many. Alexius received him warmly and offered thanksgiving to God for his deliverance.

Then he sent him on to the capital. 'Tell them,' he said, 'of your sufferings and of all that you have seen, and inform our relatives that thanks to God we are alive.' When he learnt of the killing of Ampelas and Tzipoureles, however, he was deeply grieved. 'We have lost two and gained one,' he remarked. For it was his custom, whenever he had been victorious in war, to inquire whether any of his men had been captured or slain by the enemy, and even if he had routed whole armies in triumph, but had lost one man, however low his rank, he looked upon his victory as nothing; for him it was merely a Cadmean success [19] – not a gain, but a loss. He now personally appointed military governors of the area, George Lebounes and certain others, and left them there with his soldiers while he returned with the laurels of victory to Constantinople. Kamytzes reached Damalis and boarded a small boat about the mid-watch of the night. Since he knew that the empress was in the upper part of the palace, he went there and knocked on the gate which faces the sea. The warders asked who he was, but he was unwilling to give his name; he only asked for the gate to be opened to him. After some dispute he revealed his name and was allowed to enter. The Augusta, highly delighted, received him outside the door of her bedroom (in the old days they called this balcony Aristerion). When she saw him dressed like a Turk and limping on both feet (because of his wounds in battle), her first inquiry, as she bade him sit down, was about the emperor. Then, after hearing the whole story, learning about Alexius' strange and unexpected victory and seeing the prisoner free, she was quite overcome with joy. Kamytzes was ordered to rest until daybreak and then leave the palace to announce what had happened to the people. So he rose early, mounted a horse (still dressed in the clothes in which he had arrived after his extraordinary deliverance from captivity) and rode to the Forum of Constantine. His appearance at once caused general excitement in the city. Everyone was eager to learn of his adventures; everyone longed still more to hear about the emperor. Kamytzes, surrounded by a multitude of men on

19. The equivalent of a Pyrrhic victory.

horseback and on foot, gave a full account of the war in a clear voice: he spoke of all the misfortunes of the Roman army and, more important, of all the emperor's plans against the enemy and the full vengeance he had exacted from them by his brilliant victory. Lastly he told them of his own miraculous flight from the Turks. At these words the whole populace cheered and the noise of their applause was deafening.

Such was the end of this episode. Constantinople was rife with stories of the emperor's exploits. Chance had indeed involved him in difficult situations, prejudicial both to himself and the interests of the Empire, so that he was wholly surrounded by a host of troubles. Yet every one of them was thwarted and opposed by his virtues, his vigilance, his energy. Of all the emperors who preceded him, right down to the present day, not one had to grapple with affairs so complicated, with the wickedness of men, at home and abroad, of so many types as we have seen in the lifetime of this man. Maybe it was destined that the Roman people should suffer tribulation with God's permission (for never would I attribute our fate to the movements of the stars), or perhaps Roman power declined to this decadence through the folly of previous rulers. Certain it is that in my father's reign great disorders and wave on wave of confusion united to afflict our affairs. For the Scyths from the north, the Kelts from the west and the Ishmaelites from the east were simultaneously in turmoil; there were perils, too, from the sea, not to mention the barbarians who dominated it or the countless pirate vessels launched by wrathful Saracens and sent to battle by ambitious Vetones. The latter regarded the Roman Empire with hostile eyes and all men look upon it with envy. The Romans, lording it over other peoples, are naturally hated by their subjects. Whenever they find an opportunity, all of them, by land or sea, flock from all quarters to attack us. In the old days, before our time, there was a great buoyancy about the Empire which is lacking today – the burden of government was not so heavy. But in my father's reign, as soon as he acceded to the throne, a veritable flood of dangers poured in on him from everywhere:

the Kelt was restless and pointed his spear at him; the Ishmaelite bent his bow; all the nomads and the whole Scythian nation pressed in on him with their myriad wagons. But at this stage of my history the reader perhaps will say that I am naturally biased. My answer is this: I swear by the perils the emperor endured for the well-being of the Roman people, by his sorrows and the travails he suffered on behalf of the Christians, that I am not favouring him when I say or write such things. On the contrary, where I perceive that he was wrong I deliberately transgress the law of nature and stick to the truth. I regard him as dear, but truth as dearer still. As one of the philosophers somewhere remarked, 'Both are dear, but it is best to honour truth more highly.'[20] I have followed the actual course of events, without additions of my own, without suppression, and so I speak and write. And the proof of this is near to hand. I am not writing the history of things that happened 10,000 years ago, but there are men still alive today who knew my father and tell me of his deeds. They have in fact made a not inconsiderable contribution to the history, for one reported or recalled to the best of his ability one fact, while another told me something else – but there was no discrepancy in their accounts. Most of the time, moreover, we were ourselves present, for we accompanied our father and mother. Our lives by no means revolved round the home; we did not live a sheltered, pampered existence. From my very cradle – I swear it by God and His Mother – troubles, afflictions, continual misfortunes were my lot, some from without, some from within. As to my physical characteristics, I will not speak of them – the attendants in the gynaeconitis can describe and talk of them. But if I write of the evils that befell me from without, the troubles I encountered even before I had completed my eighth year and the enemies raised up against me by the wickedness of men, I would need the Siren[21] of Isocrates,[22]

20. Aristotle, in Book I of the *Nicomachaean Ethics*.
21. The Sirens, half women, half birds, enchanted with their song.
22. Isocrates (436–338 B.C.), the Athenian orator and writer, founded a school of rhetoric.

the grandiloquence of Pindar,[23] Polemo's[24] vivacity, the Calliope[25] of Homer, Sappho's[26] lyre or some other power greater still. For no danger, great or small from near or far away, failed to attack us at once. I was truly overwhelmed by the flood and ever since, right up to the present time, even to this moment when I write these words, the sea of misfortunes advances upon me, wave after wave. But I must stop – I have inadvertently drifted away into my own troubles. Now that I have returned to my senses, I will swim against the tide, as it were, and go back to the original subject. As I was saying, some of my material is the result of my own observations; some I have gathered in various ways from the emperor's comrades-in-arms, who sent us information about the progress of the wars by people who crossed the straits. Above all I have often heard the emperor and George Palaeologus discussing these matters in my presence. Most of the evidence I collected myself, especially in the reign of the third emperor after Alexius,[27] at a time when all the flattery and lies had disappeared with his grandfather (all men flatter the current ruler, but no one makes the slightest attempt to over-praise the departed; they tell the bare facts and describe things just as they happened). As for myself, apart from the grief caused by my own misfortunes, I mourn now three rulers – my father, the emperor; my mistress and mother the empress; and (to my sorrow) the Caesar, my husband. For the most part, therefore, I pass my time in obscurity and devote myself to my books and the worship of God. Not even the less important persons are allowed to visit us, let alone those from whom we could have learnt news they happened to have heard from others, or my

---

23. Pindar (518–438 B.C.), the lyric poet, was noted for his lofty and sublime style.

24. Polemo of Laodicea (A.D. *c.* 88–145) used the so-called Asian style of oratory, impassioned and persuasive.

25. Calliope was the muse of heroic epic.

26. Sappho of Lesbos (born *c.* 612 B.C.), the famous lyric poetess, wrote with peculiar power and vivacity.

27. John II succeeded Alexius; after him came Manuel I (1143–80). Anna refers to this Manuel. She follows the usual method of counting inclusively – hence the 'third'.

father's most intimate friends. For thirty years now, I swear it by the souls of the most blessed emperors, I have not seen, I have not spoken to a friend of my father; most of them of course have passed away, but many too are prevented by fear because of the change in our fortunes. For the powers-that-be have decided that we must not be seen – an absurd decision – and have condemned us to a general execration. My material – let God and His heavenly Mother be the witnesses of this – has been gathered from insignificant writings, absolutely devoid of literary pretensions, and from old soldiers who were serving in the army at the time of my father's accession, who fell on hard times and exchanged the turmoil of the outer world for the peaceful life of monks. The documents that came into my possession were written in simple language without embellishment; they adhered closely to the truth, were distinguished by no elegance whatever, and were composed in a negligent way with no attempt at style. The accounts given by the old veterans were, in language and thought, similar to those commentaries and I based the truth of my history on them by examining their narratives and comparing them with my own writings, and again with the stories I had often heard myself, from my father in particular and from my uncles both on my father's and on my mother's side. From all these materials the whole fabric of my history – my true history – has been woven.

But I was talking of Kamytzes' escape from the barbarians and his address to the citizens. We must return to that point. Kamytzes gave an account of what had happened, just as we have described it, and told them of all the emperor's stratagems against the Ishmaelites. The inhabitants of Constantinople with one mouth and voice acclaimed Alexius, sang his praises, lauded him to the skies, blessed him for his leadership, could not contain themselves for joy because of him. They escorted Kamytzes to his home filled with happiness and a few days later welcomed the emperor as a victor crowned with laurels, an invincible general, indomitable ruler, sebastos and autocrator. So much for them. As for him, he entered the palace and after offering thanks to God and His Mother for his safe return, he resumed his normal habits. For now that the wars abroad had been settled and the rebellions of would-be emperors crushed, he turned his attention to the courts of justice and the laws. In time of peace as of war he was a first-class administrator, judging the cause of the orphan, dispensing justice to the widowed and regarding with the utmost rigour every case of wrong-doing. Only occasionally did he seek physical relaxation in the chase or other amusements; even then, as in all else, he was the true philosopher, 'bridling his body'[28] and making it more obedient to his will. For most of the day he laboured hard, but he would relax too, only his relaxation was itself a second labour – the reading of books and their study, the diligent observance of the command to 'search the Scriptures'.[29] Hunting and ball-play were of minor importance, even less, to my father – even when he was still a young man and the wild beast (the malady that affected his feet) had not yet entwined itself about him like the coils of some serpent, 'bruising his heel'[30] as the curse says. But when the disease first made its appearance and developed to its full strength, then he did devote himself to physical exercises, riding and other games, on the advice of experienced doctors. It was hoped that by constant horse-riding he would disperse some of the fluid that descended to his feet; he might be relieved of some of the weight that pressed on them. As I have remarked before, my father's affliction derived from only one external cause – the labours and fatigue he endured for the glory of Rome.

Less than a year later he heard a rumour that the Cumans had again crossed the Ister. At the beginning of the eighth indiction, therefore, he left the capital. It was early autumn in the month of November.[31] All his forces were called up and stationed at Philippopolis, Petritzos, Triaditza and in the theme of Nisos. Some were sent as far as Buranitzova on the banks of the Ister. Their instructions were to take especial

28. Epistle of James iii, 2.

29. St John v, 39.

30. Genesis iii, 15 (but Anna misquotes – instead of 'bruising' she has 'biting').

31. November 1114.

care of their horses: it was essential that they should be big and strong enough to carry riders in the event of battle. He himself remained in Philippopolis. This city is situated in the centre of Thrace. On its north side is the river Euros, which flows from the northern tip of Rhodope and after many twists and turns passes Adrianople. With the addition of several tributaries it finally enters the sea near the city of Ainos. When I mention Philip, I am not referring to the Macedonian, the son of Amyntas, for the present place is more recent than his town, but I mean the Roman Philip, a gigantic man endowed with overpowering physical strength.[32] Before his time it was a small place called Krenides,[33] though some people knew it as Trimous. However, this later Philip, the giant, made it into a large city and surrounded it with walls; it became the most famous town in Thrace, equipped with an enormous hippodrome and other buildings of note. I myself saw traces of them when I stayed there with the emperor for some reason or other. The city now stands on three hills, each enclosed by a massive high wall. Where it slopes down to the plain and level ground there is a fosse, near the Euros. Once upon a time, it seems, Philippopolis must have been a large and beautiful city, but after the Tauroi and Scyths enslaved the inhabitants in ancient times it was reduced to the condition in which we saw it during my father's reign. Even so we conjectured that it must have been, as I said, a really great city once. It had certain disadvantages; among them was the fact that many heretics lived there. Armenians had taken over the place and also the so-called Bogomils. We shall speak of the latter and of their heresy later on at the appropriate time. Apart from them there were in the city the Paulicians, an utterly godless sect were the Manichaeans.[34] As the name implies, their sect was

32. Philip II, King of Macedon and father of Alexander the Great, founded the city in 342 B.C. The Roman Philip was emperor from 244 to 249 of the Christian era.

33. It was Philippi, not Philippopolis, which was built on the site of Krenides.

34. Manichaeism originated in Persia. Mani taught that there are two opposite principles (God and Matter, or good and evil). The doctrine was refuted by John of Damascus and later by Photius, but the heresy was

founded by Paul and John, who having drunk at the well of Manes' profaneness handed on the heresy undiluted to their adherents. I would have liked to outline the Manichaean doctrine with a concise explanation and then hasten to refute their atheistic teachings, but as I know that everyone regards them as absurd and at the same time I am anxious to press on with the history, the disproof of their dogma must be omitted. In any case, I am aware that others, not only men of our own faith, but also Porphyrius,[35] our great adversary, have already refuted them. Porphyrius in several chapters reduced their foolish tenets to the point of insanity when he examined in his most learned fashion the two principles. I must add, though, that his one, absolute and supreme deity compels his readers to accept the Platonic Unity, or the One. We ourselves revere one Deity, but not a Unity limited to one Person; nor do we accept the One of Plato (the Greek *Ineffable* and the Chaldaean *Mystery*) for according to them other powers, in great numbers, are dependent on their One, powers both cosmic and supracosmic. These disciples of Manes, of Paul and John (the sons of Callinice), who were of a savage and unusually cruel disposition and were prepared to hazard all, even at the cost of bloodshed, met defeat at the hands of that admirable ruler John Tzimisces.[36] He removed them as slaves from Asia, carrying them off from the lands of the Chalybes and Armenians to Thrace. They were forced to dwell in the district of Philippopolis, for two reasons: first, Tzimisces wanted to drive them out of the heavily fortified towns and strongpoints which they ruled as tyrants; and secondly, he used them as a very efficient barrier against Scythian incursions, from which the Thracian area had often suffered. The barbarians

---

revived in the seventh century in an apparently Christian form (Paulicianism). It seems that Paul and John were brothers, who lived in Samosata, a centre of Manichaeism.

35. Porphyry (A.D. 232–*c.* 305) was a Neoplatonist and an opponent of the Christians, a voluminous writer, but not original and unimportant as a thinker.

36. John Tzimisces (969–76) was one of the greatest and most powerful of the emperors.

had been in the habit of crossing the mountain passes of
Haemus[37] and overrunning the plains below, but John
Tzimisces turned our opponents, these Manichaean heretics,
into allies; so far as fighting was concerned they formed a
considerable and powerful bulwark against the nomadic
Scyths and thereafter the cities, protected now from most of
their raids, breathed freely again. The Manichaeans, however,
being by nature an independent people, not amenable to discipline, followed their normal customs; they reverted to type.
Practically all the inhabitants of Philippopolis were in fact
Manichaeans, so that they lorded it over the Christians there
and plundered their goods, paying little or no attention to the
emperor's envoys. Their numbers increased until all the people
round the city were of their persuasion. They were joined by
another flood of immigrants. These newcomers were Armenians – a brackish stream – and they were succeeded by others
from the foulest springs of James.[38] Philippopolis was a
meeting-place, so to speak, of all polluted waters. And if the
immigrants differed from the Manichaeans in doctrine, they
agreed to join in their rebellious activities. Nevertheless my
father pitted against them his long experience of soldiering.
Some were taken without a fight; others were enslaved by
force of arms. The work that he did there and the labours he
courageously endured were truly worthy of a great apostle
– for surely there is no reason why he should not be praised.
If someone objected that he neglected his military duties, I
would point out that both East and West were the scenes of

37. This Haemus is a very long mountain range situated on a line parallel
to Rhodope. It begins at the Euxine Sea, almost touches the cataracts and
stretches right into Illyria; the Adriatic interrupts it, but I think it con-
tinues on the opposite mainland and ends as far away as the Hercynian
Forests. On either side of its slopes live numerous, extremely wealthy
tribes, Dacians and Thracians to the north and to the south Macedonians
and Thracians again. In ancient times the nomad Scyths crossed the
Haemus in full force and ravaged Roman territory, especially the nearer
towns, among which the most important was the city of Philippopolis
so renowned in those days. But that was before the might of Alexius and
his many battles brought them to extinction. (A.C.)
38. Jacob Baradaeus led the Monophysites in the sixth century.

numberless military exploits. Again, if he were blamed for treating literature with scant respect, my reply would be this: no man, I am sure, more zealously searched the Holy Scriptures than he, in order to have a ready answer in his debates with the heretics. He alone made use of arms and words alike, for with arms he conquered them and by his arguments he subdued the ungodly. On this occasion it was for an apostolic mission, not for operations of war, that he armed himself against the Manichaeans. And I myself would call him 'the thirteenth apostle' – though some ascribe that honour to Constantine the Great. However it seems to me that either Alexius ought to be ranked with the Emperor Constantine, or, if someone quarrelled with that, he should follow immediately after Constantine in both roles – as emperor and as apostle. As we were saying, Alexius arrived at Philippopolis for the reasons I gave, but as the Cumans had not yet appeared, the secondary object of the expedition became more important: he turned away the Manichaeans from their religion with its bitterness and filled them with the sweet doctrines of our Church. From early morning till afternoon or evening, sometimes till the second or third watch of the night, he invited them to visit him and he instructed them in the orthodox faith, refuting their corrupt heresy. He had with him Eustratios, the Bishop of Nicaea, and also the Archbishop of Philippopolis himself. The former was a man learned in the Scriptures and with a wide knowledge of profane literature, more confident in his powers of rhetoric than philosophers of Stoa or Academy. The emperor's chief assistant at all these interviews, however, was my husband, the Caesar Nicephorus, whom he had trained in the study of the Sacred Books. Thus many heretics at this time unhesitatingly sought out the priests in order to confess their sins and receive Holy Baptism. On the other hand, there were many at this same time who clung to their own religion with a passionate devotion surpassing that of the famous Maccabees, quoting from the Sacred Books and using them as evidence to support (as they imagined) their contemptible doctrine. Yet the majority even of these fanatics were persuaded by the emperor's untiring arguments and his frequent admonitions. They too were baptized. The talk went on often from the first appearance of the sun's rays in the east until far into the night, and for him there was no rest, generally no food, although it was summer-time and he was in an open tent.

While all this was going on and the battle of words was being fought with the Manichaeans, someone arrived from the Ister with the news that the Cumans had crossed the river. Without losing a moment Alexius drove towards the Danube with all available men. At Vidyne he found the barbarians had gone; they had retired to the further bank when they heard he was coming. A detachment of good fighters was at once ordered to pursue them. Having crossed the river they followed the Cumans for three days and nights, but when it became clear that the enemy had made their way to the far side of a tributary of the Danube on rafts (they carried these with them) they returned to the emperor. Nothing had been accomplished. He was annoyed that the barbarians had escaped, but consoled himself with the reflection that this was after all a kind of victory: they had been repelled by the mere mention of his name; moreover, he had converted many of the disciples of Manes to our faith. So a double trophy was set up: one for a victory over the Cumans by force of arms; the other for the subjection of the Manichaean heretics through theological debate. He then withdrew to Philippopolis and after a brief rest began his struggles afresh. Three champions of the Manichaeans, Kouleon, Kousinos and Pholos, were summoned to meet him every day and engage in a war of words. They were like the rest of their race in other respects, but obstinately persisted in their evil doctrine and, hard as steel, rejected all persuasion; they were also extremely clever at tearing to pieces the Holy Word. They misused their time in distorting its meaning. The contest therefore was twofold: on one side was the emperor, striving with all his might to save them; on the other, these Manichaeans arguing stubbornly to the end in order to win a proverbial Cadmean triumph. There they stood, the three of them, sharpening themselves up for the fray, as though they were boar's tusks intent on ripping to pieces the emperor's arguments. If some objection escaped Kousinos, Kouleon seized on it; and if Kouleon was in trouble, Pholos would rise up in opposition; or, one after another, they would rouse themselves to attack the emperor's propositions and refutations, like great waves succeeded by waves greater still. He demolished all their criticism as though it were nothing but a spider's web and quickly stopped their unclean mouths, but as he failed completely to convince them he despaired at last of their foolishness and sent them to the capital. There he allotted them a place to live in, the porticoes round the Great Palace. Despite them he had not been entirely unsuccessful in his hunting. For the moment the leaders had not been caught, but every day he led to God a hundred, sometimes more than a hundred, so that the sum total of those who had been caught before and those who were now won over by his words ran into thousands and tens of thousands. But why should I mention and spend time on what the whole world knows? East and West alike are witnesses, for whole cities and lands in the grip of all kinds of heresy were in various ways converted to our orthodox beliefs by him. The prominent among them were rewarded with rich gifts and made officers in the army; the converts of humbler origin, navvies, ploughmen, ox-herds and so on, he collected in one place with their wives and children and built a city for them quite near Philippopolis, on the far side of the River Euros. He settled them there. The place was called Alexiopolis, or more commonly Neocastron. To all he gave plough-land, vineyards, houses and immovable property. Unlike the gardens of Adonis, which blossom today and tomorrow fade,[39] these gifts of his were not without legal backing. They were secured by chrysobulls. Moreover, instead of confining these privileges to them alone, they could be handed down to their sons and grandsons. And if the male heirs died out, the women could inherit. This was carefully explained in the chrysobulls. I will say no more on the subject,

39. In the festival of Adonis, held at Athens in the month of April, flowers were set out on the house-tops by the women. The offerings, of course, soon died.

though most has been omitted. And let no one find fault with the history, suggesting that I am prejudiced, for there are plenty of people living today who are witnesses of these transactions; I would not be convicted of lying. The emperor, having made all necessary arrangements, left Philippopolis and came back to the capital. The theological struggles were resumed and there were unceasing polemics against Kouleon, Kousinos and their adherents. Kouleon was convinced this time – he was, I suppose, more intelligent than the others and more capable of understanding an honest argument. He became the gentlest lamb in our fold. Kousinos and Pholos, on the contrary, developed savage tendencies and in spite of the continual hammer-blows of the emperor's arguments, they remained what they were before, men of iron, unheeding and unmalleable. He committed them, therefore, to the prison called Elephantine, for of all the Manichaeans they were the most blasphemous and were clearly heading for deep melancholia. They were provided liberally with all necessities and allowed to die a lonely death in their sins.

BOOK FIFTEEN

VICTORY OVER THE TURKS – THE ORPHANAGE – HERESY OF THE BOGOMILS – ILLNESS AND DEATH OF ALEXIUS
(1116–18)

SUCH were the emperor's actions in the matter of Philip-popolis and the Manichaeans. Now the barbarians stirred up fresh trouble for him. The Sultan Sulayman[1] planned to ravage Asia once more. In order to put up a brave resistance against the emperor forces were summoned from Chorosan and Chalep.[2] Alexius had already been fully informed of the enemy's plan and decided to march himself as far as Iconium (on the borders of Kilij Arslan's sultanate) and launch a full-scale war. Foreigners were enlisted, together with a strong mercenary contingent, and his own army was everywhere called to the colours. While both generals were getting ready for the war, the emperor was attacked by the old pain in his feet. Forces continued to pour in from all directions, but only in small groups and not all at once because they lived so far away, and meanwhile the gout prevented Alexius not merely from putting his plan into operation, but even from walking at all. He was confined to his bed. He was not worried so much by the anguish he was suffering physically, however, as by the deferment of the campaign. Kilij Arslan was well aware of this and henceforward ravaged the whole of Asia at his leisure (there was nothing to stop him for the moment) and seven times he made onslaughts on the Christians. The

---

1. Anna is somewhat confused here. Sulayman ibn Kutlumish, the Sultan of Nicaea, had died in battle (1086); his son Kilij Arslan I was drowned while flying before the Seljuq emirs in 1107. The latter had two sons, Malik-Shah and Mas'ud who reigned from 1107 to 1116 and from 1116 to 1155 respectively. The Kilij Arslan of this book (whom she calls Klitziasthlan) must be Malik-Shah, the Sultan of Iconium.

2. Aleppo.

pain was afflicting the emperor as never before: hitherto it had come on only at long intervals; now it was continuous, with severe onsets following one another in quick succession. To Kilij Arslan and his friends it seemed that this suffering was a mere pretence: it was not a real illness, but a pretext for lethargy and an excuse for cowardice. Hence the mockery they indulged in at their drunken orgies. The barbarians, gifted improvisers, burlesqued his pains. The gout became a subject for comedy. They acted the parts of doctor and attendants, introduced 'the emperor' himself and putting him on a bed made fun of him. At these childish exhibitions they roared with laughter. Alexius knew what was going on and boiling with anger was more than ever determined to make war on them. Not long after there was some relief from the gout and he set out for the campaign. After reaching Damalis and sailing across the straits between Kibotos and Aigialoi, he disembarked and proceeded to Lopadion, where he awaited the arrival of his army and the mercenaries he had summoned. When all were gathered together, he moved on with the whole expeditionary force to St George's Castle, near the Lake of Nicaea, and from there to Nicaea itself. Three days later he retraced his steps and encamped on this side of the Lopadion bridge not far from the Fountain of Caryx. The plan was that the army should cross the bridge first and pitch camp in some suitable spot; then, when all was ready, he himself would cross by the same bridge and have the imperial tent pitched in the centre of the camp. The resourceful Turks, who were engaged in plundering the plain at the foot of the Lentianian hills and the place called Kotoiraekia, terrified at the news of his advance, lit numerous fires to give the impression that a great army was there. These beacons shot their flames heavenwards and scared many of the inexperienced, but had no effect whatever on Alexius. The Turks escaped with all the booty and the prisoners. Nevertheless at dawn the emperor hurried to the plain hoping to catch them somewhere in the vicinity, but he had missed the prey. However, he did find many victims still breathing, especially Romans, and many corpses too, which naturally upset him. He wanted to pursue, but as it was impossible for the whole army to overtake the runaways at speed and he was anxious not to lose all the quarry, he quickly detached some good light-armed men and after telling them what route to follow sent them off to chase the barbarian scoundrels. He himself set up camp in the neighbourhood of Poemanenon. The Turks were in fact overtaken at a place called Kellia in the native dialect, with all their plunder and captives. The Romans descended on them like a thunderbolt and soon killed most of them. Some were taken alive. The triumphant victors returned with these and every bit of the plunder. After commending their action and discovering that the enemy had been totally destroyed, Alexius went back to Lopadion and there he stayed for three whole months, partly because his intended path led through waterless tracts (it was the summer season and the heat was unbearable), partly because he was still awaiting the arrival of the mercenaries. Eventually all met at Lopadion and camp was struck. The whole army was then posted on the ridges of Olympos and the Malagni range. He himself occupied Aër. At the time the empress was residing on Prinkipo; news of the emperor's progress after his return to Lopadion would more easily reach her there. As soon as he came to Aër, he sent the imperial galley to fetch her. There were two reasons for this: in the first place he was always dreading a recurrence of the gout, and secondly he feared the domestic enemies in his entourage. Her loving care and watchful eye were both required.

Less than three days after, about dawn, the attendant in charge of the emperor's bedroom came in and stood by his bed. The empress woke up and seeing the man said, 'You have news of a Turkish attack.' When he replied that they were already at George's Fort,[3] she made a sign to him with her hand not to rouse Alexius. He had in fact heard the messenger's report, but kept absolutely still for a time and remained calm. When the sun was rising he attended to his normal tasks, although he was pondering deeply what measures ought to be taken in the circumstances. Before the third hour had passed a second messenger arrived to announce that the barbarians

3. Near Nicomedia.

were coming nearer. The empress was still with him and alarmed though she was (quite naturally) she waited for him to decide. As they hurried to a meal a third man came. Covered in blood, he threw himself at the emperor's feet and swore that danger was now imminent – the barbarians were at hand. Alexius immediately gave her permission to return to Byzantium, and she although distraught concealed her fear; there was no sign of it in word or manner. She was a brave and resolute woman. Like the famous one praised by Solomon in the Book of Proverbs, she displayed no womanly cowardice – the kind of thing we usually see in women when they hear some dreadful news: their very colour proclaims the timidity of their hearts and from their frequent shrieks and wails you would think the danger was closing in on them already. But if she feared it was for the emperor, lest he should suffer some accident; fear for herself came second. In this crisis, indeed, she acted in a manner worthy of her courage and although she parted from him reluctantly and often turned round to look at him, she pulled herself together and with a great effort, much against her will, she left him. She went down to the sea and boarded the galley reserved for empresses. It sailed past the coast of Bithynia, but was then held up by a storm and came to anchor off Helenopolis. She stayed there for some time; we must leave her and return to Alexius. With his soldiers and kinsmen he at once armed and then on horseback they all rode towards Nicaea. The barbarians had meanwhile captured an Alanian and from him learnt of the emperor's advance. They fled back along the paths by which they had just come. Strabobasileios and Michael Stypiotes (when the reader sees the name Stypiotes he must not confuse him with the half-barbarian, a slave bought for money and afterwards presented as a gift to the emperor by the Stypiotes I am speaking of here, who was a nobleman) – these two, Strabobasileios and Stypiotes, being fine soldiers with a long and honourable record, waited on the ridges of the Germioi, closely scanning the roads thereabouts, on the off-chance that the enemy might fall into their trap like some wild beast and so be captured. When they found out that they had come, they

returned to the . . .[4] plains and fought them in a fierce encounter. The Turks were thoroughly beaten. The emperor
first occupied George's Fort and then the village called
Sagoudaous by the natives, but no Turks were visible. However, he heard of their fate from the brave men I have already
mentioned, Stypiotes and Strabobasileios. He commended the
daring they had shown from the very outset of the campaign
and praised their victory. He then pitched camp close to the
walls of the fort. On the next day, having arrived at Helenopolis he met the empress, who was still bivouacking there
because of the rough seas. He gave an account of the Turkish
débâcle; he told her how in their desire for victory they had
met with disaster; how instead of being masters, as they had
imagined, they had themselves been mastered and all their
plans had gone awry. Thus he relieved her of great anxiety.
On his return to Nicaea he was informed of yet another
Turkish invasion, so he went on to Lopadion and stayed
there for a short time until news came of large-scale enemy
movements in the direction of Nicaea. He collected his forces
and turned aside to Kios, but, hearing that they were marching
all through the night on the road to Nicaea, he quickly left
and passed through that city to Miskoura. There reliable
information was received that the main body of the Turks had
not yet arrived; a few men sent by Manalugh were in the
Dolylus area and near Nicaea, watching the emperor's movements and supplying Manalugh with frequent reports about
him. Alexius accordingly sent Leo Nicerites with the troops
under his command to Lopadion. He was instructed to be
continually on his guard, to keep the roads under constant
surveillance and to report in writing whatever he discovered
about the Turks. The rest of the army was stationed at
strategic points. At this stage, he decided, it would be wiser to
abandon the attack on the sultan, for he guessed that the
survivors of the enemy would spread the news of his offensive
among all Turks in Asia; they would be told how contact had
been made on various occasions with the Romans and how
Turkish assaults had been stubbornly resisted and finally

4. The usual lacuna in the text.

defeated with heavy losses (for the great majority had been killed or captured, and only a few wounded men had got away). The barbarians hearing these reports would conclude that he intended to attack and would then retreat beyond Iconium; thus all his efforts would be in vain. Consequently he withdrew through Bithynia to Nicomedia, hoping that the enemy would imagine the danger was past and return to their old homes; thereafter with renewed courage they would disperse for plunder, in the usual Turkish way, and the sultan himself would resume his former plan. After his own men had enjoyed a brief respite and the horses and baggage-animals had built up their strength, he (Alexius) would soon begin a more vigorous campaign and launch a fierce onslaught. It was for these reasons that he made for Nicomedia. All the soldiers he had with him were quartered in the villages round about, so that the horses and pack-animals might have sufficient fodder (for Bithynia is rich in grass) and the men could get all the supplies they needed without difficulty from Byzantium and the neighbourhood by crossing the bay. They were told to lavish particular care on the animals – he emphasized this; they were not to be used for hunting or riding at all, so that when the time came they would be big and strong enough to bear their riders without distress and ready for cavalry charges against the Turks.

Having taken these precautions he settled down as a kind of observer, with guards posted on every road at some distance from Nicomedia. As he intended to stay there for several days, he sent for the Augusta; she was to remain with him until he heard of barbarian incursions and decided to leave. She came without delay. But she was annoyed and upset because she realized that some of his enemies were rejoicing over the emperor's failure to achieve his object. There were reproaches and soft whispers everywhere that after such grand preparations against the Turks and the concentration of such huge forces he had won no great success, but had retired to Nicomedia. These things, moreover, were being muttered not only in dark corners, but quite brazenly in squares, on highways and at cross-roads. Alexius himself foresaw a happy end to his campaign (and he was a good prophet in such matters). The indignant scolding of his enemies he regarded as of no importance whatever: they were childish outbursts and thoroughly despicable, the absurd outcome of puerile minds. His confidence inspired her with hope, for he assured her on oath that the very thing for which they reviled him would be the cause of a greater victory. For my part, I think that to win a victory by sound planning calls for courage; force of character and energy uninformed by thought are not enough – they end not in courage, but in foolhardiness. We are courage-ous in war against men whom we can beat; against men too strong for us we are foolhardy. Thus when danger hangs over us, being unable to make a frontal assault we change our tactics and seek to conquer without bloodshed. The prime virtue of a general is the ability to win without incurring danger – as Homer says, 'It is by skill that one charioteer beats another.' [5] Even the famous Cadmean proverb censures a victory fraught with danger. As far as I am concerned, it has always seemed best to devise some crafty strategic manoeuvre in the actual battle, if one's own army cannot match the enemy's strength. Anyone can find examples of this in the pages of history. There is no one method of achieving victory, nor one form of it, but from ancient times up to the present success has been won in different ways. 'Victory' means the same thing always, but the means by which generals attain it are varied and of intricate patterns. It appears that some of the renowned generals of old overcame their adversaries by sheer strength, whereas others prevailed on many occasions by making good use of some advantage of a different kind. In my father's case the enemy was sometimes defeated by power, sometimes by a quick-witted move, sometimes by a shrewd guess and the nerve to act on it immediately during the actual combat. There were times when he had recourse to stratagem, at others he entered the battle in person. Thus many a victory was won, often unexpectedly. He had an extraordinary love of danger, and certainly dangers continually arose. He faced them in different ways: by marching into them bare-headed

5. *Iliad* xxiii, 318.

and coming to close grips with the enemy, or on occasions by pretending to avoid conflict and feigning terror. It depended on circumstances and the situation of the moment. To put it briefly I would say this: in flight he would triumph, in pursuit conquer; falling he stood and dropping down he fell upright, like a caltrop (for however you throw it, it will always point upwards).

At this point I must again beg the reader not to rebuke me for being boastful; this is by no means the first time I have defended myself against such an accusation. It is not love for my father which prompts me to these reflections, but the course of events. In any case, there is nothing (as far as truth is concerned) to prevent a person loving his or her father and at the same time respecting veracity. I chose to write the truth about a good man, and if that man happens to be the historian's father, it is right that his name should not be omitted; it is right, too, that the historian should not be accused of *dragging in* his name. But of course the history must by its very nature be founded on truth. There are other ways in which I have demonstrated my love for him, and because of that my enemies have been inspired to sharpen sword and spear against me; everyone not ignorant of my life knows it well. The reader can rest assured that I would never betray the truth under the guise of history. There is a time for showing love for one's father, and when that time came we gave evidence of courage; there is another time for telling the truth, and now that the opportunity has arrived, I will not neglect it. If, as I said, this chance proves that I love my father as well as truth, the reader will not be able to complain that I have suppressed the facts. However, we must return to the narrative.

As long as the emperor was encamped near Nicomedia, there was nothing for him to do but enrol recruits in the main army and put them through a course of intensive training in archery, lance-fighting, riding on horseback and practising the various manoeuvres. He also taught them the new battle-formation which he himself had invented. Sometimes he rode with them, inspected the ranks and invariably made suggestions for improvement. The summer months were now over and the autumnal equinox was past: it seemed a suitable moment for expeditions. Accordingly with all his forces he drove straight for Nicaea (his original plan). On his arrival in the city, light-armed men with experienced officers were detached from the rest of the army and sent on ahead to make raids on the Turks; they were to work in small groups and forage. If they were granted victory by God and routed the enemy, they were forbidden to pursue them far; they must be content with what He had given them and make their way back in good order. These men reached a place called . . .[6] (the local name for it is Gaita) with the emperor, but after that they went their separate way at once, while he departed with the rest to the bridge near Pithekas. Then, at the end of three days, he arrived on the plain of Doryleon by way of Armenokastron and a place called Leukai. The plain was clearly large enough for manoeuvres and as he wished to review the whole army and discover its real potential, he encamped there. This was an excellent opportunity to try out effectively the battle-formation he was again considering (which he had often described on paper when making his plans)[7]. He knew from very long experience that the Turkish battle-line differs from that of other peoples. It was not arranged, as Homer says, 'buckler to buckler, helmet to helmet, man to man',[8] but their right and left wings and their centre formed separate groups with the ranks cut off, as it were, from one another; whenever an attack was made on right or left, the centre leapt into action and all the rest of the army behind it, in a whirlwind onslaught that threw into confusion the accepted tradition of battle. As for the weapons they use in war, unlike the Kelts they do not fight with lances but completely surround the enemy and shoot at him with arrows; they also defend themselves with arrows at a distance. In hot pursuit the Turk makes prisoners by using his bow; in flight he overwhelms

6. A lacuna in the text.

7. He was not unacquainted with the *Tactica* of Aelian. (A.C.)

Aelian wrote a treatise in Greek on the Macedonian phalanx, probably in the reign of Trajan. It has no great value.

8. *Iliad* xiii, 131.

his pursuer with the same weapon and when he shoots, the arrow in its course strikes either rider or horse, fired with such tremendous force that it passes clean through the body. So skilled are the Turkish archers. Now Alexius was aware of this and to counteract it he adopted his own battle formation, with the ranks so organized that the Turks would have to shoot from their right at the Roman left (which was protected by the shield); the Romans, on the contrary, would shoot *left*-handed at the Turkish exposed right.[9] After careful examination to test the impregnability of this formation he was surprised at its power: it must be, he thought, directly attributable to God – a battle-order inspired by angels. Everyone admired it and rejoiced, full of confidence in the emperor's invention. He too, as he contemplated his forces and the plain through which he was about to march, picturing to himself the solidity of his line and, calculating that it could never be broken, was full of good hopes and prayed to God that they might be fulfilled.

So, drawn up in this formation, the army reached Santabaris . . .[10] all the leaders were sent on different routes: Kamytzes was detached to march on Polybotos and Kedros (the latter a strongly fortified town held by a satrap called Poucheas); Stypiotes he ordered to attack the barbarians in Amorion. Two Scyth deserters discovered the plan, went to Poucheas and told him of Kamytzes' advance and also of the emperor's arrival. About the mid-watch of the night Poucheas left the place in abject terror with his fellow-tribesmen. As day was breaking Kamytzes arrived, but no Poucheas was to be seen – in fact no Turk whatever. Although he found the place full of booty (I am referring to Kedros)[11] he disregarded it; like a hunter who has lost the quarry which was almost in his grasp, Kamytzes was annoyed and without a moment's delay turned his horse's head in the direction of Polybotos. He fell

9. It has been suggested that Alexius drew up his line not parallel to the enemy, but at an angle; his opponents would always be faced with a shower of arrows descending on them slantwise and the Roman line would move with every change made by the enemy commander. This would certainly justify the novelty of which Anna is so proud.

10. Several words are missing in the text.

11. Anna calls it Kedrea here (not Kedros, as above).

on the barbarians suddenly, killing them beyond number. All
the booty and prisoners, moreover, were recovered. Then
camp was pitched near the place while they awaited the
emperor's coming. Stypiotes was no less successful at Poemanenon before he returned to Alexius. About sunset the emperor
reached Kedros. At once some soldiers approached him with
information that a great host of barbarians was in the small
towns of the neighbourhood, which used to owe allegiance
to the famous Burtzes [12] in the old days. The emperor acted
quickly. A descendant of this Burtzes, Bardas by name, with
George Lebounes and a Scyth, called Pitikan in the Scythian
language, were sent against them with their respective forces
(which had been built up to a considerable army). Their
instructions were to send out foragers when they got there, to
ravage all the villages in the area and to remove the inhabitants and bring them to him. These three men started on their
march without delay, but Alexius, adhering to his former plan,
was anxious to reach Polybotos and go beyond that as far as
Iconium. While he was making preparations and just about
to leave, news came that the Turks and the Sultan Malik-Shah
himself, [13] learning of his movements, had set fire to all the
crops and plains of Asia, so that there was no food whatever
for man or beast. It was said that another invasion from the
more northerly [14] regions was on its way and the rumour
spread rapidly throughout Asia. Alexius feared that on the
march to Iconium his army might perish of hunger because
food-supplies were scarce; he was also worried and suspicious
about the barbarians he expected to find there. Accordingly
he decided to do something which was both prudent and
daring – to inquire of God whether he should follow the road
to Iconium, or attack the enemy in the area of Philomelion.
He wrote his questions on two pieces of paper and placed
them on the Holy Altar. Then the whole night was spent in
singing the hymn of the day and in addressing to God fervent

12 Michael Burtzes had made a name for himself as a general in the
latter half of the tenth century.

13. Anna wrongly calls him Sulayman (see p. 471).

14. That is, from the Danishmends.

prayers. At dawn the priest went in; taking up one of the
papers from the Altar he opened it in the presence of all and
read aloud that Alexius should choose rather the road to
Philomelion. We will leave the matter there. Bardas Burtzes,
meanwhile, on his march saw a large army hurrying to join
Manalugh across the bridge at Zompe. He immediately took
up arms, attacked these Turks on the plain of Amorion and
won a complete victory. But other Turks, coming from the
east and hastening to Manalugh, chanced on his camp before
he had returned and carried off the soldiers' baggage and any
pack-animals they could find. When Burtzes came back in
triumph loaded with his spoils, he met one of the Turks
leaving the camp and learnt from him that the enemy had
plundered everything in it, including all his booty, and had
already departed. Burtzes examined the situation carefully:
he would have liked to pursue them, but they were moving
fast and his own horses were tired; so pursuit was impossible
and he abandoned the idea, lest something worse should befall
him; instead he continued his march at a slow pace and in good
order. By daybreak he had reached the towns of Burtzes (his
ancestor) and evacuated the whole population. The prisoners
were recovered and all available Turkish provisions seized.
Then, after a short interval at an appropriate spot to rest himself and his weary horses, he began the journey back to the
emperor as the sun was rising. On the way another Turkish
force met him. He plunged into battle at once and a serious
conflict flared up. However, after holding out for a reasonable
time the Turks asked for the return of their prisoners and the
booty taken from them, promising on their side that if their
demands were satisfied they would in future refrain from
attacking the Romans and go home. Burtzes refused to make
any concessions and bravely resumed the battle. On the previous day his soldiers had drunk no water at all during the
struggle; now, when they reached the bank of a river, they
quenched their burning thirst. They did it in relays: while one
party carried on fighting, another left the battle and refreshed
themselves with a drink. Burtzes was a very worried man, for
the Turks displayed great gallantry and they vastly outnum-

bered his own men. The position became desperate and a
messenger was sent to inform Alexius. The man sent was no
ordinary soldier, but George Lebounes himself. As there was no
path unoccupied by masses of Turks, Lebounes hurled himself
recklessly into their midst, pushed his way through and got
safely to the emperor. The latter, being informed of Burtzes'
plight and knowing how necessary it was to reinforce him
with men and supplies (he now had a more accurate assessment
of Turkish strength) straightway armed himself and mobilized
his troops. When all were ready in their various military
groups, he set out against the barbarians. The Basileus
Michael[15] commanded the vanguard, Bryennius the right
wing, Gabras the left and Cecaumenus the rear. As the Turks
waited for them in the distance, Nicephorus (the empress's
nephew), who was young and eager for action, rode out in
front of the line, taking with him a handful of other impatient
warriors. He fought at close quarters with the first Turk to
charge out against him and was wounded in the knee. However, he pierced his assailant's breast with his spear and the
man fell from his horse to the ground without a cry. The
barbarians behind him, seeing this, turned their backs on the
Romans and fled. The emperor, delighted with Nicephorus'
bravery, received him on the battle-field and warmly commended him. The army then marched on to Philomelion. The
lake of the Forty Martyrs was reached and on the next day a
place called Mesanakta. Later he moved on to Philomelion
and took it by assault. Subsequently various detachments
under the command of brave officers were sent out to ravage
all the small towns in the vicinity of Iconium and recover the
prisoners. They scattered all over the countryside like herds
of wild beasts hunting their prey. All the captives were in
fact released and brought back with the baggage. The native
inhabitants, Romans who were fleeing from Turkish vengeance, followed them of their own free will; there were
women with babies, even men and children, all seeking
refuge with the emperor, as if he were some kind of sanctuary.

15. The name Michael is suspect: it may have crept into the text when
a copyist was thinking of Michael Cecaumenus.

The lines were now drawn up in the new formation, with all the prisoners in the centre, as well as the women and children. The emperor retraced his steps. All along the route the march proceeded in perfect safety; in fact, if you had seen it, you would have said that these men marching in his new formation constituted a city with bastions, living and on the move.

As they went further, no barbarians appeared. But Manalugh was following with a large army and laid ambushes on either flank, and, when the emperor was going across the plain between Polybotos and the lake I have already mentioned, a detachment from the main barbarian force, all lightly-armed and bold fighters lying in wait to left and right of the Romans, suddenly became visible on the high ground above them. It was the first time that Manalugh the archsatrap had seen the new formation. He was an old man, with a vast experience of wars and armies, but he was absolutely amazed at the sight of this novel arrangement. He asked who the commanding officer was, and guessed that it must be none other than Alexius himself. He wanted to attack, but did not know how; nevertheless, he ordered the Turks to shout their war-cries. Intending to give the impression of a great army, he instructed his men not to run in close order, but in scattered groups and with no set ranks (the Turkish method described above) so as to strike terror into the Romans by the unexpectedness of the sight and the deafening noise of their horses' galloping. But Alexius at the head of the line rode on like a huge tower, or a pillar of fire, or some divine celestial apparition, encouraging his soldiers, telling them to continue in the same formation, building up their confidence. He added, moreover, that it was not for his own safety that he endured such travail, but for the honour and glory of Rome; he was quite ready, he said, to die on behalf of them all. Thus everyone was given fresh courage and each kept his place in the ranks. The march indeed went so smoothly that to the barbarians they seemed not to be moving at all. All through that day the enemy attacked, but made no progress, unable to disrupt the Roman forces in part or as a whole. In the end they ran off again to the hill-tops having achieved nothing. There they lit numerous watch-fires.

Throughout the night they were howling like wolves; occasionally they jeered at the Romans, for there were some half-breeds among them who spoke Greek. When day broke Manalugh persisted with his plan; his men were told to follow the same procedure as before. At this stage the Sultan Malik-Shah himself arrived. He was astounded at the excellent discipline of the Roman army, but in a young man's way poked fun at old Manalugh because he deferred the struggle with the emperor. 'I have put off coming to grips with him up till now, because I am old – or cowardly,' said Manalugh, 'but if you have the courage, here's your chance: try it yourself. You'll learn by experience.' The other made an immediate attack on our rearguard, while other satraps were to make a frontal assault; others again were ordered to charge against either flank. The Caesar Nicephorus Bryennius, who was in charge of the right wing, noticed the battle raging in the rear, but for all his eagerness to help checked the anger boiling up inside him, being unwilling to expose his inexperience or youth. He earnestly marched on with ranks intact and the soldiers in perfect order. As the barbarians fought with determination, the dearest of my brothers, the Porphyro-genitus Andronicus, who was in command of the left, turned about and charged violently at them on horseback. He had just reached his young manhood, the most charming time of life, a daring soldier in war, but prudent too, with a quick hand and fine intellect. Here he met his end, prematurely. In a way that none expected he left us and disappeared. His youthfulness, his physical perfection, those light vaults into the saddle – what do they mean now? My grief for him drives me to tears – but the law of history once more calls me back. It is extraordinary that nobody nowadays under the stress of great troubles is turned into stone or a bird or a tree or some inanimate object; they used to undergo such metamorphoses in ancient times (or so they say), though whether that is myth or a true story I know not. Maybe it would be better to change one's nature into something that lacks all feeling, rather than be so sensitive to evil. Had that been possible, these calamities would in all probability have turned me to stone.

When Nicephorus saw that a hand-to-hand fight had developed and there was a prospect of defeat, he wheeled about
and hurried with his own men to bring aid. Thereupon the
barbarians fled and with them the Sultan Malik-Shah. They
galloped off at full speed to the hills. Many were killed in this
battle, but the majority were captured. The survivors dispersed. The sultan himself, despairing of his life, ran off with
only one companion, his cup-bearer. They climbed up to a
chapel built on a hill-top and surrounded by rows of very tall
cypress trees. Hard on their heels came three Scyths and
Ouzas' son in hot pursuit. The sultan changed direction
slightly and since he was not recognized saved himself, but
the cup-bearer was taken prisoner by the Scyths and brought
to the emperor as a great prize of war. Alexius was delighted
that the enemy had been beaten in such a convincing manner,
but annoyed too because the sultan had not fallen into his
hands, escaping 'by the skin of his teeth' as they say. At nightfall he encamped at the place he had reached. The barbarian
survivors, climbing to the ridges above the Romans, again
lit a multitude of watch-fires and all night long bayed at them
like dogs. Meanwhile a Scythian deserter from the emperor's
army went off to the sultan. 'Never try to fight the emperor in
the daylight,' he said, 'for you will have the worst of it. Since
the plain is not large enough, he has pitched his tents very close
together. Let your light archers go down, then, and fire
volleys of arrows from the foothills at them all through the
night. They will do enormous damage to the Romans.' At
this same moment a half-barbarian came from the Turkish
camp. He slipped out unseen. Coming to the emperor he told
him all about the suggestions made by the renegade Scyth and
clearly described the whole Turkish plan for future action
against the Romans. Accordingly, Alexius divided his army
in two: one group was to remain in camp, vigilant and sober;
the rest were to arm, leave camp and anticipate the Turkish
advance – they were to engage their attackers in battle.
Throughout the hours of darkness the enemy were completely
encircling our men, making numerous charges near the foothills and continually firing volleys of arrows at them. But the

Romans, obeying the emperor's instructions, protected themselves without breaking rank and when the sun rose the whole
column set out again in the same formation, with the booty,
all the baggage, the prisoners, of course, and the women and
children in the centre. They marched on towards Ampous. A
terrible and bitter fight awaited them there, for the sultan,
drawing together his forces again and surrounding our army,
attacked fiercely from all sides. Nevertheless he was not strong
enough to disrupt the tight formation of the Romans and after
assailing what appeared to be walls of steel, he was repulsed
with nothing achieved. That night (a sleepless one) he spent
in gloomy thought. At last in desperation he took counsel with
Manalugh and the other satraps, and with their unanimous
approval at dawn he asked the emperor for terms of peace.
The emperor did not reject him – far from it. The call to halt
was sounded at once, but the whole army was instructed to
remain where it was, preserving the same formation, neither
dismounting nor removing baggage from the pack-animals;
the men were still in full armour with shield, helmet and
spear. In fact, the Romans were to follow the same orders as
on the rest of the march. The emperor had his reasons for this:
he was obviating confusion, with the subsequent break up of
the column, in which case they would probably all be captured;
he was also afraid of the Turks, who greatly outnumbered
his own men and whose attacks were coming from all
quarters. So, in a suitable place, with all his kinsmen and several
picked soldiers on either side of him,[16] he took up position at
the head of his army. The sultan then approached with his
subordinate satraps, led by Manalugh (who in age, experience
and bravery surpassed all the Turks in Asia). He met the emperor on the plain between Augustopolis and Akronion. The
satraps, seeing Alexius some way off, dismounted and made
the obeisance normally reserved for kings, but although the
sultan made several attempts to dismount the emperor would

16. On right and left were his relatives, distant or close, and next to
them selected warriors from the various contingents, all in heavy armour.
The fiery gleam from their weapons outshone the rays of the sun. (A.C.)
 Anna frequently repeats herself, often in almost identical terms.

not let him. Nevertheless he quickly leapt to the ground and kissed Alexius' foot. The latter gave him his hand, bidding him mount one of the nobles' horses. On horseback again he rode close beside Alexius, when suddenly the emperor loosed the cloak he was wearing and threw it round the Turk's shoulders. Then, after a brief pause, he made a speech, explaining his decision in full. 'If you are willing,' he said, 'to yield to the authority of Rome and to put an end to your raids on the Christians, you will enjoy favours and honour, living in freedom for the rest of your lives on lands set aside for you. I refer to the lands where you used to dwell before Romanus Diogenes became emperor and before he met the sultan in battle – an unfortunate and notorious clash which ended in the Roman's defeat and capture.[17] It would be wise, therefore, to choose peace rather than war, to refrain from crossing the frontiers of the Empire and to be content with your own territories. The advice I give is in your interests and if you listen to it you will never be sorry; in fact, you will receive liberal gifts. On the other hand, if you reject it, you can be sure of this: I will exterminate your race.' The sultan and his satraps readily accepted these terms. 'We would not have come here of our own free will,' they said, 'if we had not chosen to welcome peace with Your Majesty.' When the interview was over, Alexius allowed them to go to the tents assigned to them. He promised to ratify the agreements on the next day. At the appointed time, then, the treaty was concluded with the sultan (whose name was Saisan[18]) in the usual way. Huge sums of money were presented to him and the satraps were also rewarded generously. They departed well pleased. Meanwhile news arrived that the bastard brother of Malik-Shah, Mas'ud, jealous of his power, had plotted to murder him at the instigation of certain satraps – the kind of thing that usually happens. Alexius advised the sultan to wait

17. The Battle of Manzikert (26 August 1071) in which Romanus IV Diogenes was defeated and taken prisoner by Alp Arslan, the Seljuq leader.

18. The person Anna called Klitziasthlan in chapter I of this book. He was in fact Malik-Shah.

a little until he had more definite information about the plot;
thus he would leave in full possession of the facts and on his
guard. But Malik-Shah disregarded this advice; filled with
self-confidence he clung to his original scheme. The emperor
naturally did not wish to give the impression that he was
forcibly detaining the sultan (who had come to him voluntarily) and thereby incur reproach. He bowed to the Turk's
wishes. 'It would be well,' he said, 'to wait a little, but since
you have decided to go, you must do the next best thing, as
they say, and take with you a reasonable number of our
heavily-armed soldiers to escort you in safety as far as Iconium.' The barbarian would not even agree to this; it was
typical of his race, for the Turks are an arrogant people, with
their heads almost in the clouds. Anyway he took his leave of
the emperor and set out on his homeward path with his great
sums of money. During the night, however, he had a dream.
It was no lying vision, nor a message from Zeus, nor did it
incite the barbarian to battle 'in the guise of the son of
Neleus' (as the sweet poem says).[19] It foretold the truth. For he
dreamed that while he was breakfasting a multitude of mice
surrounded him, eager to snatch the bread from his hands;
when he treated them with contempt and tried to drive them
away in disgust, they suddenly changed into lions and over-
powered him. When he woke up, he told the emperor's
soldier-escort who was accompanying him on the journey and
asked him what was the meaning of the dream. He solved the
problem by saying that mice and lions were his enemies, but
Malik-Shah would not believe him. He went on his way,
without taking precautions. Maybe he sent out men to reconnoitre the road ahead and keep an eye open for enemies on
a plundering foray, but these scouts fell in with Mas'ud himself. He was already approaching with a great army. They
talked with him, joined in the plot against the sultan and when
they returned assured him they had seen nobody. In no doubt
that they were telling the truth, he was continuing his march
in carefree mood when Mas'ud's forces confronted him. A

19. *Iliad* ii, 20, where Agamemnon is visited by a dream sent from
Zeus. Neleus was the father of Nestor.

certain Gazes, son of the Satrap Asan Katuch (whom the
sultan had killed in the past), leapt forward from the ranks
and struck Malik-Shah with his spear. Malik turned in a flash
and as he wrenched the spear from Gazes' hands said, 'I didn't
know that women, too, are now bearing arms against us.'
With these words he fled along the road back to the emperor,
but he was stopped by Poucheas, who although he was one
of his companions had long ago favoured Mas'ud's party. He
pretended to be Malik's friend and now offered a seemingly
better plan; in reality he was laying a trap for him – digging a
pit, as it were. He advised him not to return to Alexius, but by
making a little detour to enter Tyragion, a small place quite
near Philomelion. Malik-Shah, poor fool, consented to do
this. He received a kindly welcome from the inhabitants of
Tyragion, who knew of the emperor's goodwill towards him.
But the barbarians arrived, with Mas'ud himself, and after
completely encircling the walls settled down to besiege the
town. Malik, leaning over the ramparts, uttered violent threats
against his fellow-countrymen; he went so far as to say that
Roman forces under the emperor's command were on their
way and unless the Turks stopped their activities, they would
suffer this and that punishment. The Romans in the town
bravely withstood the siege with him. But Poucheas now
dropped his mask and revealed his true character. He came
down from the walls after promising to encourage the people
to even more courageous efforts. In fact, he threatened them
and advised them to surrender and throw open the gates to the
enemy; otherwise, he said, they would be slain, for huge
forces were already on the way from as far away as Chorosan.
Partly because they were frightened by the multitude of their
enemies, partly because Poucheas had convinced them, they
allowed the Turks to come in. They arrested the sultan and
blinded him. As the instrument normally used for the purpose
was lacking, the candelabrum given to Malik-Shah by the
emperor took its place – the diffuser of light had become the
instrument of darkness and blinding. However, he could still
see a small ray of light and when he arrived at Iconium, led by
the hand of some guide, he confided this fact to his nurse and

she told his wife. In this way the story reached the ears of Mas'ud himself. He was greatly disturbed and extremely angry. Elegmon, one of the most prominent satraps, was sent to strangle the sultan with a bowstring.[20] Thus ended the career of Malik-Shah – the result of his own folly in not heeding Alexius' advice. As for the latter, he continued his march to Constantinople, maintaining the same discipline and good order to the very end.

When he hears the words 'formation', 'ranks', 'prisoners and spoils of war', 'general' and 'army commanders', the reader will probably imagine that this is the kind of thing mentioned by every historian and poet. But this formation of Alexius was unprecedented, causing universal astonishment, such as no one had ever seen before, unrecorded by any historian for the benefit of future generations. On the way to Iconium he marched in a disciplined way, keeping in step to the sound of the flute, so that an eye-witness would have said the whole army, although it was in motion, was standing immobile and when it was halting was on the march. In fact, the serried ranks of close-locked shields and marching men gave the impression of immovable mountains; and when they changed direction the whole body moved like one huge beast, animated and directed by one single mind. When the emperor reached Philomelion after rescuing prisoners everywhere from the Turks, the return journey was made slowly, in a leisurely way and at an ant's pace, so to speak, with the captives, women and children, and all the booty in the centre of the column. Many of the women were pregnant and many men were suffering from disease. When a woman was about to give birth, the emperor ordered a trumpet to sound and everyone halted; the whole army stopped at once wherever it happened to be. After hearing that a child had been born, he gave the general order to advance by another, and unusual, trumpet-blast. Again, if someone were on the point of dying, the same thing occurred. The emperor visited the dying man and priests

20. Malik-Shah was captured in 1116 and Mas'ud became sultan. He was destined to reign for almost forty years. The murder of his brother took place in 1117.

were summoned to sing the appropriate hymns and administer the last sacraments. Thus, when all the customary rites had been performed, and only when the dead had been laid in his tomb and buried, was the column allowed to move on even a short distance. At meal-times all women and men who were worn out with sickness or old age were invited to the emperor's table; most of his rations were set before them, and he incited his retinue to follow his example in giving. It was a veritable banquet of the gods, with no musical instruments, no flutes, no drums, no music at all to disturb the feasters. By such means Alexius personally supplied the needs of the marchers. On their arrival at Damalis (in the evening) he insisted that there should be no magnificent reception in the city; regal processions and flamboyant decorations were forbidden. The crossing was postponed to the next day, as indeed it had to be, but he himself immediately embarked on a small boat and reached the palace about dusk. On the following day he was wholly occupied in tending the prisoners and strangers. All children who had lost their parents and were afflicted by the grievous ills of orphanhood were committed to the care of relatives and to others who, he knew, were respectable people, as well as to the abbots of the holy monasteries, with instructions to treat them not as slaves but as free children, to see that they had a thorough education and to teach them the Sacred Scriptures. Some he introduced into the orphanage which he had personally founded, making it a school rather for those who wanted to learn; they were handed over to the directors there to receive a good general education. For in the district of the Acropolis, where the entrance to the sea grows wider, he had discovered a site near the enormous church dedicated to the great apostle Paul; here, inside the capital city, he built a second city. The sanctuary itself stood on the highest part like a citadel. This new city was laid out for so many stades in length and width – I cannot say how many, but the measurements can be verified. All round it in a circle were numerous buildings, houses for the poor and – even better proof of his humanity – dwellings for mutilated persons. One could see them coming there singly, the blind, the lame, people with

some other trouble. Seeing it full of those who were maimed
in limb or completely incapacitated, you would have said it
was Solomon's Porch. The buildings were in a double circle
and were two-storeyed, for some of these maimed persons, men
and women, live on the upper floor, while others drag themselves along below on the street level. So large was this circle
that if you wished to visit these folk and started early in the
morning, it would be evening before you finished. Such was
the city and such its inhabitants. They had no plots of ground,
no vineyards, nor any other such possession on which we
see men earning their livelihood, but like Job each of them,
man or woman, dwelt in the house built for them and everything, so far as food or clothing are concerned, was provided
for them through the emperor's generosity. The most extraordinary thing was that these poor people had as their
guardians and administrators of their means of subsistence the
emperor himself and his hard-working servants, just as if they
were lords with property and all kinds of revenue. For wherever there was an estate lying in a good situation (provided it
was easily accessible) he allotted it to these 'brethren', thus
ensuring them wine in abundance and bread and all the other
products men eat with bread. The number of persons catered
for in this way was incalculable. Rather daringly, perhaps, I
would say that the emperor's work could be compared with
my Saviour's miracle (the feeding of the seven and five
thousands).[21] In the latter case, of course, thousands were
satisfied by five loaves, for it was God who performed the
miracle, whereas here the work of charity was the result of the
Divine command; moreover, that was a miracle, but we are
dealing here with an emperor's liberality in dispensing sus-
tenance to his brethren. I myself saw an old woman being assisted by a young girl, a blind person being led by the hand by
another man who had his sight, a man without feet making use
of others' feet, a man who had no hands being aided by the
hands of his friends, babies being nursed by foster-mothers and
the paralyzed being waited on by strong, healthy men. In fact,

21. As so often in the history, Anna's references are not absolutely
accurate. She was probably relying on her memory only.

the number of people maintained there was doubled, for some were being cared for, while others looked after them. The emperor could not say to the paralytic: 'Rise up and walk!'[22] nor bid the blind man see and the man without feet walk (for that was the prerogative of the Only-begotten Son, who for our sakes became man and dwelt here on earth for us men), but he did what he could. Servants were allotted to every maimed person and the same care was lavished on the infirm as on the healthy. To describe the nature of this new city which my father built from its foundations, one might say it was four-fold, or rather multiform, for there were people living on ground level, others on the upper floor, and yet others who cared for both of them. But who could possibly number those who eat there every day, or estimate the daily expense and the forethought devoted to each individual's needs? For, in my opinion, the benefits they still enjoy after his death must be attributed to Alexius; he set aside for them the resources of land and sea, and it was he who secured for them the maximum relief from pain. One of the most distinguished men acts as guardian[23] of this city with its many thousands of inhabitants, called 'The Orphanage', because of the emperor's solicitude for orphans and ex-servicemen, but with special emphasis on the orphans. There are tribunals which deal with all these matters and accounts have to be rendered by those who administer the funds of these poor folk. Chrysobulls, moreover, are published to establish the inalienable rights of the persons maintained at the Orphanage. A large and impressive body of clergy was appointed to the church of St Paul, the great herald of our faith, and expensive lighting was provided for it. Were you to enter this church you would hear the antiphonal chants, for Alexius, after the example of Solomon, decreed that there should be both male and female choristers. The work of the deaconesses was also carefully organized and he devoted much thought to Iberian nuns who lived there; in former times it was their custom to beg from door to door whenever they visited Constantinople, but now, thanks to my

22. St Matthew ix, 5–6; St Mark ii, 9–10.
23. The *Orphanotrophos*.

father's solicitude, an enormous convent was built for them and they were provided with food and suitable clothing. The famous Alexander of Macedon might well boast of Alexandria in Egypt, Bucephale in Media and Lysimachia in Ethiopia,[24] but the Emperor Alexius found more pleasure and pride in this Orphanage than in any of the cities he founded (and we know that such cities were built by him all over the Empire). When you enter it, the sanctuaries and monasteries are on your left; on the right of the great church of St Paul stands the grammar school for orphan children drawn from all races, presided over by a master. Boys stand round him, some anxiously puzzling over grammatical questions, others writing out grammatical analyses. You might see a Latin boy being trained there; a Scyth learning Greek; a Byzantine handling Greek texts; an illiterate Greek discovering how to speak his own language correctly – all the result of Alexius' profound interest in literary studies. The technique of grammatical analysis was invented by younger men of our generation[25] (I am passing over Stylianus[26] and his school, men like Longibardus[27] and the compilers of catalogues of all kinds, the disciples of Atticus[28] and the members of the clergy at St Sophia[29] whom I will not mention by name). Today these sublime studies are considered not even of secondary importance; the poets and even the historians, together with the experience to be derived from them, are denied their rightful

24. An error for Aetolia. The place was named after Lysimachos, one of Alexander's generals, but Alexander did not in fact found this city.

25. Michael Psellus claimed that he restored grammatical analysis to the syllabus, but he was some years older than Anna. She may be referring to John Italos.

26. Stylianus was a fairly common name (Psellus had a daughter called Styliane), but no grammarian so called is known. Anna may have meant to write Syrianus, who flourished in the fifth century at Athens and wrote commentaries on Aristotle.

27. John Longibardus wrote on schedography (a contemporary of Psellus).

28. No Atticus is known to have been a grammarian, but the name was common enough.

29. At least two patriarchs between 824 and 1111 had the nickname Grammaticus.

place. Today it is the game of draughts that is all the rage – and other activities, which contravene the law.[30] I say this because it grieves me to see the total neglect of general education. It makes my blood boil, for I myself spent much time on these same exercises. After liberation from the elementary studies I devoted myself to rhetoric, touched on philosophy and in the midst of these sciences eagerly turned to the poets and historians. So the rough edges of my style were smoothed out; thereafter, with the aid of rhetoric, I condemned excessive indulgence in schedography.[31] These personal reminiscences, by the way, are not superfluous: they are intended to reinforce my argument for a general education.

Later, in the . . .[32] year of Alexius' reign there arose an extraordinary 'cloud of heretics', a new, hostile group, hitherto unknown to the Church. For two doctrines, each known to antiquity and representative of what was most evil, most worthless, now coalesced: one might say that the impiety of the Manichaeans (also known as the Paulician heresy) and the loathsome character of the Massalians were united in the Bogomils, for the dogma of the latter was an amalgam of Manichaean and Massalian teaching. Apparently it was in existence before my father's time, but was unperceived (for the Bogomil sect is most adept at feigning virtue). No worldly hairstyles are to be seen among Bogomils: their wickedness is hidden beneath cloak and cowl. Your Bogomil wears a sombre look; muffled up to the nose, he walks with a stoop, quietly muttering to himself – but inside he's a ravening wolf. This unpleasant race, like a serpent lurking in its hole, was brought to the light and lured out by my father with secret magical incantations.[33] He had recently freed himself of most of his cares in east and west, and was now turning his attention to

30. Gambling, maybe?

31. *Schedos* was a piece of paper or a tablet on which the pupil wrote analyses of sentences, definitions of words, explanations of their inflection and etymology. In other words, schedography dealt with the minutiae of scholarship. Anna was seemingly not opposed to the study in itself, but rather to its over-elaboration.

32. A lacuna in the text here.

33. Anna is of course speaking metaphorically.

things more spiritual. (For he was in everything superior to all his contemporaries: as a teacher he surpassed the educational experts, as a soldier and a general he excelled the professionals who were most admired.) The fame of the Bogomils had by now spread to all parts, for the impious sect was controlled with great cunning by a certain monk called Basil. He had twelve followers whom he called 'apostles' and also dragged along with him certain female disciples, women of bad character, utterly depraved. In all quarters he made his wicked influence felt and when the evil, like some consuming fire, devoured many souls, the emperor could no longer bear it. He instituted a thorough inquiry into the heresy. Some of the Bogomils were brought to the palace; without exception they denounced as their master, the protagonist of their heresy, a certain Basil. One of them, Diblatius, was imprisoned. Since under interrogation he was unwilling to confess, he was subjected to torture. He then admitted that Basil was the leader and he named the 'apostles' whom Basil had chosen. Several men were accordingly given the task of finding him. Basil, Archisatrap of Satanael, was brought to light, dressed in monkish garb, austere of face, with a thin beard, very tall. At once the emperor, wishing to discover from him the man's innermost thoughts, tried compulsion, but with a show of persuasion: he invited him to the palace on some righteous pretext. He even rose from his seat when Basil came in, made him sit with him and share his own table. The whole line was run out for the catch, with all kinds of tempting bait on the hooks for this voracious monster to swallow; the monk, so practised in villainy, was by every means urged to gulp down the whole treacherous offering. Alexius feigned a desire to become his disciple and maybe he was not alone in this: his brother, the Sebastocrator Isaac, also led Basil on. Alexius pretended to regard all his sayings as some divine oracle and gave way to every argument; his one hope, he said, was that the wretched Basil would effect his soul's salvation. 'I, too, most reverend father,' said he (for he smeared the cup's rim with honey-sweetness, so that the other in his lunacy might vomit forth his dark beliefs), 'I too admire you for your virtue.

497

I pray you make me understand in some degree the doctrines that Your Honour teaches, for those of our Church are all but worthless, in no way conducive to virtue.' At first Basil was coy; he wrapped close about him the lion's skin – he who was in reality an ass – and at the emperor's words shied away. Nevertheless he was filled with conceit by Alexius' praises – he had even invited Basil to share his meal. At all times Isaac was at his brother's side, play-acting with him. Finally Basil did vomit forth the Bogomil doctrine. It happened thus: a curtain divided the women's quarters from the room where the brothers were, as this loathsome creature belched out and plainly declared all his heart's secrets; meanwhile a secretary behind the curtain recorded what was said. The fool, to all appearances, was the teacher, while the emperor played the part of learner and the lesson was committed to writing by the secretary. The accursed fellow strung everything together, lawful and unlawful alike; no jot of his blasphemous doctrine was held back. Worse than that, he looked askance at our doctrine of the Divine Nature of Christ and wholly misinterpreted His human nature. He even went so far as to call the holy churches the temples of demons and treated as of little importance what among us is believed to be the consecrated Body and Blood of our first High Priest and Sacrifice. The reader will wish to know the sequel to this. Well, the emperor threw off his pretence and drew back the curtain. Then a conference was summoned of all the senate, the chief army commanders and the elders of the Church.[34] The hateful teachings of the Bogomil were read aloud. The proof was incontestable. Indeed, the accused made no attempt to dispute the charge, but at once proceeded without a blush to counter-attack, promising that he was ready to undergo fire and scourgings, to die a thousand deaths. These misguided Bogomils are persuaded, you see, that they can endure any punishment without feeling pain, for angels (they think) will pluck them from the funeral pyre itself. And although all threatened

34. The episcopal throne of Constantinople was at that time occupied by the Lord Nicolas Grammaticus, most blessed of patriarchs. (A.C.)
Nicolas III Kyrdiniates Grammaticus was patriarch from 1084 to 1111.

him and reproached him for his irreverence – even those who had shared in his ruin – he was still the same Basil, inexorable, a true Bogomil. Despite the burning and other tortures held over him, he clung with all his might to his devil, holding fast to his Satanael. He was sent to prison. Many times Alexius sent for him, many times called upon him to abjure his wickedness; but to all the emperor's pleadings he remained as deaf as ever. I must now relate the extraordinary thing which happened to this Basil before the emperor had begun to take sterner measures against him. After he had confessed his impiety, he retired temporarily to a small house newly built for him quite near the imperial palace. It was the evening after the meeting of the Synod; the stars above were shining in a cloudless sky and the moon was bright. When about midnight the monk had entered his cell, stones were thrown against it in the manner of a hailstorm. Now the stones fell automatically: they were hurled by no hand and no man was to be seen stoning this devilish abbot. Seemingly it was an act of vengeance   Satanael's demons were wrathful, outraged no doubt at the betrayal of their secrets to the emperor and the notable persecution of their heresy which followed it. Parasceviotes, the appointed guard of the diabolical old man (Basil), whose duty it was to prevent him talking with others and contaminating them with his own filth, swore with the most frightful oaths that he had heard the clatter of the stones as they were hurled on the ground and on the roof-tiles; he had seen them falling in thick showers, one after another; but he had no glimpse anywhere of a thrower. The fall of stones was followed by a sudden earthquake which rocked the ground and the roof-tiles had rattled. Nevertheless Parasceviotes, before he realized that this was devils' work, had (according to his story) been unafraid; but when he saw that the stones were raining down, as it were, from heaven and that the wretched old heresiarch had slunk inside and closed the door behind him, he decided that this was indeed the doing of demons and knew not what to make of it.

I will say no more about that miracle. It was my intention to expound the whole Bogomilian heresy, but 'modesty', as

the lovely Sappho[35] somewhere remarks, 'forbids me';
historian I may be, but I am also a woman, born in the
Porphyra, most honoured and first-born of Alexius' children;
what was common hearsay had better be passed over in
silence. Despite my desire to give a full account, I cannot – for
if I did my tongue would be sullied. However, those who
would like to know all are referred to the so-called *Dogmatic
Panoply*, a book compiled on my father's orders. He sent for a
monk named Zygabenus,[36] known to my grandmother on the
maternal side and to all the clergy, who had a great reputation
as a grammarian, was not unversed in rhetoric and had an unrivalled knowledge of dogma. Zygabenus was commanded to
publish a list of all heresies, to deal with each separately and
append in each case the refutation of it in the texts of the holy
fathers. The Bogomilian heresy was included, just as the
impious Basil had interpreted it. This book Alexius named the
Dogmatic Panoply and the volumes are so called to this day.
But we must return to Basil's downfall. From all over the
world the emperor summoned Basil's disciples and fellow-
mystics, in particular the 'twelve apostles'; their opinions were
tested and their loyalty to Basil was unimpeachable. In fact
the evil had deep roots: it had penetrated even the greatest
houses and enormous numbers were affected by this terrible
thing. Alexius condemned the heretics out of hand: chorus
and chorus-leader alike were to suffer death by burning. When

35. *Sappho, fr.* 137 (Lobel and Page ed.).
36. Euthymius Zygabenus outlived the emperor, but not much is
known of his career. He wrote extensively on religious topics: apart from
the *Panoplia*, he left commentaries on the Psalms of David and four Gospels
which are considered to be of real value. His assault on the Bogomils is
especially virulent: they were dualists; they held that the world was created
by Satanael, who will eventually be destroyed by God; their views on
the Incarnation were unorthodox; they rejected the Eucharist; they
scorned the churches as the habitation of demons; they were anti-social,
living apart from ordinary folk in a closed community; they were immoral
and performed mystic dances; they practised extreme asceticism (at least
those who claimed to be 'perfect' did so). The sect troubled Byzantium
from the tenth to the fourteenth century. Unfortunately (since 'the
winners write history') we have no Bogomil answer to these charges:
their literature was destroyed. The name Bogomil, by the way, is said to
be derived from the Slavonic *Bog* (God) and *milovi* (have pity) or *mile* (friend).

the Bogomils had been hunted down and brought together in one place, some clung to their heresy, but others denied the charges completely, protesting strongly against their accusers and rejecting the Bogomilian heresy with scorn. The emperor was not inclined to believe them and to prevent possible errors of identification he devised a novel scheme, making sure that real Christians should not be destroyed. (There was a chance that Christians might be confused with Bogomils and a Bogomil might be mistaken for a Christian and so escape.) On the next day he took his seat on the imperial throne. Many of the senators were present on this occasion, together with members of the Holy Synod and certain picked Naziraeans [37] noted for their learning. All those prosecuted for their Bogomilian beliefs were made to stand trial before this assembly; Alexius ordered them to be examined for a second time, one by one. Some admitted that they were Bogomils and vigorously clung to their heresy; others absolutely denied this and called themselves Christians. When they were challenged, they retracted nothing. The emperor glared at them and said, 'Two pyres will have to be lit today. By one a cross will be planted firmly in the ground. Then a choice will be offered to all: those who are prepared to die for their Christian faith will separate themselves from the rest and take up position by the pyre with the cross; the Bogomilian adherents will be thrown on the other. Surely it is better that even Christians should die than live to be hounded down as Bogomils and offend the conscience of the majority. Go away, then, all of you, to whichever pyre you choose.' This declaration to the Bogomils seemingly closed the case. Accordingly they were seized and led away at once. A huge crowd gathered and stood all about them. Fires were then lit, burning seven times more fiercely than usual (as the lyric poet says) [38] in the place called Tzykani-sterin. [39] The flames leapt to the heavens. By one pyre stood

37. Anna refers to monks. The name is derived from Hebrew *nazir* ('separate').

38. The words are quoted from Daniel iii, 19 (a prose writer). But the hymn writer Cosmas uses the same expression in verse when describing the fate of the Three Children of Babylon.

39. The palace polo-ground.

the cross. Each of the condemned was given his choice, for all were to be burnt. Now that escape was clearly impossible, the orthodox to a man moved over to the pyre with the cross, truly prepared to suffer martyrdom; the godless adherents of the abominable heresy went off to the other. Just as they were about to be thrown on the flames, all the bystanders broke into mourning for the Christians; they were filled with indignation against the emperor (they did not know of his plan). But an order came from him just in time to stop the executioners. Alexius had in this way obtained firm evidence of those who were really Bogomils. The Christians, who were victims of calumny, he released after giving them much advice; the rest were committed once again to prison, but the 'apostles' were kept apart. Later he sent for some of these men every day and personally taught them, with frequent exhortations to abandon their abominable cult. Certain church leaders were told to make daily visits to the rest, to instruct them in the orthodox faith and advise them to give up their heretical ideas. And some did change for the better and were freed from prison, but others died in their heresy, still incarcerated, although they were supplied with plentiful food and clothing.

As for Basil, since he was their leader and showed no sign whatever of remorse, the members of the Holy Synod, the chief monks, as well as the patriarch of that time (Nicolas) unanimously decided that he must be burnt. The emperor, who had interviewed the man at length on many occasions, cast his vote for the same verdict. He had recognized Basil's perversity and knew that his attachment to the heresy was permanent. So a huge fire was kindled in the Hippodrome. An enormous trench had been dug and a mass of logs, every one a tall tree, had piled up to a mountainous height. Then the pyre was lit and a great multitude of people quietly collected on the floor of the arena and on the steps; everybody waited impatiently to see what would happen. On the other side a cross had been set up and the godless fellow was given an opportunity to recant: if by some chance through dread of the fire he changed his mind and walked over to the cross, he

could still escape the burning. I must add that the Bogomils
were there in force, watching their leader Basil. Far from giving
way, it was obvious that he despised all punishment and
threats, and while he was still some distance from the flames
he laughed at them and boasted that angels would rescue him
from the midst of the fire. He quoted David, softly chanting,
'It shall not come nigh thee; only with thine eyes shalt thou
behold.' [40] But when the crowd stood aside and let him see
clearly that awe-inspiring sight (for even afar off he could feel
the fire and saw the flames rising and shooting out fiery sparks
with a noise like thunder, sparks which leapt high in the air
to the top of the stone obelisk which stands in the centre of
the Hippodrome), then for all his boldness he seemed to
flinch before the pyre. He was plainly troubled. Like a man at
his wits' end he darted his eyes now here, now there, struck
his hands together and beat his thighs. And yet, affected
though he was at the mere sight of it, he was still hard as steel;
his iron will was not softened by the fire, nor did the messages
sent by the emperor break his resolve. Maybe in this hour of
supreme need and misfortune a great madness possessed him,
so that he lost his mind and was utterly unable to decide what
was best for him; or perhaps – and this was more likely – the
devil that possessed his soul had shed about him a profound
darkness. There he stood, despicable, helpless before every
threat, every terror, gaping now at the pyre, now at the
spectators. Everyone thought he was quite mad, for he
neither rushed to the flames, nor did he altogether turn back,
but stayed rooted to the spot where he had first entered the
arena, motionless. Now there was much talk going on, as
everyone repeated the marvellous prophecies he had made,
and the public executioners were afraid lest somehow the
demons that protected Basil might perform some extraordinary miracle (with the permission of God) – the scoundrel
might be seen in some public place, where many people met,
coming unscathed from the midst of this tremendous fire;
thus the last error might be worse than the first. So they
decided to put him to the test. While he was talking marvels

40. Psalm 91, 7 8.

and boasting that he would be seen unharmed in the midst of
the flames, they took his woollen cloak and said, 'Let's see
if the fire will catch your clothes!' And straightway they
hurled it into the centre of the pyre. So confident was Basil in
the demon that was deluding him that he cried, 'Look! My
cloak flies up to the sky!' They saw that this was the decisive
moment,[41] lifted him up and thrust him, clothes, shoes and all,
into the fire. The flames, as if in rage against him, so thoroughly
devoured the wretch that there was no odour and nothing unusual in the smoke except one thin smoky line in the centre of
the flame. For even the elements are stirred against the wicked,
but they truly spare those who are dear to God, just as once
they yielded to those young men in Babylon [42] and submitted
to them because they were loved of God; and the fire enveloped them like some golden shrine. But on this occasion
the executioners who lifted Basil up in their arms were barely
poised for the throw when the flame seemed to leap forward
and snatch him. The crowd standing by was excited, struggling
to throw on the fire all the rest of Basil's pernicious sect, but
the emperor would not allow them. On his orders the Bogomils were kept in custody in the porticoes and colonnades of
the Great Palace. The spectators then dispersed. Later these
atheists were transferred to a prison of maximum security and
after languishing there for a long time died in their wickedness. With this act, then, this final triumph, ends the long
series of the emperor's travails and exploits. It had been a
reign of surprising boldness and novelty. I should imagine
that men who were alive then and who associated with him
must still be amazed at what was accomplished in those days.
To them it must seem unreal, like a dream or a vision. The
barbarians had gone unchecked, from the time when they

41. Anna quotes a Byzantine proverb ,'The cloak is known by its hem',
which is roughly equivalent to the Roman *ex pede Herculem* (our 'police-
men's boots'). Here it might perhaps be translated by 'the turn of the tide',
'a change of wind'; the point is that the executioners saw that Basil's
sympathizers were wavering; the crowd no longer feared his guardian
demons; there was a change of heart as they recognized him for what he
was, a charlatan and a liar. It was a decisive moment.
42. Shadrach, Meshach and Abednego.

x–xi   BOOK FIFTEEN

invaded the Empire soon after Diogenes' elevation to the
throne and his eastern campaign (which was ill-starred from
the very beginning) right down to my father's reign. Swords
and spears had been sharpened against the Christians; there
had been battles and wars and massacres. Cities were wiped
out, lands ravaged, all the territories of Rome stained with
Christian blood. Some died miserably, pierced by arrow or
lance; others were driven from their homes and carried off as
prisoners-of-war to Persian cities. Dread seized on all as they
hurried to seek refuge from impending disaster in caves,
forests, mountains and hills. There they loudly bewailed the
fate of their friends in Persia; the few others who survived in
Roman lands mourned the loss of sons or grieved for their
daughters; one wept for a brother, another for a nephew
killed before his time and like women they shed bitter tears.
In those days no walk of life was spared its tears and lamentation. Apart from a few emperors (Tzimisces, for example,
and Basil) none from that period [43] to my father's reign even
dared to set foot at all in Asia.

But why am I writing of these things? I perceive that I am
digressing from the main theme, because the subject of my
history imposes on me a two-fold duty: to relate the facts of the
emperor's life and also to expose their tragic nature. In other
words, I have to give an account of his struggles and at the
same time to do justice to all that has caused me heart-felt
sorrow. Among the latter I would count his death and the
destruction of all that I found worthwhile on earth. Yet I
remember certain remarks made by my father which discouraged me from writing history, inviting me rather to compose elegies and dirges. For I often heard him speak thus; I
even heard him once reprove the empress when she was
ordering scholars to write a history of his labours, his many
trials and tribulations, so that the record of them might be
handed down to future generations; it would be better, he

43. John I Tzimisces (969–76) and Basil II (976–1025) died long before
Romanus IV Diogenes departed for the campaign which ended at Manzikert. 'That period' is probably used loosely; she refers roughly to the
two preceding centuries.

said, to grieve for him and deplore his miseries. Less than eighteen months after his return from the Turkish campaign, he was struck down by a second terrible illness. It threatened his life; in fact it was the cause of his utter collapse and destruction. Now I have always, from my earliest years, dearly loved my father and mother, and this illness is a subject of great importance which compels me to transgress the laws of history; I am going to do, therefore, what I would certainly prefer not to do: namely, to tell the story of the emperor's death.

There had been a race-meeting, and as a result of the strong wind which was blowing at the time the humours subsided, as it were, left his extremities and settled in one of his shoulders. Most of the doctors had no idea at all of the danger with which we were threatened. But Nicolas Kallicles (for that was his name) predicted fearful troubles; he told us that he was afraid the humours, having abandoned the extremities, might move in some other direction and so endanger the patient's life. We could not believe him – because we did not wish to. At that time no one, apart from Kallicles, had dreamed of purifying his system by the use of cathartics. Alexius was not accustomed to taking purgatives; indeed, he was a total stranger to drugs. For this reason most of them (and in particular Michael Pantechnes, who was assisting them) absolutely forbade any recourse to purgatives. Kallicles foresaw what would happen and told them emphatically, 'For the time being the matter has left the extremities and attacked the shoulder and neck, but if we do not get rid of it by purging, it will move again, to some vital organ, or even to the heart itself. If that happens, the damage will be irremediable.' On the orders of the empress I was present myself at this conference, in order to act as arbiter; I heard the doctors' arguments and I personally supported the views of Kallicles; however, we were outvoted by the others. Actually on this occasion the humours, having afflicted the emperor's body for the usual number of days, gradually disappeared and the sick man recovered his health. Before six months had passed, he was assailed by a mortal sickness, probably brought on by anxiety: he was greatly affected by the pressure of daily business and the many cares of government. I often heard him telling the empress about it; in a way he was accusing the disease. 'What on earth is this trouble that affects my breathing? I want to take a deep, full breath and be rid of this anxiety that troubles me, but however often I try I can't lift even once a small fraction of the load that oppresses me. For the rest it's like a dead-weight of stone lying on my heart and cutting short my breathing. I can't understand the reason for it, nor why such pain afflicts me. And there's something else I must tell you, darling, for you share my troubles and plans: I often have fits of yawning which interrupt my breathing when I inhale and cause me awful pain. If you have any idea what this new trouble is, please tell me.' When the empress heard these words and understood what he was suffering, she was very upset; one would think that she participated in the same illness, the same asthmatic condition. She frequently summoned the best physicians and made them examine closely the nature of the disease; she begged to be told the immediate and indirect causes of it. They felt his pulse and admitted that they found in every movement evidence of all kinds of irregularities, but they were altogether unable to give a reason for this. They knew that the emperor's diet was not rich; it was indeed extremely moderate and frugal, the sort of food athletes or soldiers have, so that the question of an accumulation of humours from too rich a diet was ruled out; they attributed the difficulty in breathing to some other cause and said the main reason for his illness was overwork and the constant pressure of his worries. His heart, they said, was consequently inflamed and was attracting all the superfluous matter from the rest of his body. After this the terrible malady gave him no respite at all: it was throttling him like a halter. Every day it grew worse, attacking him no longer at intervals, but relentlessly, with no interruption. He was unable to lie on either side, so weak that every breath involved great effort. All the doctors were called to discuss his case, but they were divided in their opinions and argued; each one produced his own diagnosis with its appropriate treatment. Whatever solution was offered, his condition was serious, for never for

one moment could he breathe freely. He was forced to sit upright in order to breathe at all; if by chance he did lie on his
back or side, the suffocation was awful: to breathe in or exhale
even a tiny stream of air became impossible. When sleep in
pity overcame him, there was a danger of asphyxia, so that at
all times, asleep or awake, he was menaced by suffocation.
As purgatives were not allowed, the doctors tried phlebotomy
and made an incision at the elbow, but that also proved fruit-
less. He was just as breathless as before and there was a constant danger that he might expire in our arms. However, there
was an improvement after a pepper antidote was given. We
did not know how to contain ourselves for joy, but we offered
up prayers of thanksgiving to God. Nevertheless it was all a
delusion, for on the third or fourth day the old breathlessness
recurred, the same trouble with his lungs. I wonder if that
particular medicine did not in fact make him worse, for it
dispersed but could not control the humours; they were
driven into the cavities of the arteries and his condition
deteriorated. As a result of that, it was quite beyond our power
to find any way of making him lie down comfortably. The
disease was now at its peak: all night long, from dusk to
dawn, the emperor had no sleep; he was unable to take
nourishment properly; it was impossible to give him medicines
or other relief. I have often seen my mother spending the
whole night with him (more accurately, several consecutive
nights), seated behind him on his couch, holding him up in her
arms, encouraging him somehow to breathe. Yet she wept
copiously [44] and the care she lavished on him through whole
days and nights was indescribable; nobody could do justice
to the hard work she endured as she nursed him, changing his
position again and again, arranging and re-arranging the bed-
covers to make him comfortable. But nothing whatever
availed to give him the slightest ease; the malady tightened on
him like a noose, or rather it was his constant companion,
endlessly stifling. There was no remedy for it, so the emperor
moved to the part of the palace which faced south; oppressed
as he was, the one comfort he enjoyed was derived from move-

44. Tears more copious than the waters of the Nile. (A.C.)

ment. The empress made sure that he should have it continually, for at the head and foot of his couch she had wooden legs fitted and gave porters the job of carrying him round on it in relays. Later he was transferred to Mangana from the Great Palace. Even these precautions made no difference: there was no change for the better. When she saw that the disease was gaining ground, she despaired of all human aid. More fervently than ever she addressed her prayers to God on his behalf, had numberless candles lit at every shrine and hymns chanted without pause or intermission. She gave largess to people dwelling in every land, by every sea. All hermits living in caves or on mountains or leading their lives in solitude elsewhere were urged to make long supplications; and all those who were sick or confined in prisons and worn out with suffering were enriched by her gifts and then called upon to make intercession together for the emperor. But when his stomach was visibly enlarged to a great size and his feet also swelled up and fever laid him low, some of the doctors, with scant regard for the fever, had recourse to cauterization. Here again all attempts to cure him were vain and useless; he got no help from the cautery, for both stomach and respiratory organs were in as bad a condition as ever. The humours, as if they issued from some other source, now made their way to his uvula and seized on what the medical men [45] call the palate; his gums became swollen, his larynx congested, his tongue inflamed; the oesophagus was constricted and blocked at the end and we were now faced with the terrifying prospect of complete starvation. God knows that I took great trouble over the preparation of his food; every day I brought it to him personally and made certain that it was in an easily digested form. Anyway, every attempt to cure the inflamed tumours seemed . . .[46] whatever we and the physicians tried proved to be in vain. Eleven days passed while the disease was in its final

45. Asclepiadae, followers of Asclepius, god of medicine.
46. The text hereafter is seriously corrupted. The lacunae are not intentional, nor are they meant to convey the impression of overwhelming grief; the reason for them is merely to be found in the mutilated condition of our extant MSS.

stage; it was at its zenith and already threatening his life . . .
his condition was dangerous and diarrhoea came on. Thus at
this moment troubles one after another fell upon us. Neither
the doctors nor we who were tending him knew which way to
turn . . . but everything portended disaster. After that our
affairs were thrown into confusion and chaos; our normal
habits were disturbed; fear and danger hung over our heads.
Even in the midst of these immediate perils the Augusta's
courage never wavered and it was especially at this crisis that
she displayed her brave spirit: controlling her own bitter grief
she stood firm, like some Olympic victor, wrestling with the
cruellest pangs. She was wounded in spirit and heart-broken
as she saw him thus, but still pulled herself together and endured her sufferings; mortally wounded and pierced to the
soul by her agony, she still refused to give up. And yet the
tears flowed freely and the beauty of her face was marred; her
soul hung by a thread. It was the fifteenth day of August, a
Thursday, the day on which the Dormition of Our Lady, the
Immaculate Mother of God, is celebrated; early that morning
some of the doctors had anointed the emperor's head (they
thought it was good to do so) and they went home. It was no
hasty decision, nor was it due to any pressing need, but they
realized that the end was near. There were three principal
doctors, the admirable Nicolas Kallicles, Michael Pantechnes
(who got his surname [47] from his family) and . . . Michael the
eunuch. The whole band of relatives crowded round the
empress and forced her to take food . . . she had not slept . . .
spent several successive nights . . . in attendance on the
emperor . . . she obeyed. When the last fainting fit came on,
she again . . . having waited anxiously she perceived the . . .
life; she threw herself on the . . . began a continuous wail and
beat her breast and lamented the evils that had befallen. She
wished to breathe her last there and then, but could not. Then,
although he was on the point of death and racked by overwhelming pain, the emperor like one who masters his own
mortality . . . was distressed because of her and tried with one
of his daughters to lessen her anguish. (It was Porphyrogenita

47. Pantechnes ('wholly skilled') might have been a nickname.

Eudocia, [48] his third daughter.) The other daughter, Mary, [49] unlike that other Mary who once sat at the feet of My Lord, was busily engaged by Alexius' head, giving him water to drink from a large goblet (not from a cup – he might find it difficult to manage that) as his palate, and indeed his tongue and larynx too, were all inflamed. She was anxious to refresh him. Then in a firm, manly voice he gave the empress some advice – his last counsel: 'Why,' he said, 'why do you give yourself up so to grief at my death and force us to anticipate the end that rapidly approaches? Instead of surrendering yourself to the flood of woe that has come upon you, why not consider your own position and the dangers that now threaten you?' Such were his words, but they only reopened her wound. As for myself, I did all I could; to my friends still living and to men who in the future will read this history I swear by God who knows all things that I was no better than a mad woman, wholly wrapped up in my sorrow. I scorned philosophy and reason then, for I was busy looking after my father, carefully observing his pulse and respiration; then I would turn to my mother and comfort her as best I could. But . . . parts completely incurable . . . the emperor had fainted and we could not bring him round; the Augusta was on the verge of fainting too. They were in this condition . . . and the words of the Psalmist [50] were true indeed: 'The pains of death encompassed us.' I knew then that I had lost my mind . . . for I was mad; I did not know what was to become of me, nor where to turn. I saw the empress plunged into a sea of troubles and the emperor, lapsing into unconsciousness again and again, was being driven on to his life's end. But when my beloved sister Mary sprinkled cold water and essence of roses on him, he recovered consciousness again and bade her do the same for her mother. Then for the third time he fainted . . . it seemed a good idea to move his couch . . . those who attended him and

48. She married, but later separated from her husband and became a nun.
49. Maria (or Mary) married Nicephorus, son of Constantine Euphorbenus Catacalon.
50. Psalm 18, 4. 'The sorrows of death compassed me; the floods of ungodly men made me afraid.'

. . . we moved him to another part of the five-storeyed building, so that he might breathe fresher air and come to again (that part faced the north and there were no houses . . . to the doors). The emperor's heir [51] had already gone away to the house set apart for him, when he realized the emperor's . . . he hastened his departure and went off quickly to the Great Palace. The city was at the time . . . in a state of confusion, but there was no absolute chaos [46] . . . The empress in her wild grief said, 'Let everything be abandoned . . . the diadem, empire, authority, all power, and thrones and principalities. Let us begin the funeral dirge.' And I, heedless of all else, wailed with her and joined her in the lament . . . they tore at their hair with shrill cries of woe. But we brought her to her senses, for he was at his last gasp; he was in his 'death-struggle'. The empress had thrown herself on the ground by his head, still clothed in . . . and the purple-dyed slippers . . . deeply touched and unable to . . . the burning sorrow of her soul. Some of the medical men returned and after waiting a little felt his pulse . . . then the beating of his heart . . . nevertheless they spoke in vague terms of 'the crisis' . . . and despite appearances held out hopes of recovery. They did this deliberately, knowing that with the emperor's passing she too would die. Irene, who was an intelligent woman, did not know whether to believe or disbelieve them: she had long regarded them as expert physicians; on the other hand, she saw clearly that the emperor's life hung in the balance. She suspended judgement and kept looking at me, waiting for me to play the part of oracle (she had been wont to do that in other crises). I was expected to make some Phoebus-like prediction. Mary [52] was standing between her and the emperor; the sleeve of her robe from time to time made it impossible for Irene to look straight at him. I again held his wrist in my right hand and took his pulse . . . her putting her hands often to her head . . . the veil,

51. His son John, the future emperor. The details are to be found in Zonaras and Nicetas Choniates. The story they tell is quite different from Anna's.

52. Maria, my sovereign and dearest of my sisters, the glory of our family, steadfast, bulwark of every virtue. (A.C.)

for under the circumstances she intended to change her dress,
but I checked her every time I felt some strength in his pulse. I
was deceived . . . for apparently it was quite feeble . . . but
when the great effort of breathing . . . the working of artery
and lung ceased to function at the same time. I released the
emperor's hand and . . . to the empress . . . I again held his
wrist . . . asphyxia. She kept nudging me, urging me to tell
her about the pulse, but when . . . I touched it again and
recognized that all his strength was going and the circulation
of blood in the arteries had finally stopped, then I turned away,
exhausted and cold, my head bowed and both hands covering
my eyes. Without a word I stepped back and began to weep.
She understood what had happened. Suddenly in the depths of
her despair she emitted a loud, piercing shriek. But how can I
possibly describe the catastrophe which had overtaken the
whole world? How can I bewail my own troubles? She laid
aside her empress's veil and with a razor cut off her lovely hair
close to the skin. She threw away the purple-dyed shoes she
was wearing and asked for ordinary black sandals. But when
she wanted to exchange her purple dress for a black one, no
garment of that kind could readily be found. However, my
third sister had clothes appropriate to the occasion (she had
long before suffered widowhood herself) and the empress
accepted these and wore them. She put a simple dark veil on
her head. Meanwhile the emperor surrendered to God his
holy soul, and my sun went down . . . those who were not
overcome by their grief sang dirges, beat their breasts, raised
their voices to heaven in woeful cries . . . their benefactor who
had . . . all for them . . . weeping. Even now I cannot believe
that I am still alive and writing this account of the emperor's
death. I put my hands to my eyes, wondering if what I am
relating here is not all a dream – or maybe it is not a dream:
perhaps it is a delusion and I am mad, the victim of some
extraordinary and monstrous hallucination. How comes it that
when he is dead I am still numbered among the living? . . .
Why did I not surrender my soul too and die with him? Why
did I not lapse into unconsciousness and perish? If that could
not be, why did I not cast myself down from some high place

or throw myself into the waves of the sea? My life with its great misfortunes . . . I have recorded, but as the tragic playwright says, 'There is no suffering, no disaster sent from heaven the burden of which I could not bear.'[53] For God has indeed visited me with great calamities: I lost the shining light of the world, the great Alexius (and surely his soul was master of his poor tortured body); then there was extinguished another glorious light (or shall I rather call her the moon that brings light to all?), the pride, in name and deed, of East and West, the Empress Irene. And yet we live on, we still breathe the air of life. After that evils multiplied and we were assailed by mighty storms. Finally, the climax of all our woes, we have been forced to witness the death of the Caesar. (So tragic were the events for which we were preserved.) After a few days the evil got the upper hand and the doctors' skill failed, and I plunged into an ocean of despair; finally, only one thing irked me – that my soul still lingered on in my body. It seems to me that if I had not been made of steel, or fashioned from some other hard, tough substance . . . a stranger to myself, I would have perished at once. But living I died a thousand deaths. There is a marvellous story told of the famous Niobe [54] . . . changed to stone through her sorrow . . . . Then even after the transformation to a substance which cannot feel, her grief was still immortal. Yet I am more grief-stricken than she: after my misfortunes, great and terrible as they are, I am still alive – thus I shall experience others. Of a truth it would have been better to be metamorphosed into some unfeeling rock . . . with shedding of tears . . . I remained . . . being so insensitive to disaster . . . . To endure such dangers and to be treated in an abominable way by people in the palace is more wretched than the troubles of Niobe . . . the evil having gone so far . . . ceased thus. After the death of both rulers, the loss of the Caesar [55] and the grief caused by these events would have

53. Euripides, at the beginning of the *Orestes*.

54. Niobe was turned to stone by Zeus, according to Homer. Pausanias tells us that in his days the stone was to be seen on Mount Sipylon; it resembled a woman in some way and 'wept'.

55. Nicephorus Bryennius died in (certainly not before) 1137. The 'two rulers' (Alexius and Irene) died on 15–16 August 1118 and in 1123

sufficed to wear me out, body and soul, but now, like rivers flowing down from high mountains . . . the streams of adversity . . . united in one torrent flood my house. Let this be the end of my history, then, lest as I write of these sad events I become more embittered.

---

respectively. One could hardly regard three such bereavements in the course of some twenty years as a crushing blow. We know, moreover, that the last books of the *Alexiad* were being written thirty years after the emperor's death, when Anna must have been sixty-four years old at least. Why then her extreme bitterness in this final chapter? She had suffered disappointments: her betrothal to the young Constantine, heir-presumptive to the throne at one time, led her to believe that she might herself become empress; he died before they could be married; then again the prospects of her husband Bryennius were by no means negligible, but despite the strenuous efforts of Irene and herself to persuade the emperor on his death-bed to leave him the crown, John became emperor. Clearly there was some animosity between Anna and her brother. It seems that there was a plot, engineered by Irene and herself, to dethrone him; it failed and they found themselves disgraced and in exile. Anna herself was kept apparently under some surveillance thereafter – hence her misery. Like Psellus, who had an irritating habit of concealing names and events, Anna has left much unsaid. The historians who wrote later fill many of the gaps, but they were enthusiastic admirers of John and may have been no more impartial than she was.

APPENDIX I: GREEK FIRE

INCENDIARIES of various kinds had been used in warfare long before the time of Herodotos and these devices were duly recorded by historians. On the whole they were not very effective. The first appearance of Greek fire, however, was comparable in its demoralizing influence to the advent of the atomic bomb, at least in the limited area of Byzantine action. Both Byzantines and Arabs agree that it surpassed all other incendiary weapons in destruction and terror. It is said to have been invented by one Callinicus, a refugee from Baalbek, A.D. c. 673. His fire-ships, equipped with siphons, routed the Arabs and saved Constantinople. Thereafter it remained a closely guarded secret, so far as the composition of the fuel was concerned: liquid petroleum, naphtha, burning pitch, sulphur, pitch, resin, quicklime, bitumen have all been mentioned, together with 'some secret ingredient' (to quote J. R. Partington, whose *History of Greek Fire and Gunpowder* constitutes the best and most up-to-date examination of the whole problem). Anna's account is perhaps the most enlightening that we have, but the formula is still shrouded in mystery. Partington concludes that the Fire was 'an achievement of chemical engineering' and his work – a mine of information with extensive quotations from authorities ancient and modern and numberless references – bears witness to the confusion and contradictions of scholars.

APPENDIX II: THE BYZANTINE NAVY

THE reader will quickly realize that Anna does less than justice to her father's naval triumphs – partly, no doubt, because Alexius himself was not commanding at sea; partly because Byzantium relied on the help of Venice. Rome, both Ancient and New, took to the sea only through compulsion and one can sense a slightly derogatory tone in Anna's descriptions of naval manoeuvres: it was on land that her hero won his campaigns. Yet Alexius did much to repair the neglect of a hundred years. The imperial navy was under him united with the fleets from the provinces and the whole force was now commanded by a Grand Admiral and the Great Drungarius. Unfortunately there were too many mercenaries among the crews.

The variety of ships mentioned in the *Alexiad* is most striking: monoremes, biremes, triremes, corsairs, dromons (a generic term for warships), galleys (including one set apart for the use of empresses), merchantmen of heavy tonnage, cargo vessels, horse-transports, skiffs, dinghies, *sermones* (the exact nature of which eludes us, but they were probably fast, small craft), rowing boats, scout-ships, tiny boats for use on river or lake, fire-ships with flame-throwing apparatus and the vessel reserved for the 'Second Count' and called by the sailors *excoussaton*. The latter may refer to a ship immune from tax (the Latin *excusatum*) but there is no general agreement on that derivation.

APPENDIX III: TITLES

DURING the course of the eleventh century the relative importance of certain titles changed: in Psellus' *Chronographia* the Caesar, the Nobilissimus, the Parakoimomenus and the Orphanotrophus are persons of great consequence; there is no mention of the Domestics, the Secretici, the Catepans; but by Anna's time even the Caesar and Nobilissimus had lost some of their lustre and the rest of the old honours had, like the *nomisma*, depreciated in value. To the delight and admiration of his daughter Alexius found it necessary to invent new titles. For his brother Isaac he combined the old *sebastos* and *autocrator* (originally reserved for the emperor himself): Isaac became known as the *sebastocrator*. Meanwhile the rank of Caesar was granted to the pretender Nicephorus Melissenus. Deserving individuals were rewarded with an extraordinary range of new, high-sounding titles: *protopansebastohypertatus, protopanentimohypertatus, protonobilissimohypertatus* and so on. Those who are interested in such things can pursue the subject in *CMH* Vol. IV, Part II, pp. 18 ff.; or in Ostrogorsky, pp. 325–6. Titles were even granted to foreigners: we read of twenty honorary titles, together with their appropriate pensions, being given to Germans; the Venetian Doge became a *protosebastos*, while his patriarch received the title of *hypertimos*. Even a Turk was made Duke of Anchialus and although Bohemond was denied the Domesticate of the East which he asked for, he also became a *sebastos*. Anna emphasizes her father's generosity in such matters; no doubt the harmless sop to human vanity did in many cases achieve its purpose.

BYZANTINE RULERS

This list includes names mentioned in the *Alexiad* and is intended merely to help the reader.

Constantine VII	913–59
Romanus II	959–63
Nicephorus II Phocas	963–9
John I Tzimisces	969–76
Basil II Bulgaroktonos	976–1025
Constantine VIII	1025–8
Romanus III Argyrus	1028–34
Michael IV Paphlagon	1034–41
Michael V Calaphates	1041–2
Theodora and Zoe	1042
Constantine IX Monomachus	1042–55
Theodora (for a second time)	1055–6
Michael VI Stratioticus	1056–7
Isaac I Comnenus	1057–9
Constantine X Ducas	1059–67
Eudocia	1067
Romanus IV Diogenes	1068–71
Eudocia (for a second Time)	1071
Michael VII Ducas	1071–8
Nicephorus III Botaniates	1078–81
Alexius I Comnenus	1081–1118
John II Comnenus	1118–43
Manuel I Comnenus	1143–80

Popes of Rome

The following occupied the throne of St Peter during the period covered by the *Alexiad*:

Gregory VII	1073–85
Victor III	1086–7
Urban II	1088–99
Paschal II	1099–1118

Patriarchs of Constantinople

Cosmas I	1075–81
Eustratius Garidas	1081–4
Nicolas III Kyrdiniates	1084–1111
John IX Agapetus	1111–34

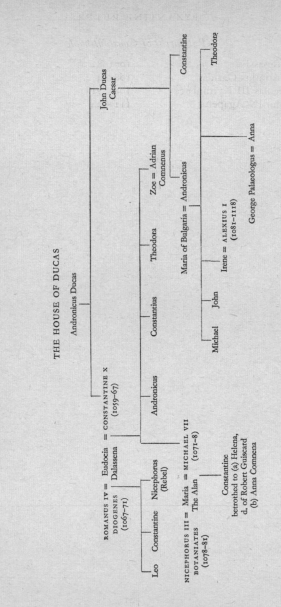

THE HOUSE OF DUCAS

THE HOUSE OF COMNENUS

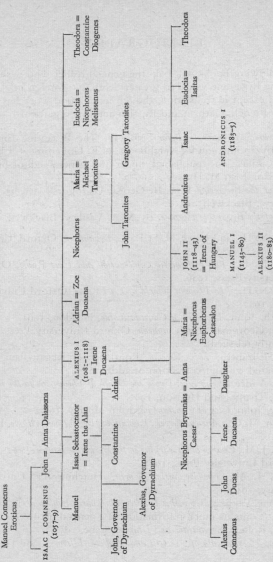

BIBLIOGRAPHY

THE following books will help the general reader who wishes to study the Byzantine world in greater depth. No foreign books are included except in translation, though much good work has been done by French, German and Russian authors in particular.

The Cambridge Medieval History, vol. iv: The Byzantine Empire, pt i: Byzantium and its Neighbours, pt ii: Government, Church and Civilization; published under the general editorship of Professor Joan M. Hussey, 1966–7.

History of the Byzantine State. By George Ostrogorsky (tr. by J. M. Hussey). Blackwell, 1956.

History of the Byzantine Empire. By A. A. Vasiliev. Blackwell, 1952.

Baynes, N. H., and Moss, H. St L. B., *Byzantium*, Oxford University Press, 1948.

Baynes, N. H., *The Hellenistic Civilization and East Rome*, Oxford University Press, 1946.

Baynes, N. H., *The Thought World of East Rome*, Oxford University Press, 1947.

Beckwith, John, *The Art of Constantinople*, Phaidon, 1961.

Buckler, Georgina, *Anna Comnena*, Oxford University Press, 1929 (recently reissued).

Dawes, Elizabeth, *The Alexiad*, Routledge & Kegan Paul, 1967 (reprinted without correction or addition).

Grabar, André, *Byzantium: From the Death of Theodosius to the Rise of Islam*, Thames and Hudson, 1966.

Hearsey, John, *City of Constantine*, John Murray, 1963.

Houston, M. G., *Ancient Greek, Roman and Byzantine Costume*, Black, 1947.

Hussey, J. M., *Church and Learning in the Byzantine Empire, 867–1185*, Oxford University Press, 1937.

Hussey, J. M., *The Byzantine World*, Hutchinson's University Library, 1957.

Johnstone, Pauline, *Byzantine Tradition in Church Embroidery*, Tiranti, 1967. (Contains much information of a general nature.)

Liddell, Robert, *Byzantium and Istanbul*, Cape, 1958.

Larousse *Encyclopedia of Ancient and Medieval History*, Paul Hamlyn, 1963.

BIBLIOGRAPHY

Maclagan, Michael, *The City of Constantinople*, Thames and Hudson, 1968.

Mathew, Gervase, *Byzantine Aesthetics*, John Murray, 1963.

Ostrogorsky, George, *History of the Byzantine State*, Basil Blackwell, 2nd edition (revised and enlarged), 1968.

Partington, J. R., *A History of Greek Fire and Gunpowder*, Heffer, 1960.

Polemis, Demetrios I., *The Doukai*, Athlone Press, 1968.

Rice, D. Talbot, *Art of the Byzantine Era*, Thames and Hudson, 1963.

Rice, D. Talbot, *Byzantine Art*, Penguin Books, 1961.

Rice, D. Talbot, *The Art of Byzantium*, Thames and Hudson, 1959.

Rice, D. Talbot, *The Byzantines*, Thames and Hudson, 1962.

Runciman, Steven, *Byzantine Civilization*, Arnold, 1933.

Runciman, Steven, *A History of the Crusades*, Penguin Books, 1965.

Sewter, E. R. A., *Michael Psellus: Fourteen Byzantine Rulers*, Penguin Books, 1966.

Sherrard, Philip, *Constantinople: Iconography of a Sacred City*, Oxford University Press, 1965.

Stewart, Cecil, *Byzantine Legacy*, Allen & Unwin, 1949.

Zernow, N., *Eastern Christendom*, Weidenfeld & Nicolson, 1961.

GLOSSARY

CATAPHRACT See p. 94, n. 31.

CATEPAN During the Comnenian period the themes (or provinces) of the Empire were governed by dukes, assisted by catepans.

CHRYSOBULL (or Golden Bull) An imperial decree, written in purple ink, with a golden seal.

DOMESTIC There was a Domestic for the East, another for the West – military commanders-in-chief (sometimes known as Great Domestics). There was also a Domestic of the *Scholae* (or *Scholarii*), mounted troops whose duty it was to guard the imperial palace.

DRUNGARIUS Although it is difficult to be precise, for military and naval titles changed their meaning during the centuries, one might equate a *drungarius* with a modern battalion commander (i.e. an officer in charge of roughly 1,000 men), but the naval *drungarius* was rather more important – he was an admiral.

EPARCH See p. 103, n. 2.

EXCUBITAE See p. 141, n. 6.

HELEPOLIS An engine for sieges, said to have been invented by Demetrius Poliorcetes. It took various forms, but seems to have been mounted on wheels.

INDICTION (originally meaning an announcement of a levy of foodstuffs to be delivered to the imperial government) became a chronological term for the first time in A.D. 312. It referred to a cycle of fifteen years and from 537 all documents had to be dated by the indiction number. By itself this number means little and has, of course, to be related to other systems of dating. See *Chronology of the Ancient World* (E. J. Bickerman, London, 1968).

LOGOTHETE See p. 103, n. 1. The civil service in Alexius's day was controlled by the logothete of the *secreta* (or Grand Logothete).

MAGISTROS A high court official. The title was conferred on many persons, each with his own sphere of action, but like many others its importance gradually declined.

MONOTHELETE One who maintained that Christ had two natures, human and divine, united in one Person, but with only one will. The heresy was condemned by the sixth oecumenical Council (A.D. 680–81).

MONOPHYSITE One who believes that Christ had only one nature (divine).

OBOL A small Greek coin (a farthing, a sou, a cent).

PELTAST See p. 94, n. 30.

PRIMICERIUS An official in the palace.

PROEDROS A high senatorial dignitary.

PROTOVESTIARIUS The officer in charge of the imperial wardrobe and the money concerned with it.

SATRAP An ancient Persian title. Satraps governed provinces. The Turks took over the title, but it was much more widely used; it often designated nothing more than a local governor.

SECRETA See p. 103, n. 1.

STADE A Greek measurement, a furlong (approximately).

STATER A Greek coin, of gold or silver, of a fixed weight.

STRATEGAT A military district.

TAGMATARCH Anna, who had a nice appreciation of the meaning of titles, uses various terms for army officers: *decurion*, e.g. is the equivalent of *dekarch*, the leader of the smallest army unit (ten men); the *turmarch* commanded a division; the *phalangarch* or *protrostrator* was of even higher rank. The *tagma*'s strength has been estimated roughly at 3,000; in other words, a *tagma* would be described in modern terms as a brigade and the *tagmatarch* as a brigadier. For some clarification of these and other titles see *CMH*, vol. iv, pt. ii.

'TORTOISE' A well known Roman military formation, but later used of portable mantlets or sheds which could give shelter to sappers or other soldiers on the battle-field or near the walls of enemy towns.

INDEX OF EVENTS

BOOK ONE

BOOK TWO

BOOK TWELVE

BOOK THIRTEEN

INDEX OF NAMES